THE AMERICAS
AND CIVILIZATION

By Darcy Ribeiro

THE CIVILIZATIONAL PROCESS
THE AMERICAS AND CIVILIZATION

The Americas
and
Civilization

by DARCY RIBEIRO

Translated from the Portuguese by
LINTON LOMAS BARRETT
and
MARIE MC DAVID BARRETT

New York   E. P. DUTTON & CO., INC.   1971

First Edition

Copyright©1969 Centro Editor de América Latina, S.A.
English translation Copyright©1971 by E. P. Dutton & Co., Inc.
All rights reserved
Printed in the U.S.A. by Vail-Ballou Press, Inc.

Published simultaneously in Canada by
Clarke, Irwin & Company Limited, Toronto and Vancouver

Library of Congress Catalog Card Number: 76-95479

SBN 0–525–05460–X

Contents

Translators' Preface

THE AUTHOR'S FOOTNOTES are numbered consecutively in each chapter and in the introduction. To distinguish our notes from his, an asterisk, not number, system is used. Wherever brevity permitted us to insert an explanatory phrase or an addition to some footnote by the author seemed necessary, brackets are used to enclose the material.

Midway in the work of translation we discovered Dr. Meggers' translation of the first book in Dr. Ribeiro's series (the present book being the second). Grateful acknowledgment is hereby made to her work for guidance in many details of terminology. Some terms used by the author do not figure in Brazilian dictionaries and are susceptible of various renderings; it is in this area that we have been particularly careful to follow Dr. Meggers, a noted anthropologist, in order to make the Ribeiro series more coherent in the English version.

L. L. B.
M. M. B.

Lexington, Virginia
December 25, 1969

Preface

THIS BOOK, an entity in itself, is one in a series of four studies in which I have attempted to rethink the paths by which the peoples of America have come to be what they are today and to discern the prospects for development open to them. The first study, *The Civilizational Process,** is an outline of the sociocultural evolution of the past ten millennia. Its purpose is to establish a classification of the developmental stages of the American peoples, past and present. The second and present book, *The Americas and Civilization,* attempts an anthropological interpretation of the social, cultural, and economic factors that have influenced the formation of the American national ethnic groups and an analysis of the causes of their uneven development. The third, *The Dilemma of Latin America,* analyzes present conditions and relationships between the rich Americas and the poor Americas within the world framework, with the aim of determining their prospects for progress, as well as identifying the power structures existing

* Translated, and with a foreword, by Betty J. Meggers (Washington, D.C.: Smithsonian Institution, 1968).

in Latin America and the virtually insurgent forces rising against them. The fourth, *Emergent Brazil,* a case study in which the general conceptual framework developed in the previous studies is applied to Brazil, seeks to explore the explicative value of the Brazilians' effort to form themselves into a modern nation.

The execution of so extensive an undertaking has, of course, presented enormous difficulties. The first arose from the limitations of the available scientific disciplines. Social scientists are trained to carry out precise, painstaking studies on narrowly delimited, unimportant subjects; but whenever one exceeds these limits by choosing subjects for their social significance, one also exceeds one's capacity to treat them "scientifically." What are scholars to do in this dilemma? Keep on accumulating research data that may, at some unforeseeable future time, allow us to work out a significant synthesis? Or take the risk of error to which pioneering attempts are liable in dealing with broad, complex topics that we are not equipped to treat as systematically as could be desired?

In societies facing grave social crises, the demands of practical action leave no room for doubt about what should be done. Among people content with their lot, scientists are able to devote their time to researches valid in themselves as contributions to knowledge about man and his world. But scientists belonging to countries dissatisfied with their lot are urged to use the tools of science to explain what their people can do to combat backwardness and ignorance. They must make the most of scientific methodology, and do so urgently, in order to discover everything tactically and strategically important to that struggle.

In our underdeveloped—and therefore dissatisfied—societies everything should be subject to question. Everyone should inquire into everything, asking whether this or that institution, or form of struggle, or even each person contributes to the perpetuation of the existing social order or toward its transformation and the establishment of a better social order. Such a better social order implies no entelechy. It is simply that social order that will enable the greatest number of people to eat more, live decently, and get an education. When such levels of abundance, health, and education are reached, we shall be able to join in the discussions of the rich on what makes prosperous societies so "unhappy." But for the present we are engaged in our war on poverty and on all those who, from within or without, whatever their motives, wish to keep our underdeveloped societies just as they are. In this war the social sciences, like all disciplines, are drafted, and intentionally or not they serve one of the warring factions.

This study attempts to integrate the anthropological, economic, sociological, historical, and political approaches in an effort to comprehend today's

American reality. Each approach would gain in cohesion but would lose in explanatory potential if isolated from the rest. Moreover, there are already too many partial studies of this sort, either grouped in generally related works or published in scattered articles, that attack the varied problems dealt with here. Organic integrations of these studies are our great lack. They are needed in order to find out what contributions the social sciences can make to our knowledge of the reality in which we live and to determine prospects for our future development. As an anthropologist I am assuming that such an integration can best be achieved from the anthropological angle. In my view, anthropology, owing to the breadth of its concerns and its methodological flexibility, is best equipped to undertake works of synthesis.

Many will think such an undertaking premature; others will say that it can be carried out only by a team, in an interdisciplinary study. The former are willing to await the accumulation of piecemeal studies that some day will make macroanalysis feasible. On the contrary, I believe that such an effort cannot be postponed.

I fully agree that it would be desirable to have such an analysis done by a team. It is nonetheless unlikely that the rich institutions dedicated to social research in Latin America will turn to that task. Their inclination will always be to undertake microstudies with scientific pretensions and to issue programmatic reports that are meant to contribute to the maintenance of the status quo. I am aware that my contribution is limited by being the work of a single individual and that it suffers from an "anthropologistical" bias; it must be viewed as such.

In the present study a historicocultural typology is used that groups the American peoples into three general categories to explain their way of life and analyze their developmental prospects. This typology makes it possible to transcend historical analysis and to focus on each people in a broader and more coherent way than would be practical using the usual anthropological and sociological approaches.

In case studies made in the light of this typology the most recommendable procedure would be an analysis of each people on the basis of the same scheme, thereby allowing systematic comparisons. However, this method would make the whole text highly repetitive and explore in equal depth both outstanding and commonplace situations. To obviate this problem I have oriented my case studies toward the analysis of those aspects of sociocultural actuality offering the highest explicative value. For example, in the case of Venezuela I examine in detail the mechanisms of economic domination exercise by U.S. firms. For the same reasons I study most closely, in the case of Colombia, the social functions of violence. As for the Antilles, I study interracial relations and the effects of colonial domination through the plantation system, as well as the first American socialist experiment. In the case of Brazil I analyze the agrarian structure—particularly the role and function of the *fazenda* [large farm] as an institution governing social life, and proceed to a deeper examination of recolonizing industrialization. In all the other cases, I have selected the significant aspects for a more detailed analysis.

By combining that historicocultural typology with this thematic treatment, I have been able to study exhaustively diverse specimen situations, preserving their concrete characteristics and integrating all these analyses at the end of the book in an over-all interpretation of models of autonomous development and patterns of historical retardation. I am quite aware that this is exceedingly ambitious. For that very reason this work aspires only to initiate a dialogue on the quality of the American peoples' self-knowledge and on their developmental problems. I hope that this general discussion will stimulate more detailed studies in the light of which this work can be revised at some future date with greater knowledge and artistry.

This series of studies has been made possible by a combination of several factors. Outstanding among them is the welcome extended by the University of Uruguay in appointing me a full-time professor of anthropology. Another factor is my status as a political exile, which explains my obsession—common to all expatriates—with understanding my country's problems. No less important, and certainly more elucidative, is my dual experience as anthropologist and politician. After ten years of scientific research on Brazil's Indians and *sertanejos* [backwoodsmen], I was called upon to perform political and advisory functions for ten more years, the last ones as minister of state in the Goulart administration. This personal experience is responsible for both the subject matter of these studies and my attitude. It explains my interest in understanding the sociocultural processes in the life of the American peoples, leading some of these to full development while condemning others to backwardness. It is my personal experience likewise that justifies the attitude with which these analyses were made: not as a merely academic exercise but as an intentional effort to contribute to an active awareness of the causes of underdevelopment.

Many of my colleagues in the social sciences would wish me to limit myself to studies of no social importance, in which the twin virtues of methodological virtuosity and scientific objectivity are displayed. Many political cohorts would like a still more militantly *engagé* book, at once a testimony to my experiences, a denunciation, and a normative program. Faithful to some of the loyalties professed by both groups, I have sought to use

my fund of anthropological and sociological knowledge in the analysis of
the problems with which the American peoples are struggling. But I have
sought equally to choose subjects for their social importance and to study
them with the purpose of influencing the current political process. Probably I have not satisfied either group. It is my hope, however, that these
studies will be of some use to a particular type of reader, more ambitious
on the comprehensive plane and more exigent as far as action is concerned
because of being inclined to understand in order to act and to act so as to
understand.

I owe a word of gratitude to my fellow countrymen in exile and to my
colleagues in Uruguayan and Argentine universities who have helped me
with suggestions over the three years devoted to these studies. To my
wife I owe the collaboration that has made them possible.

Darcy Ribeiro

Montevideo
March, 1968

INTRODUCTION:

Theories of Backwardness and Progress

"This is a critical time for the social sciences, not a time for courtesies."

— ROBERT LYND

MOST STUDIES of the uneven development of American societies are inspired by two conceptual frameworks, deeply interwoven yet opposite in orientation, especially on the prospective plane: one, that of academic sociology and anthropology; the other, dogmatic Marxism.

The first is based on the idea of a natural process of transition between archaic and modern formations, a passage from economies based on agriculture and crafts to industry-based economies, and on the idea that in this transition progressive and retrograde areas and sectors take shape in every society, interaction being the last dynamic factor in the process. "Structural duality," "reflexive modernization," "social mobility" are the familiar terms of this conceptual scheme, expressing the transition from the "traditional mode" to the "industrial mode" of societies.[1]

---

[1] On the theoretical plane this orientation is exemplified by the works of S. M. Lipset (1959), J. A. Boecke (1953), K. H. Silvert (1961), Gino Germani (1965), Jacques Lambert (1958), C. Morazé (1954), A. O. Hirschman (1961), D. Lerner

In the most extreme formulation of this concept the underdeveloped societies are described as hybrid or dual entities, characterized by the coexistence of two economies and two social structures centuries apart in development. One of them, traditionalism, would be characterized by stability, backwardness, and isolation from the contemporary world. The other, modernity, would be characterized by its synchronization with the world of its time and by its industrializing and capitalistic tendencies, for which it would be the center of diffusion.[2]

The most elaborate works on the opposition between the two poles reach extremes of descriptive virtuosity. However, lacking a theory that explains the selection of facts examined, these apparently factual descriptions are mystifying, particularly when applied to the Americas. Anthropological studies set in opposition, on the socioeconomic plane, folk societies—with predominantly rural, subsistence-level economies and motivated by traditional values—and modern societies—with predominantly urban, mercantile economies and activated by a strong entrepreneurial spirit (R. Redfield, 1941; J. Gillin, 1955; J. Steward, 1950).

Some sociologically oriented studies identify a modern model of Latin American nations as one characterized by the presence of broad middle-class sectors, whose progressive action impels the societies to a spontaneous development (J. Johnson, 1958; E. Lieuwen, 1961; K. H. Silvert, 1961; R. N. Adams, 1960; C. Wagley, n.d.). Other studies (principally G. Germani, 1965) mention multiple factors, but always attribute Latin American backwardness to the lack of qualities found in North American society, namely, certain bodies of values, types of personality, social strata, or sociopolitical institutions. For example, such studies refer to the lack of an entrepreneurial spirit, forgetting that the retarded nations of the Americas were born within the framework of mercantile economies producing

---

(1958), Bert Hoselitz (1959), A. Gershenkron (1962), S. N. Eisenstadt (1966), Peter Heinz (1965), and F. Bourricaud (1967).

Bibliographical references will follow the foregoing pattern, with the addition of page numbers only when works are textually quoted. Full bibliographical data will be found at the end of the book and is grouped according to chapters.

[2] The classic interpretations of Latin America are not analyzed here because they do not articulate a theory of social change. Taking a fatalist attitude as a point of departure, some of them attribute backwardness to climate or to race (D. F. Sarmiento, 1915; C. O. Bunge, 1903; Oliveira Vianna, 1952; A. Arguedas, 1937) and some, to negative qualities of the colonizer (M. Bomfim, 1929; J. Ingenieros, 1913; S. Ramos, 1951). Others question those determinisms, but fail to offer any congruent theory in opposition (J. B. Alberdi, 1943; E. da Cunha, 1911; G. Freyre, 1954; S. Buarque de Holanda, 1956; E. Martínez Estrada, 1933; Octavio Paz, 1950; H. A. Murena, 1964).

export goods and that their ruling castes never lacked a keen entrepreneurial spirit.

Technologically, such studies counterpose productive systems based on human and animal muscular energy and on craftsman procedures with industrial systems based on the conversion of inanimate energy and on mechanized procedures. Moreover, they omit the fact that it was the mastery of a more advanced technology (especially at the military and maritime levels) that permitted the installation of American factories,* as well as that these establishments always employed the highest technology in producing export articles or preserving the colonial system. Thus they conceal the fact that the Latin American peoples, like other backward peoples, underwent the impact of the Industrial Revolution as consumers of the products of alien industrialization. These products were introduced in sufficient quantity to enable their economies to produce raw materials more efficiently, but with the ever-present intention of keeping those economies dependent.

Structurally, such studies of Latin America focus on the presence of the middle classes and, according to each society's proportion of these, explain their relative success in modernizing political institutions. In this case we are dealing with a projection—in the form of a reactionary political doctrine—of Marx's observations on the major role of the industrial proletariat in social evolution for the intermediate sectors.

On the level of family organization, these analyses place two hypothetical models in opposition: kinship-based societies structured in extensive stable, solidary families venerating blood ties and segmented into immiscible castes versus societies founded on contractual relations, structured in conjugal, unstable families stratified along open class lines and activated by the most intense social mobility. These models describe the family systems of the dominant castes of the colonial and modern models of the Latin American societies. They say nothing of the family structure of the majority classes of their populations, which have never had the opportunity to constitute families with either group of characteristics.

On the motivational plane, the studies also contrapose the characteristics of these two models. The archaic one is characterized as a traditionalist order, based on customs, impregnated with sacred and mystical concepts, fearful of any change, and resistant to progress. The modern one is characterized by its progressive spirit, the proponent of change, the secularizer of institutions and customs. Here once again can be seen the Eu-

---

* The word is here used in the older sense of factors' stations, trading posts, and the like, rather than "manufactories."

ropean habit of confusing medievalist images with American societies both past and present. That is why their descriptions portray nothing of the Americas of yesterday and today, with their populations first massively degraded by slavery and forceably deculturated and then removed from the productive system and immersed in a "poverty culture." Such conditions have never allowed free popular cultivation of original beliefs or of traditionalism, except through secret cults or redefinitions of religious beliefs which could serve as bases for messianic rebellions.

In all the cases examined it is not a question of simple error. What is proposed through such comparisons is the thesis that a spontaneous form of development exists whereby the underdeveloped peoples' condition of backwardness, as a point of departure, would progress by addition of modernizing traits until they attained the present situation of the industrial capitalistic societies, viewed as ideal models of social order. When used to explain the poverty and wealth of the American peoples, such works describe the prosperity of the North Americans and Canadians as historical anticipations of a common spontaneous development. Such a development, still under way, is seen as affecting, at different rates, all the American peoples and therefore foreordains their homogenization at some future time. The United States and Canada represent paradigms of sociocultural evolution toward which all other peoples of the hemisphere are heading, however haltingly. Within this line of reasoning the forms of production, organization of work, regulation of social life, and world view existing in these countries emerge as normative patterns of this justificatory sociology.[3]

This approach lends itself admirably to two purposes. First, it supports a type of scientific research satisfied with copiously documenting the differences between backward and advanced societies and with recording in equal detail the contrasts of modernity and traditionalism so evident within the underdeveloped societies. Its conformist nature naturally satisfies the intellectual demands of nations content with the system being studied; they therefore do not expect their scholars to contribute toward transforming it (L. Bramson, 1961; M. Stein, 1960). Second, these studies lend themselves to the advanced nations' efforts to induce in backward nations an attitude of resignation to poverty or the equivalent thereof, that is, belief that backwardness may possibly be overcome spontaneously. In this way such studies operate as ideological forms that argue against any attempt to diagnose

[3] Examples of reaction against academic sociology can be found in the critical works of Robert Lynd (1964), C. Wright Mills (1959), Gunnar Myrdal (1944, 1954), L. A. Costa Pinto (1963), P. González Casanova (1965), A. Gunder Frank (1967), R. Stavenhagen (1965), Florestan Fernandes (1963), Fernando Henrique Cardoso (1964), and Octavio Ianni (1965, 1966).

the real causes of retardation and formulate deliberate plans for mobilizing the people for development.

Rooted in the idea of a historical progression from traditionalism to modernism, scholars of this school are unable to investigate the nature of that progression or the causal factors that activate it for two good reasons: (1) this would be feasible only on the basis of a broad historical approach with a general theory of the evolution of human societies, a theory that academic sociology abstains from formulating explicitly; (2) the admission of determining and conditioning factors, and of necessary historical sequences, would render impracticable the exercise of its paramount function, that of contributing to the perpetuation of the status quo.[4]

Confined in this ideological framework, academic sociology reduces its researches, on the explicative plane, to mere descriptions of contrasts and, on the normative plane, to the formulation of developmental doctrines advocating limited intervention in the economic system, designed to preserve rather than transform it.[5] The theoretical horizon of this approach rarely goes beyond a search for psychological, cultural, and economic factors more or less propitious to the introduction of technological innovations or to the emergence of innovative entrepreneurs.[6]

Most anthropological studies of cultural dynamics also conform to the academic attitude. Indeed, anthropologists—like all social scientists— seem prepared to undertake minute researches on restricted and socially unimportant problems, but appear incapable of focusing on the crucial issues confronting modern societies, even those questions squarely within their chosen field of scientific interest.

The current explanation for this sterility is expressed in terms of the scientist's unequivocal commitment to the advancement of knowledge. He would carry it so far as to choose his research subjects solely on the basis of their explicative value and to tackle a theme only when he has at hand a

[4] These limitations refer to those sociological studies generally considered as serious. Aside from them, a whole army of spy-investigators is conducting research in Latin America and the rest of the underdeveloped world, subsidized by organizations as alien to the academic world as the C.I.A. and the U.S. Departments of Defense and State. The best-known example is Project Camelot. Dozens of other such projects, however, have been or are currently being carried on (G. Selser, 1966).

[5] The principal fruit of this orientation is "developmentalism." In its most cautious official form it may be exemplified by the production of experts of the E.C.L.A. [United Nations Economic Commission on Latin America] and other international agencies. In its boldest reformist version it is exemplified by H. Jaguaribe (1962), Lebret (1961), C. Furtado (1961), J. Medina Echevarría (1964), Anibal Pinto (1965), and K. H. Silvert (1965).

[6] The best examples of such economic studies are those of W. W. Rostow (1960, 1960a) and E. Staley (1961) and of such sociological studies, R. Lippit (1958).

methodology capable of offering full assurance of scientific exactness and impartiality. In this case, the preference for microstudies and the distaste for bolder theories would be attributed to methodological contingencies and would be a necessary step in the maturation of the social sciences, which in this way would gather the empirical material indispensable for handling more ambitious themes (Talcott Parsons, 1951).

Other explanations relate the thematic line of these studies to extra-scientific factors. Outstanding among the latter are the ideological impregnation and the social and political involvement to which scientists are liable as members of their societies. These ties frequently make scholars mere agents for the propagation of political doctrines aimed solely at the perpetuation of the established order.

The scientific ideal of most anthropological acculturation studies seems to be the transfer of the methodology developed in ethnology to national societies. If the magnitude and complexity of a new study goes beyond these limits, the researchers arbitrarily narrow their field of observation. To do so they select concrete contact situations in which archaic and modern representatives of the national society's ethnic stocks are contraposed. Such situations are the object of exhaustive, painstaking observations, which are expected to aid in the formulation of a general theory of cultural change. In point of actual fact, however, having been isolated previously from the historical sequences in which they were shaped, from the national context into which they are introduced, and from the world economic system in which they arise, these situations cannot contribute to explaining even themselves.

Adherence to taxonomic concerns—justifiable in ethnographic research —frequently turns these acculturation studies into mere lists of exotic habits and customs. In the light of these lists scholars seek to demonstrate the necessary character of the backwardness of the communities studied and, by extension, of the rural masses or of the mestizo strata of American national societies. The lack of a theory that considers the factors actually in operation reduces such studies to a spurious psychologism, false because unacceptable to psychology proper. But it permits anthropologists to serve as advisors to welfare programs that are content to reveal the negative role of cultural traits and norms without ever exposing the compulsions of colonialism, slavery, the latifundian system, and exploitation by the patron— the owner, the master, the boss—as causal factors of backwardness.[7]

[7] Exceptions to this orientation are the anthropological studies that regain the evolutionist perspective (Gordon Childe, 1939, 1964; Leslie White, 1958; Julian H. Steward, 1955), the studies by Robert Redfield (1953, 1956), that by George Foster (1960) on the Iberian cultural matrix, the attempts at construction of typologies of today's American peoples (R. N. Adams, 1965), the sociological studies of decoloni-

These limitations are epitomized by studies in applied anthropology, the colonialist nature of which shames scholars with even a minimal sense of self-criticism. Less disgraceful examples of the same kind are found in acculturation studies carried out as part of developmental programs. Entangled in webs of not always explicit commitments, these studies are producing a vast practical store of formulas that at one and the same time deny the disinterestedness of those researches and prove their involvement in the most retrogressive programs.[8]

Good illustrations of the explicative value of this kind of study are to be seen in the anthropological essays that seek to explain Latin Americans' backwardness in terms of attributes peculiar to their character and culture. Frequently cited among these peculiarities are the cults of *machismo* and *caudillismo,** the *compadre* relationship,† the enjoyment of sadness, the exacerbation of the sentiments of honor and personal dignity, aversion to work, dread of death, and fear of specters (Gillin, 1955).

The second conceptual framework, dogmatic Marxism, is based on the idea that the differences in development of modern societies can be explained as steps in an evolutionary process, unilinear and irreversible, common to all human societies. From this point of view the backward nations would be those with the greatest sum total of the contents of past stages of human evolution, such as the slavistic and the feudal.

Studies based on this view rarely do more than mechanically apply Marxian interpretative systems to the Americas. They are thereby reduced to mere illustrations, with local examples, of classic Marxist theses on the development of capitalism in Europe. Applied to Latin America, such works emphasize the feudal residues in the past or present of different countries seeing these as the cause of backwardness. Because each region

---

zation (G. Balandier, 1955), and the recent investigations in the field of the culture of poverty by Oscar Lewis (1961, 1966).

[8] See especially G. Foster (1962), E. H. Spicer (1952), R. N. Adams (1960), and S. Andreski (1966).

Machismo is the Latin American male's obsession with the necessity of constantly parading his male sexual virility. *Caudilhismo* (Portuguese form, pronounced very nearly the same as the Spanish *caudillismo*) is the aspect of Latin American culture that produces *caudillos,* military and/or political men whose forceful personality—"charisma" is the popular term today—makes them recognized by the rank and file as natural leaders.

† *Compadrío* is the complex of relationships between *compadres*. In the original religious context, *compadre* means simply a godfather, the baptismal sponsor of an infant. This makes the father the compadre of the godfather, too. The spiritual and emotional bonds thus established extend beyond the religious context into all phases of life: two compadres are the closest of friends, and if one becomes politically powerful he feels obligated to appoint his compadre to some lucrative position. Hence the additional meaning of "excessive favoritism" in *compadrío*.

has a record of slave labor as well as of capitalistic work for wages, the scheme expands at times into such hybrid categories as feudal-slave, semi-feudal, semicolonial, and feudal-capitalist formations.

The basic presupposition of this approach is, as we have seen, a unili-near evolutionism according to which the Latin American societies are au-tarchic entities experiencing, centuries late, the same evolutionary steps already experienced by advanced societies. In its most extreme formula-tions this perspective does not account for the texture of economic, social, and cultural interrelations, in itself an impediment to the reproduction of archaic stages in their original form. Nor does this approach make an au-thentic effort to indicate the causal and conditioning factors of social dy-namics.

Paradoxically, this nominally revolutionary theory frequently turns out to be ultraconservative. Abandoning the analytic perspective of the Marxist classics, such studies become mere puerile exercises demonstrating the uni-versality of Marx's theses, and thereby not only impoverish them but ac-tually make them, willy-nilly, an ideological system indirectly supporting the status quo. Examples of such studies are those that advocate—as a strategy in the struggle against underdevelopment and toward socialism— the rooting out of the remains of feudalism, if not the consolidation of the capitalistic contents, as a necessary step in the evolution of Latin Ameri-can societies.[9]

The two approaches are both unsuccessful in explaining the unequal de-velopment of contemporary societies and in formulating strategies condu-cive to a break with backwardness. Sunk in myopic objectivism, academic sociology and anthropology content themselves with accumulating empiri-cal data without formulating a scientific theory that can explain these data in all their dynamism and variety. Dogmatic Marxism, even though it starts from an explicative theory and a fecund historical perspective, loses itself in the search for evidence of a cyclic reiteration of stages or else gets off the track in vain attempts to fit reality into formal antinomies. Both ap-proaches prove to be doctrinaire. Academic sociology and anthropology do, however, function as an instrument for maintenance of the status quo. Dogmatic Marxism, on the other hand, fails to fulfill its special vocation of providing a theory to explain social processes or a strategy for the planned transformation of Latin American societies within any foreseeable time.

---

[9] Works written with this perspective include N. W. Sodré (1944, 1963), Rodney Arismendi (1962), and Rodolfo Puiggros (1945); critical of this approach are Cáio Prado, Jr. (1966), Wanderley Guilherme (1963), Paul Baran (1964), and A. Gunder Frank (1966).

Progress and Causality

To explain change in human societies, it is necessary, therefore, to invert the analytic view of academic sociology and anthropology and critically reevaluate the Marxist approach in order to bring into focus (1) the dynamic factors in the evolution of human societies over long periods of time and (2) the conditions under which these factors operate. This is what I tried to do in a general study of sociocultural evolution during the past ten millennia.[10] My purpose here is to analyze the formative processes and developmental problems of the American nations, based on the generalizations reached in *The Civilizational Process*. In this way I hope to arrive at a better understanding of the disparities in the development of the Americas and also at significant new generalizations on the nature of dynamic social processes.

My point of departure is the generally accepted assumption that the unequal development of contemporary nations results from general historical processes of change affecting them all in differing degrees. These processes have engendered, simultaneously and correlatively, the metropolitan and the colonial economies. These processes have shaped the underdeveloped societies, not as replicas of past stages of the developed ones, but as counterparts necessary to the maintenance of the system containing both.

In view of the developmental disparities it is fitting to observe, first, that many of the nations today identified as underdeveloped have in the past known periods of splendor and prosperity as highly developed civilizations. Second, the European countries first manifesting an industrial civilization included, until the seventeenth century, backward areas notable for their mediocrity rather than for their progress. This indicates that we are faced with divergent effects of a general civilizational process that manifests itself in some cases as stagnation and regression and in others as development and progress.

In the presence of these disparities it is well to observe, further, that contemporary societies are not isolated entities but rich and poor components of a worldwide economic system in which each of them plays prescribed roles, mutually complementary and tending to perpetuate reciprocal relations. I shall try to show that the situations of backwardness or progress of the different nations result from the impacts of successive technological revolutions that have transformed human societies. These revolutions, affecting the nations differentially and altering each of their parts in

[10] Darcy Ribeiro, *The Civilizational Process*, Betty J. Meggers, trans. (Washington, D.C.: The Smithsonian Institution, 1968).

different ways, generate dephasings between societies as well as regional and sectoral asynchronisms. Because each of these processes began at a certain moment of history and continued to operate even after others were set in motion, it logically follows that we are faced as much with a historical continuity of successively unleashed effects as with simultaneous interactive functional contrasts.

Within this perspective the explanation of the unequal development of human societies must be sought along three lines of analysis. The task of the first, socioeconomic, approach is to identify the causal or conditioning factors in the transformation of human societies. This analysis allows us to record regularities and define them in terms of sociocultural processes.

The second—historicocultural—approach reconstitutes the process by which modern peoples have come to be what they are, depicting it in terms of sequences seen as antecedents and consequences, and permits elaboration of an arrangement of the evolutionary stages and their crystallization into sociocultural formations. In analyses of medium scope on the formative process of national ethnic communities, this approach engenders typologies of historicocultural configurations.

In the third or conjunctural approach, it is essential to analyze the interactive situations, explicable as balanced or irruptive tensions involving opposing elements within each social context. This analysis explains the interaction between developed and underdeveloped societies—expansion, domination—as well as the modes of influence exerted among the sectors and areas of each society—power structures, insurgent forces—in order to determine the effects of acceleration and retardation of progress deriving from these two kinds of interaction.

Only the combination of these three approaches in the form of a dialectic generates a theory of sociocultural development in terms of a historical process, set in motion by causal and conditioning factors, unleashed, accelerated, or retarded in given situations, and having foreseeable effects through its present and future action on human societies.

The principal methodological approaches available for the study of the causal factors of social development are functionalism and Marxism. The former—committed to conservative attitudes and cultivated mainly in developed, self-satisfied countries—converts the study of social dynamics into mere efforts to characterize the way by which the existing contents of each given situation contribute to the perpetuation of forms of social life. Although these efforts are concerned, fortuitously, with change factors (dysfunction, latent function), they are almost always reduced to demonstrations of functional interdependencies. They describe social systems as configurations of cultural patterns or of social institutions in which every component is equally capable of acting as a causal factor. In this view any understanding of social life becomes impossible, except as the residue of multiple independent sequences of phenomena that move arbitrarily and in which regularities of succession, causality, or conditioning cannot be distinguished.[11]

Marxism, explicitly committed to the planned reorganization of human societies, is founded on a general explicative theory of sociocultural evolution, understood as a genetic sequence of stages or economicosocial formations. Its point of departure is the postulate that the mode of production of a society (technology plus labor force) determines, at each moment of its evolution, the institutional superstructures and the forms of consciousness observed in it, with the additional postulate that, in a given situation, conflicts arise between the degree of development of the productive forces and the institutional superstructures erected on them, unleashing movements of social change. These movements are polarizations in which contrary forces collide through efforts to overcome their contradictions. The principal contradiction is the opposition of the interests of one social class—defined by the mode of institutionalization of property—and the interests of the other classes. Such contradictions generate conflicts that operate as the principal dynamic factor of human history.

It is plain that, contrary to functionalism, Marxism possesses a theory of social causation, a far-reaching historical framework explicative of sociocultural evolution, and a diagnostic approach to social praxis. This last consists of a method for analyzing the contradictions operative within each particular historical situation, permitting identification of the complexes of opposing interests to distinguish among them the contradiction responsible for the direction of the process. These contradictions cover quite varied fields, such as the oppositions between international economic systems, or between national entities, or between structural components within a society. In every concrete situation, however, are discernible the basic structural contradictions that motivate the actions most replete with consequences. Knowledge of these contradictions, besides its explicative value, has for Marxists a notable practical importance because it permits formulating strategies of intervention in the flow of social events with the objective of orienting them toward courses most propitious for the initiation of social revolution.

It was through this dialectic that Marx tried to explain the processes of transformation achieved by human societies of the past and to foresee

---

[11] Its most ambitious theoretic fruits are the "theories of medium scope" derived from the works of Talcott Parsons (1951), R. K. Merton (1957), and M. J. Levy (1952).

emergent stages. He always saw these processes as the product of a confrontation of innumerable forces with multiple developmental possibilities. They were not merely interactive forces, with equal potentialities of determination, nor were they an arbitrary flow, unsusceptible to scientific interpretation and therefore to being foreseen and even disciplined, within limits, by the human will (C. Wright Mills, 1963; L. Althusser, 1967).

Some scholars following Marx have applied the same approach in fecund form, both in the study of new situations and in the reexamination of old problems. They have thus contributed simultaneously to reaching a better understanding of these problems and to enriching the Marxist conceptual scheme itself.[12] Others, however, more faithful to the philosophical language of Marx's time than to his manner of analyzing social reality, rebuilt Marxist concepts in the form of mystic categories and formal antagonisms.[13] We have already tried to show that their role is nearly as unwholesome as that of academic sociology and anthropology.

Indeed, the social sciences do not offer any theory of broad historical scope, explicitly formulated, to oppose that of Marx—except perhaps functionalism, which is not a general theory of social dynamics because it concerns stability more than change. So the academic opposition to Marxist conceptions offers no consistent alternative for the analysis of the motive forces of social change. But since in many instances an over-all conception of society and of sociocultural evolution is indispensable, all social scientists resort frequently, albeit reluctantly, to Marxism as the unconfessed source of their best inspirations. This is the case of what has been called "critical sociology," responsible for the works that have come closest to an approach capable of treating human societies as coherent structures susceptible of being studied with scientific exactness.[14]

Considering the paralyzing opposition between the academized social sciences and dogmatic Marxism, those who need to understand social reality in order to act on it must rise above both positions. They must surmount the false sciences of man and society, unmasking their ineptitude at formulating any theory of social reality because they are committed to perpetuation of the status quo; they must go beyond dogmatic Marxism, denouncing its true nature as a school of exegetes of classic texts, incapable of focusing on social reality itself.

[12] V. I. Lenin (1932, 1965), L. Trotsky (1957), A. Gramsci (1958, 1960), G. Luckacs (1960), K. Kosik (1965), J.-P. Sartre (1963), H. Marcuse (1964), P. A. Baran and P. Sweezy (1965), L. Althusser (1967), and D. I. Chesnokov (1967).

[13] F. V. Konstantinov et al. (1960), O. V. Kuusinen et al. (1964), O. Yajot (1965), A. Viatkin et al. (1965), and A. Makarov et al. (1965).

[14] These efforts are exemplified by Max Weber (1968), K. Mannheim (1955), T. Veblen (1954), R. Lynd (1964), C. Wright Mills (1956, 1959, 1963), F. Lundberg (1960), D. Riesman (1950), E. Shils (1956), and I. L. Horowitz (1966).

This dual effort is important in the return to the Marxist investigative attitude and scientific methodology. But it is of great concern also to the desanctification of his texts: the most important were written precisely a century ago and cannot provide a current explanation for the whole of to-day's reality. We must bear in mind that Marx did not seek to create a new philosophical doctrine but to fix the bases of a scientific theory of society, founded on the meticulous study of all manifestations of social life; we must also remember that by virtue of this effort he became the founder of modern social sciences. As such, he demands three kinds of commitment by those who wish to comprehend his work: (1) to treat his propositions as any scientific statement, that is, by submitting them permanently to criticism in view of facts, accepting them as valid only by continual reformulation; (2) to carry on his effort, not through the exegesis of the texts he left, but by observing social reality in order to infer from its apparent forms, by means of systematic analysis, the structures that shape it and the processes that activate it; (3) to treat Marx himself as the founder of the social sciences, neither greater nor less than Newton or Einstein in physics and for that very reason equally incorporated into the history of science, which cannot be confused with science itself.

The science that has inherited the theme and methodology of historical materialism is anthropology (J.-P. Sartre, 1963), inasmuch as it constitutes the broadest effort at explaining how human societies came to be what they are now and the prospects they face in the immediate future. That inheritance, however, does not belong to any of the anthropologies labeled as cultural, social, or structural; such anthropologies have suffered an abrasion similar to that of academic sociology. It belongs to a new anthropology that will be distinguished by (1) a multilinear evolutionary perspective assigning each people of the present or past to a scale of sociocultural development; (2) a notion of necessary causality based on the recognition of the different determinative capacity of the various sociocultural components; (3) an attitude deliberately participant in social life and trained to judge it lucidly, like a science committed to human destiny.

It is to this dialectical anthropology that I am seeking to contribute with my effort to understand the American sociocultural reality, to formulate some principles explaining the causes of unequal development, and to determine the courses by which underdeveloped nations may overcome backwardness.

To begin with, it is necessary to state that the principal characteristic of social reality is that it is the historical product of a process of humanization. By this process man has been constructing himself through the creation of standardized forms of cultural conduct, transmissible from generation to generation, crystallized in societies with their respective cultures.

This process unfolds in several stages corresponding to the unleashing of successive technological revolutions (Agricultural, Urban, Irrigation, Metallurgical, Pastoral, Mercantile, Industrial, Thermonuclear) and of correlative movements that reorganize human societies into tribes, national ethnic groups, regional civilizations, or world civilizations. Each society is a result of these civilizational processes, which have left their imprint in differing degrees according to their reordinating capacity and the way by which they attained it.

Marxist-inspired studies generally split this reality into an infrastructure of technoeconomic content and a superstructure of sociocultural content. Although this division may be suitable in the case of highly abstract analyses, for the type of study here proposed it is more appropriate to distinguish three basic spheres of social reality, namely, the adaptive, the associative, and the ideological. Each is sufficiently integrated to be legitimately treated as a system and sufficiently differentiated from the rest to be taken as a distinct conceptual entity.

The adaptive system covers all those practices through which a society acts on nature in the effort to provide its subsistence and to reproduce the totality of goods and furnishings at its disposal. The associative system covers the complex of norms and institutions that organize social life, discipline human coexistence, regulate the work force, and govern political life. Finally, the ideological system is the body of knowledge, beliefs, and values generated in the adaptive and associative efforts.

These three systems are stratified. On the bottom is the adaptive system, which concerns the basic requisites, material and biological, of human survival. On the intermediate level is the associative system, responsible for the forms of discipline of social life for productive work. And at the apex is the ideological system, strongly molded by the others and capable of altering social life only by means of introducing innovations in the adaptive or associative forms of action.

In synchronic analyses the whole and the integration of the three systems is designated as "structure" when it is desirable to stress the forms of association (L. A. Costa Pinto, 1965). The same whole is designated as "culture" when attention is focused principally on the character of standardized guidelines of conduct, transmitted socially through symbolic interaction, modes of adaptation, norms of association, and explanations and values (Leslie White, 1958). In diachronic analyses, the whole of the three systems is called "formation" when one wishes to indicate a complex of societies representative of a stage of human evolution (D. Ribeiro, 1968).

The essential content of the adaptive system is technology; the basic element of the associative, in complex societies, is the form of social stratification in economic classes; and in the ideological, the crucial components are the bodies of knowledge, values, and beliefs developed in each group's effort to understand its own experience and to organize its social conduct.

The three systems maintain necessary connections with one another and act on social life as integrated complexes. Thus technology does not act on society directly, but by establishing the limits within which the available resources can be exploited. The effective exploitation of these resources, as well as their distribution, is carried out by means of specific forms of organization of human relations for the utilization of technology through work, and the whole process takes place in accord with the body of knowledge, values, and beliefs that motivate personal conduct (R. MacIver, 1942).

Consequently, each stage in human evolution is intelligible only in terms of the productive technology, the existent manner of regulating human relations, and the ideology that explains and qualifies the conduct of its members. The understanding of social life and its dynamics demands, however, that abstract analysis of each of these factors refer always to the integrated complexes in which they coexist and act jointly. These complexes not only combine but also oppose, at every moment, certain contents of productive technology with preexisting forms of social organization and with given bodies of beliefs and values. Tensions are generated and accumulated by the introduction of technological innovations, by the opposition of group interests, and by changes occurring in one sector and not in others. These innovations, oppositions, and redefinitions are the causes of social dynamics; they act within complexes that they set in motion but that, in turn, condition them.

Examining these interactions synchronically, the fact emerges that, in a given instance, any factor may play a causal role. By examining not merely cuts in the historical continuum but the continuum itself through diachronic analyses, the determinant position of the technological factor can be verified. In analyses of average scope the conditioning capacity of the social structure stands out as a form of organization of relationships for the purposes of production of goods, reproduction of humanity, and satisfaction of the fundamental necessities of associative life. A notorious example is the conditioning power of the latifundian form of property-holding in regard to agricultural technology and to the way of life in underdeveloped societies. Also in the synchronic analyses it is observed that the ideological contents of a culture, represented by the mental products generated in the adaptive and associative effort, or inherited from other cultural patrimonies, operate as fecund or limiting factors of social dynamics. In other words, they have the power to retard or to accelerate renovation according to their spurious or authentic character and their synchronism or dephasing in relation to changes in other spheres.

These generalizations about differences in the determinative power of the adaptive, associative, and ideological contents of sociocultural structures are not merely classificatory. In the chapters that follow they will be used to explain the differences in development of the American peoples. My hypothesis is that the present mode of existence (basic causal factor) of the peoples of the modern world has its origin in the impact of two technological revolutions, the Mercantile and the Industrial, which produced "western European civilization" first in its capitalistic-mercantile aspect and later in its imperialistic-industrial aspect. Further, both technological revolutions, operating differentially on diverse national contexts—as a process of autonomous evolution or as a reflex action of previously developed nuclei—invested some peoples with the power to dominate and exploit others and degraded those others, reducing them to dependency on the former.

The conditioning power of the associative factors will be examined by studying the way in which the new technology is incorporated into the productive system of the dominated societies. Here we shall be able to see how control of this modernization, exercised by the agents of colonial domination in association with the local privileged strata, conditioned the potentialities of the new technology to maintain external connections and perpetuate minority interests. Under these conditions, industrial technology was only partially absorbed by the dependent societies, modifying the way of life of great segments of their population but incorporating only a part of that population into the work force of the modernized sectors. In this way antagonistic situations were established: privileges given to those sectors integrated into the industrial civilization and still greater wretchedness, to those left out.

Finally, the limiting or fecund power of the ideology contributed to shaping the picture of modern American societies. I shall seek to show this by examining the role of cultural alienation imposed on the underdeveloped peoples of America by their dominators and through analysis of their own efforts to redefine the spurious contents of their culture and to formulate their own projects for development, as a means of overcoming dependency and backwardness.

Evolutionary Acceleration and Historical Incorporation

The study of the ethnic formation of the American peoples and their current problems of development demands that we first analyze the great historicocultural sequences in which they began—the technological revolutions and the civilizational processes, which correspond to the principal movements of human evolution.

We regard techological revolutions as prodigious innovations. New physical means for acting on nature and the use of new sources of energy, once attained by society, raise it to a higher stage in the evolutionary process. This occurs because the society's productive capacity expands, with consequent enlargement and changes in the distribution and composition of the population; because previous forms of social stratification are rearranged; and because the ideological contents of culture are redefined. There is also a parallel increase in the society's power to dominate and exploit the peoples within its range who have not experienced the same technological progress.

Every technological revolution spreads via successive civilizational processes that promote ethnic transfigurations of the peoples affected, remodeling them by fusion of races, confluence of culture, and economic integration to incorporate them into new ethnic conformations and into new historicocultural configurations.

The civilizational processes operate in one of two opposing ways, depending on whether the affected peoples become active instruments or passive recipients of the civilizational expansion. The first way is evolutionary acceleration, which occurs in the case of those societies that, autonomously dominating the new technology, progress socially, preserving their ethnocultural profile and, sometimes, expanding it to other peoples in the form of macroethnic groups. The second way, that of historical incorporation, occurs among peoples subjugated by societies with a more highly developed technology, thus losing their autonomy and in danger of having their culture traumatized and their ethnic profile denaturalized.

From the sixteenth century on, there have been two technological revolutions responsible for setting in motion four successive civilizational processes. The Mercantile Revolution, in an initial salvationistic-mercantile impulse, activated the Iberian peoples and the Russians and drove the former to overseas conquests and the latter to continental expansion over Eurasia. In a second impulse, more maturely capitalistic, the Mercantile Revolution, after breaking down feudal stagnation in certain areas of Europe, drove the Dutch, English, and French to overseas colonial expansion. There followed the Industrial Revolution, which, beginning in the eighteenth century, rearranged the world under the aegis of the pioneer industrial nations through two civilizational processes: imperialistic expansion and socialism.

At the same time that these successive processes commenced, the societies affected by them, either actively or passively, took shape as unequal components of different sociocultural formations, according to whether they experienced an evolutionary acceleration or a historical incorporation. So it is that, in consequence of the salvationistic-mercantile expansion, the salvationistic mercantile empires were modeled by evolutionary acceleration and their slavistic-colonial contexts, by historical incorporation. Later, in consequence of the second civilizational process, the capitalistic mercantile formations were crystallized by acceleration and their slavistic colonial, trading colonial, and immigrant colonial dependencies, by incorporation. Finally, as the fruit of the first civilizational process initiated by the Industrial Revolution, the imperialistic industrial formations emerged through acceleration and their neocolonial counterpart, by incorporation; immediately afterwards, as the result of a second civilizational process, the socialistic revolutionary, socialistic evolutionary, and nationalistic modernizing formations appeared, generated as evolutionary accelerations, although with different capacities for progress.

Historical incorporation operates by means of the domination and enslavement of alien peoples, followed by the socioeconomic structuring of the nuclei into which the dominated contingents congregate, in order to install new forms of production or exploit former productive activities. The fundamental objective of this structuring is to bind the new nuclei to the expansionist society as a part of its productive system and as an object of the intentional diffusion of its cultural tradition.

In the first stage of this process the purposeful decimation of parcels of the attacked population and the deculturation of the enslaved contingents are common. In the second stage a certain cultural creativity occurs, which permits shaping, with elements taken both from the master culture and from the subjugated, a body of common understandings, indispensable to successful coexistence and work orientation. Ethnic protocells combine fragments of the two patrimonies within the framework of domination. In a third stage these protocells enculturate persons torn from their original societies, including the native population, those transferred as slaves, and, further, the very agents of domination, and the descendants of all of them.

These new cultural cells tend to mature as protoethnic groups and to crystallize as the national identity of the area's population. In a more advanced stage of the process, the protoethnos struggles for independence in order to rise from its status as a spurious cultural variant and an exotic, subordinate component of the colonialist society to that of an autonomous society served by an authentic culture.

This restoration and emancipation are won only through a process of extreme conflict in which cultural as well as social and economic factors are conjoined. It is guided by a persistent effort at political self-affirmation on the part of the protoethnos, which hopes to win autonomy. That goal attained, a national ethnos makes itself evident—or, in other terms, the group identifies itself as a human community different from all others, with its own state and government, within which framework it lives out its destiny.

When these national ethnic groups enter in their turn on expansion into vast areas, perhaps colonizing other peoples toward whom they play a dominant role, it is possible to speak of a macroethnos. However, once a certain level of ethnoimperial expansion has been attained over a dominion, the enculturative effects and the spread of the technoscientific resources on which the domination is based tend to mature the subjugated ethnic entities, giving them the capacity for autonomous life. Thus once again the satellite turns against the ruling center, breaking the bonds of domination.

The result is autonomous national ethnic groups in interaction with one another and susceptible to the impact of new technological revolutions. These national ethnic groups display a series of discrepancies and uniformities that are highly significant in understanding their subsequent life. They vary in two basic lines: (1) according to their degree of sophistication of the productive technology and the broader or more limited prospect of development thus opened to them; (2) according to the nature of the ethnic remodeling they may have experienced and that shaped them into different historicocultural configurations, that is, into different groups that, over and above specific ethnic differences, display uniformities stemming from their parallel development. In the case of the European civilizational processes, these configurations contrast and approximate peoples according to the basic profile of European or Europeanized societies.

Classic examples of civilizational processes responsible for the rise of different historicocultural configurations are to be found in the expansion of irrigation civilizations, of such thalassocracies as the Phoenician and the Carthaginian, and of the Greek and Roman slavistic-mercantile empires, all of them responsible for the transfiguration and remodeling of innumerable peoples. More recent examples are the Islamic and Ottoman expansion and, above all, the European expansion itself, both in its Iberian salvationistic-mercantile cycle and in its capitalistic-mercantile and imperialistic-industrial cycles thereafter.

Within this perspective, studies of acculturation gain a new dimension. Instead of being limited to the results of the conjunction between autonomous cultural entities, they focus on the process whereby ethnic groups are formed in the course of imperial expansion. This process can be studied wherever the colonialist agencies of expanding societies, served by a more advanced technology and by a higher culture, act on alien sociocultural contexts. Such agencies reflect the high culture only in its instrumental, normative, and ideological aspects, which are indispensable to economic exploitation, political domination, ethnic expansion, and cultural diffusion. They generally act on more backward populations that are profoundly different culturally, socially, and, at times, racially from the dominant society. In the course of subjugation, the colonialist agencies also incorporate cultural elements from the dominated people, principally the local subsistence techniques. But essentially the new nuclei take shape as variants of the expansionist national society, whose language and culture are imposed on them. A new culture is formed, tending on the one hand to perpetuate itself as a spurious culture of a dominated society, but on the other to attend to its specific needs for survival and growth and in this way to structure itself as an autonomous ethnos.

Clearly this is not a question of autonomous cultural entities influencing each other, as in the classic studies of acculturation. What we find here is the unilateral domination of the society in expansion and the cultural asynchronism or dephasing between the colonialists and the contexts in which they implant themselves. Only in the case of interaction at the tribal level can one speak of acculturation as a process in which the respective patrimonies allow a free choice of the traits to be adopted, autonomous control of these traits, and their full integration into the old context.

The very concept of cultural autonomy requires redefinition, because one can speak of independence only in certain circumstances when it is a matter of societies affected as agents or patients in the course of civilizational processes. Neither a colonialist agency situated outside its society nor the population on which it acts constitutes an entity served by really autonomous cultures; each depends on the other and both compose, together with the metropolitan ruling center, an interdependent whole. It is hardly possible to talk of autonomy as control of one's own fate in the case of entities practicing domination, and even they, as a general thing, are part of broad sociocultural constellations whose components only partially preserve their independence. In the conjunctions resulting from ethnic expansion, there is a marked difference between the dominating entity's power to impose its tradition and the dominated subject's power to resist ethnic and cultural denaturing.

We use the term "deculturation" to designate the process operating in situations where human contingents, torn from their society (and consequently from their cultural context) through enslavement or mass removal, and hired as unskilled labor for alien enterprises, find themselves obliged to learn new ways. In these cases the emphasis is on eradicating the original culture and on the traumas that result, rather than on cultural interaction. Deculturation, in this instance, is nearly always prerequisite to the process of enculturation. Enculturation crystallizes a new body of understanding between dominators and dominated that makes social coexistence and economic exploitation viable. It expands when the socialization of the new generations of the nascent society and the assimilation of the immigrants are brought about by incorporation into the body of customs, beliefs, and values of the ethnic protocell.

Finally, we use the concept of "assimilation" to signify the processes of integration of the European into the neo-American societies whose linguistic and cultural similarities—in regard to their world view and work experiences—do not justify employing the concepts of acculturation and deculturation. Obviously, it is assumed that this participation will be limited at first and that it may be completed in one or two generations, when the immigrant descendant is an undifferentiated member of the national ethnos. As such ethnic entities admit variable forms and degrees of participation—deriving, for example, from socialization in different cultural areas or from more or less recent immigration—these differences in degree of assimilation may assume the character of different expressions of self-identification with the national ethnos.

Another concept that we have had to reformulate is that of "genuine culture" and "spurious culture," inspired by Edward Sapir (1924) but here used in the sense of cultures more integrated internally and more autonomous in the command of their development (authentic) in opposition to traumatized cultures corresponding to dominated societies dependent on alien decisions. The members of such societies tend toward cultural alientation or, rather, toward internalization of the dominator's view of the world and themselves (spurious).

These contrasting cultural profiles are the natural and necessary results of the civilizational process itself, which, in cases of evolutionary acceleration, preserves and strengthens cultural authenticity and, in cases of historical incorporation, frustrates the preservation of the original ethos or of its redefinition—on its own terms—of the innovations coming from the colonialist entity. The destruction of the original ethos causes, irremediably, a breakdown in cultural integration, which falls below minimum levels of internal congruence, passing into alienation through feeding on undigested ideas not pertinent to its own experience but only to the efforts at self-justification of the colonial power.

Critical Awareness and Underdevelopment

Within the civilizational processes described and through historical incorporation American societies on the tribal level, those already structured in rural-craftsman states, and even the theocratic irrigation empires (Inca,

Maya, Aztec) were enslaved and integrated into the worldwide economic system. It was thus that American natives and also the African Negroes brought to America leaped to a technologically more complex stage of human evolution—as participants in mercantile formations—but they were being simultaneously involved as "external proletariats" of the metropolitan economies. This progression, taking place by way of historical incorporation, was important in the loss of their ethnic autonomy and in the denaturing of their cultures, and, finally, in their conversion into ancillary components of imperial complexes modeled as slavistic-colonial areas of salvationistic-mercantile formation or of mercantile capitalism.

Humanity must have experienced similar crises while in transition between basic evolutionary stages, such as the passing from the level of tribal societies of hunters and gatherers to the horticultural villages during the Agricultural Revolution; and the evolution of the villages to the first rural craftsman states during the Urban Revolution. Some societies of these times experienced the impact of technological innovation directly as an acceleration. Others, by reflex, as an incorporation. In both cases strong tensions were generated. In the first case, however, these tensions took shape as a growth crisis that inflicted on the societies the disruptive effects of demographic explosion, structural renovation, division of men into rural and urban statuses, and stratification into castes or social classes. But they retained the requisites to renovate their societies, making them homogeneous even though inegalitarian. In the second case, that of incorporation, these tensions were enormously greater, condemning societies retarded in history to ethnic decomposition through having their populations enslaved or turned into purveyors of goods and services for the more advanced, without being able to overcome this subordination.

This condition can be changed only through long processes of ethnic reconstitution, bloody conflicts to win emancipation from the yoke of the parasitic ethnos, and the proscription of internal agents committed to the former system. In any case, however, the new ethnos will emerge traumatized because it bears within itself conflicting traditions that must be resolved, interests of social groups and strata that are contradictory, and external dependencies that in some fashion will have to be taken into account.

In the new configuration, following subjugation, certain cultural characteristics are notable. First is the presence of elements of the higher technology. These elements do not, however, make up a technological infrastructure of an autonomous economy, but are auxiliary implantations from the ruling center, dependent on it for their renovation and refinement. Second are the planned forms of social order, molded to perpetuate colonial rule and the privileges of the narrow native stratum of agents and associates of domination. Third are the syncretic bodies of beliefs and values surviving from the old patrimony or absorbed during the domination. These last operate, principally, as beguilements and justifications in defense of the colonial yoke.

Faced with this contradictory heritage, the backward peoples must master the new technological elements and augment autonomous use of them so that they may one day rise from a system supporting their inegalitarian complementary status to an economic system answering the needs of their own populations, a system of international exchange conditioned to the imperatives of their autonomy and growth. They must also remake the whole institutional system in order to eliminate from it the contingent factors of foreign domination and, as far as possible, the forms preserving minority interests opposed to technological renovation. For some peoples it is also necessary to intervene in language and in redefining values, continuing in the process of Europeanization if it has gone too far to turn back—as in the case of the Mexicans and the Andeans—or undertaking technological and institutional renovation based on the respective cultural patrimonies.

Only through a deliberate effort can this self-perpetuating chain of domination be broken. The economic crises of the system offer major opportunities to attempt that break because they weaken the dominating nucleus and compel it to exert more despotic forms of plundering with the aim of transferring the tensions afflicting it. On the other hand, when these crises coincide with the emergence of new civilizational processes, leading to the rise of other ruling centers, they run the risk that the break with one sphere of domination may only result in transference to another, as happened with the impact of the Industrial Revolution and the wars of independence that it unleashed in the Americas.

In the course of these struggles most of the neo-American societies experienced a new process of historical incorporation. Through it they only succeeded in ascending from the condition of slave colonies of the Iberian mother countries to become subject to the neocolonial exploitation of industrial imperialism. In this condition they have experienced much modernization of their sociopolitical institutions and their productive systems, but they have remained dependent on centers of foreign power.

A colonial area can emancipate itself by an evolutionary acceleration that enables it to develop autonomously as a new focus of expansion, as happened with the United States. Or it may become formally independent and, by way of historical incorporation, rise from colonial to neocolonial status. Simultaneously the internal structures undergo two opposite types of change: (1) what was a dominant colonialist class—and therefore a part of the over-all complex—turns into an autonomous national dominant class; (2) as occurred in the other American countries, the dominant strata scarcely changed function, but became attached to new spheres of external power for which they then played the role of agents of neocolonial exploitation. Correlatively, the attributes of the subaltern classes also change. In the first case, what was an external proletariat of another society, created and maintained to provide certain articles and services, may become a national proletariat desirous of ties with the outside world in a less spoliative interchange. In the second case, the status of external proletariat continues, and with it a type of neocolonial connection that limits the possibilities for autonomous development.

As we have seen, in all these cases strong tensions operate. In the former, however, these tensions are mollified because they are problems of a transitional phase or of a growth crisis. In the opposite case, in which innovations are introduced to serve alien needs, these tensions assume a traumatic form insurmountable by the simple unfolding of the process. They are no longer growth crises, but are deviations that instead of leading to independent and self-sustained development lead only to the formation of ancillary economic structures capable of experiencing only the reflexive effects of the progress attained elsewhere.

This is underdevelopment. It cannot be explained as a polarity of interactive contrasts, as the dualist theorists try to prove, nor as a crisis of transition between feudalism and capitalism that uniformly affects all the peoples immersed in that stage of evolution, as dogmatic Marxism would have it. Underdevelopment is really the result of processes of historical incorporation only explicable by foreign domination and by the constricting role of the internal dominant classes who deform the very process of renovation, transforming it from an evolutionary crisis into a paralyzing trauma.[15]

Developing within this framework, most American nations have evolved as incorporated structures: first, on being integrated into mercantile capitalism as colonial formations of various kinds; later, on being incorporated into industrial imperialism as neocolonial areas. In all the stages of this progression they were poorer and more backward than the societies that preyed on them, and also poorer and more backward than they are today.

Society as a whole, however, was passive in the face of this state of affairs. It explained poverty and wealth by mystic concepts capable of infusing an attitude of resignation into certain strata. This situation could not be altered owing to the community of interests of the dominant classes and the external agents of exploitation, both intent on maintaining slavery, the

[15] Marxist studies of industrial-imperialist expansion and its effects, under the name of "unequal and combined development" (V. I. Lenin, 1965; L. Trotsky, 1957; Paul Baran, 1965) focus on problems here studied as effects of processes of historical incorporation.

latifundias, and the monoculture on which, after all, they lived. Only in the inferior strata did the spirit of rebellion against the social order boil, especially among Negro slaves and exploited Indians who periodically revolted. These uprisings generally took on a utopian aspect, their sole standard of social reorganization being an idealization of the remote past in which neither masters nor slaves existed. Even when victorious they could not restructure their society along lines that would make it economically viable and progressive.

Neither was the system in force capable of evolving toward autonomy and progress. When living conditions in an area reached excessively low levels, desperate, mysticoreligious acts were hatched and promptly crushed in the name of order. The excess population engendered in each region was distributed among other areas, penetrating into unexplored territories, or regressed into a subsistence level economy, structured as a poverty culture. These escape valves diminished the pressures on the social structure, which remained incapable of involving the whole populace in the economic system or of incorporating a more highly productive technology. But the system was sufficiently powerful to assure its perpetuation, as well as adequately integrated to admit no doubts about the legitimacy of the prerogatives enjoyed by the dominant classes.

Only with the incubation of new civilizational processes that occasioned over-all reorganizations of society and that interested both certain sectors of the superior castes and broad bases in the subaltern classes did historical conditions arise for the breakdown of the traditional structure. Then these societies ceased to be merely backward, and became underdeveloped. This is what happened in the Bolivarian period and is the present state of affairs.

The situations of historical retardation differ, then, essentially from the state of underdevelopment by this ideological characteristic: the relative conformity and resignation to backwardness and poverty that is successfully instilled into broad strata of the population in contrast to the awareness that poverty and backwardness are curable ills.

This perception of the social system as a problem is probably an ideological subproduct of the forces acting on the productive system and demanding correlative changes in the social order. When human societies were emerging into the Mercantile Revolution there arose an equivalent critical awareness: the intellectual flourishing of the Renaissance. The same occurred with the Industrial Revolution, which engendered the libertarian ideology of the bourgeois revolutions and emancipation movements of the past century. In all these cases we encounter broadening of possible awareness of social reality as an ideological outgrowth of profound alterations in modes of adaptation and association (Marx, 1956).

Nowadays a new tide of intellectual creativity, a new broadening of possible awareness, is sweeping over the world of the disinherited peoples. It is seen in their refusal to conform to their place in the world system and in their awareness of their social structures as problems. This is occurring concomitantly with an extraordinary acceleration of the innovations made during the course of the Industrial Revolution that are causing the irruption of a new renovating impetus, the Thermonuclear Revolution, destined to affect human societies with even more far-reaching power. It is a question, probably, of a reiterative effect of the same structural processes that, altering the forms of production of human societies, compels institutional renovation and provides an opportunity for ideological inventiveness.

Seen from this angle, the opposition between a nominally scientific literature about social dynamics, produced mainly in prosperous countries and characterized by its despondency and conservatism, and the efforts made in the underdeveloped countries to create conceptual frameworks adequate to the analysis of their problems, are both products of conditions external to awareness. In the first case they are mystifications intended to replace antiquated studies of Latin America with a sophisticated but equally conformist discourse. In the second they are efforts to unmask this ideological tissue and are occasioned by a critical awareness deriving from the profound, though reflexive, restructurings experienced in recent decades by the underdeveloped societies.

Such awareness is naturally not confined to intellectual circles but reaches out over broad sectors—such as certain religious groups until recently engaged in defending the status quo—kindling them all with a progressive view of their societies and confident of the human future. In this state of affairs, chronic and silent misery is opposed by aspirations for better living conditions; independence of thought replaces resignation; and reformist or evolutionary ideals stand against conservatism.

The fundamental differences between the old situation and the new do not lie, therefore, in the wretchedness and backwardness present in both and looming even larger before than now. They are found in the new social dynamics, characterized by awareness that the over-all system is incapable of solving the problems generated by reflexive modernization and of satisfying the level of the population's aspirations. This difference separates backward societies from the underdeveloped. Some, sunken in their want, produce a bitter and reactionary body of writings; others, inspired by bold new drives, see the historical possibilities of breaking with the causes of their backwardness and are represented on the ideological plane by a revolutionary intellectuality.

The fundamental element in this creation of awareness is the concept of underdevelopment as the product of other nations' development, attained through the spoliation of others and as the effect of appropriation of the results of technological progress by privileged minorities in the underdeveloped society itself. It is, moreover, the comprehension that, as long as they remain in this framework, the dependent societies will experience only a reflexive, partial, and deformed modernization engendering demographic and social crises impossible to overcome within existing structures. It is, finally, the perception that this backwardness can only be overcome through revolution and that, in consequence, the crucial mission of social scientists in underdeveloped societies is to study the nature of social revolution and to search for ways to set it in motion.

PART I

Western Civilization and the New World

"One of the consequences of the expansion of the West was to place all the eggs of humanity in the same precious basket."

—ARNOLD J. TOYNBEE

1. The European Expansion

THE HISTORY OF man in these last centuries is principally the history of the expansion of Western Europe, which, constituting the nucleus of a new civilizational process, launched itself on all peoples in successive waves of violence, cupidity, and oppression. In this movement the whole world was shaken up and rearranged according to European designs and in conformity with European interests. Each people, even each human being, was affected and caught up in the European economic system or in the ideals of wealth, power, justice, or health inspired by it.

No previous civilizational process had showed itself so vigorous in its expansionist energy, so contradictory in its motivations, so dynamic in its capacity for renovation, so efficacious in its destructive action, or so fecund in engendering peoples and nationalities. The breadth and depth of its impact was so great that one may well ask, with regard to all that has happened in the world in these last centuries, what sprang from humankind in its diverse social and cultural configurations and what from this expansive, dominating, insatiable variant that is Western European civilization.

The European peoples that have taken the leading part in modern history as civilizing agents have been in the vanguard of two technological revolutions, the Mercantile and the Industrial, which placed them in the vanguard of sociocultural evolution as well. As such, they were pioneers in experiencing and formulating the social and ideological changes stemming from new stages of the evolution on which humanity was entering. Their discoveries, their beliefs, their ideals are for that very reason less the expressions of European creativity than necessary products of human evolution itself.

The European feudal world had been enjoying cumulative technological and social innovations for centuries; these finally restored the mercantile system and shaped the new civilization. The Renaissance was the dramatic period during which this new civilization was revealed to the European, who saw the world doubled with the discovery of the Americas, the conception of the universe redefined, the Roman Church split asunder, the Ottoman empire installed in Constantinople, and the bases of the Russian empire fixed.

A single generation during the 1500's knew such explorers as Columbus, Vasco da Gama, Cabral, and Vespucci; such conquistadores as Cortés, Pizarro, and Jiménez; such humanists as Thomas More, Erasmus of Rotterdam, Machiavelli, Luis Vives, and De Las Casas; such writers as Ariosto and Rabelais; such poets as Garcilaso de la Vega and Gil Vicente; such epic poets as Camoens; such mystics as Saint Teresa; such religiously possessed preachers and inquisitors as Savonarola and Torquemada; such reformers and restorers as Luther, Calvin, John Knox, Huldreich Zwingli, Münzer, and Saint Ignatius of Loyola; such artists of genius as Leonardo da Vinci, Raphael, Michelangelo, Botticelli, Titian, Correggio, Dürer, and Holbein; such astronomers and geographers as Copernicus and Behaim; such naturalists as Paracelsus and Vesalius; worldly popes; Florentine Maecenases; and the first modern financial enterprises.

An entire revolution took place in learning, religion, the arts, all stripped of theological shackles and turned toward the cult of classic antiquity. A new interest was initiated in empirical-inductive learning, in the observation of nature, in the understanding of society, in scientific experimentation, and in the mechanical arts.

In one part of Europe the search for religious *ascesis* and mystic ecstasy had given way to parallel movements for religious reform, secularization of customs, scientific experimentation, rationalistic speculation, and philosophic inquiry, which in the following centuries would profoundly modify the modes of doing, living, and thinking of all. In another part of Europe religious fervor was rekindled, firing peoples previously apart from Christianity into zealous guardians of the faith and extemporaneous crusaders for the expansion of a missionary and conquering Catholicism. Such were the Iberian and the Russian peoples, through whose ardor Europe burst forth, creating the bases of the first world civilization.

The Iberians, as peninsular peoples, launched themselves into overseas expansion, discovering, conquering, and subjugating new worlds, causing the division of them between Portugal and Spain to be sanctified by the pope. The Russians, as continental peoples, entered into expansion over the Eurasian subcontinent. Setting out from their original base on the Dnieper, they launched themselves into the west, over the Slavic and Balkan Europe dominated by the Ottomans; into the east and north, over the Eurasian world of the Tartar-Mongol forays, extending their frontiers as far as China and also appropriating a slice of America—Alaska—at the end of their territory.

Iberians and Russians had in common the fundamental challenge of reconquest of their own territory, which was dominated by foreign peoples of other religions. The kindling of the mission of reconquest, achieved by appeal to religious values, ripened them for external expansion by making them attack—once unification had been accomplished—all the minority ethnic groups in their territory and, beyond its borders, undertake the domination of other peoples, neighboring or distant.

The interpretations of this historical movement of crucial import for human destiny, as elaborated by central and northern Europeans, suffer two types of deformation: (1) being converted into a link in the chain of historical antecedents that led England and Holland, and later France, to become structured as capitalistic-mercantile formations; (2) being formulated as epics justifying the English, Dutch, and French imperialist domination of the world.

Within this framework the progress of the European peoples is seen as an internal rupture with feudalism, laboriously effected through centuries of technological and cultural creativity of the Italians, Dutch, and English, which finally matured with the Industrial Revolution. The role of the Iberian peoples in the extra-European context is seen as passive, and consisting, principally, in providing an area of plunder that made possible the accumulation of capital.

This approach does not explain why the first renovating impulses occurred precisely in the areas marginal to those that later figured as the capitalistic-mercantile powers of Europe and imperialistic industrial powers. Nor does it explain how societies immersed in feudalism could cement the political and economic unity necessary to undertake European expansion over the world. If feudalism signifies political departure from former imperial structures, and economic separation from former mercantile systems, such as the deterioration of the slavistic methods of production, the concept is not applicable to sixteenth-century Iberia or Russia. Both are characterized by precisely opposite attributes: political and bureaucratic centralism, the implantation of vast mercantile systems, and the initiation of vigorous movements of conquest and external colonization.

All these facts lead us to suppose that before the maturation of capitalistic-mercantile formations another civilizational process—the salvationistic-mercantile—took place, the first to afford a break with European feudalism and the emergence of a new sociocultural formation. Its technological foundation, provided by the Mercantile Revolution, was based on oceanic navigation, firearms, forged iron, and other factors that put an end to the war cavalry that had been dominant for a millennium, and permitted the beginning of a new cycle of maritime mercantile expansion.

It is true that, simultaneously, some Italian ports were vitalized as mercantile nuclei (no longer mere entrepôts of Byzantium), and some Dutch and English ports became active as poles of a European mercantile network. Even so, the expansion of these nuclei, and their maturing as cells of a capitalist formation, was made viable only by the previous expansion of Iberia and the fantastic sum of resources in the form of plundered goods and enslaved populations in America, Africa, and Asia.

This transcendental event is generally referred to in historical theories as a mere contributing factor to the civilizational process that started and developed out of the implantation of the European mercantile system. Supporters of this thesis assume that before the Industrial Revolution an impulse of autonomous technological creativity had occurred in Europe, but forget that the decisive innovations in the techniques of navigation, production, and war, on which the Iberian expansion was to be based, came from the extra-European world through the Arabs. Another consequence of this Eurocentrism is a conception of feudalism so ambiguous that it becomes applicable to any historical situation of backwardness with respect to capitalism.

A more satisfactory explanation of these same facts can be given starting with the declaration that what we are discussing here is a technological revolution earlier than the Industrial Revolution, namely, the Mercantile Revolution, founded principally on ocean navigation and firearms, which set in motion two civilizational processes crystallized as dual sociocultural formations: (1) the salvationistic mercantile and slavistic colonial; (2) the capitalistic mercantile and the trading colonial. These dual formations were produced by the same renovating forces that, acting on different contexts, permitted some peoples to rise from feudalism to a superior stage (salvationistic mercantile and capitalistic mercantile) through an evolutionary acceleration and subjected other peoples to external domination (slavistic colonial and trading colonial) through historical incorporation.

The competition and conflict between these two formations and between their components would come to favor the more progressive formation, which ended by being able to undertake the Industrial Revolution and thus outstrip the other, finally subordinating all peoples to its domination. In this new phase the capitalistic mercantile nuclei evolved toward imperialistic industrial formations; the salvationistic mercantile formations, like their colonial contexts, were modernized partially and reflexively through historical incorporation and were converted into areas of neocolonial exploitation.[1]

The Salvationistic Cycle

The European expansion of the fifteenth and sixteenth centuries started from two marginal bases, both subjected to foreign domination, Islamic in the case of the Iberian peoples, and Tartar-Mongol in the case of the Russians. The Iberians and the Russians, though contributing to the spread of the principal technological innovations of the Mercantile Revolution, nearly all connected with seamanship and explosive weapons, ended up as mercantile, despotic, and salvationistic sociocultural formations. They became salvationistic Mercantile empires modeled on the Islamic and Ottoman empires, equally hallucinated by the epic, greedy, and mystic dimensions of the goal they proposed. Thus it is that the protagonists of the first rupture with European feudalism, the transition to mercantile capitalism, did not structure themselves in accordance with the sociocultural formation that would result therefrom. This new stage in human evolution, mercantile capitalism, was to crystallize in some of the cities that had been restoring the European mercantile system for two centuries. For this very reason, when the Mercantile Revolution—which had given precedence to Iberia and to Russia—followed a new evolutionary path, the Industrial Revolution, Iberia and Russia found themselves once again left behind. This evolutionary step would place other Europeans, until then marginal to the great currents of civilization—first the English and the Dutch, then the French and the Germans—in the center of human history as the foci from which a new civilizational process—industrial capitalism—would radiate.

Some key figures of the two salvationistic mercantile empires suggest the values that motivated and inspired them, after centuries of subjugation, to break the Moorish or the Mongol yoke and become the forerunners of the

[1] I amply discuss this theme in *The Civilizational Process*.

new civilization. The Iberian world may be represented here, in the first place, by the young king Dom Sebastian, who, inspired by religious fervor, staked the whole Lusitanian nobility in a battle against the Moors at Alcazarquivir. With his death Portugal fell under the dominion of Spain and sank into despondency. The impression caused by this tragedy and the disappearance of the young king's body has made itself felt down to our own time in Portugal and Brazil in the form of Messianic (Sebastianist) movements in which fanaticized multitudes pray, flagellate themselves, and sacrifice innocents in the hope that by so doing they can bring about the mythical return of Dom Sebastian, who, they believe, must have been "put under a spell." Another figure was Henry the Navigator, a mixture of Renaissance sage (who contributed much to oceanic navigation) and mystic-fanatic who, for the love of God, wore an abrasive sash of silicon and who founded one of the most widely spread heresies of Portuguese Christianity—the preaching of the coming of the era of the divine Holy Spirit, which would, after the time of the Father and the Son, allow man to create the Christian paradise on earth.

Another characteristic figure was Isabel the Catholic. Brought up among country people and kept close to her mad mother, she made herself the queen of unified Spain, conquering the last Moslem bastion and expelling the Moors in the same year in which America was discovered. Isabel took as her most zealous task the elimination of the remaining Moorish petty kingdoms, for the Moors had impregnated the peninsular populations through more than seven centuries of Islamic domination; she sponsored the Holy Inquisition; she piously aspired to be the protector of the subjugated heathen of the New World, but to save their souls from eternal damnation and to enrich the Spanish conquistadors she condemned them to the most hypocritical form of slavery, that of the *encomiendas.**

In the Russian world the outstanding personalities are Ivan III and Ivan IV (the Terrible). The former created the consolidated Muscovite state, bringing the principalities of Kiev, Jaroslav, Rostov, Novgorod and other territories under his rule and establishing the bases of empire. In 1480 he freed Muscovy from allegiance to the Tatars of the Golden Horde (the Kipchak khanate), smashing the foundations of the Mongol expansion into Europe. Ivan IV had himself crowned Czar of all the Russias and initiated a process of mercantile colonization and of catechesis that was to incorporate, progressively, all Eurasia into the Russian empire and religion. By terrorism he bent the boyar feudal nobility to his will, and, finally, he instituted the Muscovite patriarchy in deference to the Russian aspiration to make Moscow a third Rome, ruler of Christianity.

* The *encomienda* was an estate of land, with the Indians living on it, granted by the crown to Spanish conquistadors and colonists for their services to Spain.

Simultaneously with these developments of marginal areas, north and central Europe continued efforts to break with feudalism by restoration of an international mercantile system. This process, initiated in the Italian, Flemish and English city-ports, which had also become centers of manufacturing, led to a new sociocultural formation, congruently mercantile capitalistic, therefore well qualified to undertake the new leap in techno-cultural evolution—the Industrial Revolution—based on mastery of new sources of energy and their application to mechanical contrivances of mass production.

The Europe that first confronted indigenous America was represented by Spain and Portugal, rigidly stratified agrarian-craftsman national societies. Their ruling caste was a priestly hierarchy rather than a hereditary nobility, inasmuch as the Church was the major proprietor of lands, slaves, and serfs and some clergy were soldier-priests. The numerically overin-flated nobility was poor, even indigent, but for that very reason extremely zealous not to be mistaken for the common people, whose lot was produc-tive work. The function of the nobility was war against the Moors, decided by the pope and the king and led by the clergy; or, siding with the Moors, against Christian-clerical expansion. Besides its major religious motivation this holy war yielded temporal fruits also, especially to the clergy by vir-tue of the prudent arrangement that all land taken from the infidels would become the property of the Church.

In the cities a stratum of craftsmen—principally Moorish—and merchants—mainly Jews—equivalent to the commercial bourgeoisie of growing influence in other nations, such as England, Germany, Holland, and France, was kept under strict control: religious control, because in a large measure it consisted of Moslems, Jews, and New Christians; social control, because the nobility was jealous of its own privileges and, above all, greedy for the appropriation of goods and lands; state control, because the crown derived its income, in great part, from the taxes on the mer-chants and the craftsmen. The primacy of the clergy and the systematic persecution of the Islamic and Jewish minorities contributed decisively to the lack of a bourgeoisie capable of vying for a place and a salient influ-ence in the state.

The population of the whole Iberian peninsula at the time of the In-dustrial Revolution has been estimated as 10 million, 1.5 million of whom were Portuguese. The English population was 5 million; the Dutch 1 mil-lion; the French 20 million; and the Germans, 12 million. Why was it pre-cisely this marginal area—Iberia—which was neither the most advanced economically nor the most populous, that undertook Western Europe's overseas expansion? There were many factors, among them the crucial fact that the Iberians had become heirs of the Islamic technology, more ad-vanced than the current European technology, especially that pertaining to oceanic navigation. Another important fact is that the Iberians had been engaged for nearly eight centuries, from 718 to 1492, in a struggle for emancipation from Saracen domination, a struggle that mobilized all the moral energies of the people. These two circumstances made the Iberians the promoters of conquest and the fathers of the Mercantile Revolution, though they did not figure in its fullest development. During the Mercantile Revolution they remained salvationistic mercantile empires and failed to develop into mercantile capitalistic formations. Even at the close of the most brilliant cycle of their history they were not integrated into the Industrial Revolution. On the contrary, they regressed, losing their slavistic colonial and mercantile empire to the new capitalistic industrialist imperialisms. Thus, both Portugal and Spain entered the world economy as dependent areas of neocolonial conformation.

It is as a salvationistic mercantile formation with the energies of an incipiently mercantile imperialism and the mobilizing forces of an expansionist missionary religion that Iberia undertook the discovery, conquest, and colonization of the New World, projecting over the whole world her national war against Moslem domination and her Holy War. In the same capacity she launched herself, throughout the sixteenth century, into European wars to restore Catholic Christianity against the Reformation; to internal convulsions slaughtering Jews and Moors, later institutionalized in the Inquisition; to the devastation of American high cultures and to the enslavement of their peoples, to whom would be added millions of African Negroes to constitute the greatest labor force known to the world until then. Absorbed later by the task of organizing the American colonies, and having become more prudent in the face of the capacity for reprisal of the emerging nations of capitalistic and Protestant Europe, Iberia moderated her evangelizing zeal in Europe and gradually restricted her salvationistic and mercantile hegemony to her overseas possessions and her purifying wrath to her own population.

Iberia thus reestablished with Europe her mercantile ties, which would continue to grow in a system of barter in which the more advanced inevitably fed on the more retarded. In this economic context Holland, England, and France, despite being disinherited in the Tordesillas division * of the New World, were already emerging as a mercantile capitalistic formation. Spain and Portugal were retarded salvationistic mercantile empires with economies founded on slavistic colonialism.

---

* In 1494 at Tordesillas, near Valladolid, Spain and Portugal signed a treaty dividing the non-Christian world between them, the demarcation line being 370 leagues west of the Cape Verde Islands and passing through both poles. The scantiness of geographic knowledge of the time contributed to Portugal's subsequent claim to what is now Brazil.

In this framework the two archaic nations became collectors of goods destined to enrich an ostentatious, lordly, and mystic nobility or to pay for the world-power projects of their Austrian kings rather than for productivity investment. Thus the gold and silver extracted in enormous quantities from America became only mediums of exchange to pay for the mother country's consumption of goods and imported manufactures and for the maintenance of armies. Spain and Portugal consequently became mere suppliers of precious metals, spices, and, later, sugar and other tropical products for the merchants of all Europe. And they did not create their own system for distribution of their colonial products in European markets, thus losing even the profits of commercialization.

In consequence this flow of goods plundered from or produced by enormous populations, whose consumption level was drastically lowered by enslavement, paid for the enrichment and particularly the industrialization of other areas. Add to this regressive tendency the fact that the Iberians had destroyed their system of handicrafted production, with the expulsion of hundreds of thousands of Moors, and likewise their mercantile system, with the expulsion of the Jews. Their very salvationistic mercantile form thrust them into an increasing impoverishment that was to be further accelerated by the costs of a nonproductive sector of gigantic proportions, made up principally of clergy. Portugal and Spain were submerged in humiliating indebtedness at the hands of European bankers and forced to every kind of lucrative expedient, such as the sale of land titles both in the peninsula and in the Americas.

During the reign of Philip II, who even more than Isabel incarnates Iberian salvationistic fanaticism, the Spanish clergy attained the fantastic proportion of twenty-five per cent of the adult population. According to Oliveira Martins (1951, p. 306): "a census taken during the reign of Philip II (1570) recorded 312,000 priests, 200,000 clerics of minor orders and 400,000 friars." At the beginning of the eighteenth century another census includes in the same parasitic stratum nearly 723,000 nobles, 277,000 servants of nobles, 70,000 bureaucrats and 2 million beggars. During the same period, in the region of Seville alone, the number of silk and wool looms had dropped from 16,000 to 400 and sheep, from 7 to 2 million. The Iberian population had declined from 10 to 8 million inhabitants. (Oliveira Martins, 1951, pp. 306–307).

On the cultural plane decadence was proportionate. The Salamanca student body had dropped from 14,000 to 7,000 by the end of the sixteenth century; the Inquisition under Torquemada seized and burned thousands of copies of the few books existing in the peninsula; censorship and the Index Librorum Prohibitorum were established, and terror was the rule. In eighteen years Torquemada brought 100,000 persons to trial; he burned in

effigy between 6,000 and 7,000, and in flesh and blood nearly 9,000. With
the Inquisition, the fanaticism and intolerance of salvationistic Iberia became instruments for terrorism, and vengeance and torture were institutional procedures in the name of the Holy War.

This Iberian Europe, its entire productive sector retarded, economically
obsolete in the face of the rise of European capitalism, and religiously salvationistic and fanatical, directed the cultural transfiguration of Latin
America, condemning it to backwardness. It is probable, however, that without the salvationism that motivated it, the Iberian expansion, and the Russian, would not have had the assimilative potential to coexist with and to
impose on the most disparate peoples their own cultural and religious
stamp.

Capitalistic Europe

The other Europe, enriched with the products of the Iberians' spoliation
and matured as a capitalistic mercantile formation, undertook the leap to a
new stage in the sociocultural evolution of man: the Industrial Revolution.
This was a natural and necessary stage, which would have started in one of
the feudal contexts. The circumstance of its having burgeoned in Europe
gave the white man his primacy in world domination, which convinced him
that he was intrinsically superior to other races and cultures and that he
was destined to tame, plunder, and civilize the peoples of the earth.

Equipped with an increasingly prodigious technology, the Europeans
broke the equilibrium and the stagnation in which they, as well as former
high civilizations, had plunged (the Arab-Moslem societies were paralyzed
by the Turkish-Ottoman expansion, and the Oriental ones immersed in
feudalism). On these peoples, and also on the Mexican and Inca civilizations and the tribal peoples of the entire world, the Europeans launched
themselves as the vanguard of a new technocultural revolution. Under its
impact the world was transformed, just as 10,000 years ago the Agricultural Revolution had transformed the life of peoples, multiplying the
human contingent, and, 5,000 years later, the Urban Revolution had split
some societies into rural and city populations, stratifying them in social
classes and creating the foundations for the first imperial expansions.

On the basis of new forms of action, new institutions, and new ideas,
the European reconstructed the world to supply him with goods and services. Plundering the wealth hoarded by all peoples, conscripting for slave
and servile work hundreds of millions of men, Europe was able to accumulate the capital necessary for the Industrial Revolution, transfiguring

her own societies, renovating and enriching her cities, adorning them with powers and glories that would induce the white European to see himself as the elect of creation.

The practice of using non-European peoples as suppliers of raw materials and consumers of manufactures was implemented over the centuries by all kinds of oppression and terrorism. The old surviving civilizations, some decadent, others alive, but all capable of ordering the life of their own societies, were gradually dominated, degraded, and conscripted into the world-wide mercantile system ruled by the Europeans. New peoples were constituted by the removal of millions of men from their original homes to distant lands where they could be more useful and productive from the European point of view. Thousands of tribal groups, resistant to servitude or hostile to the exploitation of their territories, were decimated, as much by slaughter as by the diseases transmitted by the white man, or else by the disillusionment into which they fell with the demoralization of the beliefs and values that gave meaning to life.

In their expansion the Europeans progressively imposed as compulsory values their notions of truth, justice and beauty. These were as powerful in the persuasive force of their universality as were the coercive methods used for their diffusion. At the same time the European languages (all part of the same language family) spread through the world, and came to be spoken by a creater number of persons than any previously existing group of languages. The various cults stemming from the same religion became ecumenical. European science and the technologies deriving from it were likewise spread throughout the world. Europe's artistic patrimony, with the multiplicity of styles with which it is expressed, became the universal canon of beauty. Her familiar political and juridical institutions, molded and remolded according to the same premises, became the guidelines of social life for the majority of peoples.

The following were European arms for this world exploit: a more advanced naval, military, and productive technology; a new body of social and economic institutions, which had multiplied the capacity for expansion of markets until it integrated the entire world in one mercantile system; an ever-renewed thirst for knowledge, individual self-affirmation that motivated thousands of adventurers, awakening them to the joy of earthly life, making them a bold corps of entrepreneurs; and, finally, an old corpus of traditions and beliefs, redefined to serve a society less preoccupied with the risks of eternal damnation than with the expansion of the kingdom of God, which was also the expansion of European domination.

To all these forces should be added, as one of the decisive weapons of conquest, a conglomerate of viruses, bacilli, and germs to which the Europeans, Asiatics, and Africans were adapted, but that fell on the indigenes of America and Oceania like plagues, rendering them defenseless against aggression and subjugation. It is estimated that shortly after their first encounter with white men, half and sometimes three-quarters of the aboriginal population of America, Australia, and the islands of Oceania died, victims of pulmonary diseases, venereal infections, various types of smallpox and more than a dozen other diseases unknown to them.

In the course of her world expansion Europe renewed herself continually, enriching her patrimony with productive techniques, with institutions of domination, and radically altering her own image. She was always the agent and the principal recipient of the civilizational processes she initiated and governed. The nations first transformed by the Mercantile Revolution and later by the Industrial Revolution enormously strengthened their coercive power over their neighbors and over the extra-European world. At the same time, however, they were compelled to reorganize their own societies. At a certain point in the process the Europeans themselves became human cattle to be exported, not to perform the dominating role formerly prescribed for the white man, but as simple manual labor, sometimes cheaper than and frequently as wretched as the slave labor. Thus the march of the Industrial Revolution across Europe, in its advance from people to people, is also a succession of uprootings of human masses and their exportation to all parts of the earth.

European ideals and beliefs were transmuted through the centuries. But to each generation they provide truths and faiths capable of stirring them to the most fanatic acts. And they always hold to a functional tie with the imperatives of perpetuation of the European system of domination. Thus, the missionary and catechistical zeal, while it lasts, flagellates the impious peoples of the entire world, compelling them to the Christian fold. Simultaneously, it economically and politically dominates them. When religious fervor enters its decline it turns on the European himself, to eradicate by fire and sword the heresies that multiply, dividing Christendom into groups more opposed to one another than to heretical peoples. Even then it retains its functionality. It frees capitalistic entrepreneurs from now-obsolete bonds and sanctifies the acquisitive fury, while the subordinate strata become resigned to new forms of social stratification. And it contributes with the Counter-Reformation and salvationism to preserving the traditional domination.

With the unleashing of the civilizational process propelled by the Industrial Revolution, old ideals of liberty, equality, and justice, so often expressed by the earlier civilizations and as often forgotten and abandoned as unviable utopias, were reborn in Europe as new and fresh projects, more attractive and apparently more possible than at any other time. Such is the bourgeois-liberal formulation of republican ideals, aimed wholly at the affirmation of the individual's freedom before the state, the church, and society.

This new body of ideas was formulated congruently as a system expressed in mercantile institutions (for example, the incorporated or joint-stock company and the banking technique) and in political institutions (for example, liberal democracy), capable of convincing and moving both Europeans and the dominant strata of the peoples involved in their net of economic exploitation, presenting it as the new frame within which prosperity and freedom would at last be attained. In the heat of these new liberal and laic ideologies was fused the reformist and salvationistic religious fervor that had made the European conquistador a trader-crusader, which give way to two new fervors—the entrepreneurial and the revolutionary-liberal. The foundation of both is the same with respect to the imperatives of trade and domination.

In the political field, monarchical absolutism was followed by the ideal of the republican and democratic state, which was to be concretized for the first time in an extra-European context with the American Revolution. To slavery, repeated historically on a gigantic scale in the American colonies, is contraposed the ideals of human dignity and equality, also very functional here, anticipating the social renovation imposed by the Industrial Revolution, which, by harnessing new and wondrous forms of energy, had made the slave and the serf unnecessary, opening the way to a libertarian conception of man.

Through all these ideological variations what endured, until the end of the nineteenth century, was the ruling position of Europe and the intra-European disputes for world domination. The precedence of the Iberian discoverers was put in check from the first decades after the Treaty of Tordesillas. Dutch, French, and English appropriated slices of a world that seemed condemned to the usufruct of the boldest Europeans. Subsequently, others entered the division of spoils, progressively restricting the Portuguese and Spanish possessions, which at last could maintain themselves in the overseas territories only through participation with the European peoples whose industrialization was most advanced. The English, Dutch, French, and German peoples would successively occupy the center of the European focus of world domination.

The Ibero-American peoples, molded in the course of the Mercantile Revolution, did not experience an evolutionary acceleration but a mere historical incorporation that made them ascend one degree of the sociocultural evolution at the cost of the loss of their original ethnic profiles and their involvement as external proletariats of the Iberian salvationistic mercantile empire. Confronted with the new cycle of renovation set in motion by the Industrial Revolution, these peoples again experienced a process of historical incorporation by means of which they freed themselves from one form of domination only to fall into another, always as external proletariats that exist not for themselves but for the prosperity of other peoples.

The Polycentric Civilization

At first, the Church justified the right of the Iberians to enjoy the fruits of their discoveries. Later, in the face of the polemic stirred up by Fray Bartolomé de las Casas over the natural rights of the Indians, a whole colonial doctrine was elaborated based on the European's adherence to three imperatives: (1) his mission to carry the gospel to the heathen, whose salvation depended on Christian piety; (2) the right of the Europeans, as children of God, to take their share of the common goods of the world created by divine providence but ignored or scorned by the savage peoples; and (3) their charitable duty, as more advanced peoples, to lead the more retarded ones to civilization. The best expression of this ideology is by the Spanish theologian Francisco de Vitoria who until recently remained the principal theorist of colonialism.

Subsequently, colonialism was justified as an imperative of European prosperity and of the very preservation of the internal social order of the colonialist nations. In this vein the Frenchman Ernest Renan wrote, in the middle of the past century:

A nation that does not colonialize is irremediably condemned to socialism, or to war between rich and poor. The conquest of a country of inferior race by a superior race which establishes itself in it to govern it is not at all strange. England practices this type of colonialism in India, with great profit to India, to humanity in general, and to herself. Just as conquests between equal races ought to be criticized, the regeneration of inferior or debased races by superior races is situated, on the contrary, in the providential order of humanity. . . . *Regere imperio populos* is our vocation (quoted by R. Aron, 1962, p. 145).

And the Englishman Cecil Rhodes, in the last quarter of the past century, said:

I am perfectly convinced that my idea represents the solution of the social problem, namely: to save the forty million inhabitants of the United Kingdom from a tragic civil war, we colonial politicians must dominate new territories in order to locate the surplus population in them, to find new markets in which to place the products of our factories and our mines. The empire, I have always said, is a question of stomach. If you do not want civil war, you must become imperialists (quoted by G. Behyaut, 1963, p. 5).

All this enlightenment did not, however, prevent the rebellion of the subjugated peoples and the liquidation of the bases of European supremacy. When that loss was already visible, another European sounded the alarm. It was Oswald Spengler who wrote, at the time of World War I:

Nevertheless, since the end of the century (XIX) the blind will to power has begun to commit decisive errors. Instead of keeping technical knowledge secret, the greatest treasure possessed by the "white" peoples, it has been proudly offered to the whole world in all the upper schools, orally or in writing, and the admiration of Hindus and Japanese has been accepted with proud satisfaction. The well-known "dispersion of industry" was begun as a consequence of the thought that it was a good idea to bring production closer to the consumer in order to obtain greater profits. Instead of exporting merchandise exclusively, secrets, procedures, methods, engineers and organizers began to be exported. There were even inventors who emigrated. . . . All men of color penetrated the secret of our power, understood it and profited by it. The irreplaceable privileges of the white peoples have been dilapidated, wasted and betrayed. The adversaries have succeeded in catching up with their models and perhaps surpass them with their mixture of colored races and with their supermature intelligence, proper to the very ancient civilizations (Spengler, 1932, pp. 135–136).

As a matter of fact, with the development of the civilizational process the two foundations on which the European sustained his hegemony and his wealth were broken up: his domination and exploitation of the colonial peoples and his monopoly of modern industrial technology. New nationalities emerged in the extra-European world and became not only autonomous in the political field but also autarchic and competitive through the development of their own industrial economies. At this stage, the European unicentric civilization depolarized into a polycentric system whose nuclei of power were divided over several continents. Around each nucleus, even in Europe, blatant contrasts of wealth and poverty among nations remained, according to the degree to which they incorporated modern industrial technology in their productive processes.

Every industrialized country had become a center for exploitation of backward countries, near or far, and was compelled to intensify and consolidate its domination over them, because spoliation—which had been the fundamental mechanism of its enrichment—had become a requisite of its prosperity. The new leader formations, constituted on the basis of the old capitalistic model, found themselves limited by two other imperatives: the tensions caused by the narrowness of the national frameworks, too narrow to contain economic competition and generating conflict situations that exploded in periodic wars, and the internal struggles of the subordinate classes, the victims of exploitation by economies governed in terms of unrestrained profit-seeking.

In Europe herself, the diagnosis and prognosis of the factors stifling her own civilization were formulated. This has occurred since the middle of the past century with the emergence of the social sciences and the socialist doctrines expressed, respectively, by Comte, Marx, and a whole series of thinkers who had been studying the problem. Their solutions consisted, essentially, in theories of social evolution that not only explained the past and the present of human societies but anticipated their future developments, presenting new models of economic, social, and political organization that could free man from war, want, ignorance, and oppression. Armed with these socialist theories, new political movements were dedicated to revolutionary struggles for the total reordering of societies.

Incapable of imposing a rational new order on her own societies, Europe saw the most violent social, economic, and cultural changes sweep over her peoples, aggravating old national disputes and intensifying class tensions to critical levels. Not able to shape a supranational political order and institute a more egalitarian socioeconomic regime, she tore herself to pieces in wars in which the countries least favored by worldly fortune sought to break down the system to force a redistribution of wealth. Finally, she fell into complete political and cultural deterioration, pressured by her masses—especially by the workers—to reform the bases of her social and political organization.

At this juncture a victorious revolution installed the first socialistically structured society. However, this socialist revolution was not in Western Europe but in Russia, just as a century earlier the bourgeois-liberal revolution was elsewhere, in North America. Thus a new sprout budded forth from the old European civilization, one that provoked a violent polarization of forces. Throughout the West a wave of hysterical despair pervaded the dominant strata, under the menace of proscription, and also the middle classes fearful of seeing their skimpy privileges annulled by a social reorganization that would accord special privileges to the more disinherited strata, particularly the workers.

Simultaneously the new and miraculously powerful technology began generating ideological, institutional, and political deformations that degraded all the values and ideals of Western civilization itself. The principal one of them was Nazism, created and fomented to face the threat of social revolution in Italy and Germany. Protected later by European statesmen as the castigator of socialist Russia, it became the most fearsome sociocultural regression ever known, requiring World War II to destroy it.

The war reduced the polycentric system that had been developing; only two dominant powers emerged in peacetime—the capitalist sprout planted in the United States and the socialist sprout that had flowered in the U.S.S.R. and spread over other areas. The conflict between the two new foci was shortly to transform the one-world dream of the Roosevelt idealists of the war effort into a real world divided between two opposing and overarmed powers.

On one hand, the zones of imperialist domination appeared merely as residues of the old system; on the other hand, the new revolutionary dynamism attracted new areas to an autonomous position of neutrality or frank hostility to the old order. Actually, the two spheres were contraposed by the differences of their historical roles: neocolonial imperialism, insistently repeating the liberal discourse that had become obsolete and unviable for itself, became committed to preservation of the status quo at any cost; socialist ideology, presenting itself as founded on the highest humanistic traditions, advocated a complete reorganization of societies.

Placed between the capitalist and the socialist spheres, the subjugated peoples are subjected to the greatest tensions. Some continue as the object of spoliation. Others are the natural area for expansion of the socialist ideology and of the struggle to win strategic alliances and positions. Confronted by the two great nations, the many small nations constitute a third world, characterized by the misery of its peoples and by its discontent with its allotted role in the world system. Gradually, this third world is becoming aware of its specific interests and of the nature of its battle for the attainment of economic and social progress. The three worlds ideologically pose as an antirevolutionary coalition, a revolutionary orthodoxy, and a nonconformist rebellion. The last two spheres seem compelled to become associated, less through any identity of their ideologies than by the frontal opposition of interests between centric and peripheral nations in the imperialist spectrum.

In this tripartite world, convulsed by arms and economic exploitation, three ideological complexes burgeon as bodies of beliefs and values offered to the peoples, especially to the new generations, to define the roles they are to assume in their own society and before humanity. In the capitalist world, mainly in the most advanced nations, the fear of social revolution commits all to the crusade for the maintenance of the status quo, condemning their peoples, especially their youth, to anomie and despondency because of incapacity to fix for them generous goals for the rational guidance of human destiny. The price of this fear and this adherence to obsolete forms of economic and social organization is historical sterility and moral obscurantism. The intellectuality of this new causeless and passionless West, surfeited with revolutionary ideologies, tends to look more like cynicism in the face of any conviction, like disillusionment in the face of hope, and especially like reactionarism in the face of progress.

For the peoples subjugated in history this reactionary tide signifies the option between backwardness or fighting for the right to direct their own destinies. In their societies two opposing ideologies confront each other: that of the dominant strata, superconservative because content with the world as it is and, above all, fearful of change; and that of the more enlightened sectors for whom everything is open to question. This attitude of inquiry into political ideas, social institutions, and knowledge is a permanent effort to conjecture what can contribute to change the world and society and what is committed to maintain them. The peoples' opposition to the international plot to keep them backward makes them nationalists. Their struggle against the internal agents of underdevelopment makes them antioligarchists.

In the socialist world the commitment to design and guide social transformation in order to construct free and prosperous societies has permitted the creation of a new moral order capable of infusing in its peoples the idea of the emancipatory destiny of man. The form in which this new moral order was implanted, however, surrounded by external hostility and internally hardened by doctrinaire orthodoxy, transformed it into a sectarian communion as oppressive as any fanatic cult. If it was possible in this ethic dimension to instill in multitudes a profound sentiment of human solidarity and to demand of every intellectual, artist, or ideologue a high moral responsibility, the risk was also greater that society would allow itself to be dominated by the despotism of new guardians of truth, justice, and beauty.

Dogmatic Marxism, straitjacketed by partisan sectarianism, loses a great part of its capacity to interpret social life, to understand the very experience undergone by socialist societies, and to guide the renovating forces to social revolution. The price of the uniformity thus gained was—here also —unanimously resigned to official truths for all fields of knowledge and the parching of the very creativity of the Marxist intellectual movement.

When it ceased being a method of interpreting history and of prefigurating the human future, and began to guide the renovation of Russian society, Marxism was reduced to a doctrine justifying the use of power, susceptible of contradicting its philosophical foundations and the humanistic loyalties that it professed. Revolutionary socialism, having to build itself under the conditioning of a menacing siege, succeeded in victoriously confronting the international plot to destroy it, but it turned out to be ideologically too narrow and in constant danger of turning toward despotism.

To the impact of the revelation of the Stalin era would be added, a little later, the Sino-Soviet dissidence as a factor in disarming the spirits of the socialist militants the world over. This misunderstanding, which had commenced promisingly as an ideological polemic over peaceful coexistence, the ways to world revolution, and criticisms of Stalinist errors, sharpened to the point of severe hostility.

The debates over the deformations that had taken place in the implantation of socialism and the bitterness of the confrontation between Chinese and Soviets had, in spite of everything, the positive effect of demystifying the socialist movements. The men who had, in this century, improved their understanding of the biological, cultural, and psychological nature of man, enabling them to judge their imperatives more rationally, were now better able to safeguard themselves against ideological Utopias. It is to be supposed that, matured with these lessons, those engaged in social renovation are seeking greater objectivity in the study of society, greater breadth of views, and greater tolerance in the formulation of solutions for human problems. Only along this road will the broad, solid basis for a profound fraternal understanding among the revolutionary militants be attained.

Throughout the world the fruits of this new open, inquiring, and critical attitude are beginning to appear. Liberated by the revision of Stalinism and demystified by the Sino-Soviet polemic, communist movements are resuming—although sluggishly—their capacity for self-criticism. Today they are trying to return to their humanistic and philosophical roots in order to reintegrate their revolutionary actions into the corpus of forgotten ethical obligations, so as to fulfill their destiny as forces of man's emancipation. Lamentably, they are still encountering enormous obstacles in resuming their theoretic attitudes, especially those of Marx, and in questioning them and criticizing the spurious subproducts to which they have given rise.

This self-critical effort arises also in other ideological currents, principally in the Christian socialist movements that seek to mobilize their churches for the social responsibilities they had always refused, being solely committed to safeguarding tradition and social order. Thus, the ground is laid for a fecund dialogue between the diverse humanistic currents. The social scientists and the intellectuals of the whole world (separated from the revolutionary movements by their bitterness toward sectarianism or by their commitment to conservatism) gain a new dimension and a renewed dignity in this reencounter. They commit themselves increasingly to widening the knowledge of man and society, not as the act of fruition or as an academic mission but with the aim of improving the human and aiding him to realize his most generous potentialities. The absenteeist and cynical attitudes, as well as the sectarian and fanatical, are unmasked as alliances with backwardness and obscurantism.

The rupture with the sectarianism of the leftist movements and the acceptance of revolutionary obligations through other currents are occasioning a deepening of all these approximations from which it is expected will result a wealth of economic and social experiences and of forms of political action of the greatest importance in the search for new paths and new solutions to the crucial problems of the advanced nations and, particularly, for overcoming the backwardness in which three fourths of humanity lives. It is the beginning of the ideological thaw in which the reactionary alliance is unmasked, once more freeing the potentially progressive forces of the world, principally of the third world, to rationally reconstruct society.

The Emerging Civilization

The Europe that began its expansion on the hypothesis that the earth had the form of a uninavigable globe converted widely divergent peoples and cultures into a single humanity. Only in terms of reference to this supreme adventure and misadventure of man, the Western and Christian European expansion, does the world of our time, the victim and fruit of that civilizational process, become intelligible.

Having lost world power, Western civilization survives through its fundamental contributions to knowledge and to humanistic ideals. The dispute for the domination of the world or of areas of it is tending to disappear, strangled by the will to autonomy of all peoples. New orders of nationalities will succeed each other throughout time, all of them, however, moved by the old humanistic banners that tomorrow will be no more Occidental and Christian than Moslem, American, Slavic, or Chinese. In this process, Western European civilization has ended by losing its autonomous character as conciliator of peoples for action within certain guidelines. It has assumed the form of tradition. Thus civilizations die when they cease to constitute nuclei of cultural diffusion and become mere currents of ideas and aspirations.

Western civilization is not giving way to another particularist civilization but to a civilization of human amplitude, which was already contained in the renovating impulse of the Industrial Revolution. The European nations, incapable of unifying themselves in a harmonious political system, remain divided, but they are already thrashing about in the framework of the new civilization. Between them pass the frontiers of the socialist and the capitalist orbits, combining on one side or the other the old world powers, more in consequence of their geographical positions than by acts of will. Europe, the western peninsula of Asia projected over Africa, is thus reduced to her real proportions and each of her old power centers reverts to her own island or province frontiers.

The European's own awareness of the widening of the world and the reduction of Europe to her proper dimensions has been expressed by Sartre in these words:

> It was so natural to be French. It was the simplest and most economical means of being universal. It was others who must explain by what ill luck or guilt they were not completely men. Now France is prostrate and we look on her as on a great broken machine. And we think: is it perchance a matter of some accident of terrain, some accident of history? We continue to be Frenchmen but the thing is no longer natural. An accident has happened to make us comprehend that we were accidental (quoted by L. Zea, 1957, p. 115).

Succeeding many civilizations, breaking the promises of as many more, Europe has opened paths for the creation of this new human, ecumenically based civilization. The rise of the Asiatic, African, and Latin American peoples to the autonomous guidance of their destiny is already in the framework of the new civilization. As they set themselves up against the domination and the spoliation of which they have been victims for centuries, it is no longer Western Europe that they oppose fundamentally, but the forms of imperialistic oppression inaugurated by her, nowadays in the hands of another nucleus of domination. And, however paradoxical it may seem, the struggle for the most generous ideals of liberty, fraternity, independence, and progress formulated in Europe is now going on, fundamentally, against the orbit of power that has denominated Western European civilization.

To the world galvanized by militarized powers that threaten the very survival of humanity in their madness, the backward peoples—armed with the authority of victims of the historical process—are responding with their intention to survive in order to re-create the world if necessary, but, essentially, with their challenge to both sides to participate in overcoming want, healing the wounds left by colonial spoliation, and eliminating the colonialist domination and oppression that still remain.

Probably no one among the disinherited peoples places very much confidence in this promise of harmonious collaboration for peace and human happiness. The defects of the old Western civilization, from which they all sprang, are too deep, their inhuman nature too evident, their cupidity for the vested interests of the old order too powerful to inspire confidence. In the face of these flaws it is well for the underdeveloped peoples to seek within themselves the energy necessary to refuse to continue temporizing with a system that represents for them only misery and suffering.

This confidence in the future, optimism, and faith in progress is characteristic of the peoples who are emerging to autonomy. Above all, they have a vivid memory of the tragedy of past colonial domination and of present imperialistic exploitation, which fortifies them to continue the battle for freedom and for development, for self-reconstruction as authentic societies and cultures. But these peoples also count on the increasing economic unviability of the imperialistic system of spoliation, which can be perpetuated only by wars much more onerous than all the interests they seek to preserve. Further, they count on the fact that, once peace is imposed, only the development of new systems of interchange will make the industrial gears mesh, to confront the imperatives of the new technological revolution and to restore to the youth of the developed countries a sense of dignity.

To attain this objective it is incumbent on the extra-European peoples —both the new peoples, who are subproducts of the European expansion, and the old, who bear witness to former civilizations debased by it—to rethink the civilizational process from the point of view of disinherited and oppressed peoples in order to rearrange the world according to the traditions of lost humanism and to redefine, once more, the course of humanity. This task is exclusively theirs, just as—as Hegel said—to the slave belongs the dignity of being the combatant for freedom against his enslaver, degraded as the soldier of oppression.

With humanity denuded of the old instrumental beliefs and of the new utopias, only man remains, his life and his happiness the ultimate and irreducible objective. This imposes a priority for the reduction of backwardness. The battle for this objective will warm the hearts of our generation and of the next and will teach them to march toward the morrow. Then they will congregate to carry forward, in a world at last pacified and integrated, the construction of the new civilization now announced: the human civilization that will make of earth the niche of men, at last conciliated and freed from want, fear, oppression, and racism.

2. The Cultural Transfiguration

"Each generation must write its own world history. And in what period has that been more necessary than in the present?"

—W. GOETHE

The Genuine and the Spurious

In the process of European expansion millions of men originally differentiated in language and culture, each looking at the world with his own view and governing his life by his peculiar body of customs and values, were drafted into a single economic system and uniform mode of living. The multiple faces of humanity were drastically impoverished, not integrated in a new, more advanced standard, but divested of the authority of their way of life and plunged into spurious forms of culture. Subjected to the same processes of deculturation and drafted into identical systems of production under stereotyped forms of domination, all the affected peoples became culturally impoverished, falling into incompressible conditions of wretchedness and dehumanization, which came to be the common denominator of the extra-European man.

Nevertheless, simultaneously a new basic human, common to all, gradually gained vigor, elevating and generalizing himself. The divergent aspirations of the multiplicity of differentiated peoples—each lost in an effort

more aesthetic than efficacious to shape the human according to its ideals
—joined together to incorporate all humanity in a single corpus of ideas
shared in its essential characteristics by all peoples. One and the same
view of the world, the same technology, the same methods of organizing
society, and, above all, the same essential goals of abundance, leisure, freedom, education fulfilled the basic requisite for construction of a human
civilization, no longer only European, nor even Western, nor yet merely
Christian.

Every human contingent caught up in the over-all system became simultaneously more uniform with the others and more divergent from the European model. Within the new uniformity ethnic variants much less differentiated than the earlier ones, but sufficiently marked to remain individual,
were prominent. Each, as it became capable of insight and of proposing
suitable plans for reorganizing society, progressively became capable also
of looking at the European with a fresh view. At that moment they began
to mature as national ethnic groups, breaking with the remote past and
with their subjugation to the Europeans.

Since then the colonial context has turned on the former ruling center to
inquire, not into the veracity of its truths nor into the justice of its ideals
nor into the perfection of its models of beauty, but into the capacity of the
over-all social, political, and economic system to realize for all men these
aspirations of prosperity, knowledge, justice, and beauty. The professed
but never executed designs were laid bare. The conviction spread that the
proclaimed object was associated with the profits being extracted, that
the beauty and the truth being worshipped were lures to servile engagement, destined to create and maintain a world divided between wealth and
misery.

This reductive process can be exemplified by analyzing what happened to
the American peoples during their four centuries of association with
agents of European civilization. The American peoples saw their societies
made over from the foundations, their ethnic constitution altered, and their
cultures debased by the loss of autonomy in the control of the transformations to which they were subjected. They were thus transmuted from a
multiplicity of autonomous peoples with genuine traditions into a few spurious societies of alienated cultures, explicable in the uniformity of their
new mode of being only by the dominating action exercised on them by an
external force and will.

Both the survivors of the old American civilizations and the new societies generated as subproducts of the tropical trading posts resulted from
European projects that sought to plunder accumulated riches or to exploit
new veins of precious minerals or to produce sugar or tobacco, but, in all

cases, to accumulate money. It was only incidentally, and nearly always unexpected and undesired by promoters of the colonial undertaking, that the constitution of new societies resulted from their effort. Only in the case of the colonies of settlers was there any intention of creating a new human nucleus, a decision sufficiently explicit and implemented to condition the spontaneous undertaking to the exigencies of that objective. Even in these cases, however, the new formations grew spurious like the rest, because they too resulted from alien projects and designs.

It is only through long-enduring covert effort in the least explicit spheres of life that these colonized societies have been reconstituting themselves as peoples. On these recondite levels their self-construction was practiced, as ethnic entities became differentiated from their parent populations, freed from the conditions imposed by colonial degradation, and as nationalities decided to gain control of their own destiny. This effort was being made not only far from the areas subject to control of the ruling authority but also against its operation, which was zealously dedicated to maintaining and strengthening the external bond and subjugation.

In spite of all these drawbacks the weaving of the new authentic sociocultural configuration is always continuing, as a natural and necessary reaction, within the spurious. Every step forward demands immense efforts, because everything is combining to keep it unauthentic. On the economic side, dependence on foreign trade, which coordinates the greater part of activities, is assigning nearly the entire labor force to export production. In the social orbit, the stratification is crowned by its ruling stratum, which, being at once oligarchic cupola of the new society and part of the dominant class of the colonial system, acts to maintain dependence on the metropolis, the mother country. On the ideological plane, a vast apparatus of regulating and indoctrinating institutions is being carved out, coercing all according to the religious, philosophical, and political values justifying European colonialism and ethnocultural alienation. These systems of ideological coercion become stronger through introjecting into the people, and into the elite of the subjugated society, a view of the world and of themselves serving to maintain European domination. It is this incorporation of the awareness of "the other" within oneself that determined the spurious character of the nascent cultures, impregnated in all their dimensions with exogenous values.

Besides the techniques for exploitation of gold or of sugar production, besides the installation of railroads or telegraphs, Europe exported to the peoples covered by her network of domination her whole cargo of concepts, preconceptions, and idiosyncrasies about herself and the world and even the colonial peoples themselves. The latter, not only impoverished by the plundering of their wealth and of the products of their work under the colonial regime, were also degraded when they assumed as a self-image the European view, which described them as racially inferior because they were Black, indigenous, or mestizo and condemned to backwardness as a fatality stemming from their innate laziness, lack of ambition, tendency to lasciviousness, and so on.

Lacking control on the political and economic plane, by virtue of colonial statute, these peoples likewise lacked autonomy in the control of their cultural creativity. Any possibility of digesting and integrating into their own cultural context the innovations imposed on them was frustrated, therefore, irremediably breaking down integration between the sphere of awareness and the world of reality. In these circumstances, as they fed on undigested alien ideas not corresponding to their own experience but to the European efforts to justify rapine and to base colonial domination on moral grounds, their dependence and their alienation expanded.

Even the most enlightened strata among extra-European peoples learned to view themselves and their fellow men as a subhumanity destined to a subaltern role. Only the immigrant colonies, which carried the European racial marks through the world and settled in the climates and regions most like those of the country of origin, were not alienated by these forms of moral domination. On the contrary, they actually took pride, like the Europeans, in their whiteness, their climate, their religion, their language, also explaining by these characteristics the successes finally achieved.

For the cultures built on the old American civilizations and for those emerged from diverse environments and composed of brown or Black people, these forms of alienation reinforced the backwardness from which only now is there a beginning of emancipation. In these cases the nascent culture, as far as the national ethos is concerned, was shaped by (1) the compulsory deculturation of the tribal ethnocentric concepts of the Indian and the Negro and, (2) the construction of a new conception of themselves as intrinsically inferior and therefore incapable of progress.

This spurious self-image, elaborated in the effort to find their place in the world, to explain their own experience, and to attribute to themselves a destiny, is a patchwork quilt of bits taken from their old traditions and from European beliefs, as best they could perceive them from their viewpoint as slaves or dependents.

On the plane of the national ethos this ideology explains backwardness and poverty in terms of the inclemency of the tropical climate, the inferiority of the dark races, the degradation of half-breed peoples. In the religious sphere it shapes syncretist cults in which African and native beliefs are mingled with Christianity, resulting in a variant further from the European Christian currents than any of its most combatted heresies. These cults were, nevertheless, fully satisfactory for consoling man for the misery of his earthly fate and, moreover, for maintaining the system, allegorically justifying white-European domination and inducing the multitudes to a passive and resigned attitude.

On the societal plane the new ethos induces conformist attitudes toward social stratification, which explain the nobility of the whites and the subordination of the dark, or the wealth of the rich and the poverty of the poor, as natural and necessary. In the field of family organization it contraposes two family standards: (1) the dominant class, invested with all the sacraments of legitimacy and continuity, and (2) the mass strata, degraded in successive matings to anarchic matriarchal forms. In this spurious spiritual universe the very values that give meaning to life, motivating each individual to struggle for ends prescribed as socially desirable, are elaborated as justifications of rapine and idleness on the part of the oligarchic strata and as prescriptions of humility and toil for the poor.

On the racial plane the colonialist ethos is a justification of racial hierarchization, introjecting a mystified consciousness of their subjugation into the Indian, the Negro, and the mestizo. By it the destiny of the subordinate strata is explained through its racial characteristics and not because of the exploitation of which they are victims. In this manner the colonialist not only rules but dignifies himself at the same time he subjugates the Negro, the Indian, and their mixed breeds and debases their ethnic self-images. Besides being depersonalized—because converted into mere material requisite for the existence of the dominating stratum—the subaltern strata are alienated in the depths of their consciousness by the association of "dark" with dirtiness and "white" with cleanliness. Even the white contingents that fall into poverty, confusing themselves with other strata by their mode of living, capitalize on the "nobility" of their color. The Negro and the Indian who gained their freedom, ascending to the status of workers, continue to bear within themselves this alienated consciousness, which operates insidiously, making it impossible for them to perceive the real character of the social relations that make them inferior. While this alienating ethos prevails, the Indian, the Negro, and the various mixed breeds cannot evade these postures, which compel them to behave socially in accordance with expectations that describe them as necessarily crude and inferior and to wish to "whiten" themselves, whether through the resigned conduct of one who knows his place in society or by selective crossing with Caucasoids in order to produce offspring of "cleaner blood."

For the peoples caught in the nets of European expansion these conceptions shaped the burden of the spiritual heritage of Western and Christian civilization. Acting like distorting lenses, they made it impossible for the nascent cultures to create an authentic image of the world and of themselves, and this blinded them to the most palpable realities.

Despite their evident adaptation to the American climate, the colonial elites longed for the European climate, displaying their detestation of the "stifling" heat. Notwithstanding their evident predilection for the dark-skinned woman, they longed for the whiteness of the European female, in response to the ideal of feminine beauty that had been inculcated in them.

The intellectuals of the colonial peoples, immersed in such alienation, could operate only with these concepts and idiosyncrasies to explain the backwardness of their peoples as compared with the white-European capacity for progress. They got so entangled in weaving the web of these causes of misery and ignorance that they never perceived the greatest, most significant evidence set before their eyes, the European spoliation to which they had always been yoked, itself more explicative of their way of life and their destiny than any of the supposed defects that occupied them so much.

The break with this alienation by the dark peoples of America was initiated only after centuries of pioneer efforts to unmask the intrigue. Only in our own times is the crossbred national human accepted as such; critically appreciative of his own formative process, and having regained a cultural authenticity that is commencing to make of the national ethos, in all spheres, a reflection of the real image and concrete experiences of each people and a motivator of its effort to confront the backwardness and want to which they have been condemned for centuries.

The new ethos of the extra-European peoples, founded on their own bodies of values, is gradually restoring to them the sense of their own dignity and, at the same time, the capacity to integrate all their populations into cohesive, genuine national societies. Compared with the ethos of some archaic societies that collapsed before the attack of small bands, the new formations are different in their bold self-affirmation and their capacity for defense and aggression. To perceive that difference it is enough to compare the episodes of the Spanish sixteenth-century conquest, or those of the English, Dutch, and French appropriations in Africa and Asia three centuries later, with the struggles for American peoples' independence, the struggles for freedom of the Algerians, the Congolese, the Angolans, the Mau-Mau, and especially the Vietnamese of our days, who are facing the armies of world powers and defeating them.

The emergence of that new ethos is the most conclusive symptom of the closing of the European civilizational cycle. Precisely as has happened with Roman civilization and with so many others that operated for centuries as centers of expansion over wide contexts docile to their aggression, Western civilization is seeing the peoples of these very contexts—by dint of their ethnic maturation and the adoption of techniques and values from the expansionist civilization—turn on them. This revolution is not destructive to the former ruling center, but libertarian rebellions of subjugated peoples resuming their ethnic image, proud of it, and defining their own roles in history.

In 1819 Bolivar inquired into the role of the Latin American peoples in the dawning new civilization, comparing the Hispano-American world with the European in these terms:

> When she freed herself from the Spanish monarchy, America was like the Roman Empire when that enormous mass fell dispersed in the ancient world. Each dismembering in that time formed an independent nation, in accordance with its situation or its interests. With the difference, however, that those members re-established once again their first associations. We do not even retain the vestige of what we formerly were; we are not Europeans, we are not indigenes; we are a species midway between the aboriginals and the Spaniards. Americans by birth, Europeans by right, we find ourselves in the conflict of disputing with the natives the titles of possession, and against the opposition of the invaders the right to support ourselves in the country where we were born; thus our case is all the more extraordinary and complicated (Bolivar's Angostura speech, February 15, 1819).

This inquiry well depicts the perplexity of the neo-American who, becoming the active subject of historical action, asks: What are we among the world's peoples, we who are neither Europe nor the West nor the original America?

Like the peoples of extra-European context, the Europeans emerging from the Roman domination were no longer what they had been. Centuries of occupation and acculturation had transformed them culturally, ethnically, and linguistically. France is a Roman cultural enterprise, as are the Iberian peoples, all having resulted from the subjugation of tribal peoples to the consul, the merchant, and the soldier of Rome, but also from the later barbarian invasions. The Germanic and Slavic tribes most resistant to Romanization were equally impelled by the Romans' civilizational process and changed themselves during that process.

The coercive power of European civilization over its area of expansion in the Americas, however, was much superior to that of the Romans. In all Europe non-Latin languages and cultures survived, and even within Latinized areas ethnic pockets subsist to attest the viability of resistance to Romanization. In the Americas, excepting the high indigenous civilizations and the island of isolation that Paraguay became—and these Europe could not completely assimilate—all was molded into the European linguistic-cultural pattern. Thus, the Spanish, the Portuguese, and the English spoken in the Americas are more homogeneous and undifferentiated than the speech of the Iberian peninsula and of the British Isles. This linguistic-cultural-ethnic uniformity can only be explained as the result of a much more intensive and continued civilizational process, capable of assimilating and fusing together the most disparate contingents.

The post-Roman macroethnos of the Iberian peoples, which had already endured the centuries-long domination of Moors and Blacks, becoming African both racially and culturally, faced a new ordeal in America. Confronted with millions of natives and other millions of Blacks, it was transfigured anew, becoming darker and more acculturated, enriching its biological and cultural patrimony, but imposing its language and its fundamental cultural image on the new ethnic entities to which it would give birth. This was the achievement of some 200,000 Europeans who came to the Americas during the sixteenth century and conquered millions of Indians and Negroes, fusing them into a new cultural complex that draws its uniformity principally from the Iberian cement with which it was amalgamated.

Today's Latin Americans are the offshoot of 2,000 years of Latinity, melted together with Mongol and Negroid populations, tempered with the heritage of many cultural patrimonies, and crystallized under the pressure of slavery and the Iberian salvationistic expansion. That is, they are a culturally old civilization thrust on new ethnic entities. The old patrimony is expressed socially in their worst aspects: the consular and alienated posture of the dominant classes, the caudillo habits of command and taste for personal power, the profound social discrimination between rich and poor, which separates men more than the color of their skins, the lordly customs, such as enjoyment of leisure, the cult of courtesy between patricians, scorn of work, the conformity and resignation of the poor with their poverty. The new is expressed in the assertive energy emerging from the oppressed strata, at last awakened to the unsanctified, eradicable nature of the misery in which they have always lived; in the increasingly enlightened and proud assumption of the crossbreed ethnic image; in the equating of the causes of backwardness and want, and in rebellion against the existing order.

The impact between these two conceptions of life and society is Latin American social revolution on the march—a revolution that will one day restore to the dark-skinned peoples of America the creative impetus lost centuries ago when their Iberian intruders were slow in integrating themselves into industrial civilization, thus entering into decadence, a revolution that will signify the entrance of the Latin Americans into the world as peoples who have a specific contribution to make to civilization. This contribution will be based, essentially, on their ethnic configuration and on its potentialities, which will make them more human because they have incorporated more of man's racial and cultural facets; more generous, because they remain open to all influences and have been inspired in a panracial integrationist ideology; more progressive, because their future depends on the development of knowledge and technology; more optimistic, because, emerging from exploitation and penury, they know that tomorrow will be better than today; freer because they do not base their national projects for progress on the exploitation of other peoples.

National Ethnic Typology

The extra-European peoples of the modern world can be classified in four great historicocultural configurations. Each of them comprises highly differentiated populations sufficiently homogeneous in their basic characteristics and in the developmental problems facing them to be legitimately treated as different categories. They are the "Witness Peoples," the "New Peoples," the "Transplanted Peoples," and the "Emerging Peoples."

The Witness Peoples are the modern representatives of old original civilizations conquered in the European expansion. The New Peoples are represented by the American peoples formed in these last centuries as a subproduct of the European expansion through the fusion and acculturation of indigenous, Black, and European populations. The Transplanted Peoples are the implanted European populations with their original ethnic profile, language, and culture preserved. Emerging Peoples are the new nations of Africa and Asia whose populations ascend from a tribal level or from the status of mere colonial trading posts to that of national ethnic groups.

These categories are founded on two premises: (1) the peoples composing them are what they are today in consequence of the European mercantile expansion and the reorganization of the world by industrially based civilization; (2) these peoples, formerly racially, socially, and culturally different, have a hybrid cultural inventory. They offer sufficient biological uniformity to warrant treatment as distinct configurations explicative of their mode of being.

These configurations must not be taken as independent sociocultural entities, because they lack a minimum of integration to give them internal order and permit them to act as autonomous units; nor should they be confused with econosocial formations,[1] because they do not represent neces-

---

[1] Concerning econosocial or sociocultural formations see D. Ribeiro, *The Civilizational Process.*

sary stages in the evolutionary process, but only conditions under which it operates. The positively acting entities are the particular societies and cultures composing them, and particularly the national states into which they are divided. These constitute the operative units, both for economic interaction and for social and political order, and also the real national ethnic frames within which the destiny of the peoples is fulfilled.

The sociocultural formations are categories of another type—such as mercantile capitalism and slavistic colonialism—equally meaningful but different from those here described.

It must be emphasized, even so, that the proposed historicocultural configurations constitute congruent categories of peoples, based on the parallelism of their historical process of national ethnic formation and on the uniformity of their social characteristics and the problems facing them. In terms of these broad configurations of peoples—rather than of the nationalities, or the respective racial compositions, or climatic, religious, and other differentiating factors—each extra-European people of the modern world can be explained. How did it develop in its current form? Why has it undergone such differentiated historical processes of socioeconomic development? What factors in each case have acted to accelerate or retard its integration into the life style of modern industrial societies?

The typology examined below aspires to be a classification of historical categories resulting from the civilizational processes that have been loosed on all the peoples of the earth in recent centuries. As such, it seeks to be significant and instrumental in the study of the process that has led these peoples, first, from the status of autonomous societies and cultures to that of subaltern components of economic systems of world domination activated by spurious cultures and, now, to emancipation movements tending to restore their autonomy as new ethnic entities integrated into the current civilizational process.

The first of these configurations, which we have designated as "Witness Peoples," is made up of the survivors of high autonomous civilizations that suffered the impact of European expansion. They are modern survivals of the traumatizing action of that expansion and of their efforts at ethnic reconstitution as modern national societies. Reintegrated in their independence, they did not regain their former autonomy, because they had been transformed not only by the joining of their traditions to the European but by the effort to adapt to the conditions they had to face as subordinate integrants of world-wide economic systems and also by the direct and reflexive impacts of the Mercantile and Industrial Revolutions.

Rather than peoples retarded in history, these are the plundered peoples of history. Originally possessing enormous accumulated wealth (which could be utilized, now, to defray the costs of their integration into the industrial systems of production), they saw their treasures sacked by the European. This sacking continued with the centuries-long spoliation of the work products of their peoples. Nearly all are enmeshed in the world imperialistic system, which fixes a place and a predetermined role for them, limiting their possibilities for autonomous development. Centuries of subjugation or of direct or indirect domination have deformed them, pauperizing their peoples and traumatizing their whole cultural life.

They face the basic problem of making the two cultural traditions to which they have become heirs—traditions not simply diverse but in many aspects mutually opposed—an integral part of themselves: (1) the European technology and ideology, whose incorporation into the old cultural patrimony was processed at the cost of redefinition of their whole way of life and of the alienation of their view of themselves and of the world; (2) their former cultural store, which, despite being drastically reduced and traumatized, preserved language, customs, forms of social organization, bodies of beliefs, and values deeply rooted in vast strata of the population, beside a heritage of common knowledge and of unique artistic styles that are now flourishing in an age of national self-assertion. Simultaneously attracted by the two traditions but incapable of fusing them meaningfully for the whole population, even today they bear within themselves the conflict between the original culture and the European civilization. Some of them have had their modernization guided by the European powers dominating them; others have seen themselves compelled to promote it designedly or to intensify it as a requisite to survival and progress in the face of the pillaging fury to which they were subjected, and also as a requisite to overcoming the obstacles represented by technological backwardness and the archaism of their social structures.

In this bloc of Witness Peoples are included India, China, Japan, Korea, Indochina, the Islamic countries, and a few others. In the Americas they are represented by Mexico, Guatemala, and the peoples of the Andean highlands, the two former being survivors of the Aztec and Maya civilizations, the latter of the Inca.

Among the Witness Peoples only Japan and, more recently and partially, China, have succeeded in incorporating modern industrial technology into their respective economies and in restructuring their societies on new foundations. All the rest are peoples divided into a more Europeanized dominant caste, sometimes biologically crossbred and culturally integrated in the modern life styles, opposed to great masses—particularly rural—marginalized by their adherence to archaic ways of life resistant to modernization.

The two nuclei of Witness Peoples of the Americas, as peoples conquered and subjugated, suffered a process of Europeanizing compulsion much more violent than their complete ethnic transmutation turned out to be. Their present national ethnic profiles are not the original ones. They display neo-Hispanic profiles thrust on the descendants of the former society crossbred with Europeans and Negroes. Though the other extra-European peoples of high culture, despite the domination they underwent, barely colored their original ethnocultural figure with European influences, in the Americas it is the neo-European ethnos that was colored by the old cultural traditions, extracting distinctive characteristics from them.

Compared with the other American ethnic groups, the Witness Peoples are distinguished as much by the presence of the values of the old tradition that they have preserved and that bestow on them the image they present, as by their much differentiated process of ethnic reconstitution. On the Middle American and Andean societies the Spanish conquistadors established themselves from the first as an aristocracy that, succeeding the old dominant class, immediately placed the intermediary strata and the whole servile mass at its service. They could thus live in more showy palaces than the richest of the old Spanish nobility, erect sumptuous temples such as Spain had never possessed, and, particularly, set up a compulsory system of Europeanization that, starting with the elimination of the native dominant class and its learned caste, ended by installing an enormous assimilative and repressive instrumentation that ran the gamut from mass catechism to the creation of universities and the maintenance of huge military contingents ready to crush any attempt at rebellion.

Besides the tasks of socioeconomic development common to all nations retarded in history, the contemporary representatives of the Witness Peoples are faced with specific cultural problems arising from the challenge to incorporate their marginal populations into the new national and cultural being now emerging, deflecting them from the archaic traditions least compatible with the life style of modern industrial societies. Some of their basic human contingents constitute ethnic units differing in their cultural and linguistic diversity and in being conscious of their ethnic differences from the national ethnos. Notwithstanding the centuries of oppression, both colonial and national, in the course of which every form of compulsion was used to assimilate them, these contingents remained faithful to their ethnic identity, preserving their own modes of conduct and their own conception of the world. This centuries-long resistance tells us that in all probability these contingents will remain differentiated, in the manner of the ethnic groups encysted in the majority of the present European nationalities. In the future they will probably figure as different modes of participation in the national life, like that of the Jews, or of the gypsies, in so many nations, or as disparate ethnolinguistic pockets equivalent to those surviving in Spain, in Great Britain, in France, in Czechoslovakia, or in Yugoslavia. To reach this form of integration, however, they will need a minimum of autonomy, which has always been denied them, the suppression of the compulsory mechanism designed to force their incorporation as undifferentiated contingents of the national society, and the Witness Peoples' acceptance of their character as multiethnic entities.

The second historicocultural configuration is constituted by the New Peoples, emerging from the conjunction, deculturation, and amalgamation of African, European, and indigenous ethnic stocks. They are here designated as New Peoples because of their fundamental characteristic of being *speciei novae,* ethnic entities distinct from their formative origins, and because they represent anticipations of what, probably, the human groups of a remote future, more and more crossbred and acculturated and thus racially and culturally uniformized, will be.

The New Peoples have been constituted by the confluence of contingents profoundly disparate in their racial, cultural, and linguistic characteristics, as a subproduct of European colonial projects. Bringing together Negroes, whites, and Indians to open great plantations of tropical products or for mining operations, with the sole aim of supplying European markets and making profits, the colonizing nations ended by molding peoples profoundly different from themselves and from all the other formative peoples. Placed together in the same communities, these Negroes, whites, and Indians, though performing different roles, began mingling and culturally fusing together. Thus, beside the white, the head of the enterprise (by dint of the conditions of domination), the Negro engaged in it as slave, and the Indian, also enslaved or treated as a mere obstacle to eliminate, a crossbred population gradually arose, amalgamating these peoples in varied proportions. In that encounter of peoples lingua franca emerged as an indispensable instrument of communication and syncretic cultures were molded, made of pieces taken from the different patrimonies that adjusted best to their conditions of life.

Not many decades after the colonial enterprises were begun, the new population, born and integrated in the plantations and mines, was no longer European or African or native, but a new ethnic body. Incorporating new contingents, these mixed populations progressively shaped the New Peoples, which shortly became aware of their specificity and finally composed new cultural configurations, ethnic entities aspiring to national autonomy.

The New Peoples, like the Witness Peoples, emerged within a heirarchy characterized by the enormous social distance separating the lordly class of plantation owners, exploiters of minerals, merchants, colonial officials, and clergy, from the slave mass engaged in production. Their dominant class, however, did not become a foreign aristocracy ruling the process of Europeanization, precisely because it had not found a former noble, literate caste to replace and supplant. They were rough entrepreneurs, masters of their lands and their slaves, forced to live with their businesses and run them personally with the aid of a small intermediate class of technicians, foremen, and priests. Where the enterprise prospered greatly, as in the sugar and mining zones of Brazil and the Antilles, they could afford the luxury of lordly residences, and they had to broaden the intermediate class both at the mills and in the coastal towns, busied in trade with the outside world. These towns became cities, expressing their economic opulence principally in their churches, with less ostentation than the aristocracy of the Witness Peoples but with much more brilliance and "civilization" than the Transplanted Peoples.

As the dominant class they were also rather the managers of an economic undertaking than the acme of a genuine society. Only very slowly did they become capable of assuming the role of native leadership, and when they did so it was to impose on the entire society, transformed into nationality, an oligarchic order founded on the monopoly of land, which would assure the preservation of their sovereign role and the conscription of the people as a labor force, slave or free, in the service of their privileges.

None of the peoples of this bloc constitutes a multiethnic nationality. In all cases their formative process was violent enough to compel the fusion of the original stocks into new homogeneous units. Only Chile, because of her peculiar formation, retains in the Araucanian contingent of nearly 200,000 Indians a microethnos differentiated from the national, historically claiming the right to be itself, at least as a differentiated mode of participation in the national society. The Chileans and the Paraguayans also differ from the other New Peoples by the principally indigenous ancestry of their population and by the absence of both the Negro slave element and the plantation system, which played so outstanding a part in the formation of the Brazilians, the Antilleans, the Colombians, and the Venezuelans. For this reason they constitute, together with the River Plate peoples, a variant of the New Peoples. The predominantly Indio-Spanish Witness Peoples differ from them because these former original native populations had not attained a level of cultural development comparable to that of the Mexicans or the Incas.

In their finished form these peoples are the result of, first, the selection of racial and cultural qualities from the formative populations that best adapted to the conditions imposed on them; second, their effort to adapt to the environment; and, third, the compulsive force of the socioeconomic system into which they were introduced. The decisive role in their formation was played by slavery, which, operating as a detribalizing force, broke these new peoples away from ancestral traditions to turn them into the subproletariat of the nascent society. In this sense the New Peoples are the product of the reductive deculturation of their indigenous African tribal patrimonies, of the selective acculturation of these patrimonies, and of their own creativity in the face of the new environment.

Separated from their American, African, and European cultural beginnings, deviated from their cultural traditions, today they represent disengaged, available peoples, condemned to integrate into industrial civilization as people who have a future only in the future of man. That is, their progressive integration into the civilizational process gave them birth, not as slavistic colonial areas of mercantile capitalism, nor as neocolonial dependents of industrial imperialism, but as autonomous formations, whether capitalist or socialist, capacitated to incorporate the technology of modern civilization into their societies and to attain for their whole population the level of education and consumption of the more advanced peoples.

The third historicocultural configuration, the Transplanted Peoples, embraces the modern nations created by the migration of European populations to new spaces in the world where they sought to reconstitute forms of life essentially identical to those of their origins. Each structured itself according to models of economic and social life of the nation from which it came.

At first the Transplanted Peoples were recruited from among the dissident European groups, especially the religious; later they were incremented with all kinds of maladjusted persons condemned to exile by the colonizing nations; and finally, their numbers were swelled by the huge migrations of Europeans uprooted by the Industrial Revolution from their rural and urban communities who came to try their luck in the new lands. The majority of these came to America as farm workers enticed by contracts committing them to years of servitude. But a large part of them later succeeded in coming as free farmers and independent craftsmen. Their basic characteristics are: cultural homogeneity, which they maintained from the start through the common origin of their population or else assimilated with new immigrants; the more egalitarian character of their societies, founded on democratic institutions of self-government and on the easier access of the farmhand to ownership of land; and their modernity as regards synchronization with the ways of life and the aspirations of the preindustrial capitalistic societies from which they had been separated.

The bloc of Transplanted Peoples is composed of Australia and New Zealand, and in a certain measure the neo-European pockets of Israel, the

Union of South Africa, and Rhodesia. In the Americas they are represented by the United States, Canada, Uruguay, and Argentina. In the first cases we encounter nations resulting from colonization projects in territories where tribal populations were decimated or confined to reservations so that a new society could be installed. In the case of the River Plate countries we find an extremely peculiar Creole elite—entirely alienated and hostile to its own ethnos as a New People—which adopts as a national project the replacement of its own people by white and dark Europeans, considered to be endowed with a more decisive vocation for progress. Argentina and Uruguay are thus the result of a process of ecological succession deliberately initiated by national oligarchies, and by that process a New People configuration is transformed into a Transplanted People. By this process the Ladino and gaucho population, originating in the crossbreeding of Iberian settlers with the natives, was crushed and replaced, as the basic contingent of the nation, by an avalanche of European immigrants.

Contrary to what occurred with the Witness Peoples and the New Peoples, which from their earliest years took shape as complex societies, stratified in profoundly differentiated classes ranging from a rich oligarchy of European conquistadors to the servile mass of Indians or Negroes, the majority of the Transplanted Peoples emerged as immigrant colonies, dedicated to farming, craftsmanship, and small business. They all faced long periods of privation while establishing their bases on the unpopulated land, seeking to make their existence economically viable by the production of goods for export to richer and more specialized markets. In such circumstances a local dominating minority capable of imposing an oligarchic social order does not emerge. Even though poor, even in want, they were living in a reasonably egalitarian society governed by the democratic principles of British tradition. They could not have universities or sumptuous churches or palaces; but they taught their whole population to read and write and gathered it together to read the Bible in their modest clapboard churches and to reach decisions through self-government.

In that way they were able to rise collectively, as a people, in proportion as the colony became consolidated and enriched, and finally to gain their freedom as a more homogeneous society, more capable of carrying on the Industrial Revolution. The peculiar conditions of their formation, as well as the patrimony of lands and natural resources to which they made themselves heirs, assured the Transplanted Peoples special conditions of development that, made fruitful by access to European markets and by the linguistic and cultural facilities of communication with the most progressive countries of Europe, permitted them the mastery of Industrial Revolution technology. This enabled many of them to excel their original forbears, reaching high stages of economic and social development. And it allowed all of them to progress faster than the other American nations, which were originally much more prosperous and cultured.

The fourth bloc of extra-European peoples of the modern world is the Emerging Peoples. They are the African populations nowadays rising from the tribal to the national level. In Asia there are also some cases of Emerging Peoples in transition from tribal to national status, especially in the socialist area, where a policy of greater respect for nationalities permits and stimulates their gestation.

This category has not appeared in America, in spite of the existence of thousands of tribal populations at the time of the conquest. Some of these were decimated promptly by the violence of European domination, others more slowly through subjection to slave labor, and only a few survived. These, under the most rigid forms of compulsion and national domination, have all been annulled as ethnic entities and as bases for new nationalities. Their African and Asian equivalents, on the other hand, despite the violence of the impact they experienced, are today rising to national life.

The Emerging Peoples face specific developmental problems stemming from the deformations resulting from their colonial exploitation by European powers; problems of detribalizing great segments of their population in order to incorporate them into the national life; and problems created by the imperative need to decolonize their own elites who, in the process of Westernization, became culturally alienated from their peoples or turned into local representatives of exogenous interests.

Emerging today to the status of autonomous nationalities, as the Latin Americans did a century and a half ago, these peoples are in danger of falling likewise under the yoke of new forms of economic domination. The fundamental challenge confronting them lies in compelling their elites not to make independence a selfish project by which these leaders simply replace the former foreign colonist. For this they have before them the experience of the peoples who preceded them and a more favorable world situation, which seems propitious to a more autonomous and progressive modernization process.

The four categories of peoples examined to this point, though meaningful and instrumental for the study of the modern world's populations, especially the American, do not portray pure types. Every one of the models has experienced intrusions that affected more or less extensive areas of its territory and differentiated greater or smaller parcels of its population. Thus, in the south of the United States there was a vast Negro intrusion, molded by a plantation-type productive system that gave rise to a New

People configuration. A great part of the racial integration problem confronting the United States derives from the presence of this intrusion, until now irreducible and unassimilated despite being overcome and dispersed in the body of the new formation. Brazil experienced an intrusion of Transplanted People with the massive immigration of Europeans to her southern region, which gave that area a peculiar physiognomy and occasioned a differentiated mode of being. Argentina and Uruguay, as has been shown, emerged to national existence as New Peoples, characterized by a neo-Guaraní protoethnos in the case of the original Paraguay and São Paulo areas. Nevertheless, they suffered a process of pastoral specialization and ecological succession through which the national ethnic character was transmuted, originating a new entity, basically European. So it is that both took shape as Transplanted Peoples, of a special type because hindered in their socioeconomic development by the survival of an archaic oligarchy of great rural landowners. In each of the American peoples lesser intrusions color and particularize certain segments of the national population and the regions of the country where they are most concentrated.

It is to be emphasized that some populations of the modern extra-European world seem not to fit into these categories. This is the case, essentially, of such nations as South Africa, Rhodesia, Malawi (Nyasaland), and Kenya. The classificatory difficulty in this case is that rather than being nations, they are still trading colonies ruled by white groups that entered the area tardily, and even now they remain unassimilated and incapable of molding a New People configuration. Their viability as a national formation is so incontrovertible that one can predict without risk of error the inevitable uprising of the subjugated classes and the elimination of the dominant one, incapable of integrating itself racially and culturally in its own national ethnic context.

In the case of the other extra-European peoples, the national character and the basic ethnocultural profile of each unit are explicable as the result of their over-all formation as Witness, New, Emerging, and Transplanted Peoples. This scale corresponds, by and large, to the current characterization of the American peoples as predominantly Indo-American, neo-American, or Euro-American. The two scales, however, are not equivalent because many other peoples, such as the Paraguayans and the Chileans, of basically indigenous form, became New Peoples and not Witness Peoples because they resulted from the fusion of the European with tribal groups that had not attained the level of the high civilizations. This is also the case of the Euro-Americans, present in all the ethnic formations of the continent; but only in the Transplanted Peoples did they stamp a clearly neo-European profile on the respective populations. The designation of "neo-Americans" does not adequately substitute for "New Peoples," because in many senses, particularly as successors of the original populations of the continent, all these peoples today are neo-Americans.

Fusion and Expansion of Racial Stocks

The quantitative analysis of the racial composition of the American peoples, in the past and in the present, presents enormous difficulties, obliging one to work with more or less arbitrary evaluations. Even official data, when available, merit no trust both for their lack of uniform census definitions of the racial groups and for the interference of attitudes and preconceptions of the very populations censused. This leads, in the Transplanted Peoples, for example, to confusing Negroes and mulattoes in a single group; in the New Peoples, to adding to the white-European contingent all the white-Indian crossbreeds and light mulattoes; and in the Witness Peoples, to identifying as mestizos the great number of racially pure natives incorporated into the modern modes of life through assimilation and acculturation.

With all the reservations deriving from the unreliability of the sources, it is nevertheless possible to set up an acceptable conjectural framework about the evolution of the racial contingents and their mixtures in the composition of the three great American blocs. The table on page 90 shows that the original indigenous group, which between 1500 and 1825 had suffered a reduction from 100 million to 7.8 million, in all three blocs, from 1825 to 1950 succeeded in doubling the latter figure (to 15.6 million) and even surpassing it in the Witness Peoples (from 6.1 to 13.8 million), but is headed for extinction in the New Peoples (from 1 to .5 million).[2]

The white European contingent increased in all areas between 1825 and 1950 (from 13.8 to 225 million), most explosively, however, in the Transplanted Peoples (from 10 to 163 million), which, starting with a predominantly Caucasoid population, multiplied at a rate much greater than that experienced by the other parent populations, by virtue of the heavy injections of European immigrants. Thus the United States quadrupled its population between 1800 and 1850 (5.3 to 23.3 million) and again quadrupled it from 1850 to 1900 (23.3 to 92.3 million). The same occurred in

[2] On the pre-Columbian population and its extermination, see W. Borah (1962) and Dobyns and Thompson (1966).

PROBABLE RACIAL COMPOSITION OF THE GREAT BLOCS OF AMERICAN PEOPLES: Period of Independence (1825), 1950, and Forecast for 2000, in Millions.

	Witness Peoples			New Peoples			Transplanted Peoples			Totals		
	1825	1950	2000	1825	1950	2000	1825	1950	2000	1825	1950	2000
Natives	6.1	13.8	33.0	1.1	1.0	0.5	0.6	0.8	1.5	7.8	15.6	35.0
Whites	1.8	10.2	26.0	2.0	41.8	130.0	10.0	163.0	300.0	13.8	215.0	456.0
Blacks	0.5	0.3	—	5.0	14.0	60.0	1.5	15.0	70.0	7.0	29.3	130.0
Mulattoes				3.5	32.2	150.0	1.0	3.7	20.0	7.5	72.0	320.0
Mestizos	3.0	36.1	150.0									
Totals	11.4	60.4	209.0	11.6	89.0	340.5	13.1	182.5	391.5	36.1	331.9	941.0

Sources: United Nations (1958–1965), A. Rosenblat (1954), F. Debuyst (1961), J. Steward (1949), *Statistical Abstract of the U.S.A.* (1966); and estimates of the 1950 national census data, with U.N. projections to the end of the century.

Argentina, whose population jumped from one to 4.7 million between 1850 and 1900, and to 17.2 million in 1950.

The Negro African group in the same period experienced a much slower growth rate than the Caucasoid (7 to 29.3 million), but much higher than the indigenous. In the areas of greatest concentration, those occupied by the New Peoples, the Negroes hardly tripled their contingent (5 to 14 million) between 1825 and 1950, whereas the whites-by-definition increased more than twenty times and the mestizos nearly ten. This slowness of increment is confirmed by the data referring to shorter periods and available for Brazil: they show that the Negro group actually suffered reductions in its absolute number (from 6.6 million to 5.7 million) between 1940 and 1950. This low growth index is explained rather by miscegenation than by the precariousness of living conditions to which the Negroes were subjected, considering that their total was maintained only by the continued importation of more slaves and by the obstacles they had to face in order to pass from slave status to that of free workers. Among the Witness Peoples, Negroes experienced absolute reductions (500,000 to 300,-000) explicable by the same factors and also, probably, by a more intensive process of absorption into the over-all population through crossbreeding.

The mestizo and mulatto contingent was the one that grew most since independence (7.5 to 72 million), after the Caucasoid, concentrating principally in the Witness Peoples, where it assumed an Indio-European aspect (3 to 36.1 million), and in the New Peoples (3.5 to 32.2 million), where it is predominantly mulatto.

The racial evolution of the American population is congruent with the typological analysis we have been making, and can be understood in terms of divergent processes of ecological succession. By one of them, immigrant European populations, concentrated in homogeneous nuclei structured in families and thus including the presence of women and children, impose themselves on the original populations. This is the case of the Transplanted Peoples, whose indigenous contingents are virtually decimated and Negroes and mulattoes more marginalized than integrated in the new ethnos. In the case of the New Peoples and the Witness Peoples we find a different ecological process by which a minority European nucleus, composed mainly of men separated from their communities, acts as a colonizing agent, imposing itself on the two other racial parent populations through intensive miscegenation, which provides them with an extraordinary capacity to whiten the rest, producing a vast mulatto and mestizo stratum. This proceeds to constitute the principal component of the population in the case of the Witness Peoples (36.1 million of mestizos to 10.2 million of whites-by-definition), and the second contingent very close to the first (32.2 and 41.8 million) in the case of the New Peoples.

Some projections can also be made as to the future development of the various racial stocks in the three blocs of American peoples by comparison of their present contingents with their tendencies toward increment or reduction. Having reached higher levels of development, the national societies of the Transplanted Peoples have experienced in consequence a strong compression in their population growth rate; so it is to be supposed that their future increase may be less notable than that of the other blocs. The United States, quadrupling its population every fifty years previously, did not even double it between 1900 and 1950; the same thing happened in Argentina and Uruguay during the last two decades. The other two blocs, having barely reached the threshold of development, are still experiencing a phase of demographic expansion that will make them continue accelerating in the next decades. Available statistics indicate that the populations of the Witness Peoples and the New Peoples, predominantly mestizo and mulatto, were little smaller in 1960, taken as a whole, than the total population of the Transplanted Peoples (220.5 million versus 182.8 million), but activated by an intense growth rate they will tend to exceed that difference amply in the next decades, until in the year 2000 they reach a total of 549.5 million versus 391.5 million for the Transplanted Peoples.

Those differences in the demographic growth rates are owing essentially to the fact that the Transplanted Peoples experienced their period of strongest increase starting with a relatively small population (5.3 million in 1800 to 23.3 million in 1850 in the United States), whereas the same phenomenon will probably occur now in Latin America, starting with a much superior population base (204 million in 1960), which, even if it grows at a substantially less accelerated rate, will tend to triple itself by the year 2000.

In the long run, therefore, it is dark-skinned America that tends to increase most, the fruit of crossbreeding of its basic contingents—unless the vast U.S. government programs of birth control succeed in altering these tendencies substantially. But it is improbable that such programs will ever be carried out, not only because of the difficulties in inducing backward, poor peoples to adopt habits proper to advanced societies but also because of the opposition that such a program provokes in Latin American leaderships. The latter are more and more heedful of the risks inherent in an artificial demographic containment whose inevitable consequence will be not merely the reduction of their contingent in the world, but the precocious aging of their populations in which a majority of minors eighteen years old and under (about 50 per cent) would be progressively replaced by an increasing proportion of adults of fifty years of age and over, which, in the current conditions of underdevelopment, would represent a dead weight.

This artificial aging of the Latin American population imposed by a power policy before reaching the minimum levels of economic and social development, which would naturally lead to the effect stated—as has occurred with all the fully industrialized countries—could disable Latin Americans for the tasks of development, withdrawing from its societies the basic factor of social renovation—the forces of demographic compression and the corresponding social tensions. Its accomplishment, by means of vast subsidized programs of distribution of contraceptive pills and incentive to abortion, could condemn Latin Americans to a dependence—if not permanent, of unforeseeable duration—on the protection and care of their rich neighbor to the north, with the consequent perpetuation of U.S. hegemony despite its then being flagrantly in the minority.

The unreliability of the available data on the racial composition of the American populations and the variety of factors that can intervene in the relative growth of each contingent in the next decades do not allow calculating their future increment by means of safe statistical projections. They do permit some likely hypotheses about the probable increment of each racial component of the three blocs and about the probable alterations of their proportions. First, the proportion of two to one for the white-by-definition contingent over the colored people, recorded in 1950 in the American populations, will change profoundly to achieve a colored supremacy of some 485 million over 456 million of whites by the end of the century. This, by virtue of a parallelism between whiteness and higher level of living, and consequently, a lower population growth rate.

The indigenous contingent will probably increase also in the same period to something more than double its 1950 total (15 to 35 million). Simultaneously, however, it will become culturally de-Indianized through incorporation into the ways of life of the neo-American populations in which it is inserted. In the end it will probably constitute a differentiated mode of participation in the national ethnos that will unify its members through retention of loyalties to their parent populations more than through their present ethnocultural characteristics.

The Negro group will very likely quadruple its total (29.3 million in 1950 to 130 million in 2000) for the reasons already mentioned and also because the social ascent presumably to be experienced in the next decades will furnish it with a higher survival index. Nevertheless, by dint of racial blending, it is possible that it may tend to color the white populations, augmenting the mulatto figure to the detriment of the expression of its own patrimony in greater Negro populations.

The mestizos, finally, we suppose will experience a more intensive increment than all the rest, nearly quintupling its contingent from 72 to 320 million through the conjunction of diverse factors, such as the elevation of the standard of living now just beginning, which will likely combine with a high growth rate, absorption of the product of mixed marriages, and lastly the assumption of its own ethnic figure, without the contingency of taking on ideological protective coloration in whites-by-definition.

All the foregoing propositions are based on the expectation of an intensive miscegenation that will amalgamate the American populations as a more and more homogeneous representation of humanity, and therefore better capacitated to coexist and to identify with all peoples. However, considering the various American areas, these tendencies can as well be intensified as reduced by certain factors. Thus, for example, if the racial war between Negroes and whites in the United States is settled along an integrationist path, the homogenizing tendency will be intensified. But if, on the contrary, racial segregation prevails, and especially if the Anglo-Americans are successful in their intention of reducing their Black populations and the dark-skinned contingents of Latin America by imposing a policy of demographic containment, the result will be the strengthening of heterogeneity and racism.

The growth of Latin American populations should carry them to a demographic figure of 650 million in the year 2000, according to calculations based on the expectation of a relatively low rate of increment. That expectation does not take into account the possibilities of a still greater increase through the raising of sanitation levels, medical progress in the treatment of sterilizing diseases, not to mention such social factors as the probable lowering of marrying age and the number of free unions, generally prolific. For all these reasons the hypothesis of a still greater increase should be considered. This demographic explosion is obviously not a good in itself, and will mean for Latin America a yet greater challenge in her effort to overcome her backwardness.[3]

This challenge shows the imperativeness of intensifying the developmental effort in order to attain a reduction of demographic growth and a moderate aging of the population in consequence of economic progress, not instead of it, as could happen with a birth control policy advocated and paid for by a foreign power as part of its plan for the future of Latin Americans.

[3] It is supposed that for a 2.5 per cent annual rate of growth an investment rate of nearly 10 per cent of national income is necessary, just to maintain the same proportion of productive equipment per active person.

PART II

The Witness Peoples

"[A]mong the groups in each society persons distinguish those that are my people, or are more my people, from those that are not so much my people. This distinction between *we* and *they* to a certain degree orders the human elements on the stage of the world."

—ROBERT REDFIELD

WE DESIGNATE as Witness Peoples the Mexican, Middle American, and Andean populations as survivors of ancient civilizations—Aztec, Maya, and Inca—that crumbled under the impact of European expansion, entering on a centuries-long process of acculturation and ethnic reconstitution, which is still not concluded for all of them.

Spain found those areas with much greater populations than her own, structured in totally different sociocultural formations. They were theocratic irrigation empires of the same type as those that developed the high civilizations of Mesopotamia (2350 B.C.), Egypt (2070 B.C.), China (1122 B.C.), India (327 B.C.), and Cambodia (600 A.D.). Like these civilizations, the American empires were based on an intensive irrigation agriculture with canal systems controlled by the state. The irrigation revolution permitted the creation of the greatest human concentrations known.

The population figure of the theocratic irrigation empires of the Americas has been the object of the most disparate evaluations. Among the most conservative are A. L. Kroeber's (1939), which admitted a total of 6.3

million for the Incas, Mayas, and Aztecs; A. Rosenblat's (1954), which
estimated them at 7.8 million; and J. Steward's (1949), which raised the
figure to 9.2 million. More recent studies, using new sources and more
precise criteria, have raised these figures. W. Borah and S. F. Cook (1963)
estimated the pre-Columbian population of central Mexico at 25 to 30
million, whereas H. Dobyns and P. Thompson (1966) put the total between 30 and 37.5 million for that area, to which they add 10 to 13 million for Mesoamerica and 30 to 37.5 million for the Andean region. According to these last estimates, better founded than their predecessors, it is
admissible that the population structured in the theocratic irrigation
empires of the Americas might have reached a total of 70 to 88 million inhabitants before the conquest. A century and a half later those populations
had been reduced to near 3.5 million, such was the depopulating impact to
which they were subjected.

Paralyzed by the Spanish attack, the Mexican, Mayan, and Incan societies collapsed; they saw their ruling classes replaced by foreign minorities
that compulsorily remodeled their cultures. This design was carried out by
means of various mechanisms, among them the intentional decimation of
the former governmental and sacerdotal caste, the depository of the
learned tradition of those cultures, and the depopulation provoked thereafter by the epidemics to which they were exposed, the imposition of slave
labor, and the effect of technical and agricultural innovations that upset
their former system of subsistence by altering its ecological base.

Under these conditions of social slaughter the two cultural traditions,
the European and the indigenous, merged: the first, represented by the minority of agents of external domination, maintaining itself entire and whole
and arming itself with all powers for imposing itself; the latter, stripped of
the most advanced contents of an urban society—its educated sectors—
traumatized under the pressure of the forces released by depopulation and
compulsory deculturation, despoiled of its accumulated treasures through
plundering, and deprived of its bodies of technicians and artisans by the
conversion of its whole population into an external proletariat degraded to
the status of unskilled labor in the mines and on the plantations to serve
an export economy.

For decades the Witness Peoples of America had no defined, congruent
way of life of their own. The old one had died as an integrating force and
no new one had yet emerged. Wasted by epidemics, led into despair by
slavery, they were transformed into flocks whose members were born and
died, living only to fulfill their destiny. Throughout all that time, however,
they retained and transmitted, from generation to generation, scraps of the
old values whose actualization in conduct was impracticable but that still
moved their descendants.

It was in these circumstances that the first cells of a Ladino culture struggled to take shape. These hybrid cells, half neoindigenous, half neo-European, were to act on the traumatized context, assimilating greater and greater parcels of it for a new mode of being and living. They delved continually into the original culture in this way, to come up more and more broadened and more differentiated from both the ancient tradition and the European model.

The process always operated within the framework represented by the compulsion capacity of the new civilization, whose technical, institutional, and especially mercantile apparatus was more advanced and whose dominant caste ruled society with enormous coercive power. In these conditions the effort at Ladinization was made, essentially, as a mechanism for conscription of the indigenous masses into the work force of the new productive system, a force placed at the service of the governing caste. The discipline of work, in slave or serf regime, more than acculturation or religious conversion, is what would amalgamate those peoples in the nascent society as its proletariat.

Indigenous populations in the same area that formerly maintained only intermittent or hostile contacts with the Aztec, Maya, or Inca high civilizations were also affected, little by little, and subjugated. On them were exerted the same compulsions, both in their own territories and in the new areas where they were relocated. Many of these populations, finding themselves dispersed and enslaved in the mines and on the plantations, had to acculturate themselves by learning the language and the common comprehensions of the Ladino culture in order to communicate mutually. Through all these mechanisms the cells of the new Ladino formation increased, acting on the surrounding peoples who had not succeeded in taking refuge in the jungles or deserts to reconstitute their cultural life at a distance.

All were to be involved finally in the expansive wave of the Ladino formation. Many of these would be partially integrated as vast marginalized strata of the national society, but dependent on it. In this way they ended by establishing a *modus vivendi* of separate coexistence that, if it permitted the preservation of greater contents of the traditional culture, at the same time degraded and condemned them to cultural regression and extreme want, as the most exploited strata of the system. Thus, resistant to all forms of constriction and acculturation, thanks to their very primitivism, some enclaves of tribal peoples were able to survive and preserve a certain autonomy.

Contrary to what happened in the immigrant colonies of North America, where a people grew endowed with conditions for providing their own subsistence and expressing their own conceptions of life, here enormous human contingents were utilized as fuel to operate the colonial productive system and to serve alien projects. Contrary, too, to the New Peoples who emerged from the deculturation of tribal ethnic groups with scant cultural development, here the Hispanization and the establishment of new, reorganizing institutions never succeeded in eradicating the mass of customs, beliefs, and values of the old ethos incorporated in those initial cells and still surviving today in the midst of their modernity.

Recollection of a past time of greatness, moral indignation at the drama of which they were victims, and the sheer weight of traditions of a high civilization disrupt the homogeneity of the European sociocultural configuration. In spite of all the compulsions attending their constitution, the new Ladino ethnos emerged, for that reason, marked with singularities that would in the future define their profile as Witness Peoples.

Both the Mexican and Inca being urban civilizations, their cities were the foci of the learned contents of their culture, which spread over their rural populations and over the other peoples incorporated into the imperial context. Once dominated, these focal cities in turn diffused the new culture, using for that purpose the old mechanisms of communication and control, to which more coercive ones were added.

They were thus transformed from diffusers of a homogeneous, autonomous cultural continuum into agencies of planned transformation of society and culture. For the practice of this new function the Spaniards implanted in the conquered cities two great reorganizing systems: the state and the Church. The former, with its administrations, civil and military, regulated productive activities, ordained massive relocations of populations from one zone to another and determined the creation of towns and cities. These were erected by acts of will, in appointed locales, with a prescribed physical form, their institutions shaped after uniform models. The dwellers in these cities, Spaniards or indigenes, were no longer fellow countrymen united in the identification with their native province, but agents of a superior will that regulated their life routine according to the social estate in which they happened to be situated, even prescribing the clothing and the adornments they could wear.

The Church was established as a second reorganizing power with the capacity to regulate the calendar of days of work, of rest, or of fiesta; the ritual that was to mark the life cycle of each person from baptism to the grave; the obligatory, the commendable, and the prohibited religious beliefs, including among the prohibited many peninsular heresies that the Church was trying to stamp out along with the indigenous cults. For the exercise of this last function the catechists were transplanted to America first; later, the ecclesiastical hierarchies and a huge clergy came; and finally, the tribunals of the holy office came to act in the new lands with the same corrective power and the same fanaticism as the peninsular tribunals.

In this manner both the neo-American and the Spanish populations were subjected to the panic of denunciation and persecution.

Acting jointly—as the two arms of the salvationistic mercantile empire into which Spain had turned—the state and the Church ruled the sociocultural rebuilding, intentionally orienting it to meet specific goals. These were (1) the construction of new societies as complements to the metropolis, destined to provide it with an inexhaustible source of riches, and (2) the extension of Christianity, understood more as a form of restoration of the rigidly molded class structures of medieval Europe than as a cult. In this exogenous project the conquered people was assigned the role of an external proletariat destined to engender, with its work, the riches demanded of it, and forced to conform, like modeling clay, to the subaltern functions prescribed for it.

Outside these spheres of planned action, other modes of cultural influence were operating. The Spaniards themselves brought habits, beliefs, and cupidities that did not fit into the imperial salvationistic project. The natives, too, despite being subjugated, were not so malleable as could be desired. They persisted in their customs, beliefs, tastes, and hopes, which notwithstanding all compulsions set up a certain resistance and ended by being incorporated into the new culture as the latter crystallized. At the end of five or six decades these protocells had a cultural configuration capable of absorbing the other indigenous groups incorporated by colonial expansion and the European and African contingents arriving later.

The rule of state and Church not only shaped the new societies but incorporated them into the world market as slavistic-colonial areas of the salvationistic-mercantile formation assumed by Spain. This bond powered the nascent societies, made them economically viable, and prevented them from plunging into a feudal stagnation. It justified the ways of conditioning unskilled labor for work, from the slave labor of the first days to the wage labor of today. Through all those processes of conscription a more and more vigorous capitalistic mercantile bond was to guide the American populations to world economy. At the same time it would lead them to higher stages of sociocultural evolution through historical incorporation that would convert them from autonomous societies in areas of colonial domination to societies dominated by more evolved nations.

In the production sphere the new configurations combined the old indigenous technology adapted to the local ecological conditions with a series of innovations selected from the Iberian cultural base for their capacity to raise the productivity of labor or to enrich diet, clothing, and dwellings. Among these are included, as most important, the introduction of the cultivation of cereals, legumes, and European fruits; the raising of livestock for farm work, riding, meat, wool, milk, and hides; plows and carts; tools and new techniques in carpentry, building, pottery, ropemaking, weaving, and fishing; the manufacture of alcoholic liquids and of soap. All these elements were introduced into the neo-American cultural patrimony together with the Iberian system of weights and measures, monetary economy, and private ownership of land and goods, all of which were to change the preexisting social order completely.

This combination of American and Iberian techniques, institutions, and beliefs was progressively blended until it became a cultural complex distinct from its parent populations. Even lacking autonomy in its development, because this was condemned to grow within the colonial frame, this complex was to provide the base on which the national ethnic entities of the Witness Peoples were constructed. What they all have in common today derives as much from the fact of their resulting from the encounter of high cultures—the indigenous and the European—as from the coparticipant Iberian cultural background and the also common forms of socioeconomic conditioning to which they were subjected. This multiple heritage would make them, at one and the same time, Witness Peoples, modern neo-Latin peoples, and national societies aspiring to autonomous integration into the mercantile, and later the industrial, civilization.

The conquistador's modes of conditioning the Mexican and Inca indigenous populations, and especially the mechanisms of domination used during the long colonial period, were responsible also for structural deformations visible even today—among others, the great social separation between the dominant castes and the people, and the bipartition of the former into different but mutually complementary patrician and oligarchic sectors.

The official agents of the colonial order of Middle America and the Andes very early formed a bureaucratic aristocracy—state, military, and ecclesiastic—differentiated from the local oligarchies of the conquistadores' successors. To the colonial societies this peninsular aristocracy represented the crown and the Church in whose name it exercised the political, military, and administrative powers and ruled social life, holding as its "property" the administrative, military, and religious institutions of control and colonial exploitation.

During the first years after the conquest, serious conflicts occurred between the bureaucratic aristocracy and the conquistadors, who also aspired to political power. Soon a *modus vivendi* was established that allowed each to play its part as a complementary power, the politicoreligious or the econoproductive. The crown consolidated its dominion by the implantation of a vast governmental machine of tax collection and maintenance of the system. The Church widened its controls in the spiritual field, sanctifying the social order and claiming the right to a heavy share in appropriated or created wealth. The oligarchy, divided into agrarian, mining, and commercial strata, enriched itself through the multiplication of entrepreneurial units and the compression of popular consumption and ennobled itself through the purchase of monarchic and religious titles and privileges. Thus the dominant class was divided into two sectors, one turning to the economic field, the other to the politicomilitary and ecclesiastic, but unified as a class against the common enemy, the subjugated peoples, the object of their exploitation.

For centuries the political history of the Witness Peoples was a succession of conflicts of the municipal councils with the metropolitan authorities over royal ordinances concerning the regulation of work, the creation of new monopolies (alcohol, tobacco, salt, and so forth), and the imposition of taxes. These oppositions to a tyrannical or incompetent authority, or to a hated bishop, rarely developed into rebellions. Even in the rebellions the resistance went no further than a formal declaration that such-and-such an order would be "obeyed but not carried out," or a deposing of authorities to shouts of "Long live the king, death to the tyrant!"

Simultaneously, however, there was a succession of popular rebellions by Indians, Negroes, and Ladinos drafted for the mines or cooped up on the plantations, against the oppression under which they lived. Several of these uprisings were prolonged for years, spreading over extensive regions and mobilizing tens of thousands of persons in the struggle, but were all overcome in the end. They were insurrections of subaltern classes attacking the system itself without the capacity to reorganize it even when temporarily victorious.

Only in the last decade of the eighteenth century did these popular tensions combine with the dissensions between Creoles and peninsular Iberians, both aiming at autonomism. With the victory of these movements and the proclamation of independence the Creole leaders formed a patriciate, replacing the former colonial aristocracy in the same oligarchic order. The last task of many liberators was to crush insurrections that they themselves had aroused and that continued after independence had been won, revolts made in the effort to gain a more just social order.

The division of the dominant caste into a bureaucratic patrician power, made up of politicians, religious and military men, and an economic power represented by the rural and urban proprietor class persisted after independence, assuming new external forms—now republican and liberal—but fundamentally retaining the same antipopular content. Consequently popular rebellions were renewed, the marginal classes of descendants of subjugated Indians rising up against the descendants of their conquerors.

This historical continuity of domination, first colonial and aristo-oligarchic, then national and patrician-oligarchic, but always oligarchic, and the vivid awareness of it on the part of the subjugated masses, is one of the characteristics of the Witness Peoples. Another is the popular irredentism, always ready to explode in emancipative rebellions that until recently assumed a utopian character, but that since the Mexican Revolution have come to be formulated and structured as revolutionary movements.

3. The Mesoamericans

THE CAPITAL OF Mexico is the most marvelous city on the continent. Its three-dimensional civilization—indigenous, colonial, and national —manifests itself simultaneously in a thousand ways—in the streets, the houses, the features, the clothing, and the posture of Mexicans of the most varied classes, creating a cultural atmosphere of vigor and contrast that singles it out among all the cities of the world. The indigenous dimension, which is preserved only in museums and documentation but which pulsates in the common people's ways of life, was one of the highest expressions of human creativity. The colonial dimension, more potent than any other in the Americas, expresses itself in the manner of being of the Mexicans, who, however reluctantly, reflect it in the language they speak, in the form of the family, in their religiosity, in the Iberian habits. It is outlined also in the European-style cathedrals and civil palaces, transfigured and sublimated by the native artisans who built them. The modern dimension flourishes throughout the city in the form of factories, avenues, cosmopolitan people. But it is expressed principally in the architecture of a few nuclei, such as the University City.

The present-day capital of Mexico was built on the ruins of Tenochti-tlán, the Aztec capital, the lake city constructed on natural plateaus and dirt fills between lakes and canal avenues. Its archeological reconstruction arouses greater and greater surprise at its grandeur, which Cortés found and destroyed. It was probably one of the greatest cities of the world in its time, certainly greater than Madrid.[1]

The Zócalo, the central square of the Mexican capital—"the world's navel"—paved with great black granite squares, with no benches—so that everyone may stand in it, as befits the civic center of the nation—is the symbol of Mexico. On one side of the Zócalo stands the old cathedral, solemn in the austere style with which the Catholic Church tried to express her domination over the cultures of the ancient Mexicans and gigantic, constructed on the ruins of the principal temple of Tenochtitlán. On another side of the Zócalo rises the government palace built on the residence of Cuauhtémoc, or Guatimozín, the last Aztec ruler, tortured and killed by Cortés. Inside the palace, Mexican history parades in the murals of Rivera and Orozco. In one of them Marx and Juárez are shaking hands, the European ideologue and the Mixtec lad who became president and who, in the mural, shouts the proud motto of Mexican self-destiny: "The spirit will speak for my race." Throughout the city one can sense the national problem of modern Mexicans, the North American influence expressed in the most characteristic popular phrase: "Pobre México, tan lejos de Dios, tan cerca de Norteamérica" (Poor mexico, so far from God and so close to the United States).

Aztec-Náhuatl Mexico

In the center and south of Mexico and in Guatemala flourished one of the most potent and singular of civilizations. Archeologists are reconstructing nowadays, with a wealth of detail, the history of its development, which through millennia unfolded from the most primitive levels to various apexes of civilization that burgeoned successively in several places. In Guatemala and in the Yucatan peninsula as the Mayan culture, and in

---

[1] Tenochtitlán, the capital of the Mexicans, had a population estimated by the chroniclers of the conquest at 300,000 inhabitants, and considered still larger by some modern scholars (G. C. Vaillant, 1941; J. Soustelle, 1962; W. Borah and S. F. Cook, 1963). Even allowing for exaggeration of these calculations, the ancient Aztec capital must be considered one of the greatest cities of its time. The population of Seville, largest of the Spanish cities in the sixteenth century, is estimated at 120,000 inhabitants; Lisbon's, at 100,000; and Madrid's, at 60,000.

Mexico as the Aztec culture, they reached peaks of development as urban civilizations based on irrigation agriculture, on the stratification of society in profoundly differentiated classes, and in complex forms of political organization; and they crystallized as theocratic empires that extended their suzerainty over vast regions.

In Mexico the Spanish conquistadors encountered the last focus of these civilizations, the Aztecs, whose language was Náhuatl and who were then in the full stride of their creativity and dominion. They were structured in a confederation of three peoples: Tenochtitlán, Texcoco, and Tlacopán, under the hegemony of the first-named, which led both army and religion and whose capital was the seat of decisions. Each people was divided into clans and possessed institutions of self-government. The Mexican confederation had expanded its dominion over an area corresponding to the greater part of the territories of present-day Mexico and Guatemala, whose peoples it had subjugated, forced to pay tribute in goods and persons, and unified in a common mercantile system.

Estimates of the population of pre-Columbian Mexico vary extraordinarily. It was in all probability much greater than that of the Iberian peninsula of that time, estimated at 10 million.[2] That population, living in cities and in the country, was stratified in rigidly differentiated classes. The superior stratum included a nonhereditary nobility and a patriciate of priests and high functionaries. The intermediate class was composed of merchants, whose growing importance established it as an "impresariat," a class of entrepreneurs, because of their possession of production property, including cultivation lands, precious metals, and cacao, the latter used as coin. All these strata were based on an enormous peasant mass that tilled the soil and engaged in all kinds of craftsmanship.

The Aztec civilization had its own system of writing and a perfected calendar and had reached a stage of urban development comparable to the Egyptian or the Babylonian. Its cities, endowed with broad avenues, stepped pyramids covered with monumental sculptures, and residential palaces are among the greatest architectural creations in the world. In these cities lived, besides the nobility and the priests, a great urban population of officials, merchants, and greatly skilled craftsmen whose works in stone, metal, and ceramics attained high artistic levels.

The Aztec hegemony over the other two peoples had been gained only a century before the conquest and was still on the way to consolidation in

---

[2] According to A. L. Kroeber (1939) it must have been 3.3 million; A. Rosenblat (1954) puts it at 5.3 million; K. Sapper (1924), 12 to 15 million; Borah and Cook (1963) claim 25 to 30 million; and Dobyns and Thompson (1966), 30 to 37.5 million. These last figures are probably closer to the fact, because they are based on a critical utilization of information sources and of explicit methods of evaluation.

the form of a theocratic irrigation empire founded on an agrocraftsman economy, incipiently mercantilized, and an absolutist theocratic-military state. The principal nucleus of the empire was ruled according to traditional norms developed from an ancient patrilineal clan structure, and the most recently conquered areas by means of a colonizational system under military chieftaincies.

At the time of the conquest the territory of Tenochtitlán, the Aztec capital, was divided into four major sections, which in turn were divided into twenty local units, the *calpulli*. Each had its own civil, military, and religious authorities, designated by the headquarters of the respective sections in accordance with certain clan norms and the wishes of the calpulli members, as expressed in assembly.

Civil administration was the duty of a bureaucratic nobility, nonhereditary, which received its posts, titles, and goods as recompense for services lent as judges, distributors of lands, collectors of tribute, comptrollers of warehousing and distributing harvests and craftsman production, and merchants who did business with periphery peoples. The military chieftains were occupied with policing and with training their troops for religious wars, and they, too, were paid in goods, usufruct of lands, and personal services. The clergy, besides its religious duties, educated the new generations of nobles in great boarding schools (*calmecac*) for the fulfillment of civil, religious, and military functions. In these schools the principal subjects were writing, astronomy, history, and religion. Another type of instruction, especially military and artisan, was given to the common folk.

Each civil or military post seemed to enjoy certain privileges, including not only the usufruct of cultivable lands but also the use of personal services from the local peasantry. Moreover, the authorities of the respective calpulli gave a bit of land to each man who married, for him to cultivate for the support of his family, with the obligation of paying in tribute one third of the harvest from it. Every family was obligated to perform services on the property of the clergy or on that of the civil nobility and also in the irrigation works and the building of cities and temples, in special mobilizations of labor forces.

A minority, and lower, social stratum was formed by persons degraded for crimes of treason, murder, or theft, or personal or family debts of goods or tributes; such persons were in the position of serfs placed at the service of others for life. It was with people recruited from this class and with the forced services of the members of calpulli that the areas given in usufruct to great lords were cultivated and the corps of porters in the service of the great merchants were organized. As can be seen, the Mexican society displayed a stratified social structure based principally on a vast free rural class, concentrated in villages of peasants and craftsmen who cultivated neighboring lands, produced their own tools, lived according to traditional subsistence standards, and provided a surplus of goods, as well as a human surplus available for war and for composing the urban craftsman class.

The most important integrating element of the Aztec ethos was probably the mythoreligious conception of destiny attributed to themselves as the people of the sun. According to these beliefs, solar movement, light, and heat were provided by means of human sacrifices to propitiate the Sun God. The need of victims for these numerous sacrifices motivated their war activity. These beliefs not only imbued the Aztecs with the ardor that made them capable of dominating other peoples, but also with a general world conception to which they sought to lead their subjects, and in which they were defined as supporters of the Sun and therefore of life and prosperity for all.

Besides the cult of the Sun—Tonatiuh—the religion of the Mexicans was founded on a body of beliefs and practices conducted in accordance with prophecies and auguries by means of which the priests determined the exigencies of sacrifices and offerings on behalf of other divinities such as Huitzilopochtli, the god of war, and Tlaloc, the god of rains.

Contrary to the Aztecs, obsessed as they were with the mysticobellicose view from which they derived their sense of destiny as the Sun People, the Texcoco worshipped mainly Quetzalcóatl, a more benign divinity worshipped through prayer, song, and poetry and to whom human sacrifice was repugnant. Furthermore, Quetzalcóatl was described as a man of white skin and long beard who was expected to come some day to live among men as a reformer of customs.

This belief seems to have been important in the paralysis of the Mexican warriors in the face of the Spanish attack. It is believed that the identification of the white, bewhiskered invaders—marked by such extraordinary signs as horses and firearms—with the benign divinity that their own tradition taught as the expected one, must have induced the Mexicans to confront the Spaniards less with the weapons of their armies than with the exorcisms of their priests. The Aztec tradition relates, in fact, all the zeal with which Moctezuma sought to placate the invaders, offering them jewels and feather cloaks carefully wrought by royal artisans in the manner due Quetzalcóatl.

But other more virulent factors, prostrating the Mexican people before so few invaders, acted after the combats began. Among these factors are the smallpox epidemics brought by the whites, the role played by the Aztecs' own social stratification, dominated by a narrow noble caste that concentrated the maximum power of domination over the other social strata, and, further, the ethnic tensions existing among the three confederated peoples, whose chieftaincies sought to join the conquistadors against Tenochtitlán.

The stratified social structure, evidence of the high degree of development attained by the Mexicans, was their weakest point before the attack by people so different from those previously confronted and conquered. Through an age-old process of social differentiation Mexican civilization had created an aristocratic stratum charged with the tasks of command and had conditioned the whole mass of the people to the role of a subordinate class. With the loss of the master caste—quickly crushed by the invader's daring even while it was trying to conciliate—none but the conquistadors could replace it as a new aristocracy.

Their task was facilitated by the people's centuries-long conditioning to obedience to nobles, who, being also the controllers of the divinities, were conceived of as superpowerful. The intermediate stratum of priests, officials, and military men, seeing their leader class cut off, instead of improvising themselves as new leaders to continue the fight—as had occurred with all the less culturally developed American tribal peoples—sought to make peace in order to continue to fulfill their functions in the service of new masters. Preserving some of their former privileges (such as exemption from taxation) and amplifying others—the transformation of usufruct of land into property and of the right to personal services into slavery—the Spaniards were able to place the whole population in their service.

A major role in the traumatization of the Mexican society was played by the mortality from smallpox, which affected hundreds of thousands of persons. It is easy to imagine the drama of that population, already bewildered by the sanguinary violence of the invaders, who, if they were gods, were undoubtedly not the benign Quetzalcóatl, but new Huitzilopochtlis, considering the new doom falling on them with the irruption of the epidemic. The strange, repugnant, and fatal disease, scalding them with fever and rotting their living bodies with no succor possible, had all the signs of a supernatural punishment. Besides, the rapidity of its dissemination through a defenseless populace must have decimated such huge quantities of people that there were probably no healthy hands capable of caring for the sick, of feeding the well, or of burying the dead.[3]

[3] The testimony left by Aztec contemporaries of the great epidemic describes how it began and spread: "Some it covered with kernels over all parts of the body, head, face, breast, etc. It was very destructive. Many people died of it. No one could stand, they could only lie stretched out in bed. None could move, not even his neck or any movement of the body. They could not lie face down, nor on the back; neither on one side nor on the other. And when they moved a little, they screamed. To many it brought death, that gummy, harsh disease that makes sores and gland lumps. Many died of it. But many only died of hunger, since no one could care for anybody; no one bothered with others.

The smallpox was followed by dozens of other germs, microbes, and viruses, many of them lethal, with which the white man was to contaminate indigenous America: pulmonary diseases and the intestinal infections that cost thousands of lives; dental caries that rotted their mouths; puerperal fevers that victimized mothers and their offspring; venereal diseases that, besides killing, sterilized and blinded millions; tetanus, trachoma, typhus, mumps, leprosy, yellow fever, malaria, and a long series of other fatal infections (D. Ribeiro, 1956; W. Borah, 1964).

The march of European civilization in Ibero-America was thus made on three feet: (1) this biotic aggregate of plagues to wipe out much of the population and to weaken resistance; (2) the thalassocratic and mercantile-capitalist thirst for plunder that, although incipient, inflamed the conquistador's zeal to save money by the conscription of millions of men on their own land or by bringing them from their homes to use them as fuel in his productive enterprises; (3) the missionary expansionism, typical of the salvationist mercantile empires, sparing no effort to eradicate "heathen heresies" and enlarge the kingdom of Christ. It was under these three iron gloves that, after being drastically reduced,[4] the Mexican population was transfigured as a new ethnos, more by a passive, covert resistance than by spectacular confrontations.

A European thinker, meditating on the drama of the conquest centuries later, considers that the Aztec-Náhuatl civilization disappeared,

> murdered in the full glory of its unfolding, destroyed like a sunflower whose head is struck off by one passing. All these states—including a world-power and more than one federation—with an extent and resources far superior to those of the Greek and Roman states in Hannibal's day . . . all this was not broken down in some desperate way, but washed out by a handful of bandits in a few years, and so entirely that the relics of the population retained not even a memory of it all (Oswald Spengler, *Decline of the West,* 1928, pp. 43–44).

"Some were contaminated with wide-spaced sores; these suffered less, they died in fewer numbers. But even so, many lost their faces, they were left eaten away. Others were left blind, they lost their sight.

"The time that this plague was active lasted sixty days, sixty deathly days. It began in Cuatlán; when it was realized, it was too late. As far as Chalco the plague spread. In spreading it grew milder, but did not cease completely. It appeared in the feast of Teotleco and ended with the feast of Panquetzaliztli. It was when the faces of the Mexican warriors were left clean" (quoted by M. León-Portilla, 1959, pp. 117–118).

[4] Henry F. Dobyns and Paul Thompson (1966) estimate that Mexico's depopulation was effected at the rate of 20–25 to 1, falling from 30–37.5 million at the time of the conquest to 1.5 million in 1650.

More eloquent than Spengler in appreciating the American tragedy are its native witnesses who, in narratives, poems, and songs recorded their view of the conquest. The following verses, selected and published by M. León-Portilla, are highly expressive.

> And all this happened to us
> We saw it, perplexed
> Along the roads lie the split arrows
> The scattered hair
> The houses are de-tiled
> The walls scorched
> The walls are spattered with brains
> Worms swarm in the streets and the squares
> The waters are red, tinted with blood
> and taste of niter.
>
>   . . .
>
> They set a price on us
> Price of youth, price of priest
> of baby and of maiden
> Enough: the price of a poor man
> was a handful of corn
> Ten rotten cakes
> was our price
> Twenty cakes of nitrous grass.
>
>   . . .
>
> Gold, jade, rich cloaks
> Quetzal plumage
> Everything that is precious
> was valued at nothing.
>
>   . . .
>
> Weep, my friends
> Understand that with these facts
> We lost the Mexicatl nation
> Water has turned sour, food has turned sour
> This is what Tlatelolco has done to us
> The giver of life.[5]

The Mexican national consciousness could not fail to be marked by these episodes, and its culture, centuries afterwards, was still divided in its bipartite heritage: the original civilization, crushed but surviving in every-

[5] Free translation of parts of poems of an anonymous poet of Tlatelolco, 1528 (quoted by M. León-Portilla, 1959, pp. 192–193.

thing compatible with the new life of a dominated people, and the European component that was struggling to fuse the neo-Mexicans into a modern nation. All this is what causes the average Mexican to talk about the
drama of Cuauhtémoc as if it had occurred yesterday, so heated is their
detestation of the conquistador. That, too, is why a Spanish friend would
not go strolling with me around Mexico City 150 years after independence, on the day of its commemoration, fearing that the popular resentment of the conquest might be turned on him.

Ethnic Reconstitution

The Spanish colonialists launched themselves like a curse on these Mexican populations, structured as an urban civilization and with a high level
of economic and political organization, but prostrated by the assault of
man and plague. The captains of the conquest, besides the riches plundered at the start, were rewarded by the crown with huge territories whose
indigenous populations found themselves delivered over to their masters'
greed. Later came a whole cohort of adventurers who progressively appropriated the remaining areas with their respective populations, everything
submitting to the new domination. With them came the missionaries to
yoke the natives, by fire and sword, to a new moral order, preached as a
redemptory philosophy but concretized as a justification of the conquest
and of the forced conscription of these populations into the new system.

After a century the aboriginal Mexican population had been reduced to
1.5 million. It had been worn away by contamination with the plagues
brought by the whites and by the two basic forms of subjugation: the
mita * for slave labor in mining and the encomienda for agricultural serfdom. At the cost of this human wastage and these forms of social compression 20,000 or 30,000 Spaniards made themselves the nobility of the
new Mexican society, which was reduced and transformed to a debased
shadow of what it had been.

The conditioning of indigenous labor for work under Spanish domination was achieved through several procedures: (1) the appropriation of the
cultivable lands by the conquistadors and their allies, followed by the introduction of the institution of private property, freely alienable; (2) the
conscription of the native for work, initially in the crude status of slave,
subject to the absolute power of his master, and later on under different

* *mita:* Group of Indians drafted by lot to labor on public works, especially in the
mines, for periods of six months; also means the tribute paid by those Peruvian Indians who had the means, in lieu of such service.

disguises. These were intended more to placate the conscience of the clergy and salvationistic royalty than to emancipate the peasantry in fact. Thus they were formal mechanisms of domination and exploitation rather than efforts to free the subjugated people.

With the institutionalized appropriation of the land, the free peasant, usufructuary of a plot of land on which he was to pay tribute, found himself the slave of a personal master who exercised over him the absolute rights of lordship in accordance with European tradition. These rights to enslavement would be gradually weakened in time, but never to the point of jeopardizing the power to conscript the labor force placed at the service of the dominant caste as its principal source of enrichment. In other words, never in the colonial regime and in what was to follow until the Mexican Revolution was there a restoration of the original character of the Aztec communities, which were essentially dedicated to providing their own subsistence in a stratified society but with a high degree of social responsibility toward all its members.

The populational waste caused by colonization did not worry Spain overmuch. After all, only a batch of slaves got cheaply were dying—they cost only the price of the conquest—and the supply seemed inexhaustible. Later, when it became evident that the great wealth to be exploited was not the original sources of plunder but the work force of a population that was diminishing daily, the crown decreed new labor conditions.

So it is that the system progressed from crude uninstitutionalized slavery to the encomienda, which innovated and disguised it under the nominal pretext of organizing the Indians' work in order to convert and integrate them into Christianity. It passed, then, to the regime of forced distribution, which, although nominally assuring the conscripted Indians the right to a minimum wage, made this pay so insignificant that in almost no way did it change the misery and subjugation to which they were subjected. Finally came the stage of legally free labor, but only after nearly all the land had been appropriated and divided into plantations and the Indians corraled in them. In this phase the simple indebtedness of the free worker for real or fictitious supplies kept him yoked to his work.

These different forms of social order not only placed the whole body of Mexican society at the service of their dominators, both local and metropolitan, but fulfilled the necessary conditions of a cultural transfiguration giving rise to a new ethnic aspect. The acculturative process in these circumstances does not operate as the encounter and interinfluencing of two distinct and autonomous cultural patrimonies. It operates as an intentional uprooting and cultural mutation, destined, not to mold an overseas offshoot in the Hispanic image, but to constitute a subaltern formation organized and disciplined to provide a perennial source of goods. Mexican civilization thus saw its own process of evolution choked off and integrated into a new civilization.

The fundamental mechanisms for destroying the original socioeconomic order were the conditioning of the labor force and the integration of the Mexican productive centers into the European mercantile system as providers of mineral wealth. The conversion of the former culture was impracticable and the Iberian life style was not feasible. For a long time, after the cultural traumatization following the conquest, Mexico had no life style of her own, nor an authentic culture, but contraposed currents of original and foreign traditions, some in collision with others, still incapable of crystallizing as a new viable culture.

Moved by this spurious culture, the alienated Mexican society needed two centuries to become a national ethnos aspiring to autonomy in the conduct of its own destiny. These were two centuries of subjugation by violence in order to Hispanize, Christianize, Westernize, and model the native in the form of Ladino populations, and the simultaneous resistance, creativity, and struggle on the part of the Ladinos to become a people in their own right and not the servile external proletariat of the European project that ruled them.

The resultant ethnos emerged as a new sociocultural formation, differentiated as much from the parent populations—whose modes of being and living had become unviable—as from the European model in which they were to play the subordinate role. But it was heir to the two patrimonies, not merely different but opposed, bearing within it a conflict that made its cultural life irremediably spurious.

Fusing and integrating the two civilizational patrimonies into a new genuine culture is the great challenge facing the Mexican people. They have responded, in the course of centuries, with a highly complex process of adapting the indigenous heritage to accommodate new modes of life and new conceptions brought from Europe and of redefining these same innovations to adjust them to the old, continually modified context.

Despite its Europeanization, even the dominant caste became caught up in the process of acculturation, so much had it been differentiated from its parent population in its effort to survive, grow, and enrich itself in the New World. After several generations born in America, its integrants still behaved like exiles, sighing for a Europe they had never seen. But they already sensed that they constituted a native nobility different from the continental because of the physical type, marked by crossbreeding with the Indian, but different above all because richer and more pompous than the peninsular nobility, thanks to their silver mines, the profitable royal monopolies, and, principally, plantations.

They lived on those plantations (the ownership of which passed to the first-born by virtue of the *mayorazgo* * institution) as a haughty lordly class founded on noble titles inherited or bought and on the power of life and death over Indians and Ladinos. Their business was agriculture and the raising of cattle and mules for transport and for work in the mines. Their refined tastes, demanding a great consumption of sumptuary articles, and their pride in displaying their wealth in the size and ornamentation of their mansions and private churches erected in the *casco* † of their estates always drove them into debt. In the last decade of the eighteenth century the majority of these haciendas fell under the dominion of the clergy for nonpayment of pledges of tithes and ecclesiastical fees. Many of their owners, then, became administrators of the Church's property, with the right to show off their titles and exercise their power, but with the obligation to manage the patrimony better in order to pay the revenues demanded of them.

The growing opposition of the members of this ruling class to the European agents of the colonial power, and the clashes and discriminations resulting from the differences between their way of life and that of the peninsula, soon convinced them that they already were the leaders of a new ethnos that could affirm itself only in the framework of an independent nationality. A decisive role in this process of growing awareness was played by the urban patriciate of merchants and scholars, especially the latter, who preached breaking away because of the immediate advantage: the number of partners in the exploitation of the country would be reduced. Only in this way could they aspire to profits and honors forbidden to them as natives and mestizos.

So it became evident for the whole ruling caste that independence would bring only advantages, because the social order would remain intact, with the indigenous and Ladino mass yoked to the plantations and the mines. The decadence of Spain, incapable of integrating herself into the Industrial Revolution then under way, and incapable of confronting the new centers of imperialist power—especially the English—encouraged these emancipatory movements, giving the local dominant class the opportunity to break away from colonial status and become integrated into the emergent economic system as a neocolonial area.

The bloody struggles that followed independence for decades were unleashed mainly by the conflicts arising from the division of colonial spoils. They occurred, above all, between the new governing caste and the clergy over the derogation of the near-monopoly exercised by the Church over territorial property.

---

* *mayorazgo:* primogeniture; the entailment of estate to the first-born son.

† This word means a small segment or section, as of an orange or lemon, and is thus here used in a depreciatory sense.

The old latifundian oligarchy, more involved with the ecclesiastical interests and more alienated, embarked in the mid-nineteenth century on a European adventure that imposed on Mexico a European emperor of perfect pedigree, crowned with the support of French troops. The popular reaction was headed by Benito Juárez, who not only expelled the invaders but initiated a broad program of national and popular reforms, nationalizing the property of the clergy, which was tied to the mad scheme of the French, and imposing severe restrictions on clerical meddling in the nation's life.

Decades of conflicts followed between regional caudillos, and between groups of these and the national authority, conflicts in which the common people shed blood on both sides. From all these battles resulted the transfer of ecclesiastical property to latifundian proprietors, old and new, under whom the peasantry continued to suffer the same exploitation, which actually increased with the breakup of communal lands and the expulsion of the peasants who enjoyed their usufruct. This was decreed at the same time that possession of lands by religious bodies was prohibited; this is the way one of the chapters of the liberal *idearium* was applied against the people—all Mexicans would be thenceforth free and equal before the law —even though these privileges would only enhance their wretchedness.

The one benefit gained by the Mexican people in return for their participation in the struggles between factions of the oligarchy was the awareness of the specificity of their own cause. The warring caudillos, having to raise popular banners to enlist combatants from the rural Ladino and native masses, contributed a great deal to this mobilization, from which would result the maturation of genuine peasant leaderships motivated by their own objectives.

Their counterpart was the old class that had been swelling since the conquest. To the *contemplados,* those rewarded by the Spanish crown after the conquest with lands and vassals, were subsequently added the *encomenderos,* the holders of encomiendas, to whom was entrusted the pious duty of catechising the pagan Indian, for which purpose the latter's lands were gobbled up and his person subjugated to serfdom. With independence the old class would grow richer still, first by purchase of the lands that the Church had been forced to part with, later by "purchasing" from the state the nationalized lands formerly belonging to religious corporations, and finally by "purchase" from the Indians of the communal lands that had been compulsorily divided. Besides all these forms of appropriation of the nation's land patrimony there were the shady republican "colonization deals," which delivered up to large landholders the remaining public lands and all the private properties lacking recent and clear titles.

The descendants of the contemplados of the mother country thus became beneficiaries of the republic, always finding ways to perpetuate, through monopoly of land, a social order that not only bestowed privileges on them but placed the people at their service.

Such was the situation with which Mexico entered the first decade of the twentieth century: 80 percent of her population of 15 million lived on the fields under the domination of a thousand great lords, the hacenderos, whose properties varied from 2,000 to several million hectares [5,000 acres to 10,000 square miles and more]. The small farmers, craftsmen, and free workers amounted to nearly 500,000. The mass of peons exceeded four million.

Congruent with this social stratification, the dominant caste maintained the high standard of living it had always enjoyed and the popular masses were poorer and poorer. The latter were divided into two basic castes: the Ladinos, who through their linguistic and cultural integration were better prepared to defend themselves, and the Indian mass, of different cultural origins, driven to the poorest and most barren regions, backward not just because they adhered to archaic ways of life but principally because they were overexploited as the base of the social pyramid.

Once again over Mexico spread the waves of a technological revolution occurring in Europe. The first had been the Mercantile Revolution, which brought the Spaniards to her shores. Now it was the Industrial, and once more Mexico's society was restructured, not through evolution to a more advanced stage of human progress, as an autonomous entity, but through historical incorporation as a neocolonial formation of industrial imperialism.

The Mexican Revolution

The oligarchic social order imposed after the struggles to regain independence assumed during the late 1800's the form of a yet more rigid, more markedly inegalitarian structure than the colonial. The state had become the champion of a regime that brazenly accorded special treatment to the latifundian proprietors, to foreign capital, to large-scale commerce, and to their two associates: the clergy, which again had become a powerful force in maintaining backwardness, and a clientele of politicians, literate and military men, whose hacienda was the public treasury.

Discontent with social inequality was growing in all popular sectors, expressing itself in the most dynamic way in the workmen's strikes led by anarchosyndicalists, and particularly in spontaneous uprisings of peasants, led by caudillos, both kinds of action being crushed with the most ferocious repression. The urban middle classes of employees were stirred to liberal activity, and their intellectual faction preached the socialist revolution.

A frankly revolutionary situation was created in 1910, when two new factors were added to this generalized discontent: (1) a grave dissension in the political patriciate motivated by the "continuism" of Porfirio Díaz, who at eighty was seeking reelection after five consecutive terms as president; (2) the emergence of two genuinely peasant leaderships, that of Emiliano Zapata in Morelos, in the south, and that of Francisco Villa in Chihuahua, in the north, both at the head of armies armed with machetes and shotguns, no longer merely calling for the return of the lands to their rightful owners but for the expulsion of the latifundian proprietors from their haciendas and the distribution of the land to the workers.

In the cities, libertarian proclamations against the Díaz reelection and for real suffrage followed one after another: for public liberties, for popular education, for all the social demands then in vogue, such as the eighthour work day, minimum wage payable in cash, protection of child labor, indemnification for work accidents, equality of pay for Mexicans and foreigners, and obligation of the owners to make their haciendas productive, under penalty of confiscation of their lands for distribution to the peasants.

The urban uprising swiftly overcame the resistance of Porfirio Díaz's troops, with Francisco Madero, leader of the movement for real suffrage, taking over the government. Simultaneously, however, the peasant insurrections spread, their leaders, not content to satisfy Madero's presidential aspirations, demanding agrarian reform. Zapata launched the Ayala Plan, declaring that he would not lay down his arms until the government restored to the *ejidos* [communal farmlands] and to the peasants all the lands from which they had been dispossessed by the hacenderos. That is how they initiated the real Mexican social revolution, which convulsed the whole country and was to continue in bloody fighting until 1919.

In 1914 Venustiano Carranza (succeeding Huerta, who had deposed Madero) took command of the legal troops and, estimating the vigor of the peasant struggles, sought to parley with their leaders. He went on to proclaim, in successive documents, his readiness to carry out agrarian reform. In spite of this new language, the head of the government did not inspire confidence, or contain by force of arms the nationwide revolutionary outbreak of the Zapatistas, who occupied the capital, and of the Villistas, who dominated nearly all the north. Carranza managed to defeat the two revolutionary leaders only after years of fighting, reiterating his commitments to carry out agrarian reforms and attend to all the social demands from the urban sectors. And he defeated them because he gained the alliance of the "red battalions," organized by the urban working classes under the leadership of the anarchosyndicalists, to collaborate in the fighting that put an end to the peasant insurrection.

The Mexican Revolution, then, accomplished its first stage, the pacification of the civil war by crushing the forces of Zapata and Francisco Villa, followed by the pursuit of the remains of their troops—transformed into guerrillas—in the areas where they had been most active and where they had counted on the full support of the peasantry. Only with the bloodiest repression of the peasants and the murder of the two leaders were the guerrillas put down.

The major revolutionary aspirations, however, had been satisfied by the 1917 Constitution, composed in the heat of the fight. It assured the government the power to expropriate private property for the achievement of agrarian reform; it instituted a broad social legislation of protection for the working class; it restrained the interference of the clergy in public matters; and it assigned the state the ownership of the subsoil and the control of the mineral and petroleum deposits.

Other than the land distribution made by the insurgent peasants themselves all other plans were realized only partially and over a long period. Invested with the presidency, Carranza began to resort to subterfuges and evasiveness, eventually being overthrown and killed as he fled with the state treasury. Only with President Obregón, in 1920, would compliance with the constitutional dictates regarding agrarian reform and the bases for pacification of peasant uprisings begin.

The Mexican Revolution had lasted nearly a decade; it had cost more than 1 million lives out of a population of 15 million, not to mention the enormous economic waste. At last the political demands of the people were met: since then a president never has been reelected, and the country has entered on a regime of full institutional stability. Notable, too, are the victories on the social plane, especially with the initiation of agrarian reform and economic reconstruction. This was to be carried out with President Plutarco Elías Calles, starting in 1924, when a political action plan was defined to join battle with the latifundium. A vast program of works, including irrigation, was begun and the Party of the Revolution, which was to centralize all political power in the presidency of the country, was founded.

A new ruling caste began to rise, then, recruited from the old elite of ex-latifundium proprietors, merchants, and bankers and from the recent elite of revolutionaries grown rich. This new national directorate professed its devotion to the ideas of the revolution, but it aspired above all to tranquilize the country, to assure Mexico the stability that she had never known, to structure a liberal-capitalist regime better able to face North American intervention. But the Mexicans had become so radical that the new power could never define itself as antirevolutionary, though it did everything possible to attain and consolidate that objective.

As years passed, the new dominant class expanded and became homogeneous. It was a literate, nationalist, progressive urban bourgeoisie whose interests lay principally in industry, commerce, and banks, seconded by an ample bureaucratic and military body of advisors drawn from the middle classes; it was served by the *charros* [Mexican peasants], who controlled the unions, and by a vast clientele of employees and officials. This new ruling caste occupied the power vacuum left by the caudillo type of leadership, which had been stamped out, and by the popular leaderships, sold out to or controlled by the bourgeoisie since the anarchosyndicalist leaders' agreement with Carranza. The new dominant class was to recontrive the privatist social order, the "Mexican system," always speaking in the name of the revolution, rendering homage to the irredentist virtues of not only Zapata and Villa but also of Carranza and Obregón, and, simultaneously, to take the greatest and most zealous care not to allow the rise of popular leaderships outside the institutional framework.

The 1924–1934 decade saw the consolidation of this new power and the institutionalization of the renovating energies unchained by the revolution. It accomplished little in the field of agrarian reform or in the promised social and educational reforms. Consequently the popular outcry again manifested itself in strikes and peasant agitations. Even in 1930 nearly 15,500 proprietors, less than 2 per cent of the total number, held 83 per cent of the appropriated area of the country. On the other hand, foreign investments, largely from the United States, in the name of whose interests the Yankee government had repeatedly intervened in the Mexican Revolution—by armed attack, economic pressure, threats, and supply of weapons—enormously increased, restoring their domination over the Mexican economy, which had been gravely endangered during the years of fighting.

The Mexican Revolution experienced its most dynamic period under the presidency of Lázaro Cárdenas (1934–1940), proving that under the ashes it still glowed and was capable of facing up to the new class that until then had managed to postpone the reorganizing impact on its interests. Cárdenas alone distributed nearly as many lands (17 million hectares) as those given out before and after him (36 million up to 1956). Furthermore, Cárdenas headed the first Latin American government to oppose foreign exploitation successfully, expropriating the railway enterprises (largely English) and the North American oil companies, paying for the latter the value of the original investment ($24 million) and not the demanded price ($450 million). Likewise, during Cárdenas' term of office

Mexican syndicalism was structured to assume, in the following decade, a leading role in the independent labor movement in Latin America.

Under Cárdenas the Mexican nation succeeded—as the highest result of his presidency—in restoring to the peasant and labor masses their lost confidence in the institutionalized revolution. For the accomplishment of agrarian reform against the foci of resistance, his government armed the peasants. To impose their rights granted by law but never respected, his government organized the working class into unions that, even though instituted by the state, were designed to win higher wages and better health and welfare services.

As a result of this policy the Cárdenas government, supported by the people through the peasant and labor union organizations, so strengthened the Revolutionary Party that the presidential elections and the selection of senators and state governors were confirmed by popular vote. This concentration of political power was expressed in the national congress, where government projects could always count on majority approval, and in the supreme court decisions, equally attentive to the presidential will. The same control was exercised over the state and municipal governments, politically and financially dependent on the federal executive and subject to its intervention. All this represented an extreme fortifying of the power and unity of the Mexican state, which in this way attained a much greater capacity for resisting Yankee expansionism and intervention and for carrying out national development programs.

Under Cárdenas, the Mexican Revolution reached its supreme moment of control over the two determining factors of the national destiny: (1) the internal constrictive forces, reduced to an urban bourgeoisie whose field of action was limited by the public enterprises dominating certain sectors; (2) the foreign investors, who were compelled to heed the governmental decisions, no matter how contrary to their interests,[6] and to accept innovations in the treatment they had always imposed on Latin American governments.

On the other hand, the unified power of all these forces—the only, or massive-majority, official party; governmental control over the union headquarters and the peasant movement; the control and clientelistic utilization of the powerful state machine; the disciplining of the army for its specific functions—made the Mexican state a monolithic power susceptible to the gravest deformations. This was indeed to happen after Cárdenas,

---

[6] These measures stirred the U.S. government to indignant claims through all diplomatic channels and through the world press. But these were empty claims because of the United States' total incapacity for an otherwise than disastrous confrontation with the new Mexican state, particularly because the United States was currently facing the effects of the Depression.

with the increased political influence of the new bourgeoisie, which, already controlling the economic system, was able to use the discipline imposed on the other strata to benefit from the over-all system.

In spite of these defects, Mexico succeeded in realizing her social and national revolution, becoming the first Latin American nation capable of formulating her own developmental project and of maintaining an autonomous and progressive foreign policy. She succeeded also in abolishing the political power of the old latifundian oligarchy and, further, in imbuing her people with a new, almost cathartic, attitude: a lofty assumption of their own ethnic characteristics and an identification of the nationality and the revolution as the frameworks in which the potentialities of the Mexican people would express themselves.

Anticipating the Russian Revolution, Mexico could perhaps have been the first model of socialistic society. For that it would have been necessary to have a mature revolutionary leadership, capable of laying the bases for an alliance of the peasant insurrections with the syndicalized working class. The important thing, however, is that without attaining objectives—expressed in some basic documents, especially by Zapata [7]—the Mexican Revolution turned a generalized popular insurrection into a force for revision of the whole regime, achieving results equivalent to those of the English, North American, and French revolutions. Like these, Mexico suc-

[7] Emiliano Zapata, in a letter written in 1918, compares the Mexican Revolution with the Russian in these terms: "We should gain much, and human justice would gain much, if all the peoples of our America and of all the nations of old Europe would understand that the cause of Revolutionary Mexico and the cause of Revolutionary Russia are and represent the cause of humanity, the supreme interest of all oppressed. Mr. Wilson, President of the United States, was right in recently rendering homage to the Russian Revolution, qualifying it as 'a noble effort for the advent of liberties.' . . . And it would only be desirable that, along this line, the visible analogy, the marked parallelism, the absolute parity, rather, existing between that movement and the Agrarian Revolution of Mexico should be remembered and taken into careful account. Both are directed toward what Leo Tolstoy had called 'the great crime,' the infamous usurpation of the land, which, being the property of all, like water and air, has been monopolized by a few powerful men supported by the force of armies and by the iniquity of laws. It is not to be wondered at, for that very reason, that the world proletariat applauds and admires the Russian Revolution, in the same way that it will lend its full adherence and sympathy and support to this Mexican Revolution, once it fully realizes what our objectives are. It must not be forgotten that by virtue of the effect of the solidarity among the proletariat, the emancipation of the worker cannot be achieved unless at the same time the liberation of the peasant is accomplished. Otherwise, the bourgeoisie will be able to set these two forces against each other and profit by the ignorance of the peasants to combat and restrain the impulses of the urban workers; and if the opportunity offers, it will be able to make use of the unwary workers and launch them against their country brothers" (quoted by Carlos Rama, 1962, pp. 139–140).

ceeded in reopening the debate on the old oligarchic ordination, reformulating it to eliminate the economic and political power of the latifundium, limit the domination exercised over the whole national life by the United States, institute an autonomous national state armed with considerable power of decision over everything affecting the national destiny, and integrate the majority of its population into the productive system and the cultural and political life of the country.

Like these revolutions, on the other hand, the Mexican Revolution had exhausted the two fundamental dynamic factors of social reordering, namely, agrarian reform and the capacity to confront the Yankees, without destroying the forces constricting its development. It therefore fell from an oligarchic order to a capitalist-patrician order structured as a modernizing nationalist sociocultural formation. Thenceforth, it would grow economically in form and intensity compatible with maintenance of the interests, both foreign and national, that were to rule its economic life. The preservation of these interests limits its prospects for progress by imposing a growth rate that will only within a century allow it to attain the economic and social development already reached by the more advanced nations, by which time the latter will be much further advanced. The new challenge facing Mexico consists in the forces that are combined to block the full realization of her potentialities.

What assured the Mexican Revolution a profound social significance was its nature as a movement capable of mobilizing the marginalized masses, composed principally of indigenes. From it came the incorporation of millions of Indians into the economic, social, and political life as Ladino peasants and an appreciable rise in Mexican agricultural production. In many other ways an equal increase in production could be obtained, probably, but obtained in the way it was, through the constitution of millions of farmers and the revitalization of thousands of communal villages (ejidos) throughout the country, it was a formidable integrative force, exemplary even today for nations containing great segments of the population culturally or socially marginalized from the national life. The checking of the revolutionary impetus, after Cárdenas, thanks to the force of inertia, barely allowed Mexico to continue in this process. This same impulse led to new stagnation of the emancipatory forces of the marginal masses.

The combativeness of the peasant movement having been mollified by the satisfaction of its most crying needs, and the urban proletariat taken into account and later disciplined by the bureaucratization of the syndicalist movement, a political vacuum was created that permitted the urban bourgeoisie and the middle class to take over the machinery of the state. Thus, the revolutionary energy was replaced by a purely verbal eloquence that today verges on the ridiculous. In its new aspect the Mexican Revolution is abandoning the agrarian radical banner to defend an agricultural technology. It is likewise abandoning the old nationalist banners, causing mere xenophobia to succeed antiimperialism, and xenophobia is impotent as an autonomist force of action.

Two disastrous effects stemming from this situation made themselves felt immediately. First, the invasion of Mexico by foreign capital, largely from the United States (in 1953, of the twenty-six Mexican private enterprises with more than 100 million pesos income each, nineteen were the property of U.S. Americans), deformed the industrialization of the country by the decapitalization imposed on it (from 1941 to 1961 the average remittance of profits always exceeded the investments), as well as by the substitution of a management caste representing exogenous interests for the national entrepreneurial group. Second, the growing fortification of the influence of the national patriciate and of that management caste, to the prejudice of the popular classes, represented in power only by compliant leaders.

This patrician hegemony accounts for the fact that nearly all the lands benefited by great public irrigation works were denied the peasant and handed over to private, city-oriented entrepreneurs. This situation prevented the elevation of the ejido-bound indigenes and the minifundium-bound small proprietor to a higher social status through integration in modern collectivist forms of agricultural exploitation. And, above all, a flagrant contrast was set up between the economic prosperity of the capitalist, established on good irrigated lands, ministered to with official credits, and the Indian peasant condemned to inefficacy and poverty.

Through all these circumstances the machine of the state, a result of the national mobilization fostered by the revolution, having broken with the national-emancipatory and popular-revolutionary objectives, preserved the new privatist social order. And by that time its power of coercion over the country and the people was so great that one can hardly imagine a rupture that would permit reopening the regime to question as occurred in 1910 and 1934.

Can the live coals be so hot under the ashes that a new Cárdenas could emerge in the institutional Revolutionary Party itself? Or is the only prospect for Mexicans a struggle for an opening in political life through parliamentary procedures in order to become a liberal-bourgeois republic on the classic model? Are the statist contents of the economy capable of spreading to other sectors, or will they tend progressively to remain stationary?

The major forces generating great tensions in present-day Mexican society are its marginal masses of Indians disinherited from all national progress and the growing masses of urban marginal people providing a reserve of labor in the over-all system. These masses, however, because of their cultural and social marginality and the effect of the spoliation they have endured from the rural and urban Ladino sectors, can hardly propose a redefinition of the national project that will give them better prospects for integration into the Mexican society. Until now, they seemed condemned to a merely passive role, hoping that the benevolence of the state would provide protection and money doles to raise their standard of living so that they will not continue to shame the country with the scandal of their misery. Nevertheless, everything indicates that in the future they can be activated as a potentially revolutionary force.

Only in 1960, after four centuries, did Mexico succeed in rebuilding her pre-Columbian demographic total, as she reached 35 million population. It was a new society, however, transfigured ethnically and rebuilt from its bases as a highly differentiated variant from the Hispanic macroethnos. The urban population had reached 51 per cent of the total; the per capita income was U.S. $408; literacy exceeded 62 per cent among those more than six years of age; industrialization and mechanization indexes in various sectors of the economy were also among the highest in Latin America. And yet there were still, in the Mexico of 1960, nearly 10 million Mexicans of indigenous extraction who spoke either Spanish and a tribal language or only the latter. They are illiterate and barefoot; they are not in the habit of eating wheat, bread, fish, eggs, or milk. This marginal stratum, which has been increasing in absolute numbers in these last years because its growth index is greater than its rate of integration into the national society, is the heritage from the original Mexico and from the Spanish conquest, from the deformations imposed on the Mexican people by the colonialism succeeding it, and from the progressive abandonment of the social dimension of the Mexican Revolution.

Of all the Witness Peoples of America, Mexico was the earliest to take cognizance of herself, accepting her own image, assuming a national ideological posture before the world, and drawing from the Aztec-Náhuatl heritage her principal integrating symbols. To this her very character of Witness People contributed decisively, in which the patrimonies of two high civilizations coexist, in a process of fusion. Her proximity to the United States, the long struggle to fix the respective boundaries, and the efforts to check the domination of the Mexican economy by the great U.S. corporations also contributed to this national self-awareness.

The United States that attacked Mexico in the past century already constituted a capitalistic society undergoing intensive industrialization, opposed to an agromercantile society paralyzed by the oligarchic constriction of the native seignorial class, which had succeeded the Spaniards and which was taking the first steps to overcome the conditions of backwardness to which Hispanic domination had subjected it for centuries. A national leadership was just beginning to emerge, still confused with the caudillo uprisings but trying to institutionalize the new nucleus of decisions, a nucleus transferred from Europe to Mexico, confronting the aggression from the France of Napoleon III, who wanted to impose an emperor on the country. All these difficulties were increased by the former English colony's expansionism, snatching away half of Mexico's original territory by warfare and treaties signed under pressure and bribery—the whole area from Texas to California.

Among the Witness Peoples of America, Mexico is also the one that has succeeded in integrating the greatest segment of the population into her economic life as active consumers and producers, and into social, political, and cultural life as persons, as citizens, and as neo-Mexicans. This category, which comprises 70 per cent of the population, is distributed through the most varied income levels, stratified in profoundly differentiated social classes, but united as the body and the expression of nationality. Racially they are mestizos, predominantly indigenous, but with parcels of European and African genes. Culturally they bear within them the two conflicting heritages, the Hispano-European and the native. The latter is more romantic than promotive and directive, because the neo-Mexican who assumes an Aztec-Náhuatl posture before the foreigner, when confronted by his own countrymen admits that his future lies in his compulsory de-Indianization through Europeanizing education.

This is probably a natural effect of the formative process of Mexican nationality, but not an inevitable one. It is in any case lamentable to see indigenes, numbering tens of thousands, continuing after four centuries to cling to the values of their original culture and remaining condemned by modern Mexico to be integrated into the role of non-Indians, which they never accepted and which until now they have been incapable of performing.

This stratum, which represents a third of the Mexican population, is marginal as much for its conditions of backwardness as for its Indian nature condemned to be Mexicanized. The socioeconomic resistances impeding their integration into modern Mexico's life style are enhanced by ethnocultural obstacles. The latter are probably more deep-rooted and difficult to eradicate because of the extraordinary vigor of self-preservation in the ethnos, especially when submitted to discriminations and coercions.

This Mexican indigenous contingent, which for centuries endured all the rigors of slavery, catechism, and every imaginable form of cultural oppression, may possibly find in its ethnic identification the power to continue to resist assimilation. The fate of the most populous ethnic groups will perhaps be to constitute themselves into differentiated modes of participation in the national entity, gradually growing more like the rest, but irreducibly singular through adherence to their ethnic loyalties. They will, in the future, be differentiated national parcels such as those subsisting in nearly all the European nations after millennia of uniformizing compression.

The character of Witness People is expressed in modern Mexico principally by the partition of society into three superposed segments or social strata differentiated by their ethnic identification as indigenes or as neo-Mexicans, and by their unequal participation in the access to, and control of, national wealth and political power.

The superior segment is formed by the association of the patronal class, composed of great industrial proprietors, financiers, and merchants, with the patriciate of professional politicians, military chiefs, bureaucrats, and technocrats created by the revolution. This stratum, racially and culturally more Europeanized, controls the economy and the political institutions and directs the revolutionary legend itself, proudly venerated but congealed through repression of any form of popular opposition. Without dividing the power, it engages broad sectors of the middle class in the political machine by means of the spoils system and corruption. In this class are the traditional families of the colonial aristocracy, mixed with indigenous stocks subsisting from the Aztec patriciate and amplified by all those who have grown rich. It is essentially the same class that undertook independence as its own project, reordering society in line with its interests, and that later faced great difficulties over agrarian reform, which deprived it of its fundamental instrument of domination. But it survived everything and preserved its domination, thanks to a mere enlargement by absorbing parcels of the urban population enriched within the Mexican system.

The intermediate stratum, considered mestizo, is less that racially—though it has absorbed a certain proportion of European and African blood—than through its integration into the Hispano-American culture through Hispanization, conversion to Catholicism, and organic incorporation into the national society. Originally it constituted the intermediary stratum between the Spanish aristocracy and the native masses and was recruited from the middle sector of Aztec society (functionaries, priests, merchants, craftsmen), which, as an urban and parasitic stratum, was in better condition to be Europeanized. In their effort to survive they created conciliatory mechanisms between the old and the new worlds, becoming bilingual and duocultural, shaping the model of the neo-Mexican that progressively became generalized as Ladino through the recruitment of Indians torn from their communities and integrated into the national society as a labor force for field and city. Today that vast Ladino stratum forms the largest parcel of the nation and constitutes the Mexican common people, covering the peasantry to the rural wage-earner, the urban workingman to the low strata of the rural and city middle class.

The third class is formed by the mass of those culturally marginalized as indigenes. Today they are almost as little indigenous—in the pre-Columbian sense—as the other Mexicans, so great were the cultural alterations undergone in four centuries. But they are unified ethnically as members of their tribal communities and diversified from the Ladinos by a particular body of cultural norms and loyalties, which not only distinguishes them from but opposes them to the national society as different and immiscible folk. They do not constitute the equivalent of the peasantry in an agro-craftsman society of the classic type, because this peasantry is represented by the Ladinos. They are a marginal category that has lost its ancient way of life, but has become modern indigenous instead of neo-Mexican. It faces the most difficult conditions of want and backwardness as the most exploited stratum, relegated to the most inhospitable areas.

The process of making these Indian contingents "Mexican" continues through individual access to Ladino status by those who separate from their communities. In that sense these nuclei operate as human breeding places, a part of which is seducible as a national labor force through the very conditions of want in which they live. Since the revolution became an integrationist movement, there has been a regression in the massive process of integrating these indigenous communities in national life. From that time on, the integrative energy has lain merely in the compulsions that take place over the rural communities, such as the atomization of indigenous properties into minifundia and the misery that obliges them to emigrate as manual laborers to other areas. To these forces propelling the populations outside of their communities are added the attractions of the urban nuclei, which, thanks to industrialization and the consequent expansion of services, offer increasing opportunities for work for those torn from the country. These two forces are impinging on the periphery of the metropolitan centers, marginalized masses much larger than the economy is capable of absorbing in the occupational system.

The principal balance remaining from the dynamic period of the Mexican Revolution has been the rise of the Ladino and "Ladinizable" mass to the status of Mexican people as it exists today through agrarian reform and, likewise, the national pacification, which put a stop to the caudillism that had kept Mexico in turmoil ever since independence. The Mexican national problem of our time is to take up again the revolutionary dynamic to redefine the privatist order that has implanted itself, checking the creative energies of the people and condemning millions of Mexicans to marginality. Institutionalizing itself as a modernizing nationalism, the postrevolutionary Mexican state was able to foster agrarian reform and start a

movement of substitutive industrialization. But it did not succeed in formulating an autonomous project of self-construction that would assure a
full autonomous development in foreseeable time periods. On the contrary,
it experienced a detention of integrative energies and oriented itself toward
a policy of economic complementarism with the United States, ending by
incorporating Mexico into the world economic system as an area of neocolonial exploitation.

Only by resuming the Cárdenas path and establishing herself as a socialist formation will Mexico be able to establish an industrialization that will
permit constructing the broad infrastructure indispensable to the maintenance of a progress rate necessary to overcome, in any foreseeable time,
her economic and social backwardness in relation to the fully developed
nations. Only along that path will Mexico achieve the degree of national
integration and development that can restore autonomy to her people in
the guidance of her destiny and permit her self-expression in modern industrial civilization.

Central America

Mesoamerica is the area extending from Mexico to the Colombian border and consisting today of five nations, plus a counterfeit of a nation fash-
ioned by the United States and a British colonial pocket. The whole, as
Witness Peoples, comprises Guatemala, with 56 per cent indigenous population, Honduras with 10 per cent, San Salvador with 20 per cent, and
Nicaragua with 24 per cent. To this whole are to be added two ethnic intrusions: Costa Rica, which had a New People formation through the fusion of natives with Europeans, and Panama, the U.S. American creation
snatched from Colombia in order to throw out the French builders of the
canal and take over the enterprise. The entire area contains fewer than 10
million inhabitants (1960). Two and a half million are indigenes bound to
their original culture and concentrated mainly in Guatemala, lending it a
typical Witness People physiognomy; 1.5 million light mestizos concentrated, principally, in Costa Rica; the remaining majority is formed by the
Ladinos, of more indigenous than Spanish phenotype with some Negro
seasoning, who have been blending since the conquest.

In this region burgeoned one of the highest civilizations in the world,
the Maya, which, though not reaching the urban and imperial level of the
Egyptians, the Incas, and the Aztecs, attained a high degree of development. It was an irrigation-agricultural civilization whose most notable cul-

tural achievements were a system of writing, arithmetic, a calendar excelled in precision only by our own, an architecture of stepped pyramids and sumptuous burial buildings, and an extraordinary monolithic sculpture —the stele—regarded as among the most elevated artistic expressions of man. It is probable also that the Mayas were the first civilization in the world to develop in tropical jungle areas, having created a model of urban structure adapted to these ecological conditions.

At the time of the Spanish conquest the Mayas had been in decadence for many centuries, victimized by disruptive forces that have never been precisely identified. Their population, estimated at a minimum of 2 million, lived in agricultural communities and in religious centers, where it was differentiated into strata of priests, functionaries, merchants, and craftsmen. South of the Maya area lived innumerable less evolved groups, linguistically distinct but all influenced in a certain measure by the two great civilizations of the region.

After the conquest of Mexico, bands of Spaniards coming from the Mexican territory and the Antilles fell on the survivors of the Mayas. They sacked everything that had any value and installed themselves as new seigniors, immediately afterwards, however, tearing one another to pieces in sanguinary disputes. The area was progressively divided by Spain into various provinces corresponding to the present nations, all subject to the jurisdiction of the authorities headquartered in Mexico.

During the colonial period, alongside the indigenous populations of Mesoamerica a few thousand Spaniards established themselves as encomenderos, appropriating lands and enslaving the natives who lived therein. With this forced labor the gold and silver mines were exploited, and with the same was organized, slowly, an export agricultural exploitation of cacao, tobacco, indigo, and cochineal. The relative success of this spoliation was manifested in the rise of a network of new towns and cities and, with them, of increasingly efficacious mechanisms of exploiting the natives, whose uprisings followed one after the other.

Far from the Spanish military and administrative center, the region fell easy prey to aggressors and smugglers, principally Englishmen who settled at some points along the coast and finally possessed themselves of two areas: the Mosquito Coast and British Honduras, the latter of which they still control today.

The formation of the modern peoples of Central America followed the Mexican in general lines, creating likewise an alienated oligarchy and patriciate and a caste committed to their service, all living on the exploitation of the indigenous populations. The one exception is Costa Rica, where the Spaniard, establishing himself with more backward populations and remaining for a long time in isolated conditions, formed a patriarchal society of small proprietors, more Europeanized than the other peoples of the region.

Independence came with a Mexican unionist project that proposed to emancipate and organize as a single state all the former provinces of the viceroyalty of New Spain. The plan was frustrated, however, by the provinces' opposition to unification under the command of the former colonial center, and because of the internal conflicts that followed Mexican independence. Then a federal republic of the Central American peoples was formed, directed by a triumvirate, which could not impose its authority, either, conflicts breaking out between the former provinces until the breakup occurred.

A vivid Central American federalist aspiration still lingers on today. It remains unattainable, however, owing to the opposition of the foreign interests invested in that area, principally U.S. American and English, who feel better protected by the division into small republics.

Formal independence was followed by decades of French and English imperialistic domination through the usual mechanism of concessions of loans, construction of railways, ports, and telegraph services, which had been proved a more efficacious form of monopolistic control and exploitation than the colonial statute itself. The last vestiges of national respectability were annulled by the United States, which, in the name of the Monroe Doctrine, of the maintenance of order, of the defense of its citizens' lives and property, or with no justification whatever, established a regime of guardianship over Central America, only allowing the English to associate in its domination.

It was in these conditions that in the last years of the past century (1899) the United Fruit Company installed itself in the area and became the real center of decisions for the whole region, commanding the economic, political, and social life of Guatemala, Honduras, Costa Rica, and Panama. United Fruit appropriated 35 per cent of the cultivable lands and nearly all the lands suited to the cultivation of bananas and pineapple in these countries, establishing itself as a monopolistic corporation of production, transportation, and commerce that permitted it to dominate the world market of tropical fruits. Thus, passing over Mexico, which she could not swallow—after appropriating all her peripheral territories—the United States attacked the countries of the isthmus, installing in them Yankee order and peace in their most elaborated form.

The republics of Central America therefore, in their backwardness and poverty, are one of the most expressive examples of the potentialities of the U.S. model of ancillary development under the aegis of its corporations. Together with the installation of these companies, the United States set up an intervention machine that conferred on Yankee embassies the power to legislate, to elect parliaments and presidents, to appoint and overthrow dictators, to enrich, to impoverish, to exile, to incarcerate, and to murder any citizen. There too, on extremely fertile lands, U.S. agricultural enterprises had every freedom of action and movement for which they strove in other areas of the globe, as an indispensable condition for the fostering of progress. Because of all this, the "banana republics"—as the Yankees called them—portrayed to the world, in the form of a concrete, visible, measurable experiment, what the U.S.-advocated developmental model can offer.

The Central American nations are the perfect kingdom of stable currency, free trade, free international exchange, private initiative, and even regional economic integration, instituted for the first time in Latin America through the Central American Common Market. They evidence, therefore, all the prerequisites of the U.S. economic ideology for guaranteeing a high rate of progress and all the political and institutional bases for developing perfect democracies. The results are the Ubicos, the Martínez, the Somozas, and others. Can the Middle American Indians and mestizos be in a conspiracy to discredit the Yankee proponents of democracy and development in the eyes of the world? Or can that sublimate of oppression, ignorance, obscurantism, and want be the natural and necessary product of the free congregation of Latin American economies with Yankee enterprises?

Every time a Central American nation finds a breach to rebel against this system of spoliation, which has turned it into the most retrograde zone on the continent, it is the United States that restores peace and order by restoring the privileges of its enterprises and of the local oligarchies. It happened with the guerrilla insurrection of Sandino; the same thing occurred when, after a student revolt had been crushed with much bloodshed, a governmental junta was set up that promoted the first election in El Salvador. This also happened when the C.I.A., in a painstaking military coup, deposed President Jacobo Arbenz.

Like the Antillean nations, the isthmus republics have been the victims of successive invasions by the United States. These interventions culminated during the first decades of the present century with the Mexican Revolution, which, rising up against the imperialist interests and the privileges of the native minorities, threatened Yankee hegemony in the Caribbean. They were repeated with the Castro revolution for fear the Cuban example find propitious terrain to subvert Yankee order throughout the region.

A series of American invasions and interventions began in Nicaragua in 1909, over the refusal to grant the United States the right to construct a canal linking the Atlantic with the Pacific. Each landing was followed by a loan to the Nicaraguan government by means of which the Americans were indemnified for the costs of the war operations and were permitted to appropriate the most lucrative sectors of the national economy. The canal concession was finally obtained in 1914, and its Nicaraguan negotiator was elected president, governing the country with the support of U.S. troops, either directly or through intermediaries, until 1925.

In 1926 the marines again invaded Nicaragua to combat an uprising led by Sandino. Son of the proprietor of a medium-sized hacienda and a peasant woman of Indian stock, Augusto César Sandino, mechanic and farmer, was to become the symbol of anti-Yankee resistance in Central America and one of the precursors of guerrilla warfare. His cause was originally the reconstitutionalization of the country, but after the intensification of American intervention it turned into a war against the foreign invader. This is why it awakened the sympathy and the adhesion of all the libertarian movements in Latin America, especially the Apristas,* whose ideals Sandino at the time regarded more highly than did Haya de la Torre himself.

Starting with twenty-nine men, the Nicaraguan caudillo gathered together, at the height of the struggle, nearly 3,000 combatants, among them volunteers from several American countries. This army was able to oppose 12,000 invaders and the local troops supporting the government; the larger forces, equipped with the most modern military resources, never succeeded in defeating and subjugating him. Sandino laid down his arms only after achieving the repatriation of the U.S. troops, the principal motivation for his fighting. As we have seen, this struggle was characterized by a nationalist ideology that had its keynote in the awareness of the indigenous ancestry of the Nicaraguan populace; the Nicaraguans identified with the Indo-American community in opposition to the oppressive *gringo* † America. It is from that ethnic consciousness of Sandino—in flagrant contrast to the alienation of the Central American dominant classes, English-speaking and submissive to their Yankee masters—that his power as a caudillo came, the leader of men who called one another "brothers" among themselves and none of whom received pay or had any other ambition than to oust the invader. This identification with the national ethnos assured Sandino of the support of the rural masses, predominantly mestizo, affording him successive victories and domination of vast areas of the country's interior.

---

* *Aprista:* member of the political party known as A.P.R.A. (see Chapter 4, n.3).

† Most often used in Spanish America as a term derogatory to U.S. Americans, *gringo* means any foreigner of Anglo-Saxon or European descent.

Without a specific project to take over the presidency and to rebuild society on new bases, Sandino's struggle could not last indefinitely. After
seven years of fighting, he was finally betrayed and assassinated by the
chief of the national guard—which had been created by the Americans as
shock troops in the defense of the foreign interests.

The second episode in the struggle for Central American freedom that
galvanized world opinion was the overthrow of the Guatemalan government of Jacobo Arbenz in 1954, when it was initiating agrarian reform
with the distribution of lands, legally owned but not utilized by the United
Fruit Company and other North American one-product enterprises, to the
Indians and peasants. The crudely reactionary nature of the military coup,
and the fact that it had been planned and directed by the C.I.A., reiterated
before the world the weight of the U.S. veto of any progressive government in the Caribbean and the untouchability of its entrepreneurial interests in the area. Only Cuba has been capable of confronting and overriding
this veto.

The disillusionment of the Guatemalans over the outcome of the Arbenz
reformist action led to the radicalization of its more combative sectors,
summoning the peasant population, predominantly indigenous and until
then resigned to its poverty, to the struggle. Thus, in 1962, after a frustrated military movement with redemocratizing and antiimperialist objectives, the guerrilla fighting began. This came about with new programmatic
aims, socialistic in character, resulting from the conviction that no government of reformist conciliation offered a minimum guarantee of victory and
progress to the Central American peoples.

Despite their contrasts, the Central American nations must be classified as
Witness Peoples because of the decisive influence of the Maya in the formation of their Ladino populations and, in the majority of them, because of
the survival of great marginal indigenous contingents. These contingents
are found principally in Guatemala, where more than 1 million Indians are
monolingual and, with basis in the old Mayan cultural patrimony, are living at a bare subsistence level.

Two nations contrast with the rest as ethnic intrusions. (1) Costa Rica,
whose population is of predominantly Spanish descent, is concentrated on
the central plateau and is distinguished by her high index of education (a
scant 21 per cent illiteracy) and by having been institutionalized as a representative democracy based on a broad stratum of farmers, merchants,
and functionaries. Besides this population of whites-by-definition, the
country contains only an Antillean Negro contingent brought in for the
construction of a railroad and compelled to settle on the coast as a marginal nucleus, discriminated against as an ethnic cyst and as a labor re-

serve for the great United Fruit plantations. (2) Panama is not really a nation because of her artificial creation and the coercion exerted over her by the United States making impossible any effort at national integration. Her population is divided into four distinct segments, segregated from and hostile to one another. The Negroes, also brought from the West Indies for work on the canal, speak English and are separated from the rest of the population by racial discrimination. The original Ladino society, with its mulatto descendants, stratified in classes from a local oligarchy of powerful merchants and large landowners to a broad intermediate stratum of public employees and clerks in urban services, down to a vast mass of the disinherited, struggling against underemployment and unemployment in the cities and the rural zones. Dominating this structure of Indians, Negro immigrants, and Ladinos hovers the U.S. American elite, exploiters of the canal and of military command. They live segregated in so conspicuously privileged a situation that no manner of violence can prevent manifestations of discontent and growing political consciousness of the Panamanians.

4. The Andeans

IN THE MOUNTAINOUS area 3,000 kilometers in length, extending from northern Chile to southern Colombia and covering the present territories of Bolivia, Peru, and Ecuador, and on the slopes descending to the Pacific, we find the second bloc of Witness Peoples of the Americas living on the plateaus, in the high Andean valleys and on the coast. They are the contemporary witnesses to the Inca civilization. They speak Aymará and Quechua, they work the land, they produce handicrafts, and they structure themselves in communities and in families for work, leisure, and worship, according to a combination of new techniques, norms, and values of European origin and old ones surviving from the original indigenous cultures. This cultural complex was redefined in view of the living conditions that it had to take into account in the course of the last four centuries, and today constitutes one of the most marked facets of the human phenomenon.

The total population of the area was estimated in 1960 at about 15.5 million: 7.5 million indigenous, 3 million whites-by-self-definition, and 5 million *cholos* [Andean equivalent of mestizo]. The predominance of the indigenous contingent is obvious, and adding in the cholos, it amounts to 80 per cent of the total population. In spite of the linguistic differentiations and the cultural and national variants, the entire bloc must be regarded as a single historicocultural complex and a single macroethnos, the neo-Inca. Its division into three nationalities—Peruvian, Bolivian, Ecuadoran—can be explained only by the fortunes of Hispanic colonization and the oligarchic order that followed independence, with the domination of Madrid replaced by the directorate of oligarchic groups.

Within the neo-Inca context, whites-by-self-definition are the Hispano-indigenous mestizos of the middle and upper class, originating principally from the racial blendings of the first centuries of the conquest. Cholos are Ladinos predominantly indigenous from the racial point of view, but deculturated and integrated into the economic and social system as its poorest parcel. And indigenes are the contingents marginalized from national life through being bound to the rural communities that preserve the language and part of the original culture; they see themselves with their own perspective, different from and alien to the world of the whites, which established itself in their territories to dominate and exploit them, and different also from the cholos, who are the immediate agents of that domination.

The Original Inca World

The Inca civilization contrasts with the Maya and the Aztec by a less mystic image and a profound organizational sense that permitted them to structure one of the most cohesive and best integrated irrigation theocratic empires in history. They had attained an urban level of civilization, served by a magnificent transportation system that joined Cuzco, their capital, with the whole Andean highland, and permitted them to control and distribute harvests and bind together thousands of communities. Population has been estimated at more than 10 million.[1] The city of Cuzco, located in the center of the cordillera at an altitude of some 11,400 feet, was at the time of the conquest one of the four or five greatest cities in the world.

What that ultraorganized human hive was like can still be seen today in the ruins of its capital city, with its streets and roadways and its stepped terraces constructed for irrigation cultivation. These terraces descend the

[1] This figure must be taken as minimal, because the most recent and best-documented studies put it much higher: Baudin (1961) speaks of 10 to 12 million; but Dobyns and Thompson (1966), making a general revaluation of the American aboriginal population, raise this figure to a minimum of 30 million.

mountains in platforms on successive curving levels, sometimes at a forty-five-degree slope for several kilometers. They were irrigated by a great system of canals, aqueducts, and dikes, built across the series of mountain ranges, the flow of which was strictly regulated by imperial functionaries and fertilized with guano manure brought from the coast. On these beds they cultivated nearly sixty types of vegetables, the greater part of them originally domesticated by the indigenous populations of the tropical jungle and adopted by the Andean peoples. They also raised llamas and alpacas, spun fine wool, and wove probably the most elaborate textiles known to the world.

Living in an inhospitable land, to which they had to adjust painfully, not only adapting themselves biologically to survive at great altitudes but also conforming the land, which in its natural state did not lend itself to agriculture, they became terrace farmers, planting and irrigating at more than 11,000 feet altitude. Having only 2 per cent cultivable area, they made the most of every bit of fertile ground. This intensive farming, with high yield per area, maintained a great urban population exempted from tasks of subsistence and concentrated in several cities of thousands of inhabitants in addition to the capital. This population was divided into military, sacerdotal, bureaucratic, and craftsman strata, a characteristically urban civilization.

Besides textiles and ceramics, Inca craftsmen were masters of an advanced metallurgy and an architectural and sculptural art in stone, responsible for magnificent structures such as bridges, embankments, highways, temples, palaces, and megalithic sculptures that testify today to the organizing capacity and the sumptuousness of their civilization.

Archeological research has demonstrated that this extraordinary indigenous civilization developed originally, step by step, in the highland country. In that process it evolved from a tribal structure of undifferentiated horticultural villages to a system of independent agrocraftsman communities, and from that to an order of rural craftsman states governed by cities and with their populations already stratified in classes. These states finally crystallized in a theocratic imperial structure that carried the Inca domination into vast areas, covering all the peoples of the highlands and the coast of the Pacific, and projecting its influence over the lowlands of the east and south, both in the Argentine pampas and the Amazon region.

It is probable that intermittent contacts with the Aztec-Maya world would have permitted reciprocal influencing, but in fact the respective developments were made independently. For all these characteristics the Inca culture, like the Middle American, is included among the few world nuclei of autonomous development of urban civilizations based on irrigation agriculture. Its major characteristic was social organization, which was not founded on private property, slavery, or monetary economy, but on a collectivist structurization, a highly centralized theocratic state, and an irrigation agriculture, of the kind that Marx called "Asiatic formation."

The Inca empire was ruled by a hereditary nobility centered in the sacred person of the Inca, "son of the Sun," married to his blood sister. The nobility, formed by members of old Inca lineages with seats in and around Cuzco, and by the heads of conquered peoples, exercised the superior functions of administration of the empire, worship, and war. They were given the privileges of adornments of precious metals, alpaca and vicuña textiles, exquisite food, domestic servants, transport in litters, and palatial houses. All these prerogatives were theirs in recompense for services rendered, because everything nominally belonged to the Inca.

Beneath the nobles by blood came a lower-ranking stratum of priests, bureaucrats, and military chieftains, and the *curacas* [community headmen], all forming a petty nobility constituted by designation, whose privileges were not transferrable to their children. Next in the social scale came an urban class of artists, architects, doctors, artisans, and minor functionaries. Further down came the temporary conscripts (*mitayos*), recruited in the rural communities for certain periods of the year for messenger services and transportation along the highways, for mining, for building, as servants for the nobility (*yanaconas*) and as soldiers. The peasantry formed the base of the social structure. It was grouped in local communities, the *ayllus,* composed of wide degrees of kinship, highly homogeneous and solidary. The Inca social pyramid, then, comprised three distinct strata: the ruling nobility, the intermediate caste of administration and control, and the working mass of the ayllus, serving in the countryside and in the cities with the status of vassals.

The principal function integrating this stratified society was performed by the religious cult of Viracocha, the hero-civilizer, and of the sun-god Pachacámac, symbolized by the Inca, and other minor deities. There was a vast clergy, with priestesses, dedicated to the cult, to hearing confession from the common people and the nobility and meting out penances to them, and especially to regulating the agricultural work according to the ritual calendar, which followed the rhythm of the seasons as if it marked and determined them.

The Inca was the nominal owner of the land, whose possession was thus assured to the peasant communities, but whose products were subject to the appropriation taxes and the forms of distribution determined by the imperial authorities. There being no private ownership of land, no coin (every precious metal was strictly controlled), and no slavery, no conditions existed for the rise of a seignoral caste and another of slaves, or of mercantile or latifundian sectors. Within his community the peasant was a free worker because he was governed only by an over-all order embracing the whole society, personified in the Inca and represented locally by the imperial bureaucracy.

In fact, the Inca society took shape as a powerful, highly centralized state system of organization of production and collection of surpluses created in the various sectors, to defray the costs of installing and maintaining the collective services, particularly the systems of irrigation, highways, and great urban works. This impounding of surpluses was done, principally, through organization of the work force, which, with great labor reserves available and a system of education and training of specialists, was able to discipline and refine a vast mechanism for providing subsistence and sumptuary production, capable of maintaining and energizing an enormous mass of humanity and constructing a highly original civilization with it.

The crop lands in the vicinity of each community were divided into three parcels, worked in succession by the peasants: that of the Inca, that of the temple, and that of the ayllu. The produce from the first filled the public storehouses, built along the highways and destined for support of the nobility, the urban workers, the army, the indigent, widows, orphans, the aged, or victims of famine in regions where the harvest was poor. The temple lands supported the clergy and their servants. The produce from the ayllu fields was destined for peasant consumption. All the agricultural work, as regards distribution of the cultivable lands, irrigation, fertilizing, care of the llama flocks, and craftsman work, was strictly controlled by the curacas by means of a decimal statistical system and mnemonic device, the *quipu* [a set of colored cords knotted in ingeniously varied ways].

The political organization of the Incas at the time of the conquest seemed to tend toward a "geometric" structure rationally imposed by the imperial power. It was based on the ayllu as the elementary unit of the system, integrated by 100 families and holding a well-delimited territory. The higher units were the "tribe," composed of 100 ayllus; the "province," formed by four tribes; and the "states," each with four provinces in a unified administration. In each sphere religious, administrative, and military commands all acted in the name of the Inca. This ideal pattern was probably never actually practiced in all its details, but it operated as a model for the populations subject to the empire.

As can be seen, the Inca civilization was characterized by the development of a state collective system—as opposed to the slavistic mercantile and capitalistic structures—in combination with a rigid social stratification dominated by an aristocracy and a vast administrative, military, and theocratic bureaucracy.

To the Central Andean peoples forming the first nucleus of the empire many others were added through a meticulous process of conquest and integration, intended not so much to enslave as to assimilate linguistically, culturally, and socially to the Inca collectivity. A formal system of education installed in Cuzco for training the governmental and religious hierarchy guaranteed the progressive assimilation of the dominant caste of all these peoples into a single social body marked by great cohesiveness.

The Inca empire was destroyed in its expansion cycle just when it apparently enjoyed exceptional conditions for organization into a vast political system that would encompass the majority of South American peoples. For this it had broad experience in assimilating other peoples, with a most elaborate regime of work organization, production distribution, reward for military and civil merit, and an integrative religion. Likewise it had an open nobility, through designation by the Inca and through exogamy, which allowed the incorporation of the ruling sectors of the conquered peoples. Actually, the Incas were completing the fusing of all the highland peoples into their system and initiating their expansion over the outside context, both tropical and temperate, over whose inhabitants they were beginning to exert influence. Factors of internal dissension (such as the dispute between the two Inca brothers, the one in Cuzco and the one in Quito, which facilitated the Spanish conquest) proved strong enough, however, to turn them from the imperial, civilizational path into a dark age of fragmentation and feudalization, as occurred with so many civilizations of the same level. Independently of these imperial cycles of rise and fall, the Incas would have fulfilled their civilizational role if they had not been checked by a paralyzing foreign conquest such as the Spanish. It dammed their evolutionary impulse and integrated them, through historical incorporation, into the status of external proletariat of a more advanced sociocultural formation.

The Hispanic Legacy

The crumbling of the Inca empire—enormous, powerful, militarized—before a little band of 200-odd Spanish adventurers is hardly explicable except by the moral paralysis caused by the sight of those strange invaders so like the sacred figure of Viracocha, the hero-civilizer of their mythology, white and bearded, as Mexico's Quetzalcóatl. The domination of the Inca empire was accomplished through its rigid social stratification, its noble caste being easily replaced by the Spaniards in lieu of the incapacity for self-defense characteristic of the subordinate strata of despotic societies. With the Inca Atahualpa held captive, the empire was conquered. Pizarro replaced him with another Inca, and the nobility and the curacas placed themselves at the disposal of the Spaniard, the disciplined army, the humble mitayos, and the submissive peasant followed suit. Centuries of rigid hierarchic discipline prepared the Inca society for the foreign domination that they could never have foreseen, because no people known to them would have dared challenge them. In their case, not even the smallpox epidemics and other diseases so decisive in the domination of the Mexicans seem to have played an important part, because the highland peoples, so far as is known, suffered from these diseases only after the conquest, and their effects seem to have been less catastrophic. The Inca empire was depopulated, however, to the same degree as that of the Mexicans. Dobyns and Thompson (1966) estimate that it may have dropped in a ratio of twenty–twenty-five to one persons in 1650. The principal factor in this depopulation apparently was the destruction of the system of irrigation agriculture and the simultaneous constriction of the population to serve the economic objectives of the colonizer.

Indeed, the strictly regulated Inca work organization suffered terribly under the domination, proportionate to the Spaniards' demands (the gold reserves were first exhausted), which eventually penetrated the whole productive system. It was the confrontation of a collectivistic economic system, based on the organization of work and on the social distribution of production, with a system of slavistic mercantile colonization centralized in the mother country, founded on land ownership, the enslavement of labor, the mercantilization of production, and the seeking of pecuniary profit as the moving force of the whole economy.

The Inca economic system was broken down through the progressive imposition of innovations that would prepare it to operate as a colonial component of a salvationistic mercantile empire. Among these innovations were private ownership of land, orientation of production for pecuniary profit in the market, introduction of a monetary economy and of the Iberian system of weights and measures, and, above all, a series of compulsory procedures of conditioning labor, both new ones, such as the encomienda, and redefinitions of such old Inca forms as the mita and the yaconato.

The encomienda consisted of the assignment of groups of Indians or whole communities to Spanish seigniors who came to enjoy the usufruct of the Indians' work, in compensation for their duties to the crown and Church, namely, to convert the Indians to Catholicism and feed and protect them. By this justification, Christian scruples were placated and the real objective attained—the appropriation of the Indians assigned, their families and their lands, as the property and livestock of the conquistador. Integrated in the new system under the direction of the old curaca caste, the Indians were compelled to produce not only those articles with which they were familiar but also articles for the European market. Thus cattle, the cultivation of alfalfa, wheat, and wine grapes were introduced by the only practicable means in a region where land was so scarce, namely, the displacement of the Indians and their replacement by cattle and by commercial farming.

The effects of this innovation were disastrous for the Indians, all the more because they were accompanied by the destruction of the former welfare distributive system. The result was years of famine that reduced the population from a total of more than 10 million, calculated as a minimum,[2] to about 1.5 million in the fifty years following the conquest. For the Spaniard, not only were the innovations lucrative, but the depopulation itself presented no great bother because there were more than enough people for such losses and, particularly, because the system weakened the subjugated peoples, which was desirable, and expelled from the countryside the manpower to be engaged as mitayos in the exploitation of the mines and in the construction of new churches, palaces, and houses or as yanaconas for domestic service, or as slaves for the haciendas that were beginning to be opened in the highland plateau region and on the coast.

Thus the Inca population was reduced by hunger and provided vast human contingents for the feverishly intensified gold and silver mining. This satisfied the aspirations of Spain, which had come to live on the production of precious metals by the American colonies, using them to pay for her manufactured imports and even foodstuffs, defraying the costs of her army and navy, and maintaining the extravagance of the most ostentatious court in Europe. It likewise served the neo-American oligarchy that was forming with the local agents of colonial exploitation.

The major technological innovations introduced by the European were iron instruments and wheel-based apparatus, which enhanced the virtuosity of indigenous weaving, the distaff and the pedal loom; the refinement of the technique of modeled ceramics with the introduction of the potter's wheel; and the improvement of transport with the wheel. Among the positive contributions to agriculture were the introduction of the plow, wheat and barley, garlic and onion, sugar cane, some fruits, and such livestock as cows and bulls, mules, and small domestic animals—chickens, pigs, sheep, goats—which qualitatively improved the former vegetarian diet, drastically reduced. Also, the use of wool clothing and artifacts of leather became general.

The conversion of the heathen under the guidance of the Church began with the installation of Catholic symbols in the Temple of the Sun and its

---

[2] Recent sources, already cited, indicate much higher figures for the pre-Columbian Inca population.

reconsecration, accompanied by the elimination of the Inca priestly hierarchy. But it gained vigor only after the consolidation of the conquest,
through efforts to banish the cults of Pachacámac and other divinities, a
task that was never completed: syncretic cults were created in which, disguised under Christian vestments, the old deities continued to reach the
hearts of their faithful.

The introduction of the Catholic clergy resulted in new duties for the
native, in the loss of more lands and the imposition of greater tributes and
obligations for the construction of churches, the only major public works
in the new civilization. These duties and sufferings were compensated for
only with the installation of a new religious calendar, which reserved
nearly ten days a year for rest and religious festivities, the promoting of
fiestas that revitalized community life, and the organization of *cofradías,*
religious confraternities, all these composing a new cultural dimension that
would permit the mitayos and Ladinized yanaconas to participate to some
degree in a new conception of the world, one that consoled them for their
afflictions and justified their fate. It constituted thereby the least brutal
facet of colonization and the only one that provided any opening for less
inegalitarian conceptions because implicit in it was a formal recognition of
human dignity extendible in a certain measure even to the Indian.

Nevertheless, the Church as an institution was to become the greatest
associate of colonial exploitation (appropriator of lands, holder of monopolies and taxation rights) and the great agency of social coercion and
moral subjugation of the nascent society. The Inquisition's tribunals among
the Witness Peoples were comparable to those of Spain in their fanaticism,
violence, and discretionary powers of arrest, torture, expulsion, and killing. With agents and informers appointed for each town, they controlled
the entire society by threatening everyone for crimes of heresy.

Unlike the former Inca peasants, the new mitayos and yanaconas returned to their communities and, compensated with goods and work implements, were veritable slaves, being expelled from the land by the cattle and
the new commercial cultivations and forced into urban centers and mines,
or onto commercial farms and cattle-raising haciendas. From these mitayos
and yanaconas, torn from community life, and curacas the neoindigenous,
deculturated, Hispanized, Christianized contingent was gradually molded
into the new man of the highlands.

Whether the Incas were actually slaves is questionable, especially if
their servitude is compared with the Negro slavery in other American
areas. Nevertheless, working with no actual right to remuneration and no
freedom to direct one's own destiny and for the production of profits for a
master makes the social status of the mitayo and yanacona closer to Greco-
Roman slavery than to feudal serfdom. The royal regulations and the

Church's prescriptions, which bestowed on them rights and dignities never respected, were acts of pharisaical piety destined to console the Christian conscience rather than to govern production conditions. Between the moral order emanating from legal codes and papal bulls and the documented real relations between masters and subalterns lay the same distance as between abstract Christian ideals and the real Christianity of the conquistadors.

The final, post-Inca form of the Ladinos is the cholo stratum. Today it makes up nearly 35 per cent of the Witness Peoples population surviving from the Inca civilization. These cholos are marginal to the Indians, who do not recognize them as their own people and whom the cholos discriminate against, and the dominant caste, whiter, more Hispanic, more enriched, with which it wishes to be identified but which also rejects it.

Nowadays the cholos speak Spanish; half of them are literate, and frequently know an indigenous language, usually Quechua, indispensable to their role as intermediate class. They are not a closed caste because their contingent continues to be enlarged by new elements separated from the indigenous communities. Neither are they a racial segment of mestizos, as is often claimed, because their basic genetic patrimony is indigenous, even though one finds Caucasoid types among them more commonly than among the Indians, and less than in the higher strata of whites-by-definition. When among indigenes they conduct themselves as superiors because of their Westernization, their higher level of aspirations, and their loyalties placed at the service of the dominant caste. Among people of higher class, they act and are regarded as half-Indians. They predominate in the cities and on the coastal ranches, constituting the national proletariat of the Andean peoples.

A Ladino stratum, quite differentiated from the cholos and composed of an urban and a rural contingent, is characterized by its Spanish monolingualism and its more modernized customs. It is in this stratum that the mestizos are inserted who result from the crossing of Indian and cholo women with descendants of Negro slaves, Chinese and Japanese immigrants, and some whites introduced into Peru principally as labor for coastal commercial farming and for mining, and more recently on the Amazon slopes. As these three extra-American contingents were scanty in number and made up almost exclusively of men, they began early to dissolve into the population, stamping differentiating racial marks on the indigenous stock, marks that make their participation in the formative process of the modern Andean peoples perceptible even today. In certain areas they were differentiated to the point of constituting a minority neo-American class with more similarity to the Ladinos of other regions than to the cholos. This is the case of the Bolivian *cambas* [Indians of the Chaco region] and the Peruvian Oriental mestizos.

The commune Indian who succeeded in retaining a tract of land and in growing up in the solidary unity of the ayllu preserves more elements of the original culture, even though he may also have experienced profound European influences and processes of cultural change. After the drastic demographic reduction following the conquest, the original population began to recuperate progressively. In 1960 there were close to 7.5 million, making up half the population of Peru (3.7 million), 60 per cent of the Bolivian (2.2 million), and 40 per cent of the Ecuadoran (1.6 million). They live mainly on the plateaus and high valleys of the cordillera, the rural population of which is 80 per cent indigenous. The few lands left to them from colonial spoliation are not only the poorest but, burdened by the demographic growth that provoked a destructive overuse, have been split up into microparcels that in certain areas only amount on the average to 0.44 hectare per family.

Besides the Indian's cultural conservatism and profound integration into the life of the ayllu, what characterizes him in relation to the other strata is his scant degree of participation in national life, expressed in the low percentage speaking Spanish (18 per cent), in the widespread illiteracy, and in the predominantly natural subsistence economy. Above all differentiating characteristics, however, his ethnic posture stands out, opposed to the Peruvian, Bolivian, and Ecuadoran national ethnos into which he has been compulsorily incorporated. That is why the Quechua and Aymará Indians we know on the Peru-Bolivia border identified themselves as indigenes of the same stock rather than as Peruvians or Bolivians.

Indians and cholos are dominated by the more Europeanized caste, the nobles and curacas, proud of their descent from the conquistadors, cultivating manners of dress and speech, eating habits, work habits, and especially leisure customs, not to mention mystic and personal attitudes that are typically Spanish. They are the proprietors of ranches, commerce, and the small industry of the cities; they are the hierarchs, liberal professionals, political leaders, students, functionaries, and clerks. All identify so wholly with their formal role of whites-by-self-definition that they qualify the cholos as mestizos when they themselves are more mestizo. A young man from one of these countries, studying in a university in the United States, reported that only after months of residence there had it been noticed that he was phenotypically Indian, which, incidentally, caused him trauma.

That higher stratum, involved in the Bolivarian struggles for emancipation, converted independence into a project of its own, transferring the political administration from Madrid to its own capitals, maintaining, however, and in many ways strengthening, the same social order that assured domination, oppression, and exploitation over cholos and Indians. Moreover, in formally emancipating the Indian from a differentiated juridical status prevailing in the colonial period (in the name of equality of all citizens of the new republics), national independence made him in fact more vulnerable to exploitation. The division of the communal lands of the ayllus into individual, alienable parcels, encouraged in the name of these egalitarian and progressive ideals, provoked the appropriation of great portions of communal lands, either by the neighboring latifundium proprietors or for the formation of new latifundia.

This tripartite structure of Indians, cholos, and whites-by-self-definition operates more as three symbiotically organized strata than as an integrated society. Thus each individual, as a general rule, is born, lives, and dies within his own class, being able to experience variations of status only within the class. Each class has its internal stratification. In the case of the whites-by-self-definition, a stratum comprising a range from the oligarchy to the middle class and including certain segments of the working class, the stratification is more rigid, less so among the cholos, and still less among the Indians. The class lines are so rigid that there are white prostitutes for the whites, *cholas* for the cholos, and Indian women for the Indians. The three strata barely interpenetrate, because habitually the son of the urbanized Indian, or of the Indian tied to the great ranches, becomes a cholo. In the cities this segregation is drawn ecologically by superposition in topographically configured conglomerates: the whites, or *gente,* people of standing, in the center; the cholos, or *menos gente,* folk of lesser degree, in the wretched quarters on the city outskirts; and the Indians as non*gente,* no people, in the poorest areas around the cities or along the roads.

The likelihood of these Indians becoming cholos is greater than the likelihood of the cholos becoming gente, because of the rigidity of the social structure and the endogamic nature of the dominant class. The channels for ascent from the status of cholo to gente would be average education, which is not accessible to them and which they do not even claim as a right (the gente would be shocked at such audacity), or wealth, which they attain extremely rarely with their little open-air market stalls and their domestic crafts. Only the army, in its recruiting of troops, the Church, in its search for priestly vocations, and the politicoelectoral and union caudillism open up channels of mobility, all of them too exiguous to be significant.

The narrow upper class widens only through its own proliferation and is self-limiting in order not to share the already scanty social wealth. It thus constitutes a closed circle, strange and hostile to the very nation, as parasitic as the colonial elite it replaced. The result is a society formed by disparate conglomerates that integrate only through their complementary roles, but that do not fuse because they lack a common body of values and explicit national interests. In this manner they do not become peoples aware of themselves or, still less, nations among the others. They are residues of a historical process of spoliation that molded them, first, to fulfill productive functions prescribed by the colonizer and, later, to serve the subsistent oligarchy in a context of imperialistic exploitation. Freakish societies, integrating spurious cultures, Bolivia, Peru, and Ecuador, after a century and a half of independence, are still foreign entrepôts installed in the altiplano, the highland country.

The entire altiplano can be characterized as a predominantly natural economy, based on the incipiently mercantile village and on the subsistence agriculture of the indigenous communities, complemented by Indian and cholo domestic crafts—textiles, ropes, braided hats, and ceramics. The marketable production in each of these sectors barely yields enough to pay for such small amounts of commercial articles as salt, matches, a few medicines, and fuels that these people need.

The properly mercantile production is concentrated in the commercial farming haciendas (rice, wheat, potatoes and the export crops, sugar, bananas, coffee) established principally on the coast, in the mining of tin and other metals, in the fishing industry (now greatly developed in Peru), in some exports of oil and in small urban intermediate-process industries. All these, naturally, are in the hands of the white-by-self-definition class, or of foreign corporation agents.

The two systems—given the complementary nature of their roles—though nonhermetic, are self-perpetuating. The growth of the mercantile sector does not engender wealth or innovations that radiate out over the total economy, contributing to the integration of the entire people into a homogeneous society. Arrogating to themselves the total wealth created, the narrow native dominant caste uses it to maintain a high standard of lordly living, and the foreign entrepreneurs installed in the area utilize it to export profits. Their contributions to the state are insufficient even to support the most indispensable public services, such as the police and military system and the vast parasitic bureaucracy.

The economic, social, and cultural situation of the Andean altiplano is very like that of Mexico at the turn of the century, though even then the Mexicans had surpassed in higher degree the alienating colonial complex. It is equally explosive by virtue of the divorce between the confined interests of the latifundian oligarchy and the foreign enterprises and those of the whole population.

The Andean altiplano's most difficult problems derive from the need to carry out simultaneously political, socioeconomic, and cultural revolutions. It is the task of the political revolution to put a stop to the hegemony of the exogenous caste of whites-by-self-definition, integrating, however, its professional strata into the renovating process as the only sector with modern mentality and some technical qualification. The socioeconomic revolution must liquidate the latifundium and foreign exploitation in order to create new institutional bases to industrialize the area and, by way of this, to raise the standard of living of Indians and cholos without throwing them into a subsistence economy even more closed than the present one. It is up to the cultural revolution to confront the problem of ethnic diversity through recognition and evaluation of indigenous languages and traditions, so as to restructure the area as a single, multiethnic national unity. All three revolutions are important in not only integrating all the social strata into a single body, but in structuring them in accordance with a new national and antioligarchic order.

The Inca empire based its agrocraftsman economy on a regime of administrative superorganization of work, founded on collectivist institutions and a high irrigation agriculture technology. The new economies of the altiplano will be challenged to establish themselves on impoverished lands no longer irrigated or fertilized, as systems of mercantile production based on ownership of land—the Indian's "undeferrable" aspiration after centuries of exploitation. The transition to collectivist forms of agricultural work organization, which would seem to correspond better to the native's natural disposition in its historical aspect, presents special difficulties for that reason. We have never found among the peasant masses of the Americas as vivid an awareness of the latifundian exploitation as among these indigenes of the altiplano. Structured socially in ayllus that saw their lands appropriated by foreigners and, later, after centuries, watched these lands being transferred from landowner to new landowner, to whom the Indians collectively always remained yoked, they have been fully enlightened about the spoliation of which they are victims.

They want possession of the land and freedom to work it in their own way without interference from any agent of the extraindigenous order subjugating them. If this attitude, on the one hand, makes their identification with any national project difficult, on the other, it makes the indigenous mass a potential revolutionary force. Nevertheless, they regarded even the Bolivian Revolution, which assured them land, as an undertaking of the whites, the city folk, whom they looked on with suspicion. Their solidarity and integration, for that reason, rarely went beyond defending at any cost the possession of the land they had won. These circumstances place enormous obstacles in the way of creating a national project with which all the differentiated bodies of society can identify themselves.

The ayllus, which for centuries kept alive the memory of the eras antedating the arrival of the Europeans as a time of plenty, and also the memory of the conquistadors' expropriation of lands and enslavement of the people, are emerging again with full vindictive vigor. Their aim is not to reconstruct the past, but to assure themselves both land and liberty. The national problem, however, goes beyond these demands because it requires a productive efficacy in agriculture attainable only through the incorporation of new forms of work organization, a more advanced technology, and an intensive industrialization to overcome the historical retardation of the Andean altiplano in the modern world.

In the cities and the mines, especially in the latter, across the centuries social strata were generating independent of the colonial oligarchy. They were formed by the working masses and by intellectualized sectors of the middle classes uprooted from traditional cultural contents, modernized by their historical posture, which makes them see the people as the nation, and demystified by the direct confrontation of the oligarchic exploitation and oppression. It is these strata that are called today to formulate a new self-image of their peoples, as the only ones sufficiently enlightened to overcome alienation and to lead the emancipatory struggles to win for themselves their own nations, occupied since their birth by agents of foreign domination and domestic exploitation.

This is the challenge facing the Witness Peoples of the Andean altiplano, precluded until now from overcoming it by virtue of the irreducible opposition between the national and popular interests and two lines of colluded interests: (1) the oligarchic and patrician strata, which ordered the state and society as their own project and reduced political life to a power dispute among their civilian and military leaders; (2) the fact that all Latin America has been doomed to keep trotting along the route of backwardness and want by the imperialistic system of continental domination. This system, ruled today by the United States, after controlling the sources of wealth in the Andean countries, has transformed their armed forces to maintain the patrician oligarchic order in the name of the fight against subversion. In recent years it even tries to define the peasant struggles of the altiplano, with their centuries-long history of rebelliousness, as subversive movements inspired by communists, in order to maintain the old order of popular misery, which is still lucrative for the local dominant castes, and to preserve a subjugated, and also lucrative, continental context.

Revivalism and Revolution

It is not only the Indians who are touched and incited by nostalgia for the Inca world, but also the cholos, an almost equally exploited and discriminated caste, and the intellectualized middle class of the altiplano, maturing gradually to become the conscience of its people. Passively, this nostalgia manifests itself as an idealization of the past in which the people's happiness was assured by the goodness and justice of the Cuzco Incas; actively, as the project of reordering social life through the restoration of the Inca complex. Both manifestations have been fruitful throughout the area since colonial times, assuming varied forms, from literary creations and political manifestoes to rebellions of the lower classes aimed at restoring the golden age.

There have been dozens of these insurrections, small and great, based on this body of revivalist beliefs. A few years after the conquest the first broke out (1564), all southern Peru clamoring for the restoration of the former monarchs in the person of an Inca who must have survived by taking refuge in the eastern forests. This legend has continued kindling the combative spirit and hopes of Ladinos and Indians. Thereafter it took the form of a miraculous kingdom located at some point in the distant east, from the banks of the Beni to the Guianas. It is the legend of Manoa, the golden kingdom of the Incas, which the adventurer Raleigh, among others, proposed to restore in all its ancient splendor, with England's protection assured by payment of an annual tribute of 300,000 pounds to the crown.

Later the legend was redefined and activated with the Oruro Plot (1739), which also sought to restore the Inca complex by crowning as Inca a Ladino named Juan Vélez. This carefully prepared rebellion, aborted before it spread, involved dozens of caciques of the highlands and the coast. It was based solely on the notion of restoration of the Inca complex. A new messianic insurrection broke out not long after (1742), centered on a runaway Indian, Juan Santos Atahualpa, who managed to remain active under arms for thirteen years at the head of a great number of followers ready to die for him. When he was finally conquered, his legend survived for decades with the promise that he would return, reincarnated as the Inca, to save his people from oppression.

The greatest of these rebellions started in Cuzco, headed by a Ladino descendant of the old Inca lineage, who named himself Túpac Amaru II. Nearly the whole indigenous and cholo altiplano responded to his summons, if not with acts of war, at least with the warmth of their hope. Beaten after years of fighting, he was killed, quartered, and exhibited in different cities as a warning to the people. His fight, like the others, was a messianic uprising of masses revolting against colonial exploitation, dreaming of a world without hacenderos, laws, magistrates, or merchants, in short, an idyllic society from which everything would be extirpated that oppressed and enslaved those masses.

Túpac Amaru II therefore directed his struggle against the social system, which he aspired to reform from top to bottom. His reordering project, however, was unable to go beyond the idea of restoring the old laws and the old, clearly unviable order. And in this lay a fundamental weakness common to all movements of this nature, which, though victorious in assault on the constituted power, do not know how to consolidate victory and still less how to guide it toward a rational reordering of society. It was only much later, with the rise of socialist doctrines, that the first theoretical instruments susceptible of orienting popular revolts were to be wrought, when a strategy for the struggles of the subordinate classes was determined and an alternative model of social order more favorable to the majority interests was created.

After independence, movements of the same nature continued to explode periodically in the Andean highlands, all of them, because of weaknesses intrinsic in the uprisings, crushed with greater or less trouble by the repressive forces. Being insurrections of subaltern classes, they were incapable of victory, but they were also inevitable, because they expressed the revolt against an insupportable social situation. It was this situation that in every generation produced new leaderships acting in the name of the old revivalist legend to keep awareness of spoliation alive. Thus was engendered an endemic state of social unrest and incipient rebellion that never became victorious but that succeeded in strengthening the bonds of ethnic cohesion, preserving its view of the conquest and the hope of a *revanche* that would restore to the highland population its lost autonomy and dignity. Even the modern guerrillas, like offshoots of the Cuban model of revolution and, consequently, formulated in accordance with a viable project of social reorder, have recourse to the convocative power of the old legend in the eyes of the Indians and cholos, who even now are warmed by hope for the restoration of the miraculous past.

The first modern and original ideological expression of the Andean altiplano peoples' complex of problems comes from Haya de la Torres, founder of *Aprismo*.[3] It began as an irredentist intellectual movement, Marxist-inspired but subsequently redefined by several other ideological

[3] A.P.R.A. (*Alianza Popular Revolucionaria Americana*) was founded in Mexico in 1924, becoming the *Partido Aprista Peruano* in 1931, under which name it exists now. [Its over-all philosophy and tenets are therefore called *Aprismo* in Spanish and Portuguese.]

influences. It originated in Mexico with the aspiration of making itself an antiimperialistic continental political front on the order of the Chinese Kuomintang and the Congress Party in India, but it was fated to survive only in Peru. There it was structured as a political party, experiencing all kinds of deformations until it turned into just another conservative party, striving for power through alliances and coups. Its influence on the Latin American populist movements from 1930 to 1945 was so great [4] that it can only be compared to that of the communists, with whom, as a matter of fact, it started disputing from the first, ending by becoming out-and-out anticommunist.

Its role in Peruvian life has also been decisive, for it can be stated that all the elections, government programs, and intellectual currents of the country have had to define themselves as aprista or antiaprista. In his political career Haya de la Torre succeeded in mobilizing Peruvian public opinion many times and attracting thousands of militants who, fighting under his direction, struggled for decades to gain power and reorder Peruvian society by aprista ideals.

The aprista ideology reveals a keen perception of Latin America's problems and of the conditions peculiar to the altiplano, and a theoretical basis drawn from the most diverse contexts, from Hegel and Marx to Spengler, Einstein, and Toynbee. However, it is fundamentally from Marx that Haya de la Torre draws his theories of society, the state, and social revolution, applying them creatively to Latin American conditions and particularly to the singularities of the Peruvian situation. Aprismo also picks up the Bolivarian unionist ideals, revitalizing them to unmask the artificial nature of the national entities resulting from independence.

It is in his view of the indigenous humanity of the Andean altiplano, degraded by European domination, and in his theme of its elevation to the status of a new civilization that Haya de la Torre attains greatest originality, creating the term "Indoamérica" as the banner of this restorational aspiration.

> The nations that erected Chichén Itzá, Uxmal, Palenque, Machu Picchu, Tiahuanaco, and San Agustín stand there beside their works. Those who mastered the altitude in order to rule over it, adapting their lungs and their hearts to live to the full on the cordilleras and the plateaus, also stand there on the very stage which the destroyers of their civilization have not succeeded in supplanting or excelling in grandeur.

[4] Parties inspired by Aprismo have consolidated in Bolivia, Ecuador, Venezuela, Costa Rica, and Cuba, thus demonstrating its extraregional transcendence as an antiimperialistic movement of Latin American unity.

But he does not look only backward: when he calls attention to "the presence of the past," so decisive in the highland peoples, it is to analyze objectively the world system of interests that has condemned them to backwardness and to seek the ways to emancipation.

The theoretic themes handled by Haya de la Torre permitted him, the first in Latin America, to reach an objective understanding of the two orders of subordination that most weighed upon its peoples, condemning them to backwardness—the exporting latifundium and the imperialistic exploitation—and to understand the nexuses that link these two orders of interests, making them act as one order that, by means of regulatory institutions and repressive forces, perpetuates the regime and maintains misery.

This understanding has been decisively furthered by the very crudity of the Peruvian social structure, displaying in every way the exotic and antipopular character of the native elite and its brazen association with foreign interests established in the country. This old aristocracy, as ostentatious and proud as the Mexican, had the same origin. It was born of the concessions of fiefs granted by the Spanish crown to the conquistadors; it grew with the courtiers rewarded with encomiendas of lands and Indians; it broadened its domain with the appropriation of the Jesuits' haciendas in the secularization period; and it grew still richer with the "civil equality" decreed by the republicans, which placed the communal lands on the market. Its first association with foreign enterprises occurred with the exploitation of guano manure, which for decades constituted the principal income of the Peruvian republic. It continued with the exploitation of copper, silver, gold, and oil deposits. The modernization of Peru by means of the construction of railroads and other systems of communication, paid for with the resources generated by the extractive economy with the exploitation of new regions, opened the market for export crops, with which foreign enterprises also busied themselves. The native aristocracy, associated in all these nonagrarian undertakings as a minor shareholder, had to allow foreign entrepreneurs into their old business of exploiting the land and the peasants. It ended by forming with them a solidarity that was to become the greatest impediment to the social and economic progress of the country.

Opposing the unilinear evolutionism of the communists, aprismo asserts that the peculiarities of Latin American historical development demand a redefinition of the Marxist theory, of the objectives of social revolution, and of the composition of forces that are to carry it out and reintegrate the new power:

That is why, if—according to the neo-Marxist thesis—"imperialism is the last stage of capitalism" (Lenin, 1917), this statement cannot be applied to all the regions of the earth. Indeed it is "that last stage," but only for the industrialized countries that have completed the whole process of negation and succession of the preceding stages. But for the countries of primitive or retarded economy, for whom capitalism arrives under the form of imperialism, this is their first stage (Haya de la Torre, 1936, p. 21).

Haya de la Torre seeks to show that for a long time it has been imperialism that has controlled the Latin American economy, as the actual fomenter of the exploitation of natural riches with the object of exporting them, and as the coordinator of the continental work force for the production of agricultural goods, also destined for the world market.

In these conditions, imperialism arrogates to itself the most profitable sectors of the national economies, deforming them in such a way as to prevent the rise of an internal market, an independent enterprise, or centers of power capable of orienting investments to the benefit of these economies. In spite of this, structuring itself as the most progressive sector, imperialism fosters modernization of the techniques of production, of transportation, and of financial and administrative procedures. Growing under this external domination, the national economic sectors are condemned to be only auxiliary forces, operating on the periphery of imperialistic interests. The freeing of national energies, thus contained, and of the native capitalists themselves, could in Haya de la Torre's view be achieved only by a rupture with imperialism through the common struggle of the whole continent's progressive forces and the installation of a broad common regional market.

Analyzing in 1923 the relations of Latin America with the United States, Haya de la Torre produced a document that caused a tremendous repercussion in the continent because it constituted one of the first realistic critical evaluations of the spoliation inflicted on the Latin American peoples.

[E]xperience of the political and economic relations between Latin America and the United States, especially the experience of the Mexican Revolution, leads us to the following conclusions: (1) The ruling classes of the Latin American countries, great landowners, great merchants, and incipient bourgeoisies, are allies of imperialism; (2) these classes concentrate the government of our countries in their hands in exchange for a policy of concessions, loans, or other operations that the landowners, bourgeois, great merchants, caudillos, or political groups of these classes negotiate or share with imperialism; (3) as a result of that alliance of classes, the natural wealth of our countries is mortgaged or sold, the fiscal policy of our governments is reduced to a mad succession of large loans, and our working classes, which have to produce for their masters, are brutally exploited; (4) our countries' progressive economic submission to imperialism is transformed into political subordination, loss of national sovereignty, armed invasions by soldiers and marines of imperialism, purchase of Creole caudillos, etc. . . . Panama, Nicaragua, Cuba, Santo Domingo, and Haiti, for example, are veritable Yankee colonies or protectorates as a consequence of the "policy of penetration" of imperialism (Haya de la Torre, 1927, pp. 189–190).

Through the analysis of those theories and facts Haya de la Torre concludes that the fundamental revolutionary task in Latin America is the unification of all progressive forces for the fight against imperialism as the root of their backwardness. That is why, too, rather than a socialist revolution under the hegemony of a proletariat too incipient to carry it out, what would fit the case is an emancipatory national revolution to be waged on the continental scale against imperialism and local oligarchies simultaneously.

He adds that, for such a struggle, all the exploited classes must be organized into a single front, in which the social precedence of the peasantry and the leadership of the middle-class intellectuals would be recognized, and which should be structured like the communist system of cells, under militant discipline. The programmatic objectives, to be accomplished gradually by revolutionary power, once won, would be nationalization of the land, to free the peasantry from archaic "boss" exploitation, and organization of a strong, cooperative type of state economy that could foster independent industrialization and liquidate foreign monopolies to recover national domination of natural wealth. All these goals would be attained under two alluring slogans: "It is not a question of taking wealth away from him that has, but of creating new wealth for those that have not" and "We do not want bread without freedom, nor freedom without bread; we want bread with freedom."

Aprismo was the first national political movement in Latin America that was not structured as a patrician elite of intermediaries between the people and power, but as a centralized organization of thousands of small nuclei of militants. For this purpose it enlisted the majority of its political, revolutionary, and union teams outside of the dominant class, from among the mass of modern Ladinos and cholos of the cities, which enabled it to mobilize huge contingents for the elections, for street demonstrations, and also for conspiracy.

Through this organization and its influence on the intellectual, student,

and labor union movements of the country, the Aprista banners were un-
furled for thirty-five years of tenacious struggle, two thirds of that time il-
legally, which cost the lives of thousands of its militants and prison terms,
beatings, and proscriptions of many others, as well as long years of exile
for Haya de la Torre and various of his companions. Captivating multitudes with its reforming mystique, Aprismo had become the one party of
the masses of Peru, winning successive electoral victories through the candidacy of Haya de la Torre or allies of his for the presidency (1931, 1936,
1941, and 1962). But all these were snatched away by military coups without the incumbents ever taking office. Aprismo's very success among the
people had become a liability because it frightened the oligarchy, making
them interrupt their liberal game to resort to military coups. The armed
forces thus became the one real political "party" in opposition to the
Aprista wave. With armed intervention before or after each Aprista victory, they came to perform functions of guardianship over all the political
life of the country. This is the situation today.

Although aiming at the acquisition of power for the reordination of Peruvian society, Haya de la Torre never came to be a revolutionary leader,
ready to unleash popular insurrection. His radicalism only went so far as a
middle-class conspirative opportunism. Faced with the oligarchic veto, he
merely redefined his own political slogans in an effort to win the consent of
the dominant class to his participation in power. In this process Aprismo
finally became demoralized in the view of great segments of its partisans
because of its spurious alliances, shady procedures, and successive revi-
sions.

In 1960, groups of Aprista militants, mainly youths, broke with the
party to form an Apra Rebelde [rebel A.P.R.A.] on the Castro model,
which, operating with other leftist groups, particularly the M.I.R. [Revo-
lutionary Leftist Movement], was to bring about the first spurts of guerrilla fighting in Peru. These "new profile" Apristas in recent years have
been joined by various nuclei that propose the revolutionary takeover of
power for a socialist reordering of Peruvian society. Today they operate
especially in the universities as a radical force that will be able to attract
increasing numbers of students to a vanguard position in the Peruvian social revolution.

The worsening of living conditions among the indigenous population,
the repercussion of the Bolivian agrarian reform throughout the altiplano,
and in some measure the long proselyting work of the Apristas and the
leftists, have all ended by making the Peruvian peasants conscious of the
eradicable nature of their poverty. The last electoral campaign, between
Haya de la Torre and Belaúnde Terry—won by the latter—with its still
more radical political debates, helped to generalize among the peasants,

and particularly among the Indians of the communal lands, the conviction that the hour of agrarian reform had finally struck. In fact, right after the elections there began a very widespread spontaneous invasion of the latifundia created by usurpation of Indian lands. Spreading rapidly throughout the cordillera, in each locality the movement mobilized thousands of indigenes, adults and children, who, carrying national flags and beating drums, advanced on the ranches, tearing out boundary markers and fences and installing themselves on the conquered lands. They threatened the ranchers with violence, allowing them to remain in their homes and witness the occupation of their crop lands by the Indians, who immediately set about cultivating them for themselves on the justification that they were simply taking back what had always belonged to them.

A great segment of the millions of indigenous Peruvians, agglutinated in the ayllus, took part in the invasion, dramatically demonstrating the gravity of the social problem represented by land monopoly. In spite of the repeated reformist statements by the new president, his government's reaction was to subdue the rebelling Indians by violence, forcing them back to the status of captive manual labor for the latifundia, to wait in that condition for the state to proceed to the legal distribution of lands. Meanwhile, the national congress refused to approve the government's proposed reforms, imposing so many modifications that they deprived them of any instrumentality.

Thus it is that Belaúnde, using repressive force to check the spontaneous movement for recovery of the land by the peasant Indians, and seeing himself disarmed by a landowner-dominated congress that denied him the legal means for the well-conducted reform he wished to implant, found himself on the crest of a new reactionary movement that forced university youth and the most authentic leaders of the Peruvian people to take up arms for social renovation.

With the frustration of the revolutionary orientation of the Indians' spontaneous movement and with the government's reformist intentions unmasked, the most combative sectors of the Peruvian left fell into conspiracy. Some of them installed themselves in the sierra as guerrilla nuclei, facing on one side persecution by the "interamerican" repressive forces and on the other the centuries-old Indian and cholo suspicion of city folk, of whom they expected only treachery. To win their trust these urban students and combatants, now guerrillas, resorted to all the symbols that might bring the Indians to regard them as allies and liberators. Therefore, they took names reminiscent of the old irredentist, messianic traditions— for example, Túpac Amaru, Atahualpa, Manco Inca, and Pachacútec— and earnestly tried to be accepted as a genuine leadership.

Between Indians and guerrillas, however, lay the distances and discriminations accumulated in centuries of ethnic oppression. Yet when these leaderships become capable of inspiring confidence, of directing the contained rebelliousness of the indigenous masses of the cordillera, nothing will stop the social revolution that will restore to the Witness People of the Inca civilization the capacity to resume the guidance of its own destiny, to free it from the parasitic castes that have always battened on its misery, and to recover its creative capacity in a new civilization.

If this mobilization of the indigene and the cholo for social revolution is not accomplished, owing to the cultural distances and to police repression, the form of the future Peruvian society will depend on the assimilative and deculturative capacity of its cities and on the modernizing power of the economy that is installed in the rural areas. The Indians will become solidly cholos, and the cholos more and more modern Ladinos, to fulfill the function of proletariat of a frankly inegalitarian society.

Today that process is already accelerating. Thus, Lima grew between 1940 and 1961 from 520,000 to 1.428 million, or 174 per cent. Measured in other terms, this abrupt urbanization reveals that 84 per cent of the Limans of 1960 had entered the city during the preceding ten years. A great part of these urbanized masses, in Lima and other nuclei of the coast, is made up of indigenes driven out of the countryside by the latifundium or attracted by promises of better living and working conditions in the city. Industrialization and the amplification of services, however, did not increase at a rate corresponding to the rural exodus, with the result that human masses still more wretched than the peasants have accumulated in the urban periphery. These masses are viewed with growing apprehension by the ruling caste, fearful of the threat represented by their advance on the seignioral homes, luxury restaurants, and department stores. Still, it is a known fact that the urban revolts can be put down more easily than rural ones, for police efficacy is enhanced by the submissive spirit of these marginal strata, not clamoring for land or other people's property but for simple social protection and for opportunities to work, to survive as the poorest of citizens.

It must be borne in mind that all industrialized societies at certain stages of their development have confronted these problems of chaotic urbanization and that they have been able to check potential revolution only by exporting their population surpluses to colonize virgin lands, or to other countries, or to be used up in wars. In Peru, if the effects of the rural exodus continue to be intense, and if it is not possible to relocate the surplus population in the eastern forest areas, this massive presence of poverty face to face with wealth will tend to operate as a revolutionary force that, acting conjointly with the peasant struggles, will overturn the existing social structure. The organization and coalition of these two forces is the great challenge facing the Peruvian revolutionary leaderships.

Revolutionary Bolivia

Among the Witness Peoples of the Andean altiplano only the Bolivians have succeeded in initiating a genuine social revolution, which, between advances and retreats, has been going on for more than fifteen years. Here, too, the revolution was incubated precisely in the poorest area, and brought to a head as much by popular revolt against misery as by the mineworkers' capacity for autonomous revolutionary action and, further, by the militant intellectuals' will to national assertion. The Bolivian Revolution is the fruit of those dynamic factors and also of the incapacity for social reordering of an extremely rigid political structure ruled by the interests of international corporations, exploiters of the minerals, and by the latifundian oligarchy.

Ever since independence, Bolivia has developed as the model of a nation dominated by a one-product entrepreneurial sector controlled from abroad. Such is the mining economy, exploited by native entrepreneurs turned partners of the international tin monopoly, whose central offices and plants benefiting from the mineral are located abroad. Entering into the pool of mineral commercialization by virtue of the value of the deposits under their control and the amount of capital at their disposal, these Bolivian entrepreneurs were able also to exploit deposits in other areas, even though they had to share, simultaneously, their own area with the associates of the international monopoly.

The whole republican life of Bolivia, ruled more by military men than by civilians, has been processed as part of the tin business, whose exigencies were strictly heeded. The national ruling class therefore emerges as a local bureaucracy of these entrepreneurial interests, imposed or deposed by them according to their efficacy in maintaining the "climate of tranquility indispensable to productive work." In the offices of the three great mining companies (Patiño, Hochschild, and Aramayo), much more than in the parliament, is where public works programs (railroads or telegraphs intended to facilitate mining exploitation), financial and public welfare planning, and urban modernization services are debated.

Given the chronic insolvency of the Bolivian state, it was likewise through these enterprises that periodic loans were obtained to pay for the most indispensable imports, the public bureaucracy, and the army as a machine of repression. In these conditions the Bolivian political patriciate, bureaucratic and subsidized, found its authority annulled in negotiating with the mining firms to make them contribute greater amounts from their profits to defray the costs of public services. Direct dependents on the enterprises, these "public men" only vied with one another in demonstrations of loyalty to the system and in eagerness to respond to the entrepreneurial demands.

The mining economy employed in 1960 nearly 90,000 workmen to produce 95 per cent of the national export. That this export value was considerable may be seen in the fact that Bolivia contributed about 30 per cent of the world tin production and that the annual profits of the enterprises exploiting the tin deposits is estimated at $100 million. These profits were systematically siphoned abroad by dint of two factors: the international policy of producing only the single product, considered indispensable to the preservation of the system, and the cosmopolitanism of the Bolivian entrepreneurs.

Subsistence economy, which was to feed and clothe the Bolivians, as well as its commercial network, became deformed because of the deliberate emphasis on one product and the monopoly of land in the hands of a narrow latifundian caste. These two sectors of the economy, if they were not mutually sustaining—owing to the exogenous character of the mining and the autarchic nature of the agricultural production—complemented each other as a single social order in the maintenance of which they were equally interested, and which they defined as the paramount task of the state and the armed forces. The high command of this social order— popularly known as the *rosca* [coil]—was composed of the proprietors of the great mining enterprises and their local agents, generals, and professional politicians recruited from the latifundian oligarchy, with a broad clientele of minor servants from the urban middle classes.

Under the domination of the rosca, public institutions functioned for decades to the satisfaction of the ruling class, and the army efficiently performed its repressive role, each contributing to perpetuating the Indian's and the peasant's servitude to the hacendero and to leading the populational surpluses—which the ayllu could not contain and the hacienda would not employ—to work in the mines, where they were worn out in very few years under the most inhuman conditions. The periodic wrangles among patrician leaderships over the distribution of favors from the corporations and over access to state revenues never went so far as to affect the system. However, in the mines, which deculturated and proletarianized masses of Indians and cholos, a new social class was engendered in opposition to the interests of the enterprises and likewise irreducibly opposed to the over-all political system set up to assure the tranquil functioning of the mining economy.

The urban middle class, confined in the narrow limits of this structure, vainly strove, by means of their intellectuals and the student movement, to develop an authentic national consciousness. But it had grown alienated through the introduction of debasing European stereotypes, and traumatized by the national complexes resulting from the defeat by Chilean invaders who had snatched from Bolivia all her coast. Thus, the national consciousness easily fell into sterile pseudopatriotism or into anomie and despair. With this, it became vulnerable to service as a maneuverable mass for such international adventurers as those who unleashed the Chaco War.

In this war Bolivia and Paraguay were maneuvered by the great oil companies. The reciprocal territorial claims interested only the Standard Oil and Royal Dutch corporations, whose purpose was to situate the oil-rich zones inside the countries in which each had influence. Bolivia lost the war, and consequently her enormous Chaco territory (250,000 square kilometers), but the oil deposits remained within her boundaries, in the power of Standard Oil, the only winner.

The Bolivians suffered a frustration that was to have cathartic effects on the middle-class intellectuals, compelling them to seek a broader comprehension of the national drama. The same effect would be projected on the people, who had seen the oligarchic war machine demoralized and the partisan system upset.

The result of this imperialistic war was the beginning of a process of national ethnic creativity that would end by liberating the Bolivian people from the alien projects imposed on them, allowing them to formulate a project of their own. From the war, then, a new Bolivia emerged, depressed by defeat but prepared now to find herself. The close association and consequent solidarity created in the struggle among Indians, cholos, and whites-by-self-definition banished, even if only episodically, the barriers between ethnically stratified classes in the face of common objectives. Those who came back questioned society and the nation; they knew that combined action is possible; they knew military techniques. From that time on, two social movements have decisively influenced Bolivians: (1) the leftist movements that create genuine union teams among the mine workers and devote themselves to an intensive propaganda of agrarian reform; (2) a strong reformist, antiimperialist rightist movement. These irredentist tendencies were fortified in the following years by the impact on Bolivian military men by the antiimperialist—above all, anti-British—propaganda spread abroad by the Nazis. Bolivia represented so unmistakably an area of exploitation by British financiers, and her national drama was explained so fully by spoliation on the part of the three great mining enterprises headquartered in London, that this new antiimperialism, detached from leftist socialistic theories, was widely accepted in military circles.

Thus, alongside the leftists who were organizing the workmen in unions and attracting the peasantry with the slogan of land distribution, new political groups emerged, deriving from the right but won over to antiimperialism. The new movements won their first positions of power in the army and the state machine. The most powerful of these organizations was the Movimiento Nationalista Revolutionario (M.N.R.), which had recruited its first militant crews among veterans of the Chaco War and had consolidated itself as a political organization in the leadership of the miners' movements for higher wages. They came to share the power in Villarroel's presidency (1943), which instituted the first national-reformist government Bolivia had known. With the fall of this government, an event dramatically underlined by the hanging of Villarroel (1946), the M.N.R. went underground, devoting itself to intensive conspiracy.

In the following years the M.N.R. fomented dozens of wild plots that cost thousands of lives in a desperate, persistent effort to gain power. Finally, in 1951, they succeeded in forcing the government to hold general elections, with their candidate, Víctor Paz Estenssoro, being elected president by an absolute majority. As was inevitable, another coup by the rosca [the reactionary vested interests] followed, annulling the elections and restoring power to the military junta. But this episode had warned the oligarchy of the risks run by their interests.

The old cosmopolitan elite reacted on two fronts: (1) the bloodiest repression of the insurgent forces; (2) bringing in the United Nations through the mediation of the United States, assuming the obligation to plan and direct (with international technicians from its diverse agencies) the modernization of Bolivian society, preserving, naturally, the interests of the rosca and maintaining the old oligarchic order.

The Bolivian people had matured enough, however, to carry on their own fight by means of successive uprisings. In 1952 the M.N.R. led an insurrection supported by the soldiers of La Paz. The uprising mobilized the urban cholos, who attacked the city, creating an inflammatory situation that the repressive army apparatus could not master. The dictatorship having been overthrown, Víctor Paz Estenssoro assumed the presidency and the popular leader Siles Zuazo, the vice-presidency, both elected by majority vote a year before.

Heading the common people under arms—the insurgent cholos, miners, and Indians—the new government abolished the old oligarchic power, replaced the antinational, antipopular elite of the mining rosca, and restructured the army. Then in succession it decreed nationalization of the tin mines, agrarian reform, every Bolivian's right to vote, and the labor unions' cogovernment of the expropriated enterprises. To carry out these decrees, which would liquidate the economic bases of the former power, the government organized an armed workers' and peasants' militia, basing the nascent state on the popular masses until then marginalized from the national life.

The revolutionary government could not have been more radical in its plans. The difficulty was to put them into practice and make the new sociopolitical system and its political leadership self-sustaining. These tasks, in themselves complex, were made more difficult because they had to be performed under conditions of near-inviability of the Bolivian nation, isolated in the middle of the continent, depending on a monopolized export market for its minerals, and plagued with poverty and illiteracy, thanks to centuries of colonialist spoliation and oligarchic oppression.

All these difficulties were enhanced by dissensions among the revolutionary forces themselves, quarrels over the theories that should orient the new power. The result was the breakup of the victorious leftist front into various competitive blocs, sometimes more opposed to one another than to the common enemy.

The most dangerous of these arguments was the one that opened between the union headquarters controlled by the mine leaders (for example, Lechín) and the military-bureaucratic nucleus of the M.N.R. with its principally peasant and middle-class bases. Conceiving of the new power as a cogovernment, intrinsically dual in nature, the syndicate leadership gradually divested itself of responsibility for the fate of the revolution and only campaigned for wage increases.

The vacuum created by the workers' withdrawal was filled by leaders from the middle class who had risen socially with the revolution as a new type of parasitic clientele, not only antiunitary but also antiworker. In this way the government became involved in diversionary maneuvers of nominally radical groups, all conspiring against the furtherance of the revolutionary process.

In this conspiracy the contention among the revolutionary forces was preached by some as an imperative for the survival of the revolution itself, owing to the unviability of a socialist Bolivian state, and by others as the preliminary stage necessary to the evolution of the national society from its technological and cultural primitivism to a modern industrial society aspiring to socialism. The inexplicit pact that resulted doomed the Bolivian Revolution to a grange agrarianism, complemented by a mineral export economy, thrust into the world capitalist system, in other words, a revolutionary project so timid that it ended by meriting the support and protection of even the United States.

Thus, the very guardian of the capitalistic order on the continent, the principal partner in the mining exploitation that had made Bolivia what she had been, coexisted with the revolution, strengthened its petty bourgeois and reformist contents, and, finally, led to failure the first genuine effort to establish a socialist republic in South America.

The agrarian reform, which constituted the structural basis of the new regime, was carried out because the armed peasant militia took care to do so directly, by taking over the lands on which they were working. Spontaneously, they also revitalized their ayllus, transforming them into centers of a new power that directed the collective tasks of construction: roads, schools, hospital wards, as well as the commercialization of their crops.

Emerging from centuries of extreme oppression, which compelled him to work on the haciendas, the Bolivian Indian now proprietor of a plot of land naturally reacted by gobbling up larger parcels of land than he could harvest and by taking it easy, unable to adapt to a work routine and a new life rhythm. The inevitable immediate effect of such absenteeism, and of the simultaneous drop in productivity in the areas still dominated by the haciendas, was lack of foodstuffs, a rise in prices, and speculation. The peasant Indians' entry into the mercantile economy was also made in the most anachronistic forms, transforming them frequently into food traffickers in the black market. Where proper planning would have reserved land for collectivist development, and enlarged the land plots distributed to the peasants, in this case the agrarian reform was left to the impulse of direct actions.

The national institution directing agrarian reform became bureaucratic when confronted with the enormity of its task and the lack of preparation of its political leaders and its technical teams. Where the agricultural economy should have been oriented toward new entrepreneurial models and the installation of great irrigation works, which required a centralized authority endowed with enormous resources, there was only the official bureaucracy, capable of establishing the territorial reserves but unable to organize efficacious productive models.

The total lands distributed to the Indians from 1953 to 1963 amounted to 4.4 million hectares, or nearly 60 per cent of the area formerly possessed by the ayllus, and benefited 134,000 families. It left the majority of the indigenes in their former condition, as can be seen, liberated only legally from their obligations to gratuitous services on the haciendas. Thus, the new agrarian structure was based on an incipient grange system, incapable of giving occupation to the whole of the peasant Indian mass and unable to raise the technical level of production, to fulfill the urban demand for food, or to improve substantially the standard of living of the rural masses.

Another unfortunate aspect of the state control of reform was its propensity to establish new agricultural nuclei in the lowlands with Indians and peasants displaced from the altiplano. This procedure, which would be an escape solution for Peru, for example (because it would reduce the demographic compression braking the principal motor of agrarian reform), in the case of Bolivia was an agrarian diversion. Besides generating social tensions between the former population of the jungle areas and the indigenous emigrants taken there, this internal colonization retarded the awakening to consciousness by the altiplano indigenes as a nucleus of the national ethnos.

In spite of these weaknesses the agrarian reform, as it was carried out in Bolivia, profoundly altered the basic social strata: (1) by overthrowing the hacienda oligarchy from its position as both proprietor and mediating patriciate between the Indians and the nation; (2) by integrating huge masses of Indians into the body of the nation through raising their living conditions and their very dignity by proclaiming their right to own the lands on which they lived and to exercise their rights as citizens; (3) by demarginalizing the cholos, who, as an intermediate stratum, could ascend in the social scale through channels opened by the emergence of innumerable parasitic functions, among others the roles of political petty leaders, militiamen, and black market traffickers in agricultural crops and in industrial articles in the rural areas; (4) by creating a new middle-class urban elite, detached from the latifundian interests and for that very reason more acceptable to the cholos and Indians, though these continued to regard it as "the other," now more just but still representing the foreigner who in the past had enslaved and degraded them.

The social problems of the Bolivian Revolution, grave enough in the agrarian sector, worsened further with the international boycott of Bolivian tin, which lasted nearly two years. This boycott, blocking the country's only source of foreign exchange, prevented the complementary importing of foodstuffs. To break this economic siege the Bolivian government decided to yield the commercialization of tin to the same monopolies that formerly exploited it directly, being obliged to accept, on every ton sold, the discount of an amount destined to amortize the value of the nationalized mines. Besides these conditions, the mines had to face a drastic price reduction artificially provoked by the dumping of the U.S. strategic reserves on the market. In consequence, the government was deprived of resources even to replace worn-out equipment, with a substantial drop in mining production that affected the whole economy of the country.

When the crisis worsened, the government was forced to redefine its economic policy in order to raise mining production. The solution found by the U.S. advisors was to induce the government to new concessions, more and more onerous for the national economy. It was thus that the state monopoly over oil developments was suspended (1955), and thereafter over various other minerals, and finally over tin itself, through the cession of deposits to the direct administration of international consortia.

Among these concessions, the workers' control over the management of the enterprises collapsed, this being a prerequisite for obtaining supervised loans from U.S. and German bankers.

This policy resulted in unhampered international commercialization of mining production and in subjecting it to the onus of processing its minerals in Texas foundries, thus continuing to deprive the economy of the foreign-exchange resources indispensable to industrialization and defrayal of the costs of the country's modernizing reforms. Later on, as a final consequence of this orientation, it had to follow a policy of confiscation of personal income through inflation and wage reductions, which were to obstruct still further the formation of an internal market and which created an atmosphere of widespread discontent, causing constant agitation among the wage-earners.

The failure of the mining sector, the only one capable of generating resources to pay for the establishment of an industrial infrastructure, extremely limited the potentialities of the Bolivian Revolution. It ended by condemning the revolution to a situation even graver than the one it sought to remedy, carrying to catastrophic levels the problems of inflation, of high prices, of unemployment, and of the economic crisis that would turn it further and further away from the original objectives. Bolivia had paid the whole price in blood, only to crystallize after all as an ancillary economy dependent on the world monopolistic system.

Despite these defects and despite the constant rise in the cost of living (thirty-five times between 1952 and 1962), the Bolivian Revolution managed to resist several counterrevolutionary attacks and to consolidate the power of the M.N.R. The latter was based, principally, on support from the peasant masses, whose armed militia was called several times to act in its defense. It was also supported by a multipartisan political front, which was to rot gradually until it constituted little opposition groups under the banner of return to the old order and, principally, of a radical revolutionary process.

Each of these opposition groups aspired to stamp its political orientation on the revolution. Some defined it as the bourgeois democratic stage of the socialist revolution, advocating "development with freedom through a parliamentary system of government" that would orient agrarian reform and free-enterprise industrialization, which in turn would engender the national bourgeoisie and the modern proletariat that should succeed it. Other currents stressed the character of "unequal and combined development" of the Bolivian economy, whose mining sector would be fully capitalistic, in opposition to the agrarian sectors submerged in feudalism or in primitive communism. These forces preached the "permanent revolution" by means of a union movement that would force the state to "leap swiftly over the stages of revolution." Completing this picture, some sectors of the middle classes, desperate because of their proscription from the orbit of political command and too alienated to be integrated into the new system, fell into pure fascist terrorism. They became agents of the counterrevolution, rejecting an order adverse to them without proposing a substitute, but ready for any desperate action.

There were many other movements. In the midst of them all President Paz Estenssoro pontificated, always conciliatory, less guided by theories than by his nostalgia for Uruguayan democracy, whose political habits, democratic educational system, and petty bourgeois prosperity he aspired to bestow, at any cost, on his Bolivian compatriots. The ideology of the M.N.R., under the command of Paz Estenssoro and Siles Zuazo, turned out to be a doctrine less revolutionary than developmental. Both men trusted that a liberal state founded on parliamentary multipartisanism, the independence of powers, and a profit economy would be able to crystallize the revolutionary aspirations of the disinherited classes and guarantee the establishment of an antiimperialist, antioligarchic society as the basis for a socialist revolution.

These doctrinaire divergences grew and became positive oppositions to the government, stimulated by the social crisis that was continually aggravated, provoked by hunger, unemployment, and speculation, in an economy laid waste by inflation and plunged into stagnation. The alliances that had enabled the revolution to be successful finally broke up entirely and the leftist syndicalist leaders established themselves in a prejudicial contraposition between the state-military bureaucracy and the progovernment peasant movement on one side and the mine unions on the other. Assailed on all sides, the government sought help in new foreign loans, in the stabilization programs of the International Monetary Fund, accepting all its demands, and in recourse to the Alliance for Progress for direct aid or foodstuffs that would be sold to gain "noninflationary resources" with which to pay the bureaucracy. The Yankee influence shortly reestablished its sovereignty. A U.S. military mission reorganized the national army, overthrown by the revolution, and enlarged it in the hands of an alienated officer class to maintain the new order.

The leftist movements, especially the workers' unions, openly attacked this policy, starting strikes, marches, and demonstrations for economic and political vindication as well as for the restoration of public freedom and union privileges. The government reacted by prosecuting and deporting some of the most prestigious leaders, such as Siles Zuazo and Lechín, companions in the struggle from the beginning. Paz Estenssoro, who was revealing continuist propensities, lost the support of the urban masses and ended by staying in office principally by means of the economic and military aid pact with the United States and the partisan militia, now frankly subsidized for putting down uprisings. He fell at last, overthrown by a coup of the new army palace guards. In the fight against the coup the government had only the support of a few partisan sectors and some of the peasant militia. Public opinion and the working class, disillusioned and hard-pressed after twelve years of frustrated revolution, witnessed his downfall without taking sides, and even rejoiced over it.

Evidence of the popular forces' defeat manifested itself slowly, and when it became manifest in action, the military junta had no difficulty in restoring order by purging the union movement of its leftist elements and handing it over to accommodating patronal organizations. Thousands of workers were simultaneously dismissed; wages were lowered; and price ceilings were removed. The junta began disarming the peasant militia and stifling the student movement. All these measures laid the ground for denationalizing the mines and negating the agrarian reform through indemnification agreements with the landowners for the lands that had been expropriated from them.

On the positive side the main contribution of the Bolivian Revolution from 1952 has been, until now, its agrarian reform, which set in motion a process of incorporation of millions of Indians and cholos into the national life. Even this gain, however, has not been consolidated because the distribution of lands barely touched a small part of the area appropriated by the latifundian system of the country (principally those marginal plots which the peasant had worked formerly as a tenant farmer), whereas the most fertile and most suited to irrigation were reserved for future collectivist forms of exploitation, which were never actually installed.

The open debate by the Bolivian dictatorial government on the revolutionary procedures of expropriation, in terms of the former owners' rights to indemnification, may question the legitimacy of the very titles of ownership of the lands occupied by the indigenes and result in the return of the former hacenderos to the areas of undistributed land reserve. Besides this threat of direct restoration of the latifundium, the mere interruption of the distribution of new lands to the peasantry will lead to the atomization of the areas that the peasants appropriated, through the successive fractioning of lots into minifundia and through the waste resultant from primitive forms of tillage.

It is to be feared, therefore, that Bolivia has started up her fundamental revolutionary motors in vain. Indeed, the Bolivian Revolution of 1952 barely reached the anteroom of a social revolution. Bolivia did not succeed in imparting to the Indians and cholos of the altiplano a revolutionary impulse of their own, capable of uniting them with their Peruvian and Ecuadoran brothers and orienting them toward the remodeling of their various ethnic groups into an authentic national ethnos of the Witness Peoples of the Inca complex, the basis for a new Andean, autonomous, fecund civilization.

Thus for the Bolivians the task of social revolution is once again posed historically. Again conspiring are the students and the miners, who now have before them, as their fundamental enemy, a repressive military regime established as a mechanism of historical regression. Their task, today as yesterday, is to kindle and spread insurgency until it bursts the Bolivian frontiers to join the struggles of the Peruvians and the Ecuadorans. To these new revolutionaries will fall the task of restoring the Inca complex and incorporating it into modern civilization.[5]

[5] This was written in 1967. Subsequent events, both in Bolivia and Peru, are described and interpreted in my book *O Dilema da América Latina.*

PART III
The New Peoples

"We are condemned to civilization. Either we progress or we disappear."

—Euclides da Cunha

THE NEW PEOPLES constitute the most characteristic historicocultural con-figuration in the Americas because they emerged throughout the continent, even though they may have been subsequently transfigured in certain areas. Their analogues are, among others, the incipient forms of certain modern European peoples that had their fundamental ethnic profiles molded by the domination and miscegenation of alien populations by slave colonizers. Thus the Iberian macroethnos and the French, Italian, and Roman na-tional ethnic groups emerged as a result of Roman mercantile colonization, which was to transfigure, culturally and linguistically, their original popu-lations through military domination, displacement of populations, enslave-ment, amalgamation, and deculturation. Other analogues are the peoples transfigured by the Moslem expansion through similar processes of colo-nial domination. These peoples total more than 300 million persons scat-tered throughout Asia and Africa. In all these cases, as in the American case, we find the emergence of new peoples through the conjunction and amalgamation of originally very differentiated ethnic groups, under conditions of despotic domination on the part of colonial agents of more developed societies, or of *Herrenvölkers,* capable of conquering and energizing societies sunk in feudalism and integrating them into imperial bodies and international mercantile systems.

The New Peoples of the Americas are also the result of specific forms of ethnic domination and productive organization under conditions of extreme social oppression and compulsory deculturation that, though exercised in other epochs and in different areas of the world, reached their fullest, most rigorous application in colonial America. Such was, first, the European colonization of the New World, by means of slavery utilized as a capitalistic mercantile process to recruit labor forces from tribal peoples, Africans and aborigines, for agrarian production and mining, and second, the establishment of the plantation as a basic social institution and as a model of capitalist entrepreneurial organization, which, combining land ownership and monopoly of labor, permitted the profitable production of articles for the world market.

The same basic model served to open great one-product economies of sugar cane and mills, to organize the great plantations of cotton, tobacco, cacao, bananas, pineapples, and other products, first within the slavocratic regime and then, after abolition, with free workers. It was also employed, with the necessary adaptations, in the extensive raising of cattle for commerce and even in commercial exploitation of vegetables. These differentiated forms of the plantation model had in common the mastery of the territory where they operated and the control of the manpower, with no respect whatever for human customs or aspirations that might obstruct the imperatives of production and profit. Another common denominator was their character as a mercantile institution that permitted linking the overseas colonies to the motherland economies.

In a certain sense the colonial plantation anticipates the modern factory in its concentration of workers under the patronal command of the owner of the means of production, hoping to profit from their work. Nevertheless, it was a strange kind of "factory," being rural and slavocratic, and therefore capacitated to isolate those who were interned therein in atypical communities, whose rhythm of work and leisure, whose customs, beliefs, family organization, and entire life were subject to the intervention of an alien will.

The natural and irreducible opposition between the patronal interests aimed at extracting maximum profit from the enterprise, on the one hand, and the proletarians seeking to obtain a greater share in the profits, is extremely restrained in the traditional plantation. The worker can only slow his work rhythm in order to wear out less quickly, or run away only to be hunted down if he is a slave, or seek another plantation of like regime if he falls into one of those spurious forms of wage serfdom that succeeded slavery.

On the plantation, under the slave regime, there was no place for the father of the family in relation to his mate and children, these being also "pieces" * belonging to the master and not to him. (Even today the citizen is not his own master, because the nation is the plantation for anyone born and living within its confines.) Between the plantation and the ouside world—of business, society, nation, religion—there was one sole mediator, the plantation owner in his roles as boss, godfather, protector, political chief, and entrepreneur.

In its slavocratic and "free" forms the plantation has been the institution shaping the profile of the New Peoples. The family, religion, and the nation itself have been modeled as projections of the plantation's elementary structure. Basic molder of society, the plantation stamped itself indelibly on the descendants of those who toiled on it as slaves or as free workmen, as it did on the dominant castes, rural and urban, all deformed by the autocratic-paternalistic spirit, seignioral tastes, and racial and social discrimination.

Established on a society thus structured, republican institutions were a sham of popular self-government, incapable of disguising the actually oligarchic nature of the power behind the show of democracy. The Industrial Revolution itself, operating on such a context, found resistances that disfigured all its potentialities for social reorder. These resistances stemmed from the exogenous character of the plantation economy, structured to attend rather to alien needs than to those of the society of which it was a part.

Being populations molded by biological amalgamation and acculturation of disparate ethnic groups within the slavocratic plantation framework, the Brazilians, Venezuelans, Colombians, Antilleans, and parts of the populations of Central America and the southern United States are New Peoples. Those of Central America and the United States experienced the same formative process, though the Central Americans are distinguished by having greater indigenous contents, and the southern United States region, not having succeeded in structuring itself as a nation, by being compelled to survive as an alien body among Transplanted Peoples. A second category of New Peoples, markedly differentiated from the first by its basically indigenotribal, national ethnic formation and by not having

---

* *Peça* [*de Indias*] was a seventeenth-century measure for classifying slaves: for example, a Negro slave fifteen to twenty-five years old was one peça; three Negro slaves from eight to fifteen or twenty-five to thirty-five, were two peças; two under eight or thirty-five to forty-five were 1 peça; suckling babies, no accounting; over forty-five or diseased, rated by arbiters.

undergone the plantation compulsions, is found in Chile and Paraguay. Uruguay and Argentina were New Peoples of the same type, though later transfigured by a process of ecological succession that solidly Europeanized them.

The cultural profiles of the New Peoples likewise differ, according to three orders of variables corresponding to the European, African, and American parent populations that blended together to form them. These variants place the diverse European peoples that promoted colonization of the Americas in opposition to one another; the principal opposition is between the Latin colonizers and the rest. These differences are relatively unimportant, as regards the formative process of the New Peoples, compared with the common denominator of slavery and the plantation system, reflected in the essential uniformity of all the New Peoples in both labor force conditioning and capitalistic mercantile entrepreneurial organization. It is true that greater institutional and economic maturity, such as the capitalistic formation of the non-Latin colonizers, added different coloring to certain areas, but did not differentiate them sufficiently to infuse characteristics opposed to the vested interests of the dominant society.

The European domination, the first variant, made each unit, linguistically, Luso-Americans, Hispano-Americans, Franco-Americans, Anglo-Americans, or Dutch-Americans and acculturated it according to Catholic or Protestant religious traditions in the spirit of the bodies of institutions, customs, and mores prevailing in the colonial metropolis. These differences, highly significant for understanding the national entities in their singularities, are unimportant in the construction of more general models. Their greatest importance lies in their general cultural frameworks, which qualify the action of each European contingent. Over these differentiating cultural factors, however, prevail the socioeconomic conditioners of the subjugation and conformation of the American populations through the slavistic colonization that characterized them as New Peoples.

In the second variant, the presence and proportion of the African contingent integrated into each neo-American population is more significant than the cultural variation of the various Negro groups brought to America. This is true because deculturation, under slave conditions, left little margin for the imprint of specific cultural traits of the African peoples on the modern national ethnic groups of the Americas. Only in the religious field are their contributions notable. Even these, syncretized, are more expressive of the Negro's protest against his oppression than of the preservation of original bodies of beliefs.

The third variant, the indigenous stock, seems to be more significant than the Negro on the cultural plane, because the native contingents found by the Europeans furnished them with the basic elements for ecological adaptation. Thus, they contributed decisively to the colonizers' protocultures. These indigenous variants present at least two basic forms: the levels of technological development attained by each aboriginal group and their respective cultural patrimonies, parts of which still survive. Included in this third variant are the Tupí-Guaraní of the South American Atlantic coast, and the Arawak and the Caribs of the Amazon jungle and the Caribbean area, all classified in terms of sociocultural evolution as "undifferentiated horticultural villages." These indigenous peoples shared the same basic form of adaptation to tropical regions, cultivating the same vegetable species and with a technology at the same developmental level. (The Araucanians of the Chilean coast and the various tribal confederations of northwestern South America and of Central America had already reached a level of "rural craftsman states" or were making progress in that direction.)

The Tupí-Guaraní peoples at the time of the discovery occupied nearly all the Atlantic coast of South America and vast interior regions, where the Portuguese and Spanish established themselves originally. From their mingling resulted not only mestizos but new cultural crystallizations, ethnocultural protocells to which these groups contributed the language that was spoken during the first centuries and nearly all the forms of subsistence technology that were used in Brazil, River Plate, and Paraguay indigenously. The Antillean Arawak and Carib peoples, which had the same level of development as the Tupí-Guaraní and the same form of ecological adaptation, constituted the basic genetic and cultural group of the first Spanish installations in that area. Despite being quickly exterminated by previously unknown diseases and by slavery, these tribal peoples gave to succeeding populations the fundamental forms of subsistence technology that would permit them to survive in the tropics.

In all these regions the primitive cultural configuration in which the indigenous contribution predominated underwent subsequent profound transformations by the introduction of European or African cultural elements and by economic specialization in tropical products and commercial cattle-raising. Only the Paraguayans, and on a lesser scale the Brazilians, still retain clear linguistic and cultural traces resulting from the Tupí-Guaraní heritage, which, owing to its pre-Columbian spatial distribution and its cultural uniformity, constituted what would come to be the national ethnic group of the Atlantic coast of South America.

On the Pacific coast the Spaniards were confronted by several indigenous groups in the south, outstanding among them the Araucanians, on whose first subjugated villages modern Chile was molded. In Venezuela and Columbia, just as in Central America, the Spaniards encountered the Chibcha, the Timoteans, and the Fincenú, Pancenú, and Cenufaná confederations, the Cuna (Panama), the Jicaque (Nicaragua), and others. All these peoples were on a higher cultural level than those of the first group. Those that were structured politically, as were the Chibcha, as rural craftsman states, having a dominant class that sought to come to terms with the invader and a dominated class already conditioned to serve any master, were quickly overcome and wiped out as ethnic entities. Those taking the first steps in this direction, such as the Araucanians, not yet with a seignioral stratum, or subaltern classes accustomed to the exploitation of their work, resisted the conquest for centuries and even today survive as ethnic minorities. All these indigenous groups, however, transmitted some traces of their cultural patrimony to the new national ethnic groups that flourished in their territories, made up largely of mestizos of Indians and European extraction. By this process also in those areas neo-American ethnic entities emerged, resulting from the multiplication of cultural protocells formed by the fusion of indigenous with European elements. In the south they formed the Chileans; in the northwest, the Venezuelans and the Colombians; and in Central America, the Panamanians and Nicaraguans, molding them all as New Peoples.

These peoples experienced profound changes in their original ethnos. In all cases, however, it is still indispensable to refer back to the indigenous ethnos, in its diverse variants, to understand the characteristics distinguishing the variants of the New Peoples and to contrapose them to the Witness and the Transplanted Peoples of the Americas.

The traits characterizing all these nations and enclaves as New Peoples are not revealed solely in their formative process. They manifest themselves also in their current profiles and in their problems of ethnonational maturation and socioeconomic development. Above all, they manifest themselves through their divorcement from any tradition, causing their most backward populations, unlike those found among the Witness Peoples, to become marginalized socially rather than culturally. The process of compulsory integration to which they were subjected deculturated these marginal peoples drastically, making them more flexible.

The New Peoples, fundamentally affected by African slavery and the plantation system, took shape according to two basic patterns. The first is distinguished by the situation in which the initial ethnic cells were generated—before the arrival of the Negro—by the miscegenation and deculturation of European and aboriginal contingents. These elementary cells were born hybrid because crossbred and heirs to the indigenous ecological adaptation and also heirs to the European ties with distant mercantile societies from which they received many cultural elements and to whose social order they had to adjust.

Only a few decades after the settlement of Europeans in each American area, these protocells had crystallized into a new cultural configuration, neither indigenous nor European. Multiplying internally they occupied large areas, forming a first social order that in the course of time would be transformed by specialization in various types of production and the simultaneous ingress of the Negro. Thus they grew, bound to the land by their indigenous inheritance and to the outside world by the mercantile forms that made viable their development as an external proletariat of European ruling centers. They developed as the result of exogenous projects, devoted to agroindustrial export activities—such as the sugar mills, mining precious metals, gathering forest products; and, finally, cattle-raising. These Indo-American protocells, the first cultural crystallizations of the New Peoples, absorbing the Black and white contingents arriving later, would be the guiding factors in the enculturation of both.

The second pattern—prevailing in some of the French and English West Indies and in southern North America—did not have this Indian-European mestizo formation, or else eradicated it through specializing in sugar or cotton plantations. The second pattern is a subproduct of capitalistic enterprises, importing human fuel in the form of Negro slaves for use on the plantations. These, directed by overseers even more efficiently capitalistic than those of the rest of the continent, attained greater yield from each "piece" from their mating to produce new slaves and from their dehumanization. Thrown into these human corrals, the tribal Negro could not preserve his language or his culture or integrate into a new culture except by parroting the ideas of his master, eating what he was given, and, particularly, training himself for the simple productive chores of the plantations and mines.

In spite of everything, the intrinsic humanity of some Creoles of the land—many of them crossbreeds of Protestant whites and Negroes—did react and master the rudiments of a greater culture, becoming afterwards agents of the enculturation of the common slave. Only in that way could their mental horizon broaden, their language (limited in vocabulary, they being newly arrived from Africa) be enriched, liberating it from its infantile simplicity—which was not the reflection of a primitive mentality, as was supposed, but of the deliberate process of making the Negro only a talking animal placed at the service of his master.

The two modalities of the New Peoples, constructed principally as slave labor brought from Africa, were thus distinguished by the presence or absence of the Indo-European cultural cell, which distinguished the New Peoples variants of Brazil, New Granada, and the Spanish West Indies from the other Antillean formations and from the southern United States. All have in common, however, certain traits from the African genetic pool and a plantation slave culture. They both represent the result of one of the greatest human undertakings, which permitted sugar, cotton clothing, tobacco, coffee, cacao, and later many other products to be used throughout the world. It was with slave labor, furthermore, that the gold mines of Brazil and other American countries were developed.

The contribution of African slave labor cannot, however, be confined to the production of those goods. From it came two other effects vitally important to civilization: first; and probably the greater, was the contribution to the formation of capital invested in Europe and in the Americas, which paid for the building of cities, the equipping of armies, and later the establishment of industrial complexes. The Negro's contribution to the formation of this capital was twofold: (1) as merchandise, inasmuch as the slave trade constituted one of the major businesses of the world for centuries; (2) as a labor force that harvested the plantations and the minerals of America, the commercialism of which made possible that fantastic accumulation of capital for productive application. The rapid maturation of mercantile capitalism, as well as the high rate of evolutionary acceleration experienced by the pioneer countries of the Industrial Revolution, became possible only thanks to the contributions of this vast external proletariat whose consumption was compressed to the biological limit in order to produce the maximum of surplus. The second vital contribution consisted in the formation of the New Peoples by the amalgamation of the Negro genetic cements with the white European and the indigenes and in the linguistic and cultural Europeanization of their descendants, which extended the European ethnos over a very broad area. Moreover, where Negro groups settled, the Europeanization of the other contingents proceeded more quickly. This power of cultural homogenization is owing to the imperative, faced by the Negro, to develop a system of common comprehensions that would permit mutual understanding between slaves of different extractions, and between them and the other contingents, an imperative that obliged them to learn the colonizer's language, thus facilitating its generalization.

The detribalization of the Negro and his blending into the neo-American societies constituted one of the most amazing population movements and the most dramatic process of deculturation in human history. To put it into effect the European uprooted from Africa, in four centuries, more than 100 million Negroes, sacrificing nearly half in capturing them and in the ocean crossing, but taking the other half to the American settlements where the attrition continued. One of the crucial effects of this displacement of Africans and their incorporation as slaves into the work force of the nascent American societies was the installation of an ethnic stratification with the tensions of racial discrimination. Above the difference between city and country folk, and even that between rich and poor, the relationships founded on slavery began to stand out. Separated by this social gulf, human relations became impregnated with the vicissitudes of an inegalitarian coexistence that divided human status into an upper category of "people" opposed to another of "animals," the first with all the rights, the latter with only duties. Much of the racial and social discrimination infecting the American peoples today has its roots in that bipartition, which fixed in whites as well as in Blacks and mulattoes rancors, reserves, fears, and repugnance not yet eradicated. Its most dramatic effect has been the introjection into the Negro of an alienated consciousness of his subjugation, assimilated from the white man's viewpoint, which associates with the color black the idea of dirt, filth, and inferiority. This alienated consciousness, not exploitation, is what explains the social inferiority of the Negro.

The Black man and his crossbreeds today account for one of the largest contingents of the New Peoples population, estimated at close to half of the total, and also a considerable part of the U.S. population. The Black is likewise the part of the population most prone to increase, and for that very reason the one that will eventually darken the Latin American peoples to the state of "colored people." Contrary to the contemporary indigenous ethnic entities, in great part unassimilated, this Black and mulatto contingent has been deculturated from its original patrimony.

Originally incorporated into their societies as slaves, Negroes emerged to freedom as the poorest and most ignorant segment, incapable of solidly integrating themselves into modern ways of life, concentrating their masses in the socially and politically most marginalized strata of national life. Miscegenation over the centuries has made the strata crossbred from Blacks and whites one of the fundamental genetic stocks of the neo-American populations. But, simultaneously, it has condemned them as mulattoes to discriminatory conditions scarcely less harsh than those burdening the Negroes, not providing them channels of ascent and social integration corresponding to those given to other strata. The eradication of these discriminations and prejudices is not a problem of the Black and mulatto contingent, but one of the fundamental challenges of the neo-American societies: only by the integration of all their parent ethnoses and by the frank acceptance of their own crossbred image will they fulfill the minimum requisites to become autonomous peoples and authentic cultures.

In some of the societies classified as new peoples we find intrusions of immigrant contingents transplanted from Europe and Asia during the last century. In certain cases they are isolated in certain regions to which they lend peculiar characteristics, such as the European zone of southern Brazil, and some areas of Central America and of Chile. In other cases they are dispersed among the national population, distinguishable from it only by their racial marks, such as the various contingents from central and northern Europe, the Japanese, Chinese, and East Indians of Brazil, Peru, and the Caribbean.

A great number of the members of these contingents, principally the Europeans, have played a dynamic role in the technological and political modernization of the New Peoples. They were prepared for this role by a series of factors. (1) They had greater professional qualifications than the local populations. In general, they included a certain proportion of craftsmen capable of creating small businesses—some of which were to become factories—or of working in the tasks of technological modernization, such as the installation of railroads and ports. (2) They retained cultural ties with more advanced societies, of whose industrial progress they could most easily inform themselves, thus creating channels of social ascent. (3) Their broad standard of consumption included various industrial articles, influencing the enlargement of the national market and the diffusion of new consumption habits. (4) They were adapted to more advanced forms of work organization, based on wage-earning, and were willing to accept manual labor chores rejected by the white segments of local populations as work proper only to slaves. (5) Their attitude as "aliens" exempt from traditional social responsibilities enabled them to exploit opportunities for enrichment not perceptible, or not acceptable, to the local workers. (6) The majority of these contingents were able to integrate homogeneously into the new societies.

Only in exceptional cases and by provocation from abroad—for example, the exploitation of national loyalties by Fascist Italy, Nazi Germany, and Imperialist Japan—have these immigrants, immersed in the New Peoples of Latin America, ever created serious problems of integration. The mass of European and Asiatic immigrants was, in general, malleable to assimilation because of their integrationist attitude. They wanted to establish a new home in Latin America, in a society more promising than the one they had left behind because it would be farther from the wars, humiliation, and oppression they had experienced. Also, they brought no marked ideology, precisely because the modern European nationalities emerged at the time of these massive migrations. They were, rather, people of certain provinces and religions, frequently as opposed to their fellow countrymen of other cults and dialects as to the people of other nationalities, and sometimes even more so. They came ready to commit themselves to the occupational hierarchy, consciously taking their place in the working class, accepting the patronal command in disciplined fashion, seeking to demonstrate their efficiency and essentially aspiring to become farmers or urban proprietors. Nevertheless, they were prompt to resent any abuse, especially the remnants of the slavocratic treatment permeating all work relationships. They contributed thus to fixing a new worker status, more independent and more self-respecting in relation to the boss class, and prepared to establish contractual rather than paternalistic relationships.

In the early days they did not involve themselves in political life, nor had they any place in it. Later on, those who won greatest economic success entered the patronal stratum, and via that ascent had access to politicopartisan life. The mass, however, was inclined to behave like a working class, not identifying itself ideologically with the formal liberalism of the local oligarchies.

Those who settled in the countryside, creating grange areas, became more and more conservative, especially those of Catholic tradition who had never learned their letters. Those who headed for the cities acted predominantly as a leftist political force and, as institutional modernizers. They created the first nuclei of radical movements in Latin America. They were anarchists, anarchosyndicalists, or socialists who opposed their bosses with strikes and depredations and were repressed with the greatest violence. For decades the whole of the Latin American left was composed essentially of European immigrants and expressed itself politically through the action of unions that they founded and led.

Their politicosocial attitude was a romantic socialism based on aversion both to the entrepreneurial bourgeoisie and to the state and its regulatory institutions, such as the army and the Church. They acted with the ingenuousness typical of socialist movements prior to the Soviet experience, when it was supposed that formal suppression of ownership of the means of production would naturally and inevitably be followed by the inauguration of a classless society, a kingdom of equality and fraternity.

After World War I the intensification of the process of industrialization and the reflexive modernization of Latin America expanded the urban wage-earner class. The descendants of immigrants who did not succeed in attaining the status of proprietors were then massively incorporated into the industrial proletariat and into the new castes of bureaucratic employes as the aristocracy of the wage-earners. They went on to follow the destiny of that stratum, being integrated into the political order through unorthodox processes such as identification with autocratic, populist, or reformist leaderships—in any case, as an antipatrician and antioligarchic electoral force.

In recent decades the solid identification of the urban strata with these renovating political positions has created a situation of political crisis, because it has made the maintenance of democratic liberal procedures impracticable for the traditional patriciate. In consequence, free and direct suffrage has been proscribed in nearly the whole of Latin America; democratic procedures have been conditioned to the control of military and civilian guardianships that make the expression of popular will unfeasible. In these circumstances the descendants of immigrants in the New Peoples, like all the populace, have been condemned to assume more radical positions because they can see only in them any prospect for rupture of the political hegemony of the traditional dominant castes.

In the following chapters the various national ethnic entities classified as New Peoples will be studied. Of the pattern constituted by the dominance of aboriginal contingents and without the impregnating presence of the plantation, we single out only Chile, because Paraguay is studied together with the River Plate countries. These last, having been transfigured into Transplanted Peoples, will be analyzed in a later chapter together with the Anglo-Americans.

5. The Brazilians[1]

BRAZIL FIGURES among the new peoples of America as the national unit with the largest territory and population, and as the only nation colonized by the Portuguese. Half the South American continent is Brazil, her territory comprising 8.5 million square kilometers and its population, 82 million (1965). Even considering Latin America as a whole, Brazil stands out with 40 per cent of the total area and 30 per cent of all the Latin American population. On the world scale Brazil is the fourth largest in uninterrupted area and seventh in population.[2]

Brazil's territory is shaped like a huge irregular lozenge with the lesser face projected toward the Atlantic in a coastline of 7,500 kilometers, and the greater separated from the Pacific and the Caribbean by a belt of seven

[1] This chapter is a synthesis of my *O Brasil Emergente*.
[2] Brazil is exceeded in uninterrupted area by the U.S.S.R. (22.4 million square kilometers), Canada (9.9 million), and China (9.8 million); and in population by China (700 million inhabitants), India (500 million), the U.S.S.R. (210 million), the United States (200 million), Japan (93 million), and Indonesia (90 million).

Hispano-American republics across 16,000 kilometers of frontiers. In South America only Chile and Ecuador do not share boundaries with Brazil.

A line running parallel to the Atlantic littoral and 500 kilometers from the ocean would encompass 60 per cent of the territory and 90 per cent of the population of the country. The remaining pocket, where the rivers Paraguay and Paraná rise, and where the Araguaia-Tocantins river is located, is the least exploited area of Brazil. The new capital, Brasília, was established in that area precisely to form a nucleus capable of promoting human occupation of the area and its full integration into the nation's social and economic life. Even today the 90 per cent of Brazilians on the Atlantic strip are concentrated in demographic islands separated from one another by broad, relatively unpopulated expanses. Only after World War II did these islands communicate regularly by land. Formerly they coexisted without coliving, a vast archipelago linked together only by means of maritime voyages or by land crossings along exceedingly precarious roads across hundreds of kilometers of virgin forest or enormous stretches of uninhabited country.

A still greater isolation prevails in relation to nearly the whole South American bloc, which despite its geographic contiguity does not offer any corresponding social and economic integration. The Hispano-American countries sharing boundaries with Brazil are separated from, rather than connected with, that nation by the thousands of kilometers of unpopulated frontiers. In fact, only Uruguay and Argentina, Paraguay and Bolivia have regular nuclei of communications with Brazil through border cities. Contact with the other countries is by sea or air, across distances equivalent to those separating Brazil from Africa or Europe or North America. In recent years air transport, increasing more and more, has seemed to shorten distances. Even so, given the vast empty spaces of Latin America, even the fastest planes can offer only flights so long and expensive that close, intimate contact remains difficult.

All these characteristics reveal how premature the installation of Latin American national projects really is. In the near future, forced by a rate of demographic increase that appears to be the highest in the world, and served by more efficient transportation systems, its populations will multiply, peopling the deserts of the interior and thus making for closer contacts and cultural interchange. Latin American unity, founded on a moral solidarity daily asserted, nevertheless has no basis in any common life together, but only in the similarity of the dominant cultural physiognomy—Hispanic or Lusitanian—and in the absence of any competition capable of generating conflicts. The famous Argentine-Brazilian rivalry, the subject of much discussion during the first decades of this century, was more like a

school exercise by idle military men than the expression of any real opposition of national interests.

To those original factors of unity three others of recent date can be
added: (1) the awareness of regional backwardness and the resolve to progress by autonomous exploitation of each country's vast resources in order
to raise its peoples' standard of living; (2) the awareness of their community of interests as exploited peoples, against the United States, which had
become an imperialistic power, especially after World War II; (3) the continental effort to attain, through planning, greater economic stability by organizing a privileged, mutually satisfactory common market. A basic obstacle to autonomous development is rupture with foreign and domestic
spoliation, and regional integration is the U.S. power policy, oriented toward perpetuating backwardness as a mechanism of domination of the
continent.

The Brazilian Protocell

The New People character of the Brazilian national ethnos is based on
its multicultural and multiracial formation in which decisive roles were
played by the Negro and the Indian as well as by the European. The processes of detribalization and deculturation of these contingents to mold the
national ethnos operated under the compulsions of slavery and, simultaneously, with the miscegenation of each contingent with the others and of all
with the Portuguese, under the domination of the latter, who imposed their
language, their religion, and a social order in conformity with their interests as colonizers.

In spite of the disparity of the original stocks and the ecological differences, a peculiar ethnos was shaped in Brazil: racially heterogeneous and
in full process of fusion, but culturally coherent through unity of language,
technology, forms of social organization, beliefs, and world views. This
was the basic formative process of all New Peoples. What is unique about
the Brazilians derives from the differentiating qualities in their indigenous,
African, and European stocks, from the particular proportion in which
these congregated in Brazil, the environmental conditions they confronted,
and, further, the nature of the production objectives that engaged and held
them together.

At what stage can one begin to speak of a neo-Brazilian culture differentiated in its developmental process? I would set that moment at the middle
of the sixteenth century, when the brazilwood commerce was dominant

and the first mills were established, and when men were still trying to conscript the Indian into slave labor. This culture must have been engendered
in the first communities on the coast of São Vicente, Bahia, Pernambuco,
and Rio de Janeiro, communities largely composed of crossbreeds from
Europeans with Indian women, and which already had a way of life of
their own, different from that of their parent populations. From these
communities came the different Brazilian sociocultural configurations,
stamping uniform traits on all of them. Their cultural bases were the Tupí
stock, found all along the coast, and the European, represented almost exclusively by the Portuguese.

These first Brazilian nuclei molded a new human type, neither indigenous nor European, that was to play the principal role in the formation of
Brazilian society—the *mameluco*,[3] identified with the Portuguese father
but speaking the maternal language better—the language of the community in which he was born—and more the heir to the indigenous culture
than to the European. These mestizos, directed by some Europeans in
charge of the trading settlements installed on the coast, drew their subsistence principally from the Indians' cultivated patches and devoted themselves to the only occupation of the land: supplying brazilwood logs to the
ships that touched at the coast in exchange for European manufactured
goods they needed and for the trinkets with which they lured the Indians
to work finding, cutting, and hauling the brazilwood.

These protocells of Brazilian culture, shaped and molded before the
Negro had arrived and when the European was still rare, were the common denominator of the popular way of life in all regions. They were integrated, principally, by the mameluco's (and, through him, the white man's
and later the Negro's) inheritance of the age-old patrimony of adaptation
to the tropical jungle and forest by the Tupí peoples. This patrimony was
a knowledge of tropical nature, a technology adjusted to it, and a characteristic world view. Indeed, these new human nuclei could only have
emerged, survived, and increased in such unviable conditions and in an environment so different from the European through their having learned
from the Indians how to master the nature of the tropics, making them
their teachers, guides, oarsmen, woodcutters, hunters, fishermen, and craftsmen, and especially through taking the Indian women to wife and engendering a vast mestizo progeny that eventually would come to people the
land.[4]

---

[3] A Brazilian term designating the crossbreed of Portuguese with Indian. It comes
from the Arabic *mamaluc,* meaning the slaves taken from European populations and
trained for maintenance of Islamic domination of those peoples.

[4] For a searching study of the Tupí-Guaraní peoples and their wars, see Florestan
Fernandes (1949).

On the scale of cultural evolution the Tupí peoples were taking the first steps in agricultural revolution, thus rising above the status of hunting and gathering tribes. They did so in their own fashion, together with various other peoples of the tropical forest who had domesticated manioc and other plants, taking them from the wild state for their cultivated fields. Besides manioc, they raised corn, beans, peanuts, tobacco, sweet potatoes, yams, squash, pumpkins and gourds, arrowwood, the annatto tree, cotton, pinguin fiber, cashews, papaya, mate [Paraguayan tea], and guaraná, among many other plants, on large farms that assured them plentiful food throughout the year and a great variety of materials for making artifacts, condiments, poisons, pigments, and stimulants. Thus they escaped the condition resultant from nutritional deficiency to which preagricultural peoples were subject in their dependence on the generosity of tropical nature, which, if it provides plenty of fruits, nuts, and tubers during one part of the year, condemns them to want in the other part. However, they did remain dependent on nature for other foods that they obtained from hunting and fishing, which were seasonal and marked by periods of abundance and want.[5]

The cultural tradition that stamped itself on the neo-Brazilian nuclei was the Tupí-Guaraní, which, together with the Carib, Arawak, and a few other groups, shared one of the most advanced adaptive technologies among tropical forest natives. From a century before the conquest, tribes of this linguisticocultural stock had occupied the Brazilian coast, with the exception of small pockets held by other indigenous peoples. The Tupí-Guaraní themselves were in upper Paraguay, where Asunción was to be established; on the islands of the River Plate, where the primitive nucleus of Buenos Aires would rise; and on tributaries of the Amazon, where the Portuguese would install themselves later. This wide distribution of the Tupí-Guaraní peoples predetermined, in a certain way, what Brazil would come to be as a national society, because it confronted the Portuguese with a uniform indigenous culture along nearly all the territorial area that the nation would eventually encompass.

The protocells of the Brazilian rustic culture were molded for this reason with an essentially Tupí feature. Later on the neo-Brazilians would seek, by preference, indigenous groups of this stock either to live with or to enslave. In their eyes these peoples were folk with whom they could get along without serious difficulties, because they all spoke variants of one and the same language, cultivated and consumed the same foods, and had a common cultural patrimony. At the end of the first century of coloniza-

[5] See Darcy Ribeiro (1955) for a study of the annual subsistence activity cycle of the tropical forest tribes.

tion, the neo-Brazilians had settled only in areas formerly dominated by the Tupí-Guaraní, spreading out over their former villages, whose inhabitants were progressively decimated by epidemics or by the hardships of slavery. Nevertheless, until their extinction they continued to contribute as a genetic and cultural stock to the formation of the Brazilian society that was to succeed it on the same territory.

Even today in Brazil the pioneers that advance on virgin areas, when they confront groups of Tupí extraction immediately recognize the essential unity of these peoples' modes of adaptation to nature and see many of their beliefs as their own. For the same reason they react against other indigenous stocks, considering them as alien, backward people because they do not raise the same plants and have food habits and contrasting customs that find no echo in their own experience.

The cane plantations and sugar production that made the Brazilian colonization project viable were initially based on these nuclei, by means of the enslavement of the indigenes, which afford the mameluco a new economic function: the capture of Indians to sell as slaves to the planters. In this way the symbiotic relations with the Indians that had made possible the first decades of peaceful coexistence and cooperation were broken off. The Indian's revolt against slavery was founded on his own egalitarian social structure, which, not differentiating a submissive stratum from a superior one, made his over-all domination insufferable.

By way of slavery and by Jesuit domestication, however, certain indigenes were compelled to integrate individually into the new nuclei, added to the mamelucos and later to the Negroes. The important fact is that, instead of the maturation of the tribal communities for civilization, through a supposed process of acculturation that would make them progress from tribal to national status, from the village to the town, as so many historians and anthropologists have supposed, the indigenous groups were simply wiped out by the death of their members in proportion as the neo-Brazilian nuclei grew. Wherever we have precise data, we can see that the coexistence of indigenous villages with new mestizo nuclei is followed by the growth of the latter and the extinction of the former, whose population decreases year after year until it disappears (Ribeiro, 1957).

The failure to draft indigenous labor for the sugar mills led to the enslavement of the African Black, equally tribal but as a general rule more evolved culturally and socially, and therefore better conditioned to serve as slave. Moreover, finding himself in a strange land, his will broken by captivity, by the ocean crossing, and by separation from people of his own community and language, the Negro felt less inclined to flee the plantation, whereas to the Indian it was merely a matter of gaining the surrounding

woods and escaping hostile tribes to find friendly Indian settlements until
he got back to his own tribe.

The new communities that were springing up in the sugar economy were
capable of sheltering far more members than the indigenous villages and
the initial protocells, because they were structured to modes of socioeconomic organization in which the interdependence of individuals ceased to
confine itself to family nuclei and extended to a complex of specialized
productive sectors, which, as peasants, craftsmen, and traders, became mutually dependent parts of a composite society. The fundamental molders of
these nuclei were slavery, as a form of conditioning the labor force, and
the plantation system, on which each new nucleus was structured.

Even with a high degree of self-sufficiency, these nuclei depended on
certain imported articles, especially metal implements, salt, gunpowder,
and a few others that they could not produce. The technology on which
their productive action was based—originally almost wholly indigenous as
regards subsistence—was enriched by European contributions that increased its productivity. These included the use of metal instruments (axes,
knives, machetes, scythes, hoes, fishhooks), firearms for war, and some mechanical contrivances little known in the first centuries, such as the press
that replaced the native *tipití* in the preparation of manioc meal; the *mon-
jolo* [a crude water-driven machine] to pound corn, the oxcart, crushers
for grinding cane, the water wheel, the compound loom, the cotton gin, the
potter's wheel, and the metal pans that replaced the ceramic toaster in
manufacturing flour and meal. An important role was played also by the
European's introduction of large livestock for meat, riding, and farm
labor; of small barnyard stock to enrich the diet, and of various cultivated
plants, both food and industrial.

Houses improved with the technique of building garden and house walls
of mud or adobe for the humbler, and of brick and lime, with tiled roofs,
for the more noble. They were enriched with more elaborate furniture, replacing sleeping hammocks with cots and bunks; braided baskets were dis-
carded for leather hampers or wood chests, and later benches, wardrobes,
and oratories were added. Still other contributions were the techniques of
preparation and use of metal tools and utensils, and of soap, alcoholic beverages, oil lamps, tanned leather, new medicines, sandals and hats, and improvements in the technique of weaving, which permitted manufacture of
better cotton cloths.

The dominant trait of the new nuclei was to have an external economic
and political command of high determinant power over their destiny. It
was this bond that was to lead the nascent communities to a new mercan-
tile-based productive system, because designed to turn a profit, and slavo-

cratically organized with the labor material brought from Africa. With economic development these characteristics would also lead to the greater differentiation of communities into a rural parcel, initially made up of peasants born on the land and occupied in the production of foodstuffs and commercial goods, and later with Negro slaves from the export plantations added, into an urban parcel of manual laborers, merchants, and craftsmen and functionaries, priests and authorities, all from the mother country, who administered and directed the undertaking technically. A stratum of specialized personnel was thus formed, aloof from the tasks of subsistence, with an educated sector exercising the functions of command, war, and social regulation, particularly on the political, entrepreneurial, and religious planes.

This higher cultural position did not represent Brazilian tribal societies' ascent to the urban, stratified status, but the simple projection on the neo-Brazilian nuclei of the advance previously achieved by the European, which shaped its American offshoots in a higher stage of sociocultural evolution. It is not a question, therefore, of a process of evolutionary acceleration but of mere historical incorporation.

What indigenous qualities were retained by the Brazilian protocell were, as we have seen, principally ecological adaptation and the language commonly spoken during the first two centuries, Tupí. Its European qualities were the ordering of the new society as a colonial component of mercantile and slavocratic capitalism; the productive technology of the exportation sector, of the building of houses, and of the manufacture of means of transport; the Portuguese language, which in the course of time imposed itself through the need of a shared system of communication; and the Catholic religion, also imposed, but, as it mingled with the new culture, so impregnated with indigenous and African beliefs that it took on a peculiar aspect, probably further from Roman Catholic orthodoxy than the heresies most rigorously combatted in the Iberian peninsula.

The culture thus molded spread from the original nuclei to the sugar mills, which multiplied along the coast. From there it passed on to the natural cattle-raising areas opening up in the interior. Afterwards, through one branch, it would shape the social life of the gold and diamond mining regions; through another it was to plunge into the Amazon jungle with the rubber-gatherers; and through a third it would affect the new pastoral areas in the extreme south. In each of these regions the new society grew, acquiring various colorations, both ecological and economic, arising from the regional variations and diversification of the productive tasks assumed. In the course of long periods it underwent continual alteration and enrichment, by spreading to new lands and humanizing them through work, but, simultaneously, transfiguring its own physiognomy and redefining its objectives and loyalties. Through all these processes the diverse forms of the Brazilians were molded, historically, which today permit distinguishing them as northeast *sertanejos, caboclos* * of the Amazon region, coastal Creoles, hillbillies of São Paulo or Minas Gerais or Goiaz, *gaúchos* † of the southern plains, gringo-Brazilians, and so on, all of them more marked by what they have in common as Brazilians than by the eventual differences of regional or functional adaptation, or of miscegenation and acculturation.

Structured socioeconomically, each of these cultural areas knew a period of splendor as long as its productive activity remained healthy through its integration into the international market. With the decline of exportable production they fell, one after the other, into long seasons of lethargy in which they regressed to a subsistence economy. Then their enterprises, cities, and plantations deteriorated, with their capital and part of their population moving to other areas in which new activities came into being. In this way the former areas retrogressed to a social and cultural condition marked by want, with degradation of the civilization levels previously achieved.

As it was rare for two cycles to occur in any given area, in each of them after the decline a residual population remained, poorer and poorer, incapable of reorganizing economic and social life, without external motivation.

That happened in the sugar area, after a little more than a century of great economic prosperity had passed (1530–1650) that had permitted the installation and maintenance of great contingents of Negroes, crossbreeds, and whites, and the creation of the first urban nuclei of the country. From the second half of the seventeenth century the sugar economy slid into decadence owing to the rise of Antillean production and the rebellions of the Negro slaves, the latter phenomena becoming chronic. The decline was to be accentuated by the emergence of the gold mining zones, which attracted a large part of the population. Then a new cycle began that was to last nearly a century (1700–1780), concentrating enormous contingents of people in the mountainous region of the center and leading a large number to the extreme west. The mining economy declined, also, when the gold and diamond deposits were exhausted, entering on the same process of regres-

---

* *Sertanejos:* people of the *sertão,* the backlands, "the bush" (to adopt an Australian close equivalent).

Caboclos: persons of copper skin, ranging from pure Indian to mestizo, or even to mulattoes with straight hair.

† The term is in the sense of cattlemen and natives of the state of Rio Grande do Sul, whether engaged in cattle-raising or not.

sion to economic forms of subsistence and a poverty culture. Only half a century later did a new economic motif emerge and establish itself in the neighboring areas with the great coffee plantations (1840–1930). Once more, parcels of the free and the slave population from the former areas of prosperity (sugar, mining, and pastoral backlands) were recruited for the new work nucleus, which would increase vastly for nearly a century, only to give way, after 1930, to the industrial economy.

Besides the major dynamic centers that dominated national economic life for long periods, some lesser nuclei appeared and declined more rapidly, enlivening some areas that afterwards also retrogressed. Such were the cotton of Maranhão (1770–1820) and the rubber of Amazônia (1880–1913), which made it possible to install civilizing nuclei in marginal areas, incorporating them into the national society.

This boom-and-bust development, occurring at different times in different areas of the country, opened the way to occupation of the immense Brazilian territory and facilitated national unity, but it also resulted in condemning to want a vast population caught up successively in each cycle. Not one of these cycles could fortify itself by economic interaction with the others. They merely complemented one another by the transfer of labor force and by constituting auxiliary nuclei of subsistence and cattle economy in the interior backlands and in the south, which served the different productive areas in succession. This pastoral expansion, though it never attained the episodic prosperity of the great cycles, permitted the formation of a mobile front responsible for the occupation of the greater part of the territory of Brazil, thus filling the empty spaces of the interior between the zones of export economies.

Only industrialization, still under way, once it is stabilized in supplying the demands of a market already nationwide in scope, will furnish the opportunity to integrate these different regions into a single economic system capable of covering the whole country, at the same time overcoming the archaic status of Brazilian society to stamp it with the characteristics of a modern nation.

On the plane of cultural development all these Brazilian forms of production and the respective socioeconomic configurations are variants of the low-energy technological system that prevailed throughout the world before the Industrial Revolution. An agromercantile civilization, it was based on farming, stock-raising, and mining with rudimentary techniques, using muscular energy, both human and animal, and apparatuses for harnessing the power of river currents, such as the water wheel, and the power of the wind, such as sailing vessels. This technology made possible the installation of the commercial enterprise from which the colonization of Brazil resulted: by making viable the removal of enormous human

masses from Africa for work on the farms and in the mines, by providing transportation for merchandise, and by establishing internal communications between the various coastal nuclei, and between them and the
European markets.

In their level of development the resultant sociocultural complexes reflected this civilizing technology, which rendered greater expansion
favorable where it was most exhaustively exploited, but which also fixed
the limits attainable by the population and the possible forms of social organization.

The prevailing mode of life was fundamentally agrarian. Nearly the
whole population lived and worked on the commercial plantations or the
subsistence farmlands dispersed over an immense territory. The urban network consisted of small port cities that, besides their basic export activity,
performed administrative, military, commercial, and religious functions.
Frequently, the government official, the soldier, the merchant, and the
priest were also planters. In any case, they lived on the surpluses produced, and the very reason for their existence lay in satisfying the needs for
order, defense, and commercialization of the agrarian and mining economy. The really creative life was in the plantations and the mines, organized to produce export goods and aspiring to satisfy autarchically the
subsistence needs of their populations.

The major imported article was slave labor, which could not multiply in
the country because of the very conditions of work to which it was subjected. Besides plantation and farm Negroes, other importations included
metal instruments, salt, and articles of consumption, particularly by the
seignioral caste. Food, clothes, and dwellings were produced on the plantation itself, except for meat, hides, and draft animals brought from the grazing zones. At times of high prices on export articles it became expedient
to buy foodstuffs and cloth goods for the slaves, activating outside the
plantation the complementary subsistence crops destined primarily for the
urban fairs.

By juggling his accounts, each planter sought to maintain his capital
against the usury of the financiers, the high cost of imported articles, and
the permanent attrition of his human and animal sources of energy. When
he accumulated sums over and above his sumptuary expenditures, he applied them to expanding the areas of cultivation, opening new plantations.

A high birth rate resulted in only a slight population increase because
of the very high death rate, both infant and general, incident to all but especially to the slave mass. This mass, used as the basic source of energy
and worn out in service, had to be replenished by the permanent flow of
the slave traffic. The nuclei of ancillary economy providing meat and
goods to the incipient domestic market, not being burdened by purchase of

slave labor and having a lower consumption of commercial articles, handled their own subsistence better, constantly increasing their population.

The first Negroes introduced into Brazil reached the coast just before the turn of the sixteenth century. They were not numerous, as is proved by historians' very insistence on documenting those first importations. With the development of the sugar economy they were brought over in great numbers. Each sugar mill owner had the royal privilege of importing 120 "pieces," but his right to buy Negroes at the slave markets was unlimited. The royal concessionaires of the slave trade had one of the most solid businesses of the colony. It lasted three centuries, permitted them to bring millions of Blacks to Brazil and in this way absorbed the largest item of the investment in sugar, gold, cotton, tobacco, cacao, and coffee enterprises: the cost of slave labor.

Compelled to integrate into the nascent society as its basic labor force, the African Negro became Brazilian as he became assimilated to the culture of those protocells, to whose forms of life, habits, and customs he had to adjust. Culturally he contributed little to them, because they had existed prior to his appearance. But he was to mark them profoundly as a genetic stock, transforming them from mameluco to mulatto. He would likewise contribute in the transition from Tupí to Portuguese as a maternal language, processed first in the areas where the Negro concentrated most, and finally embracing the whole country.

When he became the largest contingent of the agrarian population, as well as a force in Europeanizing the native populations through being subjected to the rigorous discipline of slave labor under the isolated conditions of plantation life, the Negro became a human mass more pliable to deculturation and integration into new cultural bodies than the free crossbreeds from the initial nuclei. Under conditions of compulsory deculturation the Negro was forced to immerse himself in a spurious culture based in the original protocell, to which was added an imitation of the world view, beliefs, and habits of the seignorial group, to which he contributed only a few originalities. The Negro's contribution, which could have been much greater, in the end was reduced to his role as a labor force, his racial stock, a few technological innovations, and certain survivals of a religious nature that, after the abolition of slavery, achieved freer expression.

Estimates of the Negro contingent introduced into Brazil in more than three centuries of the slave trade vary from 18 million (Calógeras, 1927) to 3.3 million (Simonsen, 1937). Almost equally varied are the estimates of the number and proportion of Negroes in the whole population during the colonial period. Artur Ramos (1944), choosing the sources he considered trustworthy, cites an estimate for the year 1800 thus: whites, 920,-

000; Negroes, 1.96 million; and "dark" (mestizos and mulattoes) persons, 1.22 million. The whites, therefore, total only a minority of 22 per cent in a Black and crossbred world.

Beginning with abolition, the Negro parcel increased in a much smaller proportion than the other two, and in more recent years has actually decreased. The fact is explained by the interruption of the slave trade and the increment in European immigration. As the proportion of this depopulation exceeds these factors, however, the drastic reduction of the Negro contingent in Brazil must be attributed principally to the precariousness of living conditions endured by the ex-slave, whose descendant faces worse conditions for survival than do the other contingents. This statistical reduction is very likely also affected by the white-oriented racial ideology that leads the common Brazilian to define the socially successful Negro as white, "light," or, at worst, "dark." Many dark ones must have passed into the enormous group of whites-by-definition, and many a Black, probably, into the residual group of the dark.

Analysis of the growth of Brazilian population and its composition according to color is highly expressive of the conditions of oppression imposed by the white on the other components. We estimate at 10 million the number of Negroes brought into Brazil as slaves until the abolition of the trade (1850); at two million the number of Indians successively faced by the frontiers of Brazilian civilization in the same period; and at 5 million, at most, the number of Europeans immigrated into Brazil up to 1950. Considering the composition of the population in 1950 (at this writing we have no 1960 census data on color composition), we learn that Indians in more or less autonomous tribal life were reduced to about 100,000 (D. Ribeiro, 1957); Negroes have probably attained a maximum of 5.6 million; those defining themselves as dark number 13.7 million; and the whites, 32 million.

Despite the definitional deformations imposed on the Negro mass by the typically Brazilian confusion of social status with color, these estimates reflect an evident progressive decrease in it, both in percentage (more than half of the population in 1800, dropping to one third in 1850 and one tenth in 1950) and in absolute numbers (after reaching 2 million in 1900 and 6.6 million in 1940, it dropped to 5.6 million in 1950, presumably falling still more thereafter).

The contrast of the Negro's progression and that of the white group is obvious. The latter jumped from 22 per cent in 1800 to 62 per cent in 1950, and numerically from 920,000 to 32 million in the same time. The high increment in the white contingent is not explicable solely by the increase in European immigration after 1800. Its volume never reached a level that could decisively influence the composition of the original population. The demographic explosion of the Brazilian whites is intelligible, then, only in terms of their fecundity and lower mortality rates, favored over the Negroes and the dark ones by their better living conditions.

The immigrant played a very considerable role in the formation of certain regional populations, especially in the south where he concentrated most, creating characteristically European countrysides and predominantly white populations. His role, though important in the racial and cultural constitution of those areas, has no great importance in explaining the evolutionary tendencies of the Brazilian population as a whole. When immigrants began arriving in larger numbers, the national population was already so numerically massive and so defined ethnically that it could absorb them culturally and racially without great changes in the whole. In Brazil, consequently, nothing occurred comparable to what happened in the River Plate countries, where a numerically weak original ethnos was submerged by the masses of immigrants, with the latter stamping a new, characteristically European physiognomy on the national population and culture.

Thus, what distinguishes the Brazilians of the different areas is cultural originalities rather than any over-all distinction capable of uniting groups that are racially, culturally, linguistically or ethnically opposed. The complex molded by so many contributions is essentially one, as regards national ethnos, leaving no room for eventual tensions to be organized around regional, racial, or cultural opposing units. One and the same culture encompasses all, and a vigorous national, increasingly Brazilian, definition animates all.

The profound differences that separate and oppose Brazilians in flagrantly contrasting strata are social in nature. They distinguish the privileged circles and secure classes that have succeeded, in a general economy of want, in achieving high standards of consumption, from the masses disinherited through living outside the productive process and the cultural, social, and political life of the nation. The reduction of these differences will only be made, however, through a reordering of the national society that permits the integration of the whole people into a modern productive system and, by this means, into the various spheres of the country's social and cultural life.

Therefore, the Brazilians of the most unmistakably Black racial physiognomy, who emerged recently from the conditions of slavery and are still concentrated in the poorest strata, are not socially and politically motivated by racial differences but by the growing consciousness of the historical and social character—therefore incidental and superable—of the factors that cast them into the poorest strata of the population; not as Negroes operating in the Brazilian framework, but as members of the poorest classes, all mobilized by equal aspirations of economic and social progress.

The very nature of racial prejudice prevailing in Brazil acts more as an integrative force than as a segregative mechanism. The Anglo-Saxon type of prejudice falls indiscriminately on every person of color, whatever his proportion of Negro blood, necessarily leading to segregation and violence because of hostility to any coexistence. The Brazilians' color prejudice (Oracy Nogueira, 1960), depending differentially on the shade of color, tending to identify the light mulatto as white, leads rather to an anticipation of miscegenation, discriminatory only insofar as it aspires to whitening the Negroes instead of accepting them as they are.

What differentiates the interracial conjunction in Brazil is the development of attitudes more encouraging than condemnatory of miscegenation. The birth of a mulatto infant in Brazil is no betrayal of either the Negro or the white stock. This integrationist ideology, stimulating to racial blending, is probably the most positive value of the Brazilian interracial conjunction. It will certainly not lead to a whitening of all Brazilian Negroes in the line of popular aspirations, but it has the virtue of repressing segregation. Also, it diffuses a racial ideology that tends to attribute the positive qualities of the Brazilian man precisely to the crossbreeding of the three elementary family trees.

The essential linguistic and cultural unity of the Brazilians of all regions is explained, principally, by two factors: (1) the exceptionally early constitution of a basic population, whose vigor and flexibility would permit it to shape all Brazilians through mere local adjustments; (2) the unity of the civilizational process, which, by integrating all those isolated implantations into a single colonial productive system governed from the metropolis, would make them grow as a single body into what would come to be modern Brazil.

With its base in those protocells the initial nucleus was formed that today we designate as "rustic Brazilian culture." [6] Throughout four centuries it diversified into several sociocultural complexes represented by the "creole culture area," which developed in the *massapé* strip * of the northeast, its fundamental institution the sugar mill; by the "caipira culture area" in the zone occupied by the mamelucos from São Paulo, first with mining activities, then with the great coffee plantations; by the "sertão culture area," which was diffused by means of the cattle ranches from the

[6] For concepts of rustic culture and *caipira* [backwoods] culture, see Antônio Cândido de Melo e Souza (1964); for peasant and folk culture, Robert Redfield (1941, 1953); for *caboclo* [copper-skinned] culture, Emílio Willems (1947); and for creole culture, Gillin (1947).

* The *massapé* (or *massapê*) is a kind of black clay soil, very fertile and good for growing sugar cane.

arid northeast to the *cerrados* * of the midwest; by the "caboclo culture area" of the Amazônia populations engaged in gathering jungle products, particularly rubber; by the "gaúcho culture area" of the south with its three variants: that of the grazing lands of the plains, the "gringo-caipira culture" of the regions colonized by immigrants—predominantly German and Italian in the southern states—and that of the *matutos,* rustic descendants of Azorians, a culture very like that of the caipira.

Each of these facets of the Brazilian traditional culture has urban and rustic features adjusting to the two fundamental human conditions. These constitute organic unities, however, because the two are mutually interdependent, being the urban and rural counterparts of one and the same society. Both are heterogeneous, deriving from their social stratification. The city facet offers a greater number of cultural and social variants for the coexistence, in the same physical space, of a heavier population, differentiated in upper, middle, and lower classes, more modern in their way of life. The rural population, isolated on the plantations, forms small, less differentiated nuclei, each divided into a small superior contingent composed of the patronal family and a few employees and the mass of dependents, formerly slaves, now servants and wage-earners.

In the Brazilian traditional structures the seignioral caste of planters, established merchants, and, sometimes, members of the liberal professions, integrates the total society as one of its constitutive elements but with a differentiated participation in cultural life. They share in the popular revelries, for example, but as benevolent, skeptical patrons rather than as participants in functional communion with popular beliefs. In fact, they constitute a closed circle, cultivating their own values, acquired in national and foreign metropolitan centers, where they become, for good or ill, heirs to literature, music, and learning; but more particularly they become alienated through the adoption of concepts and preconceptions about their own people.

Thus there are two distinct cultural circles. The popular, based on the common people's orally transmitted common knowledge, on which all productive activities are founded, forms a continuum from the city to the country and is unified by the same values and traditions, participating in the same celebrations of the religious calendar and in the weekly congregating of the market. The seignioral circle, of erudite culture—influenced by profane ideas, by new political values, and by its own forms of amusement—contrasts with the popular as modern opposed to traditional.

---

* The term means a type of land with twisted, stunted trees interspersed with grasses suitable for pasturage; it is common to the states of São Paulo, Goiaz, Minas Gerais, and Mato Grosso.

In the cities this modernity impregnates the poorer masses also, differentiating them from the rural masses by rationalistic, impersonal, and less conservative attitudes. These differentiations between the rural and the urban, the seignioral and the popular, do not, however, affect the archaic character of the whole traditional culture, or the spurious character of the world view held by the upper classes as agents of a foreign domination, yesterday colonial, today dependent or neocolonial.

The transition from the now archaic traditional standard to the modern goes on at different rates in all regions. Its basic obstacle is the opposition of the dominant caste to changes that affect its hegemonic interests. Its renovating agents are the political leaderships of the urban popular strata, independent of the traditional order, and, in certain conditions, the city entrepreneurs seeking to profit by modernization. The people, rural or urban, subjected to these opposing forces are compelled to integrate into the framework established by them. Nevertheless, they accept the innovations because they perceive that they can only gain from the changes. This attitude reflects a will for progress and constitutes, perhaps, the most remarkable characteristic of the New Peoples. The Brazilian rural populations, marginalized socially rather than culturally because of their divergence from any of the parent populations, are backward, not conservative. Every road opened to them attracts new contingents to the circuit of modern communication. Given their cultural homogeneity—resulting from the deculturation of the original populations and their consequent engagement in the local form of traditional culture—they are predisposed to accept innovations. Not being tied to a peasant traditionalism or to tribal or folkloric values, nothing attaches them to their wretched forms of life. Instead of becoming conservative, as occurs in the areas where the marginality is cultural, they show an open, receptive attitude to modernity and progress. In the humblest family of the farthest interior, the first motor truck reaching there will probably find youngsters who aspire only to drivers, who much prefer leaving to staying there, all of them ready to incorporate themselves into new ways of life.

Impoverished on the cultural plane, however, in comparison with his indigenous and African and European forebears, the rural Brazilian has become more receptive to the innovations of progress than the traditionalist peasant, the community Indian, or the tribal Negro. The future forms that Brazilian culture will probably assume with the advance of modernization will surely reinforce national ethnic unity through greater homogenization of the modes of doing, interacting, and thinking. But for a long time yet they will retain local variants, probably on the same level as the present ones by virtue of the specializing factors of environment and productive activities and because the transforming process operates on already differentiated cultural contexts. The mosaic coloration that today enriches Brazil will possibly thus be preserved.

The Oligarchic Order

The *fazenda,* the plantation, constitutes the basic institution shaping Brazilian society. Around it the whole social system is organized as a body of auxiliary institutions, norms, customs, and beliefs destined to fulfill its conditions of existence and preexistence. The family itself, the people, the nation result from the fazenda and are molded by it.

Although other systematizing models appeared later—for example, the urban nuclei founded on the factory—the fazenda still determines the destiny of the great majority of Brazilians, not merely the two thirds of the national population directly dependent on it but also those outside the fazenda whose existence is essentially conditioned by it.

Despite the installation of big industry and the rise of metropolitan centers—which is quite recent—every element of national life was reducible to the fazenda order and justified its form and existence by it alone. Today the social system is somewhat more complex because new social forces established in the cities are already asserting their interests, either unconnected with or opposed to the fazenda order, setting limits to its former hegemony. But the plantation remains the basic institution fixing the order of Brazilian society. The most eloquent expression of its power lies, probably, in its startling longevity, able to survive for four centuries and persist even when visibly obsolete and fit only to operate as the essential limiter of the popular standard of living and of the nation's greatness.

What makes that power intelligible is the fact that the fazenda system, when it was initiated, gave birth to Brazilian society. The latter developed for that very reason as a subproduct of the northeast sugar mills, the cattle ranches in the sertão, the extractive industries (forestal and mineral) structured on the same bases, and the fazendas of coffee, cotton, and cacao. In all these cases the fazenda ordered Brazilian society. Its basic formula— ownership of the agricultural or cattle *sesmaria* [royal land grant], of the *data* [mining claim], or of the forestal concession combined with control of a labor force permitted dislodging the old settler and promoting the occupation of the land; the blending and deculturating of the Black, indigenous, and European populations that shaped the Brazilian people; the structuring of families in types corresponding to the positions and social roles of their members in the fazenda economy; and an internal organizing of each new nucleus to conform with an over-all system bound to the foreign market.

The Brazilian plantation has been changing appreciably through its four centuries of history, taking on different characteristics as it adapted to new crops, with the passing from the slavocratic to the free-worker regime, and through incorporation of technological innovations deriving from the Industrial Revolution. Its basic structure, as an ordinating institution that models the social system by shaping the whole life of the nation, remains nevertheless intact.[7]

Its basic formula crystallized in the sugar mill, which inaugurated in the modern world the system of plantations [8] characterized by the slave regime and by the commercial nature of its one-product industry, as well as by the economic volume it reached as capital investment compared with the other agricultural enterprises of the period. It is configured as a community sui generis, integrated, on one hand, by the resident patron group with its small number of servants and by the slave mass, on the other: the former, living in comfortable dwellings, eating and dressing according to the lordly usage of the time; the latter, crowded into groups of huts, fed and treated like beasts of burden. It was this fantastic institution, in which were combined objectives, connections, and features of mercantile capitalism, the great economic force of the world of that day, with a new technology of agroindustrial production, the whole based on slavery, that was to make Project Brazil viable. The prior attempt to transplant a feudal system already outdated in the metropolis itself had failed. It was as a settlement of slavocratic planters that the Brazilian protosociety matured, the principal modality of New Peoples in America.

[7] Analyses and informative materials on the oligarchic order are found in Victor Nunes Leal (1948), Sérgio Buarque de Holanda (1956), Josué de Castro (1946), Nestor Duarte (1939), M. Diegues, Jr. (1959), Rui Cirne de Lima (1935), and José Maria de Paula (1944).

[8] On plantations (United States) and fazendas, see the essays of Julian H. Steward, Edgar T. Thompson, Sidney W. Wintz, and M. Diegues, Jr. (1960), Frank Tannenbaum (1947), Pierre Gourou (1959), H. W. Hutchinson (1957), Milton Santos (1955), Lynn Smith (1946), Gilberto Freyre (1954), Pierre Monbeig (1940), and Leo Waibel (1947).

Monographic studies on different types of Brazilian agrarian enterprises have been published by the Ministry of Agriculture: Manuel Diegues, Jr., "O Engenho Açucareiro" (The Sugar Mill), 1952; Dante Laytano, "A Estância Gaúcha" (The Rio Grande do Sul Ranch), 1952; José Norberto Macedo, "Fazendas de Gado do S. Francisco" (São Francisco Cattle Ranches), 1952; Arthur Cezar Ferreira Reis, "O Seringal e o Seringueiro na Amazônia" (The Rubber Trees and the Rubber Worker), 1954; Clovis Caldeira, "Fazendas de Cacau na Bahia" (Cacao Plantations in Bahia), 1954; Zedar P. da Silva, "O Vale do Itajaí" (The Itajaí Valley), 1955; Virgílio Correia Filho, "Ervais e Ervateiros" (Mate Plantations and Workers), 1957.

The national societies developing within that framework, instead of being a people sharing increasingly in the sources of power, capable of influence in making decisions affecting their destiny, constitute a mass held in ignorance and misery, governed by a patrician caste that adapts all social institutions to its designs, disguising its mastery in the most varied ways but maintaining it at all costs.

The seignioral planter caste, broadened to include politicians, lawyers, and businessmen, all supported on the same physical and social base—ownership of land exploited by others' hands—operates as a privileged group of patrons, bosses, regarding itself as the nation and seeing in the common people merely the masses indispensable to the functioning of the system. Under these conditions it is not surprising that a fazenda ideology has been created, penetrating deeply into all social strata, which seeks to explain the wealth of the wealthy and the poverty of the poor as natural and necessary expressions of intrinsic merits merely sanctioned by a wise and just order of things.

As an organizational model of social life the plantation system—by its nature as a mercantile-capitalistic enterprise intended to yield profits—contrasts with the tribal system, founded on the collective usufruct of the land by an undifferentiated community dedicated to survival through the cooperative work of all its members; the feudal system, based on the serfdom of the peasant in the service of a hereditary landlord, but essentially structured for subsistence; and the capitalistic system of granges, small farms, founded on ownership of land a family group, the major objective being the family's subsistence and progress. What contraposes the four systems, then, is the monopolistic form of land ownership and the diversity of fundamental objectives of agricultural development: patronal profit, in the case of the fazenda, and survival and reproduction of the life modes of a human community in all the other cases.

The basic prerequisites for the establishment of the plantation are, for this very reason, possession of the land and control of a work force. The first is obtained by government grant, inheritance, or purchase. The second, by control of the labor force preexistent in the area or transferred there more or less coercively. Assuming the most diverse aspects, such conditioning of the labor force made many scholars identify feudalism as the distinctive element of the plantation system.[9] In fact, several archaic

[9] The explanation of the backwardness of the Brazilian agrarian system by its feudal contents is exhaustively set forth by Nelson Werneck Sodré (1964), Moisés Vinhas (1963), and Alberto Passos Guimarães (1963). Refutations of this thesis, based on the characterization of the Brazilian agrarian structure as mercantile-capitalistic, are found in Cáio Prado Júnior (1960, 1964, 1966), Roberto Simonsen (1937), L. A. Costa Pinto (1948), and Andrew Gunder Frank (1964, 1966).

characteristics of coercion reminiscent of serfdom were, and still are, used to recruit plantation labor. But the fact that work-recruiting forms vary from slavery to wages indicates plainly the circumstantial resources of the plantation capitalistic system, capable of operating with either or both and transcending all as a new, capitalistic, mercantile organizational model. The essence of the system, then, does not lie in the slavocratic, semifeudal, or feudal character of work relationships but in the entrepreneurial organization integrating the labor force into an operative unit destined to produce for an outside market under patronal, profit-seeking direction. This quality makes it a mode of mercantile-capitalistic production within a slavistic colonial formation.

The closest analog to the plantation system established in Brazil and in other areas of the Americas is not found in the three models cited, but in the great Greek and Roman plantations in North Africa, structured to produce, with slave labor, goods for a world market. With the development of mercantile capitalism based on a broader international market and a more evolved technology, the Greco-Roman model was taken over in its mercantile and slavocratic aspect to constitute new external proletariats of greater power and at much greater distances. This took place simultaneously with the increase in manufactures and commercial crops in postfeudal Europe basic to the development of the mercantile economy. Brazil, emerging within that historical development, in passing on to the stage of industrial capitalism did not regress to a feudal order, but was led to accentuate the capitalistic attributes of the system.

When slavery, the most obsolete characteristic of the fazenda system, was abolished in Brazil, the newly freed worker did not fall to the status of a feudal land serf because this status simply did not exist. The situation is therefore completely different from that in which the old productive structures sank into feudalism by breaking with the mercantile system that energized them. The emancipated Negro found himself on a plantation where he was compelled to the status of sharecropper (*colonus*), a contender for the land he was working, like the European serf who rebelled during the phases of reestablishing the mercantile economy, to make himself a granger or wage-earner, demanding higher wages and better conditions of work. The line of Brazilian evolution, therefore, is very different because it starts with a hybrid formation based on the fazenda system, which combined the most developed capitalism of that time with the most archaic form of labor conditioning—slavery—and, particularly, because it never broke its external proletariat bonds with the world market, in the service of which it remained engaged.

The problem posed historically for Brazil by the Industrial Revolution was that of preparing herself to master the new forms of energy and the mechanical technology on which this energy was based, in order to escape the spoliation of which she was victim in the earlier system of interchange, and which would thenceforth tend to become accentuated. This would have been the Brazilian national project beginning with the mid-nineteenth century, just as it was the North American, if Brazil had by that time constituted a society formed predominantly by a free and independent population, like the farmers of the United States. Brazil, however, was not a nation but a trading colony. And the interests of the dominant castes wanted her to remain that way, latifundian and slavocratic, later latifundian and "free," but always latifundian and oligarchic. For that reason the peasant's access to land ownership, which would have formed the basis of a national society, never materialized, and independence and the republic became counterfeits for an oligarchic system that was, and wished to continue to be, the external proletariat of foreign markets.

Four other compulsions derive from the commercial nature of the plantation enterprise: (1) the monopoly of the land by a minority that compels the whole population to serve it as slave or wage labor; (2) the tendency to specialize in a single activity to attain the maximum economic yield; (3) the propensity to accumulation of goods, lands, and dependent persons in the hands of the proprietor class—the only one with monetary resources available—for the systematic appropriation of all surpluses of the economy, preventing the rise of a rural middle class capable of extending the domestic market; (4) the fractioning of the rural population into micronuclei that cannot constitute human communities because they are humble dependents on patronal whims. Imprisoned in the fazenda, where he cannot receive visitors and from which he can go out, once and for all, only to enter another, the Brazilian peasant hardly achieves the minimum conditions of social interaction, coexistence, and cultural exchange to develop a free personality capable of options and conscious of human rights. He is a pariah rather than a citizen, less for his illiteracy than for his strict dependence on a seignioral will.

The pressure of the fazenda is exerted both within the agricultural properties and on the neighboring towns and cities, and, transcending them, on the whole nation. Wherever society assents to the plantation system it is the great dominating power to whose designs and interests laws are adjusted and authorities accommodated. Producing for distant markets, foreign or national, and carrying on large-scale commerce, the plantation is able to link itself directly with the national wholesale centers, ignoring the neighboring towns and cities. These, not invigorated by the trade of the fazenda nor infused with fiscal resources by it (the planter systematically exempts himself from local taxes), are inhibited in their growth. They only attain the status of poor entrepôts, justified by a railway station or a port active only in harvest season for transporting crops. That is why cities in plantation areas regress during the same periods when new and larger cities rise in zones of grange and small ranch economies.

Brazil, as a result of colonization governed by the fazenda system, was riddled with its distinctive marks. Every person who exerts a fragment of power congruent with the system is the agent of its consolidation and perpetuation. Conversely, every person who rebels against the plantation order—the peasant who invades another's land, the intellectual who studies social problems, or the politician who fights for agrarian reform—is a subversive, attacked by the entire weight of official repression. Thus, it is clear that the fazenda order and the reigning order are one and the same, destined to self-preservation at any cost.

The dominant caste is so integrated in the system that it even expects to be considered generous, altruistic, and civilizing. It takes pride in treating its dependents with authority and protection, in having dignified the working relationships of the servitors who profess the most eloquent fidelity to it by paternalism and favoritism, and, further, in pompously practicing Christian charity.

The view of those who support the weight of the system with their labor is different. In some remote time (or even today in some of the more isolated communities) the plantation order may have been regarded by its subjects as the natural order and sacred, a divine doom of the poor. Under these conditions it was possible to expect reciprocal respect of the polar positions, each kept in its place. Social relationships could even take on a certain cordiality under the weight of oppression. A master and his peons made a plausible constellation, he standing in the center of the system as the object of the devotion and the hopes of all; the others, on the periphery, additional arms and legs in the fulfillment of his plans. Those who did not succeed in internalizing these attitudes quickly left, wandering from plantation to plantation, heading for the cities, experiencing anomie, or becoming bandits. In most cases, however, the sociocultural context was sufficiently homogeneous to induce individuals to capitulate, with only the more forceful personalities escaping, and these, for their very rebelliousness, gradually found themselves excluded from the fazendas.

This basis for work relations inside the fazenda structured the whole society. The planters of each region, connected through vicinity and kinship, formed a closed dominant group whose power, expressed in material goods and subordinates, supported the public authorities for the maintenance of order, and from their ranks the new teams of political command were recruited. The plantation, then, was the elementary cell of the national system, both economic and social and political and military.

The society resulting from this order has incurable incapacities, among them the impossibility of assuring an even modestly satisfactory standard of living for the majority of the population, the unviability of a democratic life instituted under its domination, and the impossibility of adequately industrializing productive activities and encouraging great accumulations of capital. All this characterizes it as an oligarchic organization that can maintain itself only artificially by the compression of the majority forces it condemns to backwardness and poverty. Thus, one can comprehend the reactionary consistency of the Brazilian policy, from colony to empire to republic, as an intrinsically antipopular, antidemocratic order based on monopoly of the land and of the labor force by a minority.

All Brazilian history has been woven with threads from the fazenda system, born from the transplantation of the Portuguese *sesmaria* to Brazil. The regime of the sesmaria—granted as an act of grace by the crown, or in its name by agents of the royal power—prevailed until independence. It gave way then to a more liberal rule governing access to the land, assuring ownership of the land to anyone who occupied and made it produce for a period of thirty years, and simplifying the legalizing of such occupancy insofar as it should be continued in peace (Cirne de Lima, 1935).

This liberal orientation coincides with and is explained by the period of decadence through which Brazilian agriculture was then passing—sugar had for some time been supplanted on the international markets by the Antillean production, and the gold mines had been worked out. The population of the former productive nuclei was regressing to a subsistence economy, the miners were dispensing with their slaves, and the sugar mill-plantation complexes were closing down producing only what they consumed, in order to reduce their costs. The free poor population then had begun to occupy the lands between the sesmarias, or to go beyond them to structure itself as caipira societies. Many rich men left with their slaves and cattle to open great autarchic fazendas, establishing them like islands in the wilderness, now depopulated of Indians. The venal value of the land was ridiculously low, and all wealth had come to be measured by the ownership of slaves and herds. But the free poor people could eat better and even aspire to a condition of independence and dignity.

Then a new king product, coffee, made its appearance, as exigent of land and labor as the old cane plantation-mill complex, but in the case of land, less for use than to monopolize, thus compelling the available labor force to serve the new king. In consequence the thirty-year tenure-and-title rule gave way to the 1850 Law of Lands,[10] reinforced and ratified since

[10] The U.S. Homestead Act [of 1862] had a precisely opposite aim, assuring each westward-venturing pioneer family the ownership of a quarter-section [160 acres] for developing, thus encouraging the occupation of the whole hinterland of the midwest by free farmers.

that time by abundant legislation that decreed purchase as the only form of access to the land, created a civil registration system that would make it nearly impossible for a poor farmer to legalize his land, and stipulated as the sale value of the unoccupied government lands much higher price levels than the current ones for lands already appropriated.

The following were instituted as fundamental principles of Brazilian society: the granting of lands in immeasurable expanses, not to those who worked them but to the specially privileged, controllers of the sources of political power; the guarantee, by a whole judiciary and police apparatus, of the legitimacy and inviolability of titles of ownership; the undisturbed right to hold unproductive land by virtue of the institution of proprietorship; and the control of the labor supply obliged to work within the system as the only means of survival.

The republic was to ratify all this restrictive legislation in a still more wily fashion: (1) by transferring control of unoccupied government lands to the state authority, even more submissive to the latifundian power; (2) by instituting forms of demarcation and registration of properties that prevented the small farmer from legitimizing ownership; and (3) by the promulgation of a civil code that laid on the shoulders of the rural masses the whole weight of "freedom of contract" in the name of egalitarian relations with the proprietors.

In the Brazilian historical texture these rights are the warp threads through which are woven the woof, the work relationships between masters and slaves, or patrons and dependents, always between superiors and subalterns. Over the thick material woven by the intercrossing of monopolistic land ownership and the work regime are embroidered historical and regional differences that color but do not alter the real structure of human relations in a society constituted to serve an extremely narrow, all-powerful boss caste.

Only in our own time has the fazenda order been really threatened, less because it had become socially intolerable than because new social and political metropolitan-based forces had emerged that were a new impetus for reordering society. In the rural masses there spread a more and more realistic urban image of the relations between masters and servitors, employers and wage-earners, that broke with the old notion of a moral order of subordination and condemned it as a curable evil and injustice. Society gradually came to perceive how harmful the fazenda order is, and how it constitutes the essential obstacle to abundance, progress, and democracy.

It was the alliance of the urban-based political forces with the peasant masses that for the first time in Brazil's history brought about the necessary conditions for a fight for democratization of land ownership. Through this alliance, after the last war, the struggle was begun for an agrarian reform capable of real prospects for integrating Brazilian society into industrial civilization and of assuring the majority of Brazilians the minimum requisites for the exercise of citizenship and the elevation of living standards, education, health, housing, and human dignity.

The Land Patrimony

One of the distinctive traits of the Brazilian agrarian structure is the small proportion of the country's whole area applied to agriculture and cattle-raising. Of the 8.51 million of square kilometers, only 2.65, or 31.1 per cent, are covered by rural properties. All the rest, other than small intrusions by urban areas and roads, are zones not yet reached by the national society in its long effort to open the territory. If it is true that a part of these unoccupied expanses is composed of lands impracticable for economic exploitation with available techniques, it is also true that the greater part of them is made up of lands as good as any, not developed only because they have not yet been reached.

The immediate reaction to these data is the old simplistic argument that one cannot speak of agrarian reform, and even less of land monopoly, as a crucial question in a country containing such huge expanses of idle lands. The truth, however, is that these surpluses, as far as the Brazilian rural population is concerned, might as well be in Africa, or on the moon. The rural Brazilians live hundreds of kilometers from the perimeter of these unfathomed regions, to which they cannot move and in which none could manage to survive, except as a hermit in the wilderness. Moreover, such deserts do not properly belong to anyone. Their ownership was constitutionally transferred to the states of the union as of 1891, and they have never made them accessible to the rural population.

The new frontiers by means of which Brazilian society is expanding over those empty areas like a tidal wave of millions of workers are not made up of free men's families in search of a tract of land for their own, like the pioneers who a century ago occupied the west of the United States. They are composed of *enxadeiros* [hoers, that is, unskilled field hands] under contract to serve new owners previously given possession of those lands by the registry system of the states.

In the last two decades these frontiers of pioneer natives advanced principally along the Maranhão River, over the Amazon jungle, the Paraná Valley forest, the areas of savannas and colonnaded forests in Goiaz and Mato Grosso, and the woods of the Rio Doce Valley in Minas Gerais and Espírito Santo. They added up to a human contingent of more than 2 million workers and their families. The size of their influx may be evaluated by the growth in rural population in those areas between 1950 and 1960: from 300,000 to 500,000 workers in Goiaz; from 400,000 to 1 million in Maranhão; and from 500,000 to 1.3 million in Paraná.

In nearly all cases this mass of workers advanced over already owned lands, inasmuch as legal appropriation anticipates by tens of years the actual occupation and goes hundreds of kilometers beyond the populated areas. Only in certain parts of Paraná has an island of small properties been allowed to develop, thanks to the initiative of an English company undertaking the colonization of land obtained from the state, a project imitated later by Brazilian enterprises. Even these small properties, however, were never accessible to the rural mass because of their scarcity and costliness, requiring down payments prohibitive for the majority of agricultural laborers.

The only government efforts to give access to the land in the form of small farms were the colonization programs for European immigrants. This confirmed the principle of denying ownership of land to the rural native mass in order to subject it to oligarchic exploitation, as official regulation of such programs prohibited incorporating Brazilians into the nuclei created, or else limited them to a maximum of 10 per cent.

Thus, colonial nuclei of immigrants were created in the south (Paraná, Santa Catarina, and Rio Grande do Sul), in Espírito Santo, in Minas Gerais, and in the State of Rio de Janeiro, as islands of small farms that would permit the installation of a new and improved model of rural life on Brazilian soil. Even so, they expanded very little, increasing only where private colonizing enterprises succeeded in overcoming government barriers and the opposition of the whole agrarian system to the creation of those new nuclei, in order to bring the immigrants to the fazendas. Official attempts at farm colonization with nationals were so few, so poor, and so unwillingly executed that they scarcely merit reference.

The capacity to impose the oligarchic order on the land-hungry peasant mass is conclusively demonstrated in the fact that, wherever a lawsuit has postponed for a time the authorization for legal control of land concession by the competent authority, the area is almost instantaneously invaded by the rural mass in the attempt to establish an island of small farms in it. This is what happened in the contested zone between the states of Paraná and Santa Catarina in the first decade of this century, rousing the area to a popular insurrection that the army managed to contain only after killing thousands of peasants. An abrupt invasion of the same type, which in very few years turned a desert region into a hive of people, occurred in the contested area between Minas Gerais and Espírito Santo. The same thing also happened in the old territory of Ponta Porã, in the south of Mato Grosso: in spite of being quickly put down, the insurrection caused a suspension of registry functions, which occasioned the rise of a new zone of land invasions. In this manner the colonization project of the Dourados region, which would have had the mediocre fate of the others if handled bureaucratically, established an island of progress in Mato Grosso.

In these last years the opening of great trunk highways through thousands of kilometers of uninhabited regions, such as the Belém-Brasília and the Brasília-Acre roads, offered the peasant masses the opportunity to expand into the new areas. But the expansion was limited there, too, by the oligarchy, by means of prior or posterior attribution of that land as colossal latifundia to the old proprietor class. One by one, the groups of peasants who challenged those wilderness regions, hoping to establish homes there on their own land, were expelled or forced to become sharecroppers or wage workers in the development of the new latifundia.

In the belt of appropriated lands, according to the 1960 agricultural census, 3.35 million agricultural or cattle properties were registered, with a population of nearly 38 million rural Brazilians. If we measured the density of Brazilian population by the occupation of this belt, we should find the nominal figure of 8.3 per square kilometer raised to 27.6. It is within this appropriated portion, therefore, that the Brazilian agrarian system, or the real country, is located.

Now let us see how agricultural properties are distributed under this system. For this the basic criterion of classification is the extent of the property, as much for its objectivity as for its being easily combined with other factors to define significant groups.[11] I shall start from a tripartite classification of minor properties (fewer than 100 hectares), average to large (100–1,000 hectares), and excessive or latifundian (more than 1,000 hectares).

In the group of minor properties a contingent of microenterprises, visibly incapable of operating economically, made up of establishments of fewer than ten hectares, are prominent. These are the minifundia, resulting in general from the fragmentation of larger properties. Nearly half of the 710,000 properties in this category in 1950 were therefore undeveloped or nearly unproductive in the technological level current in the country. The others were overexploited to support a population disproportionate to the area, in the majority of cases scarcely able to provide a living for the owning family.

The properties of ten to 100 hectares must be divided into two other

[11] Among others, the outstanding factors are the dominant productive activity (agricultural, livestock, forestal), the style and intensity of exploitation (degrees of technological development and volume of financial investment), and the mode of recruiting and control of labor (family, wage-paid, or sharecropping).

groups, one formed by granjas of ten to fifty hectares (36.5 per cent of the units, and 10.8 per cent of the total area, 32.3 per cent of the cultivated area of the country), distinguished by the intensity of their productive activities, principally familial in character, and a second composed of sítios of fifty to 100 hectares, distinguishable from the granjas because they add a considerable contingent of outside workers to the family group.

Within the national agrarian system, the minifundia and the granjas (under fifty hectares) perform two capital functions. They breed people exportable to the new areas on which the latifundium grows and to the cities, and they are a major national nucleus of seasonal farming (43 per cent of the total) providing the internal market with produce and vegetables, as well as dairy products (30 per cent of the dairy cattle) and a multiplicity of farm products (pigs, chickens, eggs, greens, fruits and flowers).

The living conditions of the population concentrated there, though low, are substantially higher than those of the peoples subject to the planter or the latifundium proprietor as sharecroppers or wage-workers (Clovis Caldeira, 1955, 1956; M. Diegues, Jr. 1959). Their most prized privilege is to be their own masters, for work or leisure, invested with a human dignity drastically annulled when they enter the world of the latifundium. Their fundamental problem is to halt the advance and, if possible, to smash the barriers of the latifundium and the fazenda, which surround the islands of small holdings, seeking to absorb them.

The sitios (fifty to 100 hectares) constitute a category clearly intermediary between the granjas and the fazendas, with characteristics common to both. They differ from the former in greater spatial freedom without, however, reaching sufficiently large dimensions to allow fazenda-type exploitation. According to the 1960 agricultural census there were nearly 273,000 sítios, amounting to 8.1 per cent of the number of units and to 6.6 per cent of the national appropriated area; their cultivated lands, on the other hand, made up 12.4 per cent of the cultivated area of the country. The much smaller profit potential of the sítios, as compared with that of the granjas, can probably be explained by the enormous part of them appropriated by city men for no serious purpose, often only as an ostentatious status symbol.

Granjas and sítios together (ten to 100 hectares) comprised 44.6 per cent of the nation's agricultural establishments in 1960, but they covered only 17.9 per cent of the appropriated area. Yet they constituted nearly 44.7 per cent of the country's cultivated area and absorbed half of the active rural population. This group of properties utilized in its fields 28.3 per cent of their total area, on the average, the proportion rising to 30.5 per cent on the granjas and falling to 17.3 per cent on the sítios; but on the fazendas, barely 8.4 per cent, and on the latifundia, 2.3 per cent.

The category we designate as fazendas (100–1,000 hectares) in 1960 covered 9.5 per cent of all rural establishments and absorbed 32.5 per cent of the total area owned, and 32.5 per cent of the area cultivated. In 1950 the fazendas included 23,000 of the 31,000 tillages of more than fifty hectares each, and 44.6 per cent of the national bovine herds. This intermediate category represents, as can be seen, the most potent nucleus of the nation's agrarian economy, occupying nearly half of the agricultural wageworkers and sharecroppers.

The third group of establishments with more than 1,000 hectares each is formed by properties excessively large for intensive exploitation and is the world of the Brazilian latifundium. In 1960 it represented only 0.9 per cent of the total number of establishments but contained 47.3 per cent of the country's appropriated lands, while it cultivated only 2.3 per cent of the same, equivalent to only 11.5 per cent of the nation's total farming, and occupied 7 per cent of the active rural labor force. Even in cattle-raising, its preferred activity, the latifundium is not outstanding, inasmuch as it held 60 per cent of the grazing land but raised only 35.6 per cent of the livestock. These statistics indicate that, if the latifundium should ever be developed with even the reduced intensity with which the fazenda operates, it would double the area of agricultural cultivation, and if it handled cattle-raising with the same degree of operation—which is quite low when compared with that of other countries—the herds would double also. These indices demonstrate the nature of the latifundium as land-holdings not for exploitation but for monopolizing.

Far from selling their land, the latifundium proprietors are motivated by an obsession to extend their land-holdings and to direct their entrepreneurial activity in parasitic fashion, as regards the workers retained on their latifundia in the status of sharecroppers on halves or thirds, or as regards the tenant farmers to whom they rent plots for horticultural or pastoral exploitation. In the wheat- and rice-growing regions of Rio Grande do Sul, Minas Gerais, and Goiaz, and the cotton and peanut area of São Paulo, this parasitism reaches such a level of institutionalization that the real modern agriculturists, owners of farm machines and responsible for great areas of cultivation, are not the rural proprietors but urban renters of the lands owned by the latifundia proprietors, who are not themselves capable of putting the land to use.

This is why the Brazilian agrarian structure has been defined as a system of great territorial properties and small agricultural developments (Jacques Lambert, 1959; T. Lynn Smith, 1946). This is revealed by comparison of Brazil's cultivated areas with those of other countries. The 29 million hectares cultivated in 1960 for a population of 70 million Brazilians contrasts with 40.6 million hectares for 18.6 million Canadians, with

30 million hectares for 21 million Argentinians, with the 188 million hectares for 179.6 million U.S. Americans, and with 195.8 million for 205 million Russians. These figures tell us that Brazil is not the agricultural country that so many declare her to be. And, further, if Brazil's low agricultural productivity is compared with that of the aforementioned countries, it is proved that she is more a land of latifundia proprietors than of farmers.

The ineluctable vocation of the fazenda and latifundium system for extensive or merely venture activity has certain noticeable results. First is Brazil's failure to consolidate international markets already won whenever a competitor appeared. This happened successively with sugar, cotton, rubber, tobacco, jute, the castor bean, and corn and is what is now happening with coffee and cacao.

The second concomitant is that this entrepreneurial failure, deriving from the extensive character of agrarian development, constitutes, paradoxically, one of the bases of the success of the fazenda system: its power of self-perpetuation. Basing itself on domination of the physical space—the land—to obtain control of the social space—labor—it becomes vital to the latifundium to absorb all the appropriated area in order to prevent the installation of granja or sítio nuclei that may compete for the available labor. The system operates, therefore, with its foundations in a plethoric appropriation of land, infinitely more than it can use but indispensable if it is to hold the reins of an agrarian economy and society.

Another concomitant of the system is the social precedence of the *fazendeiro,* the planter or rancher. This precedence, in force for centuries, surrounded with all the attributes of prestige, is another incentive to the accumulation of yet more land, valued not only for the power accompanying land monopoly but also for its conspicuous display as a status symbol. This is what explains the eagerness of all the Brazilian nonrich to own a fazenda, and one as extensive as possible. Thousands of merchants, industrialists, judges, doctors, lawyers, priests, government officials, and soldiers regard land as the preferred investment because of this attribute of nobility, which they would not obtain by buying a butcher shop or shares in some corporation.

This competition generates an artificial overvaluing of land property as real estate and as a simple hedge against inflation, automatically rising in value with urban growth, opening of highways, and construction of public works. To this ostentatious landowner, whose occupation is other than agriculture, add the archaic type of planter or rancher who gains his living exclusively from the land but hopes to squeeze all possible profit out of it without investing anything. Burdened by these two types of entrepreneurs, the fazenda system functions as a repository of parasites who, in spite of not making their property pay, cling to it under the protection of the institution of property and the special privilege of paying no taxes, a privilege maintained in all spheres of government.

Throughout Brazil there are zones that, by their people's mode of being and standard of living, exemplify the sítio-granja, the fazenda, or the latifundium systems. In every zone where one type predominates, the other models sometimes appear, performing complementary functions; but their character derives from the predominant type of property. Because size and productive activity naturally combine, the sítio-granja zones are structured as areas of poor farms raising greens and fruits, or small ranches of specialized stock-raising; the fazendas, as nuclei of commercial plantations, cattle ranches, and winter pastures of higher productivity; and the latifundium, as extensive, predominantly pastoral exploitations or as areas of extractive industry.[12]

The zones where the sítio-granja system predominates are densely populated, crossed by networks of roads, dotted with towns where a small active trade operates, and served by new urban networks in full tide of expansion. This situation is exemplified by all the areas in which property has been fragmented, as in the north of Paraná, certain stretches of the midwest of São Paulo, a great part of Espírito Santo, Santa Caterina, and Rio Grande do Sul, and a few patches in Minas Gerais, in the south of Mato Grosso, and in the northeast.

The human and social landscape is quite different where the fazenda predominates, and still more different where the latifundium prevails. These are immense, sluggish regions cut by railroads and highways across human deserts, having nothing to transport except certain products in harvest seasons. Towns and cities are rare, generally poor and decadent, sheltering the human debris ousted from the fazendas and latifundia after it has been worn out in work or eaten away by disease.

The active fazenda boss caste rose by 1960 to probably 100,000 persons,[13] who, added to the parasitic caste of 250,000 proprietors of under- or unexploited fazendas and latifundia, composed the apex of the dominating structure of the Brazilian agrarian system. Beneath that pinnacle are the intermediate, broader classes, formed by the small proprietors who work sítios, granjas, and minifundia. According to the 1950 census this proprietor class is divided into actives (1.3 million), lessees (176,000), and

[12] The greater part of forest products exploitation in Brazil is done in areas rented from the state, not on private properties. The major exception is the State of Acre, with its immense latifundia of rubber development.

[13] Data from the 1960 census not being available, these figures are projections from the 1950 census totals under these headings.

homesteaders or squatters (192,000), a total of 1.7 million entrepreneurs who amount to 3.3 per cent of the total population and 15.4 per cent of the active rural population. Probably their number ten years later barely exceeded 2.3 million of the 15.5 million rural workers, if proportions remained unaltered in 1960. In this stratum is found the element in the rural population with some purchasing power and some possibilities of attaining standards of comfort, health, and education comparable to the average levels of aspiration of Brazil's populations.

Below that stratum comes the marginal subworld of the Brazilian rural mass, with indexes of hunger, sickness, mortality, illiteracy, and life expectancy typical of the most wretched of earth's humanity. The number of active workers rose in 1960, again according to our calculations,[14] to 13 million, out of a total of 32.5 million rural Brazilians above the age of ten. This is the peasant mass of the country, with two basic echelons distinguished, the sharecroppers and the wage-earners.

The former, the sharecroppers, emerged in Brazil simultaneously with the sugar *engenho* [the mill-plantation complex] through the allocation of poor, crossbred manual labor to parcels of land on the engenhos where they labored as suppliers of foodstuffs, green vegetables, pigs, chickens, eggs, fruits and the like to the "big house" and also as henchmen of the master, ever ready to serve him by repressing the slaves. They later provided the same goods to the market of the nascent cities, rarely rising to become granja proprietors. With emancipation their numbers increased extraordinarily through absorption of the freed Negroes, a procedure used by the boss caste to yoke them to work and fix them as unskilled labor on the fazendas without paying them wages.

Their condition is that of renters of tracts of land by payment of half or a third of the crops they harvest. Such sharecroppers are known, respectively, as *meeiros* and *terceiros*. The patron sometimes advances seeds or furnishes other facilities, which he deducts in the annual balancing of accounts. Usually the owner of the land has the privilege of buying the whole harvest at the going rate. Generally, the half and the third are based on the sharecropper's total production, including the garden patch and the kitchen-yard animals raised for the family's food. Each privilege, especially the right to keep a riding horse, or a cow, on the fazenda pastures is specified separately, frequently putting the sharecropper under the obligation to give a certain number of days of free labor to the fazenda owner.

The historical vocation of the sharecroppers and their fundamental aspiration is to possess the land they cultivate. Their great pride is to stand out

[14] Another projection from the 1950 census, this based on the over-all figures of the 1960 census.

from the rural mass of undifferentiated hoers as small entrepreneurs who, once their deal has been made with the master of the land, run the undertaking independently, able to get credit with local merchants, paying their debts either at the year's end or after the harvest.

The whole oligarchic order, formulated in laws and guaranteed by police and armies, by assuring itself the monopoly of the land in the lands of a minority, has always conspired against their ambition to become landowners. The sharecroppers' failure in their effort to become granja proprietors represented, as we have shown, not merely the victory by the fazenda system and its latifundian concomitant, but the condemning of Brazil to backwardness. This oligarchic imposition, marginalizing the rural mass, made it impossible for the country to create the bases of a modern industrial society and of a genuine political democracy. The failure of the sharecroppers was therefore the failure of the nation.

Today the number of sharecroppers and their vanguard fronts of homesteaders and squatters (invaders of others' lands or of wastelands, estimated at 208,000 families in 1950) exceeds 2 million families, dispersed among all types of rural properties but particularly concentrated on the average fazendas in archaic fashion. They are the proletarians of patrons without capital, patrons who participate in agrarian life as landholders mounted on the backs of the mass of rural sharecroppers. They are humble dependents of the patron, master of the lands from which they draw their sustenance, master also of a substantial part of the work force of their whole family, master of their courage if that should be needed in a dispute between "colonels," * and master of their vote if they are eligible to vote.

In the new zones the sharecropper is hired to cut down virgin forests to clear the land for new, permanent cultivating or to open new areas of pasturage. Immense areas of vigorous forest in the State of Paraná, in the valleys of the Doce, the Mucurí and the Jequitinhonha rivers, and in Minas Gerais have been penetrated in this way in the last two decades. Today in Goiaz, Mato Grosso, and Maranhão other forests are being cut down and burned over, then cultivated for a year or two, only to be converted into pasture lands, in a constant expansion of the pastoral latifundium. In each of those regions the sharecroppers form masses, enormous ones, of ragged, hungry peasants engaged in the hard work of razing trackless jungles, opening new lands that they can never own. When one front is exhausted by the reduction of its woods and pastures, the sharecroppers are pushed on ahead, the rural population abruptly decays together with the agricul-

---

* Latifundia proprietors living on their fazendas become the equivalent of caudillos and in that status are called "colonels" whether they have any right to that rank or not. Colonels in dispute have often resorted to armed force and murder.

tural production, and the nascent towns and cities die, all in order to establish the latifundian world.

The second great contingent of the active rural population is formed by the wage-earners, whose numbers must have risen to 6 million in 1960. Nearly 62 per cent of them, 3.7 million, were temporary workers, that is, people available in seasons of intense rural activity, rarely totaling six months in the year. For the rest of the time they endured their misery outside the fazendas.

The mass of rural workers, according to our estimate, was distributed in 1960, by branches of production, on the following bases: of 13.5 million active persons, exclusive of proprietors but including nonpaid family members, nearly 9 million were laborers in the so-called *lavouras brancas,* poor crops such as cereals and legumes; 3 million on the large coffee, cane, cotton, cereal, and cacao plantations; 500,000 were cowboys and other workers in cattle-raising. The other 500,000 were occupied in the various complementary agricultural activities. It is to be noted that this division by branches and the categorizing by sharecropper and wage-earner conceal rather than reveal the true nature of the work of the Brazilian rural mass. In point of fact it is much more homogeneous, as the 1950 census shows when it records that 93 per cent of the rural workers are classed as unskilled manual laborers, *enxadeiros,* utilized in cutting, clearing, planting, weeding, and harvesting, trained only in the use of the hoe, the scythe, the machete, and the ax.

The widely proclaimed diversification of country work through the introduction of new technology in Brazilian agriculture has not differentiated professionally any appreciable class among the mass of enxadeiros. The value of a rural family, in the patron's eyes, is evaluated by the "number of hoes" it includes, even children who, under ten years of age, are usable in the seasons of greatest need of labor. This mass forms the census category of "unpaid family members," which in 1950 reached 16.8 per cent of the active rural labor force in Brazil, though it totaled only 1.9 per cent in the United States, a disproportion demonstrative of the degree of exploitation to which the Brazilian peasant is subjected.

Agrarian Reform

An over-all consideration of the role of agriculture in the Brazilian economy indicates that in recent years it has been losing ground in competition with industry and urban services. Farming and cattle-raising, which in 1960 occupied nearly 40 per cent of the active labor force, contributed only 30 per cent of the national product. The power and social importance of agriculture lies in the occupation of labor in a nation of rapidly growing population, and also in the export field, in which it accounts for 85 per cent of the foreign exchange credits, of which it absorbs very little directly, engendering resources for other sectors.

In the 1950–1960 decade Brazil's rural population increased from 33.1 million to 38.6 million, its percentage of the total population falling from 63.8 per cent to 54.2 per cent. On the other hand, the active rural population grew from 10.9 million to 15.5 million, experiencing a greater increment (141 on an index of 100 for 1950) than the total population of the country (136) or the rural population (116). During the same period the urban population increased from 18.7 million to 32.1 million (171 as compared with 116 rural), but the nonagricultural active population, which was was expected to rise from 7.5 million to 11.8 million,[15] apparently remained below this figure, revealing a limited capacity to absorb available labor. So the factory workers must have increased only from 1.177 million to 1.519 million during the nation's most intense period of industrialization. As can be seen, industry, by obtaining a greater and greater profit potential from its labor force through industrializing the productive process, deemphasized its capacity to absorb new contingents. Agriculture, much less technically advanced and basing production on sheer muscle power, continued operating with the supply of cheap labor in response to the demands of the growing urban market, being able thus to raise the rural population substantially.

Nevertheless, Brazil is taking long strides toward an agrarian technical advancement, with increasingly appreciable effects on the productivity of labor and on employment opportunities. Surely, about 1970, this effect will have attained all its positive and negative consequences in some regions: positive, in its promise of abundance of food for a people that has always existed on a miserably poor diet; negative, in its threat of marginalizing still larger rural contigents by throwing them off the fazendas and leading them to the periphery of the cities, where the high technical level of industrialization will be incapable of absorbing them; but positive, even so, by the pressure that these masses will inevitably exert on the socioeconomic structure to absorb the millions that will need employment.

The sole solution for this problem is a radical agrarian reform. It has been avoided in like situations by European societies only by massive exportation of their rural contingents and attrition of the population in wars. As the Brazilian patronal caste will probably not be able to count on such

[15] Definitive figures of the 1960 census on the active population are not yet known.

solutions, agrarian reform will become inexorable. The longer it is postponed, the greater the pressures that will build up, making it in that event capable of threatening the whole system, including the capitalist production regime.

In these last years broad sectors of the dominant classes—politicians, religious leaders, economists, soldiers—informed of the gravity of the problem, have taken the enlightened position of fighting for a capitalistic pattern of agrarian reform. This readiness is revealed by the fact, among other signs, that the national congress has been called on to examine more than 400 projects of agrarian reform in the past decade. Even though the great majority of them amount to no more than patching up the fazenda order, their sheer number proves the restlessness touching all social classes.

Since 1961 the reform campaign has taken on a more combative and authentic aspect, becoming one of the fundamental legislative purposes of the most progressive urban political forces that do not depend on rural votes for reelection. Its highest expression has been the Rural Worker Act, passed in May 1963, which extended the right of unionization and other special privileges of the urban worker to the agricultural wage-earner. There is also the executive branch's own project of agrarian reform, recorded in the presidential message of March 1964, which probably would have passed if the Goulart government had not fallen victim to a military coup.

The developmental theories that see in agrarian reform the fundamental mechanism for acceleration of economic progress are seeking, in the first place, to activate the economy and assure a basis for industrial development; and to cause a parcel of the rural peasantry to become small landowners integrated into the market economy as producers and consumers, maintaining the majority in the status of wage-earners, but better paid than they are now. In the second place, they seek to reduce the perilously revolutionary social tensions generated by rural misery and to ensure politico-social stability by interesting the peasants in the consolidation of the capitalistic order to defend their small properties.

The forces struggling for land reform engage in it for one or another of those objectives. Generally the urban political sectors are more interested in enlarging the domestic market and softening the demographic pressure on the cities than in land reform. For this very reason the popular mobilization of the countryside on behalf of agrarian reform was brought about in these terms. But at the level of the dominant castes it was promoted in the name of consolidation of property by means of the multiplication of the number of proprietors. The favorite watchword of the major proponent of agrarian reform, João Goulart, was the carefully worded statement that property would be better defended when, instead of 2.5 million proprietors, Brazil had 10 million.

Under such conditions the reform struggle has been carried on principally as a political mobilization of urban masses and an effort to unionize rural wage-earners, consented in and stimulated by the federal government and based on the Rural Worker Act. For this purpose the various leftist groups and the clergy itself worked jointly. In the Brazilian northeast the campaign went deeper, thanks to the cooperation of the Pernambuco government with the federal authorities, permitting massive unionization of agricultural wage-earners in the sugar mills. Organizing these masses, which made possible a substantial rise in wage levels, also was a decisive step in the mobilization of rural populations for the agrarian reform campaign.

On the other hand, almost no effort—except the work of Francisco Julião with his peasant leagues [Ligas Camponesas]—has been made to energize the true peasants in the struggle for their interests, expressed in the aspirations of the 2 million sharecroppers and of the dozens of nuclei invading lands belonging to others, scattered throughout the country, to become granja proprietors. According to the 1950 census, the number of families registered as squatters or homesteaders exceeded 200,000. Since then those nuclei have multiplied, covering broad regions where groups of such families have settled, seeking to protect themselves with arms, requiring the intervention of the army itself to expel them. The mobilization of these strata in the agrarian reform campaign would have given it a more dynamic character, freeing it from the stamp of paternalistic approval it was tending to assume. But on the other side, it would precipitate the division of the political and military forces structured until then as a system of support to the reform program.

The campaign for agrarian reform was therefore reduced in the main to an effort to clarify public opinion in the cities, to awaken and organize the masses of agricultural wage-earners and to mobilize the unions, in order to force the national congress to approve the body of reform measures proposed by the administration. These measures, tardily formulated and for that reason not widely known, are stated in President João Goulart's proposals, sent to congress in his message of March 15, 1964. Sixteen days later his government fell.

The fundamental feature of Goulart's message lay in the arrangements for progressive abolition of the oligarchic order, and for the instrumentation and self-application of the principles laid down. These would immediately assure, without need to create costly technicobureaucratic services, great gains for the two million families of sharecroppers and homesteaders. With this objective some measures of constitutional reform were proposed that would transform those two million families into an expansive stratum of *emphyteutae* * with prerogatives explicitly stated: (1) the reduction of the third and the half currently being paid for rent of the land, to a maximum of 10 per cent, which would be based on only that part of the production destined for the market; (2) the guarantee that they would not be expelled from the land occupied, except by court decision; (3) the laborers' free access (in the rent conditions stated) to the cultivatable lands kept unused or held for pasturage by their proprietors. These gains would not liberate the peasant from the patronal yoke, but would substantially better his position by guaranteeing him minimum requisites for raising his living standard and for exercising his citizenship as a voter independent of the landowner.

The immediate renovation of living and working conditions for millions of peasants was to be followed, later, by the creation of a colonization fund through expropriation of unproductive fazendas and latifundia,[16] and creating ample opportunities for ownership of land. These would, however, depend on juridical, bureaucratic, and technical measures, necessarily slow in developing.

The fundamental result of this proposed agrarian reform would possibly integrate into the nation's work force the rural labor now inactive or underutilized, plus the millions that will be added to it by the presently increasing birth rate, to form a powerful internal market capable of expanding industries and urban services, thus sponsoring, also in the cities, more ample opportunities for work and progress. It is well to recall that the interests of only 75,000 large landowners, bent on maintaining themselves in the monopolistic dominion of the immensity of lands they own but are not capable of utilizing, stand against these prospects of work, development, and vital abundance for the whole Brazilian people.

The most recent history of Brazil has been guided in great part by the battles for the accomplishment of this capitalistic agrarian reform, which, though it would consolidate the fazenda system, would open up prospects of development permitting Brazil to evolve from the trading colony she has always been into a modern nation. It is well known that, with the fall of the government that had wholeheartedly launched itself into the struggle

---

* That is, long-term lessees whose right to the possession and enjoyment of land is subject to their keeping it in cultivation and paying an annual rent.

[16] The exproporiation was to be made with partial payment in cash for the land, to permit immediate possession of the unproducing areas by the government. This act was to be subsequently followed by compensation in public bonds for the remaining value. The right was reserved to the landowner to choose and demark as his property for "licit use" an uninterrupted extent equal to double the area actually being exploited.

for reforms, the rural masses lost, and with them the people. This defeat, however, was only one episode within the long historical process, merely another battle in a war that goes on as the crucial struggle of the Brazilian people.

The campaign tactic of the reforms, based on the political mobilization of the rural and urban masses, on the effort to persuade the entrepreneurial castes, and above all on the custody of the national army, had its essential weakness in this last dependence. When the armed forces were turned aside from the nationalistic reform position, which they seemed to embody, to regress to the traditional role of maintainers of the oligarchic order and the foreign interests, this latest attempt to broaden the bases of the national society in order to integrate in it a larger part of the Brazilian people failed. Once more the club of the specially privileged prevailed over the people and the nation.

Reflexive Modernization

The network of Brazilian cities developed extremely slowly, and as long as the agromercantile economy prevailed, it never affected any considerable part of the population. At the end of the first century, Brazil had only three nuclei officially raised to the rank of cities and fourteen towns. A century later, there were seven cities and fifty-one towns. Around 1800 these had increased to ten and sixty, respectively, having a total population of 2.5 million.

With this precarious urban network Brazil rose to independence (1822) and began to undergo the impact of a new civilizational expansion—the Industrial Revolution—which, despite being reflexive, was to transform profoundly the structuring of the national society. The largest cities at that time were Rio de Janeiro (50,000 inhabitants), Salvador (45,600), Recife (30,000), São Luiz (22,000), and São Paulo (16,000).

The first effects of the Industrial Revolution were indirect and consisted of the opening of ports to free entry of industrial manufactures, especially English ones, protected by privileges imposed on the country as a condition for recognition of her independence. These consumer articles were followed, in the second half of the nineteenth century, by the importation of steam machines to turn the sugar mills of the northeast, steamboats for river and coastal shipping, and railways to penetrate the interior, linking the different productive zones to the coast. In the same period the first spinning and weaving mills were installed, located by preference in the cotton-producing rural areas. Other effects, also indirect, were the development of cotton-growing in the State of Maranhão to supply the English cotton mills and, later on, the intensive exploitation of the rubber forests of Amazônia.

This first reflexive modernization, caused by industrialization taking place outside of and far from the country, began to change the life modes of Brazilian society, causing widespread movement of fazenda families to the cities, which altered the urban network profoundly. By 1900 there were nearly 1.5 million inhabitants in only four cities, or in other words ten times the population of the large cities at the end of the colonial period. Even the quality of the national society had changed: from an area of colonial installation of agromercantile civilization, the social life of which had been established on the fazendas, it had risen to the category of a neo-colonial base for industrial civilization, introduced into a world system expressed as much in autonomous and directional industrial poles as in peripheral dependent spheres.

At the beginning of the twentieth century the first hydroelectric plants were set up in Rio de Janeiro and São Paulo, bringing electric lighting, urban transportation, the telegraph, the telephone, and mechanical equipment for the ports, all developed by foreign enterprises. Other cities preceded or followed immediately in these innovations, as well as in the installation of urban water supply, sewers, public sanitation works, and compulsory vaccination against smallpox. After 1920 use of the automobile and the truck spread everywhere.

Until then the establishment of an autonomous industry in Brazil presented almost insurmountable difficulties: (1) those of an external nature stemming from colonial subjection, which forbade any attempt at autonomous production; (2) Brazil's self-perpetuating insertion into the international market as an agrarian economy producing tropical raw materials and importing manufactures; (3) internal lacks resulting from the low level of knowledge and technology, a result of a one-crop, slavocratic economy that provided no impetus for the development of a skilled labor force.

For all these reasons, and despite the availability of capital and raw materials, as well as the existence of an incipient consumer market, little effort was made to develop autonomous industrialization, such as occurred in the United States, Japan, and other areas. Only through a slow cultural diffusion and a tardy social reordering, reflexive effects of alien industrialization, would Brazil be modernized, partially, maturing to an also reflexive urbanization that was extremely difficult because reflexive.

In the course of this process the total population of the country multiplied, rising from 10 million in 1872 to 17.4 million in 1900, and to 30.6 million in 1920. In the same proportion the urban network expanded, already including the first metropolitan areas. In 1872 the country had three cities with more than 100,000 inhabitants each, totaling 500,000; in 1930, there were six metropolitan centers with a population of 2.7 million.

This urbanization intensified the abandonment of the fazendas by the owner families and large groups of the rural population. The cities were now more inviting, defended against epidemics by public sanitation works, served by piped water, by sewers and public lighting, and endowed with educational systems. This move of the largest income groups to the cities was naturally accompanied by an intense activity in the construction of homes and commercial establishments, by amplification of transportation and communication facilities, public works, specialized labor, workshops, and domestic and auxiliary services, to serve the new permanent population, all of which employed great masses of former rural workers.

Another nonagricultural source of employment spread simultaneously throughout the country with the construction of railroads, hydroelectric plants, and factories, affording new opportunities of work, taking from the rural areas underutilized groups that, after engaging in wage-paid work, tended to become urbanized. In this way technical procedures, manufactured articles, services, and the habits of life and consumption engendered by the Industrial Revolution transformed Brazilian society, beginning to urbanize it in modern molds before industrializing it directly.

Three profound socioeconomic changes contributed to this first urban expansion. The first of the three was the abolition of slavery (1888), which brought to the cities great groups of the freed ex-slaves. The second was foreign immigration, composed of Europeans who, having already experienced metropolitanization, were more ready to be urbanized. From 1850 to 1915 Brazil received nearly 3 million immigrants, two thirds of them going to the State of São Paulo. The third factor was the inflationary process unleashed during the first decades of the twentieth century as a result of the coffee price-support policy and the state government paper currency issues, which enormously expanded the means of payment and permitted a spurt of entrepreneurial initiatives, private construction, and public works.

For those who had resources, the inflationary spur accelerated the economic process, penalizing those who held money idle and rewarding those who invested more boldly or used more credit. In an economy of colonial tradition, in which many values accumulated by grant, such as land and official privileges, the expansion of means of payment, instead of operating as a simple competition between productive factors, stimulated the transfer of income from the rich classes, more conservative and cautious, to the new ascendant castes, endowed with greater entrepreneurial capacity. Thus the European immigrants best prepared for the tasks of technological modernization were offered opportunities for enrichment and social ascent.

The three factors acted, then, as agents of modernization and accelerators of industrialization, providing the technique, capital, and skilled labor for the establishment of industries. At first these were exclusively substitutive manufactures of consumer goods habitually used but whose prices had become prohibitive for importation, thanks to the exchange devaluation intended to protect coffee. Inflation, acting along with other factors of modernization on an economy in which money had until then played little part, operated as a sieve, favoring the most enterprising and transferring to industry the resources formerly devoted to agricultural production and commerce. Industry would immediately become the principal field of application for the European immigrants' renovating vigor and for available capital, because the real products were in a state of crisis: the coffee produced was without a market, and the native Amazonian rubber had been replaced by the cultivated rubber plantations in the Orient.

In the installation of the industrialized technology in Brazil three well-differentiated periods can be distinguished. The preindustrial period of the advent of wood-burning steam engines concentrated on new means of transportation and in renovating the cane and small spinning and weaving industries. The new technology in these industries eliminated the traditional productive system and created new nuclei of work. Many factory towns of that period were transformed into regional market centers, cities articulating regional urban networks.

Railroads and steamships replaced such earlier forms of transportation as sailing vessels, mule trains, and oxcarts, providing great work opportunities during their construction and afterwards retaining some workers for operation and maintenance, opening new territories and linking them together, creating and revitalizing cities, especially those railroad centers functioning as trade centers for vast regions, hastening the decline of the old commercial and transportation centers, and creating the high-technology machine workshops that were to train the first generations of specialized workmen. These railroads, constructed by foreign enterprises by means of government-guaranteed, minimum-interest loans, not to mention other special attractions, were big business in themselves, independent of the profits they might yield. For this reason they multiplied, connecting the major productive nuclei of the interior to various ports and representing an extraordinary progress for the areas they crossed.

The second period of Brazilian industrialization began with the installation of hydroelectric plants, sufficiently large to supply power to industries. This new protoindustrialization tended to concentrate factories in the large cities, leading to the growth of suburbs to accommodate the growing labor population and the employees of the simultaneously expanding utilities.

Labor specialization, begun with the introduction of steam machines, advanced because the machines were designed only to perform prescribed tasks. Each trade became a series of simple operations and ordinary peasants quickly became factory workers. Industrial machinery, requiring more technical skill than any previous productive task, caused the formation of new technicoprofessionals. The specific needs of the hydroelectric period caused the emergence, in some urban industrial centers, of a skilled labor corps and machinery maintenance corps; this concentration of skilled labor, together with the availability of hydroelectric power, made it more and more imperative to install the new factories in the cities. Thus began the process of industrial concentration in urban centers that was to shape the whole national network of cities.

In this second period, begun with the twentieth century, Brazil's first consumer goods industrial complex was formed, created principally by occasional breakdowns in the system of providing imported manufactures. Brazil already had a consumer market for industrial manufacture, and its expansion was spurred by Brazil's incapability to produce foreign exchange balances sufficient to continue importing manufactured articles. In this way a local substitutive production emerged, precarious but fundamental for the country because it engendered a corps of industrial entrepreneurs and a specialized work force, which would join ranks to assure themselves conditions for survival and expansion. The growth of Brazilian industry in that period can be estimated by the increase in number of workmen: from 55,000 in 1890 to 160,000 in 1900, and to 275,000 in 1920.

Two factors, however, resisted industrialization: (1) the identification of the interests of export agriculture with import commerce created a hegemonic social group that, in defense of its privileges, argued the advantages of specializing Brazilian economy for production of tropical articles in exchange for manufactures; and (2) the imperialistic domination itself, the supplier of government revenues and the purchaser of agricultural harvests, defended the privileges conferred by an exclusive market for its manufactured products. Only the great international crises, temporarily numbing both sectors, permitted the industrialization, then under way, to make any progress.

During World War I the interruption of international commerce, isolating Brazil from the traditional sources of supply, liberated the nascent entrepreneurs for undertakings of wider scope, making room for the substitutive industrial surge. But peace stunned these budding efforts at autonomous industrialization, bankrupting hundreds of enterprises or forcing their mergers with international corporations. These facts operated, even so, to accelerate the maturation of the national consciousness, now awakened to the irreducible contradiction between national and foreign interests in industrialization. Thus, ideological conditions were created for instituting an official protectionist policy to safeguard the development of industry.

After World War I some sectors of the ruling classes—entrepreneurs in defense of their enterprises—and military men—preoccupied with national security—began to realize that the nation would never develop through technological modernization based on foreign supply of the machines and motors. This industry basis would make Brazil independent of the importing of some items only by importing other items, increased by remittances abroad of profits and interest. Its crucial effect would therefore be to make the national economy more efficient in the performance of its traditional function of providing raw materials, tropical products, and exportable profits. The point, then, as these men saw it, was to establish a new type of independence, more subtle and more effectual than colonial subjection and equally incompatible with a full, autonomous development.

The third period of Brazilian industrial development began in 1930 when the total industrial establishment entered on an accelerated rate of growth that quickly guaranteed the predominance of factory production over the agricultural. The 1929 crisis, drastically reducing purchasing power abroad, had provided the necessary freedom to the national entrepreneurial corps, stimulating a new effort at substitutive industrialization and with it the transition to an economy directed toward the internal market. Besides expanding the manufacturing production of articles in greatest demand—cloth, footwear, food, and drink—production started in cement, pig iron, sheet metal, paper, glass, and caustic soda.

Nearly all these industries had precarious installations and operated on a routine level of low technical standards. Many were limited to the assembling of parts or preindustrialized elements that had to be imported; all of them depended on complementary articles or on foreign tools. In many cases they had been installed as branches of large international firms, intended for simple finishing operations, and had subsequently developed local manufactures of components to obviate the increasing difficulties of importation and to discourage the emergence of local competitors protected by legislation prohibiting the importation of articles similar to those produced within the country.

Despite its being an industrialization in large measure strangled by foreign control, it would use the financial situation of the moment, which reduced the nation's capacity to import, and the inflationary pressure stemming from the government's stockpiling of coffee, to establish the bases for self-sufficiency in the production of manufactured goods.

The greatest deficiencies of this industrial spurt lay in the vital sector of sources of energy, owing to the lack of coal and oil. The usual power—hydroelectric—had begun to expand. The principal fuel continued to be wood. Industrial censuses in the following decades show great jumps in the numbers of both industrial establishments and workers, as well as in the amount of capital employed in industry and in the value of production. Industrial establishments increased from 25,000 to 50,000 between 1930 and 1940, whereas workers increased in the same period from 400,000 to 781,000.

With the great crisis past, the preparatory period for World War II began, offering Brazilian industry conditions for continuing to broaden and diversify, because of the need to substitute for articles imported from markets that would become inaccessible. Once again compulsory isolation, breaking the bonds of domination, would allow the Brazilian economy to utilize its productive resources by means of the monopoly of the domestic market and the transfer of importation funds to industry expansion.

As the war began, Brazilian industry was capable of supplying the larger part of the national consumption. Nevertheless, it depended on importing machinery, fuels and lubricants, and semiindustrialized complementary elements. In spite of the imports in the immediately preceding years, the industrial complex was in great part obsolete. A 1939 study revealed that São Paulo industry, the most advanced in the nation, was then operating with 11.3 per cent of machinery less than five years old, and with 14.2 per cent in use for five to ten years; all the rest had been in use for more than ten. Furthermore, part of the machinery considered new had been imported after long use and wear in the countries of origin, because only secondhand items could be afforded in view of the lack of revenues.

Thus, Brazil had to face isolation with a largely antiquated industry to supply her internal needs and, further, to export some articles such as textiles, which became the second export product. Compelled to improvise a whole series of materials, and having to strain its productive capacity with two or even three work shifts, Brazilian industry, in spite of the wear, came out of the war more potent and much more experienced. Naturally, it was not isolation in itself that benefited industry, but the interruption of the oppressive system of control and external interference in its expansion, on the part of foreign owners of national establishments, as well as the lack of competition from international monopolies. Isolated, industry had to improvise production, within the country, of most of the equipment and materials it was using, thus carrying out a renovation adapted to local labor and market conditions.

So it is no coincidence that the great industrial upsurge began with the 1929 crisis, which allowed the national entrepreneurs a respite almost until the opening of the war and then continuing until 1945. In these fifteen years, despite deficits in sources of electric power, in fuels of high quality, and in replacement parts, Brazilian industry progressed as never before.

The quantitative and qualitative expansion from 1930 to 1940 shows very clearly that interaction with fully developed industrial structures of the international capitalistic system has constricted the Brazilian economy. But it also shows the results of a new, frankly industrialized government policy assuring it privileged conditions for acquisition of equipment, whenever this was viable, and even placing all the capacity for political bargaining at the service of the key industry. This is the case specifically of the Volta Redonda steel works, fundamental in the country's industrial development, and of the recovery of the Minas Gerais iron deposits for the Vale do Rio Doce company, both accomplished during the war, thanks to the enlightenment of the state policy and to the competition that had started up among the great capitalist powers.

The Volta Redonda example is highly illustrative because it is the only case in which the United States, on a government-to-government level, granted a loan and furnished both great industrial installations and the technical aid needed to set them up, in order to establish a steel mill competitive with her monopolistic corporations—and, what is more, the machinery had to be produced during the war, when the U.S. industrial plants were most in demand for war production. The event was never repeated, because the United States never again found herself obliged to pay for alliance with Brazil.[17]

The resumption of international commerce after 1945 found Brazilian industry more capable of defending itself and expanding, using the import opportunities to replace its machinery and install new lines of production. During the period of isolation it had changed both quality and volume, attracting funds that made it a powerful economic sector capable of protecting its interests, and possessing great resources accumulated during the war that permitted it to compete with other importing sectors in vying for the foreign credits available for purchases abroad.

Industrialization initiated a new cycle in the postwar period, now as both agent and patient of the transformations set in motion in the country by reflexive modernization. Retreat was already impossible, as far as creation of an autonomous industrial economy was concerned. The nation's population had risen from 41.2 million to 70.9 million from 1940 to

---

[17] The U.S. financing of a large Uruguayan state hydroelectric plant, previously under contract to the Germans, was the second example of economic cooperation in the same kind of situation.

1960; industrial establishments, from 50,000 to 110,000; and workers, from 781,000 to 1.519 million. The constitution of an industrial nucleus (São Paulo, State of Rio de Janeiro, and Guanabara) capable of guiding the national economy fulfilled the basic requisite for winning full autonomy of national development. However, protected by traditional procedures, especially tariff barriers, this industrial complex was to be assaulted by a more subtle attack than it was prepared to cope with, namely the entry of the large corporations, particularly those of the United States, into the national market, no longer as exporters but through installation of local factories of consumer goods, such as household electric appliances, automobiles, chemical products, and a multiplicity of manufactured goods of popular sale. Leaping the customs barriers that prevented access to the national market, the great foreign corporations exploited it directly by placing themselves under the shelter of the national protectionist legislation and gaining access to official finances to encourage industrialization. In this way they siphoned off national funds to pay the profits on investment, royalties, know-how, insurance, and administration services, burdening the national economy, only in many cases to expand the demand for soft drinks, toilet articles, medicines, electric appliances, or foods and beverages bearing famous international brands.

The new procedure was much more lucrative than the old system of colonial export privileges, and much more tenacious because it gave the appearance of being merely competitive with the "backward" national entrepreneurs, and even progressive, thanks to the superior technical quality of its industrial plants. It presented itself, then, as the promoter of progress and industrialization, hiding the fact that it never oriented itself toward basic sectors of industrial production that could emancipate the national economy, and disguising its true nature as a suction pump draining off foreign-exchange credits.

The integration of Brazil into industrial civilization goes on reflexively, then, by means of a fourth mechanism of domination and subordination to external forces. The first had been the system of import privileges that for nearly a century had made the country a captive or preferential market for British manufactures; the second, the installation of railways, power plants and services, lights, gas, and telephones by foreign enterprises holding prior guarantee of minimum insurance charges or else monopoly of the market (certainly the most profitable method of entailment processes because, despite burdening the country, it supplied funds for development); the third, foreign control of mineral deposits, less to develop them than to exclude them from the cartelized world market in order to manipulate prices of raw materials. This process of domination allowed the English, armed with property titles, to appropriate nearly all the known mineral reserves of the nation; the fourth, industrialization, was induced by establishment of local factories of the large international corporations, principally U.S. American, and the progressive absorption of the national industrial complex through stock-sharing and technological dependence.

Of the four forms of domination, the first impeded industrialization; the second and third restricted its expansion and profit ability; the fourth absorbed and alienated Brazilian industry. The fourth is the most harmful, because it transfers abroad the centers of decision with greatest powers over the national economy; because it demands payment in foreign-exchange credits, absorbing an increasing part of the fruits of national labor; because it prevents the rise of a national entrepreneur corps by transforming the industrial bourgeoisie into a caste of managers of foreign businesses; and because it frustrates the creation of a corps of technicians that can assure autonomy to the cultural and scientific development of the nation, by transfer of the more elevated tasks of research, planning, and technological refinement to foreign laboratories.

The Brazilian Dilemma

Brazilian governmental economic policy began to be industrialist oriented through becoming conscious of the imperative need to modernize the country in order to assure its autonomy and progress. The existence by that time of a broad substitutive industrialization in Brazil, employing hundreds of thousands of workmen, and in which sectors of the bourgeoisie had invested heavily, enabled it to curb the old oligarchic domination. Then a deliberately autonomist official policy emerged that defined industrialization as the basic objective of the economy and national security.

This policy was to develop in two opposite orientations, both industrialist. The first, nationalistic and statist, aware of the constrictive role of the international monopolies, advocated the establishment of the productive infrastructure and of key industries in the form of state enterprises. The other, cosmopolitan and free-enterprise, defended the integration of the Brazilian economy in the world capitalistic market, no longer merely as the producer of tropical articles but as an industrial economy, through the introduction of the capital and know-how of the great international corporations.

These two industrialist orientations were formulated as concrete economic policies, the first with Getúlio Vargas, the second with Juscelino Kubitschek. Vargas and his nationalistic advisory board, although rightist, proposed reserving to the state the fundamental role in the installation of steel mills, in the production and refining of oil, in the production and distribution of electric power, in the prospecting for ores, in the production of acids and bases, of motors and vehicles. However, it left all other areas open and free for private enterprise, assuring it the state's protection in the form of favored financing and market reserve. Emphasis was placed, nevertheless, on the first sector, structured in state enterprises, with precedence guaranteed to them in the allotment of public moneys and in the concession of special privileges.

Juscelino Kubitschek, who succeeded Getúlio Vargas, though he held to the most irreducible nationalistic positions (such as the monopoly on exploitation of oil) because of public opinion inclined toward a contrary economic policy. He opened the Brazilian market to international companies, assuring them all the privileges that they demanded as prerequisite to their establishing themselves in the country. His objective was to instill a new dynamism in industrialization in order to raise Brazil's economy to a full maturity capable of endowing it with autarchic conditions of development. He trusted that these objectives could be achieved despite the actual sacrifice of autonomy in the conduct of development, seeing that he allowed the management of state enterprises to be transferred to international corporate control.

Nothing in Brazilian history offers a greater contrast than the economic policies of these two presidents. Vargas committed suicide in 1954, blaming foreign exploitation for the crisis into whch he had plunged the nation. His successor, Kubitschek, in order to struggle out of the crisis, resorted to an unprecedented extension of the special privileges granted to foreign capital. How can such disparity be explained? Because Vargas had regarded as unacceptable what Kubitschek saw as the way to development. A year before his suicide Vargas said:

I am being sabotaged by offended interests of private enterprises that have already gained a great deal in Brazil, that have two hundred times the capital in cruzeiros that they have invested in dollars, to carry out of the country in the guise of dividends. Instead of dollars producing cruzeiros, it is the cruzeiros that are producing dollars and emigrating.

In his testimonial he was to express in other words his condemnation of the spoliation victimizing the Brazilian people: "The profits of the foreign enterprises reach 500 per cent per year. In the declaration of value of our imports there were documented frauds of more than $100 million per year." In spite of the impact of this denunciation on public opinion, the Brazilian government was to be oriented, after Vargas' suicide, to an economic policy of unlimited concessions, resorting to an intensification of the spoliative process—supposedly transitory—as a way to overcome it.

The expedient was to grant everything to foreign capital in order to obtain, at any cost, its cooperation in a vast program of industrialization. The difficulties of the enterprise can be appreciated by the fact that Kubitschek's ambitious project of industrialization was to be carried out in an unfavorable economic situation, with insufficient capital to finance imports —in view of the decline in exports—and with national resources providing security for loans—because of the enormous deficit burdening the budget.

The financing of the program, obviously unviable in terms of traditional economic policy, required new, audacious procedures of winning and allocating foreign and domestic resources that were to weigh extremely heavily on the country. How to obtain these resources and how to stagger chronologically and distribute socially the burdens of their amortization were the fundamental questions of the Plano de Metas [Plan of Goals] that were never clarified. It was only after the program was executed that the amount could be estimated, the question of who would bear the cost verified, and the contribution it had made to the maturation of the national economy appreciated.

The solutions were, as a matter of fact, as simple as they were daring. The national and foreign entrepreneurs called on to share actively in the program were asked only to see their businesses expanded in almost ideal conditions, practically without risk and almost always subsidized to the near-total of the ventures. A reversal of criteria had taken place that, transferring to private enterprises conditions of protection and defrayal anticipated for state undertakings (which were public property), lent a new dimension to "free initiative." The new economic policy rested, likewise, on an idealization of free enterprise as the supreme form of management of property, carried to such extremes that it advocated no less than the donation of public resources to private ventures.

Probably only under these conditions would free initiative be able to act in a tributary economy where it was called on to create substitutive industries for its own exports. In the international economic context, which does not offer underdeveloped nations minimal conditions for breaking with dependence on and domination by the great industrial powers, the Plan of Goals constituted an invention: a new model of strictly capitalistic industrial development. Inevitably, it recolonized industrialization, inducing Brazil to a new historical incorporation tending to perpetuate her position as a neocolonial economy, capable only of occasioning a new surge of reflexive modernization.

Apparently unelaborated, because it consisted essentially of a report on desired objectives, the Plan of Goals resulted in an objective programming that unified in a single project the major plans of economic expansion worked out by previous governments. In its frank and open presentation it related the fundamental problems of the Brazilian economy, problems in the realms of electric power, transportation, oil production, and the industrial products that bulked largest on the national agenda of imports. The first of these it sought to handle with ample investments for the expansion and modernization of power sources available; the rest, with facilities for the installation of substitutive industries.

More important than the diagnosis and the recommendation of Plan of Goals was its calling on the country to act together for development, its capacity to treat industrialization problems as questions of national salvation, and its vigorous readiness to face and solve them promptly, resorting to any procedure that might make the projects work.

The total resources mobilized by the Plan of Goals reached 355 billion cruzeiros, 236 billion of this in national and 119 billion in foreign currency, equivalent to $2.318 billion of imported goods and services. Of this sum 43.4 per cent was distributed for amplification of electric energy generating capacity, 29.6 per cent for the national transportation system, and 20.4 per cent for key industry. The remainder had been destined for various small complementary projects of welfare and education and the construction of the new capital, Brasília.

The problem of financing in national currency was solved with the most reckless use of the government's power of issuing money for gathering funds and with the most open-handed readiness to turn them over to the enterprises that proposed to accomplish the objectives of the plan. To this end the official system of credits (through the Banco Nacional de Desenvolvimento Econômico, the Bank of Brazil, the autarchic organs of control of the Social Security Fund, and the highway, railway, and maritime national funds) negotiated advance payments for works and financing in exceptionally favorable conditions.

The moneys advanced to pay for projects permitted the contracting firms to equip themselves with machinery and services that enabled them to undertake works enormously superior to their previous capacity. The loans granted to national and foreign concerns—principally to the latter —covered nearly the whole of their expenditures in national coin for buildings and other installation expenses, guaranteeing them, moreover, subsequent banking facilities for commercial drafts. In many cases funds in cruzeiros were furnished even for purchase of foreign credits for imports. These long-term loans (frequently ten to fifteen years), at virtually no interest (9 per cent to 12 per cent) in the reigning inflationary situation, represented veritable gifts. It is estimated today that the repayment of the loans thus obtained by the private enterprises amounts to 13 to 17 per cent of the purchasing power of the money loaned to them.

The financing of the Plan of Goals in foreign money was still more generous. It offers, therefore, a measure of the conditions in which an underdeveloped nation can gain the cooperation, in substitutive industry programs, of great international corporations. Note that these corporations were asked to operate under exceptionally favorable conditions, because the establishment of industrial plants in Brazil assured them a monopoly in a national market of the greatest potential of any in the world, thanks to protectionist legislation that prohibited the importation of any articles similar to those produced in the country. It should be added that, simultaneously, the government was investing in the basic sectors that would guarantee the supply of these fundamental needs—electric power, steel, fuels, lubricants, acids, and bases—in national currency and at subsidized prices.

Even these exceptional conditions, however, proved unattractive, as can be seen from the fact that in the five years prior to the Plan of Goals the government did not induce any foreign firm to supply the basic lacks in the industrial system of the country. Indeed, the movement of foreign capital had been on the deficit side through the imbalance between the volume of remittances going abroad—interest, profits, royalties, and amortizations —and the low figure of income through new investments. With the Plan of Goals the situation changed: the entry of loan and risk capital came to exceed the outgo, thus increasing the favorable balance. This was not a real balance, naturally, because much larger amounts came into the country simultaneously as loans, which fattened the actual investments, incurring an enormous national debt to be paid by future governments.

Examination of the strong currency accounts of the Plan of Goals, totaling $2.3916 billion, shows that the sum of $1.9726 billion was covered by loans obtained abroad directly by the government or by individuals with government-endorsed backing. Foreign investments actually coming into Brazil amounted to only $419 million, or 17 per cent of the total. Of the whole amount of the loans 75 per cent, or $1.4773 billion, were transferred to the firms with priorities, that is, with special concessions and privileges in the cost of exchange in cruzeiros and in the preferential reserve of foreign credits available. In the case of the automobile industry, for example, of $685.9 million applied in the country, $200 million were represented by direct investments and $485.9 million by loans, of which $113.4 million were preferential loans.[18]

[18] These data are taken from the reports of the National Bank of Economic Development (Banco Nacional de Desenvolvimento Econômico), published directly and summarized in the Statistical Yearbooks of the Brazilian Institute of Geography and Statistics (Anuários Estatísticos do Instituto Brasileiro de Geografia e Estatística),

These figures clearly depict the conditions to which the country had to submit in order to obtain the desired collaboration of foreign capital: the ridiculous volume of actual dollar intake in comparison with the total of loans in strong currency transferred by the national economy to private enterprises for future payment in cruzeiros. As we have seen, in the majority of cases the funds in cruzeiros were also obtained through loans at negative interest granted by the official credit agencies. Thus it is plain that the foreign contribution to the establishment of their Brazilian branches represented only a preposterous fraction of the wealth turned over to them, wealth that would generate profits and be transferred abroad in dollars.

The data published by E.C.L.A. reveal a probably positive aspect of foreign private cooperation. In classifying the international bank sources of the funds obtained by Brazil to defray the costs of the Plan of Goals it shows that, of the total of $1.792 billion coming into the country as loans to finance the plan, $1.503 billion were provided by private banks. This means that only $289.3 million originated in the Eximbank (Export-Import Bank of the United States), in the B.I.D. (Inter-American Development Bank) and in other agencies nominally fostering development and capacitated to operate with the so-called "soft loans." The heavy volume of funds in strong currencies was obtained from private bankers in the practice of their occupation, dealing in money, naturally with the most rewarding rates of interest besides all sorts of official guarantees. But they were obtained, generally speaking, through the mediation of the private enterprises directly concerned in the operation.

The principal financial collaboration of foreign groups in the industrialization of Brazil, as programmed in the Plan of Goals, consisted in facilitating these arrangements. More important was their collaboration in other fields, such as the technical capacity for carrying out the undertakings, sometimes very complex, and the granting of licenses to use their patents and their prestigious trademarks—these last, of course, at the cost of huge outlays of strong currency.

Such were the actual conditions that the national economy had to accept in order to effect the program of substitutive industrialization, which in fact converted it into a recolonizing industrialization. They burdened the whole population by draining off funds through inflation, only to hand them over, almost as a gift, to private firms, especially the international corporations. They resulted, moreover, in enormously aggravating the country's indebt-

---

and the analysis made by E.C.L.A. (U.N. Economic Commission on Latin America) in "Quince Años de Política Económica en el Brasil," *Boletín Económico de América Latina,* 9, no. 2, November 1964.

edness to supply the same firms and the government's own programs with the strong currency resources indispensable to defray the costs of the program. Thus it is clear that the assurance of monopolies in a great national market, with guarantees of freedom for free-enterprise operation, and even the warmest protection and encouragement, are not sufficient to assure international cooperation in developmental programs. In addition to all this, it was necessary to practice a policy of concessions exceeding everything that could be foreseen as ideal conditions of operation of the capitalistic entrepreneurial economy.

An evaluation of the principal economic result of the Plan of Goals shows that from 1955 to 1960 the electric power capacity production rose 154 per cent; oil production, 468 per cent; refining, 247 per cent; cement production, 161 per cent. Other gains of the plan are in the establishment of capital goods industry represented by the production of automobiles, ships, mechanical construction, and heavy electric material. The automobile industry, starting from all but zero, attained in 1960 the establishment of twelve large plants and 1,200 auxiliary factories employing more than 150,000 workmen and producing 133,000 vehicles. In 1963 this last figure rose to 185,000 (86,023 automobiles, 20,546 utilitarian vehicles, 3,478 trucks, 13,922 Jeeps, and 9,908 tractors). Shipbuilding in the period reached a nominal capacity of production of 158,000 tons per year, initiating the production of dredges and equipping for major repair works. The machine- and equipment-producing industry doubled its capacity and the heavy electric material industry increased by 200 per cent, both becoming capacitated to produce two thirds of the industrial goods formerly imported.

It is pertinent to ask whether the same results—granted that these are highly positive for the new quality they add to the nation's economy— could have been accomplished by other less onerous ways. The proof that an option is virtually impossible can be found in the fact that no underdeveloped economy has succeeded in finding or innovating an alternative within the world capitalistic structure.

On the other hand, the principal economic effect of the Plan of Goals, which can only be measured as of 1965,[19] consisted in the appropriation of Brazilian industry by the international corporations and in the transformation of the Brazilian entrepreneurial corps into a cosmopolitan industrial bourgeoisie. Examining the register of private industrial firms with capital of more than 4 billion cruzeiros, one learns that 60.6 per cent of

[19] These data come from the legal regulation compelling the revaluation of the assets of these enterprises (see *Conjuntura Econômica,* February 1965; *Banas Informa,* 1965; and Carta SPED, 2-3-4/1965).

the firms and 71 per cent of their capital funds belong to international consortia, mostly of the United States. When it is considered that even in the residual parcel of nominally national firms there is an appreciable foreign element in the form of stocks and bonds, contracts for exploiting patents, technical aid, royalties, know-how and other mechanisms of exploitation and control, it must be concluded that in point of fact Brazil has no national complex of key industries but a system of foreign industrial installations.

This throws light on many apparently strange facts, such as the absence of a combative entrepreneurial bourgeoisie in Brazil, prepared to defend its expansion interests in the face of foreign domination and internal oligarchic constriction. In fact, the authentically Brazilian industrial bourgeoisie, smothered by the wave of huge international corporations, had its growth checked and in greater part was compelled to join the foreign interests in order to survive. For that reason it never attained the minimum critical mass necessary to confront the huge bulk of exogenous interests and to develop an autonomist conduct. A mere associate in foreign exploitation, it does not assume an independent posture that can enable it to demand hegemonic control of the internal factors of power, preferring to appease the traditional latifundian interests, in one way more authentically national because they do not possess the management character of this industrial bourgeoisie.

Only when one considers the total capital of the state enterprises (659.2 billion cruzeiros), adding that of the great private industrial enterprises belonging to Brazilians (428.7 billion) do we reach a majority of national capital funds (1.0879 trillion) as against foreign investments of 1.0526 trillion cruzeiros. This scant majority, however, is purely statistical, because the large national private consortia tend to side with foreign capital funds rather than with the state enterprises or the small national industries to pressure the government for all kinds of action. Thus, the powerful entrepreneurial action of the political, economic, and financial life of the nation, exerted through various mechanisms, tends to operate against autonomous development and toward an increasingly greater dependence on the world powers.

The national entrepreneurial corps, operating its enterprises (or that part of them under its control) according to technical plans imported along with machinery, ends by defining its class interests by the same criteria. They become foreigners in their own country. Keeping two sets of books on their businesses in order to have a point of reference in dollars for their progress, reducing all their reserves to dollars the better to protect against the attrition of inflation, they wind up operating their firms in an extranational circuit. Today they are citizens of the capitalistic world, and as such, more uncompromising in defense of the spoliation system than the foreigners themselves; the latter retain at least a certain fundamental loyalty to their own nations.

It was in this situation that it became the "normal" safety and precautionary procedure of many Brazilian capitalists to exchange controlling stock in their firms for common stock in the international corporations. Thus the owner of a company producing plate glass, for example, who exchanges control of his national enterprise for shares of equivalent value in some international branches of Pittsburgh Glass proceeds with complete tranquility, conceiving the trade in terms of the following advantages: he avoids a competition that could be disastrous to him; he assures himself of a highly advantageous mechanism of technical aid; he diminishes his margin of risk before any eventuality, because a revolution, a war, or an earthquake in Brazil or Germany would be counterbalanced by the preservation of his interests in Australia or France or elsewhere. By such internationalizing, Brazilian entrepreneurs sublimate their very status as capitalists, setting it on a supranational plane of solidarity to which their loyalties also revert.

Nevertheless, this is the typical native businessman found today in big industry, all of it directly or indirectly controlled by the international corporations. Their domination is so oppressive that arguments about the Latin American common market take place in the field of action of their interests and with the plain purpose of serving them rather than the national economies engaged in the system. Thus the Latin American Free Trade Association tends to be a captive market of the corporations already established in the region, who will divide among themselves the productive sectors and the market areas.

In these circumstances even the most successful economic operations in exploiting opportunities for negotiation within the area with local currencies will come out with profits that, in the final analysis, will be sent abroad in dollars. Let it be noted that even the national portion of these undertakings, which could produce new funds for investment if transformed into shares in the home corporation, will only generate more dollar profits, which will overload the commercial balance, and the return of which to Brazil will be made only under the same conditions for the ingress of any foreign capital.

Therefore, the greater the efficiency attained by this internationalization of the Latin American economies, the more harmful it tends to become. It will end by making the board meetings of the great international corporation executives with interests in the area the most powerful institution in the determination of national destinies; against its decisions there will be no power of appeal. Probably this threshold has already been crossed.

It now becomes necessary to make a final estimate of the financial results of the free-enterprise economic policy made viable by the Plan of Goals. This can be done through analyzing the results achieved by Brazil in her foreign exchange in recent years. For the purpose we have the records of the International Monetary Fund, published by the E.C.L.A.[20] for the whole postwar period, 1945–1960.

Examination of the operations in current account shows that the interchange of merchandise (import and export) left to Brazil a favorable balance of $2.7165 billion in these fifteen years. The operations classified as services, however, cost the nation $5.6017 billion, of which $2.4399 billion were for freight charges, insurance, and tourism, and $3.1618 billion for profits, amortizations, and loans or other services pertaining to foreign capital. This deficit in services, much higher than the favorable balance gained in merchandise, caused an imbalance in the current account scandalously unfavorable to the country, Brazil at the end of the period having a deficit of $2.8852 billion which had to be met by foreign indebtedness.

Considering the whole postwar period, it can be concluded that the fundamental factors of the disequilibrium in the balance of payments (the deficit of $2.8852 billion mentioned above) are, first, the deterioration of exchange relations, which permitted gaining commercial balances capable of confronting import needs only through constant increase of export tonnage; second, the onus of the so-called services, among which the cost of money remittances going out of the country and the cost of the foreign debt ($3.1618 billion), plus the burden of transportation costs, freights, and insurance ($2.1399 billion) paid to international companies can be singled out as the basic factor of ruin.

The remittance of profits during the 1945–1960 period cost the country $1.1058 billion, a sum more than doubled by payments of commissions, fees, and royalties that amounted to $1.2 billion. If we add to these figures the amortizations of the foreign debt, some $818 million, and the small private remittances of foreign exchange for vacations abroad and the like, we find in this account alone the already mentioned deficit of $3.1 billion in fifteen years, exceeding by itself the total balance of exports.

So it becomes evident that Brazil worked during the postwar period principally to pay for this drain of profit remittances and service costs, budgeted at $5.6 billion. It was covered by the export balances ($2.7 billion) and new investment of capital and new indebtedness ($1.3 billion). As all this was not enough, because there remained a deficit (to be more exact) of $1.5346 billion, it was necessary to resort to still more onerous

[20] O.N.U. [United Nations], *El financiamiento externo de la América Latina* (New York: 1964).

forms of compensation for the imbalance, through emergency loans. In other words, defrayal of the profits in capital funds introduced into Brazil not only consumed a considerable part of the result of exportation but obliged the country to plunge deeper into debt.

The available data for the subsequent five-year period (1960–1965) indicate that the situation worsened appreciably. They demonstrate the unviability of an industrial economy based on enterprises belonging to international companies whose remittances of profits absorb half the total capacity of Brazil's economy to produce foreign-exchange credits. In such circumstances, economic exploitation will have to generate its own remedy, which can only be some form of freezing of foreign profits or subsidizing the national economy to pay them without ceasing to supply the irreducible import needs. The alternative, probably inevitable, is nationalization of foreign capital.

The problem is not confined to Brazil, inasmuch as, according to Raul Prebitsch's estimates (1964), all Latin America will reach a position of absolute insolvency around 1970, the annual deficit of commercial balances by that time being on the order of $20 billion. At that stage the unviability of the U.S. corporations' empire, capable of yielding fabulous export profits but incapable of producing the internal income indispensable to cover them, will be still more evident to all, including the United States. Its value will then be principally that of an instrument for international blackmail against economically weak nations fated to be slow in paying their debts and the larger and larger amounts that they will come to owe to the headquarters of the system.

This whole analysis demonstrates the conditions under which Brazil has succeeded in initiating an accelerated process of industrialization. They have resulted in replacement of the former colonial pact by new mechanisms of historical incorporation that, though permitting the nation to produce much more than it used to import, keep it in the same state of dependency. It remains thus the tributary of foreign economies, whose standards of living and progress it helps to maintain at the cost of perpetuating its own underdevelopment and dependence on foreign decisions about all national problems.

Thus the internal spoliation of the one-crop latifundium, which controls a third of the tillable land for subsidized production of export articles, is enhanced by a new "plantation," for that is what a foreign-owned industry and commerce amount to: a plantation that, exploiting the potentialities of the domestic market, places more than half of the Brazilian workers in the service of producing foreign-exchange credits for its profit remittances.

In recent years rising inflationary pressure, with a consequent rise in prices, has created great discontent among the wage-earners. A vicious circle of wage hikes to compensate for higher prices started, which produced new rises in the cost of living. The accelerated rate of the inflationary spiral demanded urgent and radical measures. The struggle then began between the different economic sectors, each seeking to escape the cost of readjustment. The popular strata, which had already paid the principal cost of the investments by way of the indirect tax inherent in issues of paper money, defended themselves by means of wage strikes. The entrepreneurial class, which until then had benefited from the inflation, sought to escape the pressure of wage increases by raising prices and by access to the financial system of the government through generous loans. Various attempts were initiated to contain the inflation, only to cause waves of unemployment even more serious than inflation itself in an expanding economy that no longer met the minimum needs of work opportunity for a population increasing by more than three per cent annually. Beginning with 1963, the unrest worsened and spread, especially in the middle classes, less capable of protecting their salaries and not well disposed toward a government policy that seemed to favor the working class.

The final balance in this effort was an inflationary crisis of alarming proportions, which made the entrepreneurs more fearful of inflation than of economic stagnation, and an unprecedented crisis in the balance of payments, incapable of supplying the indispensable imports and of defraying the service costs of the debt contracted abroad. But it was also an economic situation not devoid of promise, because of the addition of forces to the national economy that almost exhausted the possibilities of substitutive industrialization.

The obligation to face these dilemmas once more set the whole complex of problems that had confronted Getúlio Vargas squarely before the new government, problems aggravated by the sharpening of the differences between the integrated and the marginal sectors in the economy, plus the decision of the division of tasks in the antiinflationary effort and the no less crucial question of payment of the foreign debt. Ought its cost to revert on the people, who had already paid, through inflation, the price of both subsidized industrialization and the coffee stockpiling so highly favorable to the producers? Or should it be distributed through all sectors, weighing most on the privileged classes? The response to this question is the whole later history of the nation, now more political than economic.

Besides the acceleration of the inflationary process and the foreign indebtedness of Brazil, which definitely stopped any possibility of continuing to use the printing of paper money and the issuance of government *avals* as a means of appropriating and distributing funds, two other negative effects of the national effort at industrialization stand out. First, the sectorial disparities of the national economy intensified, occasioning an even greater inequality between the living conditions of those engaged in urban and industrial services, on the one hand, and those of the immense majority yoked to agricultural labor, on the other. The unilaterally industrial orientation had resulted in this intensification, because the whole expansion of food production had remained entrusted to the old latifundian system, only capable of increasing through expanding the area cultivated, always keeping the same rudimentary technology and condemning the rural population to the lowest levels of life.

Second, there was a disparity of development between the industrial nucleus concentrated around São Paulo, Rio de Janeiro State, and Guanabara, on the one hand, and the rest of the country, on the other, whose reciprocal relations had created still more plainly a picture of internal colonization. This industrial nucleus, which in 1960 contained 26.4 per cent of the nation's population, had 41.8 per cent of the urban population, 61.1 per cent of the factory workmen, 71 per cent of the value of industrial production; 52 per cent of the persons who had finished primary schooling, 60 per cent of those who had average level education, and 61 per cent of those who had graduated from university schools.[21] Other illustrations of the concentration attained by this prime nucleus are found in its share of the national taxes collected: 50–60 per cent of the state taxes and 72 per cent of the federal. Further, it absorbs 67 per cent of the internal commerce and 84 per cent of the nation's imports, though it contributes only 44 per cent of the exports.

It is well known that metropolitan nuclei of this nature, once constituted, exert two lines of action on its market and influence areas. One induces technological renovations and technical progress, which turns the archaic productive processes to modern economy. The second is a complementary action, which induces and deepens the sectorial and regional imbalances, always bestowing privileges on the guiding centers and dooming the other areas to backwardness.[22] If the process is left to the simple collision of economic forces, the preponderance of the second effect becomes inevitable, provoking a greater and more intense dissociation rather than reorder, through the absorption of the few capital funds generated in the peripheral areas and through the increasing marginalization of the peripheral population, always the least capable and the most aged.

These effects derive, in fact, from the integration of the entire country into a single productive system, divided into specialized areas, each compatible with a different living standard, all inferior to the prime center.

[21] The data on educational levels are taken from the 1950 national census; the others, from the 1960 census.

[22] Some economic and social aspects of this process have been studied by Gunnar Myrdal (1957) as "backward effects" and "spread effects."

This imbalance is, surely, a first indispensable step toward a subsequent, less deformed, reorder. The tendency of the process, however, insofar as it acts spontaneously, is to accentuate the regional differences rather than to minimize them. Thus the international constellation of ruling nuclei and peripheral areas finds on the national plane a similar configuration, both tending to the perpetuation of the differences.

The governmental efforts to confront these regional imbalances, such as the Superintendência do Plano de Valorização Econômica da Amazônia (SPEVEA), the Superintendência do Desenvolvimento do Nordeste (SU-DENE),* and other organs of regional development have been able to serve only as mere palliatives because of the conditioning of their action to the preservation of the social structure, especially of land monopoly in the case of the northeast.

As is clear, this colonialist form of induced industrialization, by its distinct dissociative effects, had accentuated the old structural disorders, which had reached the level of acute social problems. In these circumstances it was no longer possible to postpone the confrontation of the structural problems by resorting to artificial expedients as had always been done. It was imperative to face them, opting between favoring privatism, which put all public power in the service of enriching a minority, and the never-before-practiced alternative, a courageous policy of structural reforms capable of substantially attenuating or annulling the deforming effects of the oligarchic order and foreign exploitation of society, the nation, and the national economy. Hesitating between the two projects, Jânio Quadros resigned. Opting for the nationalistic, popular solution, João Goulart was overthrown. A military dictatorship was imposed on the nation to execute a policy of contrary orientation, a policy of betrayal and privatism, and the dictatorship is making an effort to carry out this lugubrious task.

We have examined the Goulart administration's program for agrarian reform. Let us now see their solution for the problem of foreign spoliation. This was based, essentially, on a body of measures instituted by the Law of Profit Remittances and regulated by decree of the executive power, destined to control the total amount and movement of funds of the foreign enterprises.

It consisted in making a legal distinction concerning foreign capital that was employed in Brazil: foreign capital, per se, assured the right to remit profits abroad up to the limit of 10 per cent per year and privilege of re-

* *Superintendência* is the equivalent of our agency or bureau. SPEVEA is the Bureau of the Plan for Economic Valorization of Amazonia and SUDENE, the Bureau for the Development of the Northeast.

turn (the figure for money in any currency or for goods transferred at any time to the country) versus national capital belonging to foreigners, formed by the result, in cruzeiros, of their operations in Brazil, of the reinvestments effected by means of loans made abroad, or any operations not involving the ingress of funds originating abroad. This second category of capital remained wholly owned by the enterprises, which would go on handling it with complete autonomy, just as the national capitalists operate, but it would not have the right to remit profits, because it was a question of goods created in the country with the aid of national banking and thanks to the privileged protection assured by the law to national entrepreneurs.

The execution of this law of profit remittance and its regulation was hardly initiated when the coup d'état supervened. After less than a month the military dictatorship revoked both the law and the regulation, substituting for it statutes and treaties still more concessionary than any of the preceding ones.

The fundamental effect of the Goulart solution to the problem of foreign spoliation was to oblige enterprises to record the amounts of their actual investments, restricting only to these the special prerogatives given to foreign capital actually brought into Brazil to collaborate with the national economy. As for the capital funds arising from their operations in Brazil, these were assured the same guarantees granted to all national entrepreneurs. The solution was, then, plainly capitalistic, but national-capitalistic, because it safeguarded the country's interests.

The studies that preceded the aforementioned legislation demonstrated that the majority of the large firms classed as foreign invested in the country sums that rarely amounted to 20 per cent of their nominal capital. This proportion would be the criterion for restricting their profit remittances, which today cost Brazil, as has been shown, an increasing erosion of the national work product. Another effect would be to deter the U.S. government in its new policy of pressuring Brazil to buy the most obsolete, least profitable enterprises. This effect would be obtained through limiting the "nationalizable" portion to genuine foreign holdings. The military dictatorship's acquisition of one of the electric power plants for nearly $500 million would not have been made if that legislation had been in force, or else would have been done at a fifth of the cost.

The greatest drawback in the foreign capital legislation that was repealed by the dictatorship lay in its having little or no attraction for new private investments, because obviously private investors are not going to be content with a maximum of 10 per cent profit annually when they operate below the Rio Grande. In reality the conditions required to obtain foreign industrial investments are so onerous that it is better to get along without them. And the problem of Latin America these days is to uproot the foreign interests already installed in those countries rather than to facilitate the installation of new ones.

The disparaged legislation was clothed in legal, democratic, and even capitalistic attributes that made any formal protest by the U.S. government impossible. Naturally, in the eyes of the Johnson administration no Latin American government was acceptable if it advocated such attractive solutions for other plundered countries. Quite the contrary, it constituted the fundamental factor in the U.S. deliberation to conspire by all means for the overthrow of the Goulart regime, especially because, besides this law, the Goulart administration was taking measures to strengthen the state monopoly of petroleum products; recover the mineral deposits from foreign firms; amplify state enterprises for mineral exports; establish a siderurgical network that would make Brazil, in a decade, an exporter of steel and not of raw materials; and effectively control the nation's foreign commerce.

The accomplishment of agrarian reform, of the new policy of control of foreign capital funds, and of the whole program of economic emancipation under way would have set Brazil on the road to the status of accelerated and self-sustained development. For a nation that will have 100 million inhabitants by 1970—250 million by the year 2000—and that has great natural resources of every kind available, this policy would result in a great independent nation founded on an autonomous, prosperous economy.

This was what the United States prevented, in defense of her power policy and of the interests of her corporations. To justify the coup she resorted to all sorts of arguments, the major one being anticommunism. The truth, however, is that the United States never feared the Goulart administration as a threat of communist revolution. Quite the reverse, she was perfectly aware that he represented an attempt at a peaceful evolution within capitalistic frameworks.

The United States feared that the nationalist-reformist alliance would assure conditions of progress and independence to the largest of Latin American nations. Even though Goulart's reformism was the only way to preserve the democratic regime and capitalism in Brazil, the U.S. government preferred the alternative of a dictatorship that would assure the Yankees that, as long as it held power, no economic, politically independent power would emerge in Latin America. On the other hand, if a dictatorship can postpone the Brazilian revolution—as Franco did in Spain—the obstruction of ways to a peaceful evolution will also make radicalization inevitable.

The two bodies of solutions advocated by the Goulart administration for the basic problems of Brazil—agrarian reform and the disciplining of foreign business activity—can only be explained by three kinds of circumstantial factors that made their practical execution viable: (1) the international situation marked by Pope John XXIII's and President Kennedy's thought and action; (2) the precedence gained in the Brazilian armed forces by contingents of democratically and nationalistically inclined officers, following the crisis of Jânio Quadros' resignation in 1961; (3) the support given by the popular, especially labor, classes to President Goulart as the continuer of the worker policy of Getúlio Vargas. Only in these circumstances could solutions of this kind, never put into practice except by revolutionary governments, possibly be carried out.

President Goulart's measures were a mature, responsible attempt to find a peaceable way out—through persuasion and within the framework of democratic institutions and capitalistic regime—for Brazil's developmental problems. Goulart's overthrow, precisely when his popular support was at its peak, show, however, that some of those circumstantial conditions had deteriorated. It likewise shows the intrinsic weaknesses of the reformist policy. These stem from the contradiction between the revolutionary character of the socioeconomic reorder, antioligarchic and antiimperialist, that those governments propose and the unstable, merely conciliatory character of the power structure on which they are based.

The reordering measures of Goulart's reformist regime, even before they started operating, provoked the counterrevolution without the administration's being armed to confront it. In these circumstances a victorious conspiracy of ambassadors, U.S.-indoctrinated military hierarchs, and reactionary governors imposed a regressive dictatorship, which proscribed the reform policy, abandoned the nationalist orientation, and executed an external and internal veto against Brazil's development.

For Brazil, as for all Latin America, the challenge posed is the confrontation of these forces as a prior condition to the break with underdevelopment. Only through the elimination of the traditional power structure, which for centuries has failed to lead the country to autonomous development and to democracy, will Brazil be able to realize her potential as a leading American nation.

6. The Gran-Colombians

ON THE NORTHWEST coast of South America we find the second bloc of New Peoples, represented by 15 million Colombians and 8 million Venezuelans. Their New Peoples' character derives from their profoundly different cultural and racial heritages and from their history of deculturation and miscegenation under conditions of extreme compulsion—colonial domination and slavery—to form a new ethnos neither indigenous nor African nor Spanish.

The northwest coast was one of the first areas in Latin America where the Spaniards established themselves, fixing the nuclei from which they set out to conquer the continent and initiate the civilizational process from which the American peoples resulted. The initial cycle of that process consisted of the subjugation of the Indians and their conscription into mining labor, through the mita, and into agricultural production, through the encomienda. A second cycle began when, after local labor had worn out, the massive shipping of Negro slaves from Africa started, first for the mines and later for the great export agricultural enterprises and for all heavy service. The third cycle took place when the crossbred societies, subprod-ucts of those undertakings and resultant from the amalgamation of those human contingents, won their independence from Spain only to fall under the dominion of England, and later of the United States, as the production of the area came to consist mainly of oil, other minerals, and modern trop-ical products.

The last cycle is developing in our own days. It is the cycle of rebellion against the social order imposed by the local oligarchies, sustained by the foreign interests installed in the region, in order to perpetuate themselves as superwealthy in the sea of Latin American poverty. This situation is ex-pressed in many ways: in political instability, in *golpismo*,* in dictator-ships and in guerrillas. But its principal manifestation is the irruption of violence in the bloodiest forms, in which people tear each other to pieces by hundreds of thousands, apparently for futile quarrels but in fact to maintain the oligarchies.

In the following analysis of the New Peoples of New Granada and of the developmental problems facing them, we shall focus on two aspects in particular: (1) violence to maintain the oligarchic dominion, exemplified by the Colombian case; (2) the mode of operation and the fundamental characteristics of the U.S. corporation system for dominating dependent economies shown through detailed examination of the case best exemplify-ing it, the Venezuelan.

In no area of the world have U.S. entrepreneurs and their government advisors had such complete freedom of action, unless perhaps in Central America. In Venezuela they actually drew up the legislation pertaining to oil concessions and movement of capital and have always had the deciding word in the passage of any constitutional reform and all government pro-grams. Also, no Latin American nation has experienced such long periods of political stability, under the iron glove of the most cruel dictatorships, to be sure, whose titular heads were decorated by the United States. Nor can any government compare with the Venezuelan one throughout its his-tory in the amplitude of its use of U.S. aid and technical advice, under contract with planning organizations, banks, and universities or through inter-American institutions such as Eximbank, AID (Agency for Interna-tional Development), and BID, controlled from Washington. Venezuela is a living and measurable demonstration of the model of economic and so-cial development advocated by the United States for the underdeveloped world, and the most expressive illustration of the U.S. American way of progress proposed for all Latin American nations, especially those of the Caribbean, but there imposed in ideal conditions.

* The policy of resorting to coups d'état to solve problems of dissatisfaction.

Her natural wealth, discovered and under exploitation, makes Venezuela the richest land on earth, and in Latin America the one that attracts the largest U.S. investments (35 per cent of the total, or nearly $3 billion), in operational conditions systematically recommended as the freest, the most advanced, and the best suited to the unhampered exercise of free enterprise. There are not even any venture groups that have come in to exploit the deposits of oil, iron and aluminum, and banks, commerce and industry —none at all. In Venezuela the great corporations dominate, backed by the renown of the Rockefellers, the Morgans, the du Ponts, and the Mellons. The enterprises of these groups and other equally honorable ones of the United States control the whole Venezuelan economy, allowing only a minority share in the oil exploitation to the Royal Dutch Shell (26 per cent).

The Rockefeller interests in Venezuela are the largest producers of oil (60 per cent) and iron (30 per cent). They control banks and insurance, but they do not scorn collaboration also in lesser affairs. With equal zeal they devote themselves to the development of the major supermarket network and have made themselves the largest Venezuelan producers of meat, milk, chickens, and eggs. The president of Standard Oil of New Jersey himself stated in 1962 that half the corporation's profits came from Venezuela. These profits annually reach a figure of more than $600 million.

It so happens that the Venezuelan people are one of the poorest, sickest, and most ignorant people in all of impoverished Latin America. Has free enterprise failed in such propitious—and, for it, such lucrative— conditions? Or can it be the Venezuelan common people, characterized as a tropical, crossbred, lazy, ignorant people with no initiative who are responsible for their own backwardness in spite of the huge civilizational effort of the corporations?

Litters for Spaniards

The major indigenous populations encountered by the Spanish conquistador in what is now the territory of Colombia and Venezuela—the Chibcha, the Timote, and others—by their level of cultural development were above the undifferentiated horticultural villages of the tropical forest and halfway between the clan protostates of the Araucanos and the urban civilizations of Mexico and the Andean altiplano. They were already stratified in classes of farmers, craftsmen, and nobles, agglutinated in rural craftsman states,[1] whose chiefs disputed the central power. They were

---

[1] On rural craftsman states, see Ribeiro, *The Civilizational Process.*

members of a mercantile economy in which the different strata of producers traded agricultural products, ceramics, textiles, salt, precious stones, and gold, the last probably serving as coin. However, they lived in villages of only a few thousand inhabitants. They had an intensive agriculture—though not irrigated—thanks to the quality of the soil, the favorable climatic conditions, and their high horticultural technology. They planted corn, white potatoes, pigweed (quinoa, common goosefoot), manioc, green beans, tomatoes, pepper, coca, and tobacco, and they raised ducks, guinea pigs, and turkeys.

The Chibcha Indians of Colombia, estimated at some 600,000 at the time of the conquest, were concentrated principally on the fertile lands of the plateaus and valleys of the highlands. One of their major nuclei stood where Bogotá is today. Chibcha craftsmen reached a high degree of mastery in ceramics, metal work, and preparation of salt from underground deposits. Their ornaments of *repoussé* gold reveal a great virtuosity and are among the most beautiful metal objects of indigenous America.

The nobles formed a privileged caste, busied in religion, war, administration, and tax collection from the farmers and craftsmen. They were served by slaves and exacted reverence from the common people, who were forbidden to look them in the face and obliged to burn aromatic resins and strew flowers at their passing. They were transported in litters bedecked with gold and fine cloths. When they died, they were buried with their wives (sacrificed after being drugged) and their treasures of gold and silver, in order to be assured of the same status beyond the grave.

The Spaniards who penetrated the Chibcha world, dislodging the native nobility, were not content with the veneration expressed in flowers and incense or with gifts of jewels. They immediately tried to round up all the objects of precious metals and stones treasured by the natives, ransacking homes and even cemeteries for the purpose. Once this accumulated wealth was exhausted, they dedicated themselves actively to the exploitation of alluvial gold and auriferous veins, drafting all the Indians they could capture for this work.

The conquest of the Chibcha, the Timote, and the other peoples on the same level of development was rapid. The first principates surrendered almost without struggle in hopes of gaining the alliance of the Spanish, with their horses and guns, to subdue rival factions, Spaniards simply replacing the local nobility. Two years after the first encounter where was only a guerrilla resistance left in the forests where the Spanish dared not penetrate. All the population of the Chibcha and Timote rural craftsmen states had been enslaved and divided into groups to become mitayos or the property of encomenderos, rewarded by the crown and by the Church, who were to minister to their material and spiritual well-being. Some indigenous groups marginal to the great Chibcha and Timote, clung to the lands of their ancestors and succeeded in getting them recognized as *resguardos* [lands reserved for security] by paying tithes to the Church and assessments to the crown. With the tribal community thus maintained, they managed to survive a little longer.

Before the end of the sixteenth century the indigenous survivors had been deculturated, losing their language, their crafts techniques, and their culture, all superfluous in their new life. The crossbreeds, of Spanish male and Indian woman, began to surpass them in numbers and had already supplanted them as agents of a new culture, composed of a combination of elements selected from the indigenous patrimonies (principally the specialized modes of adaptation to local conditions for agricultural and crafts production) and from Hispanic contributions, elements that stamped the new culture with its basic characteristics, binding the new nuclei to European mercantile civilization.

Into this ethnos were integrated the other indigenous groups, the African Blacks, and the new Spanish immigrants, to form the modern peoples of New Granada. The Africans were incorporated in it only after being detribalized and deculturated through slavery, and contributed little to alter the protostock. The Spaniards strengthened its Hispanic cultural content to the detriment of the indigenes and the Africans.

The ruling stratum of the new society was composed of the descendants of the Spanish adventurers and the officials and clergy sent out from the kingdom to direct and sanctify the rapine. The subordinate class was the mass of enslaved Indians and the free halfbreeds, engaged for the most part in the production of metals. The African slave began to be imported only when the decimation of the mitayo Indians threatened to paralyze the mining industry and thus halt production, despite the regulations that fixed strict limits for agricultural activity in order to assure sufficient labor for mining. The flow of slaves grew constantly. From the mines they went into transportation services, and later into cultivation for export and into every economic sector where hard work wore out men most rapidly.

Mixed with whites, Indians, and the offspring of those two stocks, the Negro produced masses of mulattoes and *zambos* [offspring of Negro men and Indian women]. These new masses, liberated from the harshness of slave labor, survived and joined the new ethnic stock, multiplying as neo-Americans and molding the Colombians and Venezuelans. The whitest caste, owning the properties and managing colonial administration, was installed in the cities; the refugee Indians, in more and more distant territories, survived as ethnic groups only in the Amazon belt; the mestizos, mulattoes, and zambos, scattered throughout the area embraced by the new mercantile economy, serving as its labor force, were the most numerous contingent.

Venezuela, as an area poorer in gold or silver than other Spanish dominions, even Colombia, remained marginal to the effort of establishing the colonial empire. It was left largely to itself. The Spaniards disembarking on its shores had little resources for enrichment other than their own initiative and the Indian labor force. Some of the Indians, such as the Timotes, figured socially as rural craftsmen states on the same level as the Chibcha of Colombia. They were similarly divided into autonomous, hostile states and were for this very reason easily overcome. They also had a dominant caste desirous of allying with the Spanish and easy to replace, and a caste of horticulturists and craftsmen conditioned to subordination and therefore predisposed to enslavement.

What was to be done with so many people in a land so poor in precious metals? The solution found by the Spaniards was to become exporters of Indian slaves to the mines in Colombia. Later on they began to cultivate spices and to raise cattle for distant markets. Naturally, they busied themselves also in producing people, resulting in the emergence of a vast stratum of mestizos Hispanized by identification with the dominating father, who could extend some of his privileges to them.

In this fashion a natural subsistence economy was complemented by an export sector. The Indian masses were used up in this hard labor, in the slave trade, and in the expeditions into the Andean summits, into cliff lands and lowlands in search of gold, under the command of Spaniards fired by the idea that somewhere one more enchanted kingdom was hiding.

The crown, disappointed in the poverty of those lands, mortgaged them to a German banking house, the Welsers, who proposed risking their money in seeking the gold that the Spaniards had not found. After enormous efforts the Welsers went into bankruptcy, returning the Orinoco Valley and adjacent lands of the coast and the sierra to Spain's control.

Colonization proceeded with the subjugation of the Indian to agricultural work. At the end of the seventeenth century there were nearly twenty nuclei of Indians, Spaniards, and their mestizo offspring who were cultivating tobacco, cacao, indigo, and sugar; to these nuclei were later added Negro slaves imported from the African coast. The economic volume of these enterprises, however, was so small that Spanish ships rarely touched the Venezuelan coast, so that commerce came to be carried on, in the main, with English, French, and Dutch smugglers. Saltpeter, exploited on the coast, and the hides of the cattle that had multiplied prodigiously on the Venezuelan plains were subsequently added to the tropical products for export.

At the beginning of the eighteenth century Spain awoke to the value of her abandoned colony, which was in danger of being lost to European competitors. To block this danger the Compañía Guipuzcoana was established, with royal privileges giving the company the monopoly of trade and administrative control of the colony. However, the enterprise was to find itself confronted there by stiff-necked people accustomed to freely trading their tropical products, increasing in value, and indisposed to letting themselves be ruled by the strict Spanish colonial system. It all ended in a *modus vivendi* far more liberal than in any other Hispano-American area. It even admitted a certain interchange with smugglers in the long periods when Spanish maritime commerce was paralyzed by European wars. The colonial company itself would at such times negotiate with the contrabandists to provide the population with indispensable industrial articles.

In these circumstances, little by little, an autonomic attitude was born that was to assert itself more and more with the growing enrichment of the tropical crops and the reordering of the area along the line of a one-crop economy based on slave labor.

It was in this framework that the Venezuelan people was molded. The Indian-Spanish mestizos of the first century were joined by the mulattoes, who themselves merged, forming a population equally linked with the three stocks. The Spanish physiognomy of European natives and of Creoles born of Spaniards in the New World, but principally of the Hispanized mestizos, was imposed on the new contingents. The Negro was deculturated under the pressure of slavery, and in living alongside the linguistically Hispanized mestizo he was gradually integrated into the new society. The resulting ethnos, however, differed almost equally from the three parent ethnoses. They were no longer Indian, or European, or African, but another ethnic entity that was to constitute itself as the Venezuelan aspect of the Latin American: A New People by all its characteristics of deculturation, crossbreeding, and availability for progress because of not being tied to any conservative tradition. Although racially still blending, therefore permitting the predominantly white to be distinguished from the dominantly Black or Indian, culturally the unity had already been achieved.

This, like all the ethnic groups in the new peoples, represented a reduction of the cultural patrimonies of origin to what was compatible under the pressure of two basic modeling forces: (1) the Spanish domination with the power to impose the greatest mass of values, and the corresponding flexibility of the dominated strata of indigenes and Africans, which lacked unity because derived from very different tribal and mutually hostile peoples; (2) the conditioning for adaptation to the environment and life modes as producers of tropical articles, in the status of slave or serf populations within the rigid framework of the fazenda system.

Thus a stratified society was built up, closer to the caste than to the class system. The upper caste of native Spaniards composed the bureaucracy and the clergy, which governed the colonial enterprise on the planes of civil and ecclesiastical government. The Creole stratum, colored with indigenous and sometimes Negro genes (frequently classed as white by royal certificates of "clean blood," extending the white Spaniards' privileges to them), held the major part of the agricultural and commercial properties. The mass of *pardos* ["dark"] by preference devoted itself to craftsmanship and to herding. To the Negroes fell the farm manual labor, with the hardest tasks in the fields and in transport. The surviving Indians, still prisoners of the tribal ethnos, were marginalized under the Jesuit missionaries' control, if near at hand, or lived independent in the unexplored areas, especially in the tropical jungle where they took refuge. The most prolific contingent was that of the dark ones—predominantly mulattoes—which increased by the intercrossing and constant absorption of new injections of white, Negro, and Indian genes.

Socially, the Colombian and Venezuelan populations also settled in strata identifiable by the color of the skin, corresponding, by and large, to the poorest classes if the skin was dark, and to the dominant classes if the skin was light. This social scale of pigmentation was scarcely affected by foreign immigration, diminutive in comparison with the total population. For this very reason the social struggles in Colombia and Venezuela are sometimes erroneously interpreted as racial conflicts of Negroes, mulattoes, and mestizos against whites. In point of fact, the whole people of the two nations is mestizo, dominated by predominantly whitish oligarchies. What gives rise to the oppositions between these segments of the same ethnic group is not their racial origins but the contradictions of interests between the cosmopolitan oligarchies benefiting from the status quo and doing all they can to maintain the dominant order, on the one side, and on the other the common people, resistant to their role of beast of burden with no expectation of progress and liberty.

The frightful violence that periodically explodes in Colombian political fighting, as well as the bloody nature of the Venezuelan dictatorships, are dramatic and disordered expressions of this frontal opposition, reducible only by revolution, between the national oligarchies and the deculturated descendants of Indians and Negro slaves. It was they who, after centuries of effort, constructed the two national ethnic entities of the new peoples type that will find the requisites for their liberation only in pursuing the civilizational process that engendered them, by means of the integration of the whole Venezuelan and Colombian society in the life molds of modern industrial societies through a social reorganization that permits the people to take over the nation's destinies and the fruits of its own work.

Irredentism and Emancipation

At the end of the eighteenth century the production of tropical products had reached high levels, taking the form of a commercial agriculture of the plantation type combined with cultivation of foodstuffs and extensive cattle-raising. Together they configured a balanced economy, capable of providing the subsistence of the whole population and also funds to pay for its major import, slave labor.

All these peculiar conditions of relative autonomy, of easier contact with extra-Iberian Europe, of greater economic success than the other Spanish colonies had—their extractive mining economy had ended in collapse—placed New Granada at the forefront of the emancipation movement. That is why the principal center of Hispano-American independence conspiracy was installed there.

The struggle for independence in such inegalitarian societies naturally assumes two distinct and even opposing features. On one side were irredentist popular movements of subjugated masses aiming at freeing themselves not only from colonial oppression but from every kind of exploitation. On the other were struggles of the native dominant classes, which, aspiring to enjoy the privileges exclusively reserved for European-born Spaniards, let themselves be fired by European liberal ideology and North American "illuminism." They proposed to build utopian republics with the human masses resultant from the European tropical enterprises, making them leap from trading colonies to nations founded on liberty, equality, and fraternity. But they wanted to perform this miracle by promoting themselves, simultaneously, as the civilizational elite of the new republics. The best example of New Granadan irredentist struggles was led by the mestizo Galán—"a man of the most obscure origin," according to Archbishop Góngora—who, at the head of the Comuneros Revolution of 1781, symbolized all the contradictions of the Colombian people's struggle for their own liberation. Like Túpac Amaru in Peru (1781) and Tiradentes in Brazil (1789), Galán put himself at the head of the people, to be defeated and killed by the agents of colonial power. All three were hanged, quartered, salted, and exhibited for public execration in the places where they had preached sedition. In the three cases, moreover, the popular revolt resulted from the promulgation of new, ruinous collections by the colonial tax department.

Galán led the farmers and craftsmen, mulattoes and Indians, who were fighting against the spirits and tobacco monopoly (*estanco*) and for tax reduction and restoration to the Indians of their lands and salinas. Marching on the capital, he succeeded in rousing the whole people as he passed, subduing the colonial troops, which surrendered almost without a fight, and placing new chiefs, chosen from the people, to head the cities and towns and free the slaves. For the first time in Colombian history the Indians regained the government of their own communities, poor mestizos composed the public power, and Negroes became acquainted with freedom en masse. Thus the colonial structure was done away with, and a new power began to emerge. The task, however, was too complex for these *comuneros,* commoners in whose cultural heritage there was no precedent of social order that permitted replacing the old oligarchic rule with another kind, capable of expressing the popular interests. Its opposition was not to outrages by specific authorities or to certain forms of colonial exploitation, but to the over-all social organization, which they would have to subvert from base to summit, to institute a new regime. Like all irredentist popular movements, Galán's was successful in attacking barracks and garrisons, overthrowing authorities, and even dominating power temporarily, but it was incapable of instituting a new social order.

As was inevitable, Galán and his comuneros committed the fatal error of accepting the participation of rich merchants in their fight, giving the chieftaincy of their troops to one Berbeo. These allies, even though they, too, were adversely affected by the new taxes, were aware that the Spanish rule served their interests better than a popular government would. They acted in consequence, accepting the command of the comuneros, but secretly drawing up, before a notary, a formal declaration of the involuntary character of their alliance with the irredentist movement and a reiteration of their fidelity to the viceroy. Immediately, they sent their agents on ahead of the troops to appeal to the rich men and the clergy to join likewise, as a way of saving their property and restoring their order. Thus the popular movement won, but under the leadership of the merchants. The viceroy fled, but the archbishop assured the comuneros of satisfaction of their claims.

Faced with unexpected victory, the people celebrated, and Galán demobilized his troops. When he was informed that the viceroy had not ratified the archbishop's arrangements it was too late to reorganize the insurrection. He was captured, condemned, hanged, quartered, exhibited. "His head," the sentence read, "will be taken to Guadrias; his right hand placed in Socorro; his left, in the Villa de San Gil; his right foot, in Chavala, and

his left, in Mogotes. . . ." The tradesman Berbeo was made corregidor
and Archbishop Góngora, viceroy.

The other battlefront for independence was led by the nascent Venezuelan
and Colombian patriciates. It aspired to expel the Spaniard in order to
take control of the customs, gain access to the duties and privileges exclusive to the Spaniard, and appropriate the income received by the metropolis. This front, however, clothed itself in all the brilliant garments of European liberal ideology and displayed the emerging national pride of the
most enlightened classes. The major impediment was in the masses of poor
pardos and Negroes, subjected always to the native seignioral class, which
in their view was no better than the Iberian. For long years the essential
dispute was based on gaining the support or the neutralization of these
masses, which behaved as if they had nothing to gain with freedom, precisely because they would remain slaves or subject to as much exploitation
by the bosses. The Iberian Spaniards played off these contradictions judiciously, turning the poor Creoles against the rich, that is, the darker
against the lighter, in bloody fights that cost a fifth of the population and
created an atmosphere loaded with hostility.

Only after successive failures did Bolívar mature for his historical task,
while still a refugee in independent Haiti. There he learned to respect the
Negro and the mulatto, to recognize their role in the struggles for freedom,
and to take account of their aspirations. The new campaign for emancipation that he undertook was therefore organized on other bases. He began
by freeing the slaves on his own lands and promising general abolition of
slavery. In this way he won the support of Negro slaves. The peons of the
plains were attracted by the promise of receiving land and herbs belonging
to antirevolutionists. Speaking this new language, he achieved the support
of the Black and the dark masses, which, together with English aid in ar-
mament and troops, would enable him to inflict the first defeats on the
Spanish, and, with them as a starting point, to undertake the campaign to
liberate all Spanish America.

Even so, independence took shape as a struggle between the enriched
Creoles and the Iberian Spaniards, a fight for which the people was tardily
mobilized and from which it was jettisoned hard on the heels of victory.
Contrary to the Galán insurrection, which proposed reorder in the whole
society in accordance with the interests of the people, the struggles for political emancipation resulted in a simple change of ruling class, which became native instead of colonial. Bolívar's unitarian, generous utopia gave
way to atomization. In every port, with the sole purpose of controlling the
marketing of local products and the importation of manufactured goods,
emerged a plan for a nation. The richest stratum of the Creole population,
banned until then from high civil and ecclesiastical dignities and prohib-

ited from exercise of power and from the special privileges and profits therefrom, rose to the status of ruling class. It divided among itself the latifundia of the exiled Spaniards, appropriated the metal and saltpeter mines and the other "mines" represented by the revenues from customs and estancos [monopolies on tobacco and so forth]. It invested itself with political, judiciary, and ecclesiastical dignities and distributed the minor bureaucratic posts among its protégés, who began multiplying as the clientele of the new power.

In this pattern the national states of all Hispano-America were formed after independence. They do not represent the victory of capitalistic, mature national bourgeoisies, opposing retrograde social forces, nor the victory of the people against the oligarchy, but the Creole patriciate's appropriation of the machine of dominion and colonial extortion set up by Spain, and now obsolete and unnecessary. The objective of the directors of the emancipatory revolution was to substitute themselves for the Spanish agents, to grow rich with the usufruct of the same machine by means of the same techniques for exploiting the working mass and the same regime of slavocratic oppression.

The new ruling classes placed in command of their national societies were, in the world of things, the expression of these interests and appetites. But in the world of ideas, embodied in the enlightened sector, they professed the greatest devotion to Rousseauian ideas, to Catholic dogmas, to popular sovereignty, and to slavery, generating a formally contradictory ideology, though capable of rationalizing the new oligarchic order. Thus it is that the republic maintained the institutions of the *mayorazgo* ['primogeniture'], the tithe, and the estancos; in the name of equality and liberty initiated an unremitting fight against the resguardo of the communal lands; and in the name of progress and free trade, against the special privileges assured to the craftsmanship productions. Thousands of Indians and artisans were robbed by these procedures: first, the Indians, most helpless against the machine of liberty; then the craftsmen, who could hold out a little longer, being organized in associations and allied with other classes.

Behind these struggles stood the new patron, England. No longer colonial, but imperialist, England financed the wars for independence, creating and multiplying national states that emerged mortgaged to her bankers.[2] Through these mechanisms, industrial and banking England was replacing

[2] Not one of the Latin American countries escaped this international baptismal certificate: a first heavy loan in pounds sterling. Despite being loaded with high interest rates, these loans further suffered ruinous discounts. Rarely did the borrower receive more than sixty pounds of every 100 borrowed, and ordinarily a large part of the loan was tied to delivery of English arms and merchandise at onerous prices. The contract for payment contained the pledging of the principal sources of income of the newborn nations, such as customs receipts.

agrarian and mercantile Spain in the Latin American world, gaining privileged markets for her manufactures and at the same time captive suppliers of raw materials.

The Industrial Revolution that was going on elsewhere affected Columbia and Venezuela through a reflexive modernization, which in the following years would transmute their ways of life with the construction of railroads, ports, and telegraphs and with flooding the market with all kinds of English manufactures. Contributing decisively to economic progress, this modernization under the financial domination of England would only make those countries more efficacious providers of raw materials, more indebted and docile to imperialistic sacking. Simultaneously, however, the national associates in foreign exploitation were fattening their bank accounts in strong currencies, refining their tastes and their education and sending their children to Europe for polishing. As the younger generation grew more alienated because of their interests, attitudes, and loyalties, which were identified with the foreigner, they ended by composing a patrician-patronal caste, alienated because of their European postures, their distaste for their own racial characters as testimonies to their American and African ancestry, and their bizarre tastes. That is, they became as divorced from their people as those Chibcha nobles in their gilded litters, eager to win the Spaniard's alliance for their little wars of expansion against the nobles of other indigenous entities.

Colombia's liberal reforms were carried out in the middle of the nineteenth century with the emancipation of slaves, elimination of the tithe, and the mayorazgo, distribution to the Indians of the communal lands which they still held as private properties, liquidation of the estancos, and suspension of protectionist tariffs. Years of social unrest followed, brought about by the economic and social readjustments imposed by the reforms. The latifundia expanded, swallowing up indigenous lands, and their productive system was reorganized, substituting sharecropping for slave labor. The whole legal revolution, implicit in this transformation, was reduced to the simple expedient of turning the Negro slave into a renter, a tenant whose work is paid with the right to live on the plantation and cultivate a previously designated patch of ground for his subsistence crops and for raising a few pigs and chickens. The Negro rose from slave to the status in which the displaced Indian and the free mestizo found themselves earlier. He became responsible for his own support and free to sell his labor to any employer.

The Colombian people reached the twentieth century differentiated into economically determined social strata. The largest human segment would continue to vegetate under the domination of the hacienda system in the status of *agregados* * yoked to the latifundium. A French traveler in 1897 left a vivid picture of it:

> I have just witnessed the peons' reception of their master: I saw them with their clumsy hands touching their hatbrims, happy to offer the master—who had been away for a year and a half—their modest gifts, humbly presented: a chicken, or a few well-wrapped eggs, all accompanied by emotional blessings for "my master." I saw—will you believe me?—old women, grandmothers, kneel, join their poor cracked hands and stretch them out as if in prayer to him who is the intermediary between Heaven and the disinherited of this world. And I also watched the hacendero look away, fearing to yield to an imperceptible emotion, as if to commend to Heaven all these poor people, so loving, so submissive, so filial (D. M. Cuéllar, 1963, p. 27).

In certain more desolate regions many peasants were able to start little tobacco fields, and later coffee, on bits of land wrested from the tropical forest. They multiplied in this way as small granja farmers, enjoying some measure of tranquility until their land made valuable through their labor, stirred ambitions of others. Then the legal owners came to evict them with the apparatus of the law.

On the plains, formed by the low flatlands of the littoral—where the cattle brought by the Spaniard had multiplied inordinately—the Colombian cowboy, the *llanero,* emerged. Living on his horse, used as a means of transport, work, and war, he developed a spirit of independence based on the specialized character of his occupation, which requires skill and courage, and on the freedom he enjoyed, handling wild herds in ownerless lands. Yet he, too, would be enmeshed in the nets of social order, when the cattle belonging to none were appropriated by the new legal owners of the land where the animals had grown up wild. The llanero then became a herder of another's cattle.

In the cities there had grown up an extremely poor mestizo population of craftsmen and odd-jobmen who made their living in service to the rich city folk. They were divided into two strata, each with its own life: the common people, tied to national traditions and customs that they performed under the complacent eye of their "betters," and the latter, cultivating European habits, studying Latin and French, writing verses, playing the piano, and aspiring to the baccalaureate as the sublime ideal—and maybe even to obtaining a post in the magistrate.

Thus the rural proprietors, the men of letters, the merchants, and functionaries formed one band against the riffraff, the common people. They

* The general term for nonslave farmhands, renters, or sharecroppers.

made up different strata in the urban world, living in different cultural spheres: one, spurious, imitating European values; the other, inauthentic because it was formed on the model of servant classes in a profoundly inegalitarian society.

It was on this archaically styled society, rigidly stratified, that the reflexive pressures of the industrializational process developing elsewhere would be exerted. These would show their effects not only through consumer merchandise but also in the establishment of ports, urban services, telegraphs, and railroads, all of which, besides modifying the whole economic life of the nation, would enlarge the opportunities for work by creating more independent middle and working classes, by encouraging urbanization, and especially by demanding increased production to pay for these modern things at a cost of their weight in gold.

The republican governments of Colombia at the close of the nineteenth century were composed predominantly of the elite of Bogotá, families based on latifundian property, control of commerce, and exploitation of the public treasury, but taking great pride in their abilities as Latinists, grammarians, and poets. These urban patricians, ideologically alienated from their people and their time, looked on themselves as consuls exiled in America among the populace, called on to join in modernity, to mature for freedom, and to prepare for an extremely remote equality.

These learned men abruptly found themselves launched into the midst of the diplomatic intrigue of post-Victorian imperialist Europe when the project of an interocean canal was broached—a canal to be dug on Colombian territory, across the isthmus of Panama. Years of negotiation and intrigue followed, in which Colombia, trusting in the validity of international law, sought to protect herself in the conflicting interests of France, England, and the United States, sure that in this way she could finance the opening, maintenance, and administration of a canal equally accessible to all peoples.

Theodore Roosevelt responded to the Colombian hopes of equity with the Big Stick. He came to an understanding with the English about custody of the canal, and bought from the French, for $40 million, the rights of the canal's construction concession. Armed with these trumps, he sent to the Colombian parliament for its approval a treaty transferring to the Yankees the rights, privileges, properties, and concessions previously guaranteed to the New Canal Company and amplification of these with yet other prerogatives. He warned at once that approval was urgent and that he would allow no changes in the treaty provisions: a term of 100 years, total subordination of the area to U.S. sovereignty, and payment of $10 million—one fourth of what he had paid the French concessioners for merely desisting.

Colombia could not possibly consent to those conditions. Her refusal was followed, as had been foreseen, by a separatist movement of the population of Panama, prepared in advance, and the new "nation" was immediately recognized by the United States. A new state came in this way to figure on the continental map (1903), one with which the United States would negotiate canal matters. The Colombians, described by Roosevelt as "enemies of the human race and of civilization because of their opposition to the opening of the canal," had no other recourse than to present the most vehement verbal protests. Her army, like all Latin American armies, being organized exclusively to put down popular uprisings, was incapable of resisting the robbery.

Bitter years of national frustration followed. But no bitterness obfuscated the necessity and expediency of resuming relations with the colossus of the north, for the advantages that its rich capital funds, its progressive entrepreneurs, and its democratic way of life could bring to Colombia. Even so, only in 1921 was commerce reestablished, by means of a treaty recording the "sincere regret" of the Yankees and promising to compensate Colombia with an indemnification of $25 million. The payment of this indemnification was to cost Colombia another "Panama," because it was on condition that U.S. firms be granted the right to develop the immense oil deposits of the country. Because Colombian law defined subsoil wealth as inalienable national property, which made U.S. access impossible, payment of the indemnification was delayed until native jurists found ways to remove the obstacle.

From that point Colombia was transformed into U.S. America's greatest petroleum reserve. U.S. firms today control all the nation's vast oil fields, less than 10 per cent of which are being developed, leaving the rest as reserve in captive soil by virtue of the concessions. Even so, the business as it goes today is not to be scorned: from 1921 to 1957 U.S. companies invested $127 million in the exploitation of Colombian oil, producing in the same period $1.137 billion in profits.

Columbia's third "Panama" is United Fruit. As with other countries, this company is making Colombia a "banana republic" through constituting that country's largest latifundium. Other Yankee "Panamas" in Colombia are in the entrepreneurial sector, where U.S. interests control more than 89 per cent of the oil business, 80 per cent of banana exports, 89 per cent of the gold, silver, and platinum mining, 98 per cent of the production and distribution of electricity and gas, and 68 per cent of iron and steel production. The sectors still open to Colombian initiative are the manufactures of biscuits, bread, spaghetti, beer, and fats, the textile industry, civil construction, and coffee production.

Accounts for the ten-year period 1952–1961 reveal that the total remittance of funds abroad exceeded revenues from exports by $500 million. This deficit had to be compensated by loans, which mortgaged the national economy still further and which already amounted to more than $2 billion. The U.S. investments in the aforementioned sectors, and in banks and commercial enterprises connected with import and export, as well as the loans tied to purchases in the United States or the contracting of her firms' services, are structured as a gigantic system of drains on the national economy. By this means U.S. firms are appropriating the greater part of Colombian export production. Its effects can be measured macroscopically by the fact that the annual growth in the Colombian population (2.9 per cent), by surpassing the national income rate of growth (2.1 per cent), is sentencing the people to an ever-worsening poverty.

The situation is not at all objectionable to the oligarchy of the nation, whose income levels, when they do not remain stable, are augmented still more through inflationary mechanisms of wage confiscation. The concentration of wealth in the hands of this oligarchy can be appreciated by a glance at certain indexes. Thus, 70 per cent of the rural proprietors own 7 per cent of the land (1.9 million hectares), whereas 0.9 per cent of the proprietors own 40.9 per cent (11.2 million hectares). In the business world, in 1961, a minority of 6.1 per cent of the stockholders in corporations and joint-stock companies held 54 per cent of the capital, whereas 68 per cent of the stockholders owned only 2.5 per cent. In the distribution of national income 5.6 per cent of the Colombians earned in that same year 40 per cent of the national product, leaving the rest to all the others.

Industrial development through installation of factories by the great monopolies not only permitted annulling the effectiveness of customs barriers but turned protectionism upside down, making it serve foreign interests. For lack of any control over the movement of capital funds and profits, this mechanism transforms even the natural progress of the country into merely added efficacy in spoliative drain.

It thus becomes plain how a peripheral national economy can be at once highly lucrative for foreign investors and their local associates, and visibly disproportioned, spoliative, and deficit-making for its own population. It is likewise clear that the people's poverty and the nation's backwardness, as conditions necessary to oligarchic and imperialistic plundering, are therefore profitable. This situation, apparently unviable because of the small numbers in the privileged caste as compared with the massive size of the plundered, has been maintained by dint of a social order that straitjackets the nation, allowing it only a deformed growth, at the cost of much greater sacrifices than penury and backwardness per se.

The Barracks State

In Venezuela, as in Colombia, the people waged and won the war of independence, but peace and freedom were regulated by the oligarchy in the shape of a social, economic, and political order that subjected everything to its interests. Remaining latifundian and slavocratic, the dominant caste appropriated everything it desired, and more, of the properties promised to the combatants, who were cheated of them by their own leaders, who in turn joined the oligarchy.

Bolívar, removed from political command, died after seeing the frustration of his plans to establish the Patria Grande, embracing all Latin Americans, and after the fragmentation of even the dreamed-of confederation of Gran Colombia (1821–1830), which was to unite in a single national state what are now Ecuador, Colombia, and Venezuela. Throughout Spanish America, in every economically configured region, in nearly every port and its neighboring commercial area, an unviable nation was installed, dominated by the rich Creoles, now the heroes of independence and its masters, now richer and more powerful, and even more voracious in exploitation of the Negro and crossbred mass. Instead of the single nation dreamed of by the liberator, a constellation of precarious nationalities was formed, incapable of opposing growing imperialistic exploitation and of carrying out the gigantic task of ending backwardness and poverty.

With independence, political command lay in the hands of caudillos and economic power in the oligarchy of import-export merchants, coffee planters in the Andean zone, cacao and tobacco and cotton and sugar planters along the coast, and cattle producers on the plains. All added up to one and the same power structure. Contrary to what happened in Colombia, in Venezuela there was no conflict between the caudillos and the proprietors. (Colombia's government was structured as a republican regime, but antipopular; "democratic," but oligarchic; "free," but slavocratic and governed by a system of indirect elections; with the right to vote tied to ownership of real estate; with the death penalty for political crimes; but with full liberty to buy and sell.)

In Venezuela autocratic governments were installed, which ruled national life for 150 years. Different caudillo-led bands, agglutinated by areas—such as the Andean, those of the littoral, and the llaneros— disputed for power, each with its own troops for the maintenance of the oligarchic order against the malcontents of the respective regions. For example, a caudillo of the plains, José Antonio Páez, one of Bolívar's companions in war, imposed himself first (1830), holding power either personally or through intermediaries until 1863. Various military dictatorships followed that turned the national army into a terrorist police guard, its fidelity assured by means of all sorts of bribery to the officers. Supported by this military apparatus, governments could keep themselves in power in spite of the state of intermittent civil war represented by thirty-eight revolutions in Venezuela during the past century.

In these circumstances the state plan actually put into effect in Venezuela had the army as the only political institution, and made a kind of giant hacienda out of the public treasury, more lucrative than agriculture, cattle-raising, or commerce, and the domination over which had come to be the natural aspiration of the most powerful caudillos. Governed *manu militari* by these agents of the oligarchy, Venezuela grew sickly, with an increasingly powerful rich caste ashamed of its color, yearning to import light-skinned husbands for its daughters, opposed to the great oppressed, exploited masses of pardos and Blacks.

Periodically some liberty was permitted, like the abolition of slavery when few slaves were left and further importing of them had become impracticable, or a more liberal regulating of the right to vote in elections which were always being postponed.

At the close of the century another caudillo, Castro, took over the presidency (1899–1908). Under his rule, deterioration reached an extreme, occasioned by ruinous loans from European bankers, by the most prejudicial concessions, and by generalized corruption. The English at that time took possession of 200,000 square kilometers of Venezuela's Guiana territory. U.S. firms disputed concessions and financed revolts. British, Dutch, German, French, and Italian ships blockaded Venezuela, bombarding her ports and fortresses in 1903 and 1908, demanding payment of overdue monies. The United States, busy at the moment with the appropriation of Panama, acquiesced in the attack, alleging that the Monroe Doctrine did not apply to defaulted debtors. Besides, the Yankees had complaints about the treatment accorded their own companies.

In 1908 the presidency was seized by the caudillo Juan Vicente Gómez, also from the mountain state of Tachira, the man who was to become notorious as the most infamous of Latin American dictators. He was to remain in power until 1935, with the constant support of the United States, enforced by the guns of a cruiser and two dreadnoughts.

Gómez inaugurated a new style of understanding with the imperialist powers, yielding to all their claims and demands. His shady dealings were not in oil or imports but in the purchase of latifundia and the multiplication of herds of cattle, sectors in which his only competition came from nationals who could be jailed if he wished. To guarantee his hold on power he reorganized the army, giving posts of command to men in his confidence from his own state, and restructured the police to avoid possible rebellions, thus stamping out any attempt at sedition.

The foreign oil firms, with the setback their affairs had suffered in revolutionary, increasingly haughty, and nationalistic Mexico, approached Venezuela, attracted by her boundless oil reserves. Gómez welcomed them, putting the trusts' lawyers in charge not only of preparing the contracts for concessions but also of the wording of the very legislation regulating the exploitation. In such fashion was created a land of promise for Standard Oil and Royal Dutch Shell, which in a few years lifted Venezuela from an insignificant position to rank as the second largest oil producer in the world in 1928. By that time the sales of concessions for oil exploitation made up half of the Venezuelan budget.

With these funds Gómez paid off the foreign debt, established a strong currency, put together a personal fortune of more than $200 million, largely in lands, cattle, and coffee plantations, and enriched his whole family, including his 100 bastard children and the officers of his forces of repression. Simultaneously, however, the Venezuelan economy, deformed by the impact of the oil exploitation, fell into collapse. The "prosperity" had amounted to a rise in wages and costs that thrust agriculture and the cattle industry into a permanent crisis, above all in the production of foodstuffs, making the nation more and more dependent on imports and marginalizing the rural population. To maintain the regime in power, still greater repression became necessary, first against students and nationalistic intellectuals, and later, increasingly, against the unemployed masses seeking opportunities for work in order to live.

Jails were filled, some of them notorious, such as La Rotunda. Venezuelan jailers became celebrated torturers and murderers. The best of the country's intellectual class was imprisoned, subjected to forced labor, or exiled. Another product of the Gómez dictatorship was the emergence of a vast following of adventurers and adulators, made fat by the government and the oil firms. They trampled on one another in their eagerness to flatter, in order to merit the gratuities, consisting of shares in foreign enterprises and bills of exchange, which Gómez always carried in his pockets to distribute among the most servile. One of them made himself outstanding in his effort to supply an ideological basis for the dictatorship, terming it "democratic Caesarism" and characterizing it as both necessary and ideal for a mestizo, primitive, backward race whose innate lack of discipline required a strong hand and whose childishness demanded an energetic, castigating, but benevolent and generous father. Venezuela reached its nadir under the dictatorship of Gómez, who sickened, degraded, and rotted the whole nation.

In the same period, however, the financial success of the oil firms reached its apogee. Their happiness knew no limits, precisely because Gómez was the reverse of President Cárdenas of Mexico, who in those same years had deprived them of their domination of the Mexican oil fields. In consequence the U.S. government heaped decorations on Gómez and placed all the Yankee police forces in all areas of the world at his service, to keep watch over and persecute Venezuelan exiles who might conspire against the dictatorship.

From the United States point of view this economy, dominated by her oil corporations, represented the ideal pattern of entrepreneurial relations with the state. Nor did the army officer caste, growing richer and richer, or the Gómez oligarchy, nourished on the leftovers, have any reason to oppose it. The only flaw in the system was the Venezuelan people, which, to the displeasure of the rest, continued in spite of everything to multiply hugely and to ask for jobs that did not exist and were growing even scarcer. The ideal thing, perhaps, would be to eliminate Venezuelans from Venezuela, leaving only 100,000 well-subsidized residents who could lead a pampered existence. This being impracticable, only the alternative of the whip, the jail, and terror was left to maintain the wealth of the most lucrative corporations in the world.

In this period of economic euphoria and superprofits for the U.S. firms and the opulent national oligarchy, the Venezuelan common people suffered the most terrible burdens of hunger, all the concomitant diseases resulting from want, and infant mortality and illiteracy. Thrust into the cities by the abandonment of agricultural utilization—land had become an object of speculation, and whether it produced or not mattered little—the peasant masses crowded together in slums that contrasted with the old residential sections like cancerous sores. Without piped water, electric light, sewers, foods, schools, or hospitals, the "sovereign people" lived and died under police surveillance, while power was exercised in the name of that people, revising laws and formalizing new contracts of concessions. The economic statistics published at that time (on heavy glossy paper) demonstrated, nevertheless, that this people enjoyed one of the highest living standards in the world, if measured by per capita national income.

Gómez being mortal, at the age of seventy-seven and after more than a quarter of a century of dictatorship, died one day in his palace. His satellites concealed his death as best they could, fearing the consequences of its becoming known. Despite precautions taken to restrain the populace, when the news was divulged the rebellion exploded, spreading and invading everything like the waters from a burst dam. The multitude took to the streets possessed by an unconfined sense of freedom. After years of silence and terror, the unarmed people confronted the repressive troops and put them to flight; it improvised public rallies; it attacked homes of those who had collaborated with the dictatorship, killing the occupants found there; it burned buildings of oil companies; it assaulted prisons, freeing the political prisoners who had survived; it destroyed foreign clubs and business houses. The U.S. employees of the oil fields and their families were rounded up and hastily put aboard the tankers anchored off the coast. The U.S.-backed dictator had fallen, and the Venezuelan people, freed at last, wanted revenge for years of oppression, misery, and torture.

While the people in the streets were giving anarchic vent to their feeling of liberation, the oligarchy was conspiring to some purpose. Before the popular animus cooled down, Gómez's own minister of war, from the same State of Tachira, was installing himself as president, with control of the whole machine of repression. Very soon the renovating wave was being contained by troops in all regions. The popular movements became more disciplined, and the oligarchy made concessions in the form of constitutional guarantees, a new electoral system, and freedom to organize unions. As a pledge of democratizing intentions, some exiled leaders were called to take part in the government.

Through all these maneuvers, when the announced elections came around, another Gómez official, General Medina, also from Tachira and also a former minister of war, took the presidency. Perceiving that it was no longer possible to hold back the wave of popular hopes for liberty and progress with simple police repression, the new president moved away from the right, assumed democratic attitudes, and announced an ambitious developmental plan. The government's iron hand relaxed, permitting leftist parties to organize. These soon polarized in two hostile groups: the communists, who supported the government on the principle of sacrificing everything to the anti-Nazi war effort, and the Partisans of Democratic Action [Acción Democrática], led by Rómulo Betancourt, who won an ever-growing support from the masses.

The military government was transformed, taking a more responsible attitude. Medina accomplished the revision of the oil contracts, initiating negotiations which later established an arrangement of fifty-fifty sharing in the liquid profits and required the companies to install refineries on Venezuelan soil, to put an end to the shame of one of the world's greatest oil producers having to import refined products from the neighboring island of Curaçao. The terms were accepted, the companies receiving in compensation a forty-year extension of their concessions and the granting of new areas, which raised their dominions from 4.4 million to 9.9 million hectares. Nevertheless, the fact is memorable, because for decades Venezuela had obtained only a maximum of 17 per cent of the profits. But for the companies the new arrangement represented the consolidation of the legislation regulating oil exploitation and the express guarantee that the government was desisting from any future judicial action against abuses previously committed.

Medina was preparing to carry out an ambitious program of works when he was overthrown by a military coup. This time young officers of professional mentality entered the political arena and delivered the coup, led by Pérez Jiménez and A. D. Challaud, with the collaboration of reformist politicians.

A government junta took office, presided over by Rómulo Betancourt and composed of four other civilians and two officers. Betancourt had prepared himself from youth, as a student leader and later in exile and conspiracy, for the struggle against the Gómez dictatorship and for the exercise of power. Beginning his career as a militant communist, he separated from that party later on to form another leftist faction, "national and independent." This is what emerged as the Acción Democrática. Public opinion was quickly won over—especially the middle classes and the unionized workers in the great enterprises—by its program of administrative austerity, representative government, electoral reform, and public well-being. Simultaneously it attracted the good will of Washington as a democratic party capable of competing with the communists for the support of the masses and of orienting the social reforms toward a liberal, conciliatory direction. The Acción Democrática won the victory sooner than it had expected, because the young officers who had deposed Medina called on the party to govern, though they remained as guardians of the new administration.

Equipped with the voluminous funds of the fifty-fifty agreement, the government junta was able to launch a broad program of national renovation that gave the Acción Democrática high accreditation in the public eye. It began by sanitizing the political milieu, freezing the assets of 150 collaborators in former administrations in order to ascertain how much they had stolen, and by reducing the salaries of high officials; it augmented the collection of taxes, and created organs of economic planning and stimulation of production. It instituted the Ministry of Labor and reorganized the unions democratically. Immediately it proceeded to public works, building low-cost homes in the capital and in the interior, opening highways, constructing irrigation systems, encouraging the mechanization of farming, improving urban services, promoting malaria eradication campaigns, and organizing a national merchant fleet. It devoted itself particularly to the enlargement and improvement of the primary, intermediate, and higher education systems.

Aiming at political consolidation, the Acción Democrática opened war on the communists, calling them inapt for democracy, and agents of the Soviets. Simultaneously it heaped attentions on the armed forces official-dom, increasing salaries and assuring it of special prerogatives. With all these credentials the Acción Democrática went into the first direct elections ever held in Venezuela with suffrage granted to all over eighteen years of age (1948). Its candidate for the presidency was Rómulo Gallegos, the most celebrated Venezuelan intellectual and a veteran democratic combatant. The people gave him 85 per cent of their votes. That majority expressed their wish to see the government's progressive policy and popular orientation continued and amplified, and the agrarian reform carried out, as the major theme of the electoral campaign.

A few months later another military coup supervened, brought about by the same group of young officers who had composed the junta, in spite of all efforts by Betancourt and Gallegos to win their support. Planned in Washington (which was worried by the democratic agitation in Venezuela), the coup was executed within a few hours without resistance. There was no general workers' strike and no revolt by a million peasants armed with machetes, both of which were used by reformist leaders to threaten the oligarchy. Comporting themselves as "saviors" who proposed leading the nation to abundance and to freedom, the Acción Democrática leaders found themselves cast out of the populist government without the people manifesting any reaction to the "loss" of the power exercised in its name.

Pérez Jiménez ended by imposing himself as dictator and inaugurating terrorism, alleging that the regime was incapable of preventing the extremist infiltration that threatened institutions. The United States instantly recognized the new administration, whose titular head would be decorated a year later by Eisenhower himself with the highest Yankee honor.

Once more the oil companies had won, ridding themselves of the worry represented by a democratic regime that assured the people an increasingly active part in political life. Performing its function as an instrument of foreign domination, the new military regime derogated freedom of union organization, substituting for it an accommodating syndicalism, and it handed over to the Rockefeller and Morgan groups, practically free, the country's iron mining, which would supply U.S. foundries.

Venezuela thus returned to the Gómez policy. Besides the concessions of mineral deposits without reciprocal compensation, the foreign firms were assured of the exploitation of national labor through work contracts fixed by the government itself. Moreover, they were guaranteed, by means of police repression, the desired atmosphere of "social tranquility indispensable to productive work."

The Pérez Jiménez dictatorship lasted for ten years, restoring in every way the Gómez style: press censorship, persecution of the student movement, and police terrorism against the workers, the leftists, and the manifestations of despair by the starving and unemployed. According to its own phrasing, it had in view the preparation of the people for self-government, "depolitizing" the nation and freeing it from the dominion of demagogues and communists.

Another characteristic of this dictatorship was its pharaohism, its love of display, expressed in the caricaturish exaggeration of taste for public sumptuary works. In Pérez Jiménez's decade of power Caracas was transformed by the quantity of buildings, from luxury hotels to sumptuous military clubs, schools, and hospitals. All this was constructed in the capital, where more than half of the public expenditures was concentrated, and to appease a privileged minority. Trotting in the tracks of Gómez, this latest dictator amassed a fortune of more than $250 million, with which he fled the country on being overthrown in 1958.

His outrages finally unified against him all the political sectors of Venezuela, even the Church, so indisposed as a rule to move against dictatorships. At the last even the armed forces officers—those not involved in the repressive activities—joined in the fight against the dictatorship. Pérez Jiménez was overthrown by the union of these forces under the leadership of a Junta Patriótica made up of civilians, which called a general strike simultaneously with *pronunciamentos* by military groups. In January 1959 Admiral Larrazábal assumed the presidency, seeking to organize the government and tackle national problems, appealing to all sectors and restoring the climate of freedom.

The Venezuelan people had the opportunity to demonstrate against Yankee spoliation when Richard Nixon came to visit. His escort was received by an indignant multitude that stoned, spat, and jeered at him from Marquetía Airport to Caracas. Another crowd awaited him later at Bolívar's tomb, where he was to lay the conventional wreath of flowers, and prevented him from getting out of the car. Eisenhower, angered at the treatment accorded his vice-president, mobilized paratroopers and marine infantry from the Puerto Rico and Trinidad bases. Admiral Larrazábal's firm attitude, however, dissuaded the Americans from any attempt at disembarking. Nixon continued his trip amid other but less energetic booing, because in no other Latin American nation is Yankee domination so deep and conspicuous.

The 1960 elections put Rómulo Betancourt in the presidency. Ten years after his first installation he was returning to power, not only older but transfigured. He had finally convinced the United States that he and his party represented its ideal allies in Venezuela. He returned with the popular majority vote, which reflected trust in the reformist program of the Acción Democrática, but Betancourt was committed to precisely those same entrepreneurial groups and the oligarchy that had deposed him before and that he was now wooing assiduously as the real power that could not be ignored. From reformist, the Acción Democrática had become patrician.

Bitterly marked by the experience of his deposition and his ten years of exile, Betancourt would thenceforth do everything to remain in power and finish his term. He began by trying to match the prestige of Fidel Castro, whose revolutionary figure had roused the enthusiasm of the multitudes of Latin America. He went so far as to present himself and to be depicted abroad as "the democratic Fidel," as the champion of Kennedy's Alliance for Progress, as the liberal reformer.

The Acción Democrática, appearing after a century and a half of caudillo despotism, took on the profile of a national reform movement devoted to the struggle for development. Once consolidated in power, it revealed its true face, that of a belated patriciate, capable only of acting as agent of the oligarchic and imperialistic domination. The new Betancourt, elevated to the presidency, quickly dropped all disguises to drown in blood, to silence with censorship, and to check with jail and torture the national emancipation movements that he himself had helped mature and unleash.[3]

In all these decades of military pronouncements, coups, and revolutions, an antipopular order always prevailed in Venezuela, first in a caudillo, but national, aspect that took possession of power when the republic was promulgated; then as a cosmopolitan-caudillo when, to enrich itself and hold on to power, it became an imperialist instrument of containment of its people; and finally as a patrician-cosmopolite, initiated with the two administrations of Rómulo Betancourt (made president by officers who always remained his guardians) and continued until now.

Since independence, with this conspiracy a natural division of work has been established between the latifundian oligarchy—which wanted to take care of its lands and the bovine and human cattle living on them—and the soldiers and their patrician associates who aspired to political power, moved by the ideals of also becoming coffee planters and cattle ranchers or, through the same route, enjoying the privilege of exploiting the other "hacienda"—the public treasury. Then, as now, the objective of the caudillo and patrician governments has been the perpetuation of the old

[3] Rómulo Betancourt's political about-face is depicted by a U.S. American delighted with his "understanding" and "democratic" figure: "In sharp contrast with his sectarian political attitude of the 1945–1948 period, the 1959 Betancourt revealed a spirit of compromise and cooperation in his dealings with other political parties. . . . He is not abandoning the Acción Democrática program, but applying it more slowly and cautiously, using the methods of diplomacy and persuasion" (E. Lieuwen, 1965, p. 129).

oligarchic order, submissive to the foreign interests that guarantee their social precedence based on wealth and political power against any uprising that might endanger it.

The Republic, born of the essential opposition of interests between the native-born Spaniards and the Creole patriciate, with both sides disputing economic opportunities, positions, and honors, was structured as a mechanism to perpetuate privilege. The few thousand large proprietors, obviously unable to direct the nation within the framework of a democratic order that permitted questioning the validity of the bases of the regime, required the dominating presence of military power to impose the oligarchic will and maintain its domination over the people. This was all the more necessary in the first decades after independence, when popular rebellions caused by the oligarchic groups disputing colonial spoils put the system in imminent peril. And it became even more imperative when other "haciendas" came into the economic picture: the administration of the foreign oil businesses and the public treasury.

The military performed its subjugating role, but exacted payment for it by joining, with its families, the dominant group. This could go on expanding up to a certain limit, through enlargement of the area of agricultural and pastoral exploitation and the simultaneous increase in available labor for production. At first the system had the advantage of also permitting utilization of the increasing common people through multiplication of the units of agropastoral exploitation on the new economic frontiers. When the abolition of slavery altered labor relations, small innovations made it possible to integrate the freed Negro into the mass of free people, disciplining him to the status of renter by the imperative of working for a master as the requisite for survival.

But what was to be done after exhausting these possibilities of broadening the social structure by amplifying the exploited areas? And, above all, when would the installation of an economic enclave of high dynamic power, such as oil production, lead the whole agrarian system into a crisis? Preserving the monopoly of land and regulating petroleum exploitation by foreign enterprises became more and more difficult on the emergence of reformist and revolutionary popular leaders aware of the causes of national backwardness and determined to attack them.

Thus the dilemma recurred that had been posed since the first years of national life by the opposition between the reordinating, radical project of the irredentist popular struggles and the objective of political emancipation as the project of the native oligarchy and patriciate. The struggles were renewed in the most barbarous forms for the Venezuelan people. In these circumstances it became clear that the only chance of survival for the oligarchy and the patriciate was maintenance of the status quo by repression and terror, in the profound conviction that any liberalness toward the people would inevitably eliminate the elite from the national political picture.

The Yankee Showcase

The extractive oil industry emerged in Venezuela as a new business that would generate customs revenues and fees that could enable the system to continue operating after reaching the limits of expansion of the oligarchic caste, by opening new areas. Requiring still greater care by the administration to protect foreign interests and maintain the discipline and social peace indispensable to their work, this new sector turned corrupter from the very first. In the end it was revealed as the most profitable business in the nation, but too complicated for natives to handle. For the military and the oligarchy it came to represent the hen that laid golden eggs.

The oil development was to generate, besides taxes and fees, other products that gradually changed the archaic nature of the social structure. New strata were added, some integrated into its productive system as the working class and the white-collar class; others entered the ranks of urban employees required for the functions of the state, of commerce, and of the enormously amplified services; still others constituted a vast marginalized urban mass.

The schedule of imports was enlarged simultaneously, thanks to the exemption of funds in strong currencies, which permitted expanded use of industrial manufactures. Thus crafts production for popular consumption was wiped out, dislocating other masses from the productive system. The oil economy contributed, moreover, to the stagnation of the agricultural exploitation system, limited in its capacity for technological renovation and structurally frozen by the regime of property, which reached the labor saturation point. The people, displaced from the country as no longer necessary to the productive system, were attracted to the cities in increasingly larger masses.

The system was incapable of integrating the multiplying urban population into the economy and society. The people became mired in want and disillusionment. The growth of these contingents was to result in new demands on the machinery of repression, the only recourse available to silence their hunger and despair. In consequence, the armed forces performing this task became still more valuable.

The present dominant class of Venezuela is composed of two mutually complementary bodies: the patronate, the boss class, of latifundian and urban large proprietors and the patriciate of high-ranking military officers, political leaders, and the upper hierarchy of the Church. Together with these castes a new class, incorrectly designated as the national bourgeoisie, makes up the dominant team. This is the bureaucratic patronate, created by substitutive industrialization financed by the state through its program of "sowing industries" throughout the country and enriched as the promoters of public works. Its very origin, artificial and particularly ambivalent—being created by the donation of public funds and motivated by a falsely free-enterprise privatist ideology—does not allow it an independent posture in national political life. For the same reason, practically it is confused with the "management class," composed principally of foreigners, which administers the great oil and iron entrepreneurial interests. The bureaucratic patronate is a clientele of henchmen of the patriciate; the managers, scrupulously selected administrators trained and controlled by their employers to look after the latter's money, are characterized by fidelity to the system that permits them to rise socially and, in consequence of that, total adherence to the free-enterprise system and to external economic dependency.

The bureaucratic caste's privatism is the best expression of the ideological alienation of Venezuelan underdevelopment, which, persuaded of the superiority of private over state management, permits donating public funds to privileged individuals chosen for their servility or their political connections, enriching them with what belongs to the nation. Once this bureaucratic ideology is implanted, even when the state finds itself obliged to organize public enterprises in those sectors where it is impossible to attract any private participation, it does so provisionally, declaring its readiness to transfer the investment at the earliest opportunity. Thus the bureaucratic patronate is identified with the management class, and both with the political patriciate of the powerful directors of public services and state financial and producing agencies, in an antinational complot to support foreign spoliation and maintain the latifundian oligarchy.

To round out the picture of the Venezuelan dominant class, other categories differentiated by their functions but unified in their antinational attitude must be added to the bureaucratic caste. These include the cohort of administrative lawyers, technocrats who operate as intermediaries between the private enterprises and the government bureaus; the populist politicians, who pin their hopes of power and enrichment on riding the crest of the popular movements; and the middle class of bureaucrats, members of the liberal professions, middling and small proprietors, public officials and employees, also beneficiaries of the system of exploitation. All of them, as long as they are university students, permit themselves free political activity, induced by dissatisfaction with the backwardness and poverty to which the system condemns the majority of their fellow countrymen. After graduation, however, most settle into their social functions and into roles befitting maintainers of the regime.

The people, in city and country, dichotomizes into profoundly different strata, one integrated into the productive system, the other marginalized from it. The former is made up of the petty number who succeed in getting jobs in the large corporations, where they earn high wages and enjoy certain privileges; it is the proletariat which has waged its own "revolution" by having put an enormous distance between it and the living conditions of the disinherited masses. It is characterized by the fear of being cast into the outer darkness of the marginal mass. To this relatively privileged stratum is opposed another urban contingent, poorer and much more numerous—the occasional workers or underemployed in the middling and small enterprises.

This first stratum is paralleled in agricultural economy by the mass of rural laborers, both the stable, yoked to the latifundium, and the occasional, who work only seasonally in the coffee and cacao harvests, in cutting cane, and in other such tasks.

The second stratum is formed by those driven from the haciendas who fail to establish themselves as *conuqueros* (renters or owners of tiny patches of the latifundia) and concentrate in the rural vacant lands, from which they are progressively ousted, on which they turn to the spreading outskirts of the cities, especially Caracas. There they are herded into the most wretched living conditions, working now and then at odd jobs, surviving almost by a miracle. This contingent, marginal to the economy and to society because it is illiterate, undernourished, unprepared for urban life, and underemployed, is the principal product of an exogenous economic system, incapable of assuring employment for this mass because it is not structured to serve the Venezuelan people but a narrow, privileged caste.

The whole petroleum industry, which produces 15 per cent of the world's consumption, employs only 35,000 workers, and this number is constantly decreasing despite the increase in production, owing to the technical level of the extractive process and auxiliary services. Wages, though high in comparison to the local ones, are plainly stratified by nationality, the foreigners' pay being much higher. So, of the 1,629 employees receiving more than 4,000 bolívares, only 314 are Venezuelans. That is not just because some functions require greater training and qualifications, but because of the management policy of prohibiting the mastery of processing techniques to Venezuelans, so that for lack of technical personnel the country can never take over the enterprises.

Oil exploitation produces 60 per cent of Venezuela's state revenues, bearing practically alone the cost of national imports. It affects the economy negatively, however, by the volume of imports required and especially by the introduction of a pattern of outstanding consumption that absorbs all the revenues, leading the nation to a deficit in foreign-exchange credits that has to be covered with foreign loans.

To illustrate: Venezuela annually exports $1.5 billion in petroleum, most of it for the U.S. market, but she also imports annually $1 billion in automobiles, refrigerators, machines, materials for industry and construction, and foodstuffs, constituting the United States's best customer. Furthermore, Venezuela pays $500 million annually on amortization of loans, subsidizations of transport, insurance, royalties, and technical aid. It is therefore a high-yield economy for the foreign investor, but extortionate for the Venezuelan people, whose government is frequently obliged to go to the international bankers to apply for new loans to pay the old. In recent years the imbalance of payments has been covered principally by the sale of new concessions to the same firms, in spite of the fact that the existing reserves are only sufficient for eighteen years of production at the 1959 rate, which has subsequently been increased.

A U.S. specialist gives the following balance of accounts of the Venezuelan economy in this sector:

In 1957 government sale of petroleum amounted to $1.23 billion, a great part of which came from the sale of new concessions, while the liquid profits of the corporations totaled $829 million. The liquid investment of those corporations to the end of 1957 would reach $2.578 billion, so that the profit on the capital investment was 32.5 per cent (E. Lieuwen, 1965, p. 143).

Venezuelan economists add a third to that estimate of the profits going out of the country in the form of payments of transport, insurance, and royalties, not to mention bookkeeping manipulations of the petroleum companies. For example, the Banco Central de Venezuela showed that with the liquid profits earned in 1954 alone these enterprises amortized all the investments made up to that year.

More shocking still is the situation of the iron mining exploitations by U.S. corporations. In this case, as occurs in oil, the Yankees prefer to leave their own ore deposits as reserves and develop the Venezuelan natural resources, for two reasons: (1) in the case of the oil, because each well in Venezuela yields fifteen times the profit, and as regards the iron, because the iron content of the ore is much higher; (2) because they providently consider it better to conserve their natural riches for future use, at least as long as there are plunderable peoples in the outside world. To make the exploitation possible, the Venezuelan government not only conceded, nearly gratis, ore beds later evaluated at more than $10 billion, but also installed new electric plants that cost more than the whole investment in all of Venezuelan iron mining, to make the foreign deal viable.

The exploitation of those enormous ore deposits dates from only a few years back, but it has grown at a dizzying rate, jumping from 199,000 tons in 1950 to 17 million in 1959. All this ore is extracted in the open air by the most modern techniques, employing only 4,000 national workmen. It is transported on the companies' own railroads and ships directly to the steel works of Bethlehem Steel (Rockefeller) and U.S. Steel (Morgan). From 1950 to 1962, 126 million metric tons of iron ore were exported by that route, with an approximate value of $1 billion, more than half of which remained in the United States, the rest being retained to cover investments, wages, and taxes. These last are ridiculous, for they reach only some 85 million bolívares annually, that is, less than half of the revenue from tobacco taxes. The underbilling of this exportation—quoted at $8.17 per ton, when international prices run about $19.53—became evident when it was known that the Yankees were collecting more in Panama Canal tolls per ton of iron ore from Japanese ships than was registered as the export value with the Venezuelan government. In such circumstances, it is estimated that the profit obtained in this sector by the Yankee monopolistic enterprises covers annually, from 1957 on, half of the investment.

The two extractive industries, absorbing 90 per cent of the foreign investments—$5.4 billion—employed fewer than 40,000 Venezuelans, or 1.8 per cent of the working population, accounting, even so, for 96.7 per cent of the value of the national exports. The local substitutive industry— textiles, foodstuffs, beverages, cement, steel, tobacco, rubber, and other products—employs 300,000 workers, or 17 per cent of the working population.

This industry is almost exclusively the product of state investments, although privatized by the transfer of the public funds used for that purpose to private groups through favored financing and other special privileges. To the manufacturing sectors for production of general consumer goods were added, in recent years, systems of production of hydroelectric power, transport, warehousing, packing houses, mills, a siderurgical plant, and the beginnings of petrochemistry, which could lay the foundations for an autonomous Venezuelan industrial development. Meanwhile, the free-enterprise mentality permeating all the state bureaus and departments has threatened to transfer these undertakings to private hands also, even if their surrender to foreign firms results in losing whatever possibilities they offer for keeping within the country some centers of decision-making about national development.

The cultivating of tropical products (coffee, cacao), despite accounting for only 3.3 per cent of the value of exports, employs ten times more labor than mineral extraction does. The twelve principal sugar mills alone give more work opportunities than the whole great extractive industry. The essential characteristic of Venezuelan industry is its high operational cost, which for the people results in increasingly high prices, and for the economy, in high production costs, practicable only by means of continual subsidies and an increasingly burdensome customs protection. This is the result of the ancillary character assumed by the whole national subsistence production in relation to the export economy.

Such is the exogenous economy of Venezuela and the society it has engendered, marked by a discriminatory and antipopular social order, originally dictated by the old oligarchy's interests and modified only to accord with and facilitate foreign exploitation. Obviously, the foreign entrepreneur and his local associates profit by it, but the Venezuelan people has neither role nor function in it. The people, in fact, persist in increasing in number, annoying the owners of the country by compelling them to invent artificial distributive mechanisms to employ the populace somehow, and likewise to maintain perilous repressive systems that some day may bring about their own ruin.

Venezuela, never a target for immigrants, after the war came to receive considerable contingents, estimated at .5 million, for the most part European refugees. They were attracted by successive governments preoccupied with "improving the race" and establishing a new society. For a nation in which the greatest surplus was people, this immigration policy, besides being extremely onerous, represented the most odious discrimination against the Venezuelan people, which saw the best work opportunities escape to foreign competitors, artificially attracted at the nation's expense for principally racist motives.

The whole system has no future simply because the Venezuelans exceed 9 million already, and, in spite of misery or in consequence of it, they are increasing at the rate of 3.66 per cent per year, concentrating mainly in the cities, where the population doubles every ten years. Despite being marginalized, they are not blind to the fact that their misery is highly lucrative for the great world of the rich. And inevitably they will mature to impose, some day, a reorganization of the social order that will give them, too, a place in the sun.

Agrarian reform, the subject of much debate during the last decade, has already made the peasant conscious about his right to the land he works, consequently about the spoliative nature of the regime to which he is subject, and, further, about the iniquity and abuse inherent in owning the land and not using it or letting others use it. Hence the present real estate speculation that they call "agrarian reform"—paying such compensatory prices for the "appropriated" lands that the latifundia proprietors are rushing to the government bureaus, vying with each other to be dispossessed —will be followed one day by a real agrarian reform, capable of guaranteeing the land to him who works it and of eliminating the latifundian oligarchy from the Venezuelan social landscape.

A reversion of the armed forces to an autonomous nationalist position with respect to the oligarchy and opposed to imperialist spoliation—a position that seemed to be announced in the action of the Medina administration and of the young officers who succeeded it in power, motivated by the democratic ideals of the last years of World War II—aborted lamentably. By that time the international conjuncture of the imperialistic powers in dispute, which had permitted some military autocracies to play the part of emancipatory forces, had been replaced by the hegemony of the United States as the imperialistic superpower. In the frustration of that attempt the Yankeefication of the army thus had a decisive part. The training was carried on by means of military missions of cold war indoctrination with the aim of orienting the Venezuelan armed forces for the role of guardians of world order according to the designs and interests of the United States.

The inauguration of a democratic administration in 1958 (free elections, open to the entire adult population, resulted in the victory of opposition leaders who had suffered years of imprisonment and exile) was hailed by the Venezuelans as the long-awaited prerequisite for overcoming deformations accumulated over decades of despotism and for vanquishing underdevelopment. But the hopes thus awakened were short-lived. It soon became clear that the new leaders were nothing more than a patriciate of professional politicians and, as such, incapable of promoting indispensable structural reforms and confronting the rural and urban patronal class. It was powerless to end foreign spoliation because it had promised, as a condition of winning office, to safeguard North American interests. Corruption and favoritism worsened. Just as with the military dictatorships, public funds became the principal source of bribery and enriched the patriciate's clienteles.

Disenchantment spread rapidly, undermining ideological support of the new regime among intellectuals, students, and, later, unionized workers. This ebb of the tide came precisely when the Cuban revolution, in establishing a new way to overcome backwardness for Latin Americans, challenged both the Venezuelan left and the Venezuelan right to consider new options. The left was challenged to abandon its reformist policy of conciliation and devote itself to the revolutionary struggle for power. The right was challenged to demonstrate that it was able to attain development through an effort of self-support carried out within institutional frameworks. The

United States, in its turn, being vitally interested in the rivalry between Venezuelan and Cuban models of development, encouraged Rómulo Betancourt to set himself up as the standard-bearer of the Alliance for Progress and as the Latin American anti-Fidel who would point the way to development for the area where the major American investments were concentrated.

In the midst of this international struggle the various ideological currents within the Democratic Action Party, now in power, came into conflict. The most nationalistic faction finally left the government party to form a new one, the Leftist Revolutionary Movement (MIR). The bulk of the Democratic Action Party gradually moved further and further to the right, until it was confused with its former antagonists, who came to look on it as a new political elite, more efficacious and worthy of trust than the military dictatorships which had preceded it.

In 1961 an insurrectional movement broke out, first through military sedition and then with rural guerrillas, a movement that disturbed the country until 1964. Those combats were the bloodiest and most widespread fighting recorded in all Latin America during the 1960's, and also the only ones that united the leftist factions into a National Liberation Front, the only ones that had ample support from both intermediate sectors and the common people. The movement failed, however, for these reasons: the difficulty of reproducing the Cuban model of social revolution begun by guerrilla units; the wealth of the Venezuelan state, which enabled it to endure years of war without a crisis supervening; aid from the United States, both material and technical, in the organization and training of anti-guerrilla forces in the armed services and of police organs of anti-subversive repression; and, finally, the sagacity of the patrician elites. These last, preserving a simulacrum of representative government while working hand-in-hand with a mechanism of ferocious repression, put down the guerrillas while at the same time they awakened an eagerness for peace at any price in the majority of the populace. Isolated from their popular bases of support, the combatant units were defeated time after time, until at last they had to retreat.

At this point the unity of the leftists was broken. Arguments over revolutionary strategy broke out in Venezuela. On one side were mainly the communists, urging pacification in order to reorganize the revolutionary forces, and emphasizing the need to resume contact with the people by means of institutional mechanisms, both political and syndical. On the opposite side, the radical groups, polarized around a few guerrilla commanders who had survived, urged the prosecution of the war, even though they no longer entertained any hope of gaining power. The guerrilla had been turned, in fact, into a form of protest by which the extreme left declared its convictions while it waited for a new revolutionary strategy to be defined.

The Venezuelan revolution thus collapsed. At the same time the reflex modernization of the economy and of Venezuelan society proceeded at an accelerated pace. Branches of the great multinational enterprises, principally North American, came to produce every kind of consumer goods within the country; and the cities grew, their sumptuous buildings multiplying, giving the impression of extraordinary progress. And yet the irreducibly dependent character of the new economy perverted the very industrialization and technicalization of the other productive sectors, converting them into analogous mechanisms for strengthening foreign ties and neocolonial spoliation.

At this juncture the old problems of an economy prodigiously lucrative for foreign investors and their local associates, but an economy whose prosperity could not reach the whole of the population, once more arose, and in a still sharper form. The high indexes of demographic increment—higher than the rate of economic increment—caused the cities to burgeon beyond the affluent urbanized zones. Clusters of shacks and shantytowns multiplied and caused the marginalized contingent—because it did not succeed in integrating into the regular work force—to increase faster than the strata incorporated into the new, reflexly modernized economy.

For the privileged minority the marginalized people are a "super-population," an excess of labor which the minority seeks to eliminate progressively through programs of birth control subsidized by the United States government. However, as that periphery of the marginalized (now concentrated in the cities and prone to aspire to the consumption levels of the integrated sectors) continues to swell,[4] the tendency grows to regard it not merely as a miserable mass without regular employment, but as a menace to the system itself, because the system is not capable of absorbing these people into the national work force. Thus a demographic increment which, in relation to Venezuela's size and potential and to its low index of occupation of its own territory, would be highly welcome is actually regarded as catastrophic because it is incompatible with the maintenance of the current socioeconomic order.

In consequence, the Venezuelan elites find themselves confronted with the dilemma of choosing between two alternatives. First, to safeguard the existing order by moving from the practice of complaisant planned parenthood to compulsory birth control, which is to say, reaching the extreme of genocide. Second, to break the constrictions inherent in the system in order to allow the Venezuelan people to increase normally and to achieve its immense potential. Each group of interests, each ideological current with the capacity to exert any influence on the national life, has made its choice. The ideo-

---

[4] Recent studies indicate that the Venezuelan population will triple in the next few decades, rising to nearly 30 million in the year 2000. The population of Caracas will increase from 2 million to 6 million. The agricultural work force, barely 25% of the active population, will drop to 10% in the same period.

logues of the privileged members of the system, who seek to preserve it at all costs, see in the intensification of dependence and in the limitation of population growth the solution most favorable to themselves. That solution, if carried to the extreme of its possibilities, will lead to the "Puerto-Ricanization" of Venezuela. The most enlightened sectors, those most sensitive to their national identification, are becoming convinced that the preservation of Venezuela for itself, and the realization of its people's potential, cannot take place within the existing system. These goals will be attained only by means of a revolutionary and socialist rupture.

The Sociology of Violence

The maintenance of the oligarchic social order in collusion with foreign associates is accomplished in Colombia only by means of the most savage, bloody violence. Even in a convulsed area such as Latin America, where the misery and the backwardness of the masses and the alienation of the elites perpetuate institutional instability and periodic rebellions, Colombian violence stands out as a terrifying social "dysfunction." According to Diego Montaña Cuéllar (1963, p. 27), from 1830 to 1903 Colombia experienced twenty-nine constitutional alterations, nine great national civil wars, and fourteen local ones, two wars with Ecuador, three mutinies, and one unsuccessful conspiracy. In each of these confrontations the conquered were left to the mercy of the conquerors, who confiscated their property and compelled them to move elsewhere with their families in search of refuge. These cases of violence, engendering a heritage of hatred and resentment, a spirit of revenge and vendetta that passes from generation to generation, aggravate and worsen a climate already tense because of conflicting interests, spoliation, and revolt.

All these conflicts, however, were mere preambles to the unleashing of the unbridled violence that was to follow. The first of these conflicts exploded in 1903, nominally between the allies of the two great patrician political parties, the Liberals and the Conservatives, extending through 1,000 days of terror and costing the lives of 100,000 Colombians. These two parties are essentially identical in orientation, both having defended, at different times, the same position in regard to all questions debated in national politics; they have always been solidly in agreement about the maintenance of oligarchic privileges, on which they systematically united whenever a real threat of reform arose. But they are also the most differentiated, the most important, and also the most sinister national institutions. A Colombian, be he rich or poor, is born either Liberal or Conservative. A frightfully large number of Colombians literally die for their party affiliations, or at least on account of them, or are despoiled of their property, exiled, beaten, and humiliated because of them. This does not happen to the leaders of these parties, who put into them more ambition for a career than any real partisanship; it affects the humbler people of Colombia, massively mobilized for politicopartisan identifications that polarize all their loyalties and direct them into the byways of violence. These struggles therefore turn the people's attention away from their real executioners and exploiters to focus them on phantasmagoria. By marshaling the heritage of hatred and resentment pulsing in everyone for relatives and friends decapitated, ruthlessly murdered, violated, gutted, flayed, maimed by one or the other side, the waves of violence follow one on the other. This situation has already reached such grave heights that it is affecting the very solidarity of the nation, making loyalty to the party stronger than loyalty to the country; deeply undermining the most elementary ties of human coexistence; brutalizing character through familiarization with violence and through the massive introjection of the spirit of vendetta.

The most dreadful thing about Colombian violence is that it is not a transitional phenomenon of the fall of traditional values and the emergence of new, as yet undefined, values incapable of motivating and disciplining social conduct. It is a regular mechanism, a normal function, so to speak, of political institutions that, instead of bettering the structural forms in which it originated, only contributes to perpetuating them.

Profound historicosocial eruptions, such as those experienced by so many peoples between the colonial and the national status, between the feudal and the bourgeois society, between the capitalistic and the socialistic regime, never assumed the character of chronic eruption of violence we find in Colombia. All those cases were clearly dissociative, but also self-corrective because they contributed to eliminate one order and substitute another. Here, on the contrary, the military and political institutions plunge into violence to perpetuate the over-all social order.

The very nature of the Colombian dominant class seems to play a decisive role in this process. The ruling class emerged from the conquest, in which the Spaniard raged over the indigenous peoples like a scourge, never identifying with the vassal or slave mass placed at the service of his greed. Arising out of poverty and colonial oppression, this class lured the people into the struggle for independence only to rule it afterwards under the same exploitative regime. Later, enriched, it imposed itself on the people, growing alienated both ideologically and through its economic interests, to become the native agent of the foreign exploiters. Faced with the robbery of the panama province, it was unable to react and felt guilty. In this context the manifest reluctance of the Colombian dominant caste to examine the problem of violence is symptomatic. Such avoidance reveals its fear of baring its own leading role in the implantation of violence and the nature of the violence as a defuser of social struggles.

Of all the centuries-long forms of spoliation and deformation with which the Colombian people has been cursed since the conquest, at the hands of all those who grew rich with its misery, violence is the most harmful. It has touched every Colombian like a disease. It contaminates every home, integrating all in a heritage of hate and inducing all to glorification of the criminals in their own party. This heritage, which scourges the Colombians, is on the other hand one of the fundamental pieces in the mechanism required to maintain the oligarchic domination. Surely it cannot be eradicated except by a profound structural renovation that will suppress the whole dominant caste, causing another national leadership to emerge. However, a basic requisite for this social restructuring is the capacity to polarize the combative ardor and the clamor for justice currently dividing Colombians into two fratricidal parties, in order to unify them on common revolutionary objectives to overcome the causes of backwardness and want, which are also the causes of violence.[5]

The decade 1946–1956 illustrates how a period of economic euphoria for the dominant classes can coincide with the explosion of the most terrible wave of violence among the people. Throughout this period, by means of inflation, extraordinary profits, confiscation of wages through high prices, and absorption by the public treasury of the losses in the balance of payments caused by speculation, the rich got richer, financial and industrial corporations grew and merged, the latifundium expanded, and imperialism consolidated its domination in Colombia still further. In the same period, strikes for wage raises, upsurgings by landless peasants, attempts to break the bipartisan framework of political domination were all put down with the greatest savagery and violence. It is estimated that in the course of that decade of high entrepreneurial profits and of rivers of blood and terror, more than 300,000 Colombians lost their lives.

A first, preparatory phase began with the accession to the presidency by the Conservative leader Ospina Pérez, who released a wave of terror on the people, especially the peasants, on the pretext of retaliating for violences committed against the Liberals in 1930, when an armed rebellion of the Conservatives had been violently suppressed. In point of fact, the purpose was to give the local "kinglets" of the government party the opportunity to impose their dominion on their districts by fire and sword, rewarding their devotion with the lands of peasants dislodged from their granjas and with the property of despoiled small businessmen.

[5] These problems have been studied in a profound and courageous sociological research project under the direction of Monsignor G. Guzmán Campos (1962–1964).

The terrorist confraternities of the Pagaros, bands organized by Conservative leaders and trained by Falangists to act as a frightful mestizo Ku Klux Klan, were created in 1947 to carry out this program of "political homogenization." In collusion with the police, they would rush to the townships at the call from local petty chiefs to terrorize Liberal party peasants, in order to change the local political composition by forcing mass exodus. Besides the political objectives of their masters, the bands of Pagaros and police accomplished their own designs through sadistic use of violence and plundering. They carried out genocides, on more than one occasion murdering more than 100 persons in a single night. Terror spread throughout the country, helped on by official and unofficial banditry: in the country, against the poor peasants; in cities, against the workers who dared strike, against the students who protested, and against the intellectuals who unmasked the interests that motivated violence.

Then Jorge Eliécer Gaitán rose to prominence, a populist leader with an extraordinary capacity to communicate with the masses. He was a new, educated, urban Galán, a brilliant lawyer who had become a popular orator and political leader. His prestige grew day by day, and with it the threat of checkmating patrician domination, because he refused to be identified with either Liberals or Conservatives. He called for a *Gaitanismo* not harnessed to the traditional political parties and struggled to enlist the people in an independent fight. This was Gaitán's capital sin. He was attacked by the leaderships of both parties in proportion to his growing prestige with the common classes, both Liberal and Conservative.

On April 9, 1948, Gaitán was murdered. On that day and in those following, the people burst forth in tumultuous rebellion, with world public opinion sympathetic principally because the New Panamerican Conference was currently being held in Bogotá under the presidency of General Marshall. The slaughter came to be known as the *bogotazo,* the Bogotá coup. In one night and two days the center of the city was reduced to smoking ashes: churches, government offices, banks, stores, residences—all was smashed and burned. The army, in defense of the administration, which had taken refuge in the palace, besieged by the howling mob, decimated thousands. All through the interior of the country the Gaitanists and the Liberals who still had the power and unity to do so took over local governments and unleashed violence, committing outrages and bloody vengeance against their oppressors of yesterday.

After the first days of confusion the government recovered control of the machinery of repression and spread terror over the country, thenceforth in the charge of the army instead of the police. The Liberals who had begun by collaborating in hopes of a political about-face were then forced into opposition before the determination of the Conservatives to repress or stir up violence, depending on whether it would be of service or disservice to the candidacy of Laureano Gómez. The two parties virtually waged open war, with the consequent circumstance that it was the Liberal leaders' task to incite or condemn violent acts on moral grounds, as the case might call for, while to the rank and file of Liberals, especially the peasants, fell the lot of suffering violence on their very flesh.

Laureano Gómez was elected president unanimously, such was the panic to which the people had been driven and such was the readiness of the Conservatives and their agents to kill a Liberal rather than to let him come near a polling booth. Violence only worsened with the new administration, gaining the encouragement that was never failing, given Laureano's Nazi sympathies and Falangist position, stimulated by U.S. support through loans and honors with which they rewarded him for his fidelity to their interests and for his government's having been the only one in Latin America to send troops for the Korean War.

The Colombian guerrillas then started up. They were not politically motivated, but emerged as natural and inevitable fruits of the violence unleashed on the peasants, gathering the most desperate of them together in search of refuge or vengeance. These groups were composed, in the main, of Liberal peasants unprepared militarily and ideologically for the struggle, but thrust into the guerrilla bands because they had nowhere to go, and no way to defend their surviving relatives against the Pagaros or the police.

At first the guerrillas sought to approach the army, asking its support, trusting in the Liberal leaders who dreamed of a military coup. However, making clear by their very mode of action the irreducible opposition of interests between the peasant mass and the latifundium proprietors, between the have-nots and the oligarchy, the guerrillas began to postulate social claims: better living conditions for the llaneros, restoration of their lands to the dispossessed peasants, guarantees against police terrorism, and justice. As was to be expected, they promptly lost the support of the Liberal hacenderos who joined the chorus of the Conservatives in characterizing the guerrillas as groups of communist bandits who should be eradicated by fire and sword from the jungles and the mountains.

The masters of both political parties then began suborning officers and soldiers to spur them on to further fighting and violence. In this process the guerrillas, being hunted down and harassed, were forced to organize themselves better, learning to fight and equip themselves with weapons taken in combat. They gradually succeeded in forming ties with the peasant populations, assuring them of protection against police assaults. In the regions most affected by violence some guerrilla groups managed to impose a new order on the chaos, establishing people's organizations of self-defense, structuring a local power, and promulgating "laws of the plans" to protect lives and property and to punish criminals.

Simultaneously, however, groups of adventurers multiplied who made of guerrilla warfare a way of life, debasing it into pure banditry. These groups were joined by innumerable bands of adolescents, male and female, displaced and desperate. Extremely aggressive, they would fall upon the rural populace, killing, robbing, maiming, committing violence for the sheer joy of violence. These squads of juvenile delinquents at times reached such depths of sadistic fury that they would cut to pieces ten, twenty, thirty, even forty defenseless persons at a time with indescribable refinements of perversity. The political guerrillas from that time on had to confront simultaneously the antirevolutionary government forces, these subproducts of oppression and violence, and the static defense of the liberated "islands."

By the time such extremes were reached, violence had already spread through all strata, degrading both those who had committed it originally and those who had claimed to combat it. Thus in the course of the fighting the army officers themselves came to learn that they stood to gain more from these campaigns than from their official salaries and gratuities. They began to deal in plains cattle, to take for themselves the lands from which the dwellers were evicted, to make themselves the intermediaries of commercialization of the coffee crops. In this way the army officer corps came to be hacienda proprietors, ending by setting a scale for the military hierarchy, allotting so many hectares for each rank, in the Prussian fashion. Another cause of deterioration of the regular troops was their recent association with the Pagaros terrorist bands, with the police deformed as torturers, and, finally, with the condemned prisoners taken from the jails and pitted against the guerrillas.

In 1953 the process had advanced so far that the officers actually found the patrician politicians also superfluous. In the name of social peace General Rojas Pinilla assumed power directly. His soothing proclamation, calling on all Colombians for harmony, convinced the majority of the guerrilla fighters. Trusting in the outstretched hand of the dictator, they laid down their arms and started returning to their destroyed homes to make an effort to begin the old peaceful life. The truce did not last a year, however; violence broke out again with the massacre of dozens of students.

The conflicts exploded again. Former guerrillas were reestablished and new groups organized, all of them combatted by regular troops with the use of tanks, heavy artillery and planes, machine-gunning multitudes and burning villages with napalm bombs under the technical guidance of U.S. advisors. The failure of the war machine against guerrillas, unreachable on the crests of the hills or in the depths of the forests, progressively demoralized the troops, who compensated for their frustration by slaughtering defenseless peasants, oppressing urban workmen, and persecuting students. The generals then revived the old repressive machinery of the Falangist Pagaros, and of bands of prisoners freed on condition that they engage in counterrevolution. To this phase, perhaps, belong the most atrocious acts of sanguinary fury and sexual crimes, including per capita payment for dead guerrilla fighters or any "communists," proved by exhibiting the ears in barracks.

The violence let loose by the military dictatorship never moved the Colombian oligarchy sufficiently to lead it to a pacifying action until the economic and financial crisis disturbed it. After a decade of inflationary euphoria, of favored loans, of corruption of the financial machine and shady deals, the crisis supervened. Only then did the political patriciate bestir itself, and then only because Rojas Pinilla had taken it on himself to proclaim that neither Liberals nor Conservatives separately would assure the social peace longed for by Colombians. They joined together then to conspire, those immutable enemies of yesterday, with the counsel of those who financed their campaigns.

The Liberal Alberto Lleras Camargo, notorious as the most yielding of Colombians (or the most enthusiastic of the Latin American leaders about free enterprise, cogovernment by industrial entrepreneurs with patrician politicians, integration of producers of raw materials into international economy, and U.S. union organization), became the dove of peace. He flew to Spain, where he reached an agreement with Laureano Gómez, the instigator of terrorism against Lleras' party, on a truce between Conservatives and Liberals, or, in his words, "a parenthesis of concord in the ardor of their combats." With this patrician-oligarchy entente established, the dictatorship was overthrown by a mixture of general strike and lockout.

The pact signed in Spain, and later approved in a plebiscite, instituted the Frente Nacional, which was to guarantee the condominion of the two patrician parties over the whole machinery of the state, alternating the presidency every four years and sharing equally in all public offices, in the legislative and judicial branches, regional legislatures and municipal councils. Lleras Camargo assumed the presidency in accord with the desire of Laureano Gómez, who recommended him to the nation as the statesman with "the most capable hands and the most enlightened intelligence."

In power, Lleras Camargo would accomplish what the oligarchy most hoped for from him: U.S. loans, indispensable to the rebalancing of finances. Violence, however, although with less intensity, continued because its roots lay in deep structural causes that no summit accord could affect.

Ten years of ferocious violence, hundreds of thousands of victims was the price the Colombian people paid for a civil war, and it all resulted in this spurious fruit: an entente between the two grim patrician institutions for the oligarchic domination and the foreign exploitation to continue ruling the country.

Just as some patients exemplify clinically a pathological process, Colombia exemplifies a disease that can attack any nation whose social development is constricted by a pact of the national oligarchies with imperialistic interests implanted in them.

Because of their fundamental interests, people and oligarchy oppose each other in Colombia with such severity that the analysis of that opposition, the study of the techniques of subjugating the people, of containment of reformist impulses, of liquidation of renovating forces, casts light on the problems of social development, just as clinical studies aid in understanding the pathological processes.

The Revolution of 1,000 Days and subsequent convulsions such as those from 1930 to 1946 fall into the category of civil wars and social conflicts of the type that so many countries have experienced. The unhappily notorious Bogotazo of 1948, considering the spontaneity of its eruption following Gaitán's assassination, hardly belongs in this classification. It reveals a state of frustration of immense multitudes that can be explained only by special conditions of social compression and spoliation. The events of the so-called "homogenization" of 1950–1953, when every local despot felt encouraged to decimate the Liberals in his district, also exceeded the norm in regard to local initiative, diffusion throughout the country, and protection from the central government.

The violence that followed in still graver forms in the dictatorial period of 1955–1958 reached a climax only describable as a generalized process of dissociation and anomie. It does not end there, because violence continued after 1959 in acts apparently isolated but revealing the degree of insanity reached. Figures based on statistics of recent years show that in 1960 Colombia had a rate of death by homicide of 33.8 per 100,000 inhabitants, whereas that of the United States, by no means a tranquil nation, had 4.5, and Peru, 2.2 (Guzmán Campos, 1964, vol. 2, pp. 407–410).

These facts are explicable only by special conditions obstructing historical development, conditions that led to a structural crisis expressed in the most lawless ways. The dephasing in the development of social institutions, which normally takes place at different rates, engendering disharmonies, led Colombia not only to the usual dephasements but to a veritable social trauma. This trauma expressed structural contradictions maintained by dint of ferocious repression during long decades in order to perpetuate the archaic social stratification and the privilege system for the dominant caste. Repressing any tendencies toward change in the social structure, the Colombian oligarchy shut off all escape valves of social tensions and all the alternative paths that would permit a progressive transformation, other than the path of formal politicopartisan disputes. In the circumstances the accumulated tensions, instead of leading to authentically renovating movements, exploded in anarchic acts and initiated pathological processes as an indirect expression of the structural contradictions and as mechanisms for perpetuating the oligarchic order.

The irruption of violence en masse—with its 300,000 officially admitted murders and surely more than 1 million wounded, exiled, robbed, crippled, in one decade—occurs when the over-all order represented by the regulative institutions of national scope (government, Church, justice, army, police, parties, press) becomes confused with local order in the exacerbation of partisan hatreds, everything becoming fused and swallowed up in the same generalized dysfunction. In these circumstances the violence of the municipal petty rulers, a violence generally more discriminatory and more odious, is moved and capitalized by the high national oligarchies in their insane desire to command and control political power at all costs. And the whole social structure comes to operate as the generator of lawless forms of conduct on the individual or the family plane, forms that constitute, even so, the regular modes of maintaining the over-all regime, or in other words the very function of the institutions.

Violence thus penetrates all social strata like an endemic disease: manifesting itself in some sectors by concrete acts of terrorism, in others by complicity in crime or in more subtle forms of covering up or of justification, such as the avoidance of any polemic about the subject as a shameful, filthy thing that ought not to be mentioned, or the attitude of apparently detached cynicism that frequently fills the place of constructive self-criticism for guilt that pertains to all, but essentially to the social structure and to those interested in its maintenance. Through all these forms of participation the various sectors of Colombian society scheme together to assure impunity and encourage the perpetuation of violence.

This phenomenon is extremely serious because it affects an entire society, in contrast to other dysfunctions of the same character, such as the terrorism of the Ku Klux Klan in the United States or the mass murders by the Nazis, which were always the responsibility of a few and always directed against minorities defined ethnically as "the other." And it is especially serious because it exemplifies a consequence of the social hardening that can explode tomorrow in any of the Latin American nations deformed by the same constrictions, that is, by economicosocial orders that restrict their development to appease the interests of privileged minorities. It is a question, then, not only of lamenting what is happening to the Colombians but of avoiding a reproduction of that unleashing of violence in other areas, motivated by simple-minded provocations of the forces fighting for social renovation, or purposely inflamed by the oligarchies in their desperate efforts to maintain their interests and in their indifference to the fate of the people.

Among the factors, if not causal, at least concomitant with the violence in Colombia, are, as Monsignor Guzmán's studies point out, a series of traits that we could identify in the majority of Latin American societies: the demeaning of the governing powers in the eyes of the people, the cruelly repressive character of the armed forces as maintainers of the regime, partisanship carried to extremes, degradation of politically maneuvered justice, clientelism and corruption of the bureaucracy, deterioration of the electoral system by fraud and coercion, verbal virulence and irresponsibility of the organs of information, disparagement of the religious leaders engaged in petty political activity, racial and social prejudice, discrimination against mestizos and Negroes, and the generalized misery of the newly urbanized populations.

Any country where an equivalent oligarchic regime exists, and where the same concomitants are present (and which of the New Peoples could be excluded?) is subject to the initiation of an identical process, in the measure in which the dominant interests tend to be substantially affected. When exacerbated hatred becomes contagious, when social cohesion and national fraternity are broken down, when every family and group starts arming itself against its neighbor and taking justice into its own hands, when the fundamental values of human solidarity and mutual respect no longer motivate many or touch the emotions of anyone at sight of a mangled enemy—then the requisites are filled for a climate of terror and retaliation, which is the most terrible curse that can fall on a people. It is a disease more deadly, more deforming, and more serious than any epidemic—worse even than war between nations, because it is open, barbarous war within the nation, war that strikes down women, the aged, babies and that rots and defiles everything. The recovery of human values after this hecatomb has been unchained is more difficult than the cicatrization of war wounds, because it requires the restoration of the most delicate mechanisms of motivation or of moral restraint about which very little is known and which escape any possibility of rational, planned restoration.

That was what happened in Colombia, "infected with conspiracy," engaged in a civil war with no program, which differs from a social revolution as much as butchering differs from a surgical operation. The Colombian people, bled by its oligarchy, permeated with political hate, split into two murdering parties, was thus led to its own decimation. And the worst is that by this deviation it only helped consolidate the patrician-oligarchic antipopular order and the imperialistic spoliation, by retarding the people's consciousness of its problems, making impossible the formulation of its own project for autonomous development and, by all these means, making more difficult the unification of the common people in the struggle for their own causes.

Even the armed groups resultant from the fights between Liberals and Conservatives and later structured as "peasant republics," which in some instances embraced extensive areas of the country, ended in many cases by being wiped out. It was on the experiences of their failures that new guerrilla foci were later organized, uninvolved with the responsibilities of defending the local populations from the army's attacks and of governing them precariously. Through their struggle the Colombian revolutionary vanguards are polarizing to release generalized insurgent movements that will eradicate the structure of existing power and make possible the reordering of society according to the interests of its majority.

7. The Antilleans

THE ANTILLES FORM an enormous arc composed of thousands of islands extending from the Guianas to Florida. They include the Dutch (Surinam, Curaçao, Aruba, and the like), the British (British Guiana, Trinidad, Barbados, Bermuda, Bahamas, and so on), the French (French Guiana, Martinique, Guadaloupe, and so on), and the U.S. Antilles (Puerto Rico, Virgin Islands, and so on). Within the arc formed by the Lesser Antilles and the other outer islands (Bahamas and so on) are the three great independent antilles: Jamaica, Hispaniola—divided between the Dominican Republic and Haiti—and Cuba, the largest.

The terms "Antilles," "West Indies," and "Caribbean" are generic names employed, respectively, by the French, the English, and the United States to designate the myriad islands of the great archipelago. The term "Antilles" frequently extends to the Guianas, and the term "Caribbean" to the area embraced by the islands and the continental areas adjacent to them that received large contingents of Negroes: the south of the United States, Central America, Colombia, Venezuela and the Guianas.

These Antilles were the America that Columbus saw, since his ships touched the mainland only on the Venezuelan and Central American coasts. It is to these islands, therefore, that we just attribute his fascination with the tropical world, described sometimes in his diaries as a vision of the lost paradise.

Even today many think of the Antilles as a sun-gilded kingdom of palm trees, of beaches with clean sand, of crystalline waters and mulatto Aphrodites. So they may be for the tourist who goes direct from the airport to his air-conditioned hotel, with its private beach and its own casino. In reality no climatic amenity can conceal the sour stench of misery and the sight of ragamuffins and diseases of privation, stamped on peoples as famished as the Antilleans. Only a very few white families and a mestizo elite, also scanty, live in a segregated world of modern comfort, situated in a few privileged urban sections. The bulk of the people, whose shacks are scattered around the fringes of the cities, climbs the hills or goes down into the valleys where the plantations lie, and vegetates in conditions of the direst poverty.

The Antillean population exceeded 22 million in 1960, which makes it one of the principal American demographic blocs. It is also the densest population in relation to area in the Americas, even in the world, if one considers its enormous proportion of mountainous, volcanic, uncultivable lands. It is, moreover, the most afflicted by colonialist domination, exercised there even today by four imperialisms: the United States, the British, the French, and the Dutch. It is, finally, the least matured in its national ethnic formations and the most segmented by racial and social discrimination. In many areas Negroes, mulattoes, East Indians, and poor whites are divided by greater hostilities toward each other than toward their foreign dominators.

Emerging as subproducts of slavistic mercantile undertakings, producers of sugar and other tropical articles, the Antillean peoples only now are beginning to define themselves as American nations, aspiring to autonomy and as worthy as any others. On them, perhaps more than on any other American peoples, were stamped the psychological, social, and cultural marks of the colonial pact, which impoverished them culturally and infused and generalized in them all a denigrating image of themselves.

The Millionaire Plantations

The study of the Antilles is of particular interest because they are, in a pure and amplified state, the effects of European colonization through the plantation system, no matter which country undertook the exploitation. They also copiously exemplify how little political independence means when unaccompanied by economic autonomy, a situation conducive only to the substitution of new forms of colonial domination. They are, moreover, a testimony to how progressive peoples, proud of themselves, like the modern Cubans, can be molded out of these human masses.

This study is also of special interest for the understanding of the formative process of the American peoples because, in their poverty, the Antilles created the very rich, proud Yankee republic, whose success is owing principally to the economic viability that the sugar islands provided it, as a market for its production. Without so many slaves to feed while they produced, an immigrant colonization would have been unviable, based on small landholding and a family economy devoted primarily to production of subsistence articles. The Antilles are therefore the counterpart, Black and slave, poor and wretched, of the United States, white, rich, and free.

The one-crop economy of sugar production in its heyday provided an enormously greater profit potential than did the immigrant colonies of the English, Dutch, and French. The sugar producers were more prosperous and more advanced economies, technologically, and by their high degree of specialization they challenged other forms of agricultural production. They were also conducive to a high concentration of revenue that permitted abundant rewards from invested capital. However, they engendered some of the most wretched communities known, characterized by the contrast between the wealth of the resident owners, who reproduced European conditions of comfort and even surpassed them at very high cost on their plantations, and the indigence of the human mass engaged in the productive process.

The Antillean economy, based on the plantation, and the white U.S. American, based on a farm and crafts system, historically oppose each other as the concretization of different models ordering social life for productive effects. Economically speaking, in the seventeenth and eighteenth centuries progress and prosperity were not found in the North American immigrant colonies, but in the slavocratic plantations of the Antilles. Their economy was so prosperous that it permitted the luxury of importing Black slaves from Africa, more efficient and more expensive than the white workers engaged as temporary serfs in the North American system. In the case of the Antilles, however, all the profits of the exploitation to go abroad were drained off, only what was indispensable to replace the slave labor worn out in work or crushed by inhuman treatment and to enlarge the plantations and multiply the machinery was invested. The immigrant colonies, operating as an autonomous economic system, by trading their agricultural production with the Antillean area obtained the funds needed to cover the cost of their imports of European manufactures, and especially to invest in a multiform economy that was to become more and more autarchic and fecund.

The two complementary economies grew up together, each incorporating its own potentialities. On the continent it was an autonomous society producing cereals: it was to grow freely, generating a series of entrepreneurial models of agricultural and crafts production and of commerce and a self-government in which the people's interests made themselves heard and which allowed the incorporation of increasing masses of immigrants into a land of all but infinite extent. In the islands, captive societies emerged in which, beside a handful of rich planters, the slave people multiplied, exploited like beasts of burden, subjected to conditions of oppression that only guaranteed detribalization and deculturation of the descendants of African Negroes, to integrate them into a spurious, extremely rudimentary cultural complex.

But on the North American continent an "Antillean" content was also implanted—suitably segregated from the free society of the Transplanted Peoples of the settlement colonies. It was the southern world of the slavocratic plantations, with characteristics common to the New Peoples, based on Black slavery, miscegenation and compulsory deculturation. The victory of the north over the south, decisive in the final conformation of the nation, was to give the supremacy to the east, which had profited from the economic complementarism with the two prosperous slavocratic economies, the domestic and foreign, enriching the precarious farm economy of the Atlantic coast, making possible the grain and cattle installation of the west, and creating the foundations for U.S. industrialization.

On the North American plantations as on the Antillean, the European languages underwent change and damage, less by enrichment with African expressions or invention or new words than by the rusticity of spoken communication and by the alterations of sounds by new mouths accustomed to other languages. It was in the effort to master an instrument of communication between persons displaced from their origins, and between all of them and the world of the whites, that this changed mode of speech arose. A major factor in its conformation was that slaves learned through the harshness of work orders the most elementary technical instructions, and a system of rewards and punishments, particularly punishments, intended to make every "talking animal" produce the maximum.

Simultaneously with the emergence of these dialects, the various nuclei of Afro-Americans re-created a folklore, a music, and new bodies of beliefs, a new view of the world, which colored the cultural substratum of European origin with bits taken from the tribal cultures of all Africa, and above all with products of their own creativity. This protoculture was to serve as a source of motivation for the day-to-day struggle and a philosophy of life.

The principally spiritual contents of the African heritage in this protoculture emergent in all the areas and populations that grew from slave stocks probably do not indicate a special propensity for music, rhythm, or spectacular religiosity. Rather, they reveal the weight of their oppression as slaves, which prevented them from expressing their creativity in any other field than the sportive or intellectual ones allowed in their few hours of leisure. Having to learn to live in a strange new world where the land, the flora, and fauna were unknown to them; obliged to adapt to the food distributed to them; trained to the work techniques indispensable to produce sugar or cotton and other export products, they were despoiled of nearly everything that their cultural patrimony had prepared them to do and to create in the fields of production, institutionalization, and art. They were not human communities in a struggle to create and re-create their mode of being, their culture; they were conglomerates of "pieces" belonging to plantations and posts, condemned to produce the living conditions and mercantile products of a slavocratic society into which they were thrust as a labor force. In the circumstances their compressed creativity found its only possible outlets in the ideological, artistic, and religious expression of their drama of men turned into beasts.

The Anglo-Saxon colonization of North America turned out to be, from the first years on, a losing, unsuccessful venture for its backers, as well as competitive with the mother country's economy. It was able to continue, even so, as a form of occupation of the American lands and as an outlet for the surplus of people in the British Isles and, later on, in the continent of Europe. Thus it contributed to lessen the demographic pressures that could have led to reform of the agrarian structure, and by way of that to the explosion of the whole European social system.

It survived and grew, however, by virtue of its association with the Antilles and the southern plantations, as permanent food providers for the English islands and occasional but very frequent suppliers for the others. This supplying was done either through contraband or legally, because of the constant interruptions of commerce occasioned by the intermittent wars between European powers, which made strict monopoly of colonial commerce an impossibility.

The Antilles emerged originally as a Spanish, and later a French, effort to foster a strategic European settlement to safeguard the exceedingly rich colonial exploitation of Hispano-America or to dispute it. Thus Hispaniola, Cuba, Puerto Rico, and Jamaica were established as a mediocre farming society producing a few minor tropical articles. They were later modified as a new area of cane plantations and sugar mills by the initiative of the Dutch, expelled from the sugar regions of Brazil's northeast (1654). It was in this capacity that they grew and were populated by swarms of Negro slaves, and in less than a decade came to figure importantly in the European sugar markets, which they finally dominated.

In the Antilles, instead of the conquest they had attempted against Portugal, the Dutch preferred to carry on business, interesting the French and English colonists resident there in sugar production. Already holding control of the European sugar market as intermediaries for the sale of Brazil's production, they thus made themselves the financiers of the new enterprise, facilitating technical aid, slaves, and machinery.

The first effect of the new form of colonization was to replace white farmers and their Indian mestizo offspring with Negro slaves. The small farmers, both Spanish and French, installed in the islands, when confronted with the wave of Africans, moved en masse to the colonies on the continent by means of selling their lands, made more valuable by the new exploitation. Thus the cultivation of indigo, cacao, ginger, cotton, and subsistence crops were replaced by a sea of sugar cane.

Crossbreeding took place in all the Antilles with the greatest intensity. It began with the crossing of Europeans with the Carib and Arawak Indians they found there. It was carried on, particularly, with the Spaniards concentrated in the islands, first for the assault on Mexico, and later as the nucleus of loyal forces that Spain sought to maintain there for immediate action against any uprising of the dominated peoples. According to contemporary depositions, the Spaniards' eagerness to take Indian women as concubines went to such extremes that it became all but impossible for an Indian male to find a wife, which contributed to the extermination of the tribal ethnic entities.

As agents of miscegenation the Spaniards were succeeded by the French and English buccaneers and corsairs swarming in the islands not occupied by the Spanish. When these new European contingents installed themselves as permanent settlements, by the middle of the eighteenth century when there were still very few European women there, the blending went on with surviving Indian women and with mestizo women from the first cross-breedings. In this way a basic mestizo stratum was formed, on which the African contingents would operate, darkening it more and more.

From the beginning, miscegenation was openly practiced between Europeans and Negro women, and between the descendants of these crossbreedings and more imported Negroes. Thus a mulatto caste was constituted, for this reason alone, generally, freed from slave status but surplus in the one-crop economy and marginal to both the world of servants and the world of the truly free. The women, being more attractive concubines for the whites' taste, served in the overseers' homes and new, lighter-skinned mulattoes multiplied. The men became overseers or skilled, better-trained servants, and went back to the Negro women, attractive in the latter's eyes because of their seigniorially light skin, thus increasing the crossbreeding.

In the islands colonized by the Spanish, which continued to receive white settlers because there the one-crop domination was less, the population has a less plainly Negroid phenotype. In the French and English islands, whose original white and mestizo population moved away, fleeing the advance of the slavocratic sugar economy, the Negro and the mulatto predominate. In the British Antilles the Negro predominates, the whites reaching a maximum of 4 per cent of the population. Haiti is the extreme case of Negro homogeneity attained by this original succession and by the extermination of the local whites in the wars of independence: Haiti has only 10 per cent mulatto population. Cuba, with a lighter-skinned population, has a Negro contingent of 33 per cent.

This alteration of the original colonization projects in the Antilles was to have profound consequences in the formation of their populations. It would occasion two flagrantly contraposed variants: the Hispanio-Antillean and the Negro-Antillean. In the Spanish Antilles, from the earliest decades, a mestizo stratum took shape, heir to the genetic patrimony of its Arawak and Carib mothers and its Iberian fathers. They were not really Americans, nor yet Europeans, but they would act as colonizational agents, first over the Indians, later over the foreigners. It was these initial cells of a neo-American culture that were to integrate the new Negro contingents in the language, the knowledge, and the habits of the land. So it is that through sharing a body of common understandings that defined their mode of being and life style, both the descendants of slaves and the descendants of the colonizers were welded together, all incorporated into a new cultural complex, still spurious because of its character of exogenous implantation, which bound it to the outside world, but increasingly capacitated to go on formulating its own ethnonational projects, as future autonomous cultural entities.

In the other Antilles, from which these original mestizo cells were eradicated, or in which they never came to take shape, the Negro slave conscripted for mercantile production saw himself torn from his own people and placed under overseers. In these circumstances, in the non-Spanish Antilles as in the south of the United States, Black slaves found themselves obliged to re-create, under the most unfavorable conditions, a protoculture that filled their elementary need for human communication and for exercise of their role as talking tools. Even though the English, Dutch, and French, while separated from their families, customarily had intercourse with Negro women, also engendering multitudes of mulattoes, these of course lacked the heritage of the native mother as the repository of the age-old adaptive knowledge of the tribe, the taste for creating, and the sense of human dignity that nonstratified societies possess in such great degree. Their relations with their own fathers would always lack the easy adaptability present in those symbiotic, precapitalistic, hybrid communities of Europeans and Indians, settled on the land as more homogeneous societies and more authentic cultures.

The contraposition of the two Antillean profiles—the Hispano-Catholic, on one side, and the French, the Anglo-Saxon, and the Dutch, on the other —reflects essentially the presence or the absence of those cells that generate the Westernized protoculture. But they also reflect, in a certain measure, the difference of the ethos or the moral posture of the Iberians— mestizos themselves from centuries-old blendings with Negroes and Moors —and the principally Protestant North Europeans, with their pharisaical strictness, who allowed themselves to miscegenate but could not forgive themselves for it, and were predisposed to segregation and to prejudice against everything that seemed strange to them, even their own half-breed children.

In the areas where these contingents were present, the whites and mulattoes and Negroes were contraposed on each island not only as different social strata distinguished by their incomes and privileges but as racial blocs separated by hatred. Everything, however, was to the advantage of the white and mulatto majority, whose economic and ideological dominance was overwhelming, except in the moments of great tension when social revolts turned into race wars.

Interracial comportment in the Antillean zones had a certain archaic tinge for that reason. It seemed to evidence postabolitionist contrapositions, long since superseded in all the New Peoples: on one side, fluidity of sexual relations existed, and the Negro women's pleasure in having lighter-skinned children, which reflected a prejudiced ideal of "whitening," which in turn only admits the Negro as a future mulatto or white, but realistic, too, because of the clear social predominance of the dark over the Blacks; on the other side, the role of the mulatto, always capitalizing his paleness and his city speech, his education and his urbanity, as instruments of social ascent, doing all in his power to place himself on the white man's team and against the vastly superior numbers of his own Black peoples. In this effort the mulatto became an arrogant snob, internalizing a greater and more odious Negrophobia than that of the white man, expressed in the fear of being identified as a Negro and in the revolt of the Negro against the oppressor, whose self-proclaimed whiteness makes him identify the mulatto and the white, rather than the system of exploitation, as an enemy. Social stratification is juxtaposed so precisely to the color line that this identification becomes inevitable, involving the mulatto as much for the privileges he enjoys as for the arrogance that he develops in the service of the oppressor and as the fruit of the very trauma deriving from his marginality.

The most painful aspect of the problem is, probably, the introjection of the white man's discriminatory values and the cult of his superiority in the

Negro and the mulatto. The white man's obvious efficiency in the economic world, his notorious domination in the social, political, and educational fields, confer on him a de facto superiority that, inexorably, comes to be regarded as natural and necessary. Furthermore, it is marked by ideas, beliefs, and values that have impregnated the whole population in the most brutal and subtle ways, making the Negroes in their own eyes as second-class people, a less noble subhumanity not made in the image of the white divinity or endowed by it with the same resources of ingenuity and expertise or the same "beauty." Therefore, looking at themselves with a repulsion based on a white aesthetic ideal, speaking a language considered a patois as compared with the mother tongue, worshiping syncretic divinities of a persecuted religion, the Negro mass can move only between rebellion and resignation without finding a dignifying self-definition or a road to emancipation.

This is the heritage of the colonization that, besides wearing out millions of Negroes in work, led their free descendants to a psychological trauma that paralyzed their creativity. Segregated as castes, the light and dark Antilleans of all the islands coexist without coliving, divided into differing and socially immiscible cultural spheres. The light-skinned live in their seignioral homes, gathering in private clubs, worshiping in churches of various denominations according to the tastes of the area's colonizers, persisting in their efforts to perform every rite or gesture of etiquette perfectly or to utter some witticism in continental European fashion. The dark are bowed under the burden of work, their only opportunity for social gathering being the secret cults. Their conversion, secret and superficial, to Christianity, had only added new values to the traditions that they managed to preserve. Voodoo, Afro-Antillean *xangô,* with its patron saints syncretized from Catholic saints mixed with African divinities, with their white-hot rhythms, their alternation of sacred ceremonies and sports festivals, constituted the sole refuge of the Negro mass. Only there could the Black man forget the privations of a life of misery and humiliations, and, above all, enjoy an egalitarian "togetherness," in communion with a collectivity that made him feel more human, more dignified, expressing a culture of his own, markedly antiwhite and instrinsically subversive, because at least in the cult language he was opposing all the reigning order, in spite of the European values that filled that language. For this very reason the cults were always persecuted, not only by the piety of the religious who wished to deliver the Negro from such heresy, but also by the dominant power, colonial or national, disturbed by its irredentist nature.

Against the self-flagellating image that the Negro eventually made of himself and that operated to reinforce the economic and political domination by the white man, in recent years an irredentist movement has arisen among the intellectuals of all the Antilles, which has come to express itself in literature and political militancy with increasing vigor. It is the so-called "Antillean renaissance," [5] which is expressing itself in the three languages, motivated by the same passion to create an authentically Antillean motivated and integrated culture. It is fighting on all fronts: from the effort to mold new aesthetic canons that will free the Negro from the preoccupation with straightening his hair and lightening his skin, to the rehabilitation of Créole as a language of literary expression [in Haiti], to the reform of the educational system to de-Europeanize it; from the dignification of voodoo to the appreciative revaluation of the historical role of the Negro in the New World, his decisive contribution to making nearly everything that exists here, and the dignity with which he has borne centuries of slavery without resigning himself to it. Through all these paths they are seeking to set the Negro on his feet again, and restore his pride in himself as a human being and as a civilizer. In the zeal with which they are fighting for their new aesthetic and for creating their own world view, many of these leaders risk falling into a new racism, that is, negritude, a reaction not only explicable but even necessary to reestablish the equilibrium of a scale that for so many centuries had been tilted by a tare of whititude.

Archipelago of Four Empires

A fundamental distinction essential to the comprehension of the Antillean world of our time derives from the political statute dividing it into colonies and independent countries, despite the formal, precarious nature of the latter entities' autonomy and the disguises that attempt to conceal the dependence of the former. The dependents include the British Antilles,[6] the French,[7] the Dutch,[8] and the "free associated state" [self-gov-

[5] Among many others, outstanding in the political and intellectual world are Aimé Césaire, Eric Williams, Dantès Bellegarde, Michel Leiris, Eugène Revert, Frantz Fanon, Jacques Romain, and Jean Price-Mars.

[6] These include the Bahamas, Bermuda, some of the Leeward and Windward Islands, Turks, Caicos (two of the Leewards are now self-governing, and three of the Windwards, all five with the official status of associated states). Guyana (700,000), Trinidad, and Tobago (1 million), and Jamaica (1.9 million) are officially independent (1968 population figures).

[7] Martinique (340,000 in 1967) and Guadeloupe (320,000 in 1967) are now officially *départements* of France. French Guiana (37,000 in 1966) has shown no desire for independence, and there are several small islands still territories of France.

[8] They include Surinam (377,000 in 1968), Curaçao, Aruba, and some small islands (215,000 in 1968), all components of the Netherlands and not overseas territories—officially.

erning commonwealth] of Puerto Rico,[9] all of these containing about a third of the 24.5 million inhabitants of the area.* In all of them the plantation sugar economy predominates, which in some cases, as in Trinidad and Aruba, combines with oil and other mineral development.

It is the world of "caneocracy" with the inegalitarian, rigid social and political structures characteristic of one-crop economies, results of the wretchedness of economies deformed by the unilaterality of commercial farming, which leaves no room for subsistence cultures and organizes all social life in terms of foreign wills and needs. The French Antilles are the poorest and most backward, with their incredible combination of latifundium and minifundium and the onus of chronic underemployment. The British are a little more prosperous and combative, probably because of the presence and actuation of Negroes returning from the United States after periods of seasonal work with a higher level of aspirations.

The emancipation of the new African nations has contributed decisively to the liberation of Antillean national energies. The news of a rebellious, proud Africa emerging from its colonial yoke exploded on the Antilleans with a cathartic effect, reviving both pride in their Black humanity, humbled for centuries, and combative ardor against their old masters.

In the British Antilles, after explosions of simple undisciplined revolt, the freedom struggle assumed the form of regimentation within the English trade-union traditions. In the French islands it took a more radical form under leftist leaders. The English islands, through the creation of sham parliamentary institutions (a lower chamber with a presiding officer in robe and wig), admit a certain degree of self-government but maintain dependence on the metropolis. The French did so through a departmentalization that satisfies the aspiration of only the most alienated Antilleans who yearn for identification with the citizens of France and with the French national ethnos. All this procedure has resulted in transforming the colonies into overseas *départements* of the French republic, bastard in character with no prospect of equalization with the metropolitan French citizen in political, and more particularly in social, rights.

In the Dutch Antilles there is also an effort to simulate independence, which, though counterfeit, is better than the histrionic elevation of Puerto Rico to the category of "associate state" in the union of the United States

[9] In 1961 Puerto Rico had 2.349 million inhabitants. The 1968 forecast predicted 2.697 million.

* The translators have taken the liberty of substituting 1968 statistics for the author's 1960 figures, and in footnotes 6–9 have also tried to bring up to date the facts, figures, and official terminology as nearly as available statistics and information permit.

—entitled to one congressman without a vote—which goes against the grain of Puerto Rican national sentiment and was imposed under the pressure of Muñoz Marín's blackmailing campaign with the slogan "Association or ruin." Both the moderates of the island and the violent partisans of the late Albizu Campos are rebelling against that arrangement, the latter faction carrying their terrorism even to the U.S. proper.[10]

Of the four forms of transition to independence, the British has the advantage of creating opportunities for maturing a national political leadership and, especially implicit in it, for an evolutionary line of increasing autarchization. On the other hand, the pressure of these last years to include British Guiana, which was seeking its own paths of development and integration into Latin America, has discredited the effort, indicating that the English limits to Antillean autonomy merge with the Yankee veto to any progressive order. The independence finally granted maintains the maximum connection and dependence practicable in the irredentist atmosphere that has been created. *

In the French area, in the English, and in Puerto Rico the social situation is explosive on account of the evident incapability of the productive system to support the population and assure it a more decent living standard. In some islands the demographic concentration reaches extremes and is constantly augmented by a high birth rate.[11] In the circumstances the hope of every youth who gets an elementary education is to emigrate. The metropolises, however, set barriers to this emigration, and the U.S. labor market is barred to them by legislation of quotas destined to prevent the entrance of new "colored" contingents.

All this results in an increasing social tension that will inevitably explode in search of a social order structured to provide better utilization of the available resources. That is the model created, close at hand, by their Cuban neighbors. To the Antilleans the Cuban Revolution was a revelation comparable only to the catharsis brought on by the emancipation of the African nations. And it added to the ethnonational consciousness, given them by that emancipation, a political dimension that is turning more and more toward socialism as the solution of their problems. This

---

* On January 1, 1969, Guyana (the new official name) became at least nominally a republic, but whether it can survive may be another question, depending on whether racial friction can be eliminated between the Negro and the East Indian parties.

[10] The United States took Puerto Rico away from Spain as spoils of war in 1898, with payment of an indemnification in dollars. On the same occasion the "liberation" of Cuba and the appropriation of Guam and the Philippines were carried out.

[11] For example, 480 inhabitants per square kilometer in Barbados; 270, in Martinique; 170, in Puerto Rico; 120, in Guadeloupe. Jamaica has a demographic increment of 3.4, and Trinidad, 3.2.

rising tide of revolutionary feeling, diagnosed by the United States as "dangerous Castro-communist infection," is that nation's greatest worry in the Caribbean today.

The history of the independent Antilles is essentially the analysis of their relations with the United States and of their rebellion against that yoke. The group includes Haiti, the Dominican Republic, and Cuba, making up nearly 17 of the 24.5 million in the Antilles.[12]

As we have seen, the interplay of the Antillean sugar economy with the economy of the food-producing colonies of North America operated with the former acting as the dynamic center of the symbiotic system. This symbiosis (Celso Furtado, 1959, pp. 41–42) permitted channeling a part of the sugar economy revenues to subsidize the food-providing economy of North America, elevating it to a superior stage. So an economy emerged in America similar to that of contemporary Europe, that is, directed from the inside out, producing principally for the domestic market without a fundamental separation between the productive activities destined for export and those connected with the internal market.

This conjunction, this interplay, of capital importance to the North American settlers' economy directly challenged, however, the interests of the colonial powers, bent on forcing monopoly of commerce on their colonies, especially with respect to provisions competing with their own domestic production. Thus, the first serious tensions between England and her North American colonial nuclei stemmed from her reiterated attempts to prevent their trading with the French Antilles and her own islands there.

With U.S. independence, the Spanish and the French Antilles were disputed by the Yankees and the English, no longer competing just for the market but for economic domination. The first action of any scope by the United States was the war on Spain in which the object of dispute was the cane fields of Cuba and Puerto Rico. The leaders of U.S. independence clearly and repeatedly expressed the national aspiration of incorporating the great island into the union. They did not succeed because of the nationalistic vigor of the Hispanic Antilles, but they gained the same results by other techniques of domination: investments and interventions.

At the time of independence (1791) Haiti had a slave population of .5 million, perhaps with another 10 per cent of free mulattoes, the *affranchis,*

[12] The respective populations were, by 1968 estimates: Haiti, 4.7 million; Dominican Republic, 4 million; Cuba, 8.2 million. [Again the translators have substituted 1968 figures for the author's 1960 data in text and footnote.]

who enjoyed a privileged social position as intermediaries of the domination by a tiny caste of whites. It was the richest of the French colonies, and in those days probably one of the most profitable European possessions in the world. The latent revolt against colonial oppression, expressed overtly in the libertarian language of the leaders of the French Revolution, unified all Haitians in an irresistible emancipatory movement, permitting them to win independence before any other Latin American nation.

Nevertheless, years of internal struggle followed, the Negroes and affranchis against the whites, who sought to divide them in order to shape independence to their own ends. After the expulsion of the whites, with the extermination of those who resisted, fighting began between the mulattoes and the Negroes. It continues today in a succession of bloody episodes and periods of accommodation, always under strong tension.

These struggles made it impossible for an elite to emerge with the ability to formulate an integrative national policy and to order the new state, because of the immutable division between the Negroes, newly risen from slavery, and the better educated mulatto affranchis, who could perform this function. Haiti has thus been led for decades into a state of convulsion in which dual, disputed governments, the most ferocious dictatorships, and social regressions, such as temporary reestablishment of slavery, have succeeded each other.

This situation of anarchy has been aggravated by the very profundity of the Haitian Revolution, which, as it destroyed the bases of colonial exploitation, mortally affected the economic system itself without being capable of restoring or installing a new order of it. Only a century later, and within the socialist model, would a revolutionary vanguard lead a victorious popular insurrection to the creation of a new socioeconomic regime.

In the face of the generalized state of conflict and the aggressiveness of the Haitian against the white, the colonial powers kept their distance. However, they established a blockade around Haiti, declaring the country outlawed. The situation was further aggravated by the burden of the eviction compensation collected by France, absorbing the revenues that the Haitian governments managed to produce by means of exports.

Torn by internal racial conflict, paralyzed by the antiwhite trauma—produced by one of the most iniquitous forms of slavery the world has ever known—Haiti succeeded in surviving independent for more than a century. In this period the international financiers found ways to conquer their aversion to the Black republic, approaching it to negotiate their loans. Thus railways were financed, and likewise the outfitting of ports, and simple loans to the government to confront the crisis. U.S. bankers ended by becoming the great creditor corps, both by lending more and by acquiring the debts contracted with European bankers.

The road to dollar diplomacy being thus prepared, Marine diplomacy comes on the scene in the performance of the role proposed by the United States as the crusader for the Monroe Doctrine, taking it on herself to compel Latin Americans to fulfill the financial obligations they had assumed. U.S. intervention then supervened with an assault by the marines. A Haitian congressman expressed his sense of outrage for the wounded national dignity:

> In the name of humanity the U.S. government . . . has carried out an armed intervention in our country. And it has presented to us, on the points of bayonets and supported by the cannon of its cruisers, a treaty that it invites us, with haughty imperialism, to sign. What is this treaty? It is a protectorate imposed on Haiti by Mr. Wilson, the same Wilson who, referring to the sister republics of Latin America, said in a speech in Mobile: "We cannot be their friends unless we treat them as equals." And now he hopes to place Haiti under U.S. protection! For how long? Only God knows, when one considers the conditions required for the withdrawal of the occupation troops and for the revocation of this instrument of shame.
>
> I am no partisan of a closed republic. I do not think that isolationism is an instrument of progress for a nation. I do not believe that the principles of patriotism lie in hatred of foreigners and in rejection of foreign aid, even when offered sincerely. Neither do I think it honorable to sacrifice the dignity of one's country, whether under compulsion or not. Sacrifice it? To what end? Order, at the price of shame? Prosperity, with golden chains? Prosperity we may obtain . . . the chains we shall certainly get.[13]

Direct intervention was to last from 1915 to 1934, and then indirectly continue to our own days through the installation of a tacit guardianship regime exercised by ambassadors, the C.I.A., and U.S. navy sea patrols, always on the watch to occupy the ports against the establishment of an independent government.

The justification of the U.S. intervention in Haiti, given by one of her most accredited official historians,[14] was made in terms of the "incapacity

[13] Speech by Raymond Cabèche in the Haitian Parliament, October 1915, in debate on legislation of the U.S.-Haitian treaty. Quoted by Dantès Bellegarde, 1937, pp. 42–43, and, in turn, by J. Halcro Ferguson, 1963, p. 100.

[14] James G. Leyburn, 1941, pp. 99–103. Cited by J. H. Ferguson, 1963, p. 97. [The author apparently was misled concerning Dr. Leyburn's profession through having had to consult his work only through another's book, and in translation at that. Dr. Leyburn, a colleague and friend of one of the translators, wishes to be

of the titular government and the oligarchy to work in harmony," of the "state of anarchy" prevailing, of the "decadence and degeneration," and, further, of the mediocrity of the Haitian statesmen, "dull and incompetent." Even this historian who makes himself judge in his own case admits the "parallel" economic interest, not only in collecting back loans but also in dominating the sugar economy of the island. And, finally, he reveals as another decisive factor the racism of the Yankees, a stimulant to the combative ardor of their white infantry:

> The important fact for this study is that the presence of white American Marines in Haiti during the next two decades had definite effects upon the social life of the country.
> One of the most immediately observable results was the termination of the long political domination by the blacks, and reëstablishment of the colored elite in government control. The four presidents since 1915, Dartiguenave (1915–22), Borno (1922–30), Roy (1930), and Vincent (1930–41), have all been light-skinned. The United States forces had a definite hand in the election of the first two of these men. America's concern was certainly not to return the government to the colored group, but rather to have as titular heads of state men who were educated, temperate of mind, civil in manners—and, of course, mentally "supple" enough to carry out policies agreeable to the State Department at Washington.

Here U.S. racial discrimination combines with the docility of the affranchis, molded since colonial times for their functions as intermediaries of white exploitation. The Haitians' animosity toward the intervention, making its maintenance impossible except by means of the harshest oppression, ended by shocking world opinion. President Roosevelt suspended it in 1934 only to substitute a better disguised tutelage for it.

The final balance of accounts on these interventions is expressive. In fact, Haiti shows one of the world's most disastrous states of want, with an annual per capita income of $20–35. The great island, which had been the richest in the Antilles, today is living under a natural economy polarized only by the intrusion of imperialistic enterprises, which emphasizes more strongly the contrast between the common people's way of life and a few oases of prosperity. In the course of the centuries, however, Haiti has at last generated a nationalistic intellectual corps, now more black than mu-

---

identified as a sociologist, not a historian, and never an "accredited official historian." His *The Haitian People,* source of the quotation given above, is a standard sociological study.]

latto, which is taking long strides toward fulfilling the requisites of national integration, indispensable for undertaking the nation's social development.

The Dominican Republic, which shares the island Hispaniola with Haiti, was dominated by the United States even before Haiti. It started with an intervention in 1903, followed by the imposition of a treaty (1907) that gave her the status of protectorate. Here, too, the justification of interventionism was the nonfulfillment of bank contracts that would create a risk of European intervention on the continent. The reasons were expressed by President Theodore Roosevelt in these terms: "Adherence to the Monroe Doctrine can force us, even against our will, to play the part of international police in cases of bad conduct and impotence." And by a secretary of state in an even more blunt fashion: "The Monroe Doctrine must not be interpreted as authorization to the weak to become insolent to the strong" (Quoted by G. Selser, 1962, pp. 29, 43).

The guardian role of the United States in the Americas is defined still more incisively in this defense by the same Roosevelt:

If a nation shows that it knows how to proceed respectably in political and industrial matters, if it maintains order and pays its debts, it need not fear any interference on the part of the United States. Acts of evil, brutalization, or any and all impotence that leads to general weakening of the ties of civilized society, will require as a last resort the intervention of some civilized nation, and in the Western Hemisphere the United States cannot forget this duty (Quoted by G. Selser, 1962, pp. 260–61).

As can be seen, the propensity of the United States for tutelage over the Antilleans is of long standing, although not at all venerable: yesterday motivated by the combination of zeal for the fulfillment of international financial contracts and the lucrative nature of interventions; today justified by all these reasons plus the pledge to save them—and, if possible, all the world's peoples, whether they will or no—from "Castro-communist infection."

Intervention in the Dominican Republic lasted until 1934 also, being followed, as in the case of Haiti, by less direct though equally effective forms of domination. The penultimate of these was the murder of the dictator Trujillo by C.I.A. agents. A creature of the Yankees, Trujillo became to much even for them when world public opinion was alerted to the dreadful character of his genocidal dictatorship, which sent his executioners to murder Dominican citizens in the city of New York.

In order to give some measure of what was represented by this dictatorship, which governed the country with an iron hand for thirty-two years, we select a few facts. Trujillo came to power by force in 1930. Until then he had been the head of the police repression machine, trained by the Americans during the intervention, to assure stability to the Dominican government. An American journalist, Laura Bergquist, of *Look* magazine, after visiting the island and witnessing the ferocity of Trujillo's police, furnished her readers with an example of the horror that the Trujillo regime had aroused in her: in jail she had met a dwarf called Bola de Nieve [Snowball], whose job was to tear off, with his teeth, the genitals of the dictator's enemies.

In 1956, under the auspices of the dictator and of His Holiness Pope Pius XII, personally represented by Cardinal Spellman, the International Congress of Catholic Culture for World Peace was held in Ciudad Trujillo. Generalíssimo Doctor Rafael Leonidas Trujillo declared in opening the Congress:

> In these years of uncertainty in which humanity is living in combat with the harshest materialistic systems . . . it is our imperative duty to mobilize the forces of the spirit, to reinforce the imponderable defenses offered us by our religion, to ratify bravely our traditional principles and to convert into a living lesson, on both the domestic and the international fronts, the Divine Word of Jesus. . . . The same Jesus Christ who spoke for all times, not merely to the Pharisees of his day, has showed us the path, in one of His statements that retains, in spite of all the transformations experienced by man and society across twenty centuries, its enduring validity: "He that is not with me is against me." (Quoted by G. Arciniegas, 1958, pp. 402–403).

Yet another fact: attempting to dislodge the Haitians who had emigrated as manual laborers to Dominican territory, Trujillo ordered his army and the Dominican hacenderos to slaughter them; the massacre lasted a whole night (October 2) and took the lives of 15,000 Haitians. Shortly afterwards the congregation of the law school of Santo Domingo presented the candidacy of the Generalíssimo, as El Benefactor of the nation, for the Nobel Peace Prize for 1956.

Until the Americans decided to liquidate Trujillo at the hands of the murderers hired by the C.I.A., he had not only received every aid and support from Washington, but was frequently praised for his ability to maintain internal order, and especially for this fidelity to the ideals of Christian civilization. With Trujillo dead, however, it was learned that during his dictatorship he had manipulated such a concentration of funds that the mere transfer of the real property belonging to him and his family —lands, mills, factories, utilities—to the state proved him the holder of more than 71 per cent of the cultivable land and of 90 per cent of the country's industry.

After a period of rebellion the government was taken over by a council, which presided over the formulation of a new constitution and the first democratic elections in the country, electing Juan Bosch to the presidency in February 1963. Seven months later he was overthrown by a coup, reestablishing a dictatorship with the same military and police as in the Trujillo era.

The last episode of Yankee interventionist policy can be read in the newspapers. In May 1965, the marines landed to smother an insurrection against the dictatorship. From the American point of view, however, the movement threatened to restore Juan Bosch to power, or some president not previously approved by the department of state. Bosch himself, in an interview published in the Italian weekly magazine *L'Espresso* (May 13, 1965), pronounced this judgment on the American government's action:

> When it tried to stifle by force the democratic revolution of a people, the United States showed that it allows only two attitudes: either to be its slaves or to be communists. . . . I am too old for even Lyndon Johnson to succeed in making me a communist. But after the events of the last two days I can no longer ask my people to have faith in democracy.

Socialist America

Cuba is the largest of the Antilles in area and population. She is also the richest and most combative. Until her revolution, she was also one of the most profitable areas of U.S. neocolonial exploitation. Her extraordinary prosperity as a neocolonial capitalistic enterprise, and the consequent penury of her people, likewise constituted one of the best Yankee models of development. She was one of the countries offering least resistance— until the revolution—to her integration as a satellite of the U.S. economy; a succession of dictators and false democratic regimes had for decades done everything possible to facilitate the investment of U.S. capital in the cane fields, the production and commerce of tobacco, and into industry and utilities, advocating this course as the basic mechanism for national development—and naturally profiting from it as minority partner and employee.

At the end of the integrationist process, which had lasted nearly a century, American investments in Cuba approximated $1 billion. These were wholly tied to the Yankee economy, receiving 79 per cent of its imports from the United States and exporting 75 per cent of its products there, the latter under "privileged" conditions. This bond was further tightened by Cuba's debt to American bankers, both official and private, amounting to twice the value of the annual exports.

All Cuba, but principally the capital, had become a recreation area for U.S. tourists, offering them the most attractive vacation conditions. The island assumed the aspect of a deluxe brothel, complementary to the economic and social system prevailing in the Latin American countries most penetrated by Yankee corporations—an economy looking abroad, prosperous for foreign investors, but ruinous for its own people.

Of the population of working age only half—nearly 2 million—was engaged in the productive system. Of these, 650,000 were seasonal laborers who worked eight months in the year, at most; 100,000 others, connected with the sugar and tobacco industries, worked even less. The number of unemployed was estimated at .5 million. The wretchedness stemming from such conditions of underemployment and unemployment contrasted, of course, with the wealth of the small native group of proprietors or managers of alien properties and by the most shameless corruption of the organs of power. All this was ruled by economic stagnation engendered by the permanently critical balance of payments and by the deformations imposed by a one-crop economy.

Cuban society was ruled by the need to maintain antipopular interests and by total dependence on an exogenous economy. To perform this function the regime had equipped itself with a legal and juridical apparatus, a machinery of subornation and degradation of the political institutions, and troops whose sole function was to maintain the status quo. The long period of Batista's domination (a gangster ex-sergeant become multimillionaire and henchman of the Cuban dominant classes) best exemplifies how the state had become the tool of foreign interests opposed to those of the nation and the people. Above all these evils stood the degradation of the Cuban people, whose inferiority to the Yankee dominator was daily proved in a thousand ways, explaining the abysmal differences between U.S. progress and prosperity and South American ignorance and want in terms of Latin laziness, mestizo apathy, and Spanish backwardness.

The volume of North American interests, which covered everything from sugar to tourism, seemed to make the Cuban people's emancipation impossible, because of the opposition of Washington to injury to U.S.

investors, the unviability of a nonsubsidized sugar economy, and the danger to Yankee foreign policy in South America represented by an example of rebellion and emancipation in the Caribbean. But precisely where everything seemed most adverse to rebellion, where imperialistic penetration was deepest, where the profit potential for its investors was highest, where investors seemed most satisfied, and where the local oligarchy was most servile the chain of domination was first broken. And it was broken because the Cuban revolutionary movement was structured from the very first as a struggle for political power, devoting itself simultaneously to open war against the dictatorship and against the whole social order. Though it accepted help from forces interested in parallel struggles, it never admitted any alliance that would obligate the new power to the old regime.

No episode of the two world wars, no international event, has for that reason made so great an impact on the United States as the Cuban Revolution. First there was surprise at the rebellion of the attractive young bearded men, to all appearance so romantic; then there was perplexity before the implacable determination of those same young men to fix popular criteria for the reorganization of the Cuban economy and society; finally, there was rancor, fanned by the great companies damaged by nationalization of their profits and by the political strategists aware of the risk that the precedent of the Cuban Revolution represented for Yankee domination over all Latin America.

The leaders of the revolution seemed, in the first months, to be searching for a new social order. Aloof from any theoretical position, supported by the whole people, they approached the problems directly, seeking to solve them as they arose and in accord with national and popular interests, in the light of good sense rather than according to any revolutionary theory. They progressed, little by little, under the increasingly intense goad of a revolutionary process, toward a socialist society, inevitably attracted by the only social order compatible with their circumstances, but also pushed into it by the U.S. defense of the privileges enjoyed by the old order of Cuban society.

Fidel Castro's victory not only overthrew the Batista dictatorship, but opened the regime itself to debate and reformulation. The old oligarchic order that had always prevailed in Cuba, as in all Latin America, had been checkmated—not by congressmen elected for yet another ineffectual constitutional reform, but by the whole people. Their action was prompt. The rural wage-earners and the skilled workers in the sugar mill complexes took control of their respective enterprises, improvising new forms of management. A new antioligarchic, antiimperialistic order was thus installed by the simultaneous action of popular initiative and government acts.

Later on, some U.S. Americans sought to formulate the social model that had been lacking in Cuba, not so much for Cuba, who had gone too far on the socialist road—and which they wanted to destroy—but to forestall the outbreak of social revolutions elsewhere in South America.

Such was the Kennedy team's Alliance for Progress. In spite of its halfheartedness, their project faced so many obstacles from the vested interests of continental exploitation that its original goals had to be abandoned within less than a year. Since then the policy has been to maintain the existing system at all costs, the Yankee administration being aware of its inability to reconcile the interests of its businessmen with Latin American aspirations for progress. But it is also convinced that relations with Latin America are lucrative and safe enough for its businessmen to justify its perpetuating that system with fire and sword.

The former Alliance for Progress advocates were either won over to the new ideology or else thrust aside, yielding to a new politicomilitary group bent on using all armed, political, economic, and psychological resources to hold back history with a barrier of dollars, intrigues and conspiracies, armed interventions, and publicity campaigns as overwhelming as the funds of the greatest capitalistic power on earth permitted.

To Cuba, then, are due the two U.S. Latin American policies. The first was the Monroe Doctrine, born of the attempt at a juridical basis for domination of the island. The second, the Alliance for Progress, formulated as a reply to the challenge of the Cuban Revolution, both in its initial reformist aspect and in its final shape as simple backer of the status quo, relying on agreements with the traditional allies of the United States, the old Latin American oligarchies for whom the current system is also highly lucrative.

Throughout the history of the United States the giant of the continent and the little rebellious island have been contraposed. Born together, and even associated through the economic viability that the prosperous sugar exploitation of the Antilles gave the poor English colonies, they are still polarized today, two historical personages in every way dissociated but complementary.

At her birth the United States, according to the statements of her most representative leaders, coveted the Cuban island. For this purpose she declared war on Spain in 1898. Incapable of swallowing Cuba up directly—as she did Puerto Rico—she finally integrated Cuba into her economic system as her richest colony. In view of Cuban combativeness, the bond could be maintained only by successive interventions, by demoralizing constitutional amendments [15] that degraded primarily those who imposed them, by assassinations, and above all by support of savage dictatorships.

This oppression, owing to the cruelly humiliating forms it assumed, was decisive in awakening the Cuban revolutionary consciousness. The most enlightened leaders of the country have always severely judged the cupidity and pusillanimity of the U.S. governing bodies and have always regarded emancipation from American domination as the most burning national question. The revolution, because of its popular, national character, naturally and necessarily opposed the forces supporting the archaic regime, and lanced the old cyst of domination. From that moment Cuba and the United States once again became polarized, the former no longer the desired morsel before the latter's jaws, but representing a new sociopolitical order for the Latin American nations confronting the guardian of the old, now obsolete system.

It was precisely the exceedingly high degree of U.S. robbery of the Cuban people that constituted the dynamic factor in the revolution. A decisive cofactor was the alliance of the local oligarchy with the imperialistic overlords; that is, the privileged strata—even those not connected with the foreign corporations—feared for their own fate, considering the growing discontent of the people, and placed their reliance on the foreign power to preserve the status quo. Under the circumstances, the antiimperialistic national revolution was transformed into a social revolution against the capitalistic regime, which was incapable of offering autonomous development to the nation. In this way the almighty foreign ally became the gravedigger for the Cuban bourgeoisie, which fell, the victim of its alienation from its own people and from national interests.

The oligarchic-imperialistic pact also played a part in uniting the middle classes, indignant at the national humiliation of Cuba at the hands of the United States—especially the professional castes, and the corps of intellectuals and university students, whose fight against Batista's tyranny had always had to face the ultimate support given him by the Americans and, internally, by the native oligarchy. In this situation the middle classes became radical, transforming their original engagement in an internal political revolution against dictatorship to an antiimperialistic national revo-

[15] The Platt Amendment, affixed by the Americans as to the Cuban Constitution in 1901 and in force until 1934, reads in part (III): "That the government of Cuba consents that the United States may exercise the right to intervene for the preservation of Cuban independence, the maintenance of a government adequate for the protection of life, property, and individual liberty, and for discharging the obligations with respect to Cuba imposed by the treaty of Paris on the United States, now to be assumed and undertaken by the government of Cuba."

lution, and from there to the active or passive acceptance of the regime-reordering social revolution. The inability of the old system to channel the nation toward social progress was too notorious, and there was likewise the severity of the people's judgment of the incapacity, venality and *entreguismo* * of the old governing class. Won over to the revolution, or neutralized as forces of reaction, the middle classes played a most important part both in the conspiratory phase and in the urban fighting that created conditions for the swift, complete victory of the peasants led by Fidel Castro.

The decisive factor, nevertheless, was the capacity of the revolutionary leadership to formulate the Cuban national problem with independence and originality, and particularly to join personally in the guerrilla fighting alongside the peasants, leading the combatants to successive victories, apparently minuscule but with catastrophic effect on the morale of the government troops. It must be pointed out, however, that the Fidel Castro who went up into the mountains was already a leader nationally respected for his previous fighting and especially for the defense he had written in the Moncada prison. This document—*History Will Absolve Me*—which is probably the most vigorous revolutionary manifesto of Latin America, distributed by every possible means to the democratic combatants in the cities, above all to the students, later facilitated identification of the little group of guerrillas in the Sierra Maestra as a responsible revolutionary leadership for the Cuban people in their struggle for national emancipation.

After the victory Fidel Castro revealed an increasing capacity to communicate with the mass and to transmit to it his emancipatory passion for the country—and likewise an extraordinary talent for meeting the problems confronting him in his transition from leader of an armed insurrection to conductor of a social revolution.

The trademark of the Cuban Revolution is its fidelity to the marginal strata of the population. Not only did the revolution seek its first political support from the rural wage-earners, and with it ascend to power, but it exercised its power in a constant effort to integrate these people into the national life. Like all New Peoples, Cuba had, besides the traditional tripartite stratification of the developed nations, a marginalized fourth stratum, pushed aside from the economic life as producer and consumer and from the social, political, and cultural life of the nation. This pocket of miserable illiterates is a human by-product of the plantation-based productive process, which, besides sugar, cotton, coffee, or cacao, produces people incapable of employment or integration into the body of the nation.

* The willingness to surrender the country's natural resources and so forth, for a price.

When the national economy diversifies, a portion of these contingents is attracted to factory work and to services, thus escaping from the condition of structural marginalization. The larger contingent, however, remains surplus, seeking work in seasonal agricultural activities or accumulating on the edges of cities in search of anything that will allow it simply to survive.

From the first, the so-called Latin American "revolutions" have been rearrangements of groups in power, the only exceptions being, first, the Mexican, which, for a time, also tried to integrate the marginalized masses into social life, and more recently the Bolivian, equally frustrated. The Cuban Revolution was born as a social revolution. From its first steps its fundamental preoccupation was to create conditions for the social ascent and political integration of precisely this fourth human contingent, the wretched rural peasants and urban unemployed.

In keeping with the exigencies of this integrative process, the reorganization of society and of the national economy was oriented. Instead of assuming the traditional paternalistic attitude of social welfare protection toward the marginalized masses, the Cuban Revolution tried to set them on their own feet, incorporate them into the national life, and imbue them with self-esteem. In terms of these masses rather than of agricultural productivity the agrarian reform was carried out. It was also in these terms that the incredible Cuban educational effort was made.

The Cuban Revolution found its own path, moved as much by its internal dynamics as by the internationalization forced on it by the United States. Step by step, the decisive stages of the revolutionary installation took place within a system of forces in which one of the determinants was the U.S. American conduct. Thus it was directed more and more congruently toward socialistic solutions as the natural and necessary ways out, considering fidelity to national and popular interests and the U.S. veto of social and economic reordering.

These are the revolutionary steps in chronological order:

• Castro announces great economicosocial reforms to affect the regime of property (February 3, 1959).
• The United States threatens suspension of the sugar quota (February 20).
• Cuba reduces telephone rates and lowers rents by 50 per cent (March 3 and 6). The agrarian reform law is promulgated (May 17) and the National Institute of Agrarian Reform (I.N.R.A.) is created (June 3). Armed forces begin occupation of the latifundia (May 24).
• The United States protests the law as prejudicial to American interests on the island (June 27).

● Prime Minister Raúl Roa of Cuba, conferring with Secretary of State Herter, announces Cuban readiness to enter into talks about the amount of admissible compensation for the expropriation of lands belonging to U.S. citizens (December 10).

● The U.S. ambassador, Bonsal, presents his government's protest concerning illegal acts against rights of ownership (January 11, 1960).

● The Cuban government rejects the note, declaring that it will not grant privileges to U.S. Americans, but will pay equal indemnifications to Cuban and American latifundia proprietors. The I.N.R.A. takes over the lands of United Fruit.

● The Cuban government intervenes in foreign refineries to force them to refine Soviet petroleum bartered for sugar (June 28); U.S. protest (July 5).

● Cuba's response is to intervene in the other industries owned by Americans.

● The United States reduces the Cuban sugar quota by 700,000 tons (July 6).

● The U.S.S.R. assumes responsibility for absorbing the quota (July 6).

● Eisenhower announces a generous program of aid to Latin American nations, stating that Cuba will be excluded until she changes her attitude (July 11).

● Cuba accuses the United States of economic aggression before the U.N. Security Council. The U.S. representative responds by reaffirming the Monroe Doctrine (July 18).

● Cuba nationalizes U.S.-owned sugar mills, oil refineries, and electric plants in order to indemnify the nation for damages caused to her economy by the economic boycott, and to assure consolidation of economic independence (August 6 and 7).

● U.S. Department of State protests "the arbitrary confiscation of U.S. properties to the value of one billion dollars."

● Cuba nationalizes the U.S.-owned nickel mines (August 14).

● Castro reiterates accusations that the United States is preparing an invasion of Cuba (January 1, 1961). Cuba demands reduction of U.S. personnel in Havana (about 100) to the proportion of the Cuban personnel in the Washington embassy, because the American Embassy in Havana has become a focus of counterrevolutionaries (January 2).

● The U.S. government breaks off relations with Cuba, asserting that this action has no effect on the legal status of the Guantánamo naval base (January 3 and 4).

● Kennedy is inaugurated President of the United States (January 20). The Cuban government announces possibilities of reconciliation with the new administration (January 23).

● Kennedy declares that the American policy toward Cuba will not be altered (January 25). Cuba accedes to Latin American mediation, proposed

by Argentina, to improve relations with the United States (February 26).
• The Cuban government declares itself ready to pay compensation for the U.S. properties nationalized, if purchase of sugar is resumed (March 7).
• The U.S. government intensifies pressure on the Latin American nations to break relations with Cuba (April and May).
• Kennedy reiterates his statement that he will not invade Cuba under any circumstances (April 12).
• U.S. planes attack Cuba (April 15). Troops trained by the United States and concentrated under C.I.A. direction invade Playa Girón, suffering utter defeat (April 16).

Responding haughtily to the American challenges, with the most enthusiastic support of the masses whose animosity toward the United States had been cultivated for decades, the Cuban government found its way toward socialistic solutions. More than merely opting for this program, the Cuban people gave full support to concrete measures for national emancipation from an oppression and spoliation long since become odious. In this way the imperialistic regime, as it crumbled, incidentally led national capitalism to ruin with it, because capitalism was too dependent on the United States, too subordinate to and trusting in Yankee might to doubt it or admit any attitude but opposition to what national capitalists regarded as the extreme rashness of revolutionary youth.

In the months following Castro's victory, nearly the whole proprietor and management class moved to the United States. In its footsteps followed the circle associated with it, liberal professionals, administrators, technicians, who in executive positions requiring loyalty to the boss ended by confusing their own with the owners' interests. Thanks to U.S. stimulus, this transfer of personnel included around 100,000 persons whom the revolutionaries refused, or probably were unable, to hold back.

That exodus represented one of the greatest challenges to the nascent economy. Deprived of technical and administrative groups, of university-level professionals—in whose education the nation had invested over the decades, through the educational system and through in-service training and granting of all kinds of privileges—it seemed impossible to direct production. And yet the exodus had its positive side, too. It freed Cuba of a counterrevolutionary contingent that might have retarded, perhaps fatally, the development of the socialist state.

The harmful effects that derived from this expropriation of human resources, subsidized by the Americans, were enormous. This human expropriation is comparable only to the losses that the U.S. Americans suffered from the expropriation of their investments. However, by improvising new technicoadministrative teams, Cuba succeeded in compensating for the exodus, not only setting the productive system in motion again, but simultaneously reconditioning it to serve new interests and disciplining it for planning.

The great works of the Cuban Revolution are precisely this reorganization of the economy on socialist lines and the educational revolution now under way, which set a world record in wiping out illiteracy in one year, in putting all children in school, in leading all youth to technical schools, in matriculating nearly 1 million adult Cubans in courses of cultural recuperation and training for work. This gigantic effort, together with the vitalization and amplification of a reformed and modernized university, is preparing a new technicoprofessional, scientific, and intellectual stratum, enormously broader and more capable than the old, besides being identified with the interests of the Cuban people.

With American hostility transformed into ammunition for the struggle to consolidate revolutionary goals, Cuba was enabled always to move forward. It even had an added advantage: the people identified counterrevolution with Yankee interventionism, an idea fed by the training of antirevolutionary groups abroad, on U.S. territory or in the Middle American countries dominated by the United States, and their patriotic fervor was kindled in defense of their country and their revolution. Thus, the successive attempts at invasion by means of guerrillas, sabotage, and finally landings have always found the people united, as never before, to confront a foreign, increasingly hated enemy.

The harsh stages of a revolutionary implantation, aggravated by lacks resulting from the blockade suffered by the island, creating the greatest difficulties and privations for the whole people, could in this way be faced with a rational zeal that otherwise could have been developed only with difficulty.

This is the reverse side of the Latin American national oligarchies' conspiracy with U.S. corporations, which, if it assures both sides the maintenance of the status quo as long as it is dominant, hardly permits one to survive without the other's protection in revolutionary conditions.

Columbus' idyllic island, with its tropical climate, the prodigious fertility of its soil, and the extraordinary creativity of its people, thus turned to socialism, utilizing its very drawbacks are motivators of revolutionary zeal, and treating domestic dominant castes and foreign interests as one and the same enemy.

If the Cubans' expectation is realized, within a few years their land will be the Antillean garden, and in that case will tell all the peoples of Latin America, in the language of observable and measurable facts, what type of regime is capable of providing abundance, cultural development, and true democracy. The vast possibilities for concretizing this aspiration are what causes so many worries and arouses such anti-Cuban hatred.

8. The Chileans

THE HISTORY OF the Chilean people brings to mind Toynbee's ideas about the stimulating or impeding factors in the burgeoning of civilizations. The fundamental factor, in his eyes, would be the challenge of the difficulties that a people has to face, neither so overwhelming that they dishearten nor so weak that they soften, but stimulating enough to spur the creative mind and maintain the effort of self-affirmation.

Confronted with a rocky land and harsh climate, hammered by Pacific billows, castigated with earthquakes, warred on by the Araucanians, the Chileans, despite all these disadvantages and drawbacks—or thanks to them—have succeeded in forming an ethnos of their own, more mature and vigorous than others based on richer soil, less scourged by so many whips.

Santiago, the capital, aged and gray, solidly built to withstand earthquakes, contrasts oddly with the cordial, colorful gaiety of the people in the streets. However, greater still is the contrast between these window-shopping strollers and the men and women to be seen in the market fairs or through fences around constructions. They contrast in height and slenderness, posture, and clothing—people of two different and distant lands.

Jorge Ahumada, expressing a national self-image typical of the most alienated Chilean intellectuals, asserts: "The majority of Chileans will energetically reject the parallel with many Asian and African peoples, and also with Indo-American peoples. We like to think that we are the English of brown America." [1] No matter how this may sadden him, the truth is that the Chileans constitute a New People, the fruit of the Spaniard's crossbreeding with the native woman. Their stock is Araucanian Indian woman, captured and impregnated by the Spaniard. It was the mestizos originating from these crossings, absorbing in their turn more Indian blood through mestizo-Indian marriage, who molded the fundamental genetic patrimony of the Chilean people. This huge mestizo mass, in the effort to survive biologically and to *be* ethnically, shaped the Chilean nation, which is now becoming self-conscious and forging an authentic self-image befitting its experience and its characteristics.

Chile never received European contingents in such considerable proportions as to permit absorption of so great an indigenous somatic content or to bury it socially, as an inferior caste, under a tidal wave of immigration. Crossbreeding continued during the whole colonial period between the Indian mass and the Hispanic minority, simultaneously with a system of sociocultural integration that, freeing the mestizo from the slavery or serfdom of the Indian, allowed him to ascend via linguistic and religious Hispanization. Naturally, it was not a question of complete assimilation fusing all mestizos in an undifferentiated amalgam. Several differentiation factors, acting in conjunction, molded a phenotypically more European dominant caste. Outstanding among these factors are the privileges conferred on the native-born Spaniard by the colonial statute, providing him with means to impose himself on the Creole, and the enriched mestizos' preference for marrying Spanish women as a way of whitening. This last tendency still persists today, as can be seen in attitudes of which Ahumada is an example, and in the Creole dominant caste's absorption of some tens of thousands of Europeans emigrating to Chile after independence.

The Chilean national self-image, tending to assume the white-European characteristic as a value, results not only in an error but in a rejection of the real national profile. It is true that Chilean literature, especially its poetry, makes the principal integrating symbol the figure of the Araucanian —the real Araucanian, after all, being accepted only as servant labor and as ethnic womb, because Chilean history is nearly always the account of

---

[1] Jorge Ahumada (1958). Similar attitudes are recorded in Nicolás Palacios (1904), Francisco Antonio Encinas (1912), and A. Edwards Vives (1952).

centuries of efforts to decimate him. The situation is curiously similar to that of the São Paulo mamelucos, also proud of their four centuries of *paulistanidade* [belonging to São Paulo], likewise mestizo and equally alienated. Both render homage, with equal respect, to the Indian whom they decimated with the same efficacy.

Could this be a trait typical of the mameluco? Marginalized between two contraposed cultures, partially integrated in both, the mameluco tended to identify himself with the European father against the indigenous mother and her people, as a condition of recognition of his assimilation and as a prerequisite of social ascent. His grandchildren, generations distant from the Indian-European conflict, still manifest that fundamental ambivalence in the extravagance of their identification with the whites and in the cult of the subjugated ancestral indigenes, in contexts that indicate the latter as their own ethnic stock.

The Neo-Araucanians

The territories of Chile and the Argentine northwest were originally occupied by three great indigenous groups profoundly influenced by the peoples of high culture on the Andean altiplano. These three were the Diaguita, the Atacameño, and the Araucanians.

The first two lived on the edge of the Atacama Desert, concentrated in oasis villages or in fishing communities on the coast. They are better known through archeological research than through historical documentation, because they quickly collapsed when faced with the Spanish invasion. Reduced to slavery, victimized by contagious diseases, and worn by combats with the colonial governments dominating the highlands, they disappeared almost totally, leaving no traces. The groups that escaped these convulsions, taking refuge on the Argentine pampas, became Indian horsemen, being affected later, and also decimated, when they came into competition, first, with the gaucho in disputing the herds and pasture lands and, then, with the national ethnic groups forming after independence.

The Araucanians constituted a larger, much more powerful group, established in the Central Andes on lands with milder climate, excellent for agriculture and cattle-raising. Their population, which at the time of the conquest probably exceeded 1.5 million, is reduced today to some 322,000 indigenes surviving as an ethnic group dispersed in hundreds of small communities to the south of the Bío-Bío River. These contemporary Araucanians are nearly all survivors of the Mapuche subgroup, which, living farther south and facing the Spanish more vigorously, escaped the fate of the others—the Picunche and the Huilliche—dominated and subjugated, surviving only in the genes which they contributed to the formation of the Chilean people.

Besides linguistic unity, the three Araucanian groups presented a great cultural homogeneity. They were all on an evolutionary level intermediate between the Chibcha type of rural craftsman states and the peoples at the stage of undifferentiated horticultural villages, such as the Guaraní. They lived in permanent villages not far apart, forming blocs of great demographic density (seven persons per square mile), based on an advanced agriculture that was already utilizing irrigation and rotation of land to cultivate the white potato (probably domesticated by them), corn, and various other plants.

They were, then, on the threshold of social stratification and political unification, ready to constitute a rural craftsman state. They had already fulfilled the preliminary requisite of being producers of food surpluses sufficient to differentiate a social stratum freed from productive tasks, devoted to war, craftsmanship, shamanism, and bureaucracy. Nevertheless, they had not taken that step toward social stratification and concentration of population in urban nuclei surrounded by rural districts.

On the plane of political organization, each of the Araucanian groups was divided into independent local communities, internally structured on a kinship foundation according to a system of clan lineages. The local leaders of these communities, in times of peace, exercised the few functions of chieftainship of a nonstratified group. For war purposes they associated in confederations, but split up again into myriads of autarchic nuclei instead of structuring themselves as states.

Given their level of cultural development and the favorable conditions of the environment, the Araucanians accumulated the advantages of a nonstratified tribal society—with neither powerful lords nor miserable pariahs —with an abundant subsistence economy that furnished much leisure time. Under these conditions they were enjoying, at the time of the conquest, a rich social environment based on equality, abundance, and joy of living, stemming from living together in large homogeneous communities unified by the same traditions and by the same world view.

To the first encounters with the Spanish cavalry and firearms the Araucanians reacted with the perplexity that such novelties aroused in all Indians. However, he soon learned that these invaders were human when they dismounted, and that they and their mounts were equally vulnerable and mortal. The groups that maintained their independence entered on a long period of intermittent fighting punctuated by intervals in which a *modus vivendi* prevailed that assured them survival, but at the same time allowed the Spaniards to fortify themselves. There was also the phase of stately ceremonies of parleying, which were annually repeated between the Spanish governor and his retinue on one side and the Araucanian chieftains on the other, to sign or ratify agreements of peaceful coexistence.

Peace being broken, centuries of bitter struggle ensued in which the Araucanians offered greater resistance to the Spaniards than did the peoples of high culture. This bellicosity is explained, probably, by the stage of cultural development they had attained. Not being unified in political units or stratified in opposing classes of masters and subalterns, no such nobility existed as the Inca, the Mexican, or even the Chibcha that could appease the enemy in order to preserve its domination and its privileges, nor any servile stratum prepared for exploitation and indifferent to the substitution of new masters for old.

The two Araucanian peoples, the Picunche and the Huilliche, who first entered in conflict with the Spanish succumbed in the end. Their subjugation, however, cost more blood and effort than all the other conquests in America. Every nucleus that was dominated after the sixteenth century underwent detribalization through recruitment of the Indians as mitayos for agricultural work or gold placer mining, and as servants of all kinds. Mining at its peak employed more than 20,000 Indians, aged fifteen to twenty-five, compelled by force of slavery to be transformed into the proletariat of the nascent society. Both these mitayos and the village Indians, handed over together with their lands to the exploitation of the encomenderos, had no chance to preserve their way of life and their social institutions, or to be integrated into the European and Christian institutions. They were nothing but muscle power, to be used up at hard labor, and wombs to produce more people. In consequence, the indigenous population was reduced to less than half (A. Lipschutz, 1956, 1963). In the new native and mestizo generations that were growing up immersed in that subworld, unacquainted with their tribal traditions and having a deformed conception of Spanish culture, a necessarily spurious protoculture began to take shape. Rather than a people, they were for centuries at the service of the foreign master, to whose habits, beliefs, and prejudices they were forced to adjust.

Alluvial gold having been exhausted, the Spaniards went on to exploit exclusively the only "mine" they had left to them: the Indian labor force. Great contingents of captured Indians continued to join the nascent society in this way, war thus becoming a business in itself. Together with the enslaved indigenous mass the mestizo class was increasing, serving as a stratum of intermediaries specializing in recruiting more Indians for the labor force and creating a hybrid culture in which the Hispanic heritage would predominate. Some of these mestizos, recognized and protected by the white father, in some cases declared white by legal disposition of the crown, became integrated in the dominant caste.

Nevertheless, the great mass of mestizos and detribalized Indians would join the national society to form the principal Chilean rural contingent, the *huaso*. Occupied in cattle herding and farming, skilled with horses and associated with the horse as an instrument of work and war, the huaso is the Chilean version of the gaucho. It was with these huasos that the haciendas expanded throughout the zone liberated from hostile Indians, shaping a patriarchal society of natural economy, dominated by latifundia proprietors, their huge body of relatives, and their henchmen. On these ranches, besides agriculture and cattle herding, the huaso worked wool, leather, and wood to produce objects for local use. Monopolizing the land, the hacendero acquired control of the herds and of the huasos as a labor force capable of making the lands productive, constructing houses and property improvements, and being the fount of energy and wealth of the nascent society. By that time the Peruvian market was absorbing the surplus agricultural production, and some copper exporting was contributing to the costs of imports, giving economic viability to the colony.

The drastic reduction in the indigenous populations also operated in clearing the fields that here, as on the altiplano, were passing into the hands of the encomenderos. They were engaged in commercial farming, which supported the local mining, permitted some export of foodstuffs, and also raised cattle, horses, and sheep.

The Mapuche, established farther south, strengthened in their determination to resist by news of the fate suffered by their brother peoples after subjugation, continued fighting nearly to our own time in defense of their autonomy. In spite of seeing their tribal world destroyed, their culture made unviable, and themselves confined to the poorest strips of lands, they stubbornly clung to their ethnic identification. Under the impact of the profound acculturation that they have undergone, however, both through the centuries of open warfare and the last decades of competitive coexistence, they retain almost nothing of their original Araucanian ethnos.

The Mapuche resistance to Spanish domination was probably the longest continued and most barbarous—on both sides—of all that were waged in America. Five old Araucanian chieftains bore witness to the indigenous view of the sanguinary war, according to the report of a Spanish leader who lived among them as a captive in 1629.[2] He describes the spirit of the Indians, their adherence to the land, and the generosity of the treatment accorded him. He sets forth the laments of the old Indians, express-

---

[2] Francisco Núñez de Pineda y Bascuñán, 1863 (quoted by Lipschutz, 1963, p. 101).

ing their stupefaction at the barbarism with which the Spaniards enslaved them, branding their faces with red-hot irons, and treating them like mad dogs; he records their shock at the sadism of the Spanish ladies who took pleasure in torturing Araucanian slaves. Finally, he explains how this treatment stirred the Indians to revolt, venting their animus in the torture administered to Pedro de Valdivia, the Spanish conquistador: to sate his thirst for gold they daubed him symbolically with gold and poured dirt into his mouth until he died.

During the first half of the eighteenth century, as the fruit of the process of subjugation and miscegenation, the fundamental cultural configuration of the Chilean people had been formed. It was composed of mestizos of various social classifications, ranging from legitimate sons of enriched Spaniards to the poorest huasos liberated from the mita and the encomienda by their status as non-Indians. Their numbers were enhanced by large contingents of deculturated Indians, forming the lowest class of the nascent society, Indians marginalized from their groups by identification with the dominator, and Indians who progressively managed to pass as non-Indians, too.

On these real and simulated mestizos fell not only the heaviest tasks but also all the burden of colonial discrimination. Passed over in favor of the native-born Spaniard, barred from the nobler occupations, from military career as regular soldiers, and from land ownership—the principal form of social ascent—they lived as a subaltern caste.

While the mestizo stratum was growing, with the deculturation and abandonment of the tribal ethnos by these contingents integrated in the new society, the Indians themselves, who held aloof and isolated farther to the south, were training for war. They adopted the riding horse, took to herding the cattle that had multiplied over the countryside, and fitted metal tips to their lances and arrows. So the combats went on, motivated by this resistance and by the pressing need to capture Indians to replace the slaves worn out in work and those who escaped the encomendero by way of mestizo classification or cultural mimetism.

Another motive for the war on the Mapuches was the need to broaden opportunities for ascent of the mestizo mass itself, constantly growing, through appropriation of new indigenous lands. This procedure prevailed to the end of the nineteenth century, established by the custom of distributing the lands conquered from wild Indians among the most outstanding soldiers, in proportion to military rank.

With Chile's independence the situation at first altered only for the worse. In the name of liberty, equality, and fraternity a great deal of libertarian legislation was promulgated, aimed at destroying the bases of tribal life founded on communal ownership of land. Nominally the Araucanian was made equal to all other Chileans, but in fact he was liquidated with the fundamental status of autonomous survival. In this way competition began between Indian and latifundium owner. The latter, with communal lands adjoining his own and thus forming his most flexible boundary, naturally had on his side all those who wanted to become proprietors of latifundia. It was the epoch of false purchases, of "free" successions and cessions of tribal territories whereby the Araucanians were deprived of nearly all their former lands and the despoiled Indians were relegated to the most wretched stratum of the rural population.

An episode that can only be explained by the oppression to which the Araucanians were subjected—the adventure of a Frenchman, self-styled Antoine I, who declared himself king of "New France" and mobilized the Indians in defense of his crown—put squarely before the Chilean authorities the necessity of integrating the Araucanians into the national society. As there was no integrational instrument in the Chilean ideological arsenal other than the practices of *force majeure,* war was once more declared. Once more, this time in 1859, adventurers were recruited under promise of indigenous lands as reward for their military exploits. New land thefts and new decimations succeeded each other for more than twenty years, reducing the Araucanian area and population still further. During the same period the Araucanian groups that had settled on the Argentine pampas, multiplying along with the wild cattle and through enculturation of other tribes, joined in the emancipatory struggle. These Argentine Araucanian reached a higher level of organization through unified political and military commands and through the confederation of tribes, which permitted long resistance to the Argentine army campaign against them. They were finally exterminated.

The two episodes are highly significant as an expression of the Araucanian will to autonomy. This ethnic bloc, aspiring to nationality, which would have been the only Emerging People of the Americas, prematurely rising in an unfavorable regional and world situation, was literally crushed.

The Araucanians of today are integrated as the most miserable contingent of the economy; they are distinguished from rural Chileans principally by retaining their mother language, as a rule spoken only in the home, and by their self-identification as indigenes, that is, as people who not only consider themselves different and inferior, but are held and treated as such by the average Chilean. Through centuries of oppression they have become a poverty culture, retrogressing from the degree of development attained long ago and losing the ethnic pride they formerly displayed, because these had become incompatible with their role as the poorest caste among the most disinherited strata of the Chilean peasantry. Those who preserve a bit of communal ground, however, have an advantage over the average tenant farmer and the *roto* [man of the lowest class]: the privilege of being able to escape periodically from latifundian exploitation by taking refuge in the tribal community. Even so, this refuge only postpones the ultimate destiny, which is submergence as an undifferentiated part in the roto subworld, to rise from it with a social revolution that will make the conditions of all Chilean country people worth living.

As we have seen, the Araucanians, because of the size of their population and their degree of cultural development at the time of the conquest, would have matured in our day to the status of Emerging Peoples, like the African and Asian tribes now being transformed into young nationalities. This did not happen because they were ruthlessly slaughtered when they were ripe for that emergence and expecially because they had experienced a more ferocious continual, efficacious subjugation than any that fell on the Africans. The comparison may seem exaggerated, in view of what is known about the harshness of the white slavocrat's treatment of the Negro. The two cases are, indeed, human dramas of unfathomable depths. The Chilean and Argentine Araucanians and so many other American peoples, however, are proof to us of how much worse were the conditions that they faced. Indeed, the formative process of many American peoples is based on the genocide of populations that went as high as or exceeded hundreds of thousands, the extermination of ethnic groups who have survived only as the genetic stock of subsequent mestizo populations.

What has been observed in all these cases in America is the contraposition of the Indians and mestizos as distinct protoethnic entities from the first. The old aboriginal ethnos diminishes to the point of extinction with the last Indian to identify himself as such, whatever might be his degree of acculturation. And the new mestizo ethnos increases across the centuries as the labor force of an exogenous enterprise. This force undermines, from within, the edifice of .European domination in proportion as it acquires self-consciousness and the capacity for self-imposition as a new national entity. That happens when the mestizo succeeds in mastering, besides the physical space he occupies, the political and cultural space, first by assuming his own image with pride in it and, later, by formulating and carrying out his own project of national order.

For many mestizo countries of America the fulfillment of the first is still far off. Few have achieved the tranquil acceptance of their own image, self-identification as a new ethnos, racially more heterogeneous than the three basic trunks but neither better nor worse than they, culturally molded by the integration of the European heritage with a patrimony forged with great difficulty under compression from the slavocratic regime and in the heat of the centuries-long effort to survive in the American lands and create here their own forms of being and thinking.

One of the very last forms of European domination, existing after independence, is the internalization by millions of mestizo Americans of aestheticohuman ideals and other values based on white European characteristics as marks of superiority. This assumption of the self-image of "the other" is manifested in many ways. In the Chilean aristocracy, for example, it is betrayed by the vanity of identification as white, made with the greatest naturalness, even with genuineness, by people who regard themselves as different and better and attribute their social precedence to their lighter skin. The age-old exercise of an uncontested social superiority, founded on monopolistic ownership of land and other forms of wealth, and the habit of bossing servile dependents, usually dark-skinned, ended by making even the aristocrats of the most clearly indigenous phenotype see themselves as white and explain their superior social status by this characteristic.

In a large number of Chilean intellectuals and in the middle class most alienated from its people, the same internalization is revealed in the attempt to identify with the white aristocracy—or white by self-definition—and in the earnest effort to disfigure the true national image verbally and ideologically by creating subtle instruments for subjugation of the more strongly mestizo popular classes. So it is that the racial marks betraying indigenous ancestry, instead of being worn with pride, continue to function as stigmas, arousing discriminatory attitudes ranging from open prejudice to self-censure.

These facts, as episodes in the Chileans' formation as a New People, have not only descriptive importance but also the value of up-to-dateness, because one of the battle lines of the oligarchy's fight to perpetuate its privileges is the sociocultural and psychological barriers deterring recognition of the mestizo masses as the true Chilean people. As long as they prevail, these values will be an obstacle to the formulation of a reordering national project whose elementary priority is the integration of all Chileans, but mainly their marginalized masses, into one and the same egalitarian society.

The most curious thing about the Chilean self-image is the combination of a series of contradictory traits: (1) the extreme literary exaltation of the virile qualities of the Araucanian, transformed into mythic ancestral hero not after his disappearance but even during the combats to exterminate him; (2) the distaste for the mestizo character of the population, contraposed to a certain pride in the beauty of Chilean women, explained in terms of the Spaniard's crossbreeding with the Indian; (3) the Anglophilia of attitudes, ideology, etiquette, as an index of attainments and whiteness; (4) even a certain anti-Hispanic animosity, revealed in the effort to depict the Iberian conquistador of Chile as a blond giant of Germanic type.

All these traits lead the Chilean—like the Brazilian—to ideals of becoming "whiter," ideals that have peculiar consequences, among them the facility with which the few European contingents immigrating into Chile after independence have risen to the dominant caste. In these castes can be found a high percentage of northern European surnames and of light-skinned persons, which is explained, at least partially, by the dark oligarchy's delight in marrying off its sons and daughters to the immigrant or his descendants, in the attempt, as touching as it is ingenuous and alienated, to become whiter and de-Americanized.[3]

Copper and Nitrate Chile

The Chile that achieved political independence had a population of about 1 million inhabitants, nearly all of them established in the agropastoral areas in the vicinity of Santiago, Valparaíso, and Concepción. Independence, like the whole of national life, was decided in terms of the dominant class of latifundia proprietors, merchants, and clerics (without any appreciable participation by the people), who wished to rid themselves of a costly, humiliating, and unnecessary protectionism on the part of Spain. After the victory of San Martín's troops over the Spanish forces (1818), which smashed the last bastion of colonial power, O'Higgins took over the government, turning his attention to the destruction of a few still-resistant pockets and to the organization of the country for autonomous life.

The new republic, proclaimed in the name of the people but organized by the dominant classes, was institutionalized in the form of an oligarchic order that preserved all the privileges of the old colonial aristocracy and amplified them by the appropriation of civil, ecclesiastical, and military positions held until then by Spaniards. To this end she retained the *mayorazgo*, which perpetuated the patriarchal system by assuring the succession of the first-born in the ownership of the latifundium. Codes were reformed to adjust to the liberal winds that were blowing over the world, the colonial coercive institutions being replaced by new, equally antipopular institutions in the name of the people and of equality and liberty.

Nevertheless, by achieving a certain degree of national integration and

[3] On the problems of mixed breeding in Chile see the excellent works by A. Lipschutz (1956, 1963), Alberto M. Salas (1960), Lewis Hanke (1959), Alvaro Jara (1965), Angel Rosenblat (1954), and Juan Comas (1961).

unity in political command earlier than the other Hispano-American republics, Chile was able to commence expansion over neighboring areas, demanding a larger share of the Spanish colonial spoils than that due her. First she busied herself with the occupation and appropriation of the Strait of Magellan, which was to mark her southern boundary. She then advanced to the north, across the Atacama Desert, with an eye to the appropriation of the copper mines. Later, she won possession of all the coastal region of Bolivia and Peru where European and Chilean enterprises were beginning to exploit immense nitrate and guano deposits.

War and military triumph quickened in Chileans the feeling of pride—so eloquently expressed in the national motto "By reason or by force"—guaranteed their supremacy in the Pacific, and assured them a great source of wealth. In spite of spoliative association with foreign companies, Chile's copper, and later nitrates, placed the country in the world market as a producer of materials of decisive war value and of fundamental economic importance to Europe, which was struggling to revive its tired soil with fertilizers. The Chileans' dominant position on the Pacific assured Valparaíso the position of obligatory port of call for all shipping through the Strait of Magellan.

During the middle of the nineteenth century the population had risen to 1.5 million, and Santiago's was approaching 200,000, both considerable numbers for that period as compared with other Latin American national figures. The availability of a labor force and national resources compensated for Chile's marginal position in relation to the great world commercial routes. This position did not make Chile an attractive ground for the application of foreign capital in agricultural undertakings or for the migration leaving Europe for the New World. In the thirty years following independence, while Argentina received nearly three million Europeans, Chile had only 50,000 immigrants. These were mostly Latins, but they also included some small northern European contingents that settled in the south, as farmers. The majority of the immigrants stayed in the cities and devoted themselves to commerce, hoping to get rich and join the dominant caste through wealth and by marriage.

Social ascent would be facilitated, as we have seen, by the rigid ethnosocial stratification that divided the Chileans into a small stratum of great landowners and the mass of poverty-stricken urban and rural workers, barely separated by a thin intermediate stratum into which the immigrant integrated immediately and from which he would ascend easily, thanks to the colonialistic hyperappreciation of the white as compared with the national mestizo. Thus, what whitens or Europeanizes in Chile is not the people—as would occur in Uruguay and Argentina, becoming Transplanted Peoples—but the "aristocratic frond." Hence the presence of so many non-Spanish foreign names in the lists of public men, entrepreneurs, and diplomats of Chile.[4]

The exploitation of the newly won territories in the north, and of the port at Valparaíso, permitted diversification of the economy through the increase in mining enterprises and port patronage, which made Chile less dependent on the latifundia and facilitated an institutional reorder. Such was the period of reforms during the second half of the nineteenth century, when a more liberal regime came in: the institution of the mayorazgo was abolished, integrating the latifundia into the national economy, and limits were imposed on clerical influence on the state.

The new economic and political motive of Chilean society came to be represented from that time on by the foreign groups connected with the development and export of minerals. Adversely affected in their interests by President Balmaceda, who demanded a greater state share in profits from the business, a series of internal struggles was unleashed that cost nearly as many lives as the Chilean wars. The wage-earners of the mining regions took the side of the mining interests in these fights, misled by the latter's liberal language. The result of the conflicts was the installation, in the name of political regeneration and electoral freedom, of an administration more docile to imperialistic exigencies. The new government achieved stability by means of an oligarchic pact unifying the powerful mining and latifundia interests and those of the upper ranks of the army for control of the machine of state. This pact found its most typical political expression in the parliamentary regime that followed, dominating the country for more than thirty years in the name of democracy and the common good, but actually in the service of the agrarian oligarchy and large mining interests.

Contrary to the other Latin American nations, which, developing their mineral wealth during the colonial period, saw nearly all the fruit of their labor hauled away to the metropolis, the Chilean mines were developed largely after independence. In these circumstances, in spite of the imperialistic spoliation of its economy, the Chilean state succeeded in gaining much larger portions of the wealth created. It was thus able to count on considerable funds for public works and services, resulting in the premature metropolitanization of Santiago, unaccompanied by an industrialization that could support it; a vast parasitic middle class of government employees and officials, merchants, soldiers, and liberal professionals, which became more and more burdensome on the public treasury; and the opportunity to establish a broad system of public education.

---

[4] In 1940 nearly 100,000 Chileans of foreign origins were located in the most favored sectors of the population, nearly all in the middle classes (F. B. Pike, 1962).

Chile succeeded in this way in excelling other Latin American nations, which, sunk in poverty, had or still have to confront the cost of education and social welfare just when the state is burdened by the demands of great infrastructural investments. The Chilean oligarchy also benefited in these circumstances, using public funds to attenuate class tensions through a patronage policy with the civilian or military sectors.

Thus, under the protection of the parliamentary patriciate, which controlled all the ministries as well as the congress, a regime of corruption and patronage guided and stimulated the rise in national politics of the middle classes of employees, practitioners of the liberal professions, bureaucrats, and the middle echelons of the armed forces officers. It was this urban stratum, mobilized by new political groups extolling austerity and social reforms for succoring the popular masses plunged into pauperism, that was to alter the power structure. In 1920, when the movement won the support of the working class, its leader, Arturo Alessandri Palma, was elected president. Thus, political teams from the urban middle classes, which would form the ministries and make their political voices heard, became a counterweight to the previous hegemonic dominion of the oligarchy.

This change in the composition of political power is expressive of the structural renovation that Chile had been experiencing for decades before. As the mining economy expanded, not only had a new branch of the oligarchy and a proletariat been created, but the middle classes also had been enormously enlarged. With the growth of the cities and of the state machine, the new middle strata of employees found conditions for still further expansion and for forcing their presence and representation in power. However, the working class had grown simultaneously, beginning, through great mass movements, to demand improved living conditions. With this, pressure was exerted on the government to attend to consumer claims rather than to those of investment.

The promulgation of a new political and social statute for wage-earners would only be achieved, however, at the cost of Alessandri's fall and the imposition of a military regime. The new legislation, assuring both freedom to organize unions and democratic guarantees to the wage class, led social struggles in Chile to a high level, placing the oligarchic dominion itself in doubt. With the question posed in these terms, the leaders of the middle classes, the natural intermediaries between the working classes and the government, began claiming their own social precedence, causing the promulgation of a vast paternalistic legislation of protection for the employees—in other words, themselves—that would transform them into a new privileged caste as compared with the mass of unskilled manual laborers. The cost of wages and benefits of this parasite class, as well as social welfare and education to which only it would have access, weighed more and more heavily on the economy, making impossible any improvement in the level of living standards of the wage-earners and the peasantry.

The 1930 world crisis had tremendous repercussions on the Chilean economy, the basic weakness of which lay in its complete dependence on the international minerals market. With this in collapse for several years, the Chileans experienced an upsurge of unemployment en masse and great popular convulsions. The military regime, which had overthrown President Alessandri's middle-class administration, but had carried out a nationalistic policy of industrialization and protection of the working man, fell.

Years of unrest followed in which the prewar problems had strong repercussions on Chilean political life, and in which the workers gained greater capacity of organization and a growing influence on political power. World War II, enhancing the value of Chilean mineral production, and, above all, restricting the importation of manufactures, led to a policy of autarchic development favoring industrialization, permitting Chile to recover the rate of spontaneous progress lost since the great crisis.

Reintegration in the world market after the conflict brought back the old problems, showing in this case also the unviability of building an autonomous, progressive industrial society in the international economic context. Naturally, the difficulty was not intrinsic in Chilean society, nor was it owing to the nature of its export products, but to the foreign appropriation of Chilean mining enterprises and to the deforming role that this exogenous nucleus of interests played in the whole economy of the country. Added to the constricting effects of the internal oligarchic order, based on the latifundium, this external restriction placed the Chilean people at the service of designs not only foreign but opposed to their own.

Political Radicalization

The most characteristic traits of modern Chile are, probably, her high degree of urbanization, her incipient industrialization, foreign domination of her mineral wealth, and her political radicalization. The precocious, profound urbanization is explicit in the facts that urban population rose from 46 per cent to 65 per cent from 1920 to 1960 and that between 1952 and 1962 the population of the three largest cities increased by 65 per cent whereas that of the rest of the country rose by only 35 per cent. In 1952, 37 per cent of the working population was engaged in nonproductive services; in 1960 this grew to 46 per cent. In the latter year only 30 per cent of the working population was engaged in mining and agriculture and

24 per cent of the labor force in manufacturing industries. These figures are indicative of an overurbanization and a structural maturation that make of Chilean society an example of contradictory socioeconomic development, because it is directed from outside by the large mining corporations that, first, have taken over the mineral reserves of the nation and, second, have promoted a substitutive industrialization through branches of international companies. Both types of firms absorb the greater part of the surpluses produced by the Chilean people, taking it out of the country.

In these circumstances urbanization (because premature), industrialization (because reflexive), and structural modernization (because incomplete and incapable of bringing the entire population into the modern world's life styles) will not produce the results that a genuinely autonomous industrialization has produced in other countries. Three internal factors have also contributed to this situation: (1) the demographic expansion of nearly 2.5 per cent per year in the last decade; (2) the domination of the rural area by the latifundium (75 per cent of the cultivable land is in the hands of 5 per cent of the rural landowners) and its miserable living and working conditions, flagrantly contrasting with those of the urban workers; and (3) the attraction of city life, more democratic and egalitarian, which offers work opportunities in expanding industry, civil construction, and broad tertiary sectors including everything from domestic service to bureaucracy.

The impact of these factors started a massive move of people from country to city, creating problems of marginality but occasioning a national integration that would not have been accomplished otherwise. The integration was facilitated by the educational effort that, by teaching the huaso to read and write, amplified his level of information and participation in national life, opening to him, besides better employment prospects, opportunities to rise to a status of human dignity that rural oppression had always denied him. So it is that, in direct proportion to urbanization, firm family structure is observable in the lower strata, the index of illegitimacy, for example, falling from 40 per cent in 1917 to 17 per cent in 1959. In the cities the huaso will also join in political life independently of the patronal institutions and of rural caudillism.

The principal deforming force in Chilean development, as we have seen, is the foreign appropriation of the country's mineral wealth, first by the English and Germans, and more recently by the U.S. companies. This foreign domination over the sector that produces two thirds of the foreign exchange credits and provides a large part of the public funds, deprives the nation of the power to decide the questions of greatest importance to its destiny. Its most harmful effect, however, is the interference with the foreign policy of Chile, given the strategic nature of the export products, and with its internal political life, through these companies' pacts with the latifundian oligarchy and the national industrial and commercial bourgeoisie to maintain the exploitative system that condemns Chile to underdevelopment.

Another fundamental characteristic of Chile, stemming from her precocious structural maturation, is the political radicalization that sets the few hundred families of the "aristocratic frond" and the urban patriciate of professional politicians and entepreneurs in opposition to the entire mass of the population, from the middle strata to the classes of common people already integrated in the political process. The latest Chilean elections were held not between factions of the oligarchy or between them and leaderships of the popular forces, but between Christian-Democrats with a leftist-reformist program and an alliance of Socialists with Communists. They were held in an atmosphere of extreme tension under the interested eyes of all Latin Americans, who saw a battle of the continent decided there. Moreover, with the active, undisguised participation by the U.S. government and other international forces, which looked on Frei's fight for victory as an international battle as much theirs as it was the Chileans'.

The Christian-Democrats triumphed doubly, not only in votes but in successfully holding the elections. Actually, the very real possibilities of a leftist victory caused the greatest panic in the most reactionary sectors, creating an imminent risk of a military coup. Few Latin American countries, perhaps none, could have endured such a test without the "preventive" rupture of democratic institutions.

The questions set before the Chilean Christian-Democrat administration under the eyes of a vigilant public opinion were profound and complex. In first place on the docket was the foreign domination of the mineral deposits, which Chileans want to see nationalized and accessible to all the world markets and which the Yankees want to control, though admittedly disguised because it constitutes the very nerve center of the antiimperialistic political campaigns. The importance of minerals in the balance of payments, the dependence on the traditional foreign markets and even the system for their improvement found in foreign countries, the lack of internal resources for investment in this field, and the strategic nature of the products make the copper question the most complex challenge confronting the Chileans. Also under debate is the agrarian structure, founded on the latifundium, incapable of raising the living standards of the rural populations, and so archaic as to be incompatible with the introduction of modern technology into agriculture. This is probably the sector most vulnerable to reorder, considering the "modernity" of Chile, whose basically mining economy created a social stratification atypical of Latin America and of the type that facilitates the confrontation of latifundian interests.

Chile undoubtedly has sufficiently compressed the rural masses and has enough support from extraagrarian sectors to oppose the old latifundian oligarchy.

The Christian-Democrats are called on to solve these problems, to renovate the entire society. The challenge is a grave one, because so few Latin American governments have reached power so committed to try to do right, or so clearly called on to confront the social restructuring of the nation under the eyes of so enlightened and acute a public opinion. In the face of these challenges the techniques of development, which Chile has pioneered for Latin America, are of no avail: it is up to her to face and refute the forces of domestic and foreign constriction that are in league to maintain the status quo.

This problem is all the more complex because the rising tide of popular aspirations for progress and development now sweeping all Latin America has reached one of its highest points in Chile. There, confronting each other undisguised, are the body of socialist solutions alleging, on the basis of many precedents, that it can lead Chile to full development in a generation; and the Christian-Democrat alternative, which declares that it can do so, too, slowly but safeguarding the political and spiritual values important to the Chilean people. The Socialists and Communists, being in the opposition, can continue their proselytizing based on the same discourse. But the Christian-Democrats, with the hot potato of power burning their fingers, have to demonstrate by concrete acts their capacity to do something about the Chilean people's will to reform and progress within the framework represented by their commitment to maintain the capitalistic regime and prevent the socialist revolution.

PART IV

The Transplanted Peoples

"The United States seems destined by Providence to lay waste America with misery in the name of freedom."

—SIMÓN BOLÍVAR

THE TRANSPLANTED PEOPLES of the Americas are the contemporary result of European migrations to the broad spaces of the New World, families hoping to resume their social life with greater freedom and better chances of prosperity.

Some, such as the colonists of North America, settled in territories either uninhabited or sparsely occupied by tribal groups with incipient agricultural culture, whom they warred against or displaced instead of living or mingling with them in the way that the European colonist, Englishman or Hollander or Portuguese or Spaniard, always did: North American colonists were integrated in family groups and accompanied by white women. Other Transplanted Peoples, such as the Argentines and Uruguayans, resulted from European migrations to the River Plate region, men who competed with Hispanized mestizo groups, previously formed, whom they also displaced or subjugated with little less violence.

The Transplanted Peoples contrast with the other sociocultural configurations of the Americas because of their characteristically European profile, expressed in the landscape that they molded, their predominantly Caucasoid racial type, their cultural configuration, and the more maturely capitalistic nature of their economy, based principally on modern industrial technology and their social structure, which incorporated nearly all their population into the productive system and the majority into the social, political, and cultural life of the nation. For this very reason their national and social problems and world view are different from the American peoples of the other categories.

Between the Transplanted Peoples, especially between the North and South Americans, lie profound differences deriving not only from their cultural stocks, predominantly Latin and Catholic in one case, Anglo-Saxon and Protestant in the other, but also from their degree of development. These discrepancies bring the Argentines and Uruguayans closer to and identify them more with the other Latin Americans, also neo-Iberian, also Catholic, and likewise poor and backward. By virtue of the majority of their other characteristics, however, they are Transplanted Peoples and, as such, show many traits in common with the colonists of North America.

It is no coincidence that these Transplanted Peoples are all found in temperate zones. Conditioned through the ages to the rigors of winter and the marked rhythm of the seasons, the European immigrant finds himself more at home in similar climates, avoiding the tropics as much as possible. The inverse occurs today with the peoples adapted to the tropics, who feel uncomfortable in cold regions.

Some authors seek to explain the differences in degree of socioeconomic development between the Transplanted Peoples and the other blocs in terms of the opposition of these differentiating factors: the predominantly white racial condition versus the greater crossbreeding with colored peoples by the Latin American populations; the European cultural homogeneity versus the heterogeneity resulting from the incorporation of indigenous traditions, as occurred with the Witness Peoples; the geographic position and its climatic consequences; the Protestant versus Catholic religious identification.

The majority of such assertions cannot withstand analysis, however. Civilizations have developed in different racial, cultural, and climatic contexts. Different aspects of Western European civilization itself have been highly manifested in combination with Catholic and Protestant cults, which after all are variants of one and the same religious tradition. Only the heading of cultural homogeneity has any causal significance. Its role as motive of development, even so, does not lie in cultural homogeneity in itself, but in the possibilities that it opens up circumstantially to emigrants from Europe at a certain period in history, with access to and mastery of the new knowledge and the new technology on which the Industrial Revolution now under way was founded.

Indeed, it is only historically and through painstaking examination of the over-all civilizational process, in which all these peoples have been caught up, and of the several factors intervening in the formation of each of them, that we can explain their form and their performance. This is what we propose to do with the Transplanted Peoples, by examining the racial and cultural composition of their formative contingents and their mode of enlistment, association, and fusion in new ethnonational entities.

First, however, we must point out other general factors of differentiation or approximation of the Transplanted Peoples in relation to the other historicocultural configurations of the Americas, probably more explicative of the respective modes of being than the oft-alleged climatic, racial, and religious differences. Among these factors, in the case of the Transplanted Peoples of North America, the fact stands out that they are resultants of projects of autocolonization of new areas, in opposition to the exogenous nature of the undertakings that gave rise to other configurations: the subjugation and enslavement of culturally very advanced societies, over which the conquistador established himself as a new dominant class, as in the case of the Witness Peoples, and the settlement through enslavement of Indians and Negroes brought in for agricultural or mining exploitation, in the case of the New Peoples.

Other factors combine with these. They are, principally, the preponderance of a process of assimilation of the new contingents on the part of the first colonial nuclei, in the case of the Transplanted Peoples, as opposed to the process of deculturation that directed the integration of the enslaved indigenous and Negro contingents, in the New Peoples, and the process of cultural disintegration and ethnic transfiguration that characterizes the Witness Peoples.

The three processes are both similar and different but the specific characteristics of each of them stamped notable differences on the resulting configurations. In the first case it was a matter of linguistically Anglicizing Europeans of different origins, or of making uniform the norms of social life or customs that differed only as variants of one and the same cultural tradition. In the second case it was a question of wiping out original cultures, too highly differentiated among themselves and from the European to admit simplified forms of coexistence and work under the pressure of slavocratic compulsion and with no other interest than exploiting the labor force to the maximum. In the third case, choking off the autonomous developmental process of high original cultures gave rise to the implantation of a spurious, alienated complex in which the learned contents and the occupational qualification of the population were lost. It is plain to see that the peoples resulting from these last two processes of cultural formation would face enormously greater difficulties for their ethnonational reconstitution and for the integration of industrial civilization's technology into their cultural patrimony.

Other factors explicative of the differences in the three configurations derive from the more maturely capitalistic mercantile character of the formation guiding the creation of the Transplanted Peoples in contrast to the other two. Most notable among them is the more egalitarian nature of the society established in North America, contrasting with the more authoritarian profile of the other configurations. This opposition was expressed in the predominance of the hacienda system based on land monopoly throughout Latin America, in contrast to the predominance of family-owned farm property in North America. The former occasioned a type of republican oligarchy that conducted national destinies after independence; the latter engendered a democratic republic based on a vast middle class, participating in political life and defending self-governmental institutions.

As cofactors of the same nature one must consider, further, the predominance of the wage-earner class—though in its most elementary forms—as a means of labor recruitment in the colonies of North America, as opposed to the slavery and serfdom dominant in other areas. These two forms of labor recruitment left deep marks on the societies resulting from them. On one side, they occasioned a dignification of manual labor, contrasted with a conception of work as denigrating, proper to the servant class only.

There is some parallelism between these attitudes toward work and certain Protestant and Catholic attitudes on the matter. Nevertheless, this does not mean that these respective religions have played a causal part in the implantation of the respective viewpoints, but that each one supported the existent system in the societies in which it predominated: more maturely capitalistic in the case of the Protestants, more backward and aristocratic in the case of the Catholics. Even so, the importance of this support is not to be scorned, nor that of other derivatives of the two religious postures, such as encouragement of teaching to read and write, in order to read the Bible, in the case of the Protestants, and conservatism, expressed in the insistence on attitudes of resignation to ignorance, backwardness, and poverty, in the traditional Catholic ideology.

More than the religious factor itself, the institutional character of the two churches that catechized the New World played a part in molding the American peoples and was a major force in profoundly differentiating them: the Catholic Church, brought to the Americas in the framework of salvationistic mercantile empires into which post-Moslem Spain and Portugal had been transformed; the Protestants, as free community cults, unburdened with the Roman hierarchy and the weight of local bishops, in the frame of capitalistic mercantile sociocultural formations. The former, for this reason, was an essential part of the machine of state, motivating the conquest and promoting its salvationistic action. Like the Moslem expansion, the Catholic one was armed with a much greater coercive power over the population it dominated, and also demanded greater shares of the productive surpluses in order to manifest its glory in temples, maintain a much more numerous clergy, and lend brilliance to episcopal dignities. It suffices to compare the number, architectural quality, bulk, and wealth of the temples of Catholic America with those of Protestant America to perceive the disproportion of economic resources appropriated for religious ends in the two areas. And this was done, obviously, to the detriment of other community expenditures, such as roads, schools, enterprises, thus operating as a cofactor of backwardness.

The Church's association with the temporal power gave religious action everything that the state could provide, but the state got the Church's cooperation in perpetuating colonial domination and maintaining the oligarchic order and in aristocratizing its upper hierarchy. This frequently placed the Church in opposition to the interests and aspirations of the humbler strata of its flock. For that reason the high clergy in Catholic America has so often found itself involved in grave political crises, giving rise to a typical militant laicism, whereas the clergy of Protestant America, excluded from the political power structure, could always safeguard itself better and exert a control that, though more informal, was more efficacious.

Religious preaching, in one case jointly with the secular arm, and in the other through stimulus to community action, brought down on the Catholic Church the accusation of terrorism and fanaticism, which, although equally present and grave in the Puritan world, dissolved there as collective responsibilities. The missionary work itself, being undertaken in Catholic America with the fervor of a religion of conquest, led to constant conflicts with the colonists' interests, which was not the situation in Protestant America, a fact tantamount to another manifestation of the salvationistic character of the imperial structure into which it was thrust.

Another expression of this opposition was the fanatic vigor of the Catholic catechistic zeal. Seeking to mold the world and men according to an idealization of Christianity, it created the Jesuit republics, as admirably generous concretizations of the Platonic utopia as they were lamentable for their ingenious, cunning nature, which only disarmed the minds of the Indians conscripted into them to live more strictly subjugated. The paradox is that religion in Protestant America became actually more orthodox than

Latin American Catholicism, generalizing as a more active popular religiosity, less impregnated with syncretisms, but also more intolerant.

Other cofactors of differentiation consequent from the ethnonational
formative process of the Transplanted Peoples are discrimination and seg-
regationism, opposed to integrationism and the expectation of assimilating
all the contingents that form the ethnos through crossbreeding in the other
two historicocultural configurations. These differences are clearly manifested today in the two types of racial prejudice prevailing in the two
areas: (1) the prejudice of origin, which hits the individual of Negro ancestry recognized no matter what his phenotype may be, as in the United
States, and (2) the prejudice of mark, which discriminates against the individual in accordance with the intensity of his Negroid traits, including the
light mulattoes in the socially white group (Oracy Nogueira, 1955), as occurs among the New Peoples. Another difference is in the proportion of
the contingents marginal to the nation's economic, social, and political life.
These marginals take on a cultural character and are principally neoindigenous or mestizo in the case of the Witness Peoples; they take on a social
character and are neo-African or mulatto in the New Peoples; but they are
present in every national ethnos, sometimes as the majority of the population, and they are well-defined racial minorities in the Transplanted Peoples.
Here, too, rather than a causal factor it is a matter of the resultants from
the formative process, concomitant but differentiated, that made the Transplanted Peoples of North America form societies more egalitarian on the
social plane, more progressive on the economic, and more democratic on
the political. But they also made them more discriminatory and segrega-
tionist on the racial plane. This last factor has not only frustrated the bases
for establishing a genuinely democratic sociopolitical system in North
America, but also, in recent decades, has unleashed a torrent of dissociative tensions that is reaching the level of an internal racial war.

These factors of development and backwardness are not, however, consolidated conquests or condemnations, but dynamic components that, by
their action, have molded the peoples of each historicocultural configuration and are making them face a specific set of problems different from the
rest. Owing to these factors the continent is polarized in a nucleus of high
development and a context of underdeveloped peoples. The interaction
within the area, for this reason, has been in the form of relations between
historically dephased societies: some situated on the industrial-imperialistic formational level, others subdued to the status of neocolonial subjection. These relations, intrinsically spoliative for the backward nations, lead
to conflicts of interests and tensions. Thus, the United States maintains a
system lucrative for its companies in the region and suited to its power
policy in the continent and in the world. The study of this polarization is

important because, whatever the Latin American peoples' paths to development, it will have decisive consequences, considering the U.S. power of intervention, the imperative nature of its commitments to world power, and the weight of its invested interests in the region.

Besides the cited ethnonational blocs in North and South America, we find throughout Latin America several pockets of other historicocultural configurations with Transplanted Peoples characteristics, among others, the considerable patches of European colonization molding certain social landscapes of the south in Brazil and Costa Rica, and a small area of German colonization in Chile. Each of these, formed predominantly by transplanted Europeans, is a variant of the respective national ethnos and has been a dynamic agent, sometimes of decisive importance, in the development of the respective peoples.

9. The Anglo-Americans

Colonists of North America

Of nearly 60 million Europeans emigrating after 1800, close to 60 per cent went to the United States. Their children and grandchildren, born there and Americanized, constitute the bulk of the population, making it the largest of the Transplanted Peoples. So voluminous was this transplanting of Europeans that the history of the world would have been different if they had stayed in their countries of origin, or if they had headed for other lands. The Transplanted Peoples character of the United States derives, essentially, from this massive immigration of Europeans and their social composition—family groups wishing to reconstitute European life forms under more favorable conditions. It derives also from its constitution as a cosmopolitan aggregate linguistically and culturally Anglicized by the dominance of the English contingent.

The colonies of North America, the first established in 1607, from the start received English, Dutch, Spanish, and Swedish adventurers, originally segregated in different nuclei but later integrated by intermarriage, cultural fusion, and commerce. They were poor people, in the majority recruited from rural workers, craftsmen, and small merchants. Each contingent reflected in its cultural and technical level the degree of development of its community of origin at the time of departure. Most were brought in under work contracts that kept them obligated for several years to the one who had paid for their travel, under conditions of temporary servitude. This immigrant colonization was carried out by degrees through the multiplication of small European nuclei over immense wildernesses. After two centuries the thirteen colonies were still scratching their livelihood from the coast, unacquainted with the interior.

Confronted with the Indian, the colonist of North America as a rule behaved with the Anglo-Saxon attitude of avoidance and repulsion. As long as there was no ecological competition for territory and for Europeanization of the landscape, the colonist allowed the Indian his tribal existence, exchanging pelts for tools. Above all, he avoided the redskin. The few whites who penetrated deeper into the country and lived with the Indians quickly became enculturated as Indians, because there was no social space for mixed forms, who were viewed by the settlers of the coast with the greatest repulsion. When competition did start, they faced each other like two autonomous, opposed ethnic entities. The good Indian came to be a dead Indian. The attitude of avoidance and refusal to mingle, to assimilate, and live together, was less proper to a standard of generous tolerance of cultural differences than to the spirit of apartheid and segregation. Thus, when the exotic nuclei gained power they eliminated indigenes as mere obstacles, to clear the way for expansion. At the end of the process, only a few groups of Indians were able to survive, confined on reservations, unassimilated but deeply acculturated, with the sole prospect of growing cysts embedded in the body of the nation without ever becoming integrated.

Negroes entered North America under conditions very different from the white contingent in spite of the relative proximity of their slave status to the temporary serfdom of the majority of the white immigrants. Both were recruited for two undertakings, not only different but by their very nature opposed. The whites were brought in principally by colonizing companies, which found them among the pauperized masses marginalized by the Mercantile and, later, Industrial Revolutions when the agrarian structure of feudal Europe was broken up. These went en masse to the transatlantic rural nuclei founded and based on small family property and on craftsmanship. The Negroes were captured in Africa and sent as slaves to the plantations of the south, destined for commercial agriculture, producing cotton and other export articles for European markets.

Alongside an immigrant colonization a slave colonial enterprise was created based on a plantation economy of the same type as the Antillean, the Brazilian, and others of Latin America. When the two sociocultural structures were later united in a single society, they gave it a duality of social facets that was to constitute the dynamic opposition energizing the historical process of the United States.

The white man came to the New World to lead a life similar to the kind he had always lived and that required of him only apprenticeship in a new language, if he was not English, and adjustment to a new cultural environment more motivating, freer, more optimistic than the one he had left behind. In the cities and in the country he was subject, during the first years, to living conditions even worse than those in Europe, only distinguishable by the vivid hope that, once freed from patronal subjection, he could begin a career of his own. Once free, he competed with the strata of older settlers, both on the economic plane and for the right of political representation and equality of treatment.

This transfer of peoples was to reach avalanche proportions. The total population leaped from 3.9 million in 1790 to 5.3 million in 1800, to 23.2 million in 1850, rising to 76.3 million in 1900 and 179.6 million in 1960. Such increment can be explained by the immigration flood. During the fifty-year period following independence nearly 25 million entered the United States, a contingent more than twice the number of the original population. At the close of the century the annual number of immigrants approximated one million, and in the early twentieth century they often exceeded that figure. By that time, other than the original stocks (English, Scottish, Irish, German, and French), Jewish, Polish, Czech, and other European ethnic groups suffering the reflexive effects of the Industrial Revolution or from racial and religious persecution were beginning to come in also. Later, great masses of Latin immigrants came, especially Italian. Many of them expected to stay only a few years in America to accumulate enough wealth to enable them to return to their land of origin and establish themselves in more favorable conditions. Two thirds of them, however, stayed permanently.

The immigration wave buried the colored populations, which, representing one million as against 4.3 million whites in 1820, saw this proportion reduced in 1900 to 8.8 million vs. 67 million whites, of whom 10.3 million were immigrants. In 1940 the colored population was nearly 13 million to 118 million whites, 11.5 million of whom had been born abroad. The latter, however, did not fuse into American society as undifferentiated parts, but stratified according to scales of ethnic prestige.

The Italians and Slavs were already arousing distaste in the Americans of Anglo-German origin, and a contingent of Chinese aroused further animosity. Subsequently the Latin American mestizos, especially Mexicans and Puerto Ricans, came to join these most discriminated strata. Even today in the United States ethnic distinctions prevail which place Negroes and mulattoes on the lowest rung of social prestige and acceptability. A little above them come the Latin Americans, followed by the Japanese and Chinese. Layered above this "nonpeople" is a stratum of "almost nonpeople" composed of Slavs, Italians, and Jews. On the top of the ethnic pyramid of prestige is the class of "people" properly speaking, which, even when poorest and least educated, is regarded and behaves as if it were better.

The Negroes brought to America were compelled to detribalization and deculturation through having to live among companions in slavery who had been captured anywhere in Africa, and who were as strange to them culturally as their white masters. They had to learn a totally strange language and adapt to a completely different way of life, as human cattle destined solely to farm labor or to the procreation of new slaves. A single road of ascent was open, that of learning the master's language faster, adapting to the new work regime and the new diet, to become a better slave, with higher monetary value in the market.

The two basic stocks in North America were constituted in different parts of the territory: the rural craftsman white stock in the colonies of the northeast and the slavocratic Negro in the south, as two different and opposed human worlds. The immigrant colonies were a subproduct of the European economic and social evolution, which, smashing the feudal-agrarian structure, had come to produce more useless and unnecessary people than merchandise. Such colonies were born as a business deal that never turned out to be very profitable, but also as a solution to the social problem represented by the starving masses concentrated in European cities and towns whose economic system could not absorb them, displaced by the use of the formerly horticultural fields as cattle-raising areas and by the substitution of factory production for crafts production in the home. They came to America to construct yet another society of the European agro-craftsman type, which in its first period of installation could employ large masses in clearing the land and in constructing the physical foundations for a new national economy, such as houses, roads, and cultivated fields.

The slavocratic enterprise was characterized by its historicosocial hybridism. It combined a mercantile capitalism capable of putting up the financial resources required by the undertaking, and the reestablishment of slavery under the form it had taken in the ancient slavistic mercantile states after the first urban revolutions, surviving until the Roman empire and giving way, with its fall, to a new social order, feudal serfdom. In the settlement of North America, therefore, distinct and successive historical stages were combined, some superseded in Europe centuries before, others only emergent. Among them the Negro's enslavement for commercial farming of the Roman type was outstanding; the temporary servitude of the European recruited by the colonization companies; the small, family type of agricultural property, in great part self-sufficient, but producing certain articles for the market; and the nascent financial capitalism, which paid the costs of American enterprises with capital received from the sale of shares.

All this historicosocial complex, the formative base of U.S. society, could not operate as an integrated unit because of the irreconcilable interests of its components. This is what happened when independence was won as a project of the whites of the north, splitting the nation into two blocs in the fight to abolish slavery. At that time the great export farming interests, based on slave labor, banded together against the society resultant from immigrant colonization and already well advanced in an industrial economy. The Civil War, fought between two fundamentally different societies and won by the more progressive of the two, only placed on new rails the old opposition between the two faces of the United States.

The ascent of the North American Negro from slave to free worker and citizen status is still going on, and is far from attaining its minimum objectives. After abolition Negroes had to realize that freedom represented principally the patron's nonresponsibility for their meager support. The majority of them continued the same life of manual laborers, merely exchanging the plantation where they were slaves for a neighboring cotton field. And when they tried to assert their most elementary rights, not as Negroes but as workers and men, the Ku Klux Klan and other local terrorist organizations arose to teach them, by means of lynchings, their place in U.S. society.

Only at the beginning of this century did the mechanization of farming, reaching also into the south, expel masses of rural Negroes to the cities. Since then large contingents have moved to the north, accumulating in Black ghettoes and working sporadically at odd jobs in the lowest services that the white immigrant succeeded in escaping. Segregated in their quarters of the city, with their own schools of inferior quality, discriminated against in factories, restaurants, public carriers, movie theaters, beaches, streets, squares, and public parks, never recognized as citizens, they were integrated into U.S. society as an unwanted historical residuum endured only with the greatest distaste. However, the Negro ghetto compared so favorably with southern despotism that for several decades emigration to the north was the rural Negro's ideal.

World War I, mobilizing the whole economy and labor force of the nation, gave Negroes their first opportunity to rise to the status of workers and citizens, not yet as electors but as soldiers. The conflict over, they lost nearly all the positions won, but they had learned a great deal about the society in which they lived, taking a more aggressive attitude that provoked new waves of despotism. After the 1929 depression, with the New Deal policy and the creation of the C.I.O. [Congress of Industrial Organizations] some prospects for the Negro were opened for socioeconomic integration, strengthening his self-confidence and giving him the opportunities to demonstrate to himself, and to all, his efficacy as a skilled worker.

World War II, mobilizing all the energies of the nation's people, gave the Negro a fresh chance, a little more egalitarian, to share in the struggle and in work. Negro youths, cast into anomie and vice and despair by the social marginality in which they had grown up, found in the army the opportunity to restore their degraded dignity. Mature men and women who had never had a regular job went into the arms factories and into the services in conditions that formerly they could not have hoped for. In the postwar years came new outbreaks of violence against the haughty Negro just out of the army or large industry. His fight took on political aspects when the administration, in an electoral campaign, insisted on civil rights for Negroes. This campaign reached its climax with the Supreme Court's decision calling for the progressive desegregation of schools.

From that time a new Negro has been emerging, hostile to the old conciliatory leaderships that preached nonviolence of the Negro against the violence of the white, and proclaimed that nothing happened to the Negro who kept his place. Aggressively vindictive, the new Negro has come to constitute the vanguard of the most active revolutionary movement in the United States today. He has taken into his own hands the fight for his rights, impelled as much by animosity to the world of the whites as by the acute perception that the ghetto, heroin, and charity were dooming him to liquidation, and likewise motivated by the stimulus that the independence of the African peoples represented for the whole world's "colored peoples."

What corresponds in the United States to the socially marginalized populations of the Latin American New Peoples is this Negro and mulatto contingent. Both are the products of violent processes of detribalization, deculturation, and miscegenation. Their principal heritage from an age-old experience of misery and exploitation is the consciousness that tomorrow can be better than today or yesterday, provided that a new social order be created. The historical heritage of suffering and persecution, together with this new awareness, arm the Negro for the struggle not merely for an accommodation in the society in which he lives, but for a revolutionary ardor brought to bear on the total reordering of society. To the extent that these struggles grow sharper, the Negro will no longer be fighting racial discrimination but the existent social order itself on which the hegemony of the whites is founded.

The new U.S. Negro is for that reason not only the vanguard of the colored people but also one of the first combat corps of all the marginalized and oppressed of the Americas. The major modern resultant of the U.S. people's formative process is the presence of the Negro contingent (a New People intrusion within a Transplanted People configuration), as Americanized as any of the national stocks, as crossbred as the other descendants of slaves in all the Americas, but as undigested and discriminated against as if he were a foreign body. His most strident expressions are the ghettos of the north, which operate to accommodate and rot the Negro, and the fossil communities of the old slavocrat world such as Little Rock, Dallas, Jackson, and Selma. Both kinds are crystallizations of an inegalitarian society.

In recent years relations between Negroes and whites have transcended an odious but viable *modus vivendi,* reaching open conflict. Incorporated compulsorily into the national society as subaltern contingents, Negroes and mulattoes are finally rebelling and attacking the over-all system as the only way of forcing their integration, which is resulting in a profound social revolution.

The tensions resulting from the ethnic duality that exploded in the war of secession of the southerners against the northerners are exploding now in a revolutionary war in which Negroes and whites confront each other as equally assimilated components of one and the same divided national ethnos, whose destiny is fusion in the course of a long and bloody process. The challenge to U.S. Americans is to integrate their colored population, estimated at 20 million, into the nation, as a part socially indistinguishable from the rest. This unavoidable aim, although unwanted, must operate in the forthcoming years as one of the most potent forces for the sociopolitical formation of the United States. The process will inevitably set Black against white, white against white, and Black against Black, until it is completed in the only possible way, that is, by integration and progressive fusion into a single body of the two disparate opposing contingents.

The Founding Fathers

Among the figures to which humanity renders homage some may be called "culture heroes," a term used by anthropologists to designate the mythical personages to whom tribal peoples attribute the introduction of innovating institutions, cultivated plants, techniques, and arts. The ecumenical civilization of which we are speaking—already commencing with the dispersion of culture centers over the entire earth and the diffusion of modern technology and of the new ideals of progress, liberty, and happiness—will be founded, like all previous civilizations, on the cult of some of these culture heroes as the personification of moral values that define it and are capable of motivating the new man's conduct.

A fundamental prerequisite for the maturation of this human civilization is the capacity to draw out of the chaos of contradictory beliefs and assertions and aspirations of the modern world an image-objective formulated as a destination, at once congruent and impassioned, capable of motivating man to new efforts to outdo himself, not against other men defined racially, socially, culturally, or nationally, but in behalf of all men.

This image-objective will necessarily be defined by invoking the figures of culture heroes, patron saints worshipped for their contribution to the humanization of man. They may be scientists and sages instead of warriors and saints, but they will also be statesmen, and among them will surely be included some of those figures to whom U.S. Americans render homage as founding fathers: George Washington, Thomas Jefferson, Abraham Lincoln, Franklin D. Roosevelt. These are not U.S. American heroes alone, but heroes of all humanity because today they are much more the political and inspirational ancestors of other peoples than they are of their own countrymen, who have become morally alienated and politically renegade to their own traditions.

The founding fathers of the United States came, nearly all of them, from the national patriciate. They were rich men by inheritance, and they were manifestations of a nascent but extraordinarily mature bourgeoisie capable of facing its tasks of self-enrichment and social ordering. What makes them outstanding among Americans and in the whole world is the foresight of their people's destiny projected on the future like a design of Providence that had entrusted to them the accomplishment of a fundamental human experiment. In all their pronouncements their progressive attitude is patent, and also their optimism, their involvement in the struggle for human rights and for the furtherance of liberties, and, above all, their boldness as reformers of the world of their time.

George Washington, with his austere, aristocratic profile, assumed the guidance of his people in the war for freedom from England and founded the first modern republic, promulgating the constitution of the United States, which provided a new model in the ordering of human relations.

Thomas Jefferson gave eloquent and precise formulation to the great human aspirations of liberty and equality in some of the basic documents of the nation's life, such as the Declaration of Independence. To Jefferson as president must be attributed, moreover, the empirical proof that in the world of things and human relations the theoretical model of a republican state, as proposed by the liberal ideologues, was viable. His most important work, however, was the establishment of the institutional conditions necessary to encourage North American industrial capitalism, until that time strangled by the English manufacturing system. To him is also credited the purchase of the huge Louisiana territory and the regulation of its settlement, not by latifundian proprietors but by families of free farmers, which would assure the U.S. people some decades more of pioneerism. He must be further credited with the incorporation of millions of Europeans into the nation's population, and the constituting of the bases for an internal market that would bring the New People of the south into the Yankee republic.

Abraham Lincoln, president of the nation when the Civil War broke out, roused his people to the cause of national unity and the abolition of slavery. He regulated the march westward, promulgating the legal instruments that assured the pioneer families possession of the virgin lands that they might occupy. He fostered the country's industrialization, both because of war needs and because he had become the leader of the progressive north against the slavery and backwardness of the south.

The boldness of the political thinking of the North American culture heroes can be explained in large measure by the libertarian role of three of their inheritances: the parliamentary and community self-government traditions so deeply rooted in the English, and the esteem for individual liberties expressed in the Magna Charta of 1215. It was in the name of these bourgeois, antifeudal values and traditions that the colonies broke with the British monarchy and took the logical, but for that time extremely daring, step of installing a republic. More than this source of inspiration, however, what permitted the implantation of an authentic democratic order was the very character of the society resulting from the immigrant colonies of the north, based on a population of farmers, merchants, and craftsmen, free and literate.

These historical circumstances strongly contrast the Anglo-Saxon Americans with the Latin American republics, bound to the Iberian peninsula where the opposite tradition of absolutism and intolerance prevailed, because they had not completed their own bourgeois-liberal revolutions, and where the leader groups and the mass, both degraded by slavery and segmented into opposing classes of oligarchs and wretched, were not successful in constituting peoples.

The North American leaders, called on to organize democratic institutions and put them into effect, were dealing with matters familiar to them

and with values already consecrated by their people, counting on a powerful consensus for their renovating initiatives, which were not merely steps
forward but the inexorable, necessary course of a coherent tradition. In
Latin America, on the contrary, these values and principles with which the
liberators armed themselves ideologically were novelties for both the elite
and the common people. They were no more than substitutes for traditions
of autocratic power, wielded by the crown's delegates, and of intolerance,
as expressed by the bishops trained in the spirit of the Counter-Reformation. Hence their lack of influence on the people, who saw in the institutional renovations implanted in their name merely the complicated new
style of sophisticated rich city folk who replaced their former masters.
These new leaders therefore behaved like conquistadors, ready to impose
the new freedoms, overvaluing the most eloquently egalitarian formula-
tions, so alien to those cultural and social latitudes, and ignoring, through
class blindness, the real problems facing the peoples they were governing.
So it is that not one of them found his inspiration in the U.S. legislation
regulating the distribution of the virgin lands, but all busied themselves
with elections and special privileges, which on being promulgated became,
in the best of cases, forms governing the succession of patrician groups to
power, in order to maintain intact the social and economic order, oligarchic to the core.

Another U.S. culture hero was Franklin D. Roosevelt, whose sophisticated air, wheelchair, and eloquence incarnated in the twentieth century
the founding father of his country. In confronting the 1929 crisis with the
New Deal, causing the state to intervene in the economy, he not only went
against the cupidity and irresponsibility of the bankers and industrialists
but established the precedent of a new social policy, the institution of
which became the fundamental aspiration of the more enlightened and progressive U.S. Americans, and the fear of the more reactionary. Relations
with Latin America under his presidency changed substantially, thanks to
the reformulation of the Monroe Doctrine and the implementation of the
Good Neighbor Policy, stimulating the democratization and checking the
spoliation of the area by the great Yankee monopolies, and effectively aiding industrialization. It is true that his action was performed in a world divided among the great powers, whose competition gave the Latin Americans the opportunity for better bargaining conditions, requiring the
greatest diligence on the part of the United States to dissuade alliances
with the Axis. The fact is that the Rooseveltian phase was to stand as a
pattern for inter-American relations never afterwards restored.

During World War II Roosevelt made himself the leader of all the peoples allied against Nazism, in providing arms and men for decisive battles,
in assuring the indispensable understanding between the allies divided by

antagonisms and suspicions, and, above all, in making an effort to safeguard the dignity of victory and guarantee preservation of the peace. His formulation of the four fundamental freedoms will always be remembered as a document that expresses all men's aspirations:

we look forward to a world founded upon four essential human freedoms. The first is freedom of speech and expression—everywhere in the world.

The second is freedom of every person to worship God in his own way—everywhere in the world.

The third is freedom from want—which, translated into world terms, means economic understandings which will secure to every nation a healthy peacetime life for its inhabitants—everywhere in the world.

The fourth is freedom from fear—which, translated into world terms, means a world-wide reduction of armaments to such a point and in such a thorough fashion that no nation will be in a position to commit an act of physical aggression against any neighbor—anywhere in the world.

That is no vision of a distant millennium. It is a definite basis for a kind of world attainable in our own time and generation (Speech, January 7, 1941).

Each of these men became the leader of his generation and imprinted his libertarian thought with a vigor seldom equaled by the ideologues of all the peoples in the world. There has been no subsequent liberal or social revolution that has not found inspiration in their exhortations, that has not appealed to their example, that has not justified itself by invoking these formulations.

In fact, only for the U.S. Americans themselves have these principles died or been mummified as history dead and buried with full funeral honors. The most disastrous thing is that the ideology that inspired these attitudes has been proscribed exactly at the moment when it has become most necessary and most vivid, when the world is being shaken by a new revolutionary wave set in motion by the technological renovations that at last placed abundance and freedom within the reach of all men, and permitted the majority of nationalities to structure themselves as democratic republics, just as the United States had done over a century and a half ago. Faced by the new liberating wave, it is the descendants of these forefathers who are sallying forth into the world to conspire, to suborn, to corrupt, so that the old oligarchic order may subsist, and with it, backwardness, oppression, and want.

In this way the world that succeeded in escaping from the Hitlerian apocalypse, which would have destroyed all its humanistic patrimony, sees itself today threatened with having political freedom stifled and its avenues of progress closed in the fight against ignorance and poverty, by a superpower degraded by a minority of potentates and structured to profit by the misery of the world. Succeeding the Nazis as heirs of the antihistorical mission of preventing at all costs the reordering of the world in accordance with the interests of the disinherited of the earth, the Yankees are clinging to the hands of time in a hysterical effort to hold back the world's evolution, to obstruct the refinement of institutions, and to frustrate social reform.

In the list of U.S. culture heroes perhaps the last great president, John F. Kennedy, ought to figure. And yet he was so evidently a deviation in the course of Yankee history of our time, so transitory was his term in office, so pusillanimous was his attitude before the C.I.A. in the shameful episode of the invasion of Cuba, and his own Alliance for Progress so unable to work with the real and potential Latin American allies of the United States, that he will stand in history as the "might-have-been," that is, what he might have been if he had decisively assumed the presidency conferred on him by his people to lead the world into the new paths that he seemed to envision.

The North American culture heroes, giving expression to the aspirations for freedom of the colonies of the north, which constituted the most progressive human nucleus of their time, founded a new form of state, formulating an ideal of open and shared, free and autonomous political community that in the course of time came to be the principal model of a federal, republican, democratic state. The English political revolution that preceded and inspired them, as well as the French Revolution that followed, together with the American Revolution stand for a stage in human emancipation: the bourgeois-liberal revolution.

The American state, however, was founded on an economic order whose very dynamic would impose two fundamental limitations on it: internal tensions of the social classes in dispute, and external expansionism over other peoples. Let us see, initially, how this expansionism took shape. The founding fathers of the U.S. Americans were both the expression of fundamental human aspirations and lucid formulators of national goals. Not only did they undertake the war of national liberation from English dominion but, simultaneously, they contraposed themselves to the colonial interests of other nations in the vicinity of their territory, even though they did so nearly always to monopolize for themselves the colonial exploitation of the Americas.

Aware of the essential opposition between the two ethnonational components into which the nation was divided, they went to war to bind the south to the federation, preventing it from becoming a competitive power. Equally conscious of the role that the immense empty or conquerable lands to the west might play, they planned and executed a progressive expansion that brought these lands into the nation. In flagrant contrast to the difficulty faced by the other American nations to become unified, to capitalize politically on external tensions and to define their national project by committing their peoples to it, the United States emerged as mature for the destination proposed.

From the first years, clearly expressed national objectives have been demanded and then persistently pursued. So it is that the thirteen original states, emancipated in 1776, by 1783 had doubled their area, pushing their frontiers as far as the Mississippi by treaty imposed on England. In 1803 they redoubled their territory by negotiating with Napoleon for former lands of Spain, the Louisiana Territory. Then they gained the Oregon territory in the northwest, amounting to a fourth of their total area, under promise of claiming nothing from the Canadian colonies. And finally they snatched from Mexico, by war and chicanery, another belt equal to triple the original territory of the thirteen colonies and to half of the Mexican land area. In that fashion they took possession of all the contiguous areas from the Atlantic to the Pacific, passing from less than 1 million square kilometers to more than 8 million, with only two adjacent neighbors, the despoiled Mexican state to the south and the semicolonized Canada to the north. Their expansionist aspirations would not stop there.

Jefferson, in his role as formulator of the American national project, left recorded in two documents the plan to appropriate Cuba, which could not be done, contrary to what happened with Puerto Rico. In a letter to President Monroe, Jefferson wrote in 1823:

> I confess in all sincerity that I have always considered Cuba the most interesting addition that could ever be made to our system of states. The control which, with Florida, that island would give us over the Gulf of Mexico, as well as over the contiguous countries and isthmus, and the lands the waters of which empty into the Gulf, would completely guarantee our security (Quoted by Selser, 1962, p. 27).

In an earlier letter to President Madison in 1807 * Jefferson had emphasized:

---

* The source used by Dr. Ribeiro may well have misled him here: if the letter is dated 1807 it was written by Jefferson while still president.

Even though with some difficulty, she [Spain] will agree to Cuba's being added to our Union, so that we will not give aid to Mexico and the other provinces. This would be a good price. Then I should cause to be erected, in the most remote place in the South of the island, a column bearing the inscription NEC PLUS ULTRA, as a token that here would be the limit beyond which our acquisitions would not go in that direction.[1]

And he adds, referring now to Canada:

The only thing, in that case, that we should lack to bring freedom to the vastest empire that the world has seen since Creation, would be to include in our Confederation the land to our North . . . (Ibid., p. 21).

The expansion to the west, by occupying the contiguous areas through autocolonization, delayed the rise of U.S. imperialistic propensities. While the English, in the second half of the past century, were imposing their domination on immense regions throughout the world, launching into the Opium and Boer Wars and others, and France and Germany were following the same road, the United States was defending and swallowing the territory she had appropriated. Nevertheless, she finally joined the imperialistic club with the attack on Spain, which, after Latin America had won its independence, had fallen prostrate and easy prey to spoliation by all. Following this war for pure plunder in 1898, the United States annexed the colonies of Puerto Rico, the Philippines, and Guam, plus Hawaii, Samoa, and several protectorates in the Caribbean. The major blow was to be struck in Panama, amputating a part of Colombia's territory in order to drive off the French, who were building the canal. The Americans took over this enterprise, decisive in the political context of the continent, and created an illusion of a nation to justify their expansion.

With the aim of providing an ideological cover for the new expansionism the celebrated Monroe Doctrine was formulated, the antithesis of the conceptions of Bolívar, who postulated the unification of all the Latin American peoples in a single federal state. The Bolivarian design having come to naught, the fragmentation of Hispano-America into a multiplicity of national states having been arranged, an inert continental context was offered to the United States, who came to rule over it with growing power in the name of the defense of hemispheric peoples against the European

---

[1] Lincoln, too, in regard to Latin America, had the same attitude, based on the vision of power over neighboring areas. Thus he approved studies and démarches aiming at the appropriation of Central America to set up there a territory nominally destined for freed Negroes.

cupidity so prevalent in the outside world. The Monroe Doctrine has for this reason been compared to the protection pacts that Rome made with weak peoples to shelter them from other ambitions. These generous treaties always resulted in the installation of Roman forts and in the concession of privileges that ended by incorporating the protected peoples into the empire at a price lower than the cost of wars of conquest.

The Monroe Doctrine had the same justificatory function of covering acts of violence and spoliation with a cloak of verbal generosity. If perchance it defended some Latin American nation against European oppression, it in fact imposed on them all a neocolonial statute that enabled the Yankee entrepreneurs to penetrate with advantages over the English, German, and French competitors. In this way the Antilles, Central America, and Venezuela were in fact made colonies, and the other republics of the continent have been and are being plundered.

Yankee expansionism was made possible by the high degree of economic development that, even in the colonial period, the dominant part of North America had achieved, and also by its character as a socially and technologically more evolved nation, unified by language and integrated by primary education open to all strata of the population, as in no other country of that time. The economic base of this expansionism was communal agricultural production, first for commerce with the Antilles and later for the export of grains, cotton, tobacco, and other products to Europe. The social base was the enormous stratum of farmers, owners of their land, constituting a domestic market for industrial manufactures under conditions favorable to fantastic expansion.

In a few years after independence the country passed from an agromercantile economy to the preindustrial stage that had not yet dawned for either the majority of the European peoples or any other people of the American continent. For this, they had the extraordinary advantage of their vast movable frontier to which the contingents of unskilled labor, freed by industrialization, could go. Thus they could not only occupy their human surpluses but even absorb the huge European contingents that came to broaden their social bases, expanding the domestic market in proportion as the older communities experienced the structural renovations stemming from industrialization. For that reason they knew only in a much more attentuated degree the social tensions deriving from demographic growth and from the rural exodus that accompanied industrialization throughout the world, generating grave social crises leading to underdevelopment in the areas of reflexive modernization and to migration and war in those of direct industrialization.

The Capitalistic Feat

The first phase of U.S. industrialization took place with the installation, in the north, of factories making footwear, glass, ceramics, kerosene lamps, clocks, and watches, and later knives, axes, farm implements, mills, and textiles, these last with water power. The production of these articles replaced English manufactures and permitted the economic integration of north and south into a single system specializing in export agriculture.

Simultaneously the autocolonization of the empty spaces of the interior was going on, with successive waves of pioneers who in a few years reached the Pacific, populating the whole country in a spontaneous, unrestrained movement by means of which all hoped to be able to enrich themselves, for no one was better than anyone else. It was the time of the cowboy and the Indian, either driven out or killed; it was the world of the revolver, the six-shooter, with the school and the village newspaper yet to be added. With the extension of the railroads and telegraph lines, the transformation of the natural fields into pastures, and the opening of the first clearings for cultivation of foodstuffs, the banker and the lawyer came to the west, initiating a great reordering of the old ways of life.

Before the end of the century those wilderness regions were peopled by 6 or 7 million persons, the majority attracted by the opportunities opened to them by Lincon's Homestead Act, which in 1862 had assured each pioneer family 160 acres. More than 96,000 square miles of land was thus distributed. The United States, with 2.5 million inhabitants at the time of independence, had begun the nineteenth century with fewer than 7 million, at mid-century reached more than 20 million, distributed over the new lands and the areas of the original colonies. These last became rapidly industrialized, and also developed their former food agriculture. The south grew rich in the same way through the growing international demand for its cotton, tobacco, and other products.

The governing center of the national economy, however, was solidly entrenched in the north, which, protected against European competition, was making the most of its opportunities for industrialization, opportunities provided by national autonomy, expansion of the domestic market, customs protectionism, theft of foreign technological innovations, and recruitment of European skilled labor. Masters of the most diverse trades were brought in to stimulate the intense industrialization taking place in the United States.

Inventions of their own or copied from Europe by any and all means, honorable and dishonorable, principally the latter, were to renovate the whole of American life in the following years, laying the bases of a truly

industrial society. It was the era of the rise of the telegraph and the telephone, which unified the whole country's communications; of the linotype,
the rotary press, and the folding machine, which permitted the rise of metropolitan newspapers of enormous circulation, shapers of public opinion
and unifiers of millions of Americans' view of the world; of the typewriter,
the adding machine, the cash register, the electric light, and the cinema. It
was the age of machines and of discipline. Order gained ground over freedom. The local newspaper yielded to the metropolitan. Communities gradually came to be structured in the nation. The people turned little by little
into the mass.

A vast educational system was to cover the entire nation: one-room
schools for the far western children; large urban schools, Americanizing
the foreign masses that continued to arrive in droves; colleges and universities dedicated to a new type of education designed to train for work rather
than for the enjoyment of leisure, an education in which mathematics and
the sciences, mechanical training and practical subjects filled the hours
formerly devoted to Latin, Greek, and theology.

At the close of the century the United States had about ten cities approximating or exceeding 1 million inhabitants, 39.5 per cent of her population urbanized, a labor force of 16.7 million working in the factories and
utilities and services, multiplying at an accelerated rate; and boasted a literacy index of 89.3 per cent, the highest in the world. This prodigious
increase illustrated the maturation of the United States as an industrial
capitalistic formation. From fifth in world industrial production in 1840 it
went into fourth place in 1860, to second in 1870, and to first place in
1895. With the objective of accomplishing this feat she had multiplied her
capacity for industrial production sevenfold between 1860 and 1895.

Since then the railroads, communications, electric power, iron and steel,
and petroleum enterprises expanded as great trusts. National banks
emerged as controllers of large industry agglutinated in enormous monopolies. At the beginning of the twentieth century the nation already possessed
the greatest manufacturing industry in the world, producing more than
England and Germany together. At that time large interest groups formed
whose financial power came to reorder society, to put it at their service:
Morgan, Mellon, Rockefeller, Carnegie, duPont, Kuhn-Loeb, Guggenheim,
and the consortia of Chicago, Cleveland, and Boston. They controlled 60
per cent of the industry, 80 per cent of the railroads, and half of the banks
and utilities. Each of these groups commanded greater riches than all the
whole country's wealth at the time of independence.

The rise, both in the United States and in the other advanced capitalistic
countries, of these great consortia jointly controlling financial capital and
industry, corresponds in the external order to the passing from colonialism

based on political domination to imperialism, which can dispense with direct intervention, substituting for it more efficacious, more subtle mechanisms of control and domination. The essential objectives remain the same: monopoly of the world sources of raw materials, principally ores, oil, and agricultural export products, and assurance of captive markets for manufactured products.

Their action mechanisms consist of obtaining concessions for the establishment of great enterprises to exploit natural resources; the installation of railroads, ports, and systems of communications, destined to facilitate the export of raw materials; the establishment of industrial plants for consumer goods wherever the national economy becomes capable of absorbing them. The subsidiary mechanism is the subjection of governments through ruinous loans, made indispensable by crises provoked or intensified by the very deformation of the national economies, oriented to supply the needs of the international market more than to assure subsistence and enlarge the national labor market. On top of all this, foreign exchange and customs freedom is imposed, in order to guarantee remittance of profits and the control of the domestic market and to prevent the rise of national industries.

U.S. relations with Latin America exemplify in copious detail all these forms of domination and demonstrate their extraordinary efficacy in the maintenance of backwardness in the areas under imperialistic exploitation. This exploitation is based on economic factors and on one fundamental political factor, which is the recruitment of small national groups for the purpose of associating them with the foreign companies, transforming them into sepoys whose duty is the internal defense of the alien interests.

The rise of the great metropolises—New York, Chicago, San Francisco, Detroit, Los Angeles, Pittsburgh, Cleveland, Boston—was simultaneous with this imperialistic expansion and with the concentration of the companies into huge monopolies. Between 1909 and 1939 enterprises with more than $1 billion production increased from 1.1 per cent to 5.2 per cent; the proportion of their employees, from 30.5 per cent to 55 per cent of the active working population; and the value of their production, from 43.8 per cent to 67.5 per cent of the total American industrial production. And this process has been accelerated. From 1940 to 1947 the companies with more than $10 billion of capital absorbed 58 per cent of the private assets, and between 1948 and 1954, 66 per cent. In this progression they came to include, in 1960, nearly 72 per cent of the entrepreneurial assets. This economic overconcentration brought about a profound social restructuring, driven forward on the domestic scene by four factors.

First was the condensation of the great urban proprietors into a national ruling class controlling the railroads across the country—a network that was to contain more than 300,000 miles of lines—the nationwide system of telegraphs and, later, telephones, and the national network of industries producing articles bearing nationally known brands. Commanding the banking system from Wall Street by means of agencies distributed throughout the country, this minority of financiers, by manipulating deposits, took control of all financial resources; and through loans it proceeded to participate lucratively in the enormous industrial expansion, the total physical plant of which doubled every ten years, as well as in all business, large and small, rural and urban. The "conquering bourgeoisie" that had constructed the American capitalistic economy disappeared, then, and was replaced by a financial plutocracy. It was the end of the self-made man, directing his own enterprise, giving way to the professional corporation executive.

Second, between this ruling class and the people an increasingly numerous intermediate stratum arose: bureaucratic and administrative functionaries, technocrats, members of the liberal professions, various agents, journalists, and many other categories of employees, medium merchants, and small autonomous producers—a stratum wholly dependent on and submissive to the upper caste, whose privileges it hoped to attain, and hostile and prejudiced toward the lower classes.

Third, a factory working class was constituted, employees of large enterprises, a class composed of ex-farm workers and immigrants, all of whom, organized in unions, acquired consciousness of their problems and of the opposition between their interests and those of the bosses, thus initiating rebellions that became more and more bitter.

Fourth came the urbanization of the freed Negro and of his descendants, expelled from the rural districts or attracted to the cities in search of a more favorable environment, with their principal prospect of integration into national life being the attainment of the status of worker. They failed, however, in the face of racial discrimination, seeing the masses of white immigrants, newcomers less skilled and much less assimilated, fill all the factory jobs because of their color. Thus compressed, they are transformed into a marginal, subproletarian stratum of odd-job workers, of employees in subaltern services, unwanted and ill paid, without possibilities of integration into the system, and for that reason destined to mature for the performance of a revolutionary role. They concentrate in slums, in the deteriorated areas of cities, where they have contact only with the most miserable Latin Americans, and where Negro and mulatto childhood and youth, under inequalitarian conditions of life and education, are cursed by juvenile delinquency and drug addiction, thereby becoming less able to compete with the new white generations, though more and more inclined to political awareness.

The 1929 crisis, by weakening patronal power, for the first time in U.S. history permitted the constitution of a free labor union system, combative and capable of opposing the regime itself. The Congress of Industrial Organizations (C.I.O), created during the Roosevelt administration, when the mass of unemployed rose to more than 17 million, was a giant stride forward in the awakening of the working class to the specificity of its interests and to the antagonism between these and those of the employers, showing what a progressive government can do for the working classes when they are organized and combative, and consequently the importance of the workers' political activity. Under the command of the C.I.O the major struggles were carried out for raises in wages, but also for not strictly economic demands, such as the democratization of working conditions in factories and workshops, the establishment of more human relations in work, the participation of Negroes and women in the union movement, the overcoming of racial and national hostilities in the heart of the proletariat.

During the years following, in consequence of the industrial expansion fostered by the war economy, Negroes were able for the first time to work in the factories in conditions more nearly equal to those of the white worker. Also, the participation of women in industrial work increased extraordinarily. The very composition of the working class was modified by the ingress into factories of large contingents of men and women of average education who aspired to go into services but were attracted to industry by the high wages and the new working conditions.

Millions of Americans, white and Black, who had not found a job since the great crisis, returned to the active proletariat by virtue of the expanded labor market, the lengthened educational process, and the drafting of young men into the overexpanded armed forces. The American labor force, which had reached 20 million in 1900, jumped to 65 million during this period. Its composition had been substantially altered by the constant increase in the proportion of wage-earners in the total population, from 75 per cent to 82 per cent between 1940 and 1950, through the conversion of autonomous intermediate sectors of members of the liberal professions and small proprietors to employees. Only the farmers, whose existence had had such great importance in the configuration of the United States as a capitalistic formation capacitated to undertake autonomous industrialization, were reduced from 17 per cent to 6 per cent of the active population between 1910 and 1956, decreasing from 6.1 million in 1920 to 5.13 million in 1940, and to 3.7 million in 1956.

Simultaneously with this "proletarization" of the middle sectors by the mobilization of labor for war, the principal gains of the union movement were greatly weakened or nullified in the name of the war effort. The interpenetration of the union leaderships with government departments and bureaus controlling production, both civilian and military boards, and with the employer confederations in entities destined to promote the war effort, ended in the bureaucratization of the workers' organizations. The C.I.O., like all the rest, was dominated by a new category of parasitic henchmen who turned from being directors of the workmen's struggles to become a new force more and more tied in with the entrepreneurial and political leaders, totally committed to accommodation with the patrons in discouraging strikes, in breaking workers' resistance to automation, and in the elimination of all radical elements from the union movement.

Thus the workers' leadership was converted into a bureaucracy inspired in officialdom, orienting its action no longer toward spurring on the workers' combativity but toward utilizing them as a means of pressuring the administration and congress in order to win special privileges in the form of subsidies for those dismissed from their jobs, and retirement pensions, and other advantages. These privileges were negotiated in exchange for the strict regulation of the right to strike and of the compulsory unionization of active workers, combined with the expulsion of the unemployed to other organizations that would take over the duty of protecting them.

The war over, as the active defense and the cold war policies maintained the patronal conquests, the C.I.O., in the name of union unity, merged with the old, retrogressive A.F.L. (American Federation of Labor) to form a single union headquarters, destined to dispute with the international leftist union movement for control of the labor bureau of the United Nations. Their interests are represented in U.S. embassies on the South American continent by labor attachés dedicated to intervention in national workers' movements, switching them over to the new worker orientation directed from Washington.

For a long time they have not identified with the American workingmen. They have simply imposed themselves on them, as a new bureaucratic power controlling the union machine. Internally, they are allies of the bosses and of the government civilian and military agents against the growing mass of unemployed and marginal individuals whom they look on as a permanent subversive menace. Internationally, they are a counterrevolutionary force, opposed to all progressive movements, itself corrupt and also corrupter of the labor union movement.

Automation and Militarism

World War II had still deeper effects on the United States by radically altering innumerable spheres of the economy, now greater than that of the rest of the world, since the United States had appropriated 60 per cent of the natural resources of the earth. To maintain this wealth—and the world political system that would permit its enjoyment—it was necessary to set up a vast military system controlling more than 3,000 bases scattered over all continents and equip an army more powerful than that of the last war.

Another fundamental effect of victory was to subvert the political institutions of the United States and redefine her role as regards the other peoples of the world, which was accomplished through the fusion of the industrial plutocracy with the higher echelons of the military, thus creating a new structure of hegemonic power above the government and congress. This new structure became the command headquarters of interests bent on maintenance of the status quo in the underdeveloped world, because it had succeeded in making other people's misery highly lucrative for its corporations.

The moving force in these transformations was a series of technological innovations designed generally as a process of automation of the productive system that revealed a renovating potential probably greater than any historical accelerator known until that moment. Originally developed to aid the expansion of industry, this having become imperative through the war effort, automation extended to other activities. When peace came, it confronted Americans with the challenge to remake their whole social organization in order to enable it to use and distribute the new flood of wealth that they had made themselves capable of producing.

In the past the United States had already revealed an extraordinary talent for industrializing productive activities, simultaneously transfiguring her own social structure. It was here, too, that the new systems of rationalized production were installed, independent of the old craftsmanship training, such as the manufacture of standardized, interchangeable parts, and later the introduction of the assembly line, first in the automotive industry and then in other productive sectors. This renovating tendency would be climaxed in the refinement of mass production techniques in war industries of the highest technicoscientific standards, necessary for the production of nuclear weapons.

After the war these innovations—especially the utilization of electronic controls in factory processing—were gradually introduced into big industry, not only dispensing with old forms of occupational skills but drastically reducing the need for workmen, that is, condemning growing masses of workers to unemployment subsidized by new welfare systems, while industry was progressing and improving. Even the nonfactory sectors, such as office work and services in general, came to take on a different aspect through massive replacement of bookkeepers, calculators, tellers, and other clerks with computing machines, electronic gadgets, and programmers.

The first waves of unemployment caused by automation naturally affected the unskilled workers and the marginal strata aspiring to jobs in that category. Thus the social maladjustments of these masses, principally Negro, were enhanced by a new factor of marginalization that would accelerate their combativity, already sharpened by racial discrimination, to extreme levels. The automation process would, however, continue operating at an increasing rate, tending to enlarge these maladjusted, discontented sectors and add other contingents to them.

Where can the displaced workers and those who have never found jobs go, if technicalized agriculture and automated industry no longer need them? How can the entire population be assured the economic benefits of the new productive revolution, which only leads to a greater concentration of wealth, to an enrichment of the superrich who control the corporations? How can the correlation between services rendered and wages be replaced with another equation that, by making survival independent of work, will, in effect, and on a large scale, subsidize generalized and compulsory unemployment? How can the new society be reorganized, its productive system no longer based on a mass of unskilled and semiskilled labor, but only on a technocracy of a few programming engineers?

It is true that to live without working productively has never constituted a problem. On the contrary, this has always been the natural pattern of persons with private income and of large proprietors. The difficulty is in generalizing this inactive status, by basing it on the right of all men to the final product of progress in the productive system, which today is making the unskilled laborer as obsolete as yesterday's beasts of burden. Certain sectors tend to continue expanding—the teaching profession, welfare services, and a few others. Surely, however, with the progress of automation it will not absorb the majority of adults in the tasks of educating the young, babysitting, and caring for the old and the sick.

These are the present problems of the new U.S. society, and the future ones of all nations of the world. The reduction of the mass of industrial workers in the United States can already be clearly seen in the fact that, in a period of full employment, only 18 per cent of the mass of 68 million workers are in industry, whereas in 1900 the proportion was 30.3 per cent; it is tending to still further reduction, both relatively and absolutely, as automation advances.

The problem of the active workers separated from production is solved by the welfare system. This problem does not constitute a major challenge because the workers had already had their personalities conformed by the discipline imposed by the regime of productive work in which they were engaged. But what is to be done with the new generations, a large proportion of which will never be able to work long enough to be integrated socially and psychologically into the category of responsible people? An army of marginals, today composed mainly of Negroes, mulattoes, Puerto

Ricans, but which will grow, tomorrow, with people of all shades, threatens to advance on the institutions and the state as the greatest transforming force ever unleashed.

The social pressure of these masses marginalized by the productive process will be exerted principally to force governmental distribution of the economic benefits deriving from automation. For this reason it ought to strengthen the state's role as collector and distributor of funds (to meet increasing social charges), which will result in an ever-greater official control of the financial and productive system.

These were the tasks of peace that, like a cataclysm, frightened the American entrepreneurial world, the workers, and the politicians, because of the menaces that they seemed to contain. If they should come to impose themselves, they would inevitably lead to a breakdown of capitalistic standards and norms, thus made obsolete. They would determine the reordering of the economy and society with its base in the state's responsibilities for all citizens. In the international context it would open the way for cooperative action with the underdeveloped world, where the needs for industrial equipment and property would permit a total mobilization of the U.S. productive system and provide it with an interim formula for its social reordering as an evolutionary socialistic structure.

The second transforming force of American society derives from the oppressive domination exercised over the people and the nation by the industrial and financial companies, whose entrepreneurial interests, phobias, and fears came to govern the internal life and the foreign relations of the United States. Expressing the Rooseveltian position toward this menace, Henry A. Wallace, Vice-President of the United States, warned the nation in September 1943 about the risks that the increasing power of international monopolies represented for public liberties and progress:

> The peoples and governments of the world, without knowing it, have allowed the cartels and monopolies to form a supergovernment by means of which they can monopolize and divide whole fields of science and the world's markets among them. The people ought to recover its power to confront this supergovernment. This supergovernment has abused the people of the United States, not only in regard to synthetic rubber . . . but also in other critical industries. These gangs have their own international government, by means of which they establish private quotas of production. Their emissaries can be found in the foreign ministries of many of the important nations of the world. They create their own system of customs tariffs and determine who will get permission to produce, to buy and sell. . . . This secret agreement (on synthetic rubber) between a U.S. monopoly and a Ger-

man cartel was not submitted to any public authority. It was much more important than the majority of treaties, but the U.S. Senate has never taken any step concerning it (S. Lilley, 1966, p. 195).

As the new power increased, the average American citizen's sense of political responsibility gradually died out, as did the capacity for action by progressive leaderships, at the same time that an alternative solution to socialization was taking shape. It would be a provisional and daring solution, as Nazism had been for Germany, when placed in an equivalent situation, but even so it would connect actions and control activities in series, all directed toward a regime incompatible with the liberal institutions and with the image that the United States had of herself.

The mortal blow to American democracy, enmeshed in this antiprogressive web already in the course of the war, was to be dealt by the collusion of corporation executives, superenriched by the war, with generals who had learned to play politics and get rich by maneuvering huge war orders, and with union leaders frightened by the prospect of unemployment and crisis inevitably consequent on disarmament, if it should be done without profound structural changes. It was the birth of a new form of state, founded on the precedence of the military over the civilian power, that would wipe out all the bases of the liberal-democratic order, turning American society into a shock force for the destruction of communism. The militaristic state was being born.

With the death of Franklin D. Roosevelt, the United States had fallen into the hands of Truman, symbol of petty bourgeois mediocrity and likewise the product of a very American tradition that was not the tradition of the founding fathers, but that of the Tylers, the Polks, the Buchanans, the Theodore Roosevelts, the Hoovers, and so many others who as presidents represented plutocratic reactionism always on the lookout to gain power and degrade it. Under Truman's presidency the Rooseveltian orientation and policies that would have permitted tackling fearlessly the problems of peace were abandoned, insofar as they resulted in internal reform for disarmament. In its Latin American relations the administration abandoned the line of government-to-government loans and of incentive to autonomous industrialization, to implant the spirit of Bretton Woods, the policy of the International Monetary Fund, and, with them, free enterprise, set up as the supreme form of fostering the progress of the backward peoples. It was the "good partner policy," supplanting the Rooseveltian Good Neighbor Policy.

Faced with the fear of communism and with a kind of inferiority complex that leads so many Americans to doubt the renovating capacity of their own social system, the U.S. administrations headed down the cold war path. This had its beginning in the hottest acts in the world's history, the bombing of Hiroshima and Nagasaki—terrible in themselves, and still more so because they were unnecessary, since the Japanese were already suing for peace, but indispensable for the affirmation of the United States as the superpower of the world.

Immediately the new power succeeded in imposing on the whole nation a crucial option regarding the problems of disarmament: the intention of maintaining the war economy instead of the alternative of a government-regulated transition to a peace economy. This was to be done by means of great national plans for works and services that would guarantee the maintenance of the employment level and the progressive rise in living standards.

The immense demands of World War II on the American economy, both in war production and in the manufacture of consumer goods to supply the world, had led to an integration never before attained between the strictly military command and the directors of the great corporations. It had simultaneously induced the formulation of a new theory of national security that placed the highest priority on the need to continue total mobilization of the entrepreneurial economy, as in wartime, and the maintenance of controls over the unions so as not to disturb the automation process in the productive system.

In this way the industrial-military entente was successful in turning the concept of war security into the theory ordering society for peace. From both the military and the business points of view this formula represented the solution for many problems, such as the continuities of the productive processes already set up and the prevention of an industry-civil government accord from replacing, with the advent of peace, the industry-military accord. Among the advantages of private order was the assurance of continuing to count on the flow of government funds destined for new industrial installations for war, in the form of subsidized orders. For these same private groups the implicit victory was decisive over the tendency to state capitalism, which threatened to revive orientations of the New Deal type that had saved the capitalist system from the great depression at the cost of state intervention, planning, social reforms, and regulation of entrepreneurial activity. Thus a war economy intended to prevent crisis also avoids reforms in the name of national defense, patriotism, and anticommunism.

The effects of this antihistorical orientation of the U.S. government are in some measure shown by the fact that, whereas Roosevelt's administration spent $39 per capita in social and educational programs (1939), Johnson's administration spent on the same projects $16 per capita. Or, in other words: the proportion of expenditures for civil works and well-being dropped from 44 per cent in 1939 to 7 per cent in 1963, when defense expenditures reached 75 per cent of the national budget (C. R. de Carlo, in E. Ginzberg, 1964).

Thus, in postwar peace a new type of war machine was established, the specific demands of which, as burdensome on American society as those of a real war, were made even worse by the demolition of civilian power and the democratic ideals that the nineteenth-century United States had championed. The country turned aside from her historical role as the focus of emancipatory institutional renovation to yield herself up to the role of maintainer of the capitalistic, imperialistic order and, with it, of all the world's surviving oligarchies.

The first warning against the militarist state menace to the United States is credited to the Yankee hero of the war, President Eisenhower, who in his farewell address—knowing better than anyone what he was saying, but fulfilling his duty to say it roundly—stated:

Until the latest of our world conflicts the United States had no armaments industry. American makers of plowshares could, with time and as required, make swords as well. But we can no longer risk emergency improvisation of national defense; we have been compelled to create a permanent arms industry of vast proportions. Added to this, three and a half million men and women are directly engaged in the defense establishment. We annually spend on military security more than the net income of all United States corporations.

This conjunction of an immense military establishment and a large arms industry is new in the American experience. The total influence —economic, political, even spiritual—is felt in every city, every state house, every office of the federal government. We recognize the imperative need for this development. Yet we must not fail to comprehend its grave implications. Our toil, resources, and livelihood are all involved; so is the very structure of our society.

In the councils of government we must guard against the acquisition of unwarranted influence, whether sought or unsought, by the military-industrial complex. The potential for the disastrous rise of misplaced power exists and will persist.

We must never let the weight of this combination endanger our liberties or democratic processes. We should take nothing for granted. Only an alert and knowledgeable citizenry can compel the proper meshing of the huge industrial and military machinery of defense with our peaceful methods and goals, so that the security and liberty may prosper together.[2]

[2] Speech delivered January 17, 1961 (Quoted by Fred J. Cook 1962, pp. 8–9).

After Eisenhower's term in office this military-industrial complex grew and grew, invading all areas of American life, enlisting officers as war propagandists, pressuring congress, molding public opinion through control of communications media, inflating the C.I.A. and the Pentagon, and bending the state department to its will, so that it carried its conspiratorial, subversive interference, using espionage, terrorism, and corruption, to all the corners of the earth.

Bertrand Russell points out in a letter in 1966 appealing to the American people against the barbarism of the Vietnam War:

> The military budget of the United States is three times the sum total of the capitals of U.S. Steel, Metropolitan Life Insurance, American Telephone and Telegraph, General Motors, and Standard Oil. The Department of Defense employs three times as many people as these great worldwide firms. Thousands of millions of dollars for military contracts are provided by the Pentagon and paid over to big industry. In 1960 twenty-one billion dollars were spent for military equipment. Of this fabulous sum, seven and a half billions were divided among ten companies and another five got nearly a billion dollars each. In the offices of those firms fourteen hundred army officers are working, including two hundred and sixty-one generals and officers on active service. On the payroll of General Dynamics one hundred and eighty-seven officers, twenty-seven generals and admirals, and an ex-Secretary of the Army are listed. All of them make up a dominant caste that remains in power even when others are those nominally elected to public offices, and all the presidents find themselves obliged to cater to the interests of that omnipotent group. Consequently, American democracy lacks reality and meaning because the people cannot discharge the men who are really running the country.[3]

Such is the Moloch that is battening on the world. Taken over by the great corporations and the military that are feeding on her, the United States, people and nation, have been transformed into a machine for repressive war. This fantastic mechanism, once started, has moved forward like an avalanche, fusing into a single body the high-ranking military with the top executives of the great corporations. Thus conceived, it is directed to the maintenance of capitalistic exploitation in the United States and throughout the world, at the cost of the values that the nation itself, in its fecund stage, had engendered and that had presided over the birth of

---

[3] Published in *Marcha,* Montevideo, August 1966.

American society as the first democracy in the modern world. The economic cost of this effort exceeds many times over, as Russell said, the capitalizations of the great corporations. The one who is paying for it, however, is the American taxpayer, financing the perpetuation of the machine in which he is caged.

With the militaristic state came mobilization for a new war, with the most fantastic squandering of funds and the most oppressive domination of public opinion. What is the purpose of it all? War, naturally, which becomes much more likely for that very fact, despite its character as a battle of seconds' duration that will put an end to life on earth. More than war, however, its purpose is to retain state control over the economy in the only way that does not collide with the private entrepreneurial interests: the mobilization of the industrial plants for war by means of astronomical military orders. Probably this, too, is the only alternative open to the United States after the overexpansion of her economy, other than a profound reordering, socializing in nature.

The paradox about this process is that the United States, through the direction she has taken, is desisting from the only path that would permit her to surpass the Soviet Union, face competition with China, and still resume the historical role of being a renovating focus, in a moment when the emergence of colonial peoples to national status and the rebellion of the peoples exploited by imperialism bring to the forefront the problem of generalizing the modern technological revolution throughout the whole world. The greatness of the infrastructure that would serve as a starting point for American socialism would allow it to effect a great historical transformation without great disintegration and would even restore the health of the democratic life that has been lost.

The Warriors of the Apocalypse

With the bases of the militaristic state planted in the United States, a series of events swayed public opinion, the governing officials, and the military, leading the whole ruling class of the country to successive crises of fright and hysteria. Those events were the socialist revolution of the Chinese; the break of the monopoly on the atomic and later the hydrogen bomb by the Russians; the first sputnik, annulling the sense of security engendered by the Atlantic and Pacific "moats," which formerly isolated the United States beyond the reach of any attack; Vice-President Nixon's disastrous visit to Latin America; the Cuban Revolution, which nationalized a tenth of the U.S. investments in the Western Hemisphere; the crisis of

October 1962, provoked by the Russian nuclear projectiles installed in Cuba; and, finally, the Chinese atomic bomb.

The response of the militaristic system was to strengthen itself and liquidate all the militant liberal currents in American political life. A new reactionary wave, which had been inaugurated with McCarthyism, assailed government officials and unionists, especially the former directors of New Deal programs, transforming that participation into evidence of national treason; scientists, beginning with Oppenheimer, creator of the first atomic bomb, proscribed and dishonored at home when his prestige was rising highest in the world; professors, journalists, and writers, both celebrated and modest, even exceedingly modest, all subject to the greatest harassment, obliged to lay bare their whole lives to police scrutiny in order to explain some chance acquaintance with a radical a decade or more before. Some were driven to suicide by despair, many lost their minds, and all were left with incurable scars.

Congressional committees were followed by exhaustive, cruel police investigations carried out by the C.I.A. and the F.B.I., the latter being converted from a bureau designed to protect the people against thieves and murderers to an organization for hunting down political phantoms. Thanks to U.S. America's habitual technical proficiency, both reached peaks of efficiency in vigilance and control of all possible suspects, imposing on the country, especially on the intellectual stratum, the terror of falling under suspicion of liberal attitudes. Thus political creativity was shriveled up among the American intellectual corps, for which a position merely approximating radicalism came to be pure temerity. The frightened middle class did not dare go near any form of literature or art that questioned the social order or long-established values.

The official organizations were increased immediately by some private ones, voluntary associations that multiplied, their expenses paid by financiers to complete the work of terrorizing and indoctrination. For example, the John Birch Society, for whom Eisenhower and Truman were communists, not to mention Kennedy and Roosevelt; the China-lobbyists, the Dixiecrats, paired together, all of them, in the fight against emancipation of the Negro, in war propaganda, and in the most loutish anticommunism. Acting under the coordination of military and police authorities, these associations attacked the popular protest movements starting up all over the country advocating a nuclear weapons ban and respect for human rights.

It was in that atmosphere that the United States undertook her crusades against Korea, the frictions in Berlin, the attacks on Cuba, the uprisings in Hungary, the repressions in Greece, the C.I.A. against Mossadegh in Iran, the mercenaries' war in the Congo, the military coups in Laos and Thailand and Brazil, the invasion of the Dominican Republic, the war in Vietnam, the overthrow of Nkrumah in Ghana, and the new policy of inciting and stimulating coups d'état in Latin America. In this manner throughout the world the United States is allying itself with the most retrograde elements everywhere, taking as its international partners Franco, Chiang Kai-shek, Singman Rhee, Tshombe, Batista, Hussein, Madame Nhu, Castelo Branco, and every dictator or shady practitioner who wants to become an agent of antipopular and antiprogressive reaction against his own people.

The America of the free colonists and the pioneers, of the founding fathers and civil liberties, of private initiative and entrepreneurial competition—that America has died. A new form of state, a new attitude toward man and the world have been implanted. On the domestic side it is the capitalism of the great corporations; on the foreign side it is imperialism. And with these is also implanted a new time of unimaginable wealth and of still greater poverty, fear, and insecurity. Their first victim is the American people, surreptitiously disinherited of its civic patrimony, hedged about in its fear of assuming political responsibility, prohibited from using its creativity to rethink the world, precisely at the time when, through its historical position, it was called on to produce new reformers and revolutionaries.

Thus, that ingenious, initiative-filled people, in which man has best expressed his quality as *homo faber,* has ended by inventing the supermachine, which, by indoctrination in schools, newspapers, radio, television, movies, theater, and books, is stupefying and convincing him every day that he is the happiest man on earth because his belly is full when it could be empty; because he can buy and trade cars and odds and ends that would make any dupe in the world happy. The supermachine says that he owes all this to the "American way of life," freedom of speech, free competition, free initiative. But beware of the machine's police, because it does not pursue thieves, but subversive ideas. Beware of the workman beside you, because he may be an agent of the C.I.A. or of the company police. Be wary of your friends, because an American patriot will denounce any person suspected of fomenting unrest or doubt to the Senate Committee on Un-American Activities or to the precinct police headquarters. Beware of the night: it is so full of idle and dangerous Negroes that a respectable American is safe only in his house after nightfall.

This supermachine, which protects the U.S. citizen against world revolution, against peace that would lead to economic crisis, against racial violence, cannot protect him against fear. Protection against all these risks costs him more than all the possible dangers, because it keeps all the rational Americans anesthetized or frightened who could contribute to "security and prosperity progressing together." The scientists and the intellectuals are frightened after McCarthyism. The politicians, leaders, preachers, and teachers are afraid, under the constant vigilance of the John Birch Society and the multiple ideological police forces.

All this system of oppression is enhanced by innumerable voluntary associations, many of them secret and terrorist like the infamous Ku Klux Klan, operating as mechanisms of psychological intimidation that exert pressure in a thousand ways on anyone who differs from the mediocre norm of apparent adjustment. The gregarious propensity so characteristic of the American, which for centuries has given him thousands of civic, fraternal, and philanthropic organizations, is being mobilized to turn against the individual, these associations being involved also in the bloodthirsty persecution of the exotic citizen because he is free and dares rethink the world and human relations.

This whole system of controls is crowned by self-censure induced by the most subtle mechanisms of indoctrination, a self-censure that, once implanted in the consciousness of each American citizen, degrades his spiritual freedom and dissolves his moral responsibility, causing him always to transfer to another—the government, the police, the senator, the boss—both judgment and criticism of political life. It is in these circumstances that, out of the background of the average American's common culture, Protestant Puritanism reemerges with its mystic, fanatical contents to explain the modern world and to justify the unjustifiable. With the liberal voices of the Deweys or the William Jameses of the past silenced or discredited, like those of Wright Mills and Erich Fromm in the present, it is in the Apocalypse that the common man must seek the explanation for the "inevitability" of the bomb hanging over his head, which must finally explode so that the Day of Judgment can dawn over this sinful world.

One of the manifestations of this obsessive preoccupation with control in recent decades is the geometric increase of American missions of all kinds abroad, transformed into world projections of the internal systems of indoctrination and police control. The traditional diplomatic personnel has been enlarged by crowds of military attachés detached from all the branches of the armed forces. Their numbers are increased by the spies from the F.B.I. and the C.I.A. by tens, hundreds, even thousands, depending on the volume of U.S. investments in the area. Likewise, the labor attachés, the counselors and the technical staff, and the welfare program attachés. Lastly, the contingents of ingenuous or fiery missionaries of the faith have come, the Peace Corps volunteers, the U.S.I.S. functionaries. Today they form multitudes in all the American countries. And in these last years their numbers have been further swelled by other categories: the scientific advisors and the new types of directors of recently improvised foundations, bent on engaging the researchers and the laboratories of the whole Western world in the American research program, at the cost of a bit of equipment and certain supplements to salaries. Finally, the doctors of eugenics and birth control, frightened by the fecundity of the dark, poor peoples who are threatening to crowd the world with more hungry mouths. They are charged with the duty of promoting contraceptive campaigns in the strictest confidence, of distributing pills and pamphlets that will guarantee the U.S. Americans the desired tranquility against the explosion of the Latin American populations.

They can be recognized anywhere by their attitude of fearful reserve, very expressive of the feeling that they are doing something filthy and of the fear of being seen consorting with natives who may not be exempt from some suspicion of leftism. More than in the case of the American who stayed at home, they feel the weight of police control over them. They feel secure only when banded together, a flock of branded sheep, bleating their nostalgia, their fear, their insecurity, and often their distaste for the sordidness of the task in which they are enmired.

In these new social conditions it is the spirit of the plate of lentils, so contrary to the spirit of the founding fathers and so mean compared with such figures as F. D. Roosevelt, that today marks the American's moral profile. He must not lose his job. He must get his promotion. He must trade in his car. He must hate that Negro. He must be grateful to his boss, to the manager, to the assistant manager, and to the foreman. He must be a nice guy. "We've got to put an end to the communists." Especially, he must not think of politics. Not be a politician. Because the good American does not even want to know whether Kennedy was assassinated. Or whether the wars and guerrillas out in the world are just or unjust. It is not his business, even if his son is fighting in Vietnam or flying across the world's skies carrying the bomb that will destroy everything, himself and all of us.

This integration of everything and everyone into the same spirit of discipline and hierarchy, this impregnation with fear and insecurity: could it be a necessary, inexorable result of American development as it has operated? Only this deterministic reasoning would permit accepting the betrayal of their own body of ideals by the Americans, our contemporaries. But it is not true. To prove it, look at those who are struggling against the tide, especially the leftist intellectuals, the university students. Not all, but many of them, and they are tending to increase. It is this contingent that, by fighting, will become the salt of American life. There are also those whose personalities crumbled under the pressure of fear and who, reacting with perplexity at what has become of their country, sink into drunkenness and psychoses and refuse to talk about it. These forms of protest, although pusillanimous, prove that not all is lost. There are, finally, the Negroes, who in their never-ceasing hand-to-hand combat are fighting not only for a place in the sun in the Yankee paradise but for human dignity, for justice, equality, and the freedoms that have been the banners of the best leaders of the America of the heroic expansion period.

What most revolts the humanists all over the world is to see the nation of Lincoln debased into a docile tool of the great industrial corporations and the most corrupt militarism, to be imposed on the world as a force for maintaining backwardness; to see its youth recruited by the millions in armies and antiguerrilla units ready to fall on any people that dares struggle for abundance and freedom. The Vietnam War shows the world that any people, even the descendants of the Mayflower pilgrims, can be led into degradations equal to or greater than those of the Nazi hosts, when it turns against history, bent on reversing it.

The resemblance of the Yankee soldier of today to the old mameluke slaves captured, fed, and trained by the Turks to maintain, by fire and sword, their domination of the peoples they were oppressing, is not a merely chance one. The American civilization, so promising in its early stages, paralyzed by materialistic indigestion and particularly by its castration by the great monopolies' hegemonic interests, as seen in this year of 1967 seems condemned to be transformed into a sterile, destructive precivilization such as the Ottoman, equally full of vigor, initiative, and efficacy, but remembered in history principally for ferocity, greed, and narrowness.

Toynbee, speaking at the University of Pennsylvania about the American betrayal of its own revolution and of the democratizing mission it had proposed for itself in the past, had this to say:

> Even so, the United States is today the head of an antirevolutionary movement operating in defense of selfish interests. The United States today stands for what Rome once stood for. Rome, consequently, supported the rich against the poor in all the foreign communities that fell under her dominion. As the poor, until now, have always been more numerous than the rich, Rome's policy fostered inequality, injustice and the least happiness for the greatest number.
>
> What happened? I suppose that the simplest explanation is that America has sided with the minority. In 1775 it fought in the ranks of the majority, and this is one of the reasons why the American Revolution aroused a universal response.
>
> I maintain that, beginning with 1917, America has inverted the role that it used to play before the world. It has turned into the archiconservative power instead of continuing to be the archirevolutionary power. Stranger still is the fact that the United States has yielded up

its glorious and outstanding role to the country that had been the archiconservative power in the nineteenth century, the country that, since 1946, the United States has considered its number one enemy. America has yielded its revolutionary role to Russia (Toynbee, 1962, pp. 34–35, 48).

This is Toynbee's conclusion, full of bitterness for this America that, frightened by the bugbear of communism, has sided with the minority, making herself the world bastion for defense of selfish interests, of wealth against poverty, of oppression against freedom.

The Canadians

Canada, as seen by the Latin Americans, is a country so hidden behind the United States, still so enfolded in the British flag and so provincial and hermetic in her intellectual life that it is difficult to evaluate. Can she become a mature national ethnos in spite of being divided into Anglo- and French-Canadians? Will she tend to unfold into two nations, or cement herself as a neo-British mass in which a Latin minority will grow embittered, always differentiated? Will she have the Irish energy or the Scottish resistance to enculturation, or will she act as a malleable mass? And finally, is Canada a nation or only a Yankee industrial outpost with a markedly managerial dominant class, and will she end by merging some day with the colossus of the north, as the American founding fathers hoped?

It is curious that we, the Latins of South America, do not identify even with the Latins of North America. They always remind us of those Martinique students in Paris who, in their alienation, took on the French ethnos and became all but exasperated when they were taken for Latin Americans. The poor things were "French." They neither knew nor felt themselves to be Americans. Their self-image was that of the old Gallic colonists deported to the islands, always yearning for the mother country.

Located between the United States and Europe, closer to the latter even geographically than to Latin America, the Canadians grew like a transplant, only incidentally American. In fact, they feel closer to the Australians and New Zealanders, even to the Rhodesians and the South Africans, than to the mestizo peoples of South America.

10. The River Plate Peoples

THE SECOND BLOC of Transplanted Peoples of the Americas is composed of the Argentines and the Uruguayans. Both had the same formative process, which bifurcated at a certain point but continued operating on parallel lines. They exhibit various characteristics common to the other Hispanic peoples, but among these they stand out because of a particular physiognomy deriving from the absorption of larger non-Iberian contingents, from their ecological settling in temperate lands, and from the higher degree of economic and social development that they achieved. Compared with the Transplanted Peoples of North America the contrasts stand out: their Latin, Hispanic formation, the predominance of the Catholic religion, and their relative historical backwardness in regard to incorporation into the ways of life of the modern industrial civilizations.

The two River Plate countries had 24 million inhabitants in 1960, or 11.6 per cent of Latin America, and were the part of the Latin continent enjoying the highest per capita income, the most favorable indexes of education on all levels, the longest life expectancy, and the highest degree of urbanization. But they, too, face grave developmental problems and are far from an adequate level of exploitation of their possibilities. But they have attained a much higher degree of development than all the other Latin American peoples taken as a whole. Only Venezuela surpasses them in certain indexes, such as the over-all value of production and the per capita income, but this is a special case of structural deformation that does not mean, as we have seen, the attainment of higher living levels for the whole population, but the presence of a foreign economic cyst in the national productive system.

The New Peoples of the South

The Transplanted Peoples of North America established themselves on American soil as nuclei of villagers, craftsmen, and farmers who were trying to reproduce the European human landscape there. They made camp in the wilderness, having to compete only with the sparse indigenous tribal level population, which, as a rule, preferred trafficking with the invader to expelling him. They reached America a century after the Iberian conquest, and gradually spread along the Atlantic coast. Only two centuries later did they muster strength to tackle the difficult job of colonizing the immense wilderness of the interior.

The Transplanted Peoples of South America derive from European immigrants who came to America only after independence. The land had already been cleared; the last Indians, corralled in the most desolate terrain, were being decimated. The conquest and domination of the valleys and pampas, their occupation by cattle and by man, the construction of the first urban nuclei, and political independence itself were being accomplished at the same time. It had all been the work of the mestizos molded in two centuries of active interaction between Spaniards detached from their cultures and the indigenous communities in which they encysted themselves—in other words, the work of an earlier protoethnos that they would supplant and succeed.

Those mestizos, fruit of the blending of a few European fathers with a multiplicity of indigenous mothers, more identified with the former than with the latter, but speaking Guaraní better than Spanish, took the form of Ladino or gaucho. Ladinos were those who, living in small country towns or devoted to farming and craftsmanship, turned out relatively less mestizo-like and more Europeanized, through the continual absorption of a small number of Spaniards who came to try their fortune in this marginal American region. These were generally men accredited by the crown or mere adventurers sent to exercise bureaucratic functions or to get rich in land and cattle deals and appropriations. For this reason they took up positions above the Creole population in the new land from the first, proud of their origin in the kingdom itself. Only in rare cases did Spain undertake immigrant colonization in this region, as in all America. These colonists did not exceed a few hundred peasants located, for the purpose of guaranteeing Spanish possession, in areas disputed by Portugal. For this very reason they ended by assimilating the habits of the land, their descendants becoming practically undifferentiated from the Ladinos, but contributing also, probably, to the Hispanization of the latter.

The Ladino nuclei of the ravines and steep banks of the River Plate received some Negro slaves as a sumptuary article for domestic and other services to which the gaucho never adapted. They were very few, however, leaving no noticeable marks on the resultant racial type and ethnos. Today their presence is felt only in the small Afro-Ladino groups in Montevideo.

Gauchos were the mestizos from Indian mother and Spanish father brought up on the broad open pastoral spaces with the cattle that had multiplied prodigiously. They retained through endogamy their original biological characteristics, and through isolation in the broad plains preserved their techniques of subsistence, forms of social organization, view of the world, habits, and language molded in the first decades by the amalgamation of the dual heritage, Guaraní and Spanish, insofar as such things were compatible with their peculiar mode of life.

The dominating influence in the Ladino's cultural formation was the port, which kept him in touch with the great outside world and made him more and more exogenous. As for the gaucho, it was the wide plains, which bound him more to the fatherland, who valued his specialized adaptation to cattle-raising. The Ladinos spoke mainly Spanish; the gauchos, until the end of the eighteenth century, must have spoken Guaraní principally, both in Uruguay and in Argentina. No other hypothesis is admissible in view of the facts that the first Buenos Aires nuclei originated in Asunción and that the settlers on the Banda Oriental, the east bank, originated in the missions* or in São Paulo—all speakers of Guaraní. This hypothesis is indirectly proved by the toponymy of the old gaucho areas, nearly all the Guaraní roots.[1]

* The Jesuit communities of Paraguay, composed of Guaraní Indians converted to Catholicism and taught by the fathers.

[1] The documentation published up to now on this subject, which seems to be a blind spot in Argentine and Uruguayan bibliography, is very precarious. The latter tends to admit the Charrúas and other non-Guaraní peoples as the forebears of the gauchos, but scholars of both countries appear to be uninterested in the subject.

The social order of the River Plate region is established within this ethnic tripartition, with its ruling stratum the Ladino patriciate, which regulated life and property, commerce and customs, and by means of it appropriated to itself the fruits of common labor. The subordinate stratum was the gaucho, originally free but later subjected to increasing compulsions that, first, engaged him in the over-all system under the domination of landowners as the peon of his "sponsor," that is, his boss in work and caudillo in war, and subsequently marginalized him, displacing him with the immigrant as a basic work force. It was in this process that the gaucho not only became disfigured but Hispanized.

It was on this ethnic complex with all the characteristics of a New People, founded on the deculturation of its population and on a creativity that lent it a peculiar profile on the plane of language and life style, that the migrations spilled. So massive were they that, instead of becoming incorporated into the forming ethnos as gauchos or Ladinos, according to whether they were ruralized or urbanized, they gave birth to a new national ethnos, dominantly European, with a Transplanted Peoples profile.

The linguistic Hispanization of these migratory contingents is owing to the fact that the new waves of immigrants, despite being predominantly Italian, included a great number of Spaniards, to the assimilative capacity of the urban and rural nuclei, as well as to the compulsory power of the hacienda system into which they were introduced and which was run by the native agrarian oligarchy. In these circumstances the Italians, like all the other Europeans, had to learn the language of the land and integrate himself into the dominant values and habits responsible for what distinguishes the Argentines and Uruguayans from the other peoples.

Thus ethnic cysts were not formed, but all merged together in proportion as they became Hispanized and assimilated to form the common people of the two nationalities. Contributing to this free assimilation was the fact that these contingents were drawn principally from rural strata speaking different dialects and not identified nationally, people who opposed one another through the strong interethnic tensions characteristic of the phases of national ethnic structuration. These internal differentiations, including the linguistic, in each group compelled them to adopt a common language of communication, which in the circumstances turned out to be Spanish rather than the modern European national languages of their country.

From the original protoethnos, which in its two basic forms, the Ladino and the gaucho, had attained singular cultural characteristics—besides the Paraguayan population—there was left in Uruguay and Argentina only a nostalgia that sometimes becomes visible in the national self-image as a source of patriotic inspiration and traditionalistic affirmation. As evidence, one need only see the nativist fervor with which Uruguayans or Argentines, of pure foreign stock, recite verses from *Martín Fierro* * or read pages from gaucho writers, in an alienation typical of those who need to adopt other people's ancestors in order to recognize and accept themselves. *Martín Fierro* is obviously a literary work of extraordinary merits that can be read with pleasure by all. Very different, however, is the worshipful attitude with which it is treated, both by the oligarchic and vocational right, naturally nostalgic and backward-looking, and by the left, equally gaucho-indoctrinated and rather gringophobic.

This attitude, for that matter, is common in the modern populations of many American peoples who render homage to falsely dignifying ancestors, such as the Americans of the United States, the Chileans, and the São Paulists. Nevertheless, it is a fact that the supposed descendants of the pilgrims who came over on the Mayflower (too small in number for so many grandchildren) value "European and Puritan ancestors in search of freedom for their faith and their business," a posture appropriate to a Transplanted People; while the literary gaucho of South America, like the indigenous lineage of the São Paulist through four centuries and the Chilean's Arauchanian ancestry, only exalts the victim of the historical process that gave them birth as peoples, rather than the real ancestors.

This ideological incongruity, even plainer in the case of the River Plate Transplanted Peoples, is an indication of how incomplete their process of national ethnic maturation really is. It can be documented not only on the literary but on many other planes, such as the educational, where the textbooks, especially in elementary and secondary schools, are impregnated with the notion of a herioc, common gaucho ancestry, ignoring rather than taking in the factor of the migratory contingents, which after all were numerous and decisive in the configuration of the two national ethnic entities of the Río de la Plata.

The assumption of a European posture is only felt, in that area, in the dominant caste's pride in everything English and French, in the cultivation of Parisian and British habits, fashions and attitudes—and lately, Yankee ones—all of which is equally artificial when compared with the real composition of the population. And it only points up the still prevailing incapacity to accept its own history and from it draw motivational forces for national integration.

In the make-up of the Transplanted Peoples of South America we find several opposing factors that explain the role played by them, successively or simultaneously, throughout the historical process. The first contraposes

---

* The Argentine gaucho epic poem by José Hernández. The two parts were published in 1872 and 1879.

the neo-American, Guaraní-speaking mestizos, offspring of European fathers and indigenous mothers, to the tribal populations. In the national-ethnic formative process it occasioned bloody battles, intended to sweep the hostile Indians from the vicinity of the neo-American establishments, and compulsive forms of ecological and exonomic competition that finally decimated the independent indigenous nuclei or confined them in the most desolate territories. Today a few deeply acculturated Indians survive only in Argentina, in marginal areas, especially in Chaco province [West of the Paraná]. All the rest were wiped out.

The second opposition contraposes mutually the three neo-American basic populations: the River Plate, the midland ones between the Paraguay and the Uruguay, and the neo-Brazilian from São Paulo to Rio Grande do Sul. Such were (1) the nucleus of Asunción and its offshoots established in the area, including Buenos Aires; (2) the Jesuit missions that were set up in Guaira, went downriver to the Tape country, and settled finally on the banks of the Uruguay; and (3) the Paulist half-breeds, the main scourge of the mission Indians and principal frontier of expansion into the southern pasture lands. All three Guaraní-speaking,[2] all genetically more indigenous than European, but all configured, too, as neo-Americans and performed the role of European shock and expansion elements of domination.[3] The conflicts between the men of Asunción and those of the missions, between both and the Paulists, and between all of them and the original occupants of the Uruguayan and Argentine territory, burst out often in bloody assaults, creating throughout the region, for long periods, an atmosphere of extreme tension and most propitious for war. The populations forged in such an atmosphere developed military attitudes, in the humblest gaucho strata as much as in the caudillo leader castes.

Another opposition progressively developed between natives and those from Spain, between sons of the soil, mestizo and Americanized in their effort to adapt to new living conditions, and the Spaniards who came, first, to occupy the posts of politicoadministrative command, and, later, to control the commerce by monopoly of exports and imports or to benefit from other privileges granted by the crown. The struggle for the reduction of these contradictions guided the campaign for independence, finally won by

[2] The Tupí language of Brazil and the *lingua franca* resultant from it differ from the Guaraní of Paraguay and from modern Guaraní in the same degree that Portuguese differs from Spanish.

[3] The designation "mameluco" for the Paulists is applied for this reason to them all, since it means despotic agent of domination over their own peoples at the service of the ones who enslaved them—which is the original sense of the term as used by Arabs and Ottomans.

the Ladinos and directed by their leaders in conformity with their interests.

Another elementary contradiction, which had been generating for a long time, was to explode after independence in the form of three opposing projects of ordering the new national society: (1) the urban patriciate's project, centralistic because it aspired to perpetuate its control of foreign commerce and customs from which it had grown rich; (2) the provincial territorial oligarchy's project, federative and advocative of a decentralization that would favor the economy of the provinces more; and (3) the autonomist-national project of Paraguay, of Francia and of López, her dictators.

In the first two cases the oppositions were resolved by a pact between the urban elites and the agrarian oligarchies in the face of the later menaces to their common interests, resulting in the consolidation of the land monopoly in the hands of the caudillos and in the political hegemony of Buenos Aires. In the case of Paraguay, the autarchic national project was concretized, raising the country to relatively high levels of development from which she would fall as a result of the War of the Triple Alliance.* In the case of Argentina and Uruguay, the conflict that seemed to typify the rural-urban opposition in all societies, went beyond that. Here the components faced each other more frontally because the cities, instead of making themselves the nuclei of autonomous command of society or the diffusing centers of an authentic civilization, had turned into mirrors reflecting the European world and into agents of foreign domination of the area.

In the center of all these oppositions another one operated, opposing on one side the Ladino patriciate, established on the banks of the River Plate, and the agrarian oligarchy, both insistent on establishing the bases of an export meat economy, and on the other the gauchos, living free in the rural districts. As long as only hides were being exported, their way of life could be tolerated, and it had a function in the economic system and a place in the nascent society as labor force and cannon fodder. In the new phase the gaucho would be marginalized and compelled to suffer the discipline of the estancias, the large ranches. The struggles engendered by this opposition were shaped by the contingency of the gaucho's having to ally himself with the landowner as the soldier of a caudillo, who would be more and more his patron, his boss, through the gaucho's historical inca-

---

* Paraguay, thanks to her dictator Francisco Solano López, fought Brazil, Argentina, and Uruguay for five years (1865–1870), until, on the dictator's death in 1870, there were fewer than 500 men left in his forces.

pacity to propose a project of struggle for himself. The gauchos ultimately became the provincial oligarchy's troops in its fights to expand the frontiers and for the federativist combats, but they survived a few more decades in the dual role of peon and soldier.

Only one of the caudillos expressed the two tensions ideologically, attempting to synthesize them in a program at once federalist, expressing the provinces' aspirations for autonomy against the port and Montevidean exploitation, and reformist, advocating an agrarian reform that would provide the plains populations with a home and means of existence. He was Artigas, made a national hero by the Uruguayans for that reason, after his death in exile. Wishing to be both chief of the provinces roused by the caudillo-latifundium proprietors and at the same time the social reformer who interpreted the aspirations of the gauchos, Artigas threatened the deepest interests of the territorial oligarchy. As was inevitable, he was finally left to his fate, with his few faithful gauchos and Indians. Against him in the end were allied the forces of the port unionists and the country federalists, withdrawing, as was to be foreseen, munitions and troops from the man actually threatening the existing order by advocating distribution of frontier lands, not to the latifundian caudillos, but to the gaucho class. When Artigas was defeated, the Ladino-commercial and latifundian-oligarchic order was progressively installed, first imposing discipline on the gauchos by all manner of compulsions and later substituting European immigrants for them as a national work force, when the export cereal economy emerged.

The opposition that followed consisted of the process of ecological succession that marginalized the gauchos and poor Ladinos by giving the immigrant all the opportunities of work and social ascent in the new productive system, pastoral and agricultural. The principal characteristic of this process is that it was deliberate. This makes it one of the rare cases, if not the only one, in history in which a national leadership gained a power of determination so imperative and alienated itself so completely from its own people that it could propose no less than to substitute people of better quality for it, as a fundamental project in construction of the nationality. In the oligarchies of the New Peoples one often finds similar attitudes, and even specific projects to attract European contingents. But not one of these oligarchies was able to carry out such projects with the congruence and depth with which that goal was reached on the River Plate.

In the eyes of the Ladino patriciate directing the process, the gaucho— "these wild men with spurs and chaps"—was not adequate material for building a nation. Muddled by European liberalistic ideology, enchanted with the formula for republic government implanted in North America, and explaining the wealth and know-how of the latter by its qualities as an

Anglo-Saxon race, they formulated, under the slogan "to civilize is to populate," the project of replacing the native gaucho mass with "people of better quality."

In the following pages we shall summarily examine the fundamental stages of the River Plate peoples' formation. We shall pause first on the development of the Paraguayan nucleus from which the original New People protoethnos derived, and then on the process of succession that transfigured it, giving rise to Argentina and Uruguay as Transplanted Peoples.

Asunción and Mission Populations

The European occupation of the River Plate was not done from nuclei established at the mouth of the river, as might have been expected. It was carried out from a point on the bank of the Paraguay River, in the interior of the continent. That point was the city of Asunción, born as a stopping place for Spanish adventurers in search of the Sierra de Plata (the Silver Range), the supposed existence of which had already given its name to the entire region. It was from there that the expeditions of Alvar Núñez (1542) and Irala (1548) were to set out into the interior, seeking the fabulous riches spoken of by the Indians and which, in the end, proved to be the Potosí mines already discovered and taken by Spain, entering from the Pacific. The original camp was transformed into a mestizo country town, and one day reversed the trail, populating the River Plate.

With Asunción the Paraguayan, the *pynambí,* emerges, through the crossing of those few Spaniards of the conquest expeditions with the Guaraní women of the region. Just as the Paulist mamelucos did, they identified with the father's ethnos and opposed the mother's. But they spoke the maternal language and provided their subsistence through essentially Guaraní techniques. They finally constituted a new ethnic entity, neither European nor indigenous, but neo-American. The Asunción nucleus lived and thrived for decades in a hybrid existence of farmers and soldiers, men always ready to leave their fields to repel wild Indians' attacks or mameluco invasions, and later the wrongful impositions by Spanish and Argentine authorities who wanted to subjugate them.

In the eastern part of Paraguay a second national ethnic stock was to form with a different profile, the result of the Jesuits' action. Their Paraguayan missions constitute the Catholic Church's most successful attempt to Christianize and assure a refuge to the indigenous populations threatened with absorption or enslavement by the various nuclei of descendants of European settlers. The Company of Jesus organized them into new bases capable of guaranteeing their subsistence and progress. When the Jesuits were expelled from Spanish territories (1767), accused of having been structuring a "Christian republic" to be given independence later, the missions would disappear in a very few years, victims of assaults by the colonial bureaucracy, by men from Asunción, and by the Paulist mamelucos and purposely broken up in order to abolish characteristics regarded as "communizing." By the end of the eighteenth century the mission Indians had been dispersed, enslaved, and carried off to distant regions, or dissolved into the world of the gauchos, or else had become refugees in the wilderness, where they struggled to reconstitute their tribal life, while their lands and their cattle passed into the hands of new owners.

The third group would be constituted of the few Spaniards and their many mestizos moved from Asunción to found Buenos Aires as a new settlement and a port of communication with Spain.

The River Plate region and all its enormous hinterland, described by the discoverers as a "land of no profit," became civilized during the last half of the sixteenth century with the introduction of cattle. The first herd was brought from São Paulo, in Brazil, across hundreds of leagues of unexplored terrain and forest to Asunción, where it grew under the close vigilance of the settlers. From those Paulist cattle, raised in Paraguay, the first breeding herds went out in 1588 to the Argentine Mesopotamia [between the Uruguay and Paraná Rivers], and a half-century later to the Jesuit missions of the upper Uruguay, spreading over the whole region and multiplying astronomically in the vastness of the natural pastures and watering places open to them.[4]

The Asunción and Buenos Aires cattle was public property of the highest value in the early decades, with the greatest disputes over ownership and usufruct of it. Only the old cows and oxen were butchered. The hide was material of a thousand uses. Tallow candles were the best lights. The work ox was used in farming and for all overland hauling and was the most valuable item. Milk yielded cheese and formed the basis of the most prized foods.

The first breeding herds grew large enough to be divided among various estancias of one-half by one and a half leagues in size, which were being granted in the country near Buenos Aires. From there and from the mission breeding grounds the herds kept on multiplying, taking to the open country where they increased and grew as *cimarrones,* wild cattle, along with horses and dogs, likewise wild. By the middle of the seventeenth cen-

---

[4] Another breeding herd, coming from Bolivia down the right bank of the Paraguay River, invaded the Chaco, where it also multiplied prodigiously.

tury they must have numbered in the millions, the greater part wild and ownerless, free to anyone for the taking: first, by roundups in order to gather and lead herds to the ranches, to *querenciarlos* (that is, domesticate them to make them feel at home there); then in great hunts solely for the hides, tallow, and grease, such was the abundance of no-man's cattle. Immense herds filled the plains in all districts from the Paraguayan Chaco and the Argentine pampa to the Uruguayan countryside, at that time known as the Vaquerías del Mar, the cattlelands of the sea.

For the Chaco Indians as for those of the undulant plains of Uruguay and the Argentine pampa, the wild cattle was new game to be hunted, prodigiously abundant, greater and better than any native game, which invaded the region like a promise of inexhaustible plenty. Some tribes saw in the new species only a richer reward in the hunt. Others, imitating the Spaniard, tamed horse and cattle after their fashion, leaping from a hunting-and-gathering economy to cattle-raising, thus surpassing all the other tribes, especially the horticultural, and dominating them. This was particularly the case with the Guaikurú groups.

With the cattle a new man would come into prominence, the gaucho, from the Asunción and Buenos Aires neo-American strata, from former nuclei and from Guaraní and Guaranized Indians. In the multiplication of the wild herds he had his status of ecological specialization and of expression as an ethnic type. Gradually he became differentiated from the pynambí of Asunción and from the Platine Ladino to constitute a new sociocultural form. He retained the Guaraní as his mother tongue, just as had occurred with the Paulista mameluco, and diffused it, giving names in that language to nearly all the rivers and mountains of the regions wherever the cattle spread, and Guaranizing the indigenous groups of other stocks with which he came into contact.

The competition and open fighting between the gauchos and the Ladinos, and between both and the mission and tribal Indians, broke out and lasted until the liquidation of the missions and the decimation of the tribes. But for a long time the three neo-American contingents grew as they fought, constituting Ladino or gaucho nuclei that originally spoke Guaraní in Buenos Aires, Entre Ríos, Corrientes, and other provinces. They were essentially indigenous communities by the language they spoke, the plants they cultivated and ate, and the craftsmanship of the cloths they wove. With time they would be increasingly Westernized by miscegenation, their historical destiny as a dissociative force of independent tribal units, speaking Spanish, Christianization, and the adoption of a whole mass of Iberian cultural elements.

Practically, these neo-Guaraní had to recoil before only two groups: (1) the Guaikurú-speaking Chaco Indians—Mbayá, Abipón, and Mocoví—

and Payaguá canoemen, who, by making themselves horsemen and exploiters of the wild herds, were able to contain the expansion of the neo-Guaraní and even defeat them, and (2) the mission Indians, as long as these were led by the Jesuits and autarchically organized in distant regions.

The liquidation of both would be accomplished only with the unsought but convenient collaboration of their Brazilian rivals, the Paulist mamelucos. As soon as the first Jesuit missions grew and became rich in the seventeenth century, the Paulists started besieging them to capture and enslave the detribalized Indians, to steal the Church jewels and the cattle. These sackings and slave captures forced the missions to move several times, at the cost of enormous sacrifices. Coming to Mato Grosso in the eighteenth century to develop the gold mines discovered in the region of Cuiabá, the same Paulists made alliances with the Guaikurú Indians, trading trinkets and alcohol for cattle and inciting them to attack Asunción, finally dominating them as they had others.

The Jesuits amassed thirty missions in Paraguay. Only a few of them, however, reached a high organizational standard, sheltering thousands of indigenes. Not only did these constitute the first economically powerful nuclei in the region, but they were the beginnings of a new sociocultural formation, the mission, which would have added another feature to the River Plate peoples if it had not been decimated and dispersed when it was in full flower.

The Indians pacified and attracted by the priests were installed in hamlets that, thanks to their labor under the Jesuits' guidance, gradually were structured as towns. Around a central open square the church and the priests' home were built, sometimes magnificent edifices of richly carved stone, the school, the general storehouse, the guest house, and the young women's house in poorer buildings. Each indigenous family lived in lodgings arranged in long buildings of wattle and daub or adobe, opening on a covered veranda.

The land was divided into lots to be worked in alternate periods, assigned to the families who were to draw their support from the fields allotted, but the harvests were to be deposited, as a security measure, in the common storehouse. The best fields were reserved as tupambae, God's thing, and worked collectively. The produce from these supported the priests, the functionaries, the craftsmen, and the needy and still served to succor the community in case of hunger. Cattle-raising, yerba mate cultivation, and textile-making also pertained to the tupambae, providing the articles traded by the padres for whatever the mission needed to import, such as tools, salt, and religious ornaments.

Each mission maintained schools for boys and girls in which the most gifted learned to read and the most skillful were trained for a trade: carpentry, pottery, ceramics, weaving, painting, sculpting, and even goldsmithery. Some indigenous children learned Spanish and a few, destined for the priesthood, also studied Latin. The whole mission economic structure—based on the collective organization of the work force and on a distributive system that rewarded or penalized devotion and productivity as merited, but with no private ownership of land or personal enslavement of the worker—approximates much more the theocratic irrigation formation of the Incas, like so many other civilizations based on irrigation agriculture, than it does the colonialist-capitalistic formations founded on private enterprise, monopoly of land, and enslavement of the labor force. The coexistence of the two formations in the same area was impracticable, motivating greed and engendering conflicts, after which the historically more advanced, though more inhuman, was to prevail.

Centrally controlling the economy of all the missions, with hundreds of thousands of Indians, the Jesuits ended by becoming great traders, holders of hundreds of thousands of head of cattle, enormous crops of mate and foodstuffs, and a great crafts production of cloth. To carry on trade, they even came to have their own seagoing vessels. Such prosperity in the ocean of Paraguayan and Platine poverty was bound to arouse powerful greed, which contributed decisively to the quicker liquidation of the Jesuit system. Besides, this system, though not motivated by irredentism or by the communizing factor of which the Jesuits were accused, was as we have seen in opposition to the character of the colonization and its dominant social order—mission Indians and Ladinos simply could not coexist.

Rather than an accumulation of riches, the missions were a productive system. Once overthrown, the mission Indians were reduced to the wretched status of those who had not been taken into the Jesuit refuges, or perhaps to even worse conditions, because as products of an artificially conducted deculturation, the mission Indians had only become Guaranized and could scarcely compete with the Ladinos even for the lowest jobs in the poor but free strata. Thus they passed from *comuneros* to slaves on the sugar cane fazendas of the Brazilian northeast, when captured and sold by the mamelucos, or to serfs under the yoke of those who took possession of the lands and cattle of the missions, or, at best, they swelled the ranks of the poorest gauchos.

The Asunción group of pynambís and the Jesuit mission Indians finally merged, constituting the modern neo-Guaraní, which has all the characteristics of a New People formed by deculturation of the original populations and by its collective involvement as an area of European mercantile domination. The survival of Guaraní as the maternal tongue, and of the indigenous slash-and-burn agriculture, in cultivation of corn, manioc, and other plants, the use of unsweetened mate, the hammock, and the preservation of a body of tribal habits and beliefs, lends the neo-Guaraní a peculiar, archaic physiognomy. To this indigenous stock should be added the European contributions, especially the breeding of cattle, several crops and new techniques, and the social reordering as a part of world economy, supplying many of its needs and demanding in exchange a mercantile production that employed a large part of its labor force.

The Paraguayan neo-Guaraní forms, with the Platine Ladino and gaucho, three variants of a single protoethnos. They are distinguished by the orientation of the neo-Guaraní principally to farming and craftsmanship, by the Ladino orientation for city life and trade, and by the gaucho inclination for specialized cattle-raising. Nevertheless, they are all connected to a common formative trunk as results of a single process of occupation and colonization of the area, involving, principally, Spaniards and deculturated Guaraní Indians, and as mutually complementary parts of one and the same society in formation. Thus they would have been a protoethnos capable of maturing as the national ethnos dominating the whole region, if later historical events had not disfigured it and submerged it under the tide of other formations.

The fighting that for decades followed independence, cutting up the viceroyalty into several autonomous provinces in permanent conflict, aggravated the isolation of the Paraguayan neo-Guaranís, already segregated naturally by their interior location. Thirty years after Argentine independence the position of Paraguay had not been defined, whether as survival of a nonexistent viceroyalty, or rebelling province, or independent nation. Finally it was affirmed as a nationality after long opposition by Rosas, who, attempting to force the Paraguayans to accept Argentine jurisdiction, created more difficulties for their access to the outside world through the River Plate.

This long isolation and a succession of patriarchalist, autarchist governments such as Francia's, followed by the equally autonomist orientation of the two Lópezes, father and son, made Paraguay a self-sufficient nation founded on small farm property and an active, incipiently mercantile craftsman class. On this natural economy, premonetary in its major productive branches, by means of official control of exports of mate, hides, and hardwoods, and by closing the country to international commerce and finance, the Francia and two López dictatorships established an autarchic state policy that converted it into an island of economic autonomism and political self-affirmation.

Taking advantage of its withdrawal, Paraguay built the first railroad and the first telegraph line in Latin America controlled by the state, contrary to similar efforts that multiplied elsewhere on the continent, organized by British concessions. On the same basis foundries, shipyards, and factories for agricultural implements, arms and munitions, textiles, and even paper were constructed. With this infrastructure the nation organized an army that was probably the largest and best equipped in South America in 1865. In peacetime the soldiers were occupied in such civil works as construction of the railroad, irrigation canals, roads and bridges, and the telegraph line, besides state industries and public works.

It is said of Francisco Solano López that he nearly eliminated illiteracy in the country, sent hundreds of young men to study or serve their internships in Europe, and hired European and American specialists, all in an extraordinary effort to create a corps of technical experts and a military command for the nation. Simultaneously he fanned the flames of the Guaraní national spirit, transforming his people into *Herrenvölkers* ready to expand across the Brazilian and Argentine borders in order to break out of their isolation and win new territory.

Paraguay launched herself into war by invading territories on the Mato Grosso border, in the hope of representing the cause of the peoples of the interior and in the expectation that they would rise up with her against Buenos Aires and Montevideo, their traditional adversaries, and against the Brazilian empire, which was also disputing control of the River Plate. But the Paraguayans fought alone, because both Argentina and Uruguay ranged themselves with Brazil. All the caudillos who for decades had fought Buenos Aires and who could stir up gaucho support of the neo-Guaraní had already disappeared as an active force capable of military reaction.

The Paraguayan people was crushed after several years of fighting. Its combativeness, spurred on by the fanatic determination of López, can be appreciated by comparison of the data from the national censuses of 1853 and 1871. In the former year, prior to the war, there were 1,337,489 Paraguayans. In 1871 there were 222,079 left, including 28,746 men—all old or disabled—106,254 women, and 86,079 infants. In addition to so many lives, Paraguay had lost half her original territory. Only in 1950, nearly a century afterwards, did she succeed in reconstituting her population. In that period the populations of Latin America had enormously increased, leaving Paraguay, which had once held a vanguard position, in unfathomed backwardness.

Nevertheless, on the social and economic plane Paraguay had been an experiment demonstrative of the potentials of the neo-American protoethnos and of what the New Peoples of Latin America could do when led by an autonomism. The isolation—as regards European imperialistic expansion—that followed Spanish colonialism did not result in poverty and backwardness but, on the contrary, in technical and economic progress and in cultural development. The civilizational capacity of the neo-Guaraní, the Ladino, the gaucho, the Venezuelan llanero, the Chilean huaso, the Andean altiplano cholo, the Mexican *cepero,* the Ecuadoran *montuvio,* and the neo-Brazilian would be demonstrated with an eloquence not to be repeated until our day. A long time afterwards, in better conditions, Japan revived the Paraguayan type of despotic, autonomist state orientation, demonstrating its viability as one of the few roads to autonomous industrialization and national emancipation within the industrial-imperialistic system of domination.

Gauchos and Ladinos

The gaucho parcel of the Platine and Paraguayan original protoethnos would have a less spectacular fate, but it, too, was to be exterminated.

The first River Plate gaucho nuclei had the same origin as the neo-Guaraní, as descendants of colonizers coming from Asunción. They grew, along with the cattle, in those first starving towns of the Buenos Aires area, serving the few Spaniards and rich Creoles, these so proud of their noble lineage or whiteness, yet not so much to deter their males from mating with all the Indian and mestizo women they could. After all, these Iberian folk could hardly be fanatically white and opposed to crossbreeding after centuries of mixture with Moors and Africans on that advance frontier of Africa in Europe, the Iberian Peninsula.

The very zeal, expressed in many sixteenth-century documents, to obtain from Spain the "remedy" of marriage with some Spaniard for the girls of the family who were becoming spinsters for lack of "good men," indicates that their brothers were finding remedies in the land, preferably with the Indian women of the Guaraní stock found by the first colonizers in the islands and ravines of the Paraguay, the Uruguay, and the Plate Rivers. To these original contingents were added the mission Indians, addicted to pastoral life even before the dispersion caused by the destruction of their Jesuit refuges. And later the peoples formed by crossbreeding with the Indians of the east bank—the Charrúa, the Minuanos, and others—who, seminomadic hunters and gatherers, made themselves horsemen and masters of the fields and cattle at the same time that they became Guaranized. Their domination in certain areas was so uncontested that at the close of the seventeenth century these Indians of the Vaquerías del Mar reached a *modus vivendi* with the neo-American exploiters of the herds, collecting skinning fees and admitting to their tents some fugitives who intermarried with them and begot new gauchos.

Tribal Indians and mission Indians, all Guaranized and their mestizos gauchized by dint of living together in the midst of wars, deeply influenced each other. Thus the gaucho must have learned the use of the bolas or *boleadora* (a leather thong with two or three round stones, wrapped in leather, attached to the ends), with which the Indian lassoed the *ñandú,* the American rhea, and which came to be one of the principal implements for hunting stray cattle.

Originating from all these stocks, the gaucho was the human counterpart of the wild cattle of the pampas and Platine countryside. He constantly roamed the pampas in cavalcades, hunting down the no-man's cattle where he pleased; butchering in order to roast what he wanted and skinning the animal to sell the hide to the *pulpero,* the country storekeeper, or to the smuggler. Sometimes he took a job as temporary peon in the free cattle roundups for collecting quantities of hides, or he would camp in the rich latifundian proprietor's ranch, for the sheer joy of the rodeo trade or sport. He could always sally out into the open country when he pleased, keeping free or else attached only as a soldier through some personal bond of loyalty, more as an acolyte than as servitor. He offered a contrast, with this independence, to the Ladino peasant who let himself be tied to the country town or the farm, or became a peon for subaltern services on the ranches.

Open fighting with the mounted Indian would become imperative only with the thinning of the herds, with the entrance of the Brazilians into the cattle and hides dispute, with the fixing of a frontier and efforts to limit the benefits according to the interests of the rural oligarchy and the patriciate.

In the first stage of the conflict all of them, Ladinos and gauchos, would attack the Indians. Then followed the bands that, in both Argentina and Uruguay, scoured the plains to assault the indigenous settlements and decimate entire groups. It was necessary to clear the countryside of the former human occupant so that the cattle could increase there more rapidly and under more control. The Indian reacted and directed his attacks on all the nuclei he could, making access to the more desolate territories and vigilance over the frontiers difficult. Some joined the Brazilians who came down from Rio Grande do Sul to the Colônia do Sacramento—used by Portugal in disputing with Spain over the domination of the area—or who crossed the border to trade hides and cattle for tools and arms.

As the fighting grew more intense, both sides specialized. The Ladinos organized regular troops and installed blockhouses as small forts at the most advanced points in order to guarantee occupation of the countryside and the pampas. The Indians, transformed by dint of systematic persecution into wandering bands, driven far beyond the pastoral frontier, sallied out in *malones,* surprise raids on border ranches, on hamlets or wagon trains crossing the plains. It was a fight to the death, without truce, in which all the Indian settlements, one by one, were decimated with no effort at pacification.

The legal regulation of human occupation, directed by Buenos Aires and Montevideo, was executed by concessions of plots of 100, 200, 300, even 500 square leagues to reputable patricians who proposed to occupy them. In point of fact, only many decades later would the actual occupation and economic stimulus of these generous donations be accomplished, partially and even socially. They operated rather as a land monopoly that would inevitably appropriate the cattle and conscript the men, placing everything at the service of those who controlled the official sources of power and the commerce of the colony. The counterpart of this latifundian appropriation was the land hunger of a population that was multiplying in the country and was forced to concentrate in nuclei confined within the unused lands, human islands in the sea of the latifundium.

The oligarchic order, however, would be carried out only on a long-term basis. For a long time the only wealth would be the wild, stray cattle growing freely in the plains, where it must be hunted down. The enjoyment of profits from it was free to him who went to take it in the wild regions where it was found, and that man was the gaucho.

The hides were traded in the country stores for the few mercantile articles that interested the gaucho—mate, salt, matches, rum, tobacco, knives, harness metals, and little else—or at the ranches of the merchant-ranchers, and finally was exported, a small part through the customs machinery of the colonial monopoly, the major portion through contraband in the posts established by the dozens along the roads that skirted the river shore and the Atlantic coast.

With the appropriation of the lands, the country population gradually accumulated in the vicinity of the *pulperías,* the country stores [usually at crossroads on the pampas]. Some grew and gained fame for their illicit trading and for the attractions offered, such as music and dancing, horse racing, card games, and the presence of *chinas* [half-breed maidservants]. Besides the commerce and the huts there was the chapel. And so, slowly, urban micronuclei emerged in competition with the latifundium, the latter always complaining that the former frightened off the cattle and deprived them of the water holes.

The Spanish colonial regulations that strictly disciplined the establishment of towns and cities—fixing the location and arrangement of the buildings around the plaza, and the zoning of the farming for subsistence provision—had almost no effect on these spontaneous nuclei encysted on private lands belonging to the latifundium, which engulfed everything in its domains. Later on, nuclei emerged founded by express order of the crown, with purposes more military than economic, to protect the colonists sent from Spain and, especially, to add to the people dispersed on the plains, restricting the gaucho in his raids and imposing the authority of the ranchers.

The mine of hides, tallow, and meat that seemed inexhaustible, unrestrainedly exploited by man and decimated by the wild dogs that multiplied also in the country, feeding on calves, finally dwindled. In the mid-eighteenth century the diminishing of the wild cattle of the old Vaquerías del Mar was already seriously worrying the authorities. They began taking steps to lead the remainder to the ranches and to exterminate the wild, ravenous dogs that were attacking the full-grown animals of the ranches and hindering the raising of sheep.

In these last roundups and in the eradication of the wild dogs the gaucho had his final economic chore that still linked him to the productive system and integrated him into the over-all society by assuring him a role and a place in it. Rounding up the wild cattle that had become the property of those who had appropriated the former government unoccupied lands, separating the cows that were good for breeding, he could butcher the rest—for a short while.

During the eighteenth century, besides the hide, tallow, and grease, the exploitation of meat began, for the production of *tassajo,* jerked beef, which was exported to feed the Antillean slaves. Then (1820) came the *saladeros,* the salting houses where jerked beef was dried and prepared, to dispute the herds and to discipline on the gaucho, who could no longer butcher an animal wherever he liked, stripping the hide, eating a roast tongue or the like, and abandoning the rest. Meat had become the most prized part of the cattle.

It would be impossible to persuade the gaucho peaceably, addicted as he was to a diet of meat and mate, to abstain from his major food item. The self-defensive reaction of continuing to butcher for food—now throwing away the hide that would betray him—turned the gaucho into a "thief and gambler, drunken and barbarous," for doing what he had always done. To put an end to this "plague of the pampas," the city authorities, hand in glove with the proprietors of the lands, decreed a regime of vigilance that obliged every rural individual not a landowner to place himself at the service of a patron. Thenceforth, anyone found on the plains without the proper pass was subject to the rigors of the law. Thus all gauchos were declared vagrants, subject to jail for traveling without documents or express order from a judge. In the implementation of the new regime a full police force was set up in the rural areas to hunt down gaucho tramps, to condemn them to years of military service on the frontier, or to place them compulsorily at the service of the ranchers.

Thus, in consequence of the dwindling of the stray cattle, the appropriation of the whole land by the *hacendados,* and the new forms of coercion, the gaucho became marginalized. From that time on he had only one of his social functions left to him, that of combatant, which he would continue to perform in the last *montoneras* (gaucho troops under arms and commanded by a caudillo) that were to convulse the countryside for decades, expressing the opposition of the interior populations to domination and exploitation by Buenos Aires and Montevideo.

These struggles followed independence, fragmentating the former viceroyalty of La Plata into several provinces, separated as a result of the opposition of interests between the patriciate of merchants and functionaries of the port cities and the people of the interior. They aimed essentially at breaking Buenos Aires' monopoly on importing; assurance of free navigation of the Paraná, Uruguay, and Paraguay Rivers; nationalization of customs houses, the income from which benefited only the people of the port; protection of the craftsmen of the interior, ruined by the free trade imposed by the merchants; and, finally, protective measures in behalf of the Ladinos and gauchos of the interior, brought to extremes of want.

The best expression of the patriciate's project would be given by the political currents that won power with Mitre, Sarmiento, and Avellaneda, planners of a new economic policy. These would become effective after 1880 through three mutually complementary procedures: (1) the utilization of the immense available fiscal lands for sale or massive grant, in the form of large properties that permitted enormous enlargement of the bases of the hacienda system; (2) the reflexive modernization, through free trade and the injection of foreign capital, principally English, that made possible the construction of railroads, systems of telegraphic communication, and port installations, which led to the implantation of an economy specializing in the export of meat and cereals; and (3) the wholesale importing of foreign labor. This economic policy, rationally and steadily conducted, would in a few decades transmute the River Plate society and assure it an intense development, but because of its dependence on European capital and markets it would also establish abroad control of the national destiny.

This project, in spite of being antinational and antipopular through its nature as a foreign undertaking on American soil, opposed to the interests of the ethnos that had formed over the centuries, had a grandeur only comparable to the feat of the conquest. Its proponents undertook the gigantic task of remaking the face and body of the nation, inspired by European ideals and the greatest antigaucho animosity, under the fist of English imperialism and based on a pact of the urban patriciate with the land oligarchy. Through free trade and concession of privileges they replaced Spanish colonial domination and exploitation with new forms, more subtle and efficacious, that transformed the River Plate nations into appendixes of the European economy.

Even today, in the divisions and differences between Federalist and Unionist parties and in many ideological expressions, visible effects survive of this polarization between urban politicians and caudillos, between gauchos and Ladinos, between rich and poor. In recent decades, however, the Buenos Aires and Montevideo patriciate, now composed more of gringos than of Creoles, experiencing the other opposition that contraposes the old native stocks to the masses of immigrants, seeks to express its nationalism in the name of an identification with the gaucho, or, in other words, with precisely the principal victim of its expansion and domination.

The truth is that the descendants of immigrants now making up nearly the whole of the population—the gaucho only survives in the most remote zones or in the poorest social strata—have not succeeded yet in leaving their mark on the national ideology. Those who rise in the social scale seek to merge into the patrician oligarchy, steeping themselves in its view of the world and its ideology. Their intellectual segment has not yet molded the nation's image as the fruit of gringo ancestors, losing only with great difficulty their feeling of inferiority before the patriciate of old extraction.

The picture is infinitely rich in nuances revealing several contradictory tendencies. Thus, for example, Sarmiento, who makes his *Recuerdos de Provincia* [*Provincial Memories*] a chant of nostalgia for the old gaucho world, in his political work was the most exogenous of Argentine statesmen. In a letter to Mitre he confessed: "I hate popular barbarism. The mob and the gaucho are hostile to us. As long as there is a *chiripá* [gaucho blanket wrapped around hips and thighs], there will be no citizens." And then he meditated: "Are the masses, perchance, the only sources of power and legitimacy?" And he responds in concern before his political chief: "You will have the glory of reestablishing throughout the republic the predominance of the cultured class, annulling the uprising of the masses." This task he would propose for himself, on personally assuming the presidency.

Even so, even under the impact of this antipopular emotional burden, Sarmiento could not fail to see the effects of the ideology he was advocating: "Let us be frank, in spite of this universal invasion from Europe being prejudicial and ruinous to our country, it is useful for civilization and commerce." Sarmiento's alienation through his intoxication with the racist literature of his time is even more clearly manifest in a letter in which he writes, commenting on a colony of emigrants from California that was being created in the Chaco: "It can be the origin of a territory, and some day of a Yankee state (language and all). With this genetic cooperation our decayed race will improve." [5]

Juan Bautista Alberdi, who had been one of the ideologues of liberalism and Europeanization, subsequently became the principal spokesman of the gaucho ethnos when he perceived that it was being condemned to extermination in the name of progress. The war against Paraguay, which alerted him to the ethnic succession that was being carried out, would, however, combine all forces in a compulsory mobilization that would make it impracticable thenceforth to turn back in its policy of disfiguring the proto-nationality.

The national self-image that was being defined in these areas, in its Argentine and Uruguayan variant, will surely continue to value the integrative content of the gaucho, though less as a common ancestor than as the former master of the land, nostalgically recalled and lamented as the victim of civilization. As the patrician and oligarchic dominance diminishes, a new ideology will bud forth, one that values the immigrants' achievement and the gringo contribution, which after all is what gave the two nations the form and figure they have today and which will refuse to be ignored or disguised much longer.

The best example of the caudillo cause was Artigas, the great leader of the men of the interior. An English traveler through the Uruguayan country in the early nineteenth century describes him thus:

What do you think I saw? The Most Excellent Protector of half of the New World, sitting on a bullock's skull by a fire burning on the floor of the hut, eating meat from a spit and drinking gin from a horn. . . .
He had nearly 1,500 ragged followers in his camp who were acting in the dual function of infantry and horsemen (J. P. and G. P. Robertson, quoted by A. J. Abelardo Ramos, 1965, p. 39).

Thus all the patricians must have seen him, too, imbued as they were with liberal ideology, dazzled by everything European, especially English, and saddled with a national ethnic inferiority complex. And yet Artigas was not only the most intrepid of the military leaders defending the cause of the provinces, but the ideologue who saw most clearly the possibilities of a River Plate nation as he proposed to institute the Patria Grande and solve the problems facing the humble folk of the plains by means of agrarian reform.

[5] All quotations from Sarmiento are taken from J. J. Hernández Arregui (1963, pp. 89–91).

His armies of chiripá and lance faced the official troops clad in Europe-an-style uniforms, as the real people contraposed the revised, European-ized people dreamed of by Mitre and Sarmiento. Over these ragged armies, less through battle than by summit agreements between Brazilians, Uruguayans, and Argentines, directed by the English, mercantile civiliza-tion would become sovereign on the River Plate. English domination was thus substituted for Spanish hegemony, with slight alterations in the inter-mediary power teams in Buenos Aires and Montevideo.

The process was completed in 1880 with the full institutionalization of the constitutional regime in both countries, the subjugation of all the prov-inces of the interior, and the installation of land monopoly. Artigas' prop-ositions had fallen, and with them the last possibilities of full capitalistic development and of industrialization of the area that only the creation of a broad rural middle class, through his reform project, would have made possible.

The Immigrations

The second cycle of Platine history, called "alluvial" (J. L. Romero, 1956), began with a spontaneous movement of European immigration in-tensified by native leaderships bent on transfiguring the nation ethnically and economically through the infusion of European blood and technologi-cal modernization. They hoped thus to conform the nation to the standards of liberal democracy and economic progress that, in the view of the La-dino leaders, would never adjust to the natural subsistence and craftsman production economy, combined with the raising of cattle and the "inferior nature" of the national mestizo populations. The solution therefore was to repopulate with Europeans, educating and vitalizing the economy by bind-ing it to the European as the producer of food in exchange for manufac-tures.

To attain the first objective, legislation was enacted that gave obvious advantages to the immigrant over the national, and the government's effort was concentrated on guiding to the River Plate a part of the migratory waves and capital funds leaving Europe, the former, expelled by the effects of industrialization and the technological renovation of agriculture; the lat-ter, in search of higher yields through concessions and loans. These hands and these funds would in a few years permit crossing the deserts with rail-roads, outfitting the ports, installing meat packing plants, electric plants, and factories, fencing the ranches, and encouraging wheat-growing by gradually mechanizing the farms.

At the end of the century Argentina and Uruguay were swarming with 1.5 million immigrants, most of them Italians and Spaniards, but also Germans, Poles, and others, and they made their presence felt in the world market as great exporters of meat and wheat. Immigrants continued to land in great numbers. This wave of immigration broke on the original demographic strata burying them and stamping its own characteristics on the nation's physiognomy.

Argentina gained her independence in 1810 with nearly 350,000 inhabitants, gauchos, and Ladinos, having incorporated by that time among the latter a parcel of Europeans who contributed further to their Europeanization. These 350,000 neo-Americans, produced in a long process of ethnic formation, would grow to nearly a million in 1850, both through natural fecundity and, principally, through the incorporation of European immigrants. Thenceforth, the process of ecological succession and ethnic transfiguration would be more and more intensified. On that original million would be poured, between 1857 and 1950, 1.8 million Italians, 1.3 million Spaniards, and nearly .5 million people from other sources. It was with this massive incorporation of immigrants that Argentina's population could leap to 4.8 million in 1900 and to 17 million in 1950.

In Uruguay the process of ecological succession is also overwhelming. Starting with 74,000 inhabitants on the eve of independence (1830), she swelled to 221,000 in 1860, 35 per cent of these being foreigners, or, to put it differently, a figure higher than the original population thirty years before. The Uruguayan population jumped thereafter to 420,000 in 1872 and to nearly 1 million in 1908. In this last year, the foreign contingent numbered 181,000 in the country's total (or 17.4 per cent) and included half of the population of Montevideo, which was 309,000. The urbanization was quite premature, caused by the land monopoly, which, in Uruguay as in Argentina, would represent the second dynamic factor—after the immigratory tide—for the conformation of the respective national societies.

So it is that, at the close of the past century, both countries had been transmuted from New Peoples to Transplanted Peoples as the result of acts of will, of deliberate policies of their Ladino elites, coincident with a chapter of European history in which its principal exports were the European himself and the funds for colonizing. The project was at first a great economic success through the addition to the system of all the immensity of new lands put into production by the immigrant, and through the modernizing effects of the complementary investments that implemented the economic infrastructure for export: railroads, packing plants, ports, banks, and so on.

With the Latin people—it was not possible to import large Anglo-German contingents—came capital from the English, true entrepreneurs of the mercantile enterprise of food exports established in the River Plate region. As World War I began, England had almost as much capital invested in Argentina (320 million pounds sterling) as in India and Ceylon (379 million), with 36 million more in Uruguay. And to these heavy investments were added the applications of American, French, and German capital.

It is this enormous investment of European capital that best enables us to measure the importance of the meat- and wheat-exporting business installed on the River Plate. Its viability depended on the availability of labor and European capital for producing foods that could be exchanged for industrial manufactured goods. This same viability, however, would render possible competitive businesses set up in Canada, Australia, and New Zealand, whose increasing production would end by establishing new price bases for such articles, making their exchange for manufactures more and more onerous and finally submerging Argentina's and Uruguay's dependent economies in successive crises in the face of their competitors, who were integrated in privileged commercial systems and better prepared for the production of the same articles, thanks to the nonoligarchic nature of their agrarian structure. Settling later in virgin lands, as societies structured principally on the basis of rural farmer nuclei, the colonizers of the southern region as well as the Canadians were better able to absorb and generalize modern agricultural technology, and thus to compete with the food prices in the importing European countries and later on with the River Plate competitors.

Argentina and Uruguay, who had greatly excelled in other export areas, knowing a long period of prosperity that permitted the establishment of the productive infrastructure and subsidization of the precocious urbanization of their rural populations, would thus begin to lose pace and finally fall increasingly behind in relation to those competitors.

The impact of the two world wars, especially the second, on English imperialism created an economic vacuum that the United States came to fill in the Río de la Plata republics by virtue of their connections with the European market and the competitive nature of their exportation with respect to that of the United States. Eventually, as the British international hegemony declined and the American grew, the United States became the new center of expansion and domination of the world capitalistic system.

Isolated during the wars and the world economic crisis, both Argentina and Uruguay had their first opportunities to resort to their own forces in initiating industrialization. This reinforced the tendencies to urbanization, since the rural populations, dominated by the latifundium, began moving to the cities, a move intensified after 1914. In this way a growing factory proletariat arose, and a larger and larger middle class of merchants, small businessmen, members of the liberal professions, technicians, bureaucrats, soldiers, professors, and employees of services. Both the working class and the middle class were recruited almost exclusively from among the immigrants, who thus absorbed all the opportunities of social ascent.

The U.S. Americans became the bankers for this renovation, as suppliers of industrial equipment, as investors, and through construction of factories by the big corporations, whose interests on the River Plate region rapidly exceeded all others. World War II over, industrialization proceeded at a less intense rate, now conducted by the American corporations, which, taking advantage of the freedom to move their capital investments, leapt the customs barriers, establishing companies of their own or associated with national capital funds to exploit the expanding domestic market. This reflexive industrialization, conducted from abroad, dominated by stockholder control, through contracts of technical aid and patent royalties came to absorb a growing part of the national income in the form of profits and royalties.

The oligarchy survived the avalanche, anchored in its real estate, especially the monopolistic ownership of land, and in the privileges it had arrogated to itself, first against the Ladinos and gauchos, later against the gringos, in assuring itself the mastery of the state machine. Armed with these complementary powers, it made the land inaccessible to the immigrants also, blocking the formation of a rural middle class that could have supported an ample subsequent development as an internal market for industry.[6]

This oligarchic order compelled the two River Plate nations to precocious, reflexive metropolitanization, with all the attendant distortions, especially the creation of vast parasitic strata whose consumer demands caused the creation of mechanisms for the redistribution of the national income, always unfavorable to expenditures in investment.

In this process the urban patriciate and patronate acquired a new aspect through mixture with the economically successful gringos, which led to the loss of the aristocratic standards least compatible with the new ways of life and the obligations of bankers, populist politicians, and industrialists. A large part of the patronal group assumed the function of mere managers of foreign interests, which contributed to maintaining and deepening their exogenous, alienated posture and to incapacitate it for the role of nationalistic and industrialized bourgeoisie that it performed in other contexts. Contrariwise, by associating itself with foreign interests, installed to absorb the

[6] Exceptional conditions permitted setting aside farm areas for immigrants in some Argentine provinces and in the neighborhood of Montevideo, as had occurred in the south of Brazil. These islands of small proprietors, however, do not alter the agrarian structure, latifundian in nature, of the three countries.

income that they helped to create, the River Plate patronate tended to become cosmopolitan and an antipopular, extranational component of the system.

The rural Ladino and the remaining gauchos, an almost insignificant minority incapable of influencing national destinies, were all marginalized. They can be identified by their more indigenous phenotype in the poorest strata of the population in the most backward zones. They are the cowhands of the new, wire-enclosed ranches, the woodcutters, the mate laborers, the miners of northwest Argentina. In the cities they are the *cabecitas negras,* the "little black heads," who are commencing ascent to the status of skilled workmen in industry; they are the beggars and the domestic servants.

As the immigrant settled in the cities, inserting himself into the new urban social structure integrated by a middle class and a proletariat, he began to struggle en masse for political representation and, on the part of those grown rich, for participation in the closed circles of the patriciate and the oligarchy. The history of these new contrapositions followed different courses in Argentina and in Uruguay. In both cases, however, it was the dynamic historical factor that, confronted by the irreducible opposition between the interests of the wage-earners and those of the oligarchy and urban patriciate, placed the whole socioeconomic system in check. The history of both nations from this time on was guided by the struggles to nullify or to win over these urban contingents, which became the common people of both countries, amid the crises of the economic system.

Argentina under Guardianship

The Argentine patriciate, wrapping itself in its privileges, opposed the gringos' aspirations to citizenship rights by regulating the electoral system so that the masses were mere followers of essentially identical partisan groups. This situation was maintained until the pressure of successive generations of descendants of immigrants broke down the barrier by winning, in 1916, the compulsory free and secret ballot, with which they placed the "radical" candidate in the presidency. His administration, however, did not satisfy the expectations of the popular electorate, newly integrated in the political system. It was characterized by maintenance of demagogic language in the campaign, to cover up a policy of privileges. However, it replaced the intermediary political staffs and the upper bureaucracy, calling up new teams from the professional middle classes to government posts. This new dominant elite, once in power, practiced the old policy of the patriciate and the oligarchy. For this purpose it repressed expression of popular hopes for social reforms, using police methods and control of the press; it availed itself of the clergy and the military hierarchs, keeping them as bulwarks for the maintenance of the regime. From all this a profound opposition resulted between middle classes and the working class, which came to remember the "government of the doctors" * as a time of repression against the unions and the prohibition of strikes, a time of clericalism and police militarism.

In this situation the traditional conservative forces ended by regaining political power, exploiting the discontent of the people through a military-oligarchic alliance that imposed on the country a decade of tutelage by the army and reinstated the old systematic veto of popular participation in political power. There ensued a retrogression of the movement for political and social integration of the urban masses, formed predominantly by the descendants of immigrants incorporated into the nation as its major labor force.

Exhausted in the summit struggles within the iron circle defined for them by the oligarchy, the political organizations fell into discredit. The people entered on a period of terror and apathy from which it was to be stirred only by new forms of action not to be processed through party teams but between military factions. This was considerably furthered by the economic crisis that started in 1914, when the terms of foreign-trade exchange began to reveal themselves as ruinous, and was aggravated still more by the 1929 crisis.

Industrialization, which had become imperative because of the impossibility of continuing to defray the cost of imports of manufactured goods, had also become impracticable, given the insertion of the River Plate economies into the international market and the lack of resources of their own for investment in heavy industry installation. The disputes between the world powers before World War II and during it, however, gave a new impetus to industrialization and permitted saving foreign-exchange credits, restoring the balance of payments in nominal terms and creating a sense of prosperity.

An opportunity was thus opened to Argentina to resume former rates of progress and excel them. Above all, the opportunity existed to constitute a regime that reintegrated the people into the political process and gave the nation a chance to review, from the ground up, the old social order based on the precedence of the oligarchic interests and on external dependence.

At that time Peronism emerged as a nationalist movement that absorbed

---

* Most university-educated Latin Americans hold some kind of doctor's degree, usually law; hence the term means "government of the educated," with a slight derogative connotation in this case.

the attention of the urban masses, from the proletariat to some sectors of the less moneyed middle classes. In spite of the dictatorial propensity of the regime, with Perón the common masses joined for the second time in active political life, at first as participants in popular demonstrations, civic acts, and marches; then in elections also, and especially in a combative syndicate that, in addition to the army, came to constitute a new basic agency of the nation's political activity.

Exploiting the hostilities between the great world powers, as Vargas was doing in Brazil, Perón assured Argentina of a frankly nationalistic and industrializing orientation, an independent policy as regards the United States and England, whose interests he blocked and to whose plundering he put limits, and a domestic policy of strengthening state controls over the economy. He nationalized the railroads and various public utilities capitalized by Americans. He controlled the money market, commenced installations of iron and steel works and heavy industry, increased tenfold the output of electric power, stimulated industrialization with national capital, and substantially increased the sharing of national income with the wage-earner. His populist-worker policy, along the lines of Batlle in Uruguay and Vargas in Brazil, instituted a new type of relations between capital and labor. He organized social security and restructured the labor union system, enabling it to expand enormously.

As a result of that orientation Perón made enemies of the whole oligarchy and the patriciate, now fused together as the dominant social stratum, but at the same time he was strongly supported by the popular strata. Thus in the next elections he received two thirds of the votes and an even larger majority in the parliament, demonstrating the depth of the dissociation between the people and the dominant caste. Like Batlle and Vargas, Perón stopped short of the agrarian problem. In a nation of fundamentally agricultural economy this orientation resulted in leaving the basic sector untouched, the only one that, given fundamental reform, would permit defraying the costs of the new social welfare policy and support the industrial expansion program.

All this nationalistic, reforming thrust, which mobilized great masses and seriously considered the social questions and the autonomy of national development that had been stifled until then by the traditional parties, at a certain point came to be self-limited by the growing influence of the most retrograde sectors of the army, clergy, and bourgeoisie. These alliances imposed on Peronism an irremediable hostility to the leftist intellectuals, who could have given it an ideological content, and impregnated its action with an aura of paternalism that sought to stamp all popular and progressive measures of the government with the impression of a messianic leader's gracious bounty.

Smothered by these allies who gave little in comparison with what they received, Peronism ended by being dethroned, the reins of power being taken over by the old oligarchic-patrician class, now under liberal disguises and with antipopular guardianship exercised by the military, clerical, and imperialistic grouping. It was fervently supported by the intellectual class, the middle class, and the press, in contrast to the bitter silence of the working class. Even when, years later, the new administration was compelled to adopt certain democratic measures, it insisted on the continued exclusion of Peronists from all participation in the government. Such a decree of civic death to Peronism, which had galvanized the vast majority of Argentines, could be enforced only with a police-military machinery that has stifled the nation's political life for more than a decade.

The Argentine leftists have done little in that period, being systematically persecuted by a violent and repressive system, the fruit of the rightist orientation of Peronist Nasserism and of its effort to control the *descamisados* * masses and eradicate all socialist influence from the popular movements and from the unions. Much of the responsibility, however, falls on the leftists themselves. (1) They split into innumerable factions more hostile to each other than to the patriciate and the oligarchy. (2) The alienation of the communists, more mindful of the international situation than of local conditions, made them combatants in world conflicts rather than political militants for their own people and their own time. (3) They shared with the Peronist right the incapacity to formulate a national project capable of winning the masses to a social revolution that would reorder the economy and the institutions so as to place them at the service of the entire people and of the social, political, and cultural progress of the nation. (4) Socialist influence declined among middle-class intellectuals and university students, who in their opposition to the dictatorial nature of the Peronism, and in the name of democratic-liberal values, were led to join in the patronal, military, and clerical conspiracies, contributing to the reinstallation and maintenance of the former antipopular, antinational order.

Entangled in all these contradictions, the Argentine left seeks its own way, allying itself now with one, now with another, of the disputing groups, but nearly always exasperated with "the political backwardness of the mass," which "persists in its Peronist messianism."

Only the syndicate created by Perón exists as an agency of popular discord or political activity, depending on circumstances. For this very reason it has not become mere syndicalism, but neither has it been able to formu-

---

* The term, adopted by Perón's followers, means "shirtless," symbolic of have-nots.

late a project of social change for Argentine society. It wears itself out in conspiracies with all the military groups and in great demonstrations of strength, permitted because innocuous, never aspiring to taking over the government or to wiping out the antipopular protectorates. From exile Perón directs the advances and retreats, alliances and ruptures, himself cultivating simultaneous conspiracy with all possible groups. In that way he retains in his own hands the uncontested leadership of the Argentine popular masses, whose entrance into politics—thanks to the oligarchic and military guardianship in effect over the decades—has been simply the acceptance of Perón's ideology.

An irreducible political impasse has thus been created: free elections, for a decade, have meant Perón's return to power, and this, in the view of broad sectors of the dominant castes, of the armed forces, and of the clergy, would proscript the civic life of the country. The political leaderships that have tried to coexist with Perónism while conciliating his opponents have all stirred up military oppositions that destroyed them. Finally, in 1966, after a politicomilitary conspiracy involving all the groups, a new solution was arrived at—a boldly antirepublican, anticivilian, antidemocratic military coup, which assumed power in the name of national salvation from political chaos and disorder, in order to direct the nation on its course to "its destiny of greatness." It is a kind of inside-out Nasserism because it is not antioligarchic or antiimperialistic, but resorts to the guiding role of the armed forces as the only institution free of leftism and liberalism, and therefore capable of managing the nation, governing only by substituting military chieftainships for political, syndicalist, teaching, and technical leaderships. And all this only to maintain the status quo and to repeat old developmental and autonomist patterns with neither content nor viability, by virtue of the very submission of the military caudillos to the oligarchic interests and to the world economic system, within which Argentina finds no solution for her underdevelopment.

Uruguay: Schumpeterian Socialism

In Uruguay the immigrant's integration into political life, as a citizen vested with all rights, proceeded along democratic paths, and did so more rapidly and completely than anywhere else in Latin America. The leader of this popular mobilization was Batlle y Ordóñez, who, first at the head of the Colorado Party * and then as president of the republic [1903–1907,

* The two traditional political parties in Uruguay are the Colorado and the Blanco, but the colors red and white have no symbolism of left and right.

1911–1915], harnessed to his political bandwagon the mass of immigrants and their descendants, thus imposing himself on the national patriciate. His reforms, initiated in 1904 with the inspiration of a progressive, democratic philosophy, institutionalized in the Constitution of 1917, was a renovating impulse, unique in the continent, that laid the foundation of the first Latin American democracy.

Batlle gave the urban worker protective social legislation, regulation of the relations between employer and employee, and a system of social security, all of which are today probably the most advanced in the Americas. His educational system provided schooling for nearly every child and played a decisive role in assimilation of the immigrant mass and in national integration, as well as in the training of technicoprofessional staffs of average and superior levels for the tasks of development. He introduced a council form of government modeled on the Swiss, and reserved to the state the functions of coordination of the national economy, which permitted him to install the first oil refinery in Latin America and to nationalize, as autarchic entities, all public utilities and nearly all the productive sectors of great economic importance: oil, alchohol, cement, railways, insurance, mortgages, and gambling. The state became an entrepreneur also in the monopoly of health services, electric power, water, telegraph, and telephones. In competition with private enterprise it maintained packing plants, dairies (including manufacture of dairy products), fishing, urban transportation, and it offered incentives to the creation of cooperatives in other fields. The Batlle program nearly exhausted the possibilities of broadening state action and control in all the nonagrarian economic sectors, and he did this with the consent, explicit or not, of the latifundian oligarchy, which, seeing its substantial interests, such as land monopoly, preserved, remained uninterested in the other areas.

Nevertheless, the fact that he did not touch the latifundium, in defense of which the whole oligarchy would have united, even those members of it in Batlle's own party, a limited national development—in a predominantly agrarian economy—that threatens to condemn the Uruguayan people to the loss of the Batlle gains through the lack of economic bases capable of maintaining and expanding them. Yet, it is necessary to recognize that, thanks to the progressive, democratic program of Batlle y Ordóñez, in spite of the nation's demographic limitations (2.5 million in 1960) and the paucity of its other than agricultural resources, he wrought an incomparable work. Among the Uruguayan successes must be counted the formulation of a national image that integrates and motivates all citizens, particularly the descendants of immigrants, making them proud of their nationality, their past and their present, in spite of the economic and institutional crisis.

Uruguayan political life is ruled by a bipartisan system with a long tradition, which in more than a century of rivalry has ended by transforming the two parties into joint masters of the political power, judiciously divided and partitioned between majority and minority. The system has assured the country a high degree of political stability, capable until now of keeping the military in its proper place, without its meddling too much in politics. Each of the two parties is differentiated in clear-cut sectors of left, center, and right. A certain partisan narrowness deriving from their very aggregative power, however, has created difficulties in the joint acting of both parties' progressive sectors, giving margin to small parliamentary representations, nominally socialist. In the present conditions of the nation this acting as a single party front probably has, as it takes shape, a far greater potential of creating a national, popular, and reformist government than do the parties themselves, or the blocs of the radical left.

Besides the parties, Uruguay has a powerful syndicalist organization, highly politic, yet lacking in explicit sociopolitical objectives. Her most noteworthy characteristic is, perhaps, the unity of the working sectors with those of the middle class, made up of bankers and public functionaries, and their unity of action with the most active strata, principally the university students.

For the Uruguayans the challenge consists in finding ways to restore the high standard of living and ample distributive system that they had in the past but that is disintegrating more and more; to maintain a democratic regime, until now almost proof against overthrow (the only dictatorial interruption in a century had to withdraw, condemned unanimously by a public opinion proud of Uruguayan democracy); to stimulate the democratic educational system and refine it, resuming the impulse that it seems to have lost for some years. How much of this stagnation results from the international economic situation? How much to internal obstacles? Among the latter can be singled out antisocial privilege, such as the pastoral and agrarian latifundium, already incapable of raising its productivity; the hypertrophied political bureaucracy, which absorbs increasing portions of the national income without offering comparable benefits; a strictly syndicalist union movement and a left with a propensity for meetings but for little else, incapable of formulating an alternative to the existing national program and winning the support of public opinion for it.

With all these characteristics Uruguay, better than any other country, exemplifies the effects of the "precocious socialism" of which Schumpeter speaks (1950, 1955), and even more, probably, the effects of a socialization not only premature but partial and tactical, because it was destined to consolidate an oligarchic economic infrastructure rather than to eradicate it.

As a matter of fact, the Uruguayan urban patriciate, led by Batlle, for decades has perpetrated a reform policy tacitly agreed on by the latifundian-rancher stratum and the popular forces during a time when the latter could exert strong pressures on the political system. This policy nearly exhausted the possibilities of state intervention in the economy, "socializing," however, everything superfluous and almost nothing substantial in an agrarian export economy of meat, wool, and grain.

Within a highly favorable international market the latifundium found this socialization its form of survival, and the patriciate used it to extract considerable funds from the agrarian patronate to finance power for production (oil, electricity, and the like) and services and a welfare state that assured the urban strata—principally the middle classes—advantages in all likelihood superior to those obtaining in any other country at that time.

In this way Uruguay faced the pressures of premature urbanization, which was provoked more by the latifundium's expulsion of the rural populace than by the attraction of better work opportunities in the cities. The Batlle governmental policy, essentially, subsidized this rural-urban transfer by creating a large stratum of functionaries and employees of state-run enterprises, all with a plethora of personnel and a lack of nearly everything else, and instituting an onerous system of pensions and retirements. Thus it broke the revolutionary ardor of the recently urbanized masses, oriented by leaderships that, at that juncture, could have led them to social revolution or, much more probably, to the toughening of the power structure, as occurred in Argentina.

The Batlle solution laid the foundations for a representative democratic system by means of clubs, public meetings, and elections that allowed the citizens to participate in the control of political power. Thus, the enlistment and neutralization of potentially revolutionary sectors was accomplished, preserving the substantial interests of the old oligarchy, including latifundian proprietorship, mechanisms of export, and the banking system.

All this was accomplished by an urban patriciate that, in directing the process, became more political than entrepreneurial, and as such, as parasitic as the overinflated middle class of government employees. The fundamental financial procedure that paid the costs of this policy was customs manipulation to collect large portions of the gross export receipts. The agricultural entrepreneur, thus burdened, was in a period of prosperity that predisposed him to accept the sacrifice, all the more because the alternative was a system of taxes and direct assessments on rural property or agrarian reform.

The first formula would subject every rural proprietor to a certain fiscal intervention in the internal workings of his business and tend to lead it to higher levels of efficiency and productivity. The second was obviously not acceptable to an old oligarchy whose social precedence, political power, and source of income to maintain a high level of living were based on the inheritance of latifundia and herds. The old class thus acquiesced in the arrangement, on condition that the new republican, democratic, liberal, interventionist, and welfare state not touch its lands and the urban sectors that furnished the most profitable business deals, groups with which the oligarchy was beginning to associate itself.

In that way a paternalistic, collector-and-distributor state was installed in Uruguay, a form of state that in a favorable international situation had ample resources to create or nationalize public enterprises and subsidize services, broadening employment opportunities in the cities and constructing multiple welfare mechanisms, both direct and indirect. Above all, it was able to establish, as the political crown of a government-controlled economic orientation, a representative democracy headed by a patrician leadership strongly linked to the popular sectors and able to remain in power for decades. In times of an unfavorable economic situation crises arose, including a more or less conciliatory, weak dictatorship. Nevertheless, the bipartisan system endured, withstanding such reverses, and consolidated itself by an accord that made the two great parties permanent joint partners in power and manipulated public funds for financing economic protectionism, political patronage, and social welfare.

Applying Schumpter's hypothesis to the Uruguayan case, even superficially, it would probably explain many of the country's characteristics as necessary effects or final derivations from precocious socialism, that is, as results of a policy that resorts to socializing procedures to satisfy welfare pressures, rather than a capitalistic policy that would enable it to exploit its real potentialities for development, a policy without that minimum congruence permitting utilization of the ordering and creative virtues of a genuine socialistic system. This policy made capitalistic solutions—such as the Canadian or the Australian—seem inapplicable to the River Plate context, because it was founded on a pact guaranteeing the land monopoly and thus the survival of the latifundian ranch, incapable of achieving high production per unit area. And it also wasted a body of socializing solutions, since they were applied not according to specific exigencies of socialism and in accord with the majority interests of the people; also, they were circumscribed within the dependent sectors of the economy.

The social effects of this orientation, evaluated now through systematic research (after decades of more or less successful application, when the Uruguayan system faced its first grave crisis), would probably explain many of the problems and perplexities confronting Uruguay today. The fundamental effect of precocious socialism was, perhaps, a deformation of the characteristics of all the social classes, whose opposing interests and reciprocal aggressiveness were weakened and masked as institutional conciliatory mechanisms, but whose dynamic roles in the developmental process were also affected.

This is why the rancher could remain tied to the most archaic methods of production. Though he has had at his disposal immense expanses of rich lands, he has been incapable of even multiplying the herds and improving their use to match the slow rate of population growth. This is proved by the fact that the bovine cattle of Uruguay, 7.8 million head in 1916, had diminished in 1930 to 7.1 million, staying practically the same up to today, while the population has increased, demanding greater productive power and greater export capacity. In more recent periods the same tendency is evident, because in dollar constants the value of exports per inhabitant has dropped from 107.1 to 50.2 between 1935 and 1960. During the same period the physical volume index of exports, taking 1961 as the 100 per cent year, dropped from 108.4 to 71.6, and the total dollar value of exports fell from 189.2 million to 125 million (dollars of 1961). It is true that during the same period the percentage of internally consumed production, compared to the exported, fell from 23.4 per cent to 12.5 per cent in the agricultural sector and from 53.5 per cent to 30.9 per cent in cattle-raising; and that the surpluses produced by the agricultural economy paid for the installation of the import substitutive industry. But it is also true that the entire economy finally stagnated because of its inability to compete with international market prices and, especially, of the insufficient growth of its dynamic sector, the creator of foreign-exchange credits.

These facts plainly show how the patronal caste, responsible for the principal productive sector, lived on the extensive exploitation of its fields and cattle with no stimulus to produce more and better. Furthermore, the oligarchic stratum does not seem to have changed substantially in all these decades in its composition, its domination, or its proportion within the national picture. That is, by exploiting the inherited herds this caste has been able to pass on to its descendants its agricultural, mercantile, industrial, and other properties—within the regime of equal inheritance among the children—providing them with the same level of living, if not higher, while the total population grew poorer or saw its consumer capacity reduced. All this indicates that the collector-and-distributor pact was substantially favorable, on the economic plane, to the old agrarian oligarchy, facilitating its expansion into other commercial and industrial sectors and allowing it a long period of social peace and tranquil usufruct of its properties.

A corresponding deformation is also observable in the urban patriciate, which became parasitic-political, and in the industrial and commercial entrepreneurial corps, both of which fattened on subsidies and which, to judge by certain symptoms, seem not to have developed the characteristic acquisitive ardor of the man of capitalistic enterprise. In Uruguay one can hardly find examples of the so-called capitalist *ascesis,* of the devotion of the proprietor to his business, for which he becomes a part, intent only on expanding it to the utmost. On the contrary, what is more frequently found in Uruguay is a cautious, even timid, entrepreneur more interested in retiring from the business to enjoy the fruits of his income than in limitless expansion. The capitalist himself thus became, in the precocious socialization context, a national dependent, begging for subsidies and favored financing, and cultivating a seignoral posture. In this way he developed a taste for sumptuary goods, withdrawing funds from his business—as if it were a ranch—to provide himself with a luxurious home, foreign travel, and all sorts of superfluous expenditures, in a proportion probably greater than big businessmen in economically richer areas do. Obviously, there is a certain wisdom of life in this attitude, but also implicit economic inefficiency in the spending of investment funds and in the petty ambitions of the businessman.

The principal structural effect of premature socialization, as we have seen, was the enlargement of the middle sectors by absorption in public enterprises. Some estimate of their bulk can be given by the fact that nearly 34 per cent of the working population in Uruguay is in the tertiary sector, vs. 29 per cent in the primary and 37 per cent in the secondary. This means, in absolute numbers, that 300,000 rural workers are producing to support the dynamic sector of the economy, as compared to 385,000 in industries and 360,000 in services. This gigantism is also portrayed in the fact that a million workers in all categories are bearing the burden of 472,000 retired ones, who represent 18.7 per cent of the total population (Solari et al., 1966, p. 63).

The labor sectors also experience deformations, probably explicable by the same factors. They frequently assume a middle-class attitude, not only because they identify themselves socially as such in the field of sociopsychological postures, but because they seek to live like a poor petty bourgeoisie lamenting its inability to save, but which essentially aspires to peace and tranquility. Its forms of class action, mainly syndicalist, make the labor class a complex of pressure groups whose essential demand is to better its consumer level. Its syndicalist action, even though combative, has no relation to its political connections, harnessed to the two great parties, trusting that party alternation and some favorable world event will spontaneously resolve the problems it is facing.

With the country in a crisis because of its very structure and its dependence on a more and more unfavorable international market, the whole institutional edifice is beginning to undergo examination. In a debate more academic than political, questions are being posed over ways to break out of economic stagnation. The ranchers clamor against what they call "detractions" from their income through fiscal control of exports, forgetting that it was on this procedure that, by tacit agreement, the very perpetuation of their land monopoly was founded. The urban enterpreneurs protest against a regime in which they see only privileges assured to labor by the paternalistic state, to the prejudice of capital, equally forgetful that they have always been one of the sectors most protected by that same state. The wage-earners are also rebelling against the confiscation of their pay through inflation and the suppression of subsidies. All sectors are agitating, now accusing the council executive regime, now the bureaucracy, now the world crisis, and advocating unviable or innocuous legal reforms in whose potential for problem-solving not even they themselves believe.

Nevertheless, the crisis worsens. To the earlier deficits that could be covered by issuing currency must be added deficits in the balance of payments that force the country to deal with creditors or any available international financiers. In this fashion a new agreement is being worked out that, in view of the unlikelihood of correcting and completing the socialist orientation or of implementing an autonomous, progressive capitalistic orientation, seems fated to political retrocession through some dictatorial solution and a condemnation to stagnation and backwardness.

The popular classes, already plunged into crisis, see themselves menaced by even worse misfortunes. But they stare perplexed at the approaching storm, without formulating a program to rearrange society, made viable by a national mobilization of will. The middle classes, even more indoctrinated than the working strata with pride in their representative democracy —although they do not want to alter their self-image as "Uruguay, the Switzerland of the Americas"—are hoping for some external solution to their ever-diminishing purchasing power.

The dominant classes, both the patriciate and the oligarchy, are trusting to their ability once more to accommodate the conflicting interests through appeasement, and to some miracle—such as the lucrative Korean War— that will assure return of their lost prosperity. Some sectors of the two parties, particularly, trust that because the crisis is worldwide and therefore of interest to the United States, the latter will find the solution, especially if they can count on the political cooperation of all the nations of the hemisphere. They go so far as to advocate a preventive dictatorship of some type (not necessarily militaristic like their neighbors', if only because Uruguay lacks certain ingredients to install it) to incorporate the country into the continental situation and to assure it the help of the U.S. government.

On the technical plane Uruguay has a carefully worked out developmental program to solve her national problems in terms of small institutional reforms and great investments in ambitious projects that no one knows how to finance. This, however, is a job for technicians, not for politicians.

Such is the Uruguay of today, more the result of her past than of the world situation, with solutions lacking political reality on the technical plane, and on the political, an ample corps of progressive forces, disjointed and lacking a common plan of action. The dominant classes, now parasitic and no longer trusting in the virtues of the system they instituted, feel more inclined to assure their social precedence even at the price of the destruction of Uruguay's political image, which was so dear to them. The middle class, product of state patronage, feeling abandoned by former sources of protection, threatens to fall into a despair conducive to support of solutions by force. The labor class seems too accommodated to trade-unionism to be capable of revolutionary mobilization. In this conjecture of reciprocal perplexities the right is conspiring, the center is becoming paralyzed and neutralized, and the left is preaching a total revolution that they cannot implement—or it, too, is paralyzed, fearful of provoking a worse political crisis. Uruguay waits and hopes.

Thanks to immigrant labor and ecological conditions highly favorable to the production of basic export articles (meat, wheat, and wool) in great demand on the world market, the two Transplanted Peoples of the South Americas have constructed in this century the most mature socioeconomic structures in Latin America. They have achieved not only the highest levels of per capita income but also a distribution of national income that has permitted a middle class estimated at more than 30 per cent of the active population and a broad factory proletariat, also with the highest wage standards on the continent, and incorporating nearly the whole population into the capitalistic production system and into the nation's educational, cultural, and political life. They do not contain, therefore, those huge marginal masses present in the new peoples and the witness peoples of Latin America, whose integration into the productive system and into social and cultural life constitutes their great national problem, but tends to generate structural tensions that make likely a revolutionary outcome.

Both Argentina and Uruguay limited their potentialities, remaining on the margin of development, in leaving the agrarian structure untouched. Nevertheless, both were able to urbanize their populations early, preventing the rise of social tensions in the rural areas. One of the visible symptoms of this precocious urbanization is the flagrant contrast between the two capitals—where the population is overconcentrated and nearly all the industry is found, and in the vicinity of which the technically most advanced agriculture and cattle-raising is carried on—and the great provincial areas, sparsely populated and much poorer. In these areas the middle and the labor classes experience much less social mobility, and the rural population confronts living difficulties that are in many cases equivalent to conditions in the poor areas of the continent. Even so, this rural population is no longer a burden on the nation's destiny.

The problems facing the two River Plate republics are, then, different from those to be found in other Latin American countries, mainly because they are in great part the problems of developed nations. However, they have two basic factors in common with all Latin American countries. On the one hand is the distortion imposed by oligarchic constriction, which, monopolizing the land in a few hands, leads to extensive agrocattle exploitation, incapable of competing in the international markets, and places the whole population at the service of an insignificant minority. On the other hand there is the imperialistic constriction, which strangles their possibilities of progress as it subjects them to a recolonizing industrialization highly spoilative in character.

Having undergone the principal transformations pertinent to industrial civilization in its occupational structure [7] through the effect of a reflexive urbanization, the two societies exhibit contradictory characteristics of backwardness and progress that are expressed in their nature as modern urban societies based on an agrarian economy of latifundian ranches devoted to export. From the moment this export economy experienced difficulty owing to competition with other similar ecological areas producing cattle, wool, and grains (Canada, Australia, New Zealand) in an atmosphere of fewer institutional obstacles—it underwent a crisis more severe than those in other parts of the continent. A greater degree of progress and a more equitably distributed wealth engender higher aspirations, which collide with the limits imposed by an unfavorable position in the world economy and with the exhaustion of the productive capacity of the existing system of rural exploitation. The tensions stemming from this tend to exert increasing force on the regime, compelling it to open new horizons of development based on the immense national possibilities.

In these circumstances the power structure of the Platine nations stands before two basic dilemmas: (1) the unviability for survival of the traditional democratic system; (2) the need for new productive fronts through industrialization, limiting imperialistic spoilation. To these a third may be added, the renovation of the agropastoral economy by means of mechanization that will substantially raise productivity and permit a better social

---

[7] Nearly 40 per cent of the population is in the work force, 31 per cent of this figure being in the middle class in Uruguay and 39 per cent in Argentina, with more than 70 per cent of the population concentrated in the cities in both nations.

distribution of agricultural income. For the middle and popular classes the government itself is called into question: if it is incapable of initiating a new stage of progress, it will have to be superseded.

These are not peaceful alternatives. The entrepreneurial patronates of both countries, and their rural oligarchies, are today integrating into a system of international interests that hopes to stake its future on a world plane. Instead of fostering the revolutionary enlargement of the bases of the social structure itself, which would limit its privileges, that system will prefer to fortify itself at the cost of the repression of popular movements. For this purpose it possesses, internally, the enormous resources of control and poisoning of public opinion, and, in the case of Argentina, the interventionist vocation of the armed forces, always docile to oligarchic interests. And, externally, it has the protection of the American partner, the United States, guardian of the status quo throughout the world.

PART V

Civilization and Development

"The fact of this universal misery has divided the world into two groups of human beings: the group of those who do not eat and the group of those who do not sleep. The group of those who do not eat inhabits the poor countries and deems itself crushed in its misery by the economic oppression of the great industrial powers. The group of those who do not sleep lives in the richest areas of the world, but they do not sleep for fear of the revolt of those who do not eat."

—JOSUÉ DE CASTRO

11. Models of Autonomous Development

THE STUDY OF THE developmental prospects open to the Latin American peoples demands a preliminary analysis of the models of the industrial development and the patterns of historical retardation. This is what we shall do below, by proposing two paradigms as coincident as possible with concrete situations but not concordant with them in their peculiarities. Through the first we shall try to establish the ways in which developed societies evolved; the second will permit focalizing the configurations of backwardness in order to determine the principal obstacles, general and particular, opposing development.

The Industrial Revolution, operating as a process of evolutionary acceleration, made the pioneer industrial nations new power centers. Around them were agglutinated neighboring and distant peoples to form great imperialistic constellations. The first of these constellations was constituted with the industrialization of England (1750–1800), France (1800–1890), the Low Countries (1800–1850), and the United States (1840–1890). As pioneers in industrialization these nations were the new centers of world domination, the early model of industrial development.[1]

The same civilizational process, operating simultaneously by way of historical incorporation, actuated three modes of reorganizing relations between peoples: (1) making obsolete the bonds between the old mercantile metropolises and their colonies, it provided the majority of the latter with political emancipation, enabling them to be areas of neocolonial exploitation; (2) projecting over areas not dominated by the earlier waves of European expansion, it subjected their peoples to the colonial yoke or imposed on them statutes of neocolonial dependence; (3) establishing a self-perpetuating world economic system, it divided the free nations into a hierarchy of industrial powers endowed with the capacity for autonomous command of their destiny and dependent nations, not only disinherited in the division of the world into areas of influence, but also condemned to merely reflexive development.

This system of self-perpetuating forces was broken first by Germany (1850–1914) and Japan (1890–1920). Both succeeded in becoming industrialized by means of deliberate efforts to achieve autonomy, a fundamental condition of survival in a world subject to the pioneer industrial powers. These countries established the late model of industrial development, the first mode of rupture with the world imperialistic complex. This way was adopted later by Italy (1920–1940) and taken as the route, with less success, by many other nations (the Turkey of Mustapha Kemal, the Egypt of Nasser, the Brazil of Vargas, the Argentina of Perón, and so on).

The second capitalist rupture with backwardness inaugurated the recent model of development with the industrialization of marginal areas, such as the Scandinavian countries (1890–1930), by a peculiar evolutionary process, or of dependent areas such as Canada (1900–1920), Australia, and

---

[1] The periods given here seek to indicate the decisive decades in the installation of heavy industry (siderurgy, manufacture of machines), considering, however, that the very content of this varies appreciably during the course of the industrialization process. For comparison, see Colin Clark (1957, p. 335) on industrial production in the world measured in "international units" (based on the purchasing power of the U.S. dollar during 1925–1934). He shows that the first billion "I.U." was reached by England before 1860, by the United States about 1870, by Germany in 1875, by France in 1870, by Japan and Italy in 1920, by the U.S.S.R., Canada, and Sweden after 1925, by Holland and Australia only in 1948, and by Brazil and India after 1950. See also W. W. Rostow (1960 a), who fixes approximate dates for what he calls "take-off,"—for England, 1783–1802, for France, 1830–1860; for the United States, 1843–1860, for Germany, 1850–1873; for Japan, 1878–1900, and for Canada, 1896–1914. Rostow warns, however, that if the criterion were the period of fastest total industrial growth, these dates would have to be later: Great Britain, 1819–1848; the United States, 1868–1893; Sweden, 1890–1920; Japan, 1900–1920; Russia, 1928–1940.

New Zealand (1930–1950). These last emerged less as fruits of deliberate projects of self-development than as effects of the periods of isolation from English domination that they experienced, isolation caused by the crisis of 1929 and the two world wars. Normally these relations would not engender autonomous progress because of the intrinsically spoliative nature of the interaction between economies historically out of phase. With the appearance of war situations, or economic crises, these nations were able to export more than they imported, accumulating foreign-exchange credits, but above all, they were able to exploit autonomously their own sources of wealth, realizing potentials of progress nullified until then. With contacts reestablished, these nations were economically strengthened and able to negotiate new forms of interchange capable of preserving national economic interests and making autonomous development viable.

The third rupture, corresponding to the socialist model of industrial development, occurred in the capacity of a new civilizational process tending not to repeat old formations through the creation of new industrial capitalistic centers, but to create a new sociocultural formation, the revolutionary socialist. This was accomplished first by the Soviet Union (1930–1940) through a socialist revolution that spurred her population to the efforts indispensable to integration into modern industrial technology. Thus, together with the fourth model of industrial development, a new way of historical acceleration was established, which was to inspire, later on, the social reordering and the industrialization of various nations of Eastern Europe, China and other countries of the Far East, and finally Cuba.

Besides these three forms of rupture with backwardness, two variant forms of socioeconomic reordering have emerged during the course of the new civilizational process: (1) the maturation of evolutionary socialist formations in some highly industrialized societies by means of structural and institutional renovations resulting from the technological process itself, from the struggle of the wage-earners to improve its living conditions, and from the emancipation movements of the colonial areas (for example, the Scandinavian countries and England); (2) the national liberation movements of former colonies and dependent nations structured as modernizing nationalisms (the major representatives of which are Egypt and Algeria). They do not, however, constitute a model of industrial development because no nation has yet achieved industrial development by these routes. They are, rather, forms of rupture with dependence on imperialism and with internal oligarchic constriction, conducive to a hybrid socioeconomic formation that seeks to harmonize socialistic procedures with the preservation of capitalistic contents. Their rise and consolidation is explained in great part by the division of the world into two great opposing camps, the socialistic and the capitalistic, which occasions these partial ruptures with privatist economy and these feeble appeals to socialistic procedures.

Autocratic Roads to Industrialization

Among the four models of industrial development, the late capitalistic and the socialistic are of special theoretic interest in their character as deliberate efforts to break with imperialistic domination and to face internal causes of backwardness.

The nations that have taken this direction face two impediments to their autonomous development: (1) foreign economic domination by industrial imperialistic economies, bent on perpetuating the advantages gained with their early development; (2) domestic constrictions, exerted by the dominant classes themselves, intent on preserving their privileges and, for that reason, ready to consort with foreign interests.

In the late model, represented by Germany and Japan, this connivance was partially broken by the pressure of aspirations to national self-affirmation in the face of the expansionism of the old imperialistic powers. The principal energizer was the arms effort, which, demanding a modern industrial infrastructure as an imperative of defense, brought about the technicalization of the economy and the resultant new social order. It was a question, in both cases, of independent nations intent on gaining autonomous mastery of their own development. That objective generated a complex of social forces strong enough to overwhelm the old power structure, designed to maintain the predominance of the oligarchic order ruled by the traditional dominant classes, principally composed of latifundian proprietors. In both cases, as occurred later with Italy, a new model of capitalist development was instituted, opposed to the early pattern because it was based on an ideology of intervention in the economy that determined the place and role of private enterprises in the united effort, and also based on an autonomist attitude toward the international market.[2]

[2] The first theorist of this alternative route of industrial development, Fredric List, wrote in 1841: "It is a rule of common prudence, when one reaches the pinnacle of greatness, to pull up the ladder by which he reached the summit, in order to deprive others of the means to rise. That is the secret of the cosmopolitan doctrine of Adam Smith, and of the cosmopolitan tendencies of his illustrious contemporary, William Pitt, as well as of all their successors. . . . The nation that, by means of protectionist tariffs and maritime restrictions, has perfected its manufacturing industry and its merchant marine to the point of no longer fearing competition from any other, cannot adopt a wiser position than to throw away the tools used for its elevation, to preach to other peoples the advent of freedom of trade, to express aloud its repentance for

The Japanese industrial development best exemplifies the late model, through the character of autonomist aspiration and deliberate national effort stamped on it from the beginning. Its fundamental stages can be summarized thus: It started with Commodore Perry's landing, in 1853, at Japanese ports and the imposing of a commercial treaty with the United States, followed by identical impositions by other industrial powers. The Japanese reaction against this threat of colonization exploded in the Meiji Revolution of 1867–1870, which wiped out the old feudal order and set up a new power structure capable of undertaking industrialization. The revolution overthrew the old aristocracy and the primitive military caste, abolished the prohibition on sale of samurai lands, and inaugurated a money tax on agricultural exploitation. These measures brought on an intense mercantilization of the agrarian economy and permitted the wide collection of public funds destined for industrialization, defined as a task basic to national security.

Ten years after the Meiji Revolution the Japanese government had three large shipyards and a powerful merchant and war fleet, a wide network of railroads and communications, ten mines in operation, and dozens of factories of arms and equipment. Most of these enterprises were subsequently transferred by favoritism to private firms. The state retained command of the economy, however. That can be inferred from the fact that, from 1896 to 1913, the government offices absorbed 85 per cent of the loans obtained abroad, at the same time that direct foreign investments accounted for only 5.5 per cent of the total in that last year. Thus, an autonomous corps of industrial entrepreneurs and a powerful nationalistic military hierarchy arose, combining to form a national plutocracy with hegemony over the power structure. As can be seen, it was a development induced by acts of will, commanded by the state, without direct participation from foreign companies.

Simultaneously with this industrialization effort, the Japanese government carried out a broad educational program at all levels with the aim of teaching the whole population to read and write and to absorb and transmit the scientific knowledge and technology of industrial civilization. This national developmental project lifted an archaic society to the status of world power in a few decades despite Japan's enormous deficiencies in natural resources and despite the linguistic and cultural barriers separating the country from the ruling centers of industrial civilization.

Moved by the same basic impulse, Bismarck's Germany and, much later, Italy, broke the encirclement of the industrial powers. They insti-

---

having gone until then along the paths of error and for having taken so long to reach knowledge of the truth. . . ." (Quoted by A. Piettre, 1962, p. 292).

tuted autocratic regimes, rigidly centralized, to prepare and mobilize all national forces for development. As their first task they proposed the construction of an autarchic economy proof against harmful international competition that undermined possibilities for expansion and progress in nations that were tardily headed toward industrial capitalistic development.

Turned back on themselves, these economies operated from that time on in accordance with procedures contrary to the classic model. Instead of free enterprise, they moved forward to a state capitalism and a planned economy that opened the way to the rise of a powerful entrepreneurial plutocracy. Instead of free foreign exchange, they imposed exchanges differentiated according to the contingencies of the moment. Instead of free trade, they resorted to bilateral agreements. Instead of stable currency on gold and silver standard, they freely manipulated the currency and utilized issues of paper and inflation with economic objectives. In place of a free market, they installed controls of stocks, prices, wages and salaries, and instituted subsidies.

By these means they succeeded in breaking the ring of industrial powers that controlled the world market, and accelerating the autonomous mechanization of their productive forces with intensive industrialization as the great national goal. The acceleration was accomplished by the countries of late industrial development through a programmed and simultaneous action of institutional renovation that trained their societies for the mechanization of the productive infrastructure, capacitated to integrate the whole population into the national labor force and to educate them in modernization, an effort that elevated a considerable part of the population to the highest levels of mastery of scientific knowledge and modern technology.

In all three cases this form of rupture with retardation—based on the installation of an entrepreneurial and militaristic plutocracy—led to imperialistic expansion in the footsteps of the older world powers. Japan attacked neighboring countries, seizing the Pescadores and Formosa (1895), the Sakhalin Islands and Port Arthur (1905), and later Manchuria (1911) and other areas of China (1937). Italy built her colonial empire by adding Eritrea and Ethiopia (1935) and finally Albania to her old possessions. Germany launched her expansion first in Africa (1884), then China (1897), and the Pacific Islands (1888–1899) in search of colonies. In a second stage Germany moved against the European nations on her borders, seeking to redistribute market areas and raw materials and to gain a physical basis in Europe to make herself *the* world power.

The collision of the old imperialism with the new caused the two world wars. In the interval between them Germany and Japan turned to the Bismarckian procedures to recover from the economic crises in which they found themselves submerged. In both cases (and likewise in that of Italy) the late route was restored with even more heterodox forms of economic mobilization and political despotism. After the last war, defeated by the alliance of all the other nations, these three countries were immersed in a new international situation, headed by the United States and the Soviet Union, within which their projects of self-affirmation as superpowers of the West and the East were made obsolete. The old international structure, based on multiple capitalistic constellations in competition with one another, gave way to a socialist-capitalist bipartition. In this new situation the opportunities for political emancipation of the colonial peoples and of development for all the backward peoples were extraordinarily enlarged, but these peoples were already orienting themselves, perforce, toward socializing forms of social restructuring. Thus the way to late industrial development had been closed, as the model that could direct the efforts of emancipation and economic growth of underdeveloped nations.

Despite the damages suffered in the war, which resulted in the destruction of their whole factory complex and their basic capital, the peoples of late industrial capitalistic development recovered the former standards of production in less than a decade, resuming and accelerating the old rate of growth. Thus for a second time they advanced against retardation, this time over the ruins of a devastating war and through a close association with the American industrial corporations, subsidized in this effort by the Marshall Plan.

It must be pointed out, however, that the challenge confronting them was much less than that of the underdeveloped peoples, who were left in their retarded condition. The fundamental factor of the German and Japanese "miracle" is that they were already autonomously integrated in industrial civilization, possessing a labor force capable of reconstituting their material property, as an indigenous village destroyed by a catastrophe can be rebuilt or as an underdeveloped people can only reproduce, in like circumstances, the forms of material expression of its backwardness. More than the injection of American capital or any other factors, it was the cultural and structural maturity of their peoples that enabled them to reconstruct their way of life, their culture, their civilization.

Intentional procedures of the same nature as the late industrial developments were adopted in two other cases: (1) by advanced nations in the effort to overcome occasional crises in the system (classic examples are the Bonapartism of Napoleon III and the Roosevelt New Deal, and in certain measure the recent economic programmings of DeGaulle and Adenauer), in all cases, however, a question of efforts to recuperate from crises or to break out of economic stagnation, not a matter of original ruptures with underdevelopment; (2) by backward nations that tried to capitalize on the international tensions between imperialistic powers to promote their industrialization by way of "state capitalism" (the Turkey of Mustapha Kemal, the Brazil of Getúlio Vargas, and the Argentina of Juan Perón), in all cases, politicomilitary groups taking over the state machine and seeking to lead their nations to autonomous development by mobilizing the populations against foreign spoliation. These latter all had to face the self-defense capacity of imperialism, which saw in them a menace to its interests. They all compromised with the traditional agrarian structure, based on the latifundium. They all failed in the end, only playing the part of more efficacious agents of reflexive modernization and political awakening of their peoples for future struggles against the system of foreign and domestic domination that keeps them underdeveloped.

The Socialist Road

The revolutionary socialistic formations are the second intentional model breaking with imperialistic domination and internal oligarchic constriction. Russia, which had the pioneer role in this model, faced probably the greatest challenge to sociocultural creativity ever recorded. It was a matter of constructing a new social order that preexisted only as theoretic formulation, elaborated more as a form of political recruitment than as a project for concrete application in the practical world. Its viability and efficacy were proved to the hilt. A turbulent period from 1917 to 1921, the consequence of the insurrection itself, of foreign invasions, of international blockade, and of the effort to control the internal dissensions of the movement followed the planned construction of the socialist economy. It proceeded intitially through trial and error, but defined industrialization as a fundamental goal, expanding available energy (electric and the like), steel-producing capacity, and all kinds of machinery.

The great jump, however, was taken between 1930 and 1940, when the U.S.S.R. recovered its prerevolution productive capacity and immediately multiplied it several times over, installing the enormous decentralized industrial system that was to enable it to face the apparently impossible challenge of Nazi invasion. Even those who lament the methods employed by the Soviets and point out deformations in the pattern of society they established, are unanimous in recognizing that the U.S.S.R reached and maintained, through the quinquennial plans initiated in 1928 and the septennial plans subsequent to 1957, the highest rates of industrial production growth ever accomplished. According to Colin Clark (1957), the value of Russian industrial production, which had reached 837 million I.U.'s in

1910–1913, dropping to 181 million from 1920 to 1924, rose to 1.401 billion in 1930–1934 and to 2.74 billion in 1935–1938. Hodgman (1954) shows that from 1928 to 1937 the Soviet Union experienced an index of industrial development of 270 per cent (Soviet statistics record 450 per cent), and points out that this progression is equivalent to an annual production increment of 15 per cent, which after the war rose to 20 per cent annually (1946–1950).

Such growth indicators defy comparison. According to the studies of S. Kuznets (1964), the annual rates of growth of the per capita national product of the periods of building modern industrial economies were: England, 2.8 from 1780 to 1881; Germany, 1.7, 1851–1875; tsarist Russia, 1.3, 1850–1913; United States, 4.3, and Japan, 4.5, 1890–1927; U.S.S.R., 10.5, 1930–1960, according to the Soviet statistics, and 5.2 according to Kuznets. The data on world industrial production published in the U.N. Statistical Yearbook for 1963 indicate that, taking 1938 as the 100 year, American industrial production progressed to 221 in 1948, 303 in 1958, and 372 in 1963, whereas the Soviet progressed in the same years to 173, 434, and 686.

A more expressive measure of the Soviet industrial expansion in comparison with the capitalist economies is given by collating the increase in value of the respective industrial productions. If we take 1929 as the 100 year for the value of the Russian industrial production, the U.S. figure for that year would be 833, the English, 325, and the German, 333. In 1955, the same proportions had been reduced to 207 in the case of the United States, which dropped from eight times greater to only twice the Soviet production; and in the case of England and Germany, to 33 and 36, respectively, or in other terms, from three times the Russian figure to one third of it (Cafagna, 1961).

This capacity to set a much more intense rate of growth is not valid only for the Soviet economy but for all socialist economies, as is demonstrated by the fact that they increased from 100 to 320 between 1950 and 1959, whereas the capitalist production grew in the same period from 100 to 155 (J. Frek, 1965).

In this fashion a preindustrial, notoriously backward country such as Russia, with great portions of the population marginalized in national life, in only three decades became the second industrial power in the world, actuated by a growth increment that brings it closer and closer to the first power, tending to surpass it in over-all and per capita production in the next decade.

Three distinctive characteristics of the revolutionary socialist model of development make it especially attractive to the underdeveloped nations, the first being the high rates of economic growth it attains. Applied to the underdeveloped nations, the socialist rates of growth of gross domestic product (G.D.P.) per capita (6 per cent to 8 per cent annually) would enable them to overtake the developed nations in three or four decades. Inversely, if these nations maintain the rates of increase of their most prosperous seasons (2.2 per cent G.D.P. per capita between 1950 and 1960, according to the United Nations), or even if they reached the rates of increase of the most developed capitalist nations (2.7 per cent, 1950–1960, according to the United Nations), their possibilities of overcoming backwardness will have to be postponed to 150 to 200 years in the future.

Another distinctive characteristic of the revolutionary socialist model is that it is the only one that has lifted great masses of people from poverty to prosperity. All the preceding processes of development covered small demographic contingents. Thus the United Kingdom, in the dawn of the Industrial Revolution, has nearly 7 million inhabitants, and the United States, fewer than twenty million. But the U.S.S.R. started with 100 million, and China, today ascending to industrial development, began with 700 million. This demographic challenge, decisively important for many of the underdeveloped nations, such as India, Indonesia, and Brazil, points up the revolutionary socialist experiment as the only one that has faced it with success.

The third characteristic of the revolutionary socialist model is that it succeeded in imprinting processes of evolutionary acceleration on rigid social structures, lifting them from the level of agrocraftsman economies to the modern industrial standard. The sole exception that succeeded in industrializing itself is Japan, equally archaic and rigidly structured. This occurred, however, in the course of the century when antidevelopmental compulsions were much less oppressive. Indeed, in no country conformed by processes of historical incorporation, and deformed by them, has a Schumpeterian bourgeoisie arisen capable of leading the fight for autonomous development. Nor have plutocracies arisen prepared to mobilize the nation autocratically to impose a national program of eliminating the obsolete structures and overcoming foreign dependence in order to foster autonomous industrialization.

All these distinctive traits of revolutionary socialism make it, with increasing probability, the natural way out for nations doomed to backwardness and want while the imperialistic domination of the world markets prevails.

In fact, in equivalent situations of condemnation to underdevelopment and oligarchic constriction Russia, China, and Cuba found socialist revolution the only way open to them for development. They were all archaic nations, with incipiently capitalistic economies and rigid social structures, which for that reason seemed furthest from socialist prospects. And yet it was in them that the new model was first established, less as an overcoming of the deficiencies inherent in industrial capitalism than as a rupture of the double antiprogressive strangulation that they experienced.

In all these cases, structural rigidity, operating as a barrier to social reforms, built up tensions that led to revolutionary outbreaks. Erupting in periods of social convulsion or of war, when the machines of police-military repression ceased to function, these explosions facilitated the installation of socialist regimes that liberated long pent-up renovating forces. Thus the very vigor of the oligarchic structure operated to condense the social tensions, permitting the release and victory of radical revolutionary movements. This happened to tsarist Russia with the social and military crisis provoked by World War I; in China, Korea, and Vietnam during the resistance against the Japanese invasion and later against restoration of imperialistic dominion; in the socialist nations of Eastern Europe in combatting Nazi domination and in fraternizing with the Red Army; and in Cuba in the insurrection of the people against the Batista dictatorship, a revolutionary leadership taking charge of the movement.

In all these cases, however, the convulsive conditions and the popular insurrection itself would not have permitted, by themselves, the installation of a new order. This happens because of the presence and action of a revolutionary vanguard equipped with a socialist ideology that theoretically prefigured the possibility of a rational reordering of society according to the majority interests of the population.

As can be seen, the smashing of structural resistances to economic development admits various degrees of intentionality. In the pioneer countries of industrialization it was spontaneous, rather, for that reason occasioning a free-enterprise ideology founded on the concept that the state, operating as a check, must abstain from intervening in the free play of social forces. Such conditions were never repeated in other areas. Even in those nations in which these criteria were present in the renovation, they were superseded later by the need to introduce coordinating mechanisms to exercise imperialist domination needed for war efforts or as a way out of grave economic crises.[3]

Only the recent model of development—Scandinavia, Canada, Australia, New Zealand—seems an evolutionary path that reproduces the classic way. Even so, it could hardly be carried out without the conditions fur-

---

[3] It must be pointed out further that even in the industrialization processes most approximating to the liberal model the state has always played an important part. In England, subsidizing the merchant marine as an expansionist instrument; in France, encouraging industrialization through privileged credits; in all of them, by means of customs protection of national manufactures.

nished to those countries by the two wars and the 1929 crisis, weakening economic domination over them, compelling them to efforts to surpass themselves and permitting them to convert their complementary economy of food production into autonomous economies prepared to undertake industrialization.

Furthermore, all those countries contained small populations in large virgin territories. The exploitation of their natural resources (especially wood in Scandinavia and gold in Australia) and the flexibility of the social structure obtaining in all of them facilitated the creation of farm economies and, consequently, of a domestic market, permitting the subsequent installation of modern industrial economies.[4]

Some of these countries, emerging from a world conjuncture totally different from that which confronted the early and the late, see their possibilities of capitalist expansion severely limited. This is the case of Australia and New Zealand, and is possibly the case of South Africa and Rhodesia, which have Asia and Africa before them as a "natural" area of imperial expansion by way of historical incorporation. They all, however, confront unbearable resistance—external in the first case, internal in the second— that prevents them from repeating the perversities of colonialist capitalism.

In the countries of late industrial development, the ones that undertook technological and social renovation by acts of will and for reasons of security, the state, called on to direct the process, identified itself so closely with the interests of the entrepreneurial stratum that it succeeded in replacing the old oligarchic structure with a power elite, plutocratic in aspect. The structural renovations in these cases were less intense, and popular participation in political life was annulled or debased. The developmental ideology was a type of chauvinistic nationalism that while proclaiming the nation's destiny to be domination over other peoples, at

---

[4] Canada, the Scandinavian countries, Australia, and New Zealand are considered here as developed economies, more because of their high per capita income than their degree of industrialization. They all represent indexes of higher development for 1930–1960 than for 1950–1960: it may be that, like other economies such as the Argentine and Uruguayan, they have entered a stagnation stage. The latter two have experienced in the past equivalent periods of prosperity deriving from favorable conjunctural situations in international commerce, thereafter falling into decline owing to other factors. According to S. Kuznets (1964), from the first period indicated to the second the ten-year index of growth of per capita income of those countries dropped thus: Australia, from 20.8 per cent to 17 per cent, and Canada, from 38.4 per cent to 37.3 per cent. In this period only New Zealand, whose first developmental impulse had been retarded in relation to the others, rose from 13.9 per cent to 17 per cent.

the same time demanded monopoly of the national market for native entrepreneurs.

In the performance of its role the state was invested with discretionary
powers over society, preparing it for the tasks of economic programming,
of training the labor force, and of guaranteeing social peace to the enterprises for the accumulation of capital funds. For this purpose a machine
was set up to repress any form of opposition, especially the rebellious
wage-earners. This whole complex of procedures was amplified with the
creation of scapegoats on which responsibility for the national problems
was placed—the Jews in Germany and communism everywhere. Once a
certain degree of progress was achieved, the developmental ideology was
transfigured to persuade the nation of the imperativeness of its imperial
and civilizing destiny over backward peoples.

In the socialist pattern of break, which begins with the takeover of
power in the name of the people's forces, the state assumes the form of
proletariat dictatorship to forge new institutional mechanisms to direct the
developmental process. In this case the degree of intentionality and the
power of rational intervention through over-all planning reach the highest
levels. What differentiates the capitalist pattern from the socialist is not,
therefore, the prevalence of spontaneity, in the first case, or of interventionism, in the last. What distinguishes them is the power structure commanding the renovating process, and the social group that imposes its hegemony on the nation, conditioning the whole institutional reordering to
the preservation and amplification of its interests. These are the interests
of the subaltern classes in the case of the socialist projects, and the interests of the entrepreneurial and military plutocracies in the case of the
model of late capitalistic development.

In the socialist model of development, with the traditional patronate and
patriciate proscribed from the very first, the basic procedures of social
reordering consist of six steps: (1) the state confiscates the larger part or
the whole of the preexisting land, financial, industrial, and commercial patrimony as the background of development; (2) it applies the surplus of
production above a previously compressed consumption to technological
renovation, priority being assigned to the installation of systems of massive
energy production and heavy industry, in order to assure autonomy of later
industrial development; (3) the state mobilizes all idle forces, including the
labor force formerly only partly utilized, to expand production; (4) it exe-
cutes an agrarian reform that, in a first stage, organizes a farm economy to
enlist the peasantry in the revolutionary effort and, in a second stage, establishes collectivist systems of work to increase agricultural productivity through large, highly mechanized plantations; (5) the school system is

expanded to recover culturally the illiterate or inadequately educated adults, and by means of a wide network of schools capacitated to enroll all children, selecting from among them the most apt for medium level courses and the ones better than these for university studies, in this way, as rapidly as practicable, and as one of the basic national efforts, constructing a highly skilled work force, incorporating the whole society into the scientific and technological knowledge of the industrial era; (6) the socioeconomic and political control of all society is achieved through a single party in association with union officials who agitate for national development, this effort being carried out through a complex of stimuli and sanctions capable of discretionary action on each individual. It is in this way that a power structure is implanted that allows substitution of a new leadership, principally working class in extraction, technically and ideologically prepared to put into practice the socialist project, for the old management and technical stratum of private companies, for the former bureaucracy and the professional sectors.

We have already referred to modernizing nationalism as one alternative path of rupture with imperialistic and oligarchic constriction and with the power structure that guarantees its perpetuation. We must point out that this formation does not constitute a model of industrial development because none of the regimes thus conformed has attained a rate of industrialization sufficient to fully develop by foreseeable dates. Besides this, in the case of some older modernizing-nationalist formations—as in Mexico, after Cárdenas—this pattern regressed to certain forms of commitment to imperialism and to new privatist strata, appearing after the revolution, that checked their already slow rates of progress.

We presume that the new modernizing-nationalist formations, growing in a more favorable world conjuncture, may achieve important degrees of progress. They were all established after victorious revolutions directed by reformist groups opposed to the former power structure and vigorously antioligarchic and antiimperialistic: the army of liberation, in the case of Algeria, and the nationalistic officialdom, in the case of Egypt. Once in power, they promoted an intense popular mobilization of the urban and rural masses for a developmental national effort and instituted a new social order that seeks to harmonize socialistic procedures in the basic sectors of the economy with capitalistic procedures in the other sectors. They are thus attempting to combine the merits of deliberate economic planning with the organizational virtues of the profit system. Their basic procedures consist in the proscription of the former power structure, too committed to the old order, from national public life; in the expropriation, negotiated or not, of the great international firms and confiscation of nonproducing latifundia; in the formulation of a plan for autonomous development through national exploitation of natural resources and broad agrarian reform; in the state's assumption of the role of direct agent of economic building and structural transfiguration; in the adoption of planning as a norm of government within applicable limits; and in the creation of a new, better trained bureaucracy to serve collective interests and to modernize the administration of public offices and state enterprises.

It is probable that the modern international situation, polarized by the capitalist-socialist opposition, besides offering the opportunity for the rise of modernizing-nationalist formations, may permit them to reach higher rates of economic growth. However, the socialist world has not yet matured enough either to cooperate in an appreciable way with the efforts at industrial development of the modernizing-nationalist formations or to compel the inperialist powers to moderate their forces of domination and exploitation.

It is to be supposed, nevertheless, that with these two requisites attended to, in the course of capitalist-socialist competition, modernizing nationalism may mature as an alternative way of autonomous development through new forms of interchange in which the poor nations are more aided than harmed in their coexistence with the prosperous nations. The likelihood of international exchange as a way of development will not be attained spontaneously. The policy of modern capitalistic nations is to replace the old forms of colonial exploitation with indirect mechanisms of control and domination, such as the European Common Market and Latin American integration into recolonializing industrialization—mechanisms all controlled by the great international corporations. As such, they tend to act to incorporate rather than to accelerate progress for the underdeveloped peoples. It is only the capitalist-socialist competition and, above all, the active will to autonomy and development of the backward peoples that will lead to a new international order favorable to development.

12. Patterns of
Historical Retardation

IN THE AREAS affected by the Industrial Revolution through the process of historical incorporation we find the peoples who are retarded in history because they are marginalized from the civilization of their time and condemned to experience only its reflexive effects. They are all framed in configurations of subordination, from open colonialism to subtle forms of dependence. Their complementary economies permit only a partial integration of modern technology into their productive process, and in consequence prevent their attaining the life styles of the industrial nations.

Within this framework a spontaneous industrialization, instead of being facilitated by the existence of models of action and of maturely experienced techniques, is enormously hindered by five factors: (1) the self-perpetuating character of underdevelopment, capable only of reproducing itself spontaneously; (2) the strengthening of the domestic oligarchic-patrician ramparts, which in the course of reflexive modernization enriches itself and gains increasing power as the agent of import-export commerce, producer of tropical articles, and associate of foreign companies; (3) the transfer abroad of products of the national work force and of economic surpluses generated internally, which prevents domestic accumulation of capital available for industrial investments; (4) the exorbitant impositions of foreign firms, raising the social cost of all modernizing undertakings to insupportable levels; (5) foreign intervention in the domestic political life, which assures political precedence to the native agents of spoliation and vetoes any possibility of breaking out of backwardness, characterizing as subversive any effort at autonomous development.

At the cost of dramatic, firsthand experience these backward peoples have gradually come to perceive that the apparent progress of their modernized cities and habits of noticeable consumption of imported goods are the counterpart of their increasing pauperized masses, of the loss of their autonomy in development, and of their subjection to oppressive bonds in the economic, political, and cultural spheres. Experiencing a modernization conditioned by these limitations, they are condemned to continue as a vast peripheral area of the industrial powers and as peoples marginalized for the civilization of their time.

The traumatic character of their societies, the deformed nature of their economies, and the spurious nature of their cultures nevertheless end by being revealed to the native leaderships who diagnose the historical and circumstantial nature of their condemnation to poverty. At that moment they cease to be historically retarded peoples to become underdeveloped peoples, which is to say, conscious that their backwardness is remediable, provided that they mobilize politically to fight for their emancipation against the domestic and foreign forces conspiring to keep them in the status of consumers of imported goods and of producers of raw materials for alien industries with no prospect of autonomous development.

In the first clashes of this emancipatory struggle these leaderships become persuaded of the complexity of the task. The struggle for development of their countries does not constitute merely an internal political process, but an effort to reorganize their relations with the world. The penury from which they want to free themselves is necessary to the maintenance of the oligarchic privileges and aids in paying for the abundance and opulence of the rich peoples. In these circumstances the struggle for development necessarily takes on a nationalistic character as a conflict for the transfer of burdens. The rich peoples, in the defense of their national interests, struggle to retain the international system of exchange as one of the basic mechanisms of their prosperity. The poor peoples, in defense of their national interests, seek to escape the spoliation of that other system in order to construct a prosperous national economy out of their very poverty. In this fight for economic and social emancipation the enemy is both outside—represented by the imperialistic nations—and inside the native dominant classes. Together they operate to maintain and tighten the external bonds and to preserve and enhance their internal privileges.

Historicocultural Configurations and Development

The obstacles to reaching an organic integration in modern industrial civilization that will permit attainment of development vary, too, in accordance with the type of historicocultural configuration in which each people is inserted. The natural difficulties of the industrialization process are enhanced by various resistances, tending to make it traumatic in the case of the Witness Peoples and to set up special difficulties in the case of the New Peoples, but to facilitate its course in a certain measure in the case of the Transplanted Peoples.

We have seen how the Witness Peoples of the Americas had their civilizations paralyzed in the course of their natural evolution, to be converted into external proletariats of Spain. The mechanisms of spoliation of these peoples, besides the conquistadors' robbery of accumulated treasures and the patronate's appropriation of the fruits of their labors for centuries, included all kinds of rapacious acts by means of which the patriciate, composed of civilian, military, and ecclesiastical agents of the colonial power, collected all they could in order to return rich to their own land. This patrician bureaucracy and this patronate, which replaced the former autochthonous seignioral caste, differed from it essentially in their alienation from the society in which they were placed and by the basic motivation of their activities—spoliation.

Emerging to independence three centuries after the conquest, the Witness Peoples of the Americas were infinitely poorer than before, and had within them so great a mass of cultural elements taken from the conqueror that they were compelled to continue the process, because only by completing their Europeanization could they achieve a certain homogeneity as a national ethnos. To the developmental problems, through integration into the capitalistic system and into industrial civilization, were added, for them, the tasks of ethnic absorption of huge socially and culturally marginalized masses.

The native dominant caste, which led these peoples to independence, fundamentally desired to substitute themselves for the mother country's agents of domination. Once in command of the new national societies, that caste sought by every possible means to accelerate the process of Europeanization, but, simultaneously, it tried to direct the processes of modernization and development under the aegis of its own interests. This constriction factor came to operate from that time on as the basic conditioner of the process of social renovation and as its deformer.

A partial break with this conspiracy was accomplished by the Mexicans by means of a long and bloody revolution (1910–1919) that enabled them to carry out their agrarian reform and initiate an autonomous industrialization. A subsequent gelling of the revolutionary process, however, came to limit these possibilities, placing Mexico in an unfavorable position in the international economic system, a position only able to set slow rates of progress and postpone to some unforeseeable future the full economic and social development of the nation, as well as the maturation of conditions for its people's self-expression.

The Bolivian Revolution, which in its first stages seemed to represent a definitive break with the stagnation to which the other Andean altiplano peoples had been condemned since the conquest, suffered a still more violent regression than the Mexican. Yesterday Bolivia seemed to have a most promising prospect of following in Mexico's steps, only to fall—if she is successful in confronting the even greater obstacles set before her—into a yet more restricted modernizing nationalist structure and, in this way, into a rhythm of retarded development, without any foreseeable possibilities of overtaking the fully matured nations. Today not even that prospect is left to her, because she has plunged into a regression from which only another revolution can save her.

The other Witness Peoples that have suffered a lesser impact than the American ones from European expansion have been able to preserve their ethnic profiles and even continue in the process of macroethnic expansion, such as Dravidian India and Moslem. Nevertheless, they have all had to face the imperative of modernization. Despite its being reflexive, modernization has profoundly altered their ways of life, and it had to have a sequel, after formal independence, as an exigency of sociocultural evolution. It has changed character, however. Instead of operating to Westernize—as occurred under conditions of colonial domination—modernization is more likely to eliminate its European cultural contents. Even so, it is homogenizing because, by diffusing the same basic technological procedures, on the structural and the institutional planes it provokes responses parallel to those experienced by Europe. This uniformity was for a long time regarded by those who confuse industrial civilization with Occidental culture as a compulsory Europeanization. Today, it can be interpreted as referring to the human imperatives, not to the ethnic, of any people or combination of peoples. In the past it was incidentally European because Europe had accidentally been first in the two technological revolutions, the Mercantile and the Industrial, which would have taken place necessarily in some other area if they had not done so there. And they would have conformed civilizations with the same essential characteristics because these correspond to intrinsic peculiarities of natural phenomena, such as the energy power of steam, coal, and oil, for example. It is these natural-physical peculiarities that make industrial civilization essentially uniform, whatever the people involved. Many of the structural consequences of industrial economy are also uniform—for example, the rise of a proletariat—and, moreover, some ideological repercussions of this development—for example, the secularization of culture.

The fact that these two revolutions originated in Europe gave that region not only four centuries of domination over the world but also the opportunity to color the new civilization with the values of its traditions, so impregnating the machine, the motor, or the factory with them that these material things came to be regarded as intrinsically Western and Christian.

The Witness Peoples who achieved development by processes of evolutionary acceleration while preserving their autonomy and their ethnic image—like the Japanese, and now the Chinese—are offered the rise to a new stage of human evolution that will permit them to experience the universal homogenizing consequences of industrial civilization, but with the capacity to eradicate from it the spurious contents that qualified it as Western European and made it operate ideologically as an alienating force.

The effects of the Industrial Revolution on the New Peoples differ from those experienced by the Witness Peoples only because in them cultural amalgamation had been completed through the compulsory deculturation of the formative ethnos. The role of native leaderships was the same, however. In both cases the elite called to direct the process of economic and social renovation after independence was configured as a patriciate that used power to establish institutional structures vigorously resistant to any changes that could affect patronal interests, and in this way open to their peoples some prospects of development and integration into modern industrial civilization.

The New Peoples and the Witness Peoples of the Americas stand out as trading colony societies, founded and remolded by acts of will of the colonizing nucleus and intentionally ordered, in all their ways of being, to serve exogenous interests and objectives. As such, they experienced a foreign domination more strongly installed and more lasting than any other area in the world. With deliberate intent it was possible to reinstall in them the Greco-Roman type of slavery, transferring to the plantations and the mines of the New Peoples areas more than 50 million Black slaves during the 300 years of slavery and using up nearly seventy million indigenes of the Witness Peoples. In both, the economic systems were never organized to create and re-create the conditions of survival and reproduction of their populations, but to produce, with the attrition of these, what they did not consume in order to supply alien needs and enrich local oligarchies. In them the colonial power installed itself in the most despotic form, never recognizing any individual rights whatever that might perchance oppose the domination. In them the oligarchic and patrician alienation was so great, in relation to the national ethnos, that the New People leaderships even proposed to replace their own population in systematic programs of racial whitening, as was attempted in Brazil and Venezuela, and as was in fact done in Argentina and Uruguay, which in this way were transfigured into Transplanted Peoples. In them, finally, democratic self-government institutions were never established, but shams destined to disguise the oligarchic-patrician domination. Nor were any mechanisms of popular participation in government ever admitted, and the social distances between free men and slaves were similar to those between men and animals, with enormous inequalities of relations between rich and poor.

Operating on that despotic, slavocratic, latifundian, and export economy, the transforming forces of the Industrial Revolution found much greater resistance to the installation of a modern economy and to a new order that assured opportunities for popular participation in the benefits of progress. In these circumstances the antagonisms that in Europe—and in the societies of European type transplanted to new spaces—only limited the potentials of industrial civilization, subjecting it to a class order or retarding its installation, here succeeded in deforming the whole process. Each industrial nucleus emerges in these areas like an enclave inslanded in the middle of a prevailing archaic economy that only permits it to expand when it does not clash with the interests invested in the latifundium and in the export economy. All political power being monopolized by the import-export sectors, which aspire only to an integration more lucrative for themselves in the world system, no modern entrepreneurial corps arises in opposition to the oligarchy. This very caste turns into an industrial entrepreneurial caste and associates itself with the modernizing undertakings sponsored by the great international corporations.

In this fashion the transition from the agromercantile economy to the industrial, difficult enough in itself, has been led to a state of trauma: underdevelopment, that is, to social dystrophy characterized by the contradiction between the potentials for abundance made possible by industrial technology and the misery provoked by its conditioning to an oligarchic social order. Its most visible syndromes are the explosive increase in population and the mass move of rural people to the cities, simultaneously with a drastic reduction of accessibility to means of work and survival, which engenders increasing marginal masses doomed to the greatest want.

Transferring to the controlling centers the opportunities for industrialization and the operational profits furnished by the mechanization of the productive system, what remains implanted in these countries is an accelerated process of socioeconomic marginalization that touches larger and larger strata of the population, with a gulf widening between a small portion of privileged and the nation.

The result is a hardening of the social order and of the political system, destined to guarantee to the native dominant class the exercise of power and the benefits of progress, as a junior partner in the imperialistic spoliation that absorbs the bulk of the national work product. The result is also the constitution of a mass of marginalized humans who concentrate in the fringes of the cities and the metropolises, uniformized culturally by the simplicity of their way of life and tending to unite some day for their common destiny, as those who will have an opportunity to integrate the occupational system and to participate in the nation's social and political life only through eradication of the existing order. Europe experienced a compulsion of the same nature during the second half of the nineteenth century when she went through a corresponding stage in the industrialization process. She was able to face it only by exporting as colonists and killing in wars nearly 100 million Europeans. The Latin American dominant classes have neither of these expedients at hand, nor the possibility of integrating these masses in the national life. The popular masses are the counterparts of the dominant classes' wealth, the opponent called by history to sweep them from the social and political panorama of their countries.

The industrialization of the New Peoples and the Witness Peoples, carried out under these conditions of domestic constriction and foreign spoliation, has been deformed and incapable of generating the renovating effects that it has brought about in other contexts (1) because it was done reflexively, by the installation of modernizing mechanisms destined to activate their role as producers of raw materials; (2) because it became principally substitutive for the former imports, produced locally by the branch factories of the great corporations; (3) because its development was strangled by various limiting procedures (These latter include foreign ownership of the majority of the industrial plants, which transforms them into mechanisms for capturing funds, the predominant nature of such industrialization, namely, industries of consumption that multiply the supply of luxury goods, draining off considerable portions of the national income for superfluous expenditures; its incapacity to assure autonomy to the process of national development precisely because it lacked key industries and those producing machinery.); (4) because the factories were operated as imported goods, fruits of technological development taking place elsewhere, on which they have always remained dependent.

Another effect of the pseudoindustrialization thus established was the substitution of a managerial class for foreign interests, more interested in the international fate of capitalism than in national development, for the national entrepreneurial corps born of industrial capitalism wherever it matured autonomously, and, further, the suppression of conditions for the rise of a national corps of scientists and technologists capable of mastering modern knowledge, owing to the transfer of their functions to the research departments of the home offices of the foreign corporations.

The difference between the effects of introducing industrial technology on those two categories of peoples and the effects on the Transplanted Peoples expresses, essentially, the structural flexibility of the latter compared to the rigidity of the former, with respect to the constricting role of their oligarchies. The United States, Canada, Australia, and New Zealand, instituted as nations by the transplanting of marginalized populations from Europe to uninhabited or sparsely populated areas, were able to structure their societies without confronting the barriers of patrician-oligarchic obstruction, in accord with the world view they possessed as populations originating in countries where industrialization was under way. They benefited, initially, from their ties with England, which, on the one hand, assured them easier mastery of the sources of modern technological knowledge and, on the other, influence of a more democratic political tradition, which permitted a certain degree of popular participation in the social order. This participation laid the bases for the policy of expropriation and distribution of the broad lands belonging to the enemy after the war of independence of the United States, and later the Homestead Acts, which opened the west to millions of farmers.

An important part in the configuration of the United States was also played by the circumstance that, as Protestant peoples, the colonists sought to teach the whole population to read, in order that everyone might read the Bible, a thing that did not happen in the Catholic countries. This fact is probably as important as the Weberian parallel of the capitalistic spirit and the Protestant Ethic (Max Weber, 1948). In fact, learning to read trained broad sectors of the U.S. population [1] to share in political life and permitted fulfilling one of the basic prerequisites for training the labor force of an industrial civilization—which is not formed by oral tradition but by written transmission of knowledge. One episode depicts the importance of this factor: the printing of 150,000 copies of the classic libertarian book by Thomas Paine in the two months following its first edition played an important part in mobilizing the people for the struggle for in-

---

[1] In 1850 the United States had a literacy of 80 per cent; at the same time France had 64.7 per cent, Russia 6 per cent and Latin America probably a similar percentage.

dependence. It would be impossible to duplicate such a fact in any other American area, because of the illiteracy prevalent throughout the population, including even the rich classes.

Comparing the progress achieved by the United States and Canada with that of Argentina and Uruguay, also Transplanted Peoples, one finds that the differences in the respective developments are explained by the existence of a latifundian oligarchy in the latter two, a caste that, even after independence, preserved land monopoly, a parasitic patronate dedicated to import and export, and a bureaucratic patriciate that limited the creative craftsmanship of the immigrants, maintaining the regime of stimulation of imports. These constrictions that strangled Argentine and Uruguayan development in comparison to that of the Transplanted nations not subject to such paralyzing controls, particularly the first of these, which made unviable in the last two decades both the Argentine and the Uruguayan economies of export of meat, wool, and grains produced on latifundia in competition with the Canadian, Australian, and New Zealand farmers.

The monopoly of land compelled the mass of European immigrants going to the River Plate countries to seek the cities after brief periods in the rural districts, because of the impossibility of becoming farmers. Thus, these societies faced a double problem: they did not have a rural middle class that could, as a market, support their industrialization, and they were undergoing a premature urbanization that reduced the demographic compression for agrarian reform and created a vast parasitic sector in their economy, represented by enormous contingents of the tertiary sector, principally bureaucrats.

The Transplanted Peoples of South America emerged from the Iberian domination only to fall under the British, exactly when the United States was winning its freedom from England, thus escaping from the colonial pact to fall into neocolonial dependence. While the Americans were devoting themselves to the expansion of their domestic frontier, by means of a small-farm agricultural economy and the installation of an autonomous industrial infrastructure already aiming at a power policy, independent Argentina and Uruguay were seeking to provide themselves with manufactured goods and struggling to enlarge their cultivated fields and cattle for export, through expansion of the latifundium and the installation of foreign enterprises. These proceeded to modernize the economy by installing rail transport, electric plants, and a high technology industry.

The developments, therefore, are opposite. In the first case we have a project for creation of an autarchic economy through the diffusion of small rural property, which permitted creating a powerful market on which later industrial development was to be based. In the second case we have the maintenance of traditional complementary functions of the economy inherited from the colonial regime and the acceptance of new external dependence, growing more and more imperative.

The archaic content of the south of the United States, which rose in rebellion against the industrializing, autonomist, democratic orientation of the north, exemplifies the role of oligarchic constriction of the plantation-slavistic economy and demonstrates how far this factor could affect the development of the countries where it prevailed in the colonial period and where it survives until today. Beaten and subdued by the Civil War, the south worsened its own backwardness in comparison with the north and the west, which progressed along new paths. Even in defeat, however, it persisted for decades as a retarded dead weight on American society. Unconquered even yet in all Latin America (except Cuba), this plantation-latifundian export economy constitutes the fundamental formative principle of the respective national societies and the basic cause of the backwardness of the whole southern continent.

World Balance of Poverty and Wealth

Recapitulating the march of the civilizational process set in motion by the Industrial Revolution over the different sociocultural contexts of the world, the following models of industrial development can be distinguished:

1. Early Capitalistic Industrial Development. Implanted originally by England, pioneer in the utilization of high energy technology and in the structural transformation corresponding to it. France followed, and later the United States. In all these cases the economic and social development occurred more or less spontaneously, in structures open to international commerce by the combination of domestic progress with exploitation of peripheral economies. All these nations preserved and refined, domestically, liberal institutions that permitted their metropolitan populations to exercise a certain degree of participation in political life. Simultaneously, however, they contributed in all ways to preventing these same conditions from maturing in their areas of political or economic domination or in the potentially competitive nations that had been held back in their industrialization.

2. Late Capitalistic Industrial Development. This is the case of Germany, Japan, and Italy, which progressed by means of autocratic regimes that structured their economies autarchically in order to escape the negative compulsions of the world market. They all slipped later into totalitar-

ian forms of government and imperialistic expansionism, in the effort to accomplish a redivision of colonial areas that would benefit them. This expansionism could be checked only through two world wars.

3. Recent Capitalistic Industrial Development. In this category fall two modalities of politicoeconomic ordination: the evolutionary-socialistic pattern of the Scandinavian peoples and the liberal-capitalistic pattern of some transplanted peoples, such as Canada and Australia. New Zealand and Israel seem to be entering this category. Argentina and Uruguay failed in their attempt to achieve it. South Africa and Rhodesia are trying to develop in the same way. However, both these last have populations divided into three immiscible castes: the oppressive white minority; the stratum associated with it, composed of crossbreeds formed in the first centuries of occupation and with Asiatic contingents added later; and the great autochthonous Black mass of the former owners of the land. This composition makes them today mere trading colonies encysted in Africa, too unviable as nations to be able to achieve stability.

4. Socialistic Industrial Development. This is represented by the U.S.S.R. and the People's Republics of Eastern Europe, China, North Vietnam, North Korea, and Cuba, the last-named inaugurating the new formation in the Americas. Even though emerging less than half a century ago, they now represent 1 billion persons and cover enormous territorial areas. The power of this model to spread is not based on imperialistic expansion, but on superior forms of association that, though affected by power politics, offer more favorable conditions of international exchange. It occasions the most intense rates of economic, social, and cultural progress known today. For this reason it represents the most direct way of inducing a process of evolutionary acceleration in underdeveloped societies with rigid social structures and large populations.

In opposition to these models of industrial development we find all the other peoples of the world in several patterns of stagnation and traumatization. Among them the European nations marginalized from the process of industrialization, such as Spain and Portugal, stand out. These are survivors of the salvationistic mercantile empires, which, not succeeding in rising to industrial capitalism and experiencing the structural transformations pertaining to it, froze as rigid structures ruled by oligarchic castes and bureaucratic patriciates, in the end being reduced to areas of neocolonial exploitation. Both were convulsed by revolutionary movements that, erupting unfavorably, were crushed. Decades of oppression followed, with police states instituted as the oppressive arms of the most retrograde castes over their peoples. Greece also ranks among the proletarian nations as a result of centuries of foreign domination during which her culture patterns were debased, and as a result of her archaic agrarian structure, comparable only to that of the other underdeveloped peoples of Europe.

The second category of peoples retarded in history is composed of the extra-European populations that, having paid most of the price of alien industrialization as areas for plundering and as external proletariats, have been relegated to backwardness and want. The principal obstacle to their progress is the poverty to which they have been reduced by the transfer of the wealth accumulated for generations, and by the centuries-long drainage —which still goes on—of the products of the national work, through their insertion by way of historical incorporation into the world economic system as producers of tropical goods and raw materials. Another obstacle lies in the conditions of cultural backwardness and stagnation to which they have been led by the oligarchic and native patrician castes that made themselves, first, agents of colonial exploitation and, later, associates of imperialistic spoliation, operating in both cases to impede the development of their peoples.

Such are the underdeveloped peoples that can be classified in three blocs according to the types of sociocultural problems facing them in their struggle for development.

1. *Emerging Peoples*. These are the new nations of tropical Africa emerging from tribal to national status, in a situation of backwardness even greater than that faced by the Latin American nations on becoming independent during the first quarter of the past century. They have, however, possibilities of a more accelerated and less dependent development, thanks to the world situation, divided by the opposition between the socialist and the capitalist camps. Some of these peoples are still under colonial domination, open or disguised, by Portuguese, Belgians, English, French, and Americans. The most developed economies in this bloc are mere foreign enclaves implanted as cysts in the nascent national societies, such as the mining enterprises in the Congo, in Southern Rhodesia, Nigeria, Katanga, and the Cameroons; the cultivation of tropical export foodstuffs in Liberia, Ghana, Nigeria, Guinea, Somaliland, Kenya, the Sudan and Tanzania, Angola and Mozambique. Also in Asia, especially in the Malayan archipelago, Indonesia, and the Philippines there are various populations enduring equivalent systems of exploitation, some of which are still under colonial subjection.

2. *Witness Peoples*. These are the modern representatives of old civilizations, such as the Moslem, the East Indian, Korean, Indochinese, Aztec, and Inca, which suffered the traumatic impact of European expansion from which they are beginning to recover now, starting from the most precarious conditions of impoverishment. In all the group only Japan and

China have succeeded in modern industrial development, the former much more mature, but the second with economically much greater potential for consolidation and expansion.

The Mexican Revolution of 1910, the action of the Cárdenas administration, and the 1952 Bolivian Revolution have gained more favorable conditions for a developmental breakthrough. On the other hand, even in the first case it is going on at a rate too slow for it to be possible to admit that it may some day overtake the fully developed nations along this path.

The Moslem countries follow, mobilized for their emancipation by broad modernizing movements that gained power through nationalistic and religious military coalitions (Turkey, Egypt, Syria, and Algeria). Some of them are polarized by the Egyptian opposition to Israel to a pan-Arabism that strongly motivates industrialization and the liquidation of the archaic agrarian system. Others incline toward an effort of national reconstruction on the socialist model; these are led by Algeria. A third group is yoked to mercantile-colonial regimes of the most backward type, servile to the imperialistic interests connected with oil exploitation (Arabia, Iran, Iraq).

Burma, Pakistan, and Afghanistan are struggling, together with India, to break with underdevelopment by maintaining a balance between the socialist and the capitalist orbits, applying for aid for both. Indonesia, Cambodia, Laos, South Vietnam, and South Korea seem more and more polarized between the new front of socializing influence, emerging in the Orient with the Chinese Revolution, and the U.S. power in the Pacific. Prohibited from opting between the capitalistic and the socialistic orders, these nations are experiencing profound traumas.

3. *New Peoples.* All located in Latin America, they fall into three large, different blocs. First, the 100 million Chileans, Brazilians, and Paraguayans who, taken together, form the most populous nucleus, the first two with an advanced and diversified industrialization that assures them certain conditions of independent development. Second, the peoples of New Granada, an area including Colombia, Venezuela, and the Guianas, with economies deeply deformed by the intervention of the great American monopolistic corporations and by the hegemony of the old dominant classes (of oligarchic-patronal, parasitic-patronal, and bureaucratic-patrician composition), all hand in glove to perpetuate backwardness and thus safeguard their minority interests. All these countries have the basic problem of emancipation from this dual domination in order to attain development. Third, the 23 million Antilleans, also polarized between two models of economic and social order: the Cuban socialistic and the U.S. imperialistic; but they are prohibited by the latter's veto from considering which road best fits their peoples.

We believe we have demonstrated that the typology of the historicocultural configurations, which proved its instrumentality in characterizing
the extra-European peoples as national ethnic entities and as racial complexes, can aid also in the understanding of the causes of the uneven development of the American nations.

Considering the peoples of each bloc as a whole with respect to the degree of development attained, it can be observed that they present
uniformities as well as significant discrepancies. Despite cultural-ethnic
similarities, they contrast flagrantly through economic dephasings that
make some of them modern because they are incorporated into the civilizational process of their time and make others archaic, underdeveloped
peoples because they were traumatized in that process. On the other hand,
certain highly significant uniformities are observable. So it is that among
the Witness Peoples only the Japanese attained full industrial development, and the Chinese, in our time, are on the way to the same achievement. Among the Transplanted Peoples a much greater number—the
United States, Canada, Australia, New Zealand, and Israel—early attained
development. Among the New Peoples not one has yet gained that level.
To what point can their differences explain these contradictory perfor-
mances?

It seems obvious that the Transplanted Peoples had advantages inherent
in their type of formation for integration into modern industrial civilization, whereas the peoples in the other categories had to face greater obstacles in their struggle for development. These obstacles derive principally
from the mode of social stratification that resulted from the form of implantation of each. This was more flexible and egalitarian in the case of
the Transplanted Peoples, more rigidly hierarchical in the others, who,
from the time of their emergence, have had the majority of their populations condemned to a cultural or social marginality that prevented their integration into modern life styles. This marginality, as has been pointed
out, takes on an especially cultural character in the case of the Witness
Peoples struggling with problems of incorporation of the most archaic contingents, nearly always monolingual and clinging to customs and values of
the old cultures. In the New Peoples it is principally social in nature, inasmuch as they result from a mercantile undertaking that, by transporting
multitudes of Africans to slavery, or by detribalizing indigenous populations for the same purpose, homogenized them through deculturation but
configuring them as subaltern strata reduced to the lowest levels of
wretchedness. To develop, some must rise from their indigenous status,
clearly differentiated from the Ladino, and others from the depths of their
penury as ex-slaves, both confronting local patronates and patriciates de-

graded by the centuries-long exercise of the slavistic yoke and bound to the foreign interests that have combined in the exploitation of misery.

To overcome these defects has until now been an insuperable challenge to the New Peoples and much more difficult for the Witness Peoples than for the Transplanted Peoples. For the first two it results in an enormous effort at reorganizing the whole society that can only be conducted intentionally, contrary to what occurred among the Transplanted Peoples where it could be done more spontaneously. To accomplish this reordering required so much effort at self-improvement that no American people— except Mexico, with her 1910 revolution, Bolivia with her 1952 uprising, and recently Cuba—has been able to face it successfully. The fundamental difficulty lies in the nature of the fabric of patrician-patronal interests directing the ordering of these highly inegalitarian societies, originally founded on the plantation system and on slavery, and lately modernized as neocolonial formations. The confrontation and overcoming of this retrograde framework cannot be done through any intensification of its reflexive modernization, because that would perpetuate the backwardness. It can be attained only through a prior restructuration of society through a social revolution capable of eradicating the existing power structure and in that fashion setting free the long-contained energies of its peoples.

Once the social order is opened and remade, these underdeveloped peoples will be able to accelerate their rate of progress to attain, in a foreseeable period, the degree of development already achieved by the advanced peoples. Paradoxically, this acceleration is at once more simple and much more complex than the developmental problems facing the peoples who have already reached this stage. More simple, because the transmutations of the productive system have long since been worked out in the developed societies through industrialization. On the other hand, it is much more complex, because a foreign and local conspiracy of vested interests in the old system opposes the indispensable prior renovation of the social structure, fearful of the damages that will be caused the centric peoples by reordering the economy of the peripheral peoples, and the local dominant classes by the loss of their privileges. Thus the basic prerequisites for an evolutionary acceleration among the underdeveloped peoples are an internal social revolution and a decisive confrontation in the international orbit, because only thus will they be able to withdraw the instruments of power from the hands of the internal dominant classes and their international associates, equally committed to their backwardness because they know how to make it profitable for themselves.

Bibliography[*]

INTRODUCTION: THEORIES OF BACKWARDNESS AND PROGRESS

Adams, Richard N. 1960. *Social Change in Latin America Today: Its Implications for United States Policy.* New York: Harper & Bros.
———, and D. B. Heath (eds.). 1965. *Contemporary Cultures and Societies of Latin America.* New York: Random House.
Alberdi, J. B. 1943. *Base y Puntos de Partida para la Organización de la República Argentina.* Buenos Aires.
Althusser, Louis. 1967. *La Revolución Teórica de Marx.* Mexico City.
Andreski, Stanislaw. 1966. *Parasitism and Subversion: the Case of Latin America.* New York: Pantheon Books.
Arguedas, Alcides. 1937. *Un Pueblo Enfermo: contribución a la psicología de los pueblos hispanoamericanos.* Santiago, Chile.
Arismendi, Rodney. 1962. *Problemas de una Revolucíon Continental.* Montevideo.

[*] Where possible the bibliographical entry is given in the language of its original publication. Otherwise the English translation is listed. In cases where no comparable English translation of the original exists, the edition listed is the one used by the author. (Ed.)

Balandier, G. 1955. *Sociologie Actuelle de l'Afrique Noire*. Paris.

Baran, Paul A. 1964. *A Economia Política do Desenvolvimento*. Rio de Janeiro.

————, and P. M. Sweezy. 1965. *Monopoly Capital*. New York: Monthly Review Press.

Beals, Ralph L. 1946. *Cheram: a Sierra Tarascan Village*. Washington, D.C.

Boeke, J. H. 1953. *Economics and Economic Policy of Dual Societies*. New York: Institute of Pacific Relations.

Bomfim, Manuel. 1929. *O Brasil na América*. Rio de Janeiro.

————. 1931. *O Brasil na História*. Rio de Janeiro.

Bourricaud, François. 1967. *Poder y Sociedad en el Perú Contemporáneo*. Buenos Aires.

Bramson, Leon D. 1961. *The Political Context of Sociology*. Princeton, N.J.: Princeton University Press.

Bunge, Carlos O. 1903. *Nuestra América*. Barcelona.

Cardoso, Fernando Henrique. 1964. *O Empresário Industrial e o Desenvolvimento Econômico no Brasil*. São Paulo.

Casanova, Pablo González. 1965. *La Democracia en México*. Mexico.

Chesnokov, D. I. 1967. *Materialismo Histórico*. Montevideo.

Childe, V. Gordon. 1939. *Man Makes Himself*. London: Oxford University Press.

————. 1964. *Social Evolution*. New York: Meridian Books.

Costa Pinto, L. A. 1965. *Sociologia e Desenvolvimento*. Rio de Janeiro.

————. 1963. *La Sociologia del Cambio y el Cambio de la Sociología*. Buenos Aires.

Cunha, Euclides da. 1911. *Os Sertões. Campanha de Canudos*. Rio de Janeiro.

Dahrendorf, Ralf. 1966. *Sociedad y Sociología*. Madrid.

Echevarría, J. Medina. 1964. *Consideraciones Sociológicas sobre el Desarrollo de América Latina*. Buenos Aires.

Eisenstadt, S. N. 1966. *Modernization: Protest and Change*. Englewood Cliffs, N.J.: Prentice-Hall.

Estrada, E. Martinez. 1933. *Radiografía de la Pampa*. Buenos Aires.

Fernandes, Florestan. 1963. *A Sociologia numa Era de Revolução Social*. São Paulo.

Foster, George M. 1960. *Culture and Conquest*. New York: Quadrangle Books.

————. 1962. *Traditional Cultures and the Impact of Technological Change*. New York: Harper & Bros.

Frank, Andrew G. 1966. *Capitalism and Underdevelopment in Latin America. The Cases of Chile and Brazil*. New York: Monthly Review Press.

————. 1967. "Sociology of Development and Underdevelopment of Sociology," *Catalyst*, No. 3 (Summer). University of Buffalo Press.

Freyre, Gilberto. 1954. *Casa Grande e Senzala*. 2 vols. Rio de Janeiro.

Furtado, Celso. 1961. *Desarrolo y Subdesarrollo*. Buenos Aires.

Germani, Gino. 1965. *Política y Sociedad en una Epoca en Transición*. Buenos Aires.

Gerschenkron, Alexander, 1962. *Economic Backwardness in Historical Perspective*. Cambridge: Harvard University Press.

Gillin, John. 1955. "Ethos Components in Modern Latin-America," in *American Anthropologist*, Vol. 57.

Gramsci, Antonio. 1958. *El Materialismo Histórico y la Filosofía de Benedetto Croce*. Buenos Aires.

————. 1960. *Los Intelectuales y la Organización de la Cultura*. Buenos Aires.

Guerreiro Ramos, Alberto. 1959. *La Reducción Sociológica*. Mexico.

Guilherme, Wanderley. 1963. *Introdução ao Estudo das Condições Sociais no Brasil*. Rio de Janeiro.

Heinz, Peter. 1965. *Sociología*. Buenos Aires.

Hirschman, Albert O. (ed.). 1961. *Latin American Issues: Essays and Comments*. New York: Twentieth Century Fund.

Holanda, Sérgio Buarque de. 1956. *Raízes do Brasil*. Rio de Janeiro.

Horowitz, Irving Louis. 1966. *Three Worlds of Development*. New York: Oxford University Press.

Hoselitz, Bert F. 1959. *Sociological Aspects of Economic Growth*. Glencoe, Ill.: The Free Press.

Ianni, Octavio. 1965. *Estado e Capitalismo*. Rio de Janeiro. 1966. *Raças e Classes Sociais no Brasil*. Rio de Janeiro.

Ingenieros, José. 1913. *Sociología Argentina*. Buenos Aires.

Jaguaribe, Hélio. 1962. *Desenvolvimento Econômico e Desenvolvimento Político*. Rio de Janeiro.

Johnson, John J. 1958. *Political Change in Latin America*. Stanford, Calif.: Stanford University Press.

———. 1964. *The Military and Society in Latin America*. Stanford, Calif.: Stanford University Press.

——— (ed). 1964a. *Continuity and Change in Latin America*. Stanford, Calif.: Stanford University Press.

Kohn, Hans. 1961. *The Idea of Nationalism*. New York: The Macmillan Co.

Konstantinov, F. V., et al. 1960. *El Materialismo Histórico*. Mexico.

Kosik, Karel. 1965. *Dialettica del Concreto*. Milan.

Kuusisen, O. V., et al. 1964. *Manual de Marxismo-Leninismo*. Buenos Aires.

Labriola, Antonio. 1947. *Del Materialismo Storico*. Bari, Italy.

Lambert, Jacques. 1958. *Os Dois Brasis*. Rio de Janeiro.

Lange, Oskar. 1966. *On Political Economy*. Vol. I, Elmsford, N.Y.: Pergamon Press.

Lebret, Louis-Joseph. 1961. *Manifiesto por una Civilización Solidaria*. Lima, Peru.

Lenin, V. I. 1932. *The State and Revolution*. New York: International Publishers.

———. 1965. *Imperialism, the Highest Stage of Capitalism*. New York: China Publications.

Lerner, Daniel. 1958. *The Passing of Traditional Society*. Glencoe, Ill.: The Free Press.

Leroi-Gourhan, André. 1945. *Milieu et Technique*. Paris.

Lévi-Strauss, Claude. 1963. *Structural Anthropology*. New York: Basic Books.

Levy, Marion J. 1952. *The Structure of Society*. Princeton, N.J.: Princeton University Press.

Lewis, Oscar. 1961. *The Children of Sanchez*. New York: Random House.

———. 1966. *La Vida, a Puerto Rican Family in the Culture of Poverty*. New York: Random House.

Lieuwen, Edwin A. 1961. *Arms and Politics in Latin America*. London: Oxford University Press.

Lippitt, Ronald, et al. 1958. *The Dynamics of Planned Change*. New York: Harcourt, Brace.

Lipset, Seymour M. 1959. *Political Man—The Social Bases of Politics*. New York: Doubleday & Co.

Luckacs, George. 1960. *Histoire et Conscience de Classe*. Paris.

Lundberg, Ferdinand. 1960. *America's Sixty Families*. New York: Citadel Press.

Luxemburg, Rosa. 1964. *The Accumulation of Capital*. New York: Monthly Review Press.

Lynd, Robert. 1964. *Knowledge for What?* New York: Grove Press.

MacIver, Robert M. 1942. *Social Causation*. Boston: Ginn & Co.

Makarov, A., et al. 1965. *Manual de Materialismo Histórico*. Buenos Aires.

Malinowski, Bronislaw. 1945. *The Dynamics of Culture Change*. New Haven, Conn.: Yale University Press.

Mannheim, Karl. 1955. *Ideology and Utopia*. New York: Harcourt, Brace.

Marcuse, Herbert. 1958. *Soviet Marxism: A Critical Analysis*. New York: Columbia University Press.

————. 1964. *One Dimensional Man*. Boston: Beacon Press.

Marshal, Juan F. 1967. *Cambio Social en América Latina*. Buenos Aires.

Marx, Karl. 1956. *El Capital*. 5 vols. Buenos Aires.

————. 1958. *La Sagrada Familia y otros escritos*. Mexico.

————. *El Modo de Producción Asiático*. Cordoba.

———— and Frederich Engels. 1958. *La Ideología Alemana*. Montevideo.

Mead, Margaret (ed.). 1955. *Cultural Patterns and Technical Change*. New York: New American Library.

Merton, Robert K. 1957. *Social Theory and Social Structure*. Glencoe, Ill.: The Free Press.

Mills, C. Wright. 1956. *The Power Elite*. New York: Oxford University Press.

————. 1959. *The Sociological Imagination*. New York: Oxford University Press.

————. 1963. *The Marxists*. New York: Dell Publishing.

Moore, Barrington, Jr. 1958. *Political Power and Social Theory*. Cambridge: Harvard University Press.

Murdock, George Peter. 1945. "The Common Denominator of Cultures" in Ralph Linton (ed.), *The Science of Man in the World Crisis*. New York: Columbia University Press.

Murena, H. A. 1964. *El Pecado Original de América*. Buenos Aires.

Myrdal, Gunnar. 1944. *An American Dilemma*. New York: Harper & Bros.

————. 1954. *The Political Element in the Development of Economic Theory*. Cambridge: Harvard University Press.

————. 1957. *Economic Theory and Underdevelopment Regions*. London: Gerald Duckworth.

Parsons, Talcott. 1951. *The Social System*. Glencoe, Ill.: The Free Press.

Paz, Octavio. 1950. *El Laberinto de la Soledad*. Mexico.

Pinto, Anibal. 1965. *Chile, una Economía Difícil*. Santiago, Chile.

Prado, Caio, Jr. 1942. *Formacão do Brasil Contemporaneo. Colonia*. São Paulo.

————. 1945. *Historia Econômica do Brasil*. São Paulo.

————. 1966. *A Revolução Brasileira*. São Paulo.

Puiggros, Rodolfo. 1945. *Historia Económica del Rio de la Plata*. Buenos Aires.

Radcliffe-Brown, A. R. 1931. *The Present Position of Anthropological Studies*. London.

Ramos, Samuel. 1951. *El Perfil de Hombre y la Cultura en México*. Buenos Aires.

Redfield, Robert. 1941. *The Folk Culture of Yucatán*. Chicago: University of Chicago Press.

————. 1953. *The Primitive World and Its Transfigurations*. Ithaca, N.Y.: Cornell University Press.

————. 1956. *Peasant Society and Culture: An Anthropological Approach to Civilization*. Chicago: University of Chicago Press.

Ribeiro, Darcy. 1968. *The Civilizational Process*. Translated by Betty Meggers. Washington, D.C.: Smithsonian Institute Press.

Riesman, David, et al. 1950. *The Lonely Crowd*. New Haven, Conn.: Yale University Press.

Rostow, Walt W. 1960. *The Stages of Economic Growth.* New York: Cambridge University Press.

———. 1960a. *The Process of Economic Growth.* New York: W. W. Norton.

Sapir, Edward. 1924. "Culture, Genuine and Spurious" in *American Journal of Sociology* (January).

Sarmiento, Domingo F. 1915. *Conflicto y Armonías de las Razas en América.* Buenos Aires.

Sartre, Jean Paul. 1963. *Crítica de la Razón Dialéctica.* 2 vols. Buenos Aires.

Selser, Gregorio. 1966. *Espionage en América Latina.* Buenos Aires.

Shils, Edward A. 1956. *The Torment of Secrecy.* Glencoe, Ill.: The Free Press.

Silvert, Kalman H. 1961. *Reaction and Revolution in Latin America. The Conflict Society.* New Orleans: Hauser Press.

———. 1963. *Expectant Peoples: Nationalism and Development.* New York: Random House.

———. 1965. *Nacionalismo y Política de Desarrollo.* Buenos Aires.

Sodré, Nelson Werneck. 1944. *Formação da Sociedade Brasileira.* Rio de Janeiro.

———. 1963. *Introdução à Revolução Brasileira.* Rio de Janeiro.

Spicer, Edward H. 1952. *Human Problems in Technological Change: A Casebook.* New York: Russell Sage Foundation.

Staley, Eugene. 1961. *The Future of Underdeveloped Countries.* New York: Harper & Bros.

Stalin, Joseph. 1937. *Le Marxisme et la Question Nationale et Coloniale.* Paris.

———. 1939. *Fundamentos del Leninismo.* Mexico.

Stavenhagen, Rodolfo. 1965. "Siete Tesis Equivocadas sobre América Latina" in *Política Exterior Independente,* No. 1. Rio de Janeiro.

Stein, Maurice R. 1960. *The Eclipse of Community: An Interpretation of American Studies.* Princeton, N. J.: Princeton University Press.

Steward, Julian H. 1950. *Area Research: Theory and Practice.* New York: Social Science Research Council.

———. 1955. *The Theory of Culture Change: The Methodology of Multilinear Evolution.* Urbana, Ill.: University of Illinois Press.

Tawney, R. H. 1947. *Religion and the Rise of Capitalism.* New York: Harcourt, Brace.

Trotsky, Leon. 1957. *The History of the Russian Revolution.* Ann Arbor, Mich.: University of Michigan Press.

Veblen, Thorstein. 1954. *The Theory of the Leisure Class.* New York: New American Library.

Vianna, Oliveira. 1952. *Populações Meridionais do Brasil.* Rio de Janeiro.

Viatkin, A. (ed.). 1965. *Comprendio de Historia y Economía.* I: *LAS Formaciones Pre-Capitalistas.* II: *La Sociedad Capitalista.* Moscow.

Wagley, Charles. n.d. *A Revolução Brasileira.* Bahía.

Weber, Max. 1964. *El Sabio y la Política.* Córdoba, Argentina.

———. 1968. *Economy and Society.* Totowa, N. J.: The Bedminster Press.

White, Leslie. 1945. "History, Evolutionism and Functionalism: Three Types of Interpretation of Culture," *Southwestern Journal of Anthropology,* Vol. I.

———. 1958. *The Science of Culture: A Study of Man and Civilization.* New York: Grove Press.

———. 1959. *The Evolution of Culture.* New York: McGraw-Hill Book Co.

Wittfogel, Karl A. 1957. *Oriental Despotism.* New Haven, Conn.: Yale University Press.

Worsley, Peter. 1965. *The Third World*. Chicago: University of Chicago Press.
Yajot, O. 1965. *Qué es el Materialismo Dialéctico*. Moscow.

1. THE EUROPEAN EXPANSION

Albornoz, C. Sánchez. 1956. *España, un Enigma Histórico*. 2 vols. Buenos Aires.
————. 1956—*La España Musulmana*. 2 vols. Buenos Aires.
Altamira, Rafael. 1949. *A History of Spain*. New York: Van Nostrand.
Ardao, Arturo. 1956. *La Filosofía en el Uruguay en el Siglo XX*. Mexico.
Armillas, Pedro. 1962. *Programa de Historia de América. Período Indígena*. Mexico.
Aron, Raymond. 1962. *Dimensiones de la Conciencia Historica*. Madrid.
Balandier, Georges. 1962. "Les Mythes Politiques de Colonisation et de Descolonisation en Afrique." *Cahiers Internationaux de Sociologie*. Vol. XXIII. Paris.
————. 1965. *Ambiguous Africa*. New York: Pantheon Books.
Bates, Marston. 1952. *Where Winter Never Comes: A Study of Man and Nature in the Tropics*. New York: Charles Scribner's Sons.
Bell, Daniel. 1959. *The End of Ideology*. Glencoe, Ill.: The Free Press.
Beyhaut, Gustavo. 1963. *Europeización e Imperialismo en América Latina durante la Segunda Mitad del Siglo XIX*. Montevideo.
————. 1964. *Raíces Contemporáneas de América Latina*. Buenos Aires.
————. 1965. *Fischer Weltgeschichte. Süd und Mittelamerica*. Vol. II. Berlin. (Author used the Spanish translation, in manuscript.)
Bloch, Marc. 1939–1940. *La Societé Feodale*. 2 vols. Paris.
Caballero Calderon, E. 1944. *Suramérica, tierra del hombre*. Medellin, Colombia.
Capdequi, J. M. Ots. 1957. *El Estado Español en las Indias*. Mexico.
Carr, Edward Hallett. 1957. *The New Society*. New York: St. Martin's Press.
Carranca y Trujillo, Raúl. 1950. *Panorama Crítico de Nuestra América*. Mexico.
Caso, Antonio. 1943. *Apuntes de Cultura Patria*. Mexico.
Chaunu, Pierre. 1964. *L'Amérique et les Amériques. De la Préhistoire a nos jours*. Paris.
Childe, V. Gordon. 1954. *What Happened in History*. London: Penguin Books.
Collingwood, R. G. 1946. *The Idea of History*. London: Oxford University Press.
Corbisier, Roland. 1958. *Formação e Problema da Cultura Brasileira*. Rio de Janeiro.
Dumont, René. 1962. *L'Afrique Noire est Mal Partie*. Paris.
Eisenstadt, S. N. 1962. *The Political Systems of Empires*. Glencoe, Ill.: The Free Press.
Emerson, Rupert. 1960. *From Empire to Nation*. Cambridge, Mass.: Harvard University Press.
Fanon, Frantz. 1963. *Los Condenados de la Tierra*. Mexico.
————. 1965. *Escucha, Blanco!* Barcelona.
Foster, George M. 1960. *Culture and Conquest*. New York: Quadrangle Books.
Frank, Waldo. 1929. *The Re-discovery of America*. New York: Charles Scribner's Sons.
————. 1931. *America Hispana: A Portrait and a Prospect*. New York: Charles Scribner's Sons.

Gourou, Pierre. 1959. *Los Países Tropicales. Xalapa.* Mexico.

Hanke, Lewis. 1949. *The Spanish Struggle for Justice in the Conquest of America.* Philadelphia: University of Pennsylvania Press.

―――. 1959. *Modern Latin America, Continent in Ferment.* 2 vols. New York: Van Nostrand.

Hardoy, J. E. 1964. *Ciudades Precolombinas.* Buenos Aires.

Haring, C. H. 1947. *The Spanish Empire in America.* New York: Harcourt, Brace.

Hegel, Georg W. F. 1928. *Filosofía de la Historia Universal. Buenos Aires.*

Holanda, Sergio Buarque de. 1956. *Raízes do Brasil.* Rio de Janeiro.

Hunter, Monica. 1936. *Reaction to Conquest: Effects of Contact with Europeans on the Pondo of South Africa.* Oxford: Oxford University Press.

Ingenieros, José. 1922. *Por la Unión Latino Americana.* Buenos Aires.

Jaguaribe, Hélio. 1958. *O Nacionalismo na Atualidade Brasileira.* Rio de Janeiro.

Kroeber, Alfred L. 1944. *Configurations of Culture Growth.* Berkeley and Los Angeles: University of California Press.

Lange, Oskar. 1963. *On Political Economy.* Vol. I. New York: The Macmillan Co.

―――. 1966. *La Economía en las Sociedades Modernas.* Mexico.

Lévi-Strauss, Claude. 1955. *Tristes Tropiques.* Paris.

Lewin, Boleslao. 1962. *La Inquisición en Hispanoamerica. Judíos, Protestantes y Patriotas.* Buenos Aires.

Linton, Ralph. 1955. *The Tree of Culture.* New York: Alfred A. Knopf.

Lipschutz, Alejandro. 1963. *El Problema Racial en la Conquista de América y el Mestizaje.* Santiago, Chile.

Luckacs, George. 1960. *Histoire et Conscience de Classe.* Paris.

Lumumba, Patrice. 1967. *Congo, My Country.* New York: Frederick A. Praeger.

Madariaga, Salvador de. 1959. *Presente y Porvenir de Hispanoamérica y otros ensayos.* Buenos Aires.

Mannheim, Karl. 1955. *Ideology and Utopia.* New York: Harcourt, Brace & World.

Mannoni, O. 1964. *Prospero and Caliban: A Study of the Psychology of Colonization.* New York: Frederick A. Praeger.

Manzoni, Aida Cometta. 1960. *El Indio en la Novela de América.* Buenos Aires.

Marx, Karl. 1956. *El Capital.* 5 vols. Buenos Aires.

―――. 1957. *Contribution à la critique de l'Economie Politique.* Paris.

―――. 1962. *Manuscritos Económico-Filosoficos.* Mexico.

――― and Frederich Engels. 1958. *La Ideología Alemana.* Montevideo.

Mauro, Fréderic. 1964. *L'Expansión Européenne (1600–1870).* Paris.

Mills, C. Wright. 1958. *The Causes of World War Three.* New York: Simon & Schuster.

Miranda, Fernando Márquez. 1958. *Pueblos y Culturas de América.* Buenos Aires.

Mumford, Lewis. 1944. *The Condition of Man.* New York: Harcourt, Brace.

Nehru, Jawaharlal. 1962. *Nehru on World History.* Bloomington, Ind.: Indiana University Press.

Nkrumah, Kwame. 1966. *Neo-colonialism: The Last Stage of Imperialism.* New York: International Publishers.

Northrop, F.S.C. 1946. *The Meeting of East and West: An Inquiry Concerning World Understanding.* New York: The Macmillan Co.

Oliveira Martins, J. P. 1951. *Historia de la Civilización Ibérica.* Buenos Aires.

Paz, Octavio. 1959. *El Laberinto de la Soledad.* Mexico.

Perez, Demetrio Ramos. 1947. *Historia de la Colonización Española en América.* Madrid.

Petit Muñoz, Eugenio. 1927. *Interpretaciones Esquemáticas sobre la Historia de la Conquista y la Colonización Españolas en América.* Montevideo.

Ramos, Artur. 1946. *As Culturas Negras no Novo Mundo—O Negro Brasileiro.* São Paulo.

Redeld, Robert. 1953. *The Primitive World and Its Transformations.* Ithaca, N.Y.: Cornell University Press.

Rosenblat, Angel. 1954. *La Población Indígena y el Mestizaje en América.* 2 vols. Buenos Aires.

Saco, J. A. 1932. *Historia de los repartimientos y Encomiendas.* Havana.

———. 1938. *Historia de la Esclavitud de la Raza Africana en el Nuevo Mundo y en Especial en los Países hispano-americanos.* Havana.

Sanchez, Luis Alberto. 1962. *Análisis Espectral de América Latina.* Buenos Aires.

Sartre, Jean-Paul. 1956. "Le Colonialisme est un Système" in *Les Temps Modernes.* (No. 123). Paris.

Schurz, William L. 1949. *Latin America: A Descriptive Survey.* New York: E. P. Dutton & Co.

———. 1954. *This New World: The Civilization of Latin America.* New York: E. P. Dutton & Co.

Senghor, Leopold S. 1964. *On African Socialism.* New York: Frederick A. Praeger.

Siegfried, André. 1934. *L'Amérique Latine.* Paris.

Silva, L. 1961. *Latinoamérica al rojo vivo.* Madrid.

Sombart, Werner. 1946. *El Apogeo del Capitalismo.* Mexico.

Sorokin, Pitirim A. 1957. *The Crisis of Our Age: the Social and Cultural Outlook.* New York: E. P. Dutton & Co.

Spengler, Oswald. 1932. *Man and Technics: a Contribution to a Philosophy of Life.* New York: Alfred A. Knopf.

———. 1945. *The Decline of the West.* 2 vols. New York: Alfred A. Knopf.

Steward, Julian H. 1946–50. *Handbook of South American Indians.* 7 vols. Washington, D.C.: Smithsonian Institution Press.

———. (ed.) 1955. *Theory of Culture Change: The Methodology of Multilinear Evolution.* Urbana, Ill.: University of Illinois Press.

Tawney, Richard H. 1926. *Religion and the Rise of Capitalism.* New York: Harcourt, Brace.

Tax, Sol (ed.). 1952. *Heritage of Conquest. The Ethnology of Middle America.* Glencoe, Ill.: The Free Press.

Teitelboim, Volodia. 1963. *El Amanecer del Capitalismo y la Conquista de América.* Buenos Aires.

Touré, Sékou. 1959. *La Guinée et l'Emancipation Africaine,* Paris.

Toynbee, Arnold J. 1947. *The Study of History* (Abridged edition). 2 vols Oxford: Oxford University Press.

Ureña, Pedro Henriquez. 1961. *Historia de la Cultura en la América Hispánica.* Mexico.

Vasconcellos, José. 1934. *La Cultura Hispanoamericana.* La Plata.

Vitoria, Francisco de. 1946. *Reflexiones sobre los Indios y el Derecho de Guerra.* Buenos Aires.

Vives, J. Vicens. 1957–1959. *Historia Social y Económica de España y América.* 5 vols. Barcelona.

Weber, Alfred. 1960. *Historia de la Cultura.* Mexico.

White, Leslie. 1959. *The Evolution of Culture.* New York: McGraw-Hill Book Co.

Whitehead, Alfred North. 1926. *Science and the Modern World.* Glencoe, Ill.: The Free Press.
Worcester, Donald E., and Wendell G. Schaeffer. 1956. *The Growth and Culture of Latin America.* London: Oxford University Press.
Worsley, Peter. 1965. *The Third World.* Chicago: University of Chicago Press.
Zavala, Silvio. 1944. *Ensayo sobre la Colonización Española en América.* Buenos Aires.
―――. 1947. *Filosofía de la Conquista.* Mexico.
Zea, Leopoldo. 1957. *América en la Historia.* Mexico.
Znaniecki, Florian. 1944. *Las Sociedades de Cultura Nacional y Sus Relaciones.* Mexico.
Zum Felde, Alberto. 1943. *El Problema de la Cultura Americana.* Buenos Aires.

2. CULTURAL TRANSFIGURATION

Adams, Richard N. 1956. *La Ladinización en Guatemala.* Guatemala.
Bagu, Sergio. 1949. *Economía de la Sociedad Colonial.* Buenos Aires.
―――. 1952. *Estructura Social de la Colonia.* Buenos Aires.
Balandier, Georges. 1955. *Sociologie Actuelle de L'Afrique Notre: Dynamique des Changements Sociaux en Afrique Centrale.* Paris.
―――. 1964. *Africa Ambigua.* Buenos Aires.
Ballesteros-Gaibrois, Manuel, and Julia Ulloa Suarez. 1961. *Indigenismo Americano.* Madrid.
Barradas, J. Pérez de. 1948. *Los Mestizos de América.* Madrid.
Bastide, Roger. 1960. *Sociologie des Regions Africaines au Brésil.* Paris.
――― and Florestan Fernandes (eds.). 1959. *Brancos e Negros em São Paulo.* São Paulo.
Beals, Ralph. 1951. "Urbanism, Urbanization and Acculturation." *American Anthropologist.* No. 53.
―――. 1953. "Acculturation" in A. L. Kroeber (ed), *Anthropology Today.* Chicago: University of Chicago Press.
Beltran, Gonzalo Aguirre. 1957. *El Proceso de Aculturación.* Mexico.
Benneth, Wendell C. 1953. "New World Culture History: South America" in A. L. Kroeber (ed.), *Anthropology Today.* Chicago: University of Chicago Press.
Borah, Woodrow. 1962. "Population Decline and the Social and Institutional Changes of New Spain in the Middle Decades of the Sixteenth Century." 34th session. *Internationalen Amerikanisten-kongresses.* Copenhagen.
―――. 1964. "America as Model: The Demographic Impact of European Expansion upon the Non-European World." 35th session. *Congreso Internacional de Americanistas.* Vol. III. Mexico.
Casanova, Pablo González. 1965. *La Democracia en México.* Mexico.
Cèpéde. M. F. Houtart, and L. Grond. 1967. *La Población Mundial y los Medios de Subsistencia.* Barcelona.
Childe, V. Gordon. 1939. *Man Makes Himself.* London: Oxford University Press.
―――. 1954. *What Happened in History?* Baltimore: Penguin Books.
―――. 1964. *Social Evolution.* New York: Meridian Books.
Comas, Juan. 1961. *Relaciones Inter-Raciales en América Latina.* Mexico.

Corbisier, Roland. 1958. *Formação e Problema da Cultura Brasileira*. Rio de Janeiro.

Costa Pinto, L. A. 1958. *O Negro no Rio de Janeiro*. Rio de Janeiro.

Debuyst, Frederico. 1961. *La Población en América Latina*. Brussels.

Dobyns, Henry F., and Paul Thompson. 1966. "Estimating Aboriginal American Population," *Current Anthropology*. Vol. VII, No. 4. Utrecht, Netherlands.

Fanon, Frantz, 1963. *Los Condenados de la Tierra*. Mexico.

————. 1965. *Escucha, Blanco!* Barcelona.

Fernandes, Florestan. 1964. *A Integração do Negro á sociedade de Classes*. São Paulo.

Foster, George M. 1953. "What is Folk-Culture?" *American Anthropologist*. No. 55.

————. 1960. *Culture and Conquest: America's Spanish Heritage*. New York: Quadrangle Books.

————. 1962. *Traditional Cultures and the Impact of Technological Change*. New York: Harper & Bros.

Freyre, Gilberto. 1951. *Sobrados e Mucambos*. Rio de Janeiro.

————. 1952. *Casa Grande e Senzala*. Rio de Janeiro.

Furtado, Celso. 1959. *Formação Econômica do Brasil*. Rio de Janeiro.

Gillin, John. 1947. "Modern Latin American Culture." *Social Forces*. No. 25.

————. 1949. "Mestizo America" in Helmut de Terra et al., *Tepexpan Man*. New York: Viking Fund.

————. 1955. "Ethos Components in Modern Latin American Culture." *American Anthropologist*. No. 57. Menasha.

Gourou, Pierre. 1947. *Los Paises Tropicales*. Mexico.

Guerreiro Ramos, Alberto. 1957. *Introdução Critica á Sociologia Brasileira*. Rio de Janeiro.

Guitard, Odette. 1962. *Bandung y el despertar de los Pueblos Coloniales*. Buenos Aires.

Hardy, Georges. 1933. *Geographie et Colonisation*. Paris.

Herskovits, Melville. 1941. *The Myth of the Negro Past*. New York: Harper & Bros.

Hollanda, Sérgio Buarque de. 1956. *Raizes do Brasil*. Rio de Janeiro.

————. 1957. *Caminhos e Fronteiras*. Rio de Janeiro.

Humphrey, Norman D. 1953. "Raza, Casta y Clases en Colombia." *Ciencias Sociales*. Vol. IV, No. 21. Washington, D.C.

Hunter, Monica. 1936. *Reaction to Conquest*. London: Oxford University Press.

Ianni, Octavio. 1966. *Raças e Classes Sociais no Brasil*. São Paulo.

Keesing, Felix. 1953. *Culture Change: An Analysis and Bibliography of Anthropological Sources to 1952*. Stanford, Calif.: Stanford University Press.

Kroeber, Alfred L. 1940. *Cultural and Natural Areas of Native North America*. Berkeley, Calif.: University of California Press.

————. 1944. *Configurations of Cultural Growth*. Berkeley, Calif.: University of California Press.

———— (ed.). 1953. *Anthropology Today*. Chicago: University of Chicago Press.

Latcham, Ricardo, Ernesto Montenegro and Manuel Vega. 1956. *El Criollismo*. Santiago, Chile.

Lewis, Oscar. 1951. *Life in a Mexican Village: Tepoztlán Restudied*. Urbana, Ill.: University of Illinois Press.

————. 1959. *Five Families: Mexican Case Studies in the Culture of Poverty*. New York: Basic Books.

————. 1963. "Nuevas Observaciones sobre el'Continuum Folk-Urbano y Urbanización." *Ciencias Políticas y Sociales.* Vol. IX, No. 3. Mexico.

Linton, Ralph (ed.). 1949. *Most of the World. The Peoples of Africa, Latin America, and the East Today.* New York: Columbia University Press.

————. 1955. *The Tree of Culture.* New York: Alfred A. Knopf.

Lipschutz, Alejandro. 1944. *El Indoamericanismo y el Problema Racial en las Americas.* Santiago.

Malinowski, Bronislaw. 1945. *The Dynamics of Culture Change.* New Haven, Conn.: Yale University Press.

Mariategui, José Carlos. 1963. *Siete Ensayos de Interpretación de la Realidad Peruana.* Havana.

Mintz, Sidney W. 1954. "Sobre la Cultura de Folk: Redfield y Fortes" in *Ciencias Sociales.* Vol. V, No. 26. Washington, D. C.

Myrdal, Gunnar, et al. 1944. *An American Dilemma: The Negro Problem and Modern Democracy.* New York: Harper & Bros.

Nogueira, Oracy. 1955. "Preconceito Racial de Marca e Preconceito Racial de Origem." 31st session. *Congresso Internacional de Americanistas.* Vol. I. São Paulo.

Ortiz, Fernando. 1940. *Contrapunteo Cubano del Tabaco y el Azúcar.* Havana.

Pan American Union. 1964. *Trabajos del Simposio sobre Población.* Washington, D.C.

Pierson, Donald. 1945. *Bracos e Pretos na Bahía.* São Paulo.

Ramos, Arthur. 1942. *Aculturação Negra no Brasil.* São Paulo.

————. n.d. *Guerra e Relacões Raciais.* Rio de Janeiro.

————. 1944–47. *Introducão à Antropologia Brasileira.* 2 vols. Rio de Janeiro.

Redfield, Robert. 1941. *The Folk Culture of Yucatán.* Chicago: University of Chicago Press.

————. 1953. *The Primitive World and Its Transformations.* Ithaca, N.Y.: Cornell University Press.

————.1956. *Peasant Society and Culture.* Chicago: University of Chicago Press.

————, Ralph Linton, and Melville J. Herskovits. 1936. "Memorandum on the Study of Acculturation." *American Anthropologist.* No. 38. Menasha.

Ribeiro, Darcy. 1956. "Convívio e Contaminação—Efeitos Dissociativos da Depopulaçao Provacada por Epidemias em Grupos Indígenas." *Sociologia.* Vol. XVIII, No. 1. São Paulo.

————. 1957. "Culturas e Línguas Indigenas do Brasil." *Educacão e Ciências Socialis.* Vol. II, No. 6. Rio de Janeiro.

————. 1958. "A Aculturação Indígena no Brasil." Condensation in Charles Wagley and Marvin Harris, *Minorities in the New World.* New York: Columbia University Press.

————. 1962. *A Política Indigenista Brasileira.* Rio de Janeiro.

Rosenblat, Angel. 1954. *La Población Indígena y el Mestizaje en América.* Buenos Aires.

Sapir, Edward. 1949. *Selected Writings of Edward Sapir in Language, Culture, and Personality.* Berkeley, Calif.: University of California Press.

Sauvy, Alfred. 1954–56. *Théorie Générale de la Population.* Paris.

————. 1958. *De Malthus à Mao Tse Toung.* Paris.

Service, Elman R. 1955. "Indian-European Relations in Colonial Latin-America." *American Anthropologist.* No. 57. Menasha.

Siegel, B. Y., et al. 1954. "Acculturation: An Explanatory Formulation." *American Anthropologist.* No. 56. Menasha.

Sireau, Alberto. 1966. *Teoria de la Población. Ecología Urbana y su aplicación a la Argentina.* Buenos Aires.

Stavenhagen, Rodolfo. 1963. "Classes, Colonialismo y Aculturación." *América Latina.* Vol. VI, No. 4. Rio de Janeiro.

————. 1965. "Siete Tesis Equivocadas sobre América Latina." *Política Exterior Independente.* No. 1. Rio de Janeiro.

Steward, Julian H. (ed.). 1946–50. *Handbook of South American Indians.* Vols. I-VI. Washington, D.C.

————. 1949. "The Native Population of South America" in *Handbook of South American Indians.* Vol. V.

————. 1950. *Area Research, Theory and Practice.* New York: Social Science Research Council.

Suret-Canale, J. 1959. *Africa Negra.* Buenos Aires.

Tannenbaum, Frank. 1947. *Slave and Citizen: The Negro in the Americas.* New York: Alfred A. Knopf.

Troncoso, Moisés Poblete. 1967. *La Explosión Demográfica en América Latina.* Buenos Aires.

United Nations. 1958. *Estudios Demográficos.* No. 28. New York: United Nations.

————. 1965. "Conferencia Mundial de Población, 1965." *Boletín Informativo.* New York: United Nations.

U.S. Census. 1966. *Statistical Abstract of the U.S.* Washington, D.C.: Government Printing Office.

Wagley, Charles, and Marvin Harris. 1955. "A Typology of Latin America Subcultures." *American Anthropologist.* No. 57. Menasha.

————. 1958. *Minorities in the New World.* New York: Columbia University Press.

Warner, W. Lloyd, and Leo Srole. 1945. *The Social Systems of American Ethnic Groups.* New Haven, Conn.: Yale University Press.

White, Leslie. 1959. *The Evolution of Culture.* New York: McGraw-Hill Book Co.

Willems, Emílio. 1946. *A Aculturação dos Alemães no Brasil.* São Paulo.

Williams, Eric. 1944. *Capitalism and Slavery.* Chapel Hill, N.C.: University of North Carolina Press.

Wolf, Eric R. 1955. "Types of Latin American Peasantry." *American Anthropologist.* No. 57. Menasha.

Zea, Leopoldo. 1957. *America en la Historia.* Mexico.

3. THE MESOAMERICANS

Adams, Richard N. 1956. *La Ladinización en Gautemala.* Guatemala.

———— (ed.). 1960. *Social Change in Latin America Today: Its Implications to United States Policy.* New York: Harper & Bros.

Aguirre Beltran, Gonzalo. 1940. *La Población Negra de México.* Mexico.

Alperovich, M. S., and B. T. Rudenko. 1960. *La Revolución Mexicana de 1910/1917 y la Política de los Estados Unidos.* Mexico.

Arciniegas, Germán. 1958. *Entre la Libertad y el Miedo.* Buenos Aires.

Bemis, Samuel F. 1943. *The Latin American Policy of the United States.* New York: Harcourt, Brace.

Borah, Woodrow. 1964. "America as Model: The Demographic Impact of European

Expansion upon the Non-European World." 35th session. *Congresso International de Americanistas*. Mexico.

———— and Sherburne F. Cook. 1963. *The Aboriginal Population of Central Mexico on the Eve of the Spanish Conquest*. Berkeley, Calif.: University of California Press.

Capdequi, Ots. J.M. 1941. *El Estado Español en las Indias*. Mexico.

Carmona, Fernando. 1964. *El Drama de América Latina: el Caso de México*. Mexico.

Casanova, Pablo González. 1962. "Sociedad plural y desarrollo: el caso de México." *América Latina*. No. 4. Río de Janeiro.

————. 1963. "Sociedad Plural, Colonialismo Interno y Desarrollo." *América Latina*. Vol. VI, No. 3. Rio de Janeiro.

————. 1965. *La Democracia en México*. Mexico.

Caso, Alfonso. 1953. *El Pueblo del Sol*. Mexico.

Cline, Howard F. 1953. *The United States and Mexico*. Cambridge, Mass.: Harvard University Press.

————. 1962. *Mexico: From Revolution to Evolution. 1940–1960*. London: Oxford University Press.

Comas, Juan. 1961. *Relaciones Inter-Raciales en América Latina. 1940–1960*. Mexico.

Davila, Carlos. 1950. *Nosotros, los de las Américas*. Santiago, Chile.

Dobyns, Henry, and Paul Thompson. 1966. "Estimating Aboriginal American Population." *Current Anthropology*. Vol. VII, No 4. Utrecht, Netherlands.

Frank, Andrew Gunder. 1964. "México: As Faces de Jano da Revolução do século XX" in *Perspectivas de América Latina*. Rio de Janeiro.

Gillin, John. 1949. "Mestizo América" in Ralph Linton (ed.), *Most of the World, the Peoples of Africa, Latin America and East Today*. New York: Columbia University Press.

Hanke, Lewis. 1959. *Aristotle and the American Indians: A Study in Race Prejudice in the Modern World*. Chicago: Henry Regnery.

Herzog, Jesus Silva. 1960–62. *Breve Historia de la Revolución Mexicana*. 2 vols. Mexico.

International Labor Office. 1953. *Poblaciones Indígenas. Condiciones de Vida y de Trabajo de los Pueblos autóctonos de los países independientes*. Geneva.

Iturriaga, José E. 1951. *La Estructura Social y Cultural de México*. Mexico.

Kepner, Charles D., and J. H. Soothill. 1935. *Banana Empire: A Case Study of Economic Imperialism*. New York: Vanguard Press.

Krehm, William. 1959. *Democracia y Tiranías en el Caribe*. Buenos Aires.

Kroeber, A. L. 1939. *Cultural and Natural Areas of Native North America*. Berkeley, Calif.: University of California Press.

Leon-Portilla, Miguel. 1959. *Visión de los Vencidos. Relaciones Indígenas de la Conquista*. Mexico.

————. 1963. *Imagen del México Antiguo*. Buenos Aires.

Lewis, Oscar. 1951. *Life in a Mexican Village: Tepoztlan Restudied*. Urbana, Ill.: University of Illinois Press.

————. 1959. *Five Families: Mexican Case Studies in the Culture of Poverty*. New York: Basic Books.

————. 1960. "México since Cárdenas" in R. N. Adams (ed.), *Social Change in Latin America Today*. New York: Harper & Bros.

Lipschutz, Alejandro. 1956. *El Problema Racial en la Conquista de América y el Mestizaje.* Santiago, Chile.

———. 1963. *La Comunidad Indígena en América y en Chile: Su Pasado histórico y sus Perspectivas.* Santiago, Chile.

Lombardo Toledano, Vicente. 1943. *Definición de la Nación Mexicana.* Mexico.

Maddox, James G. 1965. "La Revolución y la Reforma Agraria" in Oscar Delgado (ed.), *Reformas Agrarias en América Latina.* Mexico.

Mejia Nieto, Arturo. 1947. *Morazán.* Buenos Aires.

Mello, Astrogildo Rodríguez de. 1946. *O Trabalho Forçado de Indígenas nas lavouras de Nova-Espanha.* São Paulo.

Mendieta y Nuñez, Lucio. 1934. *Esbozo de la Historia de los Primeros Años de la Reforma Agraria de México (1910/1920).* Mexico.

———. 1954. *El Problema Agrario de México.* Mexico.

Moreno, Manuel M. 1962. *La Organización Política y Social de los Aztecas.* Mexico.

Morley, Silvanus. 1956. *Ancient Maya.* Stanford, Calif.: Stanford University Press.

Nearing, Scott, and Joseph Freeman. 1925. *Dollar Diplomacy: A Study in American Imperialism.* New York: Viking Press.

Palerm, Angel, and Eric Wolf. 1961. "Varios Estudios sobre la Civilización de Regadío en Mesoamérica." *Revista Interamericana de Ciencias Sociales.* Vol. I, No. 2. Washington, D.C.

———. 1961a. "La Agricultura y el Desarrollo de la Civilización en Mesoamérica." *Revista Interamericana de Ciencias Sociales.* Vol. I, No. 2. Washington, D.C.

Pan American Institute of History and Geography. 1951. *Ensayos sobre la Historia del Nuevo Mundo.* Publication 118. Mexico.

Rama, Carlos. 1962. *Revolución Social en el Siglo XX.* Buenos Aires.

Redfield, Robert. 1941. *The Folk Culture of Yucatán.* Chicago: University of Chicago Press.

Ribeiro, Darcy. 1956. "Convívio e Contaminacão—Efeitos Dissociativos da Depopulacão provocada por epidemias em grupos Indígenas." *Sociologia.* Vol. XVIII, No. 1. São Paulo.

———. 1968. *The Civilizational Process.* Washington, D.C.: Smithsonian Institute Press.

———, et al. 1960. "Un concepto de Integración Social." *América Indígena.* Vol. XX, No. 1. Mexico.

Rosenblat, Angel. 1954. *La Población Indígena y el Mestizaje en América Latina.* 2 vols. Buenos Aires.

Salas, Alberto M. 1960. *Cronica Florida del Mestizaje de las Indias.* Buenos Aires.

Sapper, Karl. 1924. "Die Zahl und die Volksdichte der Indianischen Bevolkerung in Amerika von der Conquista und in der Gegenwart." 21st session. *Congreso Internacional de Americanistas.* Leiden.

Selser, Gregorio. 1957. *Sandino, General de Hombres Libres.* 2 vols. Buenos Aires.

Soustelle, Jacques. 1962. *Daily Life Among the Aztecs.* New York: The Macmillan Co.

Spengler, Oswald. 1928. *The Decline of the West.* 2 vols. New York: Alfred A. Knopf.

Steward, Julian H. (ed.). 1949. "The Native Population of South America," in *Handbook of South American Indians.* Vol. V: *Comparative Anthropology of South American Indians.* Washington, D.C.

Tannenbaum, Frank. 1950. *México: The Struggle for Peace and Bread.* New York: Alfred A. Knopf.

Thompson, Eric J. 1934. *La Civilización Aztéque.* Paris.

Townsend, William C. 1952. *Lázaro Cardenas: Mexican Democrat.* Ann Arbor, Mich.: George Wahr.

Vaillant, George C. 1941. *The Aztecs of Mexico.* New York: Doubleday & Co.

Wittfogel, Karl. 1957. *Oriental Despotism.* New Haven, Conn.: Yale University Press.

Zavala, Silvio H. 1953. *Aproximaciones a la Historia de México.* Madrid.

4. THE ANDEANS

Arguedas, Alcides. 1937. *Un Pueblo enfermo: contribución a la psicología de los pueblos hispanoamericanos.* Santiago, Chile.

Baudin, Louis. 1961. *A Socialist Empire. The Incas of Peru.* New York: Van Nostrand.

Bourricaud, François. 1967. *Poder y Sociedad en el Perú Contemporáneo.* Buenos Aires.

Cesped, Augusto. 1966. *El Presidente Colgado.* Buenos Aires.

Dobyns, Henry F., and Paul Thompson. 1966. "Estimating Aboriginal American Population." *Current Anthropology.* Vol. VII, No. 4. Utrecht, Netherlands.

Haya de la Torre, V. R. 1927. *Por la Emancipación de América Latina.* Buenos Aires.

———. 1936. *Adónde vá Indoamérica?* Santiago, Chile.

International Labor Office. 1953. *Poblaciones Indígenas. Condiciones de Vida y de Trabajo de los Pueblos Autóctonos de los países independientes.* Geneva.

Kantor, Harry. 1958. "El Programa Aprista para Perú y Latinoamérica." *Revista Combate.* No. 3. San José, Costa Rica.

Leonard, Olen E., 1952. *Bolívia: Land, People and Institutions.* Washington, D.C.: Scarecrow Press.

Mariategui, José Carlos. 1963. *Siete Ensayos de Interpretación de la Realidad Peruana.* Havana.

Ortiz, Nuflo Chavez. 1965. *Bolivia y su posición en la Estrategia, medios y fines de la Revolución Nacional.* Montevideo.

Osborne, Harold. 1955. *Bolivia, a Land Divided.* London: Royal Institute of International Affairs.

Penaloza, Luiz. 1954. *História Económica de Bolivia.* La Paz.

Sanchez, Luiz Alberto. 1954. *Haya de la Torre y el APRA.* Santiago, Chile.

———. 1958. *El Perú: Retrato de un País Adolescente.* Buenos Aires.

Steward, Julian H. (ed.). 1946. "The Andean Civilizations" in *Handbook of South American Indians.* Vol. II. Washington, D.C.

——— and Louis C. Faron. 1959. *Native Peoples of South America.* New York: McGraw-Hill Book Co.

Tamayo, Franz. 1944. *Creación de la Pedagogía Nacional.* La Paz.

Uceda, Luis de la Puente. 1965. "La Revolución en Perú—concepciones y perspectivas" in *Monthly Review* (Selections in Spanish). Buenos Aires.

Urteaga, Horacio Villanueva. 1964. "El Incario en la Emancipación del Perú." 35th session. *Congreso Internacional de Americanistas.* Mexico.

Valcarcel, Daniel. 1965. *La Rebelión de Túpac Amaru*. Mexico.

Velarde, José Feldmann. 1954. *Victor Paz Estensoro—El Hombre y la Revolución*. La Paz.

Villanueva, Victor. 1962. *El Militarismo en el Perú*. Lima.

Vinueza, L. Benites. 1944. *Ecuador: Drama y Paradoja*. Mexico.

Zavaleta Mercado, René. 1967. *Bolivia, El desarrollo de la Conciencia Nacional*. Montevideo.

5. THE BRAZILIANS

Abreu, Capistrano de. 1934. *Capítulos da História Colonial* (1500–1800). Rio de Janeiro.

Albersheim, Ursula. 1962. *Uma Comunidade Teuto-Brasileira (Jarim)*. Rio de Janeiro.

Amaral, Azevedo. 1938. *O Estado Autoritário e a Realidade Nacional*. Rio de Janeiro.

Banas (Economic Research Organization). 1965. "As 767 Maiores Companhias do Brasil" in *Brasil 65*. São Paulo.

Bastide, Roger. 1957. *Brésil, Terre des Contrastes*. Paris.

Brazilian Institute of Geography and Statistics. 1950. *Censo Agrícola de 1950*. Rio de Janeiro.

———. 1960. *Rescenseamento Geral do Brasil*. Rio de Janeiro.

———. 1963–66. *Anuários Estatísticos de 1963, 1964, 1965, 1966*. Rio de Janeiro.

Caldeira, Clóvis. 1954. *Fazendas de Cacau na Bahia*. Rio de Janeiro.

———. 1955. *Arrendamento e Parceria*. Rio de Janeiro.

———. 1956. *Mutirão. Formas de Ajuda Mútua no meio rural*. São Paulo.

———. 1960. *Menores no Meio Rural*. Rio de Janeiro.

Calogeras, Pandiá J. 1927. *A Política Exterior do Império*. 2 vols. São Paulo.

Camargo, J. F. 1957. *Exodo Rural do Brasil*. São Paulo.

Cardoso, Fernando Henrique. 1962. *Capitalismo e Escravidão no Brasil Meridional. O Negro da sociedade escravocrata do Rio Grande do Sul*. São Paulo.

———. 1964. *Empresário Industrial e Desenvolvimento Econômico no Brasil*. São Paulo.

Castro, Josué de. 1946. *Geografía da Fome*. Rio de Janeiro.

Correia Filho, Virgílio. 1957. *Ervais do Brasil e Ervateiros*. Rio de Janeiro.

Costa Pinto, L. A. 1948. "A Estrutura da Sociedade Rural Brasileira." *Sociologia*. Vol. X, Nos. 2/3. São Paulo.

———. 1953. *O Negro no Rio de Janeiro*. Rio de Janeiro.

Cunha, Euclides da. 1911. *Os Sertões*. Rio de Janeiro.

Diegues, Manuel, Jr. 1952. *O Engenho de Acúcar no Nordeste*. Rio de Janeiro.

———. 1959. *População e Propriedade da Terra no Brasil*. Rio de Janeiro.

———. 1960. "Propriedade e Uso da Terra no 'Plantation' brasileiro" in Julian H. Steward (ed.), *Sistema de Plantaciones en el Neuvo Mundo*.

———. 1964. *Imigração, Urbanização e Industrialização*. Rio de Janeiro.

Duarte, Nestor. 1939. *Reforma Agrária*. Rio de Janeiro.

Faoro, Raymundo. 1958. *Os Donos do Poder—Formação do Patronato Político Brasileiro*. Porto Alegre.

Fernandes, Florestan. 1949. *A Organização Social dos Tupinambá*. São Paulo.

————. 1960. *Mudanças Sociais no Brasil*. São Paulo.

————. 1964. *A Integração do Negro á Sociedade de Massas*. São Paulo.

Frank, Andrew Gunder. 1964. "A Agricultura Brasileira: Capitalismo e o Mito do Feudalismo," *Revista Brasiliense*. No. 51. São Paulo.

————. 1966. *Capitalism and Underdevelopment in Latin America: The Cases of Chile and Brazil*. New York: Monthly Review Press.

Freyre, Gilberto. 1935. *Sobrados e Mucambos*. Rio de Janeiro.

————. 1954. *Casa Grande e Senzala*. 2 vols. Rio de Janeiro.

————. 1959. *Ordem e Progresso*. Rio de Janeiro.

Fundação, Getúlio Vargas. 1965. "Retrospecto 1964" in *Conjuntura Econômica*. No. 2. Rio de Janeiro.

Furtado, Celso. 1959. *Formação Econômica do Brasil*. Rio de Janeiro.

————. 1962. *A Pre-Revolução Brasileira*. Rio de Janeiro.

Geiger, Pedro Pinchas. 1963. *Evolução da Rede Urbana Brasileira*. Rio de Janeiro.

Gillin, John. 1947. *Moche: A Peruvian Coastal Community*. Washington, D.C.

————. 1947a. "Modern Latin American Culture." *Social Forces*. No. 25.

Goulart, João. 1964. *Mensagem ao Congresso Nacional*. Brasília.

Gourou, Pierre. 1959. *Los Países Tropicales. Xalapa*. Mexico.

Guerreiro Ramos, Alberto. 1957. *Condições Sociais do Poder Nacional*. Rio de Janeiro.

Guimarães, Alberto Passos. 1963. *Quatro Séculos de Latifúndio*. São Paulo.

Holanda, Sérgio Buarque de. 1956. *Raízes do Brasil*. Rio de Janeiro.

Hutchinson, Harry W. 1957. *Village and Plantation Life in Northeastern Brazil*. Seattle: University of Washington Press.

————. 1960. *Mobilidade e Trabalho—Um estudo da cidade de São Paulo*. São Paulo.

Ianni, Octavio. 1962. *As Metamorfoses do Escravo. Apogeu e crise da escravatura no Brasil Meridional*. São Paulo.

————. 1963. *Industrialização e Desenvolvimento Social no Brasil*. Rio de Janeiro.

————. 1966. *Raças e Classes Sociais no Brasil*. Rio de Janeiro.

Jaguaribe, Hélio. 1962. *Desenvolvimento econômico e Desenvolvimento Político*. Rio de Janeiro.

Kuznets, Simon, et al. (eds.). 1955. *Economic Growth: Brazil, India, Japan*. Durham, N.C.: Duke University Press.

Lambert, Jacques. 1959. *Os Dois Brasil*. Rio de Janeiro.

Laytano, Dante de. 1952. *A Estância Gaúcha*. Rio de Janeiro.

Leal, Victor Nunes. 1948. *Coronelismo, Enxada e Voto*. Rio de Janeiro.

Leite, Antonio Dias. 1966. *Caminhos do Desenvolvimento*. Rio de Janeiro.

Lessa, Carlos. 1964. "Quince Años de Política Económica en el Brasil" in *Boletin Económico de América Latina*. Santiago, Chile.

Lima, Heitor Ferreira. 1954. *Evolução Industrial de São Paulo*. São Paulo.

Lima, Rui Cirne de. 1935. *Terras Devolutas. História, Doutrina e Legislação*. Porto Alegre, Brazil.

Macedo, José Norberto. 1952. *Fazendas de Gado no Vale do São Francisco*. Rio de Janeiro.

Marchant, Alexandre. 1943. *Do Escambo à Escravidão*. São Paulo.

Melo e Souza, Antônio Cândido. 1964. *Os Parceiros do Rio Bonito. Estudo sôbre o caipira paulista e a transformação dos seus meios de vida*. Rio de Janeiro.

Mintz, Sidney W. 1960. "La Plantación como un tipo sociocultural" in J. H. Steward (ed.), *Plantaciones en el Neuvo Mundo*. Washington, D.C.

Monbeig, Pierre. 1940. *Ensaios de Geografía Humana.* São Paulo.

Morais Filho, Evaristo de. 1962. *O Sindicato Unico no Brasil.* Rio de Janeiro.

Morazé, Charles. 1954. *Les Trois Âges du Brésil.* Paris.

Moura, Aristoteles. 1956. *O Dólar no Brasil.* Rio de Janeiro.

Myrdal, Gunnar. 1957. *Economic Theory and Underdeveloped Regions.* London: Gerald Duckworth.

Nogueira, Oracy. 1960. "Côr de Pele e Classe Social" in *Sistemas de Plantaciones en el Nuevo Mundo.* Washington, D.C.

——. 1962. *Familia e Comunidade: Um Estudo Sociológico de Itapetininga.* Rio de Janeiro.

Normano, J. F. 1945. *Evolução Econômica do Brasil.* São Paulo.

Paim, Gilberto. 1957. *Industrialização e Economia Natural.* Rio de Janeiro.

Paula, José María de. 1944. *Terra dos Indios.* Rio de Janeiro.

Pedrosa, Mário. 1966. *A Opção Brasileira.* Rio de Janeiro.

——. 1966a. *A Opção Imperialista.* Rio de Janeiro.

Perdigão Malheiros, A. M. 1944. *A Escravidão no Brasil.* São Paulo.

Pierson, Donald. 1945. *Brancos e Pretos na Bahia.* São Paulo.

Pinto, Alvaro Vieira. 1956. *Ideologia e Desenvolvimento Nacional.* Rio de Janeiro.

Pinto Ferreira. 1965. *Capitais Estrangeiros e Dívida Externa no Brasil.* São Paulo.

Prado, Caio, Jr. 1942. *Formação do Brasil Contemporâneo.* São Paulo.

——. 1960. "Contribução para a análise da questão agrária no Brasil." *Revista Brasiliense.* No. 28. São Paulo.

——. 1964. "Marcha da questão agrária no Brasil." *Revista Brasiliense.* No. 51. São Paulo.

——. 1966. *A Revolução Brasileira.* Rio de Janeiro.

Ramos, Arthur. n.d. *Guerra e Relações de Raça.* Rio de Janeiro.

——. 1944–47. *Introdução á Antropologia Brasileira.* 2 vols. Rio de Janeiro.

Rangel, Inácio. 1957. *Introdução ao Estudo do Desenvolvimento Econômico Brasileiro.* Salvador, Brazil.

——. 1957a. *Dualidade Básica da Economia Brasileira.* Rio de Janeiro.

Redfield, Robert. 1941. *The Folk Culture of Yucatán.* Chicago: University of Chicago Press.

——. 1953. *The Primitive World and Its Transformations.* Ithaca, N.Y.: Cornell University Press.

Reis, Arthur Cezar Ferreira. 1954. *O Seringal e o Seringueiro da Amazônia.* Rio de Janeiro.

Ribeiro, Darcy. 1955. "Os Indios Urubus—Ciclo Anual de Atividades das Subsistência de uma Tribo na Floresta Tropical." 31st session. *Congreso Internacional de Americanistas.* São Paulo.

——. 1956. "Convívio e Contaminação—Efeitos Dissociativos da depopulacão provocada por epidemias em grupos indígenas." *Sociologia.* Vol. XVIII, No. 1. São Paulo.

——. 1957. "Culturas e Línguas Indígenas do Brasil." *Educacão e Ciências Sociais.* Vol. II, No. 6. Rio de Janeiro.

——. 1962. *Política Indigenista Brasileira.* Rio de Janeiro.

Rodrigues, Leoncio. 1966. *Conflito Industrial e Sindicalismo no Brasil.* São Paulo.

Santos, Milton. 1955. *Zona de Cacau.* Salvador, Brazil.

Silva, Zedar Perfeito da. 1955. *O Vale do Itajaí.* Rio de Janeiro.

Simonsen, Roberto. 1937. *História Econômica do Brasil (1500–1820).* São Paulo.

Smith, T. Lynn. 1946. *Brazil: People and Institutions.* Baton Rouge, La.: Louisiana State University Press.

Sodré, Nelson Werneck. 1960. *O que se deve ler para conhecer o Brasil.* Rio de Janeiro.

———. 1963. *Introdução á Revolução Brasileira.* Rio de Janeiro.

———. 1964. *História da Burguesia Nacional.* Rio de Janeiro.

SPED. Carta Económica Brasileira. 1965. "Os Grandes Grupos Econômicos no Brasil." *SPED* n.s. 2, 3, 4. Rio de Janeiro.

Steward, Julian H. 1949. "The Native Population of South America" in *Handbook of South American Indians.* Vol. V. Washington, D.C.

———. 1960. "Perspectivas de las Plantaciones" in *Sistemas de Plantaciones en el Nuevo Mundo."* Washington, D.C.: Pan American Union.

——— (ed.). 1960. *Sistemas de Plantaciones en el Nuevo Mundo.* Washington, D.C.: Pan American Union.

Tannenbaum, Frank. 1947. *Slave and Citizen: The Negro in the Americas.* New York: Alfred A. Knopf.

Tavares, María Conceição, et al. 1964. "Auge y Declinación del Proceso de Sustitución de Importaciones en el Brasil." *Boletin Económico de América Latina.* Vol. IX, No. 1. Santiago, Chile.

Teixeira, Anísio. 1957. *Educação não é Privilégio.* Rio de Janeiro.

Thompson, Edgar T. 1960. "La Plantación como Sistema Social" in *Plantaciones en el Nuevo Mundo.* Washington, D.C.: Pan American Union.

Touraine, Alain. 1961. "Industrialisation et Conscience Ouvrière a São Paulo" in *Syndicats d'Amérique Latine.* Paris.

United Nations. 1958. *Estudio Demográficos.* No. 28. New York: United Nations.

———. 1961–64. *Statistical Yearbook.* New York: United Nations.

———. 1964. *El Financiamiento Externo de América Latina.* New York: United Nations.

Valverde, Orlando. 1964. *Geografía Agrária do Brasil.* Vol. I. Rio de Janeiro.

Vianna, Oliveira. 1956. *Evolução do Povo Brasileiro.* Rio de Janeiro.

Vieira da Cunha, Mário Wagner. 1963. *O Sistema Administrativo Brasileiro 1930/1950.* Rio de Janeiro.

Vinhas, Moisés. 1963. *Operários e Camponeses na Revolução Brasileira.* São Paulo.

Wagley, Charles. n.d. *A Revolução Brasileira.* Salvador, Brazil.

Waibel, Leo. 1947. "O Sistema de Plantações Tropicais" in *Boletim Geográfico.* Vol. V, No. 56. Rio de Janeiro.

Willems, Emílio. 1947. *Cunha. Tradição e Transição em uma Cultura Rural no Brasil.* São Paulo.

6. THE GRAN-COLOMBIANS

Barradas, José Pérez de. 1948. *Los Mestizos de América.* Madrid.

Betancourt, Rómulo. 1956. *Venezuela: Política y Petróleo.* Mexico.

Bonilla, Frank, and J. A. Silva-Michelena. 1966. *Studying the Venezuelan Polity.* Boston: Massachusetts Institute of Technology.

Campos, Germán Guzman, Orlando Fals Borba, and Eduardo Umaña Luna. 1963–64. *La Violencia en Colombia. Estudio de un Proceso Social.* 2 vols.

Cuellar, Diego Montaña. 1963. *Colombia. País formal y país real.* Buenos Aires.

Damas, German Carrera. 1964. *Cuestiones de Historiografia Venezolana.* Caracas.

Donoso, Manuel Cabieses. 1963. *Venezuela, Okey! (Origen y objectivos de la lucha armada).* Santiago, Chile.

Fals Borba, Orlando. 1958. *Estudio sobre las Condiciones del Desarrollo en Colombia.* 2 vols. Bogotá.

————. 1961. *Campesinos de los Andes.* Bogotá.

Gaitan, Jorge Eliecer. 1963. *Las Ideas Socialistas en Colombia.* Bogotá.

Galbraith, W. O. 1953. *Colombia, a General Survey.* London: Royal Institute of International Affairs.

Institute of Political Studies on Latin America. 1965. *América del Sur frente al Desarrollo.* Barcelona.

Johnson, John J. 1958. *Political Change in Latin America.* Stanford, Calif.: Stanford University Press.

Kroeber, A. L. 1946. "The Chibcha" in *Handbook of South American Indians.* Vol. II: *The Andean Civilizations.* Washington, D.C.

Lieuwen, Edwin. 1965. *Venezuela.* London: Oxford University Press.

Mijares, Augusto. 1967. *La Evolución Política de Venezuela 1810/1960.* Buenos Aires.

National Council of Policy and Planning for Colombia. 1960. *Plan General de Desarrollo Económico y Social.* Bogotá.

Reichel-Dolmatoff, Geraldo. 1953. *Colombia: Programa de Historia de América. Período Indígena.* Mexico.

Rosenblat, Angel. 1954. *La Población Indígena y el Mestizaje en América.* 2 vols. Buenos Aires.

Salas, Alberto M. 1960. *Crónica Florida del Mestizaje de las Indias.* Buenos Aires.

Santa, Eduardo. 1964. *Sociología Política de Colombia.* Bogotá.

Smith, T. Lynn. 1951. "Observations on the Middle Classes in Colombia" in *Materiales para el Estudio de la Classe Média en América Latina.* Vol. VI. Washington, D.C.: Pan American Union.

Steward, Julian H., and Louis C. Faron. 1959. *Native Peoples of South America.* New York: McGraw-Hill Book Co.

Tovar, R. A. 1962. *Venezuela, País Ocupado.* Caracas.

Vallerrilla Lanz, L. 1919. *Cesarismo Democrático.* Caracas.

7. THE ANTILLEANS

Amengual, Gumersindo M. 1963. *Subdesarrollo y Revolución en Latinoamérica.* Havana.

Arciniegas, Germán. 1958. *Entre la Libertad y el Miedo.* Buenos Aires.

Baran, Paul. 1963. *Reflexiones sobre la revolución Cubana.* Buenos Aires.

Bellegarde, Dantés. 1937. *Resistence Haitienne.* París.

————. 1938. *La Nation Haitienne.* Paris.

Blas Roca. 1961. *Los Fundamentos del Socialismo en Cuba.* Havana.

Bosch, Juan. 1961. *Trujillo, causas de una tiranía sin ejemplo.* Caracas.

Castro, Fidel. 1959. *La Revolución Cubana.* Buenos Aires.

————. 1965. *El Partido Maxista-Leninista.* Buenos Aires.

Cesaire, Aimé. 1955. *Discours sur le Colonialisme*. Paris.

Chonchol, Jacques. 1965. "Cuba, el Primer Bienio de Reforma Agraria (1959/1961)" in Oscar Delgado (ed.), *Reformas Agrarias en la América Latina*. Mexico.

Cook, Mercer. 1951. *An Introduction to Haiti*. Washington, D.C.: Pan American Union.

Draper, Theodore. 1962. *Castro's Revolution:* New York: Frederick A. Praeger.

Fanon, Frantz. 1965. *Escucha, Blanco!* Barcelona.

Ferguson, J. Halcro. 1963. *El Equilibrio Racial en América Latina*. Buenos Aires.

Food and Agricultural Organization of the United Nations. 1963. "La Reforma Agraria Cubana" in *El Trimestre Económico*. Vol. XXX, No. 17. Mexico.

Friedlaender, H. E. 1944. *História Económica de Cuba*. Havana.

Frondizi, Silvio. 1961. *La Revolución Cubana: Su significación Histórica*. Montevideo.

Furtado, Celso. 1959. *Formação Econômica do Brasil*. Rio de Janeiro.

Guérin, Daniel. 1959. *Cuatro Colonialismos sobre las Antillas*. Buenos Aires.

Guevara, Ernesto Che, et al. 1967. *Cuba. Cuadernos de "Marcha."* No. 3. Montevideo.

Hanke, Lewis. 1959. *Modern Latin America*. Vol. I: *Mexico and the Caribbean*. Princeton, N.J.: Van Nostrand.

Jagan, Chedi, and Jeannete Jagan. 1964. *Guayana Inglesa*. Buenos Aires.

Jenks, Leland H. 1959. *Nuestra Colonia de Cuba*. Buenos Aires.

Jimenez, Antonio Nuñes. 1960. *Geografía de Cuba*. Havana.

Krehm, William. 1959. *Democracia y Tiranías en el Caribe*. Buenos Aires.

Mende, Tibor. 1956. *America Latina entra en Escena*. Santiago, Chile.

Metraux, Alfred. 1963. *Vodú*. Buenos Aires.

Mills, C. Wright. 1961. *Escucha, Yanqui—La Revolución en Cuba*. Mexico.

Morray, Joseph P. 1962. *The Second Revolution in Cuba*. New York: Monthly Review Press.

Omedo, José. 1963. *Cuba: La Revolución de América*. Bogotá.

Ortiz, Fernando. 1940. *Contrapunteo Cubano del Tabaco y del Azúcar*. Havana.

Pedrero, Enrique Gonzalez. 1959. *La Revolución Cubana*. Mexico.

Reno, Philip. 1965. *El drama de la Guayana Británica*. Buenos Aires.

Rodrigues, Carlos Rafael. 1965. "La Segunda Reforma agraria cubana: causas y derivaciones" in Oscar Delgado (ed.), *Reformas Agrarias en la América Latina*. Mexico.

Romain, Jacques. 1934. *Analyse Schématique*. Haiti.

Rostovsky, Miroshevsky, and Rubizov. 1941. *Nueva Historia de la América Latina*. Buenos Aires.

Sartre, Jean Paul. 1960. *Huracán sobre el Caribe*. Havana.

Selser, Gregorio. 1962. *Diplomacia, Garrote y Dolares en América Latina*. Buenos Aires.

Sweezy, Paul M., and Leo Huberman. 1961. *Cuba: Anatomy of a Revolution*. New York: Monthly Review Press.

Williams, Eric. 1942. *The Negro in the Caribbean*. Washington, D.C.: Associates in Negro Folk Education.

8. THE CHILEANS

Ahumada, Jorge. 1958. *En vez de la Miseria*. Santiago, Chile.

Basadre, Jorge. 1948. *Chile, Perú y Bolivia Independientes*. Barcelona.

Becket, James. 1965. "Problemas de la Reforma Agraria" in Oscar Delgado (ed.), *Reformas Agrarias en la América Latina*. Mexico.

Comas, Juan. 1961. *Relaciones Inter-Raciales en América Latina: 1940–1960*. Mexico.

Cunile, Pedro. 1965. *Geografía de Chile*. Santiago.

Delgado, Oscar (ed.). 1965. *Reformas Agrarias en la América Latina. Procesos y Perspectivas*. Mexico.

Donoso, Ricardo. 1946. *Las Ideas Políticas en Chile*. Mexico.

———. 1963. *Breve Historia de Chile*. Buenos Aires.

Economic Commission on Latin America. 1963. *El Desarrollo Económico de América Latina en la Post Guerra*. New York: United Nations.

———. 1964. *El Financiamiento Externo de América Latina*. New York: United Nations.

Encinas, Francisco Antonio. 1912. *Nuestra Inferioridad Económica. Sus causas, sus consecuencias*. Santiago.

———. 1954–55. *Resúmen de la Historia de Chile*. Santiago.

Espartaco. 1965. *Crítica a la Izquierda Latinoamericana*. Montevideo.

Fichter, Joseph H. 1962. *Cambio Social en Chile—Un estudio de actitudes*. Santiago.

Frank, Andrew G. 1966. *Capitalism and Underdevelopment in Latin America. The Cases of Chile and Brazil*. New York: Monthly Review Press.

Frei, Eduardo. 1951. *Sentido y Forma de una Política*. Santiago.

Hanke, Lewis. 1959. *Aristotle and the American Indians: A Study in Race Prejudice in the Modern World*. Chicago: Henry Regnery.

Jara, Alvaro. 1965. *Fuentes para la Historia del Trabajo en el Reino de Chile*. Santiago.

Johnson, John J. 1958. *Political Change in Latin America*. Stanford, Calif.: Stanford University Press.

Jovet, Julio César. 1955. *Ensayo Crítico del Desarrollo Económico y Social de Chile*. Santiago.

Lago, Tomás. 1953. *El Huaso. Ensayo de Antropología Social*. Santiago.

Lagos, Ricardo. 1961. *La Concentración del Poder Económico*. Santiago.

Lipschutz, Alejandro. 1956. *La Comunidad Indígena en América y en Chile. Su pasado histórico y sus perspectivas*. Santiago.

———. 1963. *El Problema Racial en la Conquista de América y el Mestizaje*. Santiago.

Millan, Orlando. 1964. *Los Comunistas, los Católicos y la Libertad*. Santiago.

Mostny, Greta. 1954. *Culturas Precolombinas en Chile*. Santiago.

Necochea, Hernan Ramírez. 1960. *Historia del Imperialismo en Chile*. Santiago.

Palacios, Nicolás. 1904. *Raza Chilena*. Valparaíso.

Pike, Frederick B. (ed.). 1962. *Chile and the United States, 1880–1962*. Notre Dame, Ind.: University of Notre Dame.

Pinto, Anibal. 1953. *Hacia Nuestra Independencia Económica*. Santiago.

———. 1962. *Chile, un caso de desarrollo frustrado*. Santiago.

———. 1965. *Chile, una Economía Difícil*. Santiago.

Rosenblat, Angel. 1954. *La Población Indígena de América.* 2 vols. Buenos Aires.

Salas, Alberto M. 1960. *Crónica Florida del Mestizaje de las Indias. Siglo XVI.* Buenos Aires.

Steward, Julian H. (ed.). 1946. *Handbook of South American Indians.* Vol. II: *The Andean Civilizations.* Washington, D.C.: Pan American Union.

Valenzuela, Lagos T. 1941. *Bosquejo Histórico del Movimiento Obero en Chile.* Santiago.

Villegas, Humberto F., et al. n.d. *Desarrollo de Chile en la Primera Mitad del siglo XX.* 2 vols. Santiago.

Vives, A. Edwards. 1952. *La Fronda Aristocrática. Historia Política de Chile.* Santiago.

Vuskovic, Sergio, and Oswaldo Sergio. 1964. *Teoría de la Ambiguedad. Base Ideológica de la Democracia Cristiana.* Santiago.

9. THE ANGLO-AMERICANS

Baran, Paul, and P. M. Sweezy. 1965. *Monopoly Capital.* New York: Monthly Review Press.

Bell, Daniel. 1959. *The End of Ideology.* Glencoe, Ill.: The Free Press.

Bessie, Alvah. 1957. *The Un-Americans.* New York: Cameron Associates.

Boggs, James. 1963. *The American Revolution: Pages from a Negro Worker's Notebooks.* New York: Monthly Review Press.

Braden, Anne. 1966. "Estados Unidos: el Movimiento Negro de Libración Nacional" in *Monthly Review* (in Spanish), n.s. 28–29. Buenos Aires.

Burlingame, Roger. 1953. *The Machines That Built America.* New York: Harcourt, Brace.

Cook, Fred J. 1962. *The Warfare State.* New York: The Macmillan Co.

Cuneo, Dardo. 1964. *La Batalla de América Latina.* Buenos Aires.

Davenport, Russell W. (ed.). 1952. *U.S.A., the Permanent Revolution.* New York: Prentice-Hall.

De Carlo, Charles R. 1964. "Perspectives on Technology" in Eli Ginzberg (ed.), *Technology and Social Change.* New York: Columbia University Press.

Frazier, E. Franklin. 1957. *The Negro in the United States.* New York: The Macmillan Co.

Freidel, Frank. 1965. *America in the Twentieth Century.* New York: Alfred A. Knopf.

Fromm, Erich. 1941. *Escape from Freedom.* New York: Henry Holt & Co.

Galbraith, John K. 1956. *American Capitalism.* Boston: Houghton, Mifflin.

Ginzberg, Eli (ed.). 1964. *Technology and Social Change.* New York: Columbia University Press.

Giraud, M. 1950. *Histoire du Canadá.* Paris.

Gorer, Geoffrey. 1948. *The American People: A Study in National Character.* New York: W. W. Norton.

Harrington, Michael. 1962. *The Other America.* New York: The Macmillan Co.

Henry, Jules. 1963. *Culture Against Man.* New York: Random House.

Huberman, Leo, and Paul M. Sweezy. 1963. *Teoría de la política exterior norteamericana.* Buenos Aires.

Jefferson, Thomas. 1949. *Thomas Jefferson on Democracy*. New York: New American Library.

Johnson, Charles S. 1934. *Shadow of the Plantation*. Chicago: University of Chicago Press.

Laski, Harold. 1948. *The American Democracy*. New York: Viking Press.

Lerner, Max. 1957. *America As a Civilization*. New York: Simon & Schuster.

Lilley, Sam. 1966. *Man, Machines, and History*. New York: International Publishers.

Lundberg, Ferdinand. 1960. *America's 60 Families*. New York: Citadel Press.

Martineau, Harriet. 1962. *Society in America*. Garden City, N.Y.: Doubleday & Co.

Millikan, M. F., and D.L.M. Blackmer (eds.). 1961. *Emerging Nations: Their Growth and U.S. Policy*. Boston: Little, Brown.

Mills, C. Wright. 1951. *White Collar: The American Middle Classes*. New York: Oxford University Press.

———. 1956. *The Power Elite*. New York: Oxford University Press.

Mead, Margaret. 1965. *And Keep Your Power Dry*. New York: William Morrow.

Morris, Richard B. (ed.). 1956. *Basic Documents in American History*. New York: Van Nostrand.

Myrdal, Gunnar, et al. 1944. *An American Dilemma*. New York: Harper & Bros.

Paine, Thomas. 1894–96. *The Writings of Thomas Paine*. New York: Burt Franklin.

Perlo, Victor. 1951. *American Imperialism*. New York: International Publishers.

———. 1957. *The Empire of High Finance*. New York: International Publishers.

Raymond, Jack. 1964. *Power at the Pentagon*. New York: Harper & Row.

Riesman, David, et al. 1950. *The Lonely Crowd*. New Haven, Conn.: Yale University Press.

Roussin, Marcel. 1959. *Le Canadá et le système Interamericaine*. Ottawa.

Schlesinger, Arthur M. 1964. *Rumbos de la Historia Norteamericana*. Buenos Aires.

——— and Hommer C. Hocket. 1948. *Political and Social Growth of the American People. 1865–1940*. New York: The Macmillan Co.

Selser, Gregorio. 1962. *Diplomacia, Garrote y Dólares en América Latina*. Buenos Aires.

Shils, Edward A. 1956. *The Torment of Secrecy*. Glencoe, Ill.: The Free Press.

Siegfried, André. 1956. *Panorama de los Estados Unidos*. Madrid.

Sorokin, Pitirim A. 1961. *Mutua convergencia de Estados Unidos y la URSS hacia un tipo sociocultural intermedio*. Mexico.

Staley, Eugene. 1944. *World Economic Development. Effects on Advanced Industrial Countries*. Geneva: International Labor Office.

Stampp, Kenneth M. 1956. *The Peculiar Institution: Slavery in the Ante-Bellum South*. New York: Alfred A. Knopf.

Stein, Maurice R. 1960. *The Eclipse of Community: an Interpretation of American Studies*. Princeton, N.J.: Princeton University Press.

Sternberg, Fritz. 1959. *The Military and Industrial Revolution of Our Time*. New York: Frederick Praeger.

Steward, Julian H. (ed.). 1960. *Sistemas de Plantaciones en el Nuevo Mundo*. Washington, D.C.: Pan American Union.

Stonequist, Everett V. 1937. *The Marginal Man: A Study in Personality and Culture Conflict*. New York: Charles Scribner's Sons.

Tannenbaum, Frank. 1947. *Slave and Citizen: The Negro in the Americas*. New York: Alfred A. Knopf.

Tocqueville, Alexis de. 1965. *Democracy in America*. New York: Harper & Row.

Toynbee, Arnold J. 1962. *America and the World Revolution, and Other Lectures.* London: Oxford University Press.

Tumin, Melvin M. (ed.). 1957. *Segregation and Desegration.* New York: Anti-Defamation League.

Turner, Frederick J. 1873. *The Frontier in American History.* New York: Henry Holt & Co.

U.S. Department of Commerce. 1949. *Historical Statistics of the United States* (1789–1945). Washington, D.C.: Government Printing Office.

West, James. 1945. *Plainville, USA.* New York: Columbia University Press.

Whitney, Frances. 1954. *Sintesis de la Historia de los Estados Unidos.* Mexico.

Williams, Eric. 1944. *Capitalism and Slavery.* Chapel Hill, N.C.: University of North Carolina Press.

Williams, William A. 1959. *The Tragedy of American Diplomacy.* New York: World Publishing.

10. THE RIVER PLATE PEOPLES

Acevedo, Pablo Blanco. 1955. *El Gaucho, Su Formación Social.* Montevideo.

Alberdi, Juan Bautista. 1920. *Obras Selectas.* Buenos Aires.

Araujo, Orestes. 1911. *Historia de los Charrúas y demás tribus del Uruguay.* Montevideo.

Ares Pons, Roberto. 1964. *Uruguay en el Siglo XIX. Acceso a la Modernidad.* Montevideo.

Arregui, J. J. Hernández. 1957. *Imperialismo y Cultura. La política en la inteligencia argentina.* Buenos Aires.

———. 1960. *La Formación de la Conciencia Nacional (1930/1960).* Buenos Aires.

———. 1963. *¿Qué es el Ser Nacional? La Conciencia Histórica Hispanoamericana.* Buenos Aires.

Assunção, Fernando O. 1963. *El Gaucho.* Montevideo.

Astrada, Carlos. 1964. *El Mito Gaucho.* Buenos Aires.

Bagu, Sergio. 1949. *Economía de la Sociedad Colonial. Ensayo de Historia comparada de América Latina.* Buenos Aires.

———. 1952. *Estructura Social de la Colonia.* Buenos Aires.

Barran, José P., and Benjamín Nahum. 1964. *Bases Económicas de la Revolución Artiguista.* Montevideo.

Belloni, Alberto. 1960. *Del Anarquismo al Peronismo. Historia del Movimiento Obrero Argentino.* Buenos Aires.

Benvenuto, Luis Carlos. 1967. *Breve Historia del Uruguay.* Montevideo.

Beraza, Agustín. 1964. *La Economía en la Banda Oriental. 1811/1820.* Montevideo.

Bunge, Augusto. 1919. *La Inferioridad Económica de los Argentinos Nativos.* Buenos Aires.

Campal, Esteban F. 1962. *Hombres, Tierras y Ganados.* Montevideo.

Campos, Germán J. Bidart. 1961. *Grupos de Presión y Factores de Poder.* Buenos Aires.

Cardozo, Efraim. 1959. *El Paraguay Colonial: Las Raíces de la Nacionalidad.* Buenos Aires.

Cardozo, Efraim. 1965. *Breve Historia del Paraguay*. Buenos Aires.

Coni, Emilio. 1937. *Gauchos del Uruguay*. Buenos Aires.

Cornblit, Oscar E., Ezequiel Gallo, and Alfredo A. O'Connel. 1965. "La Generación del 80 y su Proyecto: Antecedentes y Consecuencias," in Torcuato di Tella et al., *Argentina, Sociedad de Masas*. Buenos Aires.

Di Tella, Guido, and Manuel Zymelman. 1965. "Etapas del Desarrollo Económico argentino" in Torcuato di Tella et al., *Argentina, Sociedad de Masas*. Buenos Aires.

Di Tella, Torcuato S. 1964. *El Sistema Político Argentino y la Clase Obrera*. Buenos Aires.

————, Gino Germani, Jorge Graciarena, et al. 1965. *Argentina, Sociedad de Masas*. Buenos Aires.

Estrada, E. Martínez. 1933. *Radiografía de la Pampa*. Buenos Aires.

Fabregat, Enrique Rodríguez. 1942. *Batlle y Ordóñez, el Reformador*. Buenos Aires.

Faroppa, Luis A. 1965. *El Desarrollo Económico del Uruguay*. Montevideo.

Ferre, Alberto Methol. n.d. *La izquierda Nacional en la Argentina (Con textos seleccionados de varios autores)*. Buenos Aires.

Ferrer, Aldo. 1963. *La Economía Argentina—Las Etapas de su Desarrollo y Problemas Actuales*. Mexico.

Fitzgibbon, Russell H. 1954. *Uruguay—Portrait of a Democracy*. New Brunswick, N.J.: Rutgers University Press.

Frondizi, Arturo. 1955. *La Lucha Antiimperialista*. Buenos Aires.

Frondizi, Silvio. 1958. *Doce Años de Política Argentina*. Buenos Aires.

————. 1957–1960. *La Realidad Argentina*. 2 vols. Buenos Aires.

Germani, Gino. 1955. *Estructura Social de la Argentina*. Buenos Aires.

————. 1965. "Hacia una Democracia de Masas" in Torcuato di Tella et al., *Argentina, Sociedad de Masas*. Buenos Aires.

Gonzalez, J. Natalicio. 1949. *Como se construye una Nación*. Asunción, Paraguay.

Grompone, Antonio M. 1962. *La Ideología de Batlle*. Montevideo.

Halperin-Longhi, Julio. 1961. *El Río de la Plata al comenzar el Siglo XIX*. Buenos Aires.

Hernandez, José. 1967. *Martín Fierro*. Buenos Aires.

Hernandez, Pablo. 1913. *Organización Social de las Doctrinas Guaraníes de la Compania de Jesús*. Barcelona.

Imaz, José Luis de. 1964. *Los que Mandan*. Buenos Aires.

Ingenieros, José. 1918. *Sociología Argentina*. Buenos Aires.

Legizamon, Martiniano. 1961. *De Cepa Criolla*. Buenos Aires.

Maldonado, Silvio. 1952. *El Paraguay*. Mexico.

Marianetti, Benito. 1964. *Argentina, Realidad y Perspectivas*. Buenos Aires.

Martinez Ces, Ricardo. 1962. *El Uruguay Batlista*. Montevideo.

Murena, H. A. 1964. *El Pecado Original de América*. Buenos Aires.

Murray, Luis Alberto. 1960. *Pro y Contra de Alberdi*. Buenos Aires.

Oddone, Blanca M. Paris de, et al. 1966. *Cronología Comparada de la Historia del Uruguay*. Montevideo.

Odonne, Juan Antonio. 1966. *La Formación del Uruguay Moderno. La Inmigración y el desarrollo económico-social*. Buenos Aires.

Pastore, Carlos. 1949. *La Lucha por la Tierra en el Paraguay*. Montevideo.

Pena, Arturo López. 1958. *Teoría del Argentino*. Buenos Aires.

Pendle, George. 1952. *Uruguay—South America's First Welfare State.* London: Royal Institute of International Affairs.

————. 1957. *The Land and the People of Argentina.* New York: The Macmillan Co.

Pintos, Francisco R. 1960. *Historia del Movimiento Obrero del Uruguay.* Montevideo.

Pivel Devoto, Juan E. 1945. *Historia de la República Oriental del Uruguay.* Montevideo.

————. 1957. *Raíces Coloniales de la Revolución Oriental de 1811.* Montevideo.

Porta, Eliseo Salvador. 1961. *Uruguay: Realidad y Reforma Agraria.* Montevideo.

Puiggros, Rodolfo. 1965. *De la Colonia a la Revolución.* Buenos Aires.

Quijano, Carlos. 1963. *La Reforma Agraria en el Uruguay.* Montevideo.

Rama, Carlos M. 1965. *Sociología del Uruguay.* Buenos Aires.

Ramos, Jorge Abelardo. 1959. *Historia Política del Ejército Argentino.* Buenos Aires.

————. 1961. *Crisis y Resurrección de la Literatura Argentina.* Buenos Aires.

————. 1962. *El Partido Comunista en la Política Argentina. Su Historia y su Crítica.* Buenos Aires.

————. 1964. *La Lucha por un Partido Revolucionario.* Buenos Aires.

————. 1965. *Revolución y Contra-Revolución en la Argentina. (Historia de la Argentina en el Siglo XIX.)* Buenos Aires.

Real de Azua, Carlos. 1961. *El Patriciado Uruguayo.* Montevideo.

————. 1964. *Antología del Ensayo Uruguayo Contemporáneo.* 2 vols. Montevideo.

————. 1964a. *El Impulso y su Freno.* Montevideo.

Rey, Esteban. 1959. *Frigerio y la traición de la burguesía industrial.* Buenos Aires.

Rippy, J. Fred. 1947. *Latin America and the Industrial Age.* New York: G. P. Putnam's Sons.

————. 1959. *British Investments in Latin America, 1822/1949.* Minneapolis: University of Minnesota Press.

Romero, José Luis. 1956. *Argentina: Imágenes y Perspectivas.*

Sarmiento, Domingo Faustino. 1946. *Conflicto y Armonías de las Razas en América.* Buenos Aires.

Schopelocher, Roberto. 1955. *Historia de la Colonización Agrícola en Argentina.* Buenos Aires.

Schumpeter, Joseph A. 1950. *Capitalism, Socialism and Democracy.* New York: Harper & Bros.

————. 1955. *Imperialism and Social Classes.* New York: Meridian Books.

Serrano, Antonio. 1947. *Los Aborígenes Argentinos.* Buenos Aires.

Solari, Aldo E. 1958. *Sociología Rural Nacional.* Montevideo.

————. 1964. *Estudios sobre la Sociedad Uruguaya.* Montevideo.

————. 1965. *El Tercerismo en el Uruguay.* Montevideo.

————, et al. 1966. *Uruguay en Cifras.* Montevideo.

Strasser, Carlos (ed.). 1959. *Las Izquierdas en el Proceso Político Argentino.* Buenos Aires.

Trias, Vivian. 1961. *Las Montoneras y el Imperio Británico.* Montevideo.

Vanger, Milton. 1963. *José Batlle y Ordóñez of Uruguay: The Creator of His Time 1902–1906.* Cambridge, Mass.: Harvard University Press.

Vidart, Daniel. 1955. *La Vida Rural Uruguaya.* Montevideo.

Wonsewer, Israel, Enrique V. Iglesias, Mario Bucheli, and Luis A. Faroppa. 1959. *Aspectos de la Industrialización el Uruguay.* Montevideo.

Yurique, Alvaro. 1957. *Manual de Historia Argentina.* Buenos Aires.

Zum Felde, Alberto. 1945. *Evolución Histórica del Uruguay.* Montevideo.

————. 1963. *Proceso Histórico del Uruguay.* Montevideo.

11. MODELS OF AUTONOMOUS DEVELOPMENT
and
12. PATTERNS OF HISTORICAL AND RETARDATION

Agarwala, A. N., and S. P. Singh. 1963. *La Economia del Desarrollo.* Madrid.

Arnault, Jacques. 1960. *Historia del Colonialismo.* Buenos Aires.

Aron, Raymond. 1961. *Dimensions de la Conciencia Histórica.* Madrid.

Arzumanian, A. 1965. *Ideología, Revolución y Mundo Actual.* Buenos Aires.

Ashton, Thomas S. 1948. *The Industrial Revolution, 1760–1830.* London: Oxford University Press.

Balandier, G. (ed.) 1956. *Le Tiers Monde: Sous-Developemenet et Developement.* Paris.

Barre, Raymond. 1964. *El Desarrollo Económico.* Mexico.

Bauer, P. T. 1957. *Economic Analysis and Policy in Underdeveloped Countries.* Durham, N.C.: Duke University Press.

Bell, Daniel. 1959. *The End of Ideology.* Glencoe, Ill.: The Free Press.

Berle, Adolf A., Jr., and G. C. Means. 1937. *The Modern Corporation and Private Property.* New York: The Macmillan Co.

Cafagna, L. 1961. *La Economía de la Unión Soviética.* Mexico.

Cardoso, Fernando Henrique. 1964. *El proceso de desarrollo en América Latina.* Mimeographed.

Clairmonte, Frederick. 1960. *Economic Liberalism and Underdevelopment.* New York: Asia Publishing.

Clark, Colin. 1957. *The Conditions of Economic Progress.* New York: St. Martin's Press.

Dobb, Maurice. 1961. *Economía, Política y Capitalismo.* Mexico.

Domar, E. D. 1957. *Essays in the Theory of Economic Growth.* New York: Oxford University Press.

Dorselaer, J., and A. Gregory. 1962. *La Urbanización en América Latina.* 2 vols. Freiburg.

Drogat, Noël. 1964. *Los Países del Hambre.* Barcelona.

Echevarria, José Medina. 1964. *Consideraciones Sociológicas sobre el desarrollo Económico.* Buenos Aires.

————. 1967. *Filosofía, Educatión y Desarrollo.* Mexico.

Economic Commission on Latin America. 1963. *Estudio Económico de América Latina.* New York: United Nations.

————. 1963a. *El Desarrollo Económico de América Latina en la Postguerra.* New York: United Nations.

————. 1964. *Estudio Económico de América Latina.* New York: United Nations.

————. 1964a. *El Financiamiento Externo de América Latina.* New York: United Nations.

Fourastie, J. 1958. *Le Grand Espoir du XXe Siècle.* Paris.

Frank, Andrew G. 1966. *Capitalism and Underdevelopment in Latin America. The Cases of Chile and Brazil.* New York: Monthly Review Press.

Furtado, Celso. 1961. *Desarrollo y Subdesarrollo.* Buenos Aires.

————. 1966. *Subdesenvolvimento ou Estagnação na América Latina.* Rio de Janeiro.

Galbraith, John K. 1958. *The Affluent Society.* Boston: Houghton-Mifflin.

Gannage, Elié. 1962. *Economie de Developpement.* Paris.

Gerschenkron, Alexander. 1951. *A Dollar Index of the Soviet Machinery Output 1927/28 to 1937.* New York.

Guevara, Ernesto Che. 1966. *Condiciones para el Desarrollo Económico Latino Americano.* Montevideo.

Hauser, Philip (ed.). 1962. *La Urbanización en América Latina.* Paris.

Hirschman, Albert O. 1945. *National Power and the Structure of Foreign Trade.* Berkeley, Calif.: University of California Press.

————. 1958. *The Strategy of Economic Development.* New Haven: Yale University Press.

———— (ed.). 1961. *Latin American Issues: Essays and Comments.* New York: Twentieth Century Fund.

Hodgman, Donald R., and A. Bergson (eds.). 1954. *Soviet Economic Growth.* New York.

Horowitz, Irving Louis. 1966. *Three Worlds of Development.* New York: Oxford University Press.

Hoselitz, Bert F. 1960. *Sociological Aspects of Economic Growth.* Glencoe, Ill.: The Free Press.

Jaguaribe, Hélio. 1962. *Desenvolvimento Econômico e Desenvolvimento Político.* Rio de Janeiro.

Jalée, Pierre. 1966. *El Saqueo del Tercer Mundo.* Paris.

Karol, K. S. 1967. *China, the Other Communism.* New York: Hill & Wang.

Kuznets, Simon S. 1964. *Postwar Economic Growth. Four Lectures.* Cambridge, Mass.: Harvard University Press.

Lacoste, Ives. 1962. *Los Países Subdesarrollados.* Buenos Aires.

Lange, Oskar. 1963. *Political Economy.* Vol. I. New York: The Macmillan Co.

————. 1966. *La Economía en las Sociedades Modernas.* Mexico.

Lebret, Louis-Joseph. 1961. *Manifesto por una Civilización Solidaria.* Lima.

Lenin, V. I. 1941. *El Imperialismo. Fase Superior del Capitalismo. (Obras Escogidas,* Vol. II.) Moscow.

Lerner, David. 1959. *The Passing of Traditional Society.* Glencoe, Ill.: The Free Press.

Lewis, W. A. 1955. *Theory of Economic Growth.* Homewood, Ill.: Richard D. Irwin.

Luxemburg, Rosa. 1963. "Una Anticrítica" in *La Acumulación del Capital.* Buenos Aires.

Machado Neto, A. L. 1960. *As Ideologias e o Desenvolvimento.* Bahía.

Mannheim, Karl. 1955. *Ideology and Utopia.* New York: Harcourt, Brace.

Mao Tse-tung. 1963. *Obras Escogidas.* Vol. IV. Peking.

Marx, Karl. 1956. *El Capital.* 5 vols. Buenos Aires.

Mendes-France, P., and G. Ardant. 1955. *Economics and Action.* New York: UNESCO.

Moussa, Pierre. 1959. *Las Naciones Proletarias.* Madrid.

————. 1966. *Los Estados Unidos y las Naciones Proletarias.* Barcelona.

Myrdal, Gunnar. 1957. *Economic Theory and Underdevelopment Regions*. London: Gerald Duckworth.

————. 1960. *Beyond the Welfare State*. New Haven, Conn.: Yale University Press.

Nurkse, Ragnar. 1953. *Problems of Capital Formation in Underdeveloped Countries*. New York: Oxford University Press.

Perroux, François. 1958. *La Coexistence Pacifique*. Paris.

————. 1964. *La Industrialización del Siglo XX*. Buenos Aires.

Piettre, André. 1962. *Las Tres Edades de la Economía*. Mexico.

Rippy, J. Fred. 1947. *Latin America and the Industrial Age*. New York: G. P. Putnam's Sons.

Rostow, Walt W. 1960. *The Stages of Economic Growth*. New York: Cambridge University Press.

————. 1960a. *The Process of Economic Growth*. New York: W. W. Norton.

Sauvy, A. 1958. *De Malthus à Mao-Tse-Toung*. Paris.

Schemeliov, N. P. 1965. *Los Ideólogos del Imperialismo y los Problemas de los Países Subdesarrollados*. Bogotá.

Schumpeter, Joseph A. 1950. *Capitalism, Socialism and Democracy*. New York: Harper & Bros.

————. 1961. *The Theory of Economic Development*. New York: Oxford University Press.

Sédillot, René. 1961. *História de las Colonizaciones*. Barcelona.

See, Henri. 1928. *Modern Capitalism, Its Origins and Evolution*. New York: Burt Franklin.

Selser, Gregorio. 1964. *Alianza para el Progreso, La Mal Nacida*. Buenos Aires.

Snow, Edgar. 1962. *The Other Side of the River: Red China Today*. New York: Random House.

Stalin, Joseph. 1947. *El Marxismo y la Cuestión Nacional y Colonial*. Buenos Aires.

Sweezy, Paul M. 1963. *Capitalismo e Imperialismo Norteamericano*. Buenos Aires.

———— and Paul Baran. 1965. *Monopoly Capital*. New York: Monthly Review Press.

Touré, Sékou. 1959. *La Guinée et l'Emancipation Africaine*. Paris.

Trentin, Bruno. 1965. *Ideología del Neocapitalismo*. Buenos Aires.

Trias, Vivian. 1966. *La Crisis del Dolar y la Política Norteamericana*. Montevideo.

Trotsky, Leon. 1957. *The History of the Russian Revolution*. Ann Arbor, Mich.: University of Michigan Press.

Urquidi, Victor L. 1962. *Viabilidad Económica de América Latina*. Mexico.

Viatkin, A. (ed.) 1965. *Compendio de Historia y Economía*. Vol. I: *Las Formaciones Precapitalistas*. Vol. II: *La Sociedad Capitalista*. Moscow.

Viner, Jacob. 1953. *International Trade and Economic Development*. London: Oxford University Press.

Weber, Max. 1948. *The Protestant Ethic and the Spirit of Capitalism*. New York: Charles Scribner's Sons.

Index